LENIN

COLLECTED WORKS

17

THE RUSSIAN EDITION WAS PRINTED
IN ACCORDANCE WITH A DECISION
OF THE NINTH CONGRESS OF THE R.C.P.(B.)
AND THE SECOND CONGRESS OF SOVIETS
OF THE U.S.S.R.

ИНСТИТУТ МАРКСИЗМА-ЛЕНИНИЗМА при ЦК КПСС

В. И. ЛЕНИН

СОЧИНЕНИЯ

Издание четвертое

ГОСУДАРСТВЕННОЕ ИЗДАТЕЛЬСТВО
ПОЛИТИЧЕСКОЙ ЛИТЕРАТУРЫ
МОСКВА

V. I. LENIN

COLLECTED WORKS

VOLUME
17
December 1910 – April 1912

PROGRESS PUBLISHERS
MOSCOW

TRANSLATED FROM THE RUSSIAN BY D O R A C O X
EDITED BY THE LATE G E O R G E H A N N A

First printing 1963
Second printing 1968
Third printing 1974

Printed in the Union of Soviet Socialist Republics

11-17-78

CONTENTS

Page

Preface 15

1910

LETTER TO THE RUSSIAN COLLEGIUM OF THE CENTRAL COMMIT-
TEE OF THE R.S.D.L.P. 17

THE STATE OF AFFAIRS IN THE PARTY 23

CERTAIN FEATURES OF THE HISTORICAL DEVELOPMENT OF
MARXISM 39

1911

JUDAS TROTSKY'S BLUSH OF SHAME 45

THE CAREER OF A RUSSIAN TERRORIST 46

LEV TOLSTOI AND HIS EPOCH 49

MARXISM AND *NASHA ZARYA* 54

THOSE WHO WOULD LIQUIDATE US. *Re: Mr. Potresov and
V. Bazarov* 60

I 60
II 65
III 67
IV 72
V 77

THE CADETS ON "TWO CAMPS" AND "SENSIBLE COMPROMISE". 82

THE FIFTIETH ANNIVERSARY OF THE FALL OF SERFDOM . . . 87

PAUL SINGER 92

COMMENTS. *Menshikov, Gromoboi, Izgoyev.* 96

TO THE RUSSIAN COLLEGIUM OF THE C.C. 106

APROPOS OF AN ANNIVERSARY 110

"THE PEASANT REFORM" AND THE PROLETARIAN-PEASANT REVOLUTION 119

WRECKERS OF THE PARTY IN THE ROLE OF "WRECKERS OF LE-GENDS" 129

THE CADETS AND THE OCTOBRISTS 134

IN MEMORY OF THE COMMUNE 139

THE SOCIAL STRUCTURE OF STATE POWER, THE PROSPECTS AND LIQUIDATIONISM. 144

POLEMICAL NOTES 164

THE MEANING OF THE CRISIS 168

CONFERENCE OF THE BRITISH SOCIAL-DEMOCRATIC PARTY . 173

A CONVERSATION BETWEEN A LEGALIST AND AN OPPONENT OF LIQUIDATIONISM 179

"REGRET" AND "SHAME" 189

THE MEETING OF THE C.C. MEMBERS OF THE R.S.D.L.P. *May 28-June 4 (June 10-17), 1911* 195

    1. LETTER TO THE MEETING OF THE C.C. MEMBERS OF THE R.S.D.L.P. ABROAD 197

    2. SUMMARY (PLAN) FOR REPORT BY THREE BOLSHEVIK MEMBERS OF THE C.C. TO A PRIVATE MEETING OF NINE MEM-BERS OF THE CENTRAL COMMITTEE 200

    3. DRAFT RESOLUTION DEFINING TERMS OF REFERENCE . . 205

THE RESULTS OF THE DUMA SESSION. *"We Did This Together"* 206

OLD TRUTHS THAT ARE EVER NEW 211

RESOLUTION ADOPTED BY THE SECOND PARIS GROUP OF THE R.S.D.L.P. ON THE STATE OF AFFAIRS IN THE PARTY 216

Introduction 216
   I 217
  II 220
 III 221

INTRODUCTION TO THE PAMPHLET *TWO PARTIES* 225

REFORMISM IN THE RUSSIAN SOCIAL-DEMOCRATIC MOVEMENT 229

FROM THE CAMP OF THE STOLYPIN "LABOUR" PARTY. *Dedicated to Our "Conciliators" and Advocates of "Agreement".* . 242

COMMENT BY *SOTSIAL-DEMOKRAT* EDITORS ON STATEMENT BY COMMISSION CONVENING PLENARY MEETING OF C.C. . . 245

STOLYPIN AND THE REVOLUTION 247

THE NEW FACTION OF CONCILIATORS, OR THE VIRTUOUS . . 257

THE ELECTION CAMPAIGN AND THE ELECTION PLATFORM . . 278

FROM THE CAMP OF THE STOLYPIN "LABOUR" PARTY 287

THE GRAND TOTAL 292

TWO CENTRES 297

OLD AND NEW. *Notes of a Newspaper Reader* 300

SPEECH DELIVERED IN THE NAME OF THE R.S.D.L.P. AT THE FUNERAL OF PAUL AND LAURA LAFARGUE, NOVEMBER 20 (DECEMBER 3), 1911 304

HYNDMAN ON MARX 306

A LIBERAL LABOUR PARTY MANIFESTO 313

   I 313
  II 317
 III 321

THE SOCIAL-DEMOCRATIC GROUP IN THE SECOND DUMA. *An Account of the Whole Affair* 325

THE SLOGANS AND ORGANISATION OF SOCIAL-DEMOCRATIC WORK INSIDE AND OUTSIDE THE DUMA 331

AGENCY OF THE LIBERAL BOURGEOISIE 342

THE CLIMAX OF THE PARTY CRISIS 343

FROM THE CAMP OF THE STOLYPIN "LABOUR" PARTY 354

TROTSKY'S DIPLOMACY AND A CERTAIN PARTY PLATFORM . .   360

THE RESULTS OF THE ARBITRATION OF THE "TRUSTEES" . . .   365

THE CAMPAIGN FOR THE ELECTIONS TO THE FOURTH DUMA .   368

    I. Fundamental Questions of Principle   368
   II. The Role of Worker Electors in the Election Cam-
       paign   372
  III. The Peasantry and the Peasant Electors in the Elec-
      tion Campaign   380
  IV. Conclusions Based on the Experience of the Elections
      to the Third Duma   384

OLD AND NEW   388

MEETING OF THE BOLSHEVIK GROUPS ABROAD. December 14-17
(27-30), 1911   393

  1. DRAFT RESOLUTION ON THE REPORT "STATE OF AFFAIRS
     IN THE PARTY". Organisation of the Social-Democratic
     Party Forces Abroad and the Tasks of the Bolsheviks . .   393

  2. RESOLUTION ON THE RUSSIAN ORGANISING COMMISSION
     FOR THE CONVENING OF A CONFERENCE   396

FUNDAMENTAL PROBLEMS OF THE ELECTION CAMPAIGN . .   397

      I   397
     II   402
    III   405
    IV   407
     V   412
    VI   417
   VII   420

FIRST EXPOSURE OF CADET NEGOTIATIONS WITH THE
CABINET   424

THREE QUESTIONS   433

THE FAMINE AND THE REACTIONARY DUMA   446

                              1912

THE SIXTH (PRAGUE) ALL-RUSSIA CONFERENCE OF THE
R.S.D.L.P. January 5-17 (18-30), 1912   451

  1. DRAFT RESOLUTION ON THE CONSTITUTION OF THE
     CONFERENCE. Resolution on the Constitution   453

  2. DRAFT RESOLUTION ON THE TASKS OF THE PARTY IN
     THE PRESENT SITUATION   455

3. DRAFT RESOLUTION ON THE TASKS OF SOCIAL-DEMO-
CRATS IN THE STRUGGLE AGAINST THE FAMINE . . 458

4. DRAFT RESOLUTION ON LIQUIDATIONISM AND THE GROUP
OF LIQUIDATORS. *Liquidationism and the Group of Liquidators* 460

5. RESOLUTIONS OF THE CONFERENCE 462

The Russian Organising Commission for Convening the Conference 462

The Constitution of the Conference 462

The Absence of Delegates from the Non-Russian National
Centres from the General Party Conference 464

On the Reports of the Local Organisations 465

The Tasks of the Party in the Present Situation . . . 466

Elections to the Fourth Duma 468

I 468
II 469
III 470

The Social-Democratic Group in the Duma 471

The Character and Organisational Forms of Party Work 472

The Tasks of Social-Democracy in the Struggle Against the
Famine 474

The Party's Attitude to the Workers' State Insurance Duma
Bill 475

I 475
II 477

The "Petition Campaign" 479

Liquidationism and the Group of Liquidators 480

The Central Organ 482

Rabochaya Gazeta 482

Newspaper *Pravda* 482

Changes in the Organisational Rules of the Party . . . 482

Property in the Hands of the Former Trustee, and Financial Reports 483

The Red Cross 483

The Party Organisation Abroad   484

The Russian Government's Attack on Persia   484

The Chinese Revolution   485

The Policy of the Tsarist Government in Finland . . .   485

Greetings to the German Social-Democratic Party . . .   486

AN ORGAN OF A LIBERAL LABOUR POLICY   487

AGAINST UNITY—WITH THE LIQUIDATORS   491

POLITICAL PARTIES IN THE FIVE YEARS OF THE THIRD DUMA   497

        I   497
        II   500

REPORT TO THE INTERNATIONAL SOCIALIST BUREAU ON THE
ALL-RUSSIA CONFERENCE OF THE R.S.D.L.P.   . . . . . ,   503

THE ELECTION PLATFORM OF THE R.S.D.L.P. . . . . . . ,   506

TO THE EDITORIAL BOARD OF ZVEZDA. P.S. to "The Election Platform of the R.S.D.L.P."   513

PUT YOUR CARDS ON THE TABLE   514

DEPUTY T. O. BELOUSOV'S WITHDRAWAL FROM THE SOCIAL-
DEMOCRATIC GROUP IN THE DUMA   521

FAMINE   527

THE PEASANTRY AND THE ELECTIONS TO THE FOURTH DUMA .   529

THE ANONYMOUS WRITER IN VORWÄRTS AND THE STATE OF
AFFAIRS IN THE R.S.D.L.P.   533

        Preface   535

A LETTER TO HUYSMANS, SECRETARY OF THE INTERNATIONAL
SOCIALIST BUREAU   547

THE BLOC OF THE CADETS WITH THE PROGRESSISTS AND ITS
SIGNIFICANCE   551

A POOR DEFENCE OF A LIBERAL LABOUR POLICY   556

THE SECOND BALLOT IN RUSSIA AND THE TASKS OF THE WORK-
ING CLASS   562

LIBERALISM AND DEMOCRACY 569

     I 569

     II 574

Notes 579

The Life and Work of V. I. Lenin. Outstanding Dates . . . 621

ILLUSTRATIONS

Cover of *Mysl*, No. 2, for January 1911, containing Chapter II
of Lenin's "Strike Statistics in Russia" and the beginning of
the article "Those Who Would Liquidate Us (Re: Mr. Potresov
and V. Bazarov)" 63

First page of Lenin's manuscript "Put Your Cards on the Table",
March 1912 515

PREFACE

Volume Seventeen of Lenin's works covers the period December 1910 to April 1912.

The principal contents of the volume are writings reflecting the struggle for the Party, against the liquidators and their accomplices—renegades from the revolution.

In the articles "The State of Affairs in the Party", "Those Who Would Liquidate Us (Re: Mr. Potresov and V. Bazarov)", "The Social Structure of State Power, the Prospects and Liquidationism", "Wreckers of the Party in the Role of 'Wreckers of Legends'", "A Conversation Between a Legalist and an Opponent of Liquidationism", "A Liberal Labour Party Manifesto", "From the Camp of the Stolypin 'Labour' Party", Lenin uncovers the ideological roots and essence of liquidationism and exposes the liquidators' systematic wrecking of the work of the leading Party bodies.

The article "The New Faction of Conciliators, or the Virtuous" shows the unprincipled shifts of the conciliators to the side of the liquidators.

In the articles "The Cadets and the Octobrists", "First Exposure of Cadet Negotiations with the Cabinet", "Political Parties in the Five Years of the Third Duma", "The Bloc of the Cadets with the Progressists and Its Significance", Lenin illustrates the class nature of the party of counterrevolutionary liberalism—the Cadet Party.

The elections to the Fourth State Duma are dealt with in "The Election Campaign and the Election Platform", "The Campaign for the Elections to the Fourth Duma", "Fundamental Problems of the Election Campaign".

A considerable part of the volume is taken up by documents which throw light on the significance of the Prague

Party Conference which expelled Menshevik liquidators from the Party, a fact that played an outstanding role in preserving and strengthening the revolutionary party of the proletariat. These documents include the article on "The Climax of the Party Crisis", "Draft Resolution on Liquidationism and the Group of Liquidators", the resolutions of the Prague Conference, "Report to the International Socialist Bureau on the All-Russia Conference of the R.S.D.L.P.", the pamphlet "The Anonymous Writer in *Vorwärts* and the State of Affairs in the R.S.D.L.P.", "A Letter to Huysmans, Secretary of the International Socialist Bureau".

Lenin's famous article "Certain Features of the Historical Development of Marxism" is included in this volume.

In this edition two letters to the Russian Collegium of the C.C. of the R.S.D.L.P. (1910-11) are included in the *Collected Works* for the first time. In these letters Lenin shows how the liquidators, otzovists, *Vperyod* group, and Trotskyites wrecked the work of the Party, and puts forward the task of uniting Party forces in the struggle for the restoration of the Party. The following are also included in Lenin's *Collected Works* for the first time: the note "Judas Trotsky's Blush of Shame"; materials relating to the June Meeting of the members of the C.C. in 1911: "Letter to the Meeting of the C.C. Members of the R.S.D.L.P. Abroad", "Summary (Plan) for Report by Three Bolshevik Members of the C.C. to a Private Meeting of Nine Members of the Central Committee", "Draft Resolution Defining Terms of Reference"; the articles "The Social-Democratic Group in the Second Duma", "Agency of the Liberal Bourgeoisie"; documents of the meeting of the Bolshevik groups abroad: "Draft Resolution on the Report 'State of Affairs in the Party'", "Resolution on the Russian Organising Commission for the Convening of a Conference"; the documents of the Prague Conference: draft resolutions on the constitution of the Conference, on the tasks of the Party in the present situation, on the tasks of Social-Democrats in the struggle against the famine, "The Election Platform of the R.S.D.L.P.", letter "To the Editorial Board of *Zvezda*", and the article "Put Your Cards on the Table".

LETTER TO THE RUSSIAN COLLEGIUM
OF THE CENTRAL COMMITTEE OF THE R.S.D.L.P.[1]

Recent events in the life of the Russian Social-Democratic Labour Party abroad clearly show that the "unity crisis" of the Party is coming to a head. I, therefore, consider it my duty, solely by way of information, to let you know the significance of recent happenings, the denouement that may be expected (according to this course of events) and the position adopted by orthodox Bolsheviks.

In *Golos*, No. 23,[2] Martov in his article "Where Have We Landed?" gibes at the Plenary Meeting,[3] at the fact that the Russian Collegium of the Central Committee has not met once during the year, and that nothing has been done to carry out the decisions. He, of course, "forgets" to add that it is precisely the liquidator group of Potresovs that has sabotaged the work of the Russian Central Committee; we know of the non-recognition of the Central Committee by Mikhail, Roman, and Yuri,[4] and their statement that its very existence is harmful. The C.C. in Russia has been wrecked. Martov rejoices at this. It stands to reason that the *Vperyod* group[5] also rejoices, and this is reflected in the *Vperyod* symposium, No. 1. In his glee, Martov has blurted out his views prematurely. He screams with delight that "legality will finish them" (the Bolsheviks or the "Polish-Bolshevik bloc"). By this he means that *thanks to the obstruction* of the Central Committee's work by the liquidators, there is no way out of the present situation that would be *legal** from the Party point of view. Obviously, nothing

---

* See footnote to p. 29.—*Tr.*

pleases the liquidators more than a hopeless situation for
the Party.

But Martov was in too much of a hurry. The Bolsheviks
still have at their disposal an archi-legal means of emerging from this situation as foreseen by the Plenary Meeting
and published in its name in No. 11 of the Central Organ.[6]
This is the demand for the return of the funds, because the
Golos and *Vperyod* groups obviously have not abided by the
terms agreed on—to eliminate factions and to struggle
against the liquidators and the otzovists.[7] It was precisely
on these *conditions*, clearly agreed to, that the Bolsheviks
handed over their property to the Central Committee.

Then, on the 5th December, 1910 (New Style), the Bolsheviks, having signed the conditions at the Plenary Meeting[8]
applied for the return of the funds. According to legal procedure this demand must *lead to the convening of a plenary
meeting*. The decision of the Plenary Meeting states that
"should it prove impossible" (literally!) for a plenary meeting to take place within three months from the date of the
application, then a commission of five members of the C.C.—
three from the national, non-Russian, parties, one Bolshevik
and one Menshevik—is to be set up.

Immediately, the *Golos* supporters revealed themselves in
their true colours. The *Golos* supporter Igor,[9] a member of
the Central Committee Bureau Abroad,[10] conscious of the
policy of the Russian liquidators, handed in a statement
that he was against holding a plenary meeting, but was in
favour of a commission. The violation of legality by the
Golos group is thus apparent, since a plenary meeting may
be convened before the conclusion of the three-month period. Once such a request has been made it is not even permissible to raise the question of a commission.

The liquidator Igor, true servant of the Party traitors,
Messrs. Potresov and Co., calculates quite simply that the
plenary meeting is a sovereign body and consequently its
session would open the door to a solution of the whole Party
crisis. A commission, however, is not a sovereign body and
has no rights apart from the investigation into the claim
put forward in the application. (Three Germans are now
considering this claim.) Hence, having obstructed the
Russian Central Committee, the liquidators (and their lack-

eys abroad, the *Golos* group) are now trying to prevent anything in the nature of a Central Committee from working. We shall yet see whether this attempt succeeds. The Poles in the Central Committee Bureau Abroad[11] are voting for the plenary meeting. It now all depends on the Latvians and the Bund members,[12] from whom so far no reply has been received. Our representative in the Bureau Abroad has submitted and distributed a firm protest against Igor. (Copies of Igor's statement and this protest are attached herewith.)

It has become clear that the struggle for the plenary meeting is a struggle for a legal way out, a struggle for the Party. The fight of the *Golos* group against the plenary meeting is a fight against a way out of the Party crisis, is a fight against legality.

Plekhanov and his friends,[13] whom we kept informed of every step, are in complete agreement with us on the necessity for a plenary meeting. They, too, are in favour of it; the draft of our joint statement on this matter is now being considered, and in the near future we shall either come forward with a statement together with Plekhanov's group, or we shall publish an article on the question in the Central Organ.

Further, on the 26th November (N.S.), 1910, Trotsky carried through a resolution in the so-called Vienna Party Club (a circle of Trotskyites, exiles who are pawns in the hands of Trotsky) which he published as a separate leaflet. I append this leaflet.

In this resolution, open war is declared on *Rabochaya Gazeta*,[14] the organ of the Bolsheviks and Plekhanov's group. The arguments are not new. The statement that there are now "no essential grounds" for a struggle against the *Golos* and *Vperyod* groups is the height of absurdity and hypocrisy. Everybody knows that the *Golos* and *Vperyod* people had no intention of dispersing their factions and that the former in reality support the liquidators, Potresov and Co., that the *Vperyod* group organised the factional school abroad[15] (using funds of well-known origin), where they teach Machism, where they teach that otzovism is a "legal shade of opinion" (taken literally from their platform), etc., etc.

Trotsky's call for "friendly" collaboration by the Party with the *Golos* and *Vperyod* groups is disgusting hypocrisy and phrase-mongering. Everybody is aware that for the whole year since the Plenary Meeting the *Golos* and *Vperyod* groups have worked in a "friendly" manner against the Party (and were secretly supported by Trotsky). Actually, it is only the Bolsheviks and Plekhanov's group who have for a whole year carried out friendly Party work in the Central Organ, in *Rabochaya Gazeta*, and at Copenhagen,[16] as well as in the Russian legal press.

Trotsky's attacks on the bloc of Bolsheviks and Plekhanov's group are not new; what *is* new is the outcome of his resolution: the Vienna Club (read: "Trotsky") has organised a "general Party fund for the purpose of preparing and convening a conference of the R.S.D.L.P.".

This indeed is new. It is a direct step towards a split. It is a clear violation of Party legality and the start of an adventure in which Trotsky will come to grief. This is obviously a split: Trotsky's action, his "fund", is supported only by the *Golos* and *Vperyod* groups. There can be no question of participation by the Bolsheviks and Plekhanov's group. That the liquidators (of *Golos*) in Zurich have already supported Trotsky is comprehensible. It is quite possible and probable that "certain" *Vperyod* "funds" will be made available to Trotsky. You will appreciate that this will only stress the adventurist character of his undertaking.

It is clear that this undertaking violates Party legality, since not a word is said about the Central Committee, which alone can call the conference. In addition, Trotsky, having ousted the C.C. representative on *Pravda*[17] in August 1910, himself lost all trace of legality, converting *Pravda* from an organ supported by the representative of the C.C. into a purely factional organ.

Thus, the whole matter has taken on definite shape, the situation has clarified itself. The *Vperyod* group collected "certain funds" for struggle against the Party, for support of the "legal shade of opinion" (otzovism). Trotsky in the last number of *Pravda* (and in his lecture in Zurich) goes all out to flirt with *Vperyod*. The liquidators in Russia sabotaged the work of the Russian Central Committee. The liquidators abroad want to prevent a plenary meeting abroad—in other words, sabotage anything like a Central Committee. Taking advantage of this "violation of legality", Trotsky seeks an organisational split, creating "his own" fund for "his own" conference.

The roles have been assigned. The *Golos* group defend Potresov and Co., as a "legal shade of opinion", the *Vperyod* group defend otzovism, as a "legal shade of opinion". Trotsky seeks to defend both camps in a "popular fashion", and to call his conference (possibly on funds supplied by *Vperyod*). The Triple Alliance (Potresov+Trotsky+Maximov) against the Dual Alliance (Bolsheviks+Plekhanov's group). The deployment of forces has been completed and battle joined.

You will understand why I call Trotsky's move an adventure; it is an adventure in every respect.

It is an adventure in the ideological sense. Trotsky groups all the enemies of Marxism, he unites Potresov and Maximov, who detest the "Lenin-Plekhanov" bloc, as they like to call it. Trotsky unites all to whom ideological decay is dear, all who are not concerned with the defence of Marxism; all philistines who do not understand the reasons for the struggle and who do not wish to learn, think, and discover the ideological roots of the divergence of views. At this time of confusion, disintegration, and wavering it is easy for Trotsky to become the "hero of the hour" and gather all the shabby elements around himself. The more openly this attempt is made, the more spectacular will be the defeat.

It is an adventure in the party-political sense. At present everything goes to show that the real unity of the Social-Democratic Party is possible only on the basis of a sincere and unswerving repudiation of liquidationism and otzovism. It is clear that Potresov (together with *Golos*) and the *Vperyod* group have renounced neither the one nor the other. Trotsky unites them, basely deceiving himself, deceiving the Party, and deceiving the proletariat. In reality, Trotsky will achieve nothing more than the strengthening of Potresov's and Maximov's anti-Party groups. The collapse of this adventure is inevitable.

Finally, it is an organisational adventure. A conference held with Trotsky's "funds", without the Central Committee, is a split. Let the initiative remain with Trotsky. Let his be the responsibility.

Three slogans bring out the essence of the present situation within the Party:

1. Strengthen and support the unification and rallying of Plekhanov's supporters and the Bolsheviks for the defence of Marxism, for a rebuff to ideological confusion, and for the battle against liquidationism and otzovism.

2. Struggle for a plenary meeting—for a legal solution to the Party crisis.

3. Struggle against the splitting tactics and the unprincipled adventurism of Trotsky in banding Potresov and Maximov against Social-Democracy.

Written not later than
December 15 (28), 1910

First published in 1941 in
Proletarskaya Revolutsia, No. 1

Published according to
a typewritten copy

THE STATE OF AFFAIRS IN THE PARTY

The question of the crisis in our Party has again been given priority by the Social-Democratic press abroad, leading to stronger rumours, perplexity and vacillation among wide Party circles. It is, therefore, essential for the Central Organ of the Party to clarify this question in its entirety. Martov's article in *Golos*, No. 23, and Trotsky's statement of November 26, 1910 in the form of a "resolution" of the "Vienna Club", published as a separate leaflet, present the question to the reader in a manner which completely distorts the essence of the matter.

Martov's article and Trotsky's resolution conceal definite practical *actions*—actions *directed against the Party.* Martov's article is simply the literary expression of *a campaign launched by the* Golos *group to sabotage the Central Committee* of our Party. Trotsky's resolution, which calls upon organisations in the localities to prepare for a "general Party conference" independent of, and against, the Central Committee, expresses the very aim of the *Golos* group—*to destroy the central bodies so detested by the liquidators, and with them, the Party as an organisation.* It is not enough to lay bare the anti-Party activities of *Golos* and Trotsky; they must be *fought.* Comrades to whom the Party and its revival are dear must come out most resolutely against all those who, guided by purely factional and narrow circle considerations and interests, are striving to destroy the Party.

Martov's article "Where Have We Landed?" is poorly disguised mockery of the Plenary Meeting's decisions and the rejoicing of a liquidator over the adversities suffered by the Party. *"Not once* did they succeed in *convening in*

Russia the Collegium of the Central Committee although
it consists of only a few members"—this is how Martov
writes, using italics, as if bubbling over with the pleasure
all liquidators will derive from the publication of this
fact.

Unfortunately, what Martov says is true. The Russian
Central Committee has not succeeded in meeting. But Martov is mistaken if he thinks that he can evade the question
as to *who* sabotaged the work of the Central Committee in
Russia. It was not only the police who hindered the holding
of the meeting, in addition to the police there was one obstacle of a *political* nature. That obstacle was the well-
known refusal by Mikhail, Roman, and Yuri to attend a
meeting of the Central Committee even *if only* to co-opt
new members, and their statement that they "consider the
very existence of the Central Committee harmful".

It cannot be denied that refusal to attend even one meeting for the purpose of co-option, refusal to attend at the
invitation of people who carry on their work amid a host
of obstacles placed in their way by the police, means *sabotaging the work of the Central Committee*. Nor can it be denied
that this political act, accompanied by a statement that
its motives were matters of *principle*, was carried out by
members of the group of "most prominent" *Golos* contributors in Russia (the letter of the *sixteen*[18] in *Golos*,
No. 19-20), who are also members of the liquidationist *legal*
groups of Potresov and Co. All these are facts. *The group
of independent legalists, the enemies of the Social-Democratic
Party—these are the people who sabotaged the work of the
Central Committee in Russia.*

When Axelrod asserts (in *Golos*, No. 23) that the "label"
of liquidator is tacked on "indiscriminately", when he stoops
even to such nonsense as to state that we are capable of
calling a liquidator someone who is physically tired or crushed
by the struggle for his daily bread; when, indulging as he
does in this kind of infantile twaddle, he *maintains silence*
about that particular group and those very groups of liquidators who have been mentioned in the Central Organ of the
Party *by name*, then there is no need to prove the unscrupu-
lousness of such subterfuges. When Martov and other *Golos*
people pretend to "argue" in *Golos* against the liquidators

in Russia, declaring that their acts are "frivolous" (!), and "exhorting" them to wait a little longer (Martov on Levitsky in No. 23), and *at the same time work* hand in glove with them, and, together with them, form a separate *faction* abroad for the purpose of fighting the Party and lending support to its enemies, such as Mr. Potresov, we can see in this but one of many manifestations of political hypocrisy. No politically-minded person will say that Mr. Milyukov is seriously fighting the *Vekhi*[19] writers when he "argues" with them, declares them to be "frivolous", and at the same time *works* hand in glove with them politically. Everyone will see that this only proves Mr. Milyukov's hypocrisy, and by no means disproves his political solidarity with *Vekhi*. No politically-minded person will say that Mr. Stolypin and his government are seriously fighting the Black Hundreds[20] when he "argues" with them (in *Rossiya*[21]), accuses them of "frivolity", but at the same time *works* hand in glove with them. Everyone will see that Mr. Stolypin and the tsar's government thereby prove nothing but their hypocrisy, that this by no means disproves the fact of their political solidarity with the Purishkeviches.

But if everyone is clear about the political hypocrisy of *Golos*, Martov's *hint* that "legality finishes" the official representatives of the Party *cannot be clear* to 999 out of 1,000 readers, because it is a deliberately vague hint.

It is the duty of the Central Organ to disperse any haze enveloping our Party affairs, so that the substance of the differences may become clear to *everyone*.

What Martov means is that, *apart* from a decision of the Central Committee, there is *no other* way out of the crisis that would conform to Party legality. Consequently, *since* the liquidators in Russia have succeeded in sabotaging the work of the Central Committee there (*and if the liquidators abroad succeed in preventing the Central Committee from meeting even outside Russia*), there will be no legal way out of the situation. And Martov rejoices in advance: the Central Committee, he says, has been completely wrecked, there is *no* legal way out, and the liquidators, he thinks, have won their game.

Martov was in too much of a hurry. He has *blurted out* too soon what Mr. Potresov and the other enemies of the Party *have kept to themselves.*

Yes, Martov is right! The Central Committee alone can find the way out of the crisis in the Party. Hence, if, on account of police obstacles, and on account of the above-mentioned political obstacles, the Central Committee is prevented from meeting in Russia, it must be convened abroad. This is the *only* way of approaching a solution to the crisis. The Bolsheviks, one of the Party trends that concluded at the last Plenary Meeting of the Central Committee the agreement which provided for joint Party work outside the factions, took measures to hasten the only possible solution to the Party crisis. The representatives of the Bolshevik group placed its property at the disposal of the Party, *on condition* that simultaneously with the dissolution of its own group centre, those of the Mensheviks (the *Golos* group) and the otzovists (the *Vperyod* group) would also be dissolved. This *has not been done.* What is more, *Golos Sotsial-Demokrata* (the leading organ of the *Golos* group), has deliberately taken under its wing and protection the enemies within the Party, whom the Plenary Meeting of the Central Committee unanimously instructed us to fight most resolutely, as representing bourgeois and anti-Party deviations from Social-Democracy. In view of this obvious violation of the terms of the agreement concluded at the Plenary Meeting between all the Party trends and groups, in view of the obvious anti-Party policy of one of the parties to the agreement, the Bolsheviks thought it necessary to demand the return of the funds which a year before they had placed at the disposal of the Party on definite conditions. On December 5, 1910, they filed an application to this effect with the Central Committee Bureau Abroad. Whether the Bolsheviks were right or wrong in acting as they did will be determined by the body appointed by the Plenary Meeting. The point is that *now*, since the representatives of the Bolshevik trend have filed their application, it is imperative to convene a plenary meeting of the Central Committee abroad, and not only for the purpose of finding a way out of the internal crisis in the Party; it is *imperative* as a step dictated to all the trends and groups which conclud·

ed the agreement of January 6, 1910, *according to the obligation they themselves assumed, in the resolution which they themselves adopted unanimously.** The convocation of a plenary meeting of the Central Committee has become not only a necessity in the interests of the Party, it has become a *juridical obligation.* We see again that *there can be no legal way out of the situation, other than the convening of a plenary meeting of the Central Committee....*

It is on this point that the policy of the *Golos* group immediately revealed itself.

It would appear that, according to the clear and unequivocal decision of the Central Committee, the only thing for its Bureau Abroad to do, in view of the application filed by the Bolsheviks, was to call a plenary meeting; and only if the attempts to convene it in the course of three months failed, was the Bureau to resort to the other method of settling the question as provided by the Central Committee. But the *Golos* group acted differently.

On December 12, Igorev of *Golos*, a member of the Central Committee Bureau Abroad, filed a written statement in which he declared that he was *against calling a plenary meeting* and would agree only to a commission.

It is obvious wherein lies the rub: a plenary meeting is a sovereign body and, if it were convened, *could* find a *legal* way out of the crisis, a legal way out of the impossible state of affairs in Russia. A commission on the other hand, is *not* a sovereign body, it has no rights (except that of examining the Bolsheviks' claim to their funds); it *cannot* find *any legal* way out of the crisis.

---

* At the Plenary Meeting, the Central Committee entered into an agreement with certain representatives of the Bolshevik trend, providing for the *conditional* transfer of their funds to the Party. This agreement was recognised as Party *law*, as the source of Party *legality.* It was published in the Central Organ (No. 11), together with the entire procedure stipulated by the Meeting in connection with the agreement. The principal provision was, that if the Bolsheviks filed an application showing that the *Golos* and *Vperyod* trends *violated the terms* of amalgamation, *a plenary meeting was to be called* (abroad). The decision printed in No. 11 of the Central Organ, states: "Should it prove impossible for various reasons to arrange a plenary meeting within three months after the representatives of the Bolshevik trend have filed their application", a special commission "is to be set up".

The saying has proved true—he who diggeth a pit shall fall into it.

The kind-hearted Martov had hardly shown the Party the "pit" of the allegedly hopeless, from the legal point of view, situation in which the liquidators would be so happy to see the official Party, when *Igorev of* Golos *found himself in that very pit*!

The Russian liquidators have sabotaged the work of the Central Committee in Russia. Now the liquidators abroad are trying to prevent the meeting of the Central Committee outside Russia. The liquidators are happy in anticipation of that greatest of joys (for Stolypin and for the liquidators)— the absence of *any* Central Committee. What a boon that would be for the Potresovs and for the *Vperyod* faction!

We shall not dwell here on the subterfuges of Igorev of the *Golos* group and on their refutation in the counter-statement filed by a Bolshevik member of the Central Committee Bureau Abroad.* We shall only note the fact that Igorev of *Golos* obligingly and bluntly declared that he would protest against a plenary meeting *even if* it were convened *in conformity with the general Rules* (for which a unanimous decision of the Central Committee Bureau Abroad is required), and not by the adoption of a special decision based on an application. In the opinion of Igorev of *Golos* a plenary meeting is "unwieldy", etc. Naturally—since for the liquidators the very existence of our illegal Party is too "unwieldy". The other "reason" advanced by Igorev is that the plenary meeting would be made up mostly of exiles. But this does not prevent the *Golos* group from lending every support to Trotsky's *purely émigré* plan of calling a "general Party" conference independently of, and against, the Central Committee....

The *Golos* group have decided to disrupt *any and every* attempt to convene the Central Committee.

Further, we must draw the attention of Party members to a more general problem—the state of affairs in the R.S.D.L.P. Like every revolutionary party, our Party can exist and develop only if there is at least an elementary *desire*

---

* In a letter addressed to the Central Organ this comrade requests us to help him inform the Party of the *Golos* group's attempts to prevent the plenary meeting.

on the part of revolutionaries to help one another in carrying out *common* work.

If the Party Rules and decisions (the Party's "legality") do not serve to *facilitate* this joint work, but are used as *pretexts* for people in some of the most important Party bodies to *hamper* this work from within, then Party work becomes an indignified farce. In any other party the difficulties attending the convening of the Central Committee would have led at once to dozens of ways and means being found to circumvent police obstacles, they would have produced a host of new methods of work. We, however, find factionalists *inside* the Party, some of whom serve the Potresovs, and others the out-and-out otzovists and semi-anarchists, *outside* the Party. In the hands of people like Igorev of *Golos*, "legality" is converted into an instrument for damaging the Party from *within*, for hampering its work, for helping the Potresovs to destroy the Party*. This is an impossible situation. And it will not be remedied by "well-meaning resolutions" which Martov legitimately holds up to ridicule. In order to help matters, we must, first of all, *understand* them. We must understand why it is absurd, unbecoming, and ridiculous to concoct well-meaning resolutions about joint work with gentlemen like Potresov and Co. Once the Party realises that we have here two incompatible policies, that it is a question of Social-Democracy versus liberalism, it will rapidly find a way out. Then we shall succeed in creating a "legality" which the liquidators will be *unable* to use as a means of tripping up the Party.

It must be admitted that Mr. Potresov and his friends, as well as Igorev of *Golos*, deserve our *thanks* for the successful way in which they are helping the Party to *realise* this.

Trotsky's statement, though *outwardly* entirely unconnected with Martov's jeering at the adversities of the Party, and with the attempts of the *Golos* supporters to sabotage the Central Committee, is actually connected with the one

---

* When Martov jeers at official Party institutions, saying that "legality finishes them", he is *right insofar* as the fruitfulness of the work is killed by *such* "legal" (i.e., created in accordance with the Party Rules or by decisions of the Plenary Meeting) forms of these institutions as *permit* Mikhail, Roman, Yuri, the *Golos* group (as represented by Igorev), etc., to hamper the work.

and the other by inseverable ties, by the ties of "interest". There are many Party members who still fail to see this connection. The Vienna resolution of November 26, 1910, will undoubtedly help them understand the essence of the matter.

The resolution consists of three parts: (1) a declaration of war against *Rabochaya Gazeta* (a call to *"rebuff it resolutely"* as one of the "new factional group undertakings", using Trotsky's expression); (2) polemics against the line of the Bolshevik-Plekhanov "bloc"; (3) a declaration that the "meeting of the Vienna Club [i.e., Trotsky and his circle]* resolves: to organise a general Party fund for the purpose of preparing and convening a conference of the R.S.D.L.P.".

We shall not dwell on the first part at all. Trotsky is quite right in saying that *Rabochaya Gazeta* is a "private undertaking", and that *"it is not authorised to speak in the name of the Party as a whole"*.

Only Trotsky should not have forgotten to mention that he and his *Pravda* are not authorised to speak in the name of the Party *either*. In saying that the Plenary Meeting recognised the work of *Pravda* as useful, he should not have forgotten to mention that it appointed a *representative of the Central Committee* to the Editorial Board of *Pravda*. When Trotsky, in referring to the Meeting's decisions on *Pravda*, fails to mention this fact, all one can say about it is that *he is deceiving the workers*. And this deception on the part of Trotsky is all the more malicious, since in *August* 1910 Trotsky *removed* the representative of the Central Committee from *Pravda*. Since that incident, since *Pravda has severed* its relations with the Central Committee, Trotsky's paper is nothing but a "private undertaking", and one, moreover, that has failed to carry out the obligations it assumed. Until the Central Committee meets again, the *only* judge of the relations between *Pravda* and the Central Committee is the Central Committee *representative* appointed by the Plenary Meeting who has *declared that Trotsky behaved in a manner hostile to the Party*.

---

* Interpolations in square brackets (within passages quoted by Lenin) have been introduced by Lenin, unless otherwise indicated. —*Ed.*

That is what emerges from the question, so opportunely raised by Trotsky, as to who is "authorised to speak in the name of the Party as a whole".

Nor is that all. Inasmuch as (and so long as) the legalist liquidator-independents obstruct the Central Committee in Russia, and inasmuch as (and so long as) the *Golos* group obstruct the Central Committee abroad, the *sole* body authorised "to speak in the name of the Party as a whole" is the *Central Organ*.

Therefore, we declare, *in the name of the Party as a whole*, that Trotsky is pursuing an anti-Party policy; that, by failing to make the least mention of the Central Committee in his resolution (as if he had already come to an understanding with *Golos* that the work of the Central Committee would be sabotaged), and by announcing in the name of *one group abroad* the *"organisation of a fund* for the purpose of convening a conference of the R.S.D.L.P.", he is *contravening* Party *legality* and is embarking on the path of *adventurism* and a *split*. If the efforts of the liquidators to sabotage the work of the Central Committee meet with success, we, as the sole body authorised to speak in the name of the Party as a whole, will immediately declare that we take no part *whatever* in Trotsky's "fund" or in his venture, and that we shall recognise as a *general Party* conference only one convened *by the Central Organ*, not one convened by Trotsky's circle.*

But so long as events have not brought about the final wrecking of the Central Committee, there is still hope for a way out that is entirely *legal* from the Party point of view.

While calling upon Party members to fight resolutely for this solution based on Party legality, we shall try to investigate "the fundamental principles" of the differences which the *Golos* group and Trotsky are in a hurry to carry to the point of a split—the former, by obstructing the work of the Central Committee, and the latter, by ignoring it and "organising a fund" for the purpose of convening a

---

* That a general Party conference, one convened by the Central Committee of the Party, is really *needed* and should be called *as soon as possible*—of that there can be no question.

"conference of the R.S.D.L.P." (no joke!) by Trotsky's circle.

Trotsky writes in his resolution that at present "there is no basis for the struggle on principle" being waged by the "Leninists and Plekhanovites" (in thus substituting *personalities* for the *trends* of Bolshevism and pro-Party Menshevism, Trotsky aims at disparagement, but succeeds only in expressing his own lack of understanding).

It is to investigate these fundamental principles that the Central Organ calls upon Social-Democrats throughout Russia—examine this very interesting question while the "uninteresting" struggle over the convocation of the plenary meeting is still going on.

We quote in full the reasons given by Trotsky for his statement that the struggle of the Central Organ is not justified by any basic difference of principle.

"The conviction has taken firm root among *all* [Trotsky's italics] Party trends, that it is necessary to restore the illegal organisation, to combine legal with illegal work, and to pursue consistent Social-Democratic tactics. These fundamental directives were *unanimously* adopted by the last Plenary Meeting.

"The difficulty now, a year after the Meeting, is not the proclamation of these truths, but *their application in practice*. The way to achieve this is by harmonious work carried on jointly by all sections of the Party—the '*Golos*', 'Plekhanov', 'Leninist', and '*Vperyod*' groups, and the non-factionalists. The Party has already spiritually outgrown the period of its infancy, and it is time that all its members felt and acted as *revolutionary Social-Democrats*, as patriots of their Party and not as members of factions. This co-operation must take place within the framework of the Party as a whole, not around factional bodies."

That is an example of how fine words are worn into shreds by phrase-mongering intended to disguise a monstrous untruth, a monstrous deception both of those who revel in phrase-mongering and of the whole Party.

It is a plain and crying *untruth* that *all* Party trends are convinced of the need to revive the illegal organisation. Each issue of *Golos* shows that its writers regard Mr. Potresov's group as a *Party trend*, and that not only do they "regard" it as such but that they *systematically* take part in its "work". Is it not ridiculous, is it not disgraceful today, a year after the Plenary Meeting, to play at hide and seek, to deceive oneself and deceive the workers, to indulge in verbal tricks, when it is a question, not of empty phrases, but of *"application in practice"*?

Yes or no? Does Trotsky regard the Potresovs who were specifically mentioned in the Central Organ, as a "Party trend" or not? This is precisely a question of the "application in practice" of the decisions of the Plenary Meeting, and *it is now a year* since it was posed by the Central Organ clearly, bluntly, and unambiguously, so that there could be no evasions!

Trotsky is trying again and again to evade the question by passing it over in silence or by phrase-mongering; for he is concerned to keep the readers and the Party *ignorant of the truth*, namely, that Mr. Potresov's group, the group of sixteen, etc., are absolutely independent of the Party, represent expressly distinct factions, are not only doing nothing to revive the illegal organisation, but are obstructing its revival, and are *not* pursuing *any* Social-Democratic tactics. Trotsky is concerned with keeping the Party ignorant of the truth, namely, that the *Golos* group represent a faction abroad, similarly separated from the Party, and that they actually render service to the liquidators in Russia.

And what about the *Vperyod* group? Trotsky knows perfectly well that ever *since* the Plenary Meeting they have been strengthening and developing their separate faction, disposing of funds independently of the Party, and maintaining a separate factional school in which they teach, not "consistent Social-Democratic tactics", but that "otzovism is a legal shade of opinion"; in which they teach otzovist views on the role of the Third Duma, views expressed in the factional platform of *Vperyod*.

Trotsky maintains silence on this undeniable truth, because the truth is detrimental to the *real* aims of his policy. The real aims, however, are becoming clearer and more obvious even to the least far-sighted Party members. They are: *an anti-Party bloc of the Potresovs with the* Vperyod *group*—a bloc which Trotsky supports and is organising. The adoption of Trotsky's resolutions (like the "Vienna" one) by the *Golos* group, *Pravda*'s flirtation with the *Vperyod* group, *Pravda*'s allegations that only members of the *Vperyod* group and Trotsky's group are active in the localities in Russia, the publicity given by *Pravda* to the *Vperyod* factional school, Trotsky's direct assistance to this school, these are all facts which cannot long remain concealed. Murder will out.

The substance of Trotsky's policy is "harmonious work" carried on by *Pravda* together with the factions of the Potresovs and *Vperyod*. The various roles in this bloc have been clearly cast: Mr. Potresov and Co. are continuing their legalistic work, independently of the Party, work of destroying the Social-Democratic Party; the *Golos* group represent the foreign branch of this faction; and Trotsky has assumed the role of attorney, assuring the naïve public that "consistent Social-Democratic tactics" has taken "firm root among *all* Party trends". The *Vperyod* group also enjoy the services of this attorney, who pleads their right to maintain a factional school and resorts to hypocritical and formal phrases in order to gloss over their policy. Naturally, this bloc will support Trotsky's "fund" and the anti-Party conference which he is convening, for here the Potresovs and the *Vperyod* group are getting what they want, namely, freedom for their factions, blessings of the conference for those factions, a cover for their activity, and an attorney to defend that activity before the workers.

Therefore, it is from the standpoint of "fundamental principles" that we must regard this bloc as *adventurism* in the most literal meaning of the term. Trotsky *does not dare* to say that he sees in Potresov and in the otzovists real Marxists, real champions of loyalty to the principles of Social-Democracy. The essence of the position of an adventurer is that he must forever resort to evasions. For it is obvious and known to everyone that the Potresovs and the otzovists *all* have their *own* line (an anti-Social-Democratic line) and that they are *pursuing* it, while the diplomats of *Golos* and *Vperyod* only serve as a screen for them.

The most profound reason why this bloc is *doomed* to failure—no matter how great its success among the philistines and no matter how large the "funds" Trotsky may succeed in collecting with the assistance of *Vperyod* and Potresov's "sources"—is that it is an *unprincipled* bloc. The theory of Marxism, "*the fundamental principles*" of our entire world outlook and of our entire Party programme and tactics, is now in the forefront of all Party life not by mere chance, but because it is inevitable. It was no mere chance that since the failure of the revolution, *all* classes of society, the widest sections of the popular *masses*, have displayed a fresh interest in the very fundamentals of the world outlook, including the questions of religion and philosophy, and the *principles* of our Marxist doctrine *as a whole*; that was inevitable. It is no mere chance that the masses, whom the revolution drew into the sharp struggle over questions of tactics, have subsequently, in the period characterised by the absence of open struggle, shown a desire for *general theoretical* knowledge; that was inevitable. We must again explain *the fundamentals of Marxism* to these masses; the defence of Marxist theory is again on the order of the day. When Trotsky declares that the rapprochement between the pro-Party Mensheviks and the Bolsheviks is "devoid of political content" and "unstable", he is thereby merely revealing the depths of his own ignorance, he is thereby demonstrating his own complete emptiness. For it is precisely the fundamental principles of Marxism that have triumphed as a result of the struggle waged by the Bolsheviks against the non-Social-Democratic ideas of *Vperyod*, and as a result of the struggle waged by the pro-Party Mensheviks against the Potresovs and *Golos*. It was precisely this rapprochement on the question of *the fundamental principles* of Marxism that constituted *the real basis* for really harmonious work between the pro-Party Mensheviks and the Bolsheviks during the whole year following the Plenary Meeting. This is a fact—not words, nor promises, nor "well-meaning resolutions". And no matter what differences divided the Mensheviks and the Bolsheviks in the past, and will divide them in future (only adventurers are capable of attracting the crowd with *promises* that the differences would be set aside, or that they would be "liquidated" by this or that resolution)—this fact cannot be expunged from history. Only the internal development of the principal factions *themselves*, only *their own* ideological evolution, can provide the guarantee that the factions will really be abolished as a result of their drawing closer together, as a result of their being tested in joint work. This began after the Plenary Meeting. We have *so far not* seen harmonious work between Potresov and the *Vperyod* group and Trotsky; all

2*

we have seen is group diplomacy, juggling with words, solidarity in evasions. But the Party has seen the pro-Party Mensheviks and the Bolsheviks work in harmony for a whole year, and anyone who is capable of valuing *Marxism*, anyone who holds dear the "fundamental principles" of Social-Democracy, will not doubt for a moment that nine-tenths of the workers belonging to *both* groups will be fully in favour of *this* rapprochement.

It is precisely from the standpoint of "fundamental principles" that Trotsky's bloc with Potresov and the *Vperyod* group is adventurism. And it is equally so from the standpoint of the *Party's political* tasks. These tasks were indeed pointed out by the Plenary Meeting *unanimously*, but that does not mean that they can be reduced to that banal phrase—combining legal with illegal work (for the Cadets[22] also "combine" the legal *Rech*[23] with the illegal Central Committee of their party)—which Trotsky deliberately uses in order to please the Potresovs and the *Vperyod* group, who do not object to hollow phrases and platitudes.

"The historical circumstances in which the Social-Democratic movement finds itself in the period of bourgeois counter-revolution," the resolution of the Plenary Meeting states, "inevitably beget—as a manifestation of bourgeois influence upon the proletariat—on the one hand, the repudiation of the illegal Social-Democratic Party, the belittling of its role and importance, attempts to curtail the programmatical and tactical tasks and slogans of revolutionary Social-Democracy, etc.; and, on the other hand, repudiation of Social-Democratic work in the Duma and of the utilisation of opportunities for legal work, failure to appreciate the importance of the one and the other, inability to adapt revolutionary Social-Democratic tactics to the peculiar historical conditions of the present moment, etc."

After *a year's experience*, no one can evade a direct answer to the question as to the *real* meaning of these points. Nor must it be forgotten that at the Meeting *all* the representatives of the non-Russian nationalities (joined at the time by Trotsky, who is in the habit of joining *any* group that happens to be in the majority at the moment) declared in a written statement that *"in point of fact* it would be desirable to describe the trend mentioned in the resolution as liquidationism, against which it is essential to fight".

The experience of the year since the Plenary Meeting has shown in practice that it is precisely Potresov groups and the *Vperyod* faction that *are the embodiment* of this bourgeois influence upon the proletariat. The *evasion* of this obvious fact is what we call adventurism, for so far nobody has dared to say openly that the line of Potresov and his friends is *not* liquidationism, or that recognition of otzovism as "a legal shade of opinion" *conforms* to the line of the Party. The year that followed the Meeting has not been wasted on us. We have enriched our experience. We have seen the *practical* manifestation of the tendencies noted at the time. We have seen *factions* arise that embody those tendencies. And *words* about the "harmonious work" of these *anti-Party* factions in an allegedly "Party" spirit can no longer deceive any large sections of the workers.

Thirdly and lastly, Trotsky's policy is adventurism in the *organisational* sense; for, as we have already pointed out, it violates Party legality; by organising a conference in the name of one group abroad (or of a bloc of *two* anti-Party factions—the *Golos* and *Vperyod* factions), it is directly making for a split. Since we are authorised to speak in the name of the whole Party, it is our duty to uphold Party legality to the end. But we by no means want the Party membership to see only the *form* of "legality" and to overlook the *essence* of the matter. On the contrary, we draw the *main* attention of Social-Democrats to the *essence* of the matter, which consists in the *bloc* formed by the *Golos* and *Vperyod* groups—a bloc which stands for full freedom for Potresov and his friends to engage in liquidationist activity and for the otzovists to destroy the Party.

We call upon all Social-Democrats to fight resolutely for Party legality, to fight the anti-Party bloc, for the sake of the fundamental principles of Marxism, and in order to purge Social-Democracy of the taint of liberalism and anarchism.

P. S. The publication of the above article in a special edition (decided on by the vote of a majority of the Editorial Board—two representatives of the Bolshevik trend and one representative of the Polish organisation) has led to a protest (published as a separate leaflet) on the part of the two other members of the Editorial Board who belong to the *Golos* trend. The authors of the leaflet do not deal with the contents of the article, *The State of Affairs in the Party*, on their merits, but accuse the majority of the Editorial Board (1) of violating their formal rights as co-editors, and (2) of committing an act of "police informing". Since the dispute is not conducted on the plane of principles and tactics but along the lines of an organisational squabble and personal attacks, we consider that the most proper procedure is to refer it entirely to the Central Committee. We believe that, even before the Central Committee comes to a decision on this question, all *Party* comrades will be able to form a proper opinion of the "polemical" methods of the two members of the Editorial Board—Martov and Dan.

Written not later than
December 15 (28), 1910

Published on December 23 or 24, 1910
(January 5 or 6, 1911)
as a reprint from the supplement to
Sotsial-Demokrat, No. 19-20

Published according to
the text of the reprint
verified with the text
in the supplement
to *Sotsial-Demokrat*,
No. 19-20

CERTAIN FEATURES
OF THE HISTORICAL DEVELOPMENT OF MARXISM[24]

Our doctrine—said Engels, referring to himself and his famous friend—is not a dogma, but a guide to action. This classical statement stresses with remarkable force and expressiveness that aspect of Marxism which is very often lost sight of. And by losing sight of it, we turn Marxism into something one-sided, distorted and lifeless; we deprive it of its life blood; we undermine its basic theoretical foundations—dialectics, the doctrine of historical development, all-embracing and full of contradictions; we undermine its connection with the definite practical tasks of the epoch, which may change with every new turn of history.

Indeed, in our time, among those interested in the fate of Marxism in Russia, we very frequently meet with people who lose sight of just this aspect of Marxism. Yet, it must be clear to everybody that in recent years Russia has undergone changes so abrupt as to alter the situation with unusual rapidity and unusual force—the social and political situation, which in a most direct and immediate manner determines the conditions for action, and, hence, its aims. I am not referring, of course, to general and fundamental aims, which do not change with turns of history if the fundamental relation between classes remains unchanged. It is perfectly obvious that this general trend of economic (and not only economic) evolution in Russia, like the fundamental relation between the various classes of Russian society, has not changed during, say, the last six years.

But the aims of immediate and direct action changed very sharply during this period, just as the actual social

and political situation changed, and *consequently*, since
Marxism is a living doctrine, *various* aspects of it *were bound*
to become prominent.

In order to make this idea clear, let us cast a glance at
the change in the actual social and political situation over
the past six years. We immediately differentiate two three-
year periods: one ending roughly with the summer of 1907,
and the other with the summer of 1910. The first three-year
period, regarded from the purely theoretical standpoint,
is distinguished by rapid changes in the fundamental features of the state system in Russia; the course of these
changes, moreover, was very uneven and the oscillations in
both directions were of considerable amplitude. The social and
economic basis of these changes in the "superstructure" was
the action of *all* classes of Russian society in *the most diverse* fields (activity inside and outside the Duma, the press,
unions, meetings, and so forth), action so open and impressive and on a mass scale such as is rarely to be observed in
history.

The second three-year period, on the contrary, is distinguished—we repeat that we confine ourselves to the purely
theoretical "sociological" standpoint—by an evolution so
slow that it almost amounted to stagnation. There were no
changes of any importance to be observed in the state system.
There were hardly any open and diversified actions by the
classes in the majority of the "arenas" in which these actions
had developed in the preceding period.

The similarity between the two periods is that Russia
underwent capitalist evolution in both of them. The contradiction between this economic evolution and the existence
of a number of feudal and medieval institutions still remained and was not stifled, but rather aggravated, by the
fact that certain institutions assumed a partially bourgeois
character.

The difference between the two periods is that in the first
the question of exactly what form the above-mentioned
rapid and uneven changes would take was the dominant, his-
tory-making issue. The content of these changes was bound
to be bourgeois owing to the capitalist character of Russia's
evolution; but there are different kinds of bourgeoisie. The
middle and big bourgeoisie, which professes a more or less

moderate liberalism, was, owing to its very class position, afraid of abrupt changes and strove for the retention of large remnants of the old institutions both in the agrarian system and in the political "superstructure". The rural petty bourgeoisie, interwoven as it is with the peasants who live "solely by the labour of their hands", was bound to strive for bourgeois reforms of a *different* kind, reforms that would leave far less room for medieval survivals. The wage-workers, inasmuch as they consciously realised what was going on around them, were bound to work out for themselves a definite attitude towards this clash of two distinct tendencies. Both tendencies remained within the framework of the bourgeois system, determining entirely different forms of that system, entirely different rates of its development, different degrees of its progressive influence.

Thus, the first period necessarily brought to the fore— and not by chance—those problems of Marxism that are usually referred to as problems of tactics. Nothing is more erroneous than the opinion that the disputes and differences over these questions were disputes among "intellectuals", "a struggle for influence over the immature proletariat", an expression of the "adaptation of the intelligentsia to the proletariat", as *Vekhi* followers of various hues think. On the contrary, it was precisely because this class had reached maturity that it could not remain indifferent to the clash of the two different tendencies in Russia's bourgeois development, and the ideologists of this class could not avoid providing theoretical formulations corresponding (directly or indirectly, in direct or reverse reflection) to these different tendencies.

In the second period the clash between the different tendencies of bourgeois development in Russia was *not* on the order of the day, because *both* these tendencies had been crushed by the "diehards", forced back, driven inwards and, for the time being, stifled. The medieval diehards[25] not only occupied the foreground but also inspired the broadest sections of bourgeois society with the sentiments propagated by *Vekhi*, with a spirit of dejection and recantation. It was not the collision between two methods of reforming the old order that appeared on the surface, but a loss of faith in reforms of any kind, a spirit of "meekness" and "repentance", an enthusiasm for anti-social doctrines, a vogue of mysticism, and so on.

This astonishingly abrupt change was neither accidental nor the result of "external" pressure alone. The preceding period had so profoundly stirred up sections of the population who for generations and centuries had stood aloof from, and had been strangers to, political issues that it was natural and inevitable that there should emerge "a revaluation of all values", a new study of fundamental problems, a new interest in theory, in elementals, in the ABC of politics. The millions who were suddenly awakened from their long sleep and confronted with extremely important problems could not long remain on this level. They could not continue without a respite, without a return to elementary questions, without a new training which would help them "digest" lessons of unparalleled richness and make it possible for incomparably wider masses again to march forward, but now far more firmly, more consciously, more confidently and more steadfastly.

The dialectics of historical development was such that in the first period it was the attainment of immediate reforms in every sphere of the country's life that was on the order of the day. In the second period it was the critical study of experience, its assimilation by wider sections, its penetration, so to speak, into the subsoil, into the backward ranks of the various classes.

It is precisely because Marxism is not a lifeless dogma, not a completed, ready-made, immutable doctrine, but a living guide to action, that it was bound to reflect the astonishingly abrupt change in the conditions of social life. That change was reflected in profound disintegration and disunity, in every manner of vacillation, in short, in a very serious *internal* crisis of Marxism. Resolute resistance to this disintegration, a resolute and persistent struggle to uphold the *fundamentals* of Marxism, was again placed on the order of the day. In the preceding period, extremely wide sections of the classes that cannot avoid Marxism in formulating their aims had assimilated that doctrine in an extremely one-sided and mutilated fashion. They had learnt by rote certain "slogans", certain answers to tactical questions, *without having understood* the Marxist criteria for these answers. The "revaluation of all values" in the various spheres of social life led to a "revision" of the most abstract and general philosophical fundamentals of Marxism. The influence of bourgeois philosophy in its diverse idealist shades found expression in the Machist epidemic that broke out among the Marxists. The repetition of "slogans" learnt by rote but not understood and not thought out led to the widespread prevalence of empty phrase-mongering. The practical expression of this were such absolutely un-Marxist, petty-bourgeois trends as frank or shamefaced "otzovism", or the recognition of otzovism as a "legal shade" of Marxism.

On the other hand, the spirit of the magazine *Vekhi*, the spirit of renunciation which had taken possession of very wide sections of the bourgeoisie, also permeated the trend wishing to confine Marxist theory and practice to "moderate and careful" channels. All that remained of Marxism here was the phraseology used to clothe arguments about "hierarchy", "hegemony" and so forth, that were thoroughly permeated with the spirit of liberalism.

The purpose of this article is not to examine these arguments. A mere reference to them is sufficient to illustrate what has been said above regarding the depth of the crisis through which Marxism is passing and its connection with the whole social and economic situation in the present period. The questions raised by this crisis cannot be brushed aside. Nothing can be more pernicious or unprincipled than attempts to dismiss them by phrase-mongering. Nothing is more important than to rally *all* Marxists who have realised the profundity of the crisis and the necessity of combating it, for defence of the theoretical basis of Marxism and its fundamental propositions, that are being distorted from diametrically opposite sides by the spread of bourgeois influence to the various "fellow-travellers" of Marxism.

The first three years awakened wide sections to a conscious participation in social life, sections that in many cases are now for the first time beginning to acquaint themselves with Marxism in real earnest. The bourgeois press is creating far more fallacious ideas on this score than ever before, and is spreading them more widely. Under these circumstances disintegration in the Marxist ranks is particularly dangerous. Therefore, to understand the reasons for the inevitability of this disintegration at the present time and to close their ranks for consistent struggle against this disintegration is, in the most direct and precise meaning of the term, the task of the day for Marxists.

Zvezda, No. 2, December 23, 1910
          Signed: *V. Ilyin*   Published according to
                                                                the *Zvezda* text

JUDAS TROTSKY'S BLUSH OF SHAME

At the Plenary Meeting Judas Trotsky made a big show of fighting liquidationism and otzovism. He vowed and swore that he was true to the Party. He was given a subsidy.

After the Meeting the Central Committee grew weaker, the *Vperyod* group grew stronger and acquired funds. The liquidators strengthened their position and in *Nasha Zarya*[26] spat in the face of the illegal Party, before Stolypin's very eyes.

Judas expelled the representative of the Central Committee from *Pravda* and began to write liquidationist articles in *Vorwärts*.[27] In defiance of the direct decision of the School Commission[28] appointed by the Plenary Meeting to the effect that no Party lecturer may go to the *Vperyod* factional school, Judas Trotsky did go and discussed a plan for a conference with the *Vperyod* group. This plan has now been published by the *Vperyod* group in a leaflet.

And it is this Judas who beats his breast and loudly professes his loyalty to the Party, claiming that he did not grovel before the *Vperyod* group and the liquidators.

Such is Judas Trotsky's blush of shame.

Written after January 2 (15), 1911

First published on January 21.
1932, in *Pravda*, No. 21

Published according to
the manuscript

THE CAREER OF A RUSSIAN TERRORIST

The above is the subtitle of an article on the death of Karaulov, which Mr. Rubanovich, representative of the Socialist-Revolutionary Party,[29] published in the French socialist newspaper *L'Humanité*.[30] It is, indeed, an instructive career.

After the events of March 1, 1881, Karaulov arrived in Paris and offered his services to the head of the Narodnaya Volya[31] to put the organisation on its feet again. The editor of the *Vestnik Narodnoi Voli*,[32] the future renegade Tikhomirov, gave him permission. Karaulov returned to Russia with Lopatin, Sukhomlin, and others. In 1884 he was arrested in Kiev and sentenced to four years' penal servitude, although his colleagues received death sentences or penal servitude for life.

How is this "strange [in the words of Mr. Rubanovich] clemency" to be explained? Rumour had it, Mr. Rubanovich informs us, that the President of the military court was amazed by the resemblance Karaulov bore to his son, who had died in tragic circumstances. But, Mr. Rubanovich adds, "other explanations of this strange clemency" are current. However, he does not tell us what they are.*

But there are no doubts as to Karaulov's most recent "career". In 1905 he came out so brazenly against the revolutionaries, that the voters repudiated him in the elections to the First and the Second State Dumas. "If I have to choose between two camps," Karaulov said at a meeting (according to a report in *Birzheviye Vedomosti*[33]), "one of which is made

---

* He apparently refers to the current suspicion that Karaulov "made a clean breast of it" at the investigation.

up of government troops, and the other of revolutionaries with the notorious slogan of dictatorship of the proletariat, I should not hesitate to join the former against the latter." No wonder Witte interceded on behalf of this man for the reinstatement of his rights. No wonder that Karaulov gained prominence in the Third Duma as one of the most despicable counter-revolutionary Cadets, one of those who always had some hypocritical phrase ready.

The surprising thing is that there are people who consider themselves sympathisers of democracy, and who today, on the occasion of Karaulov's death, extol him as a "democrat", a "fighter", etc.

The surprising thing is that Mr. Rubanovich, who represents the Socialist-Revolutionary Party, can write in a French socialist organ that "much will be forgiven this former Socialist-Revolutionary who went over to the camp of the moderates, because he could strike the proper chord" (the reference is to the sitting of the Duma at which the Rights called Karaulov a jail-bird, and he retorted that he was proud of the fact).

To "forgive" a renegade his career because of an effective *phrase* is fully in the spirit of the Socialist-Revolutionaries. There are renegades from all revolutionary parties in all countries, and there are always some among them who are past masters in the art of playing for effect. But it is not often that revolutionaries, representatives of "revolutionary" parties, openly declare: "Much will be forgiven" a renegade for clever repartee. For such things to happen, it is necessary that the "revolutionary" party should include an enormous proportion of *liberals with bombs*. For such things to happen, it is necessary that these liberals, now left without bombs, should feel at home in "revolutionary" parties that do not in any way concern themselves with upholding revolutionary principles, revolutionary tradition, revolutionary honour and duty.

There is yet another and more profound lesson to be drawn from "the career of a Russian terrorist". It is a lesson of the class struggle; it shows that in Russia at present only revolutionary *classes* can serve as a prop for parties which are to any real extent revolutionary. Not Karaulov alone, but the *mass* of the bourgeois intelligentsia, which until recently was democratic and even revolutionary-minded, has now *turned its back* on democracy and the revolution. There is nothing accidental in this; it is the inevitable result of the development of class-consciousness on the part of the Russian bourgeoisie which has realised *through experience* how close is the moment when the "camp" of the monarchy and the camp of the revolution will confront each other and has realised through experience *which* side it will have to choose when that moment comes.

Those who want to learn from the great lessons of the Russian revolution must realise that only the development of the class-consciousness of the proletariat, only the organisation of *this* class and the exclusion of petty-bourgeois "fellow-travellers" from its party, and the elimination of the vacillation, weakness, and lack of principle, characteristic of them, *can* again lead, and surely will lead, to new victories of the people over the monarchy of the Romanovs.

Sotsial-Demokrat, No. 19-20,
January 13 (26), 1911

Published according to
the *Sotsial-Demokrat* text

LEV TOLSTOI AND HIS EPOCH

The epoch to which Lev Tolstoi belongs and which is reflected in such bold relief both in his brilliant literary works and in his teachings began after 1861 and lasted until 1905. True, Tolstoi commenced his literary career earlier and it ended later, but it was during this period, whose transitional nature gave rise to *all* the distinguishing features of Tolstoi's works and of Tolstoi-ism, that he fully matured both as an artist and as a thinker.

Through Levin, a character in *Anna Karenina*, Tolstoi very vividly expressed the nature of the turn in Russia's history that took place during this half-century.

"Talk about the harvest, hiring labourers, and so forth, which, as Levin knew, it was the custom to regard as something very low, ... now seemed to Levin to be the only important thing. 'This, perhaps, was unimportant under serfdom, or is unimportant in England. In both cases the conditions are definite; but here today, when everything has been turned upside down and is only just taking shape again, the question of how these conditions will shape is the only important question in Russia,' mused Levin." (*Collected Works*, Vol. X, p. 137.)

"Here in Russia everything has now been turned upside down and is only just taking shape", —it is difficult to imagine a more apt characterisation of the period 1861-1905. What "was turned upside down" is familiar, or at least well known, to every Russian. It was serfdom, and the whole of the "old order" that went with it. What "is just taking shape" is totally unknown, alien and incomprehensible to the broad masses of the population. Tolstoi conceived this bourgeois order which was "only just taking shape" vaguely, in the form of a bogey—England. Truly, a bogey, because Tolstoi rejects, on principle, so to speak, any attempt to investigate the features of the social system in this "England", the connection between this system and the domination of capital, the role played by money, the rise and development of exchange. Like the Narodniks,[34] he refuses to see, he shuts his eyes to, and dismisses the thought that what is "taking shape" in Russia is none other than the bourgeois system.

It is true that, if not the "only important" question, then certainly one of the most important from the standpoint of the immediate tasks of all social and political activities in Russia in the period of 1861-1905 (and in our times, too), was that of "what shape" this system would take, this bourgeois system that had assumed extremely varied forms in "England", Germany, America, France, and so forth. But such a definite, concretely historical presentation of the question was something absolutely foreign to Tolstoi. He reasons in the abstract, he recognises only the standpoint of the "eternal" principles of morality, the eternal truths of religion, failing to realise that this standpoint is merely the ideological reflection of the old ("turned upside down") order, the feudal order, the way of the life of the Oriental peoples.

In *Lucerne* (written in 1857), Tolstoi declares that to regard "civilisation" as a boon is an "imaginary concept" which "destroys in human nature the instinctive, most blissful primitive need for good". "We have only one infallible guide," exclaims Tolstoi, "the Universal Spirit that permeates us." (*Collected Works*, II, p. 125.)

In *The Slavery of Our Times* (written in 1900), Tolstoi, repeating still more zealously these appeals to the Universal Spirit, declares that political economy is a "pseudo science" because it takes as the "pattern" "little England, where conditions are most exceptional", instead of taking as a pattern "the conditions of men in the whole world throughout the whole of history". What this "whole world" is like is revealed to us in the article "Progress and the Definition of Education" (1862). Tolstoi counters the opinion of the "historians" that progress is "a general law for mankind" by referring to "the whole of what is known as the Orient" (IV, 162). "There is no general law of human progress," says Tolstoi, "and this is proved by the quiescence of the Oriental peoples."

Tolstoi-ism, in its real historical content, is an ideology of an Oriental, an Asiatic order. Hence the asceticism, the non-resistance to evil, the profound notes of pessimism, the conviction that "everything is nothing, everything is a material nothing" ("The Meaning of Life", p. 52), and faith in the "Spirit", in "the beginning of everything", and that man, in his relation to this beginning, is merely a "labourer ... allotted the task of saving his own soul", etc. Tolstoi is true to this ideology in his *Kreutzer Sonata* too when he says: "the emancipation of woman lies not in colleges and not in parliaments, but in the bedroom", and in the article written in 1862, in which he says that universities train only "irritable, debilitated liberals" for whom "the people have no use at all", who are "uselessly torn from their former environment", "find no place in life", and so forth (IV, 136-37).

Pessimism, non-resistance, appeals to the "Spirit" constitute an ideology inevitable in an epoch when the whole of the old order "has been turned upside down", and when the masses, who have been brought up under this old order, who imbibed with their mother's milk the principles, the habits, the traditions and beliefs of this order, do not and cannot see *what kind* of a new order is "taking shape", *what* social forces are "shaping" it and how, what social forces are *capable* of bringing release from the incalculable and exceptionally acute distress that is characteristic of epochs of "upheaval".

The period of 1862-1904 was just such a period of upheaval in Russia, a period in which, before everyone's eyes the old order collapsed, never to be restored, in which the new system was only just taking shape; the social forces shaping the new system first manifested themselves on a broad, nation-wide scale, in mass public action in the most varied fields only in 1905. And the 1905 events in Russia were followed by analogous events in a number of countries in that very "Orient" to the "quiescence" of which Tolstoi referred in 1862. The year 1905 marked the beginning of the end of "Oriental" quiescence. Precisely for this reason that year marked the historical end of Tolstoi-ism, the end of an epoch that could give rise to Tolstoi's teachings and in which they were inevitable, not as something individual, not as a caprice or a fad, but as the ideology of the conditions of life under which millions and millions actually found themselves for a certain period of time.

Tolstoi's doctrine is certainly utopian and in content is reactionary in the most precise and most profound sense of the word. But that certainly does not mean that the doctrine was not socialistic or that it did not contain critical elements capable of providing valuable material for the enlightenment of the advanced classes.

There are various kinds of socialism. In all countries where the capitalist mode of production prevails there is the socialism which expresses the ideology of the class that is going to take the place of the bourgeoisie; and there is the socialism that expresses the ideology of the classes that are going to be replaced by the bourgeoisie. Feudal socialism, for example, is socialism of the latter type, and the nature of *this* socialism was appraised long ago, over sixty years ago, by Marx, simultaneously with his appraisal of other types of socialism.[35]

Furthermore, critical elements are inherent in Tolstoi's utopian doctrine, just as they are inherent in many utopian systems. But we must not forget Marx's profound observation to the effect that the value of critical elements in utopian socialism "bears an inverse relation to historical development". The more the activities of the social forces which are "shaping" the new Russia and bringing release from present-day social evils develop and assume a definite character, the more rapidly is critical-utopian socialism "losing all practical value and all theoretical justification".

A quarter of a century ago, the critical elements in Tolstoi's doctrine might at times have been of practical value for some sections of the population *in spite of* its reactionary and utopian features. This could not have been the case during, say, the last decade, because historical development had made considerable progress between the eighties and the end of the last century. In our days, since the series of events mentioned above has put an end to "Oriental" quiescence, in our days, when the consciously reactionary ideas of *Vekhi* (reactionary in the narrow-class, selfishly-class sense) have become so enormously widespread among the liberal bourgeoisie and when these ideas have infected even a section of

those who were almost Marxists and have created a liquidationist trend—in our days, the most direct and most profound harm is caused by every attempt to idealise Tolstoi's
doctrine, to justify or to mitigate his "non-resistance", his
appeals to the "Spirit", his exhortations for "moral self-
perfection", his doctrine of "conscience" and universal
"love", his preaching of asceticism and quietism, and so
forth.

Zvezda, No. 6, January 22, 1911   Published according to
          Signed: *V. Ilyin*   the *Zvezda* text

MARXISM AND *NASHA ZARYA*[36]

In a review of the press appearing in *Zvezda*, No. 4, it was correctly stated that at the present moment all Marxist circles are interested in the question of liquidationism and in assessing the problem of the hegemony of the proletariat; and that if the polemics over this important question are to bear fruit, they must deal with principles, they must not be the *"ad hominem* and malicious polemics carried on by *Nasha Zarya"*.

I fully share this opinion and shall, therefore, pass over in complete silence the tricks resorted to by that magazine to imply that one can understand only *whom* the controversy is about, but not *what* it is about (*Nasha Zarya*, No. 11-12, p. 47). I shall take *Nasha Zarya* itself *for a year*—just up to its first anniversary and try to examine *what* it is about and what the magazine has to say on this score.

The first issue of *Nasha Zarya* appeared in January 1910. In the second issue, which appeared in February, Mr. Potresov already declared that the controversy between the Machians and the Marxists, and the question of liquidationism were included among the *"trivialities"*. "I ask the reader," wrote Mr. Potresov, "whether it is possible that there can exist, in this year of 1909, as something that is actually real and not a figment of a diseased imagination, a liquidationist tendency, a tendency to liquidate what is already beyond liquidation and actually no longer exists as an organised whole" (p. 61).

By this unsuccessful attempt to evade the issue, Mr. Potresov supplied the best corroboration, one startling in its Herostratean boldness, of the view which he intended to refute. In January and February 1910, Mr. Potresov must have known that his opponents would not agree with his appraisal of the actual state of affairs. Consequently, it could not be dismissed as something "which no longer exists" since the non-existent cannot be appraised. The question is not whether in actual practice one-tenth, or one-twentieth, or one-hundredth, or any other fraction equals nought, it is *whether there exists a trend* which regards that fraction as superfluous. The question is whether there is a difference in principle as to the significance of the fraction, what attitude should be taken toward it, should it be increased, etc. By replying to *this* question that there is "nothing", "nought", and that "nought is but nought", Mr. Potresov fully expressed the liquidationist trend whose existence he denies. His sally was remarkable only for its particular "malice" (as it was aptly put in the press review in *Zvezda*, No. 4), for its lack of straightforwardness and journalistic clarity. But it is precisely because it is not a matter of personalities, but of a trend, that Moscow rushed to the assistance of St. Petersburg. The Moscow *Vozrozhdeniye*,[37] No. 5, of March 30, 1910, quoted Mr. Potresov approvingly and added on its own behalf: "There is nothing to liquidate and for ourselves we may add, the dream of resuscitating that hierarchy, in its old", etc., "shape is nothing but a harmful, reactionary utopia" (p. 51).

It is quite obvious that it is not a question of the old *shape*, but of the old *substance*. It is quite obvious also that the question of "liquidating" is inseparably connected with the question of "resuscitating". *Vozrozhdeniye* went just one little step farther than Mr. Potresov; it expressed *the same* idea a little more clearly, more straightforwardly and more honestly. It dealt with trends and not with personalities. Persons may be evasive rather than straightforward, but trends are certain to reveal themselves in the most varied circumstances, shapes and forms.

Take, for instance, Mr. Bazarov, who was a Bolshevik once and perhaps still considers himself one—all kinds of strange things happen in our days. In the April issue of *Nasha Zarya* he refuted Mr. Potresov, and did this so successfully, so fortunately (for Potresov) that he declared literally that "the notorious question of hegemony" is "the biggest and yet most trivial misunderstanding" (p. 87). Note:

Mr. Bazarov refers to that question as "notorious", i.e., one that had been raised before, that was already known in April 1910! We note this fact, it is very important. We note that Mr. Bazarov's statement that "there will be no question of hegemony" (p. 88) if among the petty bourgeoisie in town and countryside there is "a sufficiently radical sentiment against political privileges", etc., and if it is "permeated with a strongly nationalistic spirit", actually amounts to a complete failure to understand the idea of hegemony and to a renunciation of this idea. It is precisely the concern of the leader to fight "nationalism" and to drive it out of those "sentiments" of which Bazarov speaks. The success of this work cannot be measured by immediate, direct results achieved today. There are times when the results of the resistance to nationalism, of resistance to the spirit of decay, and of resistance to liquidationism—which, incidentally, is as much a manifestation of bourgeois influence on the proletariat as is the nationalism which at times affects a section of the workers—there are times when these results begin to tell only after years, perhaps even after very many years. It happens that a spark merely smoulders for many years, a spark which the petty bourgeoisie regard and proclaim as non-existent, liquidated, extinguished, etc., but which actually lives and feeds the spirit of resistance to despondency and renunciation, and manifests itself after a protracted period of time. Everywhere and always, opportunism clutches at the minute, at the moment, at today, for it is unable to appreciate the connection between "yesterday" and "tomorrow". Marxism, on the other hand, *demands* a clear awareness of this connection, an awareness that expresses itself not in words alone but in deeds. That is why Marxism cannot be reconciled with the liquidationist trend in general, and particularly with the denial of hegemony.

St. Petersburg is followed by Moscow. The Menshevik, Mr. Potresov, is followed by the former Bolshevik, Mr. Bazarov. Bazarov is followed by Mr. V. Levitsky, who is a more straightforward and honest opponent than Mr. Potresov. In the July issue of *Nasha Zarya*, Mr. V. Levitsky writes: "Whereas the previous [form of organisation of the class-conscious workers] was the leadership in the national struggle for political freedom, the coming one will be the *class* [Mr. Levitsky's emphasis] party of the masses who have embarked upon their historic movement" (p. 103).

This one sentence represents a remarkably apt and concentrated expression of the *spirit* of all the writings of the Levitskys, Potresovs, Bazarovs, of the whole of *Vozrozhdeniye*, the whole of *Nasha Zarya*, and the whole of *Dyelo Zhizni*.[38] The above-quoted passage from Mr. Levitsky could be supplemented, replaced, enlarged upon and illustrated by hundreds of other quotations. It is just as "classical" a phrase as Bernstein's famous: "The movement is everything, the final aim is nothing"[39]—or like Prokopovich's (in the *Credo* of 1899)[40]: the workers should confine themselves to the economic struggle, leaving the political struggle to the liberals.

Mr. Levitsky is theoretically incorrect when he *contrasts* hegemony with a class party. This contrast alone furnishes sufficient grounds for saying that the party which *Nasha Zarya* is *in actual fact* following is not based on Marxism but on liberalism. Only the theoreticians of liberalism throughout the world (recall Sombart and Brentano) conceive of a *class* labour party in the way Mr. Levitsky "conceives" of it. From the standpoint of Marxism the class, so long as it renounces the idea of hegemony or fails to appreciate it, is not a class, or not yet a class, but a *guild*, or the sum total of various guilds.

But while Mr. Levitsky is unfaithful to Marxism, he is quite faithful to *Nasha Zarya*, i.e., to the liquidationist trend. What he said about the substance of *this* trend is the honest truth. In the past (as far as the followers of this trend are concerned) there was "hegemony"; in the future there will not be, nor should there be, any. And what about the present? At present there is the *amorphous* agglomeration which represents the circle of writers and reader friends of *Nasha Zarya*, *Vozrozhdeniye* and *Dyelo Zhizni*, who are engaged, *at present*, in this year of 1911, in advocating the necessity, the inevitability, the usefulness and the logic of a *transition* from the *past* concept of the hegemony of the proletariat to the idea of a class party in the Brentano[41] sense (or, for that matter, in the Struve or Izgoyev sense)

in the *future*. The fact that amorphism is one of the
principles of liquidationism was stated by its opponents
in so many words as far back as 1908, i.e., *a year* before
Nasha Zarya came into existence. Since Mr. Mayevsky[42]
asks, in December 1910, what is liquidationism, we can
refer him to the answer given officially exactly two years ago.
In that answer he will find an exact and complete characterisation of *Nasha Zarya*, although the latter came into
existence a year after that. How was this possible? It was
possible because it was not, nor is it, a question of personalities, but of a trend, which became apparent in 1907 (see,
if you must, the concluding part of the pamphlet by Mr.
Cherevanin himself, where he deals with the events of the
spring of 1907[43]), found patent expression in 1908, was
appraised by its opponents at the end of 1908, and in 1910
founded for itself an open press organ and organs.

When you say: in the past there was hegemony, *but* in
the future there ought to be a "class party"—you thereby
glaringly show the connection between liquidationism and
the renunciation of hegemony, and confirm the fact that
this trend has broken with Marxism. Marxism maintains:
since there was "hegemony" in the past, consequently, the
sum of trades, specialities, guilds gave rise to the class;
for it is the consciousness of the idea of hegemony and its
implementation through their own activities that converts
the guilds as a whole into a class. And once they have grown
to the level of a "class", no external conditions, no burdens,
no reduction of the whole to a fraction, no rejoicing on the
part of *Vekhi*, and no pusillanimity on the part of the opportunists, can stifle this young shoot. Even if it is not
"seen" on the surface (the Potresovs do not see it, or pretend
not to see it, *because* they do not care to see it), it is alive;
it lives, preserving the "past" in the present, and carrying
it into the future. Because there was hegemony in the past,
Marxists are *in duty bound*—despite all and sundry renuncia-
tors—to uphold its idea in the present and in the future;
and this ideological task fully corresponds to the material
conditions which have created the class out of guilds and
which continue to create, extend and consolidate it, and
which lend strength to its resistance to all "manifestations
of bourgeois influence".

The magazine *Nasha Zarya*, however, in the issues published during the year, represents, in a concentrated form, that very expression of bourgeois influence on the proletariat. Liquidationism exists not only as a trend of people who profess to be the supporters of a given class. It represents one of the minor streams in that wide torrent of "regression" which has swept up several classes, is characteristic of the three years 1908-10 and, perhaps, will remain characteristic of a few more years. In the present article I had to confine myself to a definition of this minor stream on the basis of quotations from *Nasha Zarya*, Nos. 2-7. In future articles I expect to dwell on Nos. 10, 11, and 12 of that magazine, as well as to prove in greater detail that the minor stream of liquidationism is but a part of the torrent of *Vekhi* doctrines.

Written after January 22
(February 4), 1911

First published in
Sovremennaya Zhizn (Baku),
No. 3, April 22, 1911
Signed: *V. Ilyin*

Published according to
the. *Sovremennaya Zhizn* text

THOSE WHO WOULD LIQUIDATE US
RE: MR. POTRESOV AND V. BAZAROV[44]

We sometimes come across literary efforts whose only significance lies in their Herostratean nature. A most ordinary literary work, as, for instance, Eduard Bernstein's well-known *The Premises of Socialism*, assumes outstanding political significance and becomes the manifesto of a trend amongst Marxists, although it departs from Marxism all along the line. Similar outstanding significance, by reason of their Herostratean nature, undoubtedly attaches to Mr. Potresov's article on trivialities in last year's February issue of *Nasha Zarya*, and V. Bazarov's article in reply to it in the April *Nasha Zarya*. To be sure, the questions discussed in these articles are far from being so profound or of such wide scope, and have not the same international significance, as the questions raised by Bernstein (or, rather, which he put forward after the bourgeoisie had already done so), but for us Russians, in the period of 1908-9-10-?, these are questions of tremendous and cardinal importance. That is why Mr. Potresov's and V. Bazarov's articles are *not* out of date, and it is necessary, it is our duty, to deal with them.

I

Mr. Potresov, who is fond of artificial, flowery and laboured expressions, devotes his article to "the contemporary drama of our social and political trends". Actually, there is not the slightest trace of the dramatic in what he says, or can say, of the post-revolutionary evolution of liberalism, Narodism and Marxism, which he took it upon himself to discuss. But you cannot get away from the comic in Mr. Potresov's reflections.

"It is precisely liberalism as an ideological trend," writes Mr. Potresov, "that presents a picture of the greatest degeneration and the greatest helplessness. We need only consider the widening gulf between practical liberalism and theorising liberalism"—between the "empiricism" of Milyukov's *Rech* and the theories of *Vekhi*.

Tut, tut, my dear sir! The gulf is widening between what you and semi-liberals like you said and thought of the Cadets in 1905-6-7 and what you are compelled to admit, stuttering and contradicting yourself, in 1909-10. The contradiction between the "empiricism" of the practical liberals and the theories of gentlemen *à la* Struve was fully apparent even before 1905. Just recall how the *Osvobozhdeniye*[45] of those days blundered in literally every one of its attempts at "theorising". Since you are *now* beginning to put two and two together, and find that liberalism "seems" to be "broken up" (this is yet another of your verbal tricks, an empty phrase, for *Vekhi* has *not* broken with *Rech*, or vice versa; they have been, are, and will go on living in perfect harmony with each other), that it is "sterile", "suspended in mid-air", and represents but the "least stable" (*sic!*) "section of bourgeois democrats", who are "not bad as voters", etc.—your cries about the "drama" of liberalism merely signify the tragicomedy of the collapse of your illusions. It is not at the present time, not during the three years 1908-10, but in the preceding three-year period that the liberals "seemed" to be the least stable section of bourgeois democrats. The "least stable" are those quasi-socialists who serve mustard to the public after supper. The distinguishing feature of the previous three-year period (insofar as the question examined by Mr. Potresov is concerned) was liberalism "suspended in mid-air", "sterile", "voting", etc., liberalism. *At that time* it was the political duty of the day to recognise the nature of liberalism for what it was; it was the urgent duty, not only of socialists, but also of consistent democrats, to warn the masses of this. March 1906, not February 1910—that was the time when it was important to sound the warning that the liberalism of the Cadets was suspended in mid-air, that it was sterile, that the objective

conditions reduced it to nothingness, to the farce of being
"not bad as voters"; that the victories of the Cadets represented an unstable zigzag between the "serious" constitutionalism (read: sham constitutionalism) of the Shipovs or
Guchkovs and the struggle for democracy waged by those elements that were *not* suspended in mid-air and did *not* confine
themselves to the fond contemplation of ballots. Just call
to mind, my dear sir, who it was that spoke the truth about
the liberals at the proper time, in March 1906.[46]

The distinguishing feature, the peculiar characteristic
of the three-year period (1908-10) under discussion is by no
means the "sterility" of liberalism "suspended in mid-air",
etc. Quite the contrary. Nothing has changed in the class
impotence of the liberals, in their dread of democracy, and
in their political inanity; but this impotence reached its
height at a time when there were opportunities to display
strength, when conditions made it possible for the liberals
to hold full sway in at least a certain field of action. Thus,
for instance, at the time the Cadets had a majority in the
First Duma, they were in a position to use their majority
either to serve democracy or to hamper the cause of democracy, to render assistance to democracy (even if only in
such a small matter, as, let us say, the organisation of local
land committees) or to stab democracy in the back. And
that period was *characterised* by the Cadets being "suspended
in mid-air", and those who were "not bad as voters" proving
to be nothing but inventors of instructions for the subsequent Octobrist[47] Duma.

In the three-year period that followed, the Cadets, while
remaining true to themselves, were *less* "suspended in mid-
air" than before. You, Mr. Potresov, resemble that hero of
popular lore who loudly voices his wishes and opinions at
inappropriate times. The 1909 *Vekhi* group is *less* "suspended
in mid-air" than Muromtsev was in 1906, for it is of *real*
use and renders *practical* service to the class which represents
a great power in Russia's national economy, namely, the
landowners and capitalists. The *Vekhi* group helps these
worthy gentlemen collect an armoury of weapons for their
ideological and political struggle against democracy and
socialism. This is something that *cannot* be destroyed by
dissolutions of the Duma or, in general, by any political dis-

ЦѢНА 30 КОП.

МЫСЛЬ

ЕЖЕМѢСЯЧНЫЙ
ФИЛОСОФСКІЙ и ОБЩЕСТВЕННО-ЭКОНОМИЧЕСКІЙ ЖУРНАЛЪ.

№ 2.
ЯНВАРЬ.
1911.

СОДЕРЖАНІЕ:

Г. ПЛЕХАНОВЪ. Смѣшеніе представленій (окончаніе).—
Н. Р—КОВЪ. Современная русская аграрная политика
и виды на будущее (оконч.).—В. ИЛЬИНЪ. О статистикѣ
стачекъ въ Россіи (гл. II).—Г. Ц—ЧЪ. Къ вопросу объ
иностранныхъ капиталахъ въ Россіи.—В. ИЛЬИНЪ.
Наши упразднители (о т. Потресовѣ и В. Базаровѣ).
НА ТЕМЫ ДНЯ:—ГР. Законъ о лишеніи отдыха торгово-
промышленныхъ служащихъ.— ПОЛЕМИЧЕСКІЯ ЗА-
МѢТКИ: Р.—1) «Вѣхи» о Толстомъ. 2) Благодушный
либералъ. 3) Совѣтъ г. Клейнберту.—ИНОСТРАННОЕ
ОБОЗРѢНІЕ: Х. Л. РАППОПОРТЪ. Дѣйствительность
и мечты. П ОРЛОВСКІЙ. Литературные наброски.—
ОБЩЕСТВЕННО - ЭКОНОМИЧЕСКАЯ ЖИЗНЬ. — БИ-
БЛІОГРАФІЯ.—НЕКРОЛОГЪ: П. Зингеръ.

МОСКВА.

Cover of *Mysl*, No. 2, for January 1911, containing Chapter II
of Lenin's "Strike Statistics in Russia" and the beginning of the
article "Those Who Would Liquidate Us (Re: Mr. Potresov and
V. Bazarov)"

Reduced

turbances occurring under the existing social and economic system. As long as the class of landed proprietors and capitalists exists, their hack journalists, the Izgoyevs, Struves, Franks and Co., will also exist. As far as the "work" of the Muromtsevs and, in general, of the Cadets in the First Duma is concerned, it could be "destroyed" by the dissolution of the Duma (for, in point of fact, they did not do any work; they only indulged in words which, far from serving the people, corrupted them).

The Cadets in the Third Duma are the same party, with the same ideology, the same policy, and to a large degree even the same people, as those in the First Duma. And that is precisely why the Cadets in the Third Duma are less "suspended in mid-air" than they were in the First Duma. Don't you understand this, my dear Mr. Potresov? You were wrong in undertaking a discussion of "the contemporary drama of our social and political trends"! Let me tell you, in strict confidence, that in the future, too, and probably for quite some time to come, the political activity of the Cadets will not be "sterile"—not only because of the reactionary "fecundity" of *Vekhi*, but also because so long as there are political minnows in the ranks of democracy, there will be food for the big fish of liberalism to thrive on. So long as there is the kind of instability in the ranks of the socialists, the kind of flabbiness among the representatives of democracy so vividly exemplified by figures like Potresov, the skill of the "empiricists" of liberalism will always prove sufficient to catch these minnows. Don't worry, Cadets: you'll have plenty to feed on so long as the Potresovs exist!

II

Mr. Potresov's arguments dovetail even less when he discusses Narodism. The Cadets he calls "former democrats" and even "former liberals"; of the peasantry he says: "By entering political life, the peasantry [in Mr. Potresov's opinion, they have not yet entered political life] would usher in an entirely new chapter in history, that of peasant democracy, which would spell the end of the old, intellectual, Narodnik democracy".

So the Cadets are former democrats and the peasantry are future democrats. But who, then, are the present democrats? Was there no democratic, no mass democratic, movement in Russia in 1905-07? Was there none in 1908-10? Potresov resorts to "round-about" phrases, to phrases that evade the essence of the matter, in order to throw a veil over the present. The direct and plain recognition of what indubitably exists at present flies in the face of the whole liquidationist philosophy of the Potresovs, for it would mean the plain and direct recognition of the now indubitable historical fact that the Cadets *never* represented any more or less mass democratic movement in Russia, that they never pursued a democratic policy, whereas the peasantry, the very same "peasant millions" of whom Mr. Potresov also speaks, did and do represent this bourgeois democratic movement (with all its limitations). Mr. Potresov evades this *cardinal* question precisely in order to save the liquidationist philosophy. But he cannot save it!

In trying to ignore the past and the present of the peasant democratic movement, Mr. Potresov again misses the mark when he confidently discusses the future. Late again, my dear sir! You yourself speak of the "possible consequences of the law of November 9"[48]; hence, you yourself admit the possibility (purely abstract, of course) of its success. But as a result of this success the "*new* chapter in history" may prove to be a chapter not only in the history of *peasant* democracy, but also in the history of peasant *agrarians.*

The development of peasant farming in Russia and, consequently, of peasant land tenure and peasant politics cannot proceed along any other but capitalist lines. In its essence, the agrarian programme of the Narodniks, as formulated, for instance, in the well-known Platform of the 104[49] (in the First and Second Dumas), far from contradicting this capitalist development, implies the creation of conditions for the most widespread and most rapid capitalist development. The agrarian programme now in operation, on the other hand, implies the slowest and most narrow capitalist development, one most impeded by the survivals of serfdom. Objective historical and economic conditions have not yet provided an answer to the question—which of these programmes will, in the final analysis, determine the form bourgeois agrarian relations will assume in the new Russia.

Such are the plain facts which the liquidators find it necessary to confuse.

"In face of all the changes," writes Mr. Potresov, referring to the changes in the ranks of the intellectual, Narodnik democratic movement, "one thing has remained unchanged: so far [!] the real peasantry have not introduced any corrections of their own into intellectualist ideology with its peasant trimmings."

This is a statement of the purest *Vekhi* type and it is absolutely false. In 1905, the "real" peasant masses, the rank and file themselves, acted in the open historical arena, and introduced *quite a number* of "corrections" into the "intellectualist ideology" of the Narodniks and the Narodnik parties. Not all of these corrections have been *understood* by the Narodniks, but the peasantry *did introduce* them. In 1906 and in 1907, the very "real" peasantry created the Trudovik[50] groups and the Draft Platform of the 104, thereby introducing *a number of corrections*, some of which even the Narodniks noted. It is generally recognised, for example, that the "real" peasantry revealed their *economic* aspirations, and approved private and co-operative land tenure in place of the "commune".

The *Vekhi* people who are purging liberalism of democracy, systematically converting it into a servant of the money-bags, are properly performing their mission in history when they declare that the movement of 1905-07 was one of intellectuals, and assert that the real peasantry introduced no corrections of their own into the intellectualist ideology. The tragicomedy of liquidationism is its failure to notice that its assertions have been and are simply a rehash of the *Vekhi* ideas.

III

This transformation becomes even more obvious when Mr. Potresov proceeds to discuss Marxism. The intelligentsia, he writes, "... by its organisation of party circles ... overshadowed the proletariat". You cannot deny the fact that it is the bourgeoisie that has widely circulated this idea through

Vekhi and through the entire liberal press, and has used it
against the proletariat. In the essay in which he formulated this idea, Axelrod wrote that "history in a prankish mood"
could provide bourgeois democracy with a leader from
the Marxist school. History in a prankish mood made use of
the pit which Axelrod obligingly threatened to dig for the
Bolsheviks, and has put Axelrod himself in it!

If you turn to the objective facts of history, you will find
that *all* of them, the entire period of 1905-07, even the elections to the Second Duma (to cite as an example one of the
simplest, though not one of the most important, facts),
proved conclusively that "the organisation of party circles"
did not "overshadow" the proletariat, but *developed directly*
into the organisation of the parties and trade unions of the
proletarian *masses.*

But let us pass on to the main, or "central", point of
Mr. Potresov's Herostratean effort. He claims that Marxist
thought "is doping itself with the hashish of trivialities"—
the struggle against Machism and the struggle against liquidationism, "debating anything and everything ... other than
those things that constitute the nerve of a social and political trend like Marxism, anything but questions of economics and questions of politics". And what a host there is of
such questions! exclaims Mr. Potresov. "How is the economic
development of Russia proceeding, what realignments of
forces does this development effect under the cloak of reaction, what is going on in the countryside and in the cities,
what changes does this development introduce in the social
composition of the working class of Russia, etc., etc? Where
are the answers, or even the initial attempts at answers,
to these questions, where is the economic school of Russian
Marxism?"

The answer, or at any rate an initial attempt at an answer,
is to be found in the very "hierarchy", whose existence Mr.
Potresov maliciously and hypocritically denies. The development of the Russian state system during the past three
centuries shows that its class character has been changing
in one definite direction. The monarchy of the seventeenth
century with the Boyars' Duma did not resemble the bureaucratic-aristocratic monarchy of the eighteenth century.
The monarchy of the first half of the nineteenth century was

not the same as the monarchy of 1861-1904. In the 1908-10 period a new phase was clearly outlined, marking *one more step* in the same direction, which may be described as the direction leading towards a bourgeois monarchy. The character of the Third Duma and the present agrarian policy are closely connected with this step. The new phase, therefore, is not an accident but represents a specific stage in the capitalist evolution of the country. This new phase does not solve the old problems, nor can it do so; consequently, since *it is unable to eliminate them*, it calls for the use of new methods of approach to old solutions of old problems. That is the peculiar feature of this cheerless, gloomy, difficult period, which, however, has proved to be inevitable. The particular economic and political characteristics of this period have given rise to the distinctive features of the ideological alignments in the ranks of the Marxists. Those who recognise the new methods of approach to the old solution of old problems are finding a common ground in their present joint practical tasks, although they are still divided as to how the old solutions should have been applied or advanced at one juncture or another during the preceding period. Those who deny (or who do not understand) the new methods of approach, or that we are confronted with the old problems and are heading towards the old solution of these problems, are *in fact* deserting Marxism, are *in fact* surrendering to the liberals (as Potresov, Levitsky, and others have done) or to the idealists and the syndicalists (as V. Bazarov and others have done).

Since they have surrendered themselves to alien people and alien ideas, both Potresov and Bazarov, as well as those who share their views, inevitably lose their bearings and find themselves in a most comical and false position. Mr. Potresov beats his breast and shouts: *"Where* is the *initial attempt* at an answer, and what is that *answer?"* Martov, who knows the answer just as well, tries to assure the public that that answer recognises "the bourgeoisie in power"—a common trick whereby liberals take advantage of the temporary enforced silence of their opponents! At the same time they ask us with an offended air: "What do you mean by liquidationism?" This very trick, most worthy gentlemen, is one of the methods of liquidators (if not of renegades);

people claiming allegiance to a "whole"* take advantage of
its loss of strength to assure the public that there is no
"answer", although the answer has already been given by
"the whole".

Liquidationism, writes Mr. Potresov, is "a figment of a
diseased imagination", for you cannot liquidate "what is
already beyond liquidation and actually no longer exists as
an organised whole".

I am not in a position fully to convey to the reader my
opinion of these lines; but in order to convey an approxi-
mate idea of it, let me ask the reader: What should we call
a person whose closest associates and colleagues accept
proposals favourable to them made by the "whole" (precisely as a "whole") and who the following day declares in
the press that there is no "whole"?

But, enough of that.

The following question of principle is involved: can the view
on the necessity for the old solution of the old problems change
according to the *degree* of disintegration of the "whole"?
or even, if you like, with its disappearance? It is obvious
to everyone that it cannot. If the objective conditions, if
the fundamental economic and political features of the present epoch, demand the old solution, then the greater the
disintegration, the less there is left of the "whole", the more
one must be concerned about, and the more ardently must
the publicist speak about the need for the "whole". As we
have already pointed out, we must recognise the new methods of approach; but who is to apply them? Obviously the
"whole". Obviously, the tasks of the publicist as seen by those
who understand the importance of the period we are passing
through and its basic political features, are diametrically
opposed to the *entire* line of the Potresovs. Certainly, no
one can even seriously think of denying the connection between the "answer" which I outlined above (to the question
of the economics and politics of the present period) and anti-
liquidationism.

Let us now turn from the general principles involved
in the presentation of the question to its concrete historical
aspect. That trend in Marxism which advocates the necessity

---

* i.e., the Party.—*Tr.*

of the old solution and pursues its line accordingly has fully taken shape in the 1908-10 period. Another trend has also taken shape, one which during *all these three years* has opposed the recognition of the "old solution" and the restoration of the old fundamental forms of the whole. It would be ridiculous to deny this fact. And a third trend which has taken shape has failed during all these three years to understand the new forms of approach, the importance of work in the Third Duma, etc. Such people have recognised the old solution only in words, as one that has been learned by rote but not understood, as words repeated by force of habit but not *applied* consciously and intelligently to the changed circumstances (changed at least in the sphere of work in the Duma, but, of course, not only in that sphere).

The connection between liquidationism and the general philistine mood of "weariness" is obvious. The "weary" (particularly those weary as a result of doing nothing) are making no effort to work out for themselves an exact answer to the question of the economic and political appraisal of the current moment: they all disagree with the above appraisal, formally *accepted by all* as the appraisal given on behalf of the whole; but they all fear even to think of opposing to it *their own* exact viewpoint, for instance that of the collaborators of the liquidationist *Nasha Zarya*,[51] etc. The "weary" insist: the old no longer exists, it has lost its vitality, it is lifeless, etc., etc.; but they have not the slightest intention of racking their brains for an answer, a purely political and precisely formulated answer, to the unavoidable question (unavoidable for every honest publicist): what exactly should be substituted for the old, and whether it is necessary to restore "what is [allegedly] beyond liquidation, since it is already liquidated" (according to Potresov). For three years they have been abusing the old, reviling it—especially from such platforms as are barred to the advocates of the old—and now, falling into the arms of the Izgoyevs,* they exclaim: What nonsense, what a figment of the imagination all that talk about liquidationism is!

---

* See his article in *Russkaya Mysl*,[52] 1910, on Potresov the supporter of *Vekhi* ideas. From such embraces Potresov will *never* wash himself clean.

Of *such* "weary" people, of Mr. Potresov and Co., one *cannot* say in the well-known verses of the poet: "... No traitors they—just weary carrying their cross; the fire of anger and of sorrow, while mid-way still, they lost".[53]

"Weary" persons of this kind, who ascend the rostrum of the publicist and from it justify their "weariness" of the old, their unwillingness to work on the old, belong to the category of people who are not just "weary", but are treacherous as well.

IV

The philosophical struggle of the materialists, the Marxists, against the Machists, i.e., against the idealists, is also classed by Mr. Potresov as "triviality". Mr. Potresov is highly indignant over the "orgy" of philosophising ("Oh, my friend Arkady Nikolayevich, spare me your eloquence!"[54]) and, in this connection mentioning Plekhanov and myself as representing the materialists, he describes us as *"political figures of yesterday"*. I had a good laugh over this expression. There is so much obvious and amusing boasting in this that our hare really deserves a bit of the bear's ear.* Plekhanov and others—"political figures of yesterday"! The political figures of *today* are apparently Potresov and his "gang". Charming and frank.

Whenever Arkady Nikolayevich accidentally speaks without eccentricity or grimaces, he defeats himself superbly. Just make a little effort, Arkady Nikolayevich, and try to *think*: you deny the existence of liquidationism as a *political* trend, as a trend which distinguishes, *not* Menshevism from Bolshevism, but Potresov and Co. from Plekhanov and the Bolsheviks *jointly*. And yet, while you deny this, you at the same time describe Plekhanov and myself as "political figures of yesterday". Look how clumsy you are: Plekhanov and I *together* may be called political figures of yesterday, precisely because we think that the organisation of yesterday, as a form of yesterday's movement (yesterday's in its *principles*) is necessary today. Plekhanov and

---

* The allusion is to I. A. Krylov's fable "The Hare at the Hunt", in which the hare boasts about how "we" killed the bear.—*Tr.*

I differed sharply, and we still differ on questions of what
steps *that* organisation of yesterday, working on the basis
of *that* movement of yesterday, should have taken at one
juncture or another; but we are drawn together by the
struggle against those who *today* deny the very *principles* of
yesterday's movement (this includes also the question of
hegemony, of which more later), deny the very *foundations*
of yesterday's organisation.

Well, Arkady Nikolayevich, are you still unable to understand what is meant by liquidationism? Do you still
think that Plekhanov and I have been drawn together by
some Machiavellian plot or by a malicious desire to *substitute* a "struggle on two fronts" for the "defeat" of liquidationism?

But, to return to the "orgy of philosophising".

"We know," writes Mr. Potresov, "what a deep impression
on the consciousness of German Social-Democracy was made
at the time by Engels's struggle against Dühring, and how
theses, seemingly most abstract, were actually of vital and
concrete significance to the German working-class movement...." The most abstract theses were of vital and concrete
significance! Another bit of phrase-mongering and nothing
else! Try to explain, if you "know", what was the "vital
and concrete significance" of Engels's *thesis* that Dühring's
philosophical reflections on time and space were wrong!
The trouble with you is that, like a schoolboy, you learned
by rote, that "Engels's controversy with Dühring was of
great significance"; but you have not *thought* about its meaning, and therefore you repeat what you have learned by
rote in a wrong and utterly distorted form. It is wrong to
say that "the most abstract theses [of Engels against Düh-
ring] were actually of vital and concrete significance to the
German working-class movement". The significance of
Engels's most abstract theses was that they explained to the
ideologists of the working class what was erroneous in the
shift from materialism towards positivism and idealism.
If, instead of high-sounding, but hollow, phrases about
"a deep impression" or the "vital and concrete significance"
of "the most abstract theses", you had given such an exposition (that is, one more or less definitive from the philosophical standpoint) of Engels's views, you would have seen

at once that the reference to Engels's controversy with
Dühring goes *against* you.

"We know," Mr. Potresov continues, "what part the
struggle against subjective sociology played in the history of
the formation of Russian Marxism." ... And what about
the part played by Lavrov's and Mikhailovsky's positivist
and idealist doctrines in the errors of subjective sociology?
Every shot of yours, Arkady Nikolayevich, misses its mark.
If you cite an historical parallel, you must single out and
point out exactly what is similar in the different events;
if not, what you get will not be an historical comparison but
words cast to the winds. If we take the historical parallel
you cite, we must ask: would the "formation" of *Russian*
Marxism have been possible *without* Beltov's[55] explanation
of the principles of philosophical materialism and of their
importance in refuting Lavrov and Mikhailovsky? There
can only be one answer to this question, and that answer,
if we are to use the historical parallel in order to draw conclusions with regard to the controversy with the Machists—
goes *against* Mr. Potresov.

... "But precisely because we know all this [why, of
course! haven't we just seen what it amounts to when Mr.
Potresov writes: "We know all this"?], we want to see a living
and real connection established at last between the philosophical controversy we are dealing with, and the Marxist
social and political trend, its problems and requirements.
Meanwhile"—here follows a reference to Kautsky's letter
in which it was said that Machism is a *Privatsache* (a private
affair), that the controversy over it is a "*fata morgana*", etc.

The reference to Kautsky is typical of philistine judge-
ment. The point is not that Kautsky is "unprincipled", as
Mr. Potresov remarks sarcastically (*à la* Izgoyev), but that
Kautsky *does not know*, nor does he claim to know, the state
of affairs in regard to Russian Machism. In his letter Kautsky admits that Plekhanov is well versed in Marxism, and
expresses his own conviction that idealism cannot be reconciled
with Marxism, and that Machism is not idealism (or that
not every form of Machism is idealism). It is obvious that
Kautsky is *mistaken* on the last point, particularly as regards Russian Machism. But it is a pardonable mistake on
his part, for he has *never studied* Machism as a whole, and

his opinion was expressed in a private letter obviously written as a warning against exaggerating the differences. But a *Russian* Marxist writer, who, under such circumstances, refers to Kautsky, merely betrays a philistine laziness of mind and cowardice in the fight. In 1908, when the letter was written, Kautsky *may have hoped* that in a certain interpretation Machism could be "reconciled" with *materialism*. But to refer to Kautsky in connection with this question in Russia in 1909-10 means *to undertake the task* of reconciling the Russian Machists with the materialists. Does Mr. Potresov or anybody else really undertake this task in all seriousness?

Kautsky is not unprincipled; but Potresov and Co., who want to proclaim Machism "a private affair", are *a model of unprincipledness* among Russian Marxists today. Kautsky was quite sincere and not a bit unprincipled when, in 1908, never having read the Russian Machists, he advised *them* to seek peace with Plekhanov as a man versed in Marxism, and as a materialist; for Kautsky has always declared in favour of materialism and against idealism, and he expressed the same opinion in his letter. But Potresov and Co., who in 1909-10 hide behind Kautsky, have *not a grain* of sincerity, *not a trace* of respect for principles.

You say, Mr. Potresov, that you fail to see any living and real connection between the philosophical controversy and the Marxist trend? Well, permit me, a political figure of yesterday, most respectfully to point out to you at least the following circumstances and considerations: (1) The controversy over the question as to what is philosophical materialism and why deviations from it are erroneous, dangerous and reactionary *always* has "a real and living connection" with "the Marxist social and political trend"—otherwise the latter would not be Marxist, would not be social and political, would not be a trend. Only narrow-minded "realistic politicians" of reformism or anarchism can deny the "reality" of this connection. (2) Considering the wealth and many-sidedness of the ideological content of Marxism, there is nothing surprising in the fact that in Russia, just as in other countries, various historical periods give prominence now to one, now to another particular aspect of Marxism. In Germany before 1848, the philosophical forming of Marxism was the aspect particularly stressed; in 1848 it was the political ideas of Marxism; in the fifties and sixties it was the economic doctrine of Marxism. In Russia before the revolution, the aspect that was particularly stressed was the application of the economic doctrine of Marxism to Russian reality; during the revolution, it was Marxist politics; since the revolution it is Marxist philosophy. This does not mean that any of the aspects of Marxism may at any time be ignored; it only means that the *prevalence of interest* in one aspect or another does not depend on subjective wishes, but on the totality of historical conditions. (3) It is not by mere chance that the period of social and political reaction, the period when the rich lessons of the revolution are being "digested", is also the period when the fundamental theoretical, including the philosophical, problems are of prime importance to any *living* trend. (4) The progressive trends of Russian thought cannot fall back upon a great philosophical tradition, such as that connected with the Encyclopaedists of the eighteenth century in France, or with the epoch of classical philosophy from Kant to Hegel and Feuerbach in Germany. That is why it was necessary for the advanced class of Russia to sort out its philosophy and there is nothing strange in the fact that the belated "sorting-out" came about after this advanced class had, during the recent great events, fully matured for its independent historical role. (5) This philosophic "sorting-out" had been ripening for a long time in other countries as well, because modern physics, for instance, had posed a number of new questions which dialectical materialism had to "cope with". In this respect, "our" (to use Potresov's expression) philosophical controversy is of more than just a certain, i.e., Russian, significance. Europe provided material for a "freshening" of philosophical thought; and Russia, which was lagging behind, seized upon this material with particular "eagerness" during the period of enforced lull in 1908-10. (6) Belousov recently said of the Third Duma that it is a sanctimonious body. He grasped correctly the class characteristic of the Third Duma in this respect and justly branded the hypocrisy of the Cadets.

Not accidentally, but of *necessity*, have our reactionaries in general, and the liberal (*Vekhi*, Cadet) reactionaries in particular, "pounced on" religion. The stick and knout alone are not sufficient to serve the purpose; in any case the stick is cracked. *Vekhi* is helping the advanced bourgeoisie to find a new, ideological stick, a spiritual stick. Machism, as a species of idealism, is *objectively* a weapon in the hands of the reactionaries, a vehicle of reaction. The struggle against Machism "at the bottom" is therefore not accidental but inevitable in an historical period (1908-10) when "at the top" we see not only the "sanctimonious Duma" of the Octobrists and Purishkeviches, but also sanctimonious Cadets and a sanctimonious liberal bourgeoisie.

Mr. Potresov made the "reservation" that he was "not at present touching" upon the subject of "god-building".[56] That is precisely what distinguishes the unprincipled and philistine publicist Potresov from Kautsky. Kautsky *knew nothing either* of the god-building of the Machists *or* of the god-worshipping *Vekhi* people, and therefore he *could* afford to say that not every type of Machism is idealism. But Potresov knows all this, and by "*not touching*" upon the main thing (the main thing to persons with a *narrow* "publicist" approach) acts the hypocrite. By proclaiming the struggle against Machism "a private affair" Mr. Potresov and his like are abetting *Vekhi* in the "social and political" sense.

V

In passing from Mr. Potresov to Bazarov, we must note, to begin with, that, as regards the philosophical controversy, our answers to the former also hold good for the latter. There is only one point to be added: one can quite understand V. Bazarov's tolerant attitude to Mr. Potresov, his insistence on finding "some truth" in Potresov's arguments, for Mr. Potresov (like all the liquidators), while disavowing Machism formally and in words, yields to it, *as a matter of fact*, on the most essential point. The Machists as representatives of a trend, and as a group with a "platform" of its own, have never really dared to demand anything more than that their departure from Marxism be regarded as "a private affair"! It is therefore not surprising that Potresov and Bazarov are ogling each other. The group of liquida-

tionist writers and the group of Machist writers are, in our
period of disintegration, *indeed at one* in defending the "freedom of disintegration" from the adherents of Marxism, from
the champions of the theoretical foundations of Marxism.
And, as *even* Bazarov has proved by his article, this solidarity is *not* confined to questions of philosophy.

I say "even", for Bazarov, in particular, has always been
distinguished for his very thoughtful attitude to serious
political problems. This fact must be mentioned if we are
to appreciate the meaning of the incredible vacillations of
this man, and not merely for the purpose of stressing the
very useful past activity of a writer who is now out to earn
the laurels of Herostratus.

Bazarov, for instance, made the following statement of
a Herostratean nature: "In my opinion, the biggest and
yet most trivial misunderstanding of our times is the notorious question of the hegemony of the working class". There
seems to be some fate pursuing the Machists in our midst.
Some of them defend the "freedom of disintegration", declaring that otzovism is a legal shade of opinion; others, who
see the folly and harm of otzovism, frankly hold out their
hands to the liquidators in the sphere of politics. It is the
liquidators in *Nasha Zarya*, and in *Zhizn*, and in *The Social Movement*,[57] who are waging a direct and indirect
struggle against the idea of this hegemony. We are sorry
to state that Bazarov *has joined their camp.*

What are his arguments on the substance of the matter?
Five years ago such hegemony was a fact. "At present, for
quite obvious reasons, that hegemony has disappeared.
More—it has turned into its direct opposite." The proof:
"In our days, in order to become popular in democratic
circles of society, it has become a necessity to kick at Marxism". Example: Chukovsky.

You read these lines and you can hardly believe your
eyes. Bazarov, who claimed to be a Marxist, has turned into
a has-been, into one capable of flirting with the Potresovs.

You have no fear of *God* in you, V. A. Bazarov. Chukovsky
and other liberals, as well as a host of Trudovik democrats,
have always "kicked" at Marxism, and particularly ever
since 1906; but was not "hegemony" a fact in 1906? Get out
of your liberal-journalistic cubby-hole, consider at least

the attitude of the peasant deputies in the Third Duma to the working-class deputies. The mere juxtaposition of the unquestionable facts of their political behaviour during the past three years, even a mere comparison between their formulations of motions for next business and the Cadet formulations, to say nothing of a comparison between the political declarations made in the Duma and the conditions under which the large masses of the population have been living during this period, proves incontrovertibly that even today hegemony is a fact. The hegemony of the working class is the political influence which that class (and its representatives) exercises upon other sections of the population by helping them to purge their democracy (where there is democracy) of undemocratic admixtures, by criticising the narrowness and short-sightedness of all bourgeois democracy, by carrying on the struggle against "Cadetism" (meaning the corrupting ideological content of the speeches and policy of the liberals), etc., etc. There is nothing more characteristic of our present times than the fact that Bazarov *could* write such incredible things, and that a group of journalists who also consider themselves friends of the workers and adherents of Marxism patted him indulgently on the back for this!

"It is absolutely impossible to foretell what will be the state of affairs at the moment of the coming revival," Bazarov assures the readers of the liquidationist magazine. "If the spiritual character of urban and rural democracy is approximately the same as it was five years ago, then the hegemony of Marxism will again become a fact.... But there is absolutely nothing out of the way in the supposition that the character of democracy will undergo a substantial change. Imagine, for instance, that among the petty bourgeoisie of the Russian villages and cities a sufficiently radical sentiment exists against the political privileges of the ruling classes, that it is sufficiently united and active, but is permeated with a strongly nationalistic spirit. Since Marxists, cannot think of any compromises with nationalism or anti-Semitism, it is obvious that under such circumstances there will not be even a trace of hegemony."

In addition to being wrong, all this is monstrously absurd. If certain sections of the population combine hostility to privilege with nationalist sentiments, surely it is the duty of the leader to explain to them that such a combination hinders the abolition of privilege. Can the struggle against privilege be waged *unless* it is combined with the struggle of the petty bourgeois who suffer from nationalism, against the petty bourgeois who gain from it? Every struggle of every petty bourgeois against every kind of privilege *always* bears the imprint of petty-bourgeois narrow-mindedness and half-heartedness, and it is the business of the "leader" to combat these qualities. Bazarov argues like the Cadets, like the *Vekhi* writers. Or, more correctly, Bazarov has joined the camp of Potresov and Co., who already have been arguing this way for a long time.

What cannot be seen on the surface does not exist. What the Chukovskys and Potresovs do not see is not real. Such are the premises of Bazarov's arguments, which fly in the face of Marxism. Marxism teaches us that so long as capitalism exists the petty-bourgeois masses must inevitably suffer from undemocratic privileges (theoretically, such privileges are "not indispensable" under *pure* capitalism, but the *purification* of capitalism will continue until its death), that they must suffer from economic oppression. Therefore, so long as capitalism exists it will *always* be the duty of the "leader" to explain the source of these privileges and this oppression, to expose their class roots, to provide an example of struggle against them, expose the falsity of the liberal methods of struggle, etc., etc.

That is how Marxists think. That is how they regard the duties of the "leader" in the camp of those whose condition does not permit any reconciliation with privilege, in the camp, not only of the proletarians, but also of the semi-proletarian and petty-bourgeois masses. The Chukovskys, however, think that once that camp has suffered reverses, has been hard-pressed and driven underground, "hegemony has disappeared", and the "question of hegemony has become a most trivial misunderstanding".

When I see Bazarov, who says such disgraceful things, marching hand in hand with the Potresovs, Levitskys and Co., with those who assure the working class that what it needs is not the leadership, *but* a class party; when, on the other hand, I see Plekhanov starting (to use the contemptuous expression of the magnificent Potresov) "a row" at the slightest indications of serious vacillation in the question of leadership, I say to myself, the Bolsheviks would indeed be the wild fanatics obsessed by factionalism their enemies represent them to be, if, the circumstances being as they are, they wavered even for a moment, if they doubted even for one second that their duty, the duty emanating from all the traditions of Bolshevism, from the very spirit of its teachings and policies, is to hold out their hands to Plekhanov and to express their full comradely sympathy with him. We differed, and still differ, on the questions as to how the leading classes ("hegemons") should have acted at one time or another in the past. But in the present period of disintegration, we are comrades in the struggle against those to whom the question of hegemony is nothing but "a most trivial misunderstanding". As for the Potresovs, Bazarovs, etc., they are strangers to us, no less strangers than the Chukovskys.

Let this be taken note of by those good fellows who think that the policy of rapprochement with Plekhanov is a narrow policy that "smacks of factionalism"; who would like to "extend" the policy to include a reconciliation with the Potresovs, Bazarovs, etc.; and who absolutely refuse to understand why we regard such "conciliationism" as either hopeless stupidity or abject intrigue-mongering.

Mysl, Nos. 2 and 3,
January and February 1911
Signed: *V. Ilyin*

Published according to
the text in the journal *Mysl*

THE CADETS ON "TWO CAMPS"
AND "SENSIBLE COMPROMISE"

The answer given by *Rech* to the semi-official organ of the Cabinet on the question of the "slogan" for the elections to the Fourth Duma and on the present-day political alignment represents an interesting and significant phenomenon.

Rech agrees with *Russkiye Vedomosti*[58] that "the elections to the Fourth Duma will be a contest between two camps only: the Progressists and the Rights". "Votes will have to be cast not for parties, nor for individual candidates, but for or against the consolidation of the constitutional system in Russia. ["Consolidation" is a very charming way of putting it!] The political meaning of this slogan ... is an objective acknowledgement of the indisputable fact that the line pursued by the government has again united the entire opposition, both to the right and to the left of the Cadets." The Cadets will constitute "the centre of this politically heterogeneous group", and, although they form part of it, "will renounce their former programme and tactics just as little as did the Social-Democrats when they joined the pre-October alliances" (the editorial, January 21).

"Gentlemen, we can say in reply to the semi-official and official press, it is you yourselves who have been instrumental in uniting us.... At present political trends in Russia are merging to an ever greater extent in two big camps—for and against the Constitution.... Our task at present is the same, again the same, just as it was before October 17..." (ibid.).

In assessing these observations we must distinguish between the conditions attending the elections to the Fourth Duma and the social and political meaning of the changes under discussion (the "slogan" and the alignments). The circumstances of the elections in general, in the provinces in particular, will certainly compel the "opposition" to resort to the vague non-party term "Progressists"[59] on an even wider scale than before. The refusal to legalise even such parties as the Cadets will inevitably lead to this, and the bewilderment of the semi-official organ of the Cabinet on this score is, of course, nothing but sheer hypocrisy. In the big cities, for instance, as the Cadets themselves admit in that very same editorial, independent candidates of "groups more to the left" (to use the expression of *Russkiye Vedomosti*) will stand for election. This alone shows that there can be no question of just *two* camps.

Further, *Rech* thought it best completely to forget the existence of a worker curia, as provided by the present election laws. Finally, with regard to the elections in the villages (the peasant curia) it must be said that here even the *word* "Progressists" will undoubtedly be avoided; but it will probably not be the Cadets who will constitute the *actual* "centre" of the "politically heterogeneous" or politically undefinable groups.

What, then, does the talk about *two* camps amount to? To the fact that it pleases the Cadets, in speaking of the present political situation, to narrow down their field of vision to include *only* those elements that constitute the majority in the Third Duma. The Cadet gentlemen are willing to recognise as political "camps" only that insignificant section of the population represented by these elements. Hitherto the *main* division in this small corner created by the coup d'état of June 3 has been: the Rights, the Octobrists, the Cadets. (It is well known that the character of the Third Duma was determined, in the final analysis, by two majorities: the Rights with the Octobrists and the Octobrists with the Cadets.) Now (according to the forecast of *Russkiye Vedomosti*, with which *Rech* is in agreement) *these three* elements will be divided into two "camps": the Rights and Progressists.

We fully admit that these predictions of the liberals are based not on the wishes of the liberals alone, but on objective facts as well—on the changes in the political situation and in the political sentiments of the Russian bourgeoisie. It would be impermissible, however, to forget that one can speak of *two* camps only when the field of observation is limited to the majority in the Third Duma. It would be impermissible to forget that the *actual* meaning of all this talk is nothing more than the tendency on the part of the Octobrist and the Cadet "camps" to draw closer together, merge and unite in the Progressist "camp" (with the tacit understanding, of course, that a more or less considerable section of the Octobrist camp will defect to the camp of the Rights). When the Cadets say: "we" have been united, again "we" have one task, etc., these words "we", "us", "our" *actually* mean nothing more than the Octobrists and the Cadets.

Now, what has united "them"? What is "their" task? What is "their" slogan for the elections to the Fourth Duma? "The consolidation of the Constitution", reply *Russkiye Vedomosti* and *Rech*. This reply is only seemingly definite; actually, it defines absolutely nothing; it amounts to the same, absolutely meaningless, reference to some indefinite "mean" between the Octobrists and the Cadets. For both Milyukov and Guchkov agree that "Thank God, we have a Constitution", but when they dream of making common cause, it is for the purpose of "consolidating", not what "we" *have*, but what we have not. It is also a dream, and not a very sensible one at that, that Milyukov and Guchkov, the Cadets and the Octobrists of today, and the "Progressists" of tomorrow, could agree on a definition of what should be included in the desired Constitution. They would be unable to agree either on the legal formulations expressing the Constitution, or on defining what real interests of what actual classes this Constitution should meet and safeguard. Hence, the *real* meaning of this joint slogan amounts to this: while they are being drawn more closely together by "a *negative* aim—that of the struggle against the common enemy" (as *Rech* puts it in the same editorial), the Octobrists and the Cadets cannot define their positive tasks, cannot find in their camps the forces that would be capable of emerging from the deadlock.

The observations of *Rech* on the subject of a "sensible compromise" in connection with another matter are a very clearly expressed admission that they are indeed in a state of deadlock, that it is necessary to emerge from this state, that this is necessary for both the Octobrists and the Cadets, and that, after they have emerged, both will be absolutely impotent by themselves.

"During the debate in the Duma on the St. Petersburg sewerage system," we read in an editorial in *Rech* of January 20, "the unhealthy undercurrent of the controversy was somewhat lessened, and even the Centre [i.e., the Octobrists] found it possible to accept the sensible compromise which the people's freedom group proposed and the municipality accepted; but the interference of P. A. Stolypin rudely tore away the veil [you, Messrs. Cadets, would like vexed questions to remain hidden under a veil, wouldn't you?] and revealed the same old background, with which everyone has been disgusted for some time—that of the *political* struggle of the state against the municipality."

The liberal bourgeoisie in the guise of an innocent—oh, how innocent!—person dreaming of "sensible compromises" on a businesslike, non-political basis, and the representatives of the old, "non-constitutional", principles in the role of political educators who tear down the veils and reveal the class background! A sensible compromise, the liberal muses, means that what the Cadets, the Octobrists and the non-party bigwigs of capital (the St. Petersburg municipality) have agreed upon may be conceded. There is nothing sensible in the idea of our yielding to you, the government replies; the only sensible thing is that you yield to us.

The minor question of the sanitation of St. Petersburg, of the distribution of the responsibilities and rights between local self-government and autocratic government, became the occasion for the elucidation of truths of no mean importance. What, indeed, is more "sensible"—the wishes, dreams and demands of the whole bourgeoisie, or the power of, say, the Council of the United Nobility[60]?

In the eyes of *Rech*, as well as of the whole Cadet Party, the criterion of the "wisdom" of a compromise is in its approval by men of affairs, businessmen, bigwigs, the Octobrists themselves, the wire-pullers of the St. Petersburg municipality themselves. But the *actual* state of affairs— no matter how it is furbished up with phrases like "Thank God, we have a Constitution"—unmasks these compromises and tears away these veils rather rudely.

To sum up: "You have been instrumental in uniting us", *Rech* says to the semi-official organ of the Cabinet. Who do they mean by "us"? It appears that they mean the Octobrists and the Cadets. What have they united for? For a common task, the consolidation of the Constitution. And what are we to understand by the Constitution and its consolidation? A sensible compromise between the Octobrists and the Cadets. What is the criterion of the wisdom of compromises of this kind? Their approval by the worst representatives of Russian "Kolupayev" capitalism,[61] such as the St. Petersburg municipal councillors. And what is the practical result of these sensible compromises? The result is that P. A. Stolypin, or the Council of State, or Tolmachov,[62] etc., "rudely unmask" these compromises.... Oh, these practical politicians!

But will there not be a third camp at the elections to the Fourth Duma—one that realises how senseless, ridiculous and naïve is the Cadet policy of "sensible compromise"? What do you think of that, gentlemen of *Rech* and *Russkiye Vedomosti*?

Zvezda, No. 8, February 5, 1911
Signed: V. *Ilyin*

Published according to
the *Zvezda* text

THE FIFTIETH ANNIVERSARY
OF THE FALL OF SERFDOM

February 19, 1911, marks the fiftieth anniversary of the fall of serfdom in Russia. Everywhere preparations are under way to celebrate this jubilee. The tsarist government is taking every precaution to ensure that only the most reactionary views regarding the so-called "emancipation" of the peasants are put forward in the churches and schools, in the barracks and at public lectures. Circular letters are being rushed from St. Petersburg to all parts of Russia, instructing all and sundry institutions not to order for distribution among the people any books and pamphlets other than those published by the National Club, i.e., by one of the most reactionary parties in the Third Duma. In some places overzealous governors have even gone so far as to dissolve committees organised without police "guidance" (for instance, by the Zemstvos[63]) for the celebration of the anniversary of the Peasant "Reform"; they are being dissolved for showing insufficient willingness to conduct the celebrations along the lines demanded by the Black-Hundred government.

The government is worried. It sees that no matter how downtrodden, intimidated, backward and ignorant a worker or a peasant may be, the mere mention of the fact that fifty years ago the abolition of serfdom was proclaimed nevertheless stirs and agitates people repressed by the Duma of the landlords, of the nobility, people who are suffering more than ever before from the petty tyrannies, violence and oppression of the feudal-minded landowners and of their police and bureaucrats.

In Western Europe the last survivals of serfdom were abolished by the Revolution of 1789 in France and by the revolutions of 1848 in most of the other countries. In Russia, in 1861, the people, who had for centuries been kept in slavery by the landowners, were unable to launch a widespread, open and conscious struggle for freedom. The peasant revolts of those days remained isolated, scattered, spontaneous "riots", which were easily suppressed. The abolition of serfdom was effected, not by an insurrectionary people, but by the government, which realised after its defeat in the Crimean War[64] that it was no longer possible to maintain the system of serfdom.

It was the landowners themselves, the landowning government of the autocratic tsar and his officials, that "emancipated" the peasants in Russia. And these "emancipators" manipulated matters *in such a way* that the peasants entered "freedom" stripped to the point of pauperism; they were released from slavery to the landowners to fall into bondage to the very same landowners and their flunkeys.

The noble landowners "emancipated" the Russian peasants in such a way that *more than a fifth* of all the peasant land was cut off and taken away by the landlords. The peasants were compelled to pay *redemption money*, i.e., *tribute* to the former slaveholders, for their own peasant land drenched with their sweat and blood. The peasants paid hundreds of millions of rubles in such tribute to the feudal lords, thus lapsing into ever greater poverty. Not content with grabbing peasant land and leaving to the peasants the worst and sometimes entirely worthless land, the landowners frequently laid traps for them—they divided up the land in such a way as to leave the peasants either without pastures, or without meadows, forests, or water for their animals. In *most* of the gubernias* of Russia proper the peasants, after the abolition of serfdom, remained in the same old state of hopeless bondage to the landowners. After their "emancipation" the peasants still remained the "lower" social-estate, tax-paying cattle, the common herd over whom

---

* *Gubernia, uyezd, volost*—Russian administrative-territorial units. The largest of these was the gubernia, which had its subdivisions in uyezds, which in turn were subdivided into volosts. This system of districting continued under the Soviet power until the introduction of the new system of administrative-territorial division of the country in 1929-30.—*Ed.*

the authorities set up by the landowners lorded it at will, from whom they exacted taxes, whom they flogged with birches, manhandled, and humiliated.

In no other country in the world has the peasantry, after its "emancipation", experienced such ruination, such poverty, such humiliations and such outrageous treatment as in Russia.

But the fall of serfdom stirred up the whole people, awakened it from age-long slumber, taught it to seek its own way out, to wage its own fight for complete freedom.

The fall of serfdom in Russia was followed by an increasingly rapid development of cities, and factories, mills and railways were built. Capitalist Russia was advancing to replace feudal Russia. The settled, downtrodden serf peasant who stuck firmly to his village, had implicit faith in the priests and stood in awe of the "authorities" was gradually giving way to a new generation of peasants, peasants who had worked as seasonal labourers in the cities and had learned something from their bitter experience of a life of wandering and wage-labour. The number of workers in the big towns, in the factories, was constantly on the increase. Gradually the workers began to form associations for their common struggle against the capitalists and the government. By waging this struggle the Russian working class helped the peasant millions to rise, straighten their backs and cast off serf habits.

In 1861 the peasants were only capable of "riots". In the decades that followed the Russian revolutionaries who made heroic efforts to rouse the people to struggle remained isolated figures and perished under the blows of the autocracy. By 1905 the Russian working class had gained strength and had matured as a result of the years of strike struggles and the years of propaganda, agitation and organisation carried on by the Social-Democratic Party. And the Russian working class led the whole people, the millions of peasants, *into revolution.*

The Revolution of 1905 undermined the tsarist autocracy. Out of a mob of muzhiks repressed by feudal slavery of accursed memory, this revolution created, for the first time in Russia, a people beginning to understand its rights, beginning to realise its strength. For the first time, the

Revolution of 1905 showed the tsarist government, the Russian landowners and the Russian bourgeoisie that millions and tens of millions of people were becoming *citizens*, were becoming *fighters* who would no longer permit anyone to treat them like cattle, treat them as a mob. The real emancipation of the masses from oppression and tyranny has nowhere in the world ever been effected by any other means than the independent, heroic, conscious struggle of the masses themselves.

The Revolution of 1905 only undermined the autocracy; it did not destroy it. Now the autocracy is venting its rage on the people. The landowners' Duma serves only to oppress and repress the people all the more. Discontent and anger are again rife everywhere. That first step will be followed by a second. The beginning of the struggle will have its continuation. The Revolution of 1905 will he followed by a new, a second, revolution. The anniversary of the fall of serfdom serves as a reminder of, and a call for, this second revolution.

The liberals whine: we need "another February 19". That is not true. This kind of talk is worthy only of bourgeois cowards. No second "February 19" is possible after 1905. There can be no "emancipation from above" of a people which has learned (and *is learning*—from the experience of the landowners' Third Duma) to fight from below. There can be no "emancipation from above" of a people which has been led, even if but once, by the revolutionary proletariat.

The Black Hundreds understand this, and that is why they are afraid of the anniversary of 1861. As Menshikov, that faithful watchdog of the tsar's Black Hundreds, wrote in *Novoye Vremya*: "The year 1861 *failed to prevent 1905*".

The Black-Hundred Duma and the fury with which the tsarist government is persecuting its enemies is not preventing but hastening the new revolution. The grim experience of 1908-10 has taught the people to take up the fight again. The workers' summer strikes (in 1910) have been followed by the students' winter strikes. The new struggle is gaining momentum perhaps more slowly than we would wish, but surely and inevitably.

The revolutionary Social-Democratic movement, while purging itself of the sceptics who have turned their backs on the revolution and the illegal party of the working class, is mustering its ranks and welding its forces for the impending great battles.

Rabochaya Gazeta, No. 3,
February 8 (21), 1911

Published according to
the *Rabochaya Gazeta* text

PAUL SINGER

DIED JANUARY 18 (31), 1911

On February 5, this year, the German Social-Democratic Party buried Paul Singer, one of its oldest leaders. The entire working-class population of Berlin, many hundreds of thousands of people, responded to the call of the Party and marched in the funeral procession; they came to honour the memory of a man who had devoted all his strength and all his life to the cause of the emancipation of the working class. Berlin, with its three-million population, had never seen such a multitude—at least a million people marched in or watched the procession. Never had any of the mighty of this world been honoured with such a funeral. Tens of thousands of soldiers can be ordered to line the streets during the funeral of some monarch or a general famous for the slaughter of external and internal enemies; but if the working people in their millions were not attached heart and soul to *their* leader, to the cause of the *revolutionary* struggle of these very masses against the oppression of the government and the bourgeoisie, it would be impossible to rouse the population of a huge city.

Paul Singer came of bourgeois stock, from a family of merchants, and for quite a long time was a wealthy manufacturer. At the beginning of his political career he was associated with the bourgeois democrats. But, unlike the bulk of bourgeois democrats and liberals, who very soon forget their love of liberty out of fear of the successes of the labour movement, Singer was an ardent and sincere democrat, fearless and consistent to the end. He was not caught up by the vacillations, cowardice and treachery of the bourgeois democrats which aroused in him only a feeling of repulsion and strengthened his conviction that only the party of the revolutionary working class is capable of pursuing the great struggle for liberty to its consummation.

In the sixties of the past century, when the cowardly German liberal bourgeoisie turned its back on the growing revolution in their country, was bargaining with the government of the landowners and becoming reconciled to the unlimited power of the monarchy, Singer turned resolutely toward socialism. In 1870, when the entire bourgeoisie was intoxicated by the victories over France, and when the broad masses of the population fell under the spell of the vile, misanthropic, "liberal" propaganda of nationalism and chauvinism, Singer signed a protest against the annexation of Alsace and Lorraine from France. In 1878, when the bourgeoisie helped Bismarck, that reactionary, landlords' ("Junkers'", as the Germans say) minister, to promulgate the Anti-Socialist Law,[65] to dissolve the workers' unions, ban working-class newspapers, and shower persecution upon the class-conscious proletariat, Singer finally joined the Social-Democratic Party.

Since then the history of Singer's life is inseparably bound up with that of the German Social-Democratic Party. He devoted himself heart and soul to the difficult task of building up the revolutionary organisation. He gave the Party all his energy, all his wealth, all his remarkable abilities as an organiser, all his talent as a practical worker and leader. Singer was one of those few, we might say, one of the extremely rare cases of socialists of bourgeois origin whom the long history of liberalism, the history of the treachery, cowardice, deals with the government, and sycophancy of the bourgeois politicians does not enervate and corrupt; *but it steels* and converts them into stalwart *revolutionaries*. There are few *such* socialists of bourgeois origin, and the proletariat should trust *only* these rare people, people who have been tested in the course of many years of struggle, if it desires to forge for itself a working-class party capable of overthrowing contemporary bourgeois slavery. Singer was a ruthless enemy of opportunism in the ranks of the German workers' party, and to the end of his days remained undeviatingly faithful to the uncompromising policy of revolutionary Social-Democracy.

Singer was not a theoretician, or a writer, or a brilliant orator. He was first and foremost a *practical* organiser of the *illegal* party during the period of the Anti-Socialist Law, and a member of the Berlin Municipal Council and, after the repeal of that law, of the Reichstag. And this practical organiser, who spent most of his time in minor, everyday, technical parliamentary and every kind of "executive" activity was great for the reason that he did not make a fetish of details, he did not yield to the quite usual and quite philistine tendency to keep out of any sharp struggle on questions of principle, allegedly for the sake of this "executive" or "positive" activity. On the contrary, every time a question arose concerning the fundamental nature of the revolutionary party of the working class, its ultimate aims, blocs (alliances) with the bourgeoisie, concessions to monarchism, etc., Singer, who devoted all his life to this practical activity, was always to be found at the head of the staunchest and most resolute fighters against every manifestation of opportunism. During the operation of the Anti-Socialist Law, Singer together with Engels, Liebknecht and Bebel was in the fight on two fronts: against the "young",[66] the semi-anarchists, who repudiated the parliamentary struggle, and against the moderate "legalists at any price". In later years, Singer fought just as resolutely against the revisionists.

He earned the hatred of the bourgeoisie, and it followed him to the grave. Singer's bourgeois enemies (the German liberals and our Cadets) now point out with malicious glee that his death means the passing away of one of the last representatives of the "heroic" period of German Social-Democracy, that is to say, the period when its leaders were imbued with a strong, fresh, unqualified faith in revolution and championed a principled revolutionary policy. According to these liberals, the rising generation of leaders, those who are coming to replace Singer, are moderate, punctilious "revisionists", men of modest pretensions and petty calculations. It is true that the growth of the workers' party often attracts many opportunists to its ranks. It is also true that in our day socialists of bourgeois origin most often bring to the proletariat their timidity, narrow-mindedness and love of phrase-mongering rather than firmness of revolutionary convictions. But the rejoicing of the enemies is premature! The *masses* of workers in Germany, as well as in other countries, are becoming welded ever more strongly into *an army of revolution*, and this army will deploy its forces in the not far distant future—for the revolution is gaining momentum both in Germany and in other countries.

The old revolutionary leaders are passing away; but the young army of the revolutionary proletariat is growing and gaining strength.

Rabochaya Gazeta, No. 3,
February 8 (21), 1911

Published according to
the *Rabochaya Gazeta* text

COMMENTS

MENSHIKOV, GROMOBOI, IZGOYEV[67]

The statement[68] made by sixty-six Moscow industrialists—who, according to the calculations of a certain Moscow newspaper, represent capital amounting to five hundred million rubles—has given rise to a number of extremely valuable and characteristic articles in various newspapers. In addition to casting an uncommonly glaring light on the present political situation, these articles furnish interesting material on many fundamental questions of principle relating to the entire evolution in twentieth-century Russia.

Here is Mr. Menshikov of *Novoye Vremya*, setting forth the views of the Right parties and of the government:

"How is it that all these Ryabushinskys, Morozovs, et al., fail to understand that should there be a revolution they will all hang or, at best, become paupers?"

Mr. Menshikov says (*Novoye Vremya*, No. 12549) that he quotes "these vigorous words" "from the letter of a student of a very revolutionary institute". And to this Mr. Menshikov adds his own observations:

"Despite the grim warning of the year 1905, the upper classes of Russia, including the merchant class, are extremely hazy about the impending catastrophe.... Yes, Messrs. Ryabushinsky, Morozov, and all others like you! Despite the fact that you are flirting with the revolution, and despite all the testimonials of liberalism which you are hastening to earn, it is you who are going to be the first victims of the revolution now brewing. You will be the first to hang, not for any crimes you may have committed, but for something which you consider a virtue, merely for possessing those five hundred million rubles you brag so much about.... The liberal bourgeoisie, with the middle sections of the nobility, the civil service, and the merchant class together with their titles, ranks and capital are heedlessly heading towards the brink of the revolutionary precipice. If the liberal instigators of revolution live to see the day at last when they are dragged to the gallows, let them then recall their indulgent treatment by the old state power, how considerately it listened to them, how it humoured them, and how few were the claims it made upon their empty heads. On that very day, which will be a black day for them, let them compare the blessings of the radical regime with the old, patriarchal order."

That is what the unofficially semi-official organ of the government wrote on February 17—the very same day that *Rossiya*, the officially semi-official organ of the government, was doing its utmost to prove, with the assistance of *Golos Moskvy*,[69] that the "escapade" of the sixty-six "cannot be considered as expressing the opinion of the Moscow merchants". "The Congress of the Nobility," *Rossiya* says, "is an organisation; whereas the sixty-six merchants who say that they acted as private individuals are not an organisation."

It is embarrassing to have two semi-official organs! One refutes the other. One is trying to prove that the "escapade" of the sixty-six cannot be regarded as the expression of the opinion even of the Moscow merchants alone. At the same time the other is trying to prove that the "escapade" is of much wider significance, since it expresses the opinion, not only of the Moscow merchants, and of the merchant class, but of the whole of Russia's *liberal bourgeoisie* in general. On behalf of "the old state power", Mr. Menshikov has undertaken to caution this liberal bourgeoisie: it's your interests we have at heart!

There is probably not a single country in Europe in which this call "not to instigate" addressed to the liberal bourgeoisie by the "old state power", the nobility and the reactionary publicists, did not resound hundreds of times in the course of the nineteenth century.... And never were these calls of any avail, even though the "liberal bourgeoisie", *far from wanting* to "instigate", fought against the "instigators" with the same energy and sincerity with which the sixty-six merchants condemn strikes. Both condemnations and calls are powerless when all the conditions of social life make one class or another feel that the situation is intolerable, and compel it to voice its feeling. Mr. Menshikov correctly expresses the interests and the point of view of the government and the nobility when he tries to frighten the liberal bourgeoisie with revolution and accuses it of being frivolous. The sixty-six merchants correctly express the interests and the point of view of the liberal bourgeoisie when they accuse the government and condemn the "strikers". But these mutual accusations are only a sure symptom testifying to serious deficiencies in the mechanism", to the fact that, despite all the willingness of "the old state power" to satisfy the bourgeoisie, to meet it half-way and to reserve for it a very influential place in the Duma, and despite the very strong and sincere desire on the part of the bourgeoisie to settle down, establish good relations, come to terms and adjust itself, despite all this, the "adjustment" does not make any headway! This is the substance of the matter, this is the background; the mutual accusations are nothing but trimmings.

Mr. Gromoboi, writing in *Golos Moskvy*, addresses "a necessary warning" to "the government" (*Golos Moskvy*, No. 38, of February 17, in an article entitled "A Necessary Warning"). "No displays of 'firm' rule," he writes, "no volitional impulses will give the country peace unless they go hand in hand with reforms which are long overdue." (Mr. Gromoboi is not very literate in his writings, but the meaning of his words is nevertheless quite clear.) "And the unrest caused by the protracted crisis cannot be given as a *force majeure* reason for not honouring promissory notes." (This is an awkward comparison, Mr. Publicist of the Octobrist merchants. In the first place, the notes happen to be unsigned; secondly, even if they were signed, where is the commercial court to which you could appeal and where is the sheriff, etc., who would enforce the judgement? Think it over, Mr. Gromoboi—you will see that not only the Octobrists, but the Cadets too, are a party of spurious promissory notes in politics.) "In such a case unrest will only increase ... the student riots will be followed by much that has been experienced before. If you turn the ship round you are bound to see its wake.... The bet on the weak was lost; now it may turn out that the bet on the strong will also be lost. The government will have nothing to show. Its hopes that the unrest will subside may vanish like smoke no matter what kind of elections take place." (Mr. Gromoboi is referring to the elections to the Fourth Duma.) "If the caravans of the opposition begin to move over those cliffs where only the mists of government hovered before, if the government alienates the moderate elements and remains in isolation, the elections will turn into bitter defeat, and the entire system will be shaken because it is not a system based on law."

Menshikov accuses the bourgeoisie of "instigating" "revolution"; the bourgeoisie accuses the Menshikovs of leading to an "increase of unrest". "It is an old story, but ever new."

In dealing with the same subject in the Cadet *Rech* the renegade Izgoyev attempts to draw some sociological conclusions—not realising what a rash thing it is for Cadets in general, and renegades in particular, to undertake such a task. In an article entitled "Juxtaposition" (in the issue of February 14), he draws a comparison between the Congress of the United Nobility and the statement of the sixty-six Moscow merchants. "The United Nobility," he says, "have sunk to the level of Purishkevich; the Moscow industrialists have begun to talk the language of statesmen." In the past, Mr. Izgoyev goes on to tell us, "the nobility rendered the people great services in the cultural field", but "only a minority engaged in cultural activity, while the majority kept the people down.... But such, in general, is the law of history that only the minority of a given class acts in a progressive way."

Very, very fine. "Such, in general, is the law of history." This is what the Cadet *Rech* says through the mouth of Mr. Izgoyev. On closer examination, however, we discover to our amazement that the "general laws of history" do not hold good beyond the confines of the feudal nobility and the liberal bourgeoisie. Indeed, let us recall *Vekhi*, to which the same Mr. Izgoyev contributed, and against which the most prominent Cadets carried on a polemic, but in such a way as to deal only with details, without touching upon fundamentals, principles, essentials. The essential view set forth in *Vekhi*—one shared by all the Cadets and expressed a thousand times by Messrs. Milyukov and Co.—is that, except for the reactionary nobility and the liberal bourgeoisie, each class in Russia has revealed itself (in the first decade of the present century) by the actions of a minority who succumbed to the "intoxication", were swept along by "intellectual leaders", and are unable to rise to a "statesmanlike" view of things. "We must have the courage to admit," wrote Mr. Izgoyev in *Vekhi*, "that the vast majority of members of our State Dumas, with the exception of thirty or forty Cadets and Octobrists, have not shown themselves to possess the knowledge required to undertake the job of governing and reconstructing Russia." Everybody will understand that this refers to the peasant deputies, the Trudoviks, and the workers' deputies.

Consequently, it is "in general, the law of history" that "only the minority of a given class acts in a progressive way". If it is the minority of the bourgeoisie that acts, then it is a progressive minority, justified by the "general law of history". "Once the minority obtains an opportunity to act, moral prestige extends to the entire class," Mr. Izgoyev informs us. But if it is a minority of peasants or of workers that acts, then this by no means corresponds to "the law of history", this is by no means "the progressive minority of the given class", this minority by no means possesses the "moral prestige" enabling it to speak on behalf of the "entire" class—no, nothing of the kind: this is a minority led astray by "intellectuals", it is not, according to *Vekhi*, statesmanlike, it is anti-historic, has no roots, etc.

It is a risky business for Cadets in general and for *Vekhi* writers in particular to indulge in generalisations, because every attempt they make at generalisations inevitably exposes the inherent affinity between the arguments of the Cadets and those of Menshikov.

Rossiya and *Zemshchina*[70] argue: the sixty-six merchants are a minority by no means representing the class, they have not shown themselves to possess either the knowledge or the ability "to govern and reconstruct Russia"; moreover, they are not even merchants, but "intellectuals" who have been led astray, etc., etc.

The Izgoyevs and the Milyukovs argue: the Trudoviks and the workers' deputies in our State Dumas, for example, are minorities which by no means represent their classes

(i. e., nine-tenths of the population); they have been led astray by "intellectuals", have not shown themselves to possess either the knowledge or the ability to "govern and reconstruct Russia", etc., etc.

How is this inherent affinity between the arguments of *Rossiya* and *Zemshchina*, on the one hand, and those of *Rech* and *Russkiye Vedomosti* on the other, to be accounted for? The reason is this: despite the differences in the classes represented by these two groups of newspapers, neither class is *any longer* capable of any material, independent, creative and decisive historical action that is *progressive*. Not merely the first but the second group of newspapers, not only the reactionaries, but the liberals, too, represent a class that *is afraid* of historical, independent action on the part of other, broader, sections, groups or masses of the population, of other numerically stronger classes.

Mr. Izgoyev, as a renegade "Marxist", will certainly see a crying contradiction in this: on the one hand, we recognise Russia's capitalist development and, consequently, its inherent tendency towards the fullest possible and purest possible rule of the bourgeoisie both in the economic and in the political sphere; on the other hand, we declare that the liberal bourgeoisie is *no longer* capable of independent, creative historical action!

This "contradiction" exists in real life, and is not the result of faulty reasoning. The inevitability of bourgeois rule does not in the least imply that the liberal bourgeoisie is *capable* of such displays of historical independent activity as might free it from its "enslavement" to the Purishkeviches. In the first place, history does not move along a smooth and easy road, such as would imply that every historically ripe change means *ipso facto* that precisely the class which stands to profit most by it, is mature and strong enough to carry this change into effect. Secondly, in addition to the liberal bourgeoisie, there is yet another bourgeoisie; for instance, the entire peasantry, taken in the mass, is nothing but the democratic bourgeoisie. Thirdly, the history of Europe shows us that some changes, bourgeois in their social substance, were accomplished by elements whose background was by no means bourgeois. Fourthly, we see the same thing in the history of Russia during the past half-century.

When the ideologists and leaders of the liberals begin to argue the way the Karaulovs, the Maklakovs, the Milyukovs and the *Vekhi* writers do, *that means* that a number of historical factors have caused the liberal bourgeoisie to exhibit such a pronounced tendency to "beat a retreat" and to show such dread of moving forward, that this forward movement will pass them by, will go beyond them, in spite of their fears. And an altercation such as mutual accusations of being responsible for "increasing unrest" hurled by Gromoboi at Menshikov and by Menshikov at Gromoboi,* is but a sign that this historical movement forward is beginning to be felt by all....

"Contemporary society," says Mr. Izgoyev in the same article, "based on the principle of private property, is a class society, and for the time being it cannot be anything else. Whenever one class is tottering another class is always striving to step into its place."

"What a clever chap," Mr. Milyukov must think when he reads such tirades in his *Rech*. It is rather pleasant to have a Cadet who was a Social-Democrat at the age of twenty-five and by the time he reached thirty-five had "come to his senses" and repented of his errors.

It is rash on your part, Mr. Izgoyev, to dabble in generalisations. Contemporary society is admittedly a class society. Can there be a party in a class society which does not represent a class? You have probably guessed that there cannot be. Then why make such a *faux pas*, why do you prate about a "class society" in the organ of a party which prides itself on, and sees its merit in calling itself a non-class party? (Other people who, not only in words, not merely for the sake of journalistic prattle, recognise contemporary society as a class society, regard such talk as hypocrisy or short-sightedness.)

When you turn your face to the United Nobility or to the liberal Moscow merchants you shout that contemporary society is a class society. But when you have to, when unpleasant (ah, how terribly unpleasant!) events compel you to turn around, even if for a brief moment, to face the peas-

---

* By the liberal merchants at the nobility and by the nobility at the liberal merchants.

ants or the workers, you begin to rail at the narrow, lifeless, fossilised, immoral, materialist, godless and unscientific "doctrine" of the class struggle. You would surely do better, Mr. Izgoyev, not to tackle any sociological generalisations! Don't ask for trouble.

"Whenever one class is tottering another class is always striving to step into its place."

Not always, Mr. Izgoyev. It happens at times that the two classes, the one that is tottering and the one that "is striving", are both in an advanced stage of decay—one more, the other less, of course, but both are in an advanced stage of decay. It happens that, feeling its decay, the class that "is striving" forward *is afraid* of taking a step forward, and when it does take such a step it is sure to lose no time in taking two steps back. It happens that the liberal bourgeoisie (as was the case in Germany, for instance, and particularly in Prussia) is afraid to "step into the place" of the tottering class, but exerts *every* effort to "share the place" or, rather, to obtain any kind of place, even if it be in the servants' hall—*anything* rather than *step into* the place of the "tottering", anything rather than bring matters to the point where the tottering would "fall". Such things happen, Mr. Izgoyev.

In historical periods when such things do happen, the liberals, if they succeed in passing themselves off as democrats, are liable to bring (and they do bring) the greatest harm to the entire cause of social development; for the difference between the liberals and the democrats is precisely that the former are afraid "to step into the place", while the latter are not. Both the former and the latter are engaged in accomplishing the historically ripe bourgeois change; but the former are afraid to accomplish it, are hindering it by their fear, while the latter, although they often share many illusions on the results that will derive from the bourgeois change, put all their strength and their very soul into its accomplishment.

In illustration of these general sociological reflections, I shall take the liberty of citing one example of a liberal who does not strive, but is afraid to "step into the place" of the tottering class, and who is, therefore (consciously or

unconsciously, that makes no difference), most flagrantly
deceiving the population when he calls himself a "democrat".
This liberal is the landlord A. Y. Berezovsky the First,
Member of the Third Duma, a Cadet. During the debate in
the Duma on the agrarian question (in 1908) he delivered the
following speech, which was approved of by the leader of
the Party, Mr. Milyukov, who described it as "splendid".
In view of the forthcoming elections, we make bold to think
that it will not be amiss to recall that speech.

"... It is my profound conviction," Mr. Berezovsky said
in defending the Agrarian Bill before the State Duma on
October 27, 1908, "that this Bill is much more advantageous
to the landowners, too, and I am saying this, gentlemen,
as one who knows farming, since I own land and have engaged in it all my life.... You must not seize upon the bare
fact of compulsory alienation, wax indignant over it and declare that it would be an act of violence; you must examine
what this proposition amounts to, what, for instance, the
Bill of the 42 members of the First State Duma proposed.
That Bill contained only the recognition of the necessity of
alienating in the first place the land that is not exploited
by the owners themselves, that is cultivated by peasants
using their own implements and animals, and, finally, land
that is let out to tenants. Further, the party of people's
freedom supported the proposal that committees be organised
in the localities, which, after working for some time,
perhaps even for a number of years, were to ascertain which
land was subject to alienation, which was not, and how much
land was needed to satisfy the peasants. The committees
were to be so constituted that half their membership would
have been made up of peasants, and the other half of non-
peasants; and it seems to me that in the general actual situation which would thus have been created in the localities,
it would have been possible to ascertain properly both how
much land there was that could be alienated and how much
land was needed for the peasants; and, finally, the peasants
would have seen for themselves to what extent their just
demands could be satisfied and to what extent their desire
to get a lot of land was often wrong and unjustified. Then
this material would have been referred to the Duma for further elaboration, after which it would have been referred to

the Council of State,[71] and, finally, it would have been submitted to the tsar for his sanction. That, properly speaking, was the method of procedure at which, for some unknown reason, the government took fright, dissolved the Duma, and thus brought about the present state of affairs. This systematic work would undoubtedly have had as its result, the satisfaction of the true needs of the population and consequently, its pacification, and the preservation of the efficiently run estates, which the party of people's freedom never intended to destroy unless there was an extreme need for this." (Verbatim Reports, p. 398.)

When Mr. Izgoyev, who belongs to the same party as Mr. Berezovsky, writes in his article "Juxtaposition" that "Russia is a democratic country and will not tolerate any oligarchy, either new or old", we can see quite clearly what this kind of talk really means. Russia is by no means a democratic country, nor will she ever become one so long as fairly large sections of the population regard a party like the Cadets as a democratic party. This bitter truth is a thousand times more vital to the people than the honeyed lies dispensed by the representatives of the half-hearted, spineless, and unprincipled liberal oligarchy, the Cadets. The more such "altercations" as those between the Menshikovs and the sixty-six and Gromoboi become the order of the day the more necessary it is to remind people of this bitter truth.

Zvezda, No. 11, February 26, 1911
Signed: *V. Ilyin*

Published according to
the *Zvezda* text

TO THE RUSSIAN COLLEGIUM OF THE C.C.

In view of the possibility and likelihood of the Central Committee being convened in Russia, we consider it our duty to outline our views on several important questions affecting our position as people responsible to the Party.

(1) At the January 1910 Plenary Meeting, we, responsible representatives of the Bolshevik trend, concluded an agreement with the Central Committee, published in the Central Organ, No. 11. Our application, submitted by three officials, with power of attorney from Meshkovsky,[72] is a formal cancellation of this agreement owing to the *non-fulfilment* of its clearly-defined conditions by the *Golos* and *Vperyod* groups. Naturally, it is understood that we, although compelled to submit this application because no functioning Central Committee actually exists and there is the beginning of a split abroad, will willingly withdraw it, or agree to a review of the agreement, if the Central Committee succeeds in meeting and in re-establishing Party work and the Party line violated by the afore-mentioned factions.

(2) The Party line was clearly defined by the Plenary Meeting, and it is useless for the *Golos* group and Trotsky and Co. to try to confuse the issue. The line consists in recognising that both liquidationism and otzovism are *bourgeois* theories having a fatal influence on the proletariat. After the Plenary Meeting, in violation of its decisions, these two trends have developed and taken shape in anti-Party factions—the Potresov and *Golos* groups on the one hand, and the *Vperyod* group on the other. Among the Mensheviks, support for the Party line laid down by the Meeting was forthcoming from only the so-called pro-Party or Plekhanov

group, those who have been and still are *resolutely* conducting a struggle against the Potresov and *Golos* trends.

(3) For this reason, as representatives of the Bolshevik trend, we emphatically protest against the *Golos* group's attack on *Innokenty*[73] for having refused, in the summer of 1910, to recognise as candidates for co-option those Mensheviks who remained true to *Golos* or whose actions were not fully indicative of their Party affiliation. In doing so, *Innokenty*, the chief representative of a trend in Bolshevism differing from ours, acted correctly, and we have *written* proof that precisely as its representative he defined the Party principle uniting *all* Bolsheviks, before witnesses from the P.S.D.,* in the manner shown.

(4) The attempt of the *Golos* group, in the name of the splitting faction of émigrés, to propose from abroad "their own" candidates for co-option to the C.C. cannot be regarded as anything but an unheard-of affront. While at the Plenary Meeting there may have been people who sincerely believed the pledges of the Mensheviks to struggle against the liquidators, now, a year later, it is quite clear that the *Golos* people cannot be trusted on this question. We protest resolutely against candidates being put forward for election by the émigré faction of liquidators, and demand that Plekhanov's followers *in Russia* be circularised, they can *undoubtedly* provide candidates from among the pro-Party Mensheviks.

(5) The splitting moves of the *Golos* and *Vperyod* groups and of Trotsky are now fully recognised, not only by the Bolsheviks and the Poles (in the Central Organ), but also by Plekhanov's group (see the Paris resolution of Plekhanov's group). We assert that the *first* decisive step towards a split was the announcement made by Trotsky on November 27, 1910, without the knowledge of the C.C., of the convening of a conference and of the "fund" for it. Our application (December 5, 1910) was the reply we were forced to make to that announcement. The *Vperyod* school has become one of the centres of this split; Trotsky took part in it *in defiance* of the clear decision of the Party School Commission. We were blamed *in print* by *Golos* for "disorganising" this

---

* Polish Social-Democrats.—*Ed.*

school. Considering it our duty to *disorganise* anti-Party émigré factions, we demand the appointment of a commission to *investigate* the "funds" of this school and *the help given it by Trotsky and Golos*. By shouting about expropriation, which we put an end to once and for all at the Plenary Meeting, the *Golos* group are not only blackmailing, but *are covering up* their *moral* (and not only moral) support of the *violators* of the resolution of the Meeting.

(6) Olgin,[74] a follower of Plekhanov, has disclosed that Dan frankly explained the desire of the *Golos* group to transfer the C.C. to Russia as being due to the probability (or inevitability) of its failure. The Party tribunal will have to make a pronouncement on this. Anyone who has followed the *Golos* group's policy over the past year will have no doubt that *in actual fact* they have been splitting the C.C. and hampering its work. The London candidates of *Golos* are not only alive, but carry out *political* work in an *anti-Party* spirit both *in the workers' unions and in the press*. By absenting themselves from the C.C. meeting, they confirm their liquidationism. For this reason we are in duty bound to warn the comrades on the C.C. in Russia, who are working under desperately difficult conditions (since they are *all* known to the police), that they are also threatened by an internal enemy inside the Party. We cannot manage without some sort of base abroad unless we are prepared to run the risk of a *single* failure on our part freeing the hands of the disruptive Potresovs. The Central Committee Bureau Abroad, which is *now* carrying out a policy of *aid* to the *Vperyod* and *Golos* groups and to Trotsky, cannot be allowed to remain abroad. We cannot rely on the pledged word or the "signing" of a resolution. We must, if we wish to be *realistic* politicians who are not deluded by mere formalities, study the *ideological-political trends* emanating from the working-class movement and from the counter-revolutionary influence on it.

These trends have grown and developed since 1908. They have brought Plekhanov's group and the Bolsheviks closer together, and have created a bloc between the *Golos* and *Vperyod* groups and Trotsky, who support the split while endeavouring to hide its existence. The immediate future of our Party (and it is useless closing our eyes to this) will inevitably be determined by the struggle along these lines; not the desires of individuals or groups, but the objective conditions of the epoch, as shown in the resolution of the Plenary Meeting, give rise to the struggle.

> The representatives of the Bolshevik trend, signatories to the agreement with the C.C. in January 1910 (three, and on the authority of the fourth, Meshkovsky).[75]

Written in February 1911
First published in 1931
in *Lenin Miscellany XVIII*

Published according to
the manuscript

APROPOS OF AN ANNIVERSARY

The fiftieth anniversary of the so-called Peasant Reform raises many interesting questions. Here we can touch only upon some of the economic and historical issues, deferring publicist topics in the narrower sense of the term to another occasion.

About ten or fifteen years ago, when the controversies between the Narodniks and the Marxists were first brought before the general public, the difference in the appraisal of the so-called Peasant Reform emerged time and again as one of the most important issues of that controversy. The theoreticians of Narodism, for instance, the well-known Mr. V. V., or Nikolai —on,[76] regarded the basic features of the Peasant Reform of 1861 as something fundamentally different from, and hostile to, capitalism. They said that the Regulations of February 19[77] legalised the "endowment of the producer with means of production" and sanctioned "people's production" *as distinct* from capitalist production. They regarded the Regulations of February 19 as an earnest of the *non*-capitalist evolution of Russia.

Even then the Marxists opposed a fundamentally different view to this theory. The Regulations of February 19 were one of the *episodes* in the replacement of the serf (or feudal) mode of production by the bourgeois (or capitalist) mode. According to this view, the Regulations contain *no* other historico-economic elements. "The endowment of the producer with means of production" is an empty, sentimental phrase which glosses over the plain fact that the peasants, who are small producers in agriculture, were being converted from producers engaged primarily in natural economy into producers of commodities. The precise extent to which commodity production had developed in peasant economy in various parts of Russia during that epoch is another question. But it is beyond doubt that the "emancipated" peasant was entering the sphere of commodity production and none other. "Free labour" *in place** of serf labour thus meant nothing more than the free labour of the wage-worker or small independent producer under the conditions of commodity production, i.e., of bourgeois social and economic relations. The land *redemption* payments brought out this nature of the Reform in even bolder relief, for they lent a stimulus to monetary economy, i.e., they increased the peasant's dependence on the market.

The Narodniks saw in the emancipation of the peasants with the provision of land allotments a *non*-capitalist principle, the "genesis" of what they called "people's production". In the emancipation of the peasants without land they saw the capitalist principle. The Narodniks (particularly Mr. Nikolai —on) based this view *on the teachings of Marx*, citing in its justification that the freeing of the worker from the means of production is a fundamental condition of the capitalist mode of production. A singular phenomenon: beginning with the eighties (if not still earlier) Marxism was already such an indisputable, actually dominating force among the progressive social doctrines in Western Europe, that for a long time in Russia theories hostile to Marxism could not be openly expressed. These theories made sophistry of Marxism and falsified it (sometimes unconsciously); they appeared to be Marxist and, "by referring to Marx", tried to deny the application of Marx's theory to Russia! The Narodnik theory of Mr. Nikolai —on claimed to be "Marxist" (in the 1880s and 1890s); subsequently the liberal-bourgeois theory of Messrs. Struve, Tugan-Baranovsky and Co. began by *"almost"* fully accepting Marxism, these gentlemen developed their views and preached their liberalism under the guise of "the further critical development" of Marxism. We shall probably have more than one occasion to return to this singular feature of the development of Russian social theories since the end of the nineteenth century (up to and including contemporary opportunism—liquida-

---

* Insofar as this *replacement* was going on *in actual fact*, we shall see further that it was a more complicated process than would appear on the surface.

tionism, which clings to Marxist *terminology* in order to cover up its anti-Marxist substance).

What interests us at the present moment is the Narodnik appraisal of the "great Reform". It is a radical mistake to think that the striving to deprive the peasants of land in 1861 represented a capitalist tendency, whereas the striving to endow them with land was anti-capitalist, socialist (the best among the Narodniks saw in the term "people's production" a pseudonym for socialism, a pseudonym imposed by *censorship* restrictions). This view is a great sin against historical truth; it transfers Marx's "ready-made" formula (a "formula" which is applicable only to highly developed commodity production) to the conditions of *serfdom*. Depriving the peasants of land in 1861 in most cases actually meant the creation, not of a free labourer in capitalist production, but of a *bonded* (i. e., in fact a semi-serf or even almost serf) *tenant* on the same land that belonged to the "master", the landowner. Actually, the "allotments" of 1861 meant in most cases the creation, not of a free and independent farmer, but of a tenant *bound to the land* and in fact compelled to perform the same old corvée by cultivating the landlord's land with his own farm equipment, in payment for pasture, for meadows, for the necessary arable land, etc.

The peasant entered the sphere of bourgeois social relations to the extent to which he was actually, and not merely nominally, emancipated from serf relations (the essence of these relations was "labour-rent", i. e., the labour performed for the landowner by a peasant endowed with an allotment of land). But this *real* emancipation from feudal relations was much more complicated than the Narodniks thought. *At that time* the struggle between those who were in favour of depriving the peasants of land and those in favour of "endowing" them, often expressed merely a struggle between two *feudalist* camps, a dispute over the question as to whether it was more advantageous to the landowner to have a tenant (or a peasant rendering labour service) without any land *or* with an "allotment", i. e., one bound to the locality, bound by a patch of land insufficient to provide for his living and therefore compelling him to hire himself out for a "livelihood" (selling himself into bondage to the landowner).

On the other hand, there is no doubt that the greater the amount of land the peasants received upon their emancipation, and the cheaper the price they had to pay for it, the more rapidly, fully and freely would capitalism have developed in Russia, and the sooner would the survivals of serfdom and bondage have disappeared, the larger the home market would have become, and the more certain would the development of towns, industry and trade have been.

The Narodniks made the mistake of dealing with the problem in a utopian manner, in the abstract, unrelated to the actual historic circumstances. They declared that the "allotment" was the basis for independent small-scale farming. *Insofar* as this was true, the peasant "endowed with land" became a commodity producer and found himself in the conditions of bourgeois society. *Actually*, however, the "allotment" was too often so small, so burdened with excessive payments, situated so unfavourably for the peasant and so "fortunately" for the landlord, that the "allotment" peasant inevitably found himself in a position of unredeemable bondage, his status remained, in fact, the same as under the relations of serfdom; he performed the same old corvée service (in the form of labour-service, etc.).

Thus, two tendencies were latent in Narodism, which the Marxists defined even then, when they referred to the liberal-Narodnik views, the liberal-Narodnik appraisal, etc. Insofar as the Narodniks painted the Reform of 1861 in bright colours, forgetting that in the majority of cases "endowment" actually meant that the landlords' estates were ensured a supply of cheap slave labour, a supply of cheap hands tied to the place of residence, they descended (often without being aware of it) to the point of view of liberalism, the point of view of the liberal bourgeois, or even of the liberal landowner; objectively they became the advocates of the type of capitalist evolution which is most burdened with landowner traditions, is most bound up with the feudal past, of which it is ridding itself most slowly and with the greatest difficulty.

The Narodniks, however, were bourgeois democrats to the extent that they did not idealise the Reform of 1861, but fought ardently and sincerely for the smallest payments and the largest "allotments", for "allotments" without *any* restrictions, with the utmost cultural, legal, etc., independence for the peasant. Their only shortcoming was that their democracy was by no means always consistent and determined and that, moreover, they failed to realise that it was of a bourgeois nature. Incidentally, it may be said that the most "Left" of our Social-Narodniks even to this day often conceive of the word "bourgeois" in this connotation as smacking of "politics", whereas, in point of fact, the term bourgeois democracy represents the only exact scientific definition from the Marxist point of view.

These two tendencies in Narodism—the liberal and the democratic—were already quite clearly *indicated* at the time of the Reform of 1861. We cannot dwell here in greater detail on an analysis of these tendencies, particularly on the connection between utopian socialism and the second of these tendencies. We shall merely mention the difference between the ideological and political trends of, say, Kavelin, on the one hand, and Chernyshevsky, on the other.

When we contemplate, in a general way, the change in the entire system of the Russian state in 1861, we are bound to admit that that change was a step in the transformation of feudal monarchy into a bourgeois monarchy. This is true not only from the economic, but also from the political point of view. We need only recall the nature of the reforms in the sphere of the judiciary, administration, local self-government, etc., which followed the Peasant Reform of 1861, to see the correctness of this statement. One may argue whether this "step" was a great or a small one, whether it was quick or slow, but the *direction* in which this step was taken is so clear, it has been made so clear by all the subsequent events, that there can hardly be two opinions about it. It is, however, all the more necessary to stress this *direction* because of the more frequent half-baked opinions we hear nowadays to the effect that "steps" in the transformation into a bourgeois monarchy in Russia have been taken only in very recent years.

Of the two Narodnik tendencies referred to, the democratic tendency, the tendency not based on the intelligence and initiative of landowning, bureaucratic and bourgeois circles, was extremely weak in 1861. That is why matters went no further than a very small "step" in the transforma-

APROPOS OF AN ANNIVERSARY

tion into a bourgeois monarchy. Still, this weak tendency existed even then. It showed itself subsequently too, sometimes more strongly and sometimes more feebly, both in the sphere of social ideas and in the sphere of the social movement characteristic of the *entire* post-Reform period. This tendency grew with each decade of the period, nurtured by each step in the economic evolution of the country and, consequently, also by the combination of social, juridical and cultural conditions.

These two tendencies, which were only just beginning to emerge in 1861, found a fairly full and open expression forty-four years after the Peasant Reform, in the most varied spheres of social life, in the various twists and turns of the social movement, in the activity of large masses of the population and of important political parties. The Cadets and the Trudoviks—taking each of these terms in its broadest meaning—are the direct descendants and successors, the actual vehicles of the two tendencies which were already taking shape half a century ago. The connection between 1861 and the events that took place forty-four years later is indisputable and obvious. And the fact that both tendencies have survived during half a century, that they have grown stronger, developed and expanded, unquestionably testifies to their strength; it shows that they are deeply rooted in the entire economic structure of Russia.

Menshikov, the *Novoye Vremya* writer, expressed this connection between the Peasant Reform and the events of the recent past in the following singular tirade: "The year 1861 failed to prevent 1905—hence, why shout about the *greatness* of a reform which has failed so miserably?" (*Novoye Vremya*,[78] No. 12512, of January 11, "An Unnecessary Jubilee".)

With these words Menshikov inadvertently touched upon extremely interesting scientific problems of history; first, the interrelation between reform and revolution in general, and, secondly, the connection, interdependence, and affinity between the socio-historical trends, strivings and tendencies of 1861 and the 1905-07 period.

The concept "reform", is undoubtedly the opposite of the concept "revolution". Failure to remember this contrast, failure to remember the line that divides these two

concepts, constantly leads to very serious mistakes in all
historical discussions. But this contrast is not something
absolute, this line is not something dead, but alive and changing, and one must be able to define it in each particular
case. The Reform of 1861 remained but a reform owing to
the extreme feebleness, ignorance and lack of cohesion
between the social elements for whom change was essential.

That is the reason for such marked feudal features in this
reform, that is why it was so full of bureaucratic monstros-
ities and brought the peasants such untold misfortunes.
Our peasantry has suffered much more from the inadequate
development of capitalism than it has from capitalism
itself.

Although this reform remained nothing but a reform
because of the weakness of certain social elements, it created,
despite all obstacles and hindrances, conditions for the further
development of those elements; these conditions expanded
the area in which the old contradictions came into play
and extended the number of groups, strata and classes of the
population that took a conscious part in "the play" of contradictions. That is why the followers of the democratic tendency that was hostile to liberalism at the time of the 1861
Reform, those who then (and for a long time after) appeared
to be mere individuals with no ground under their feet—that
is why those people *proved* actually to be on incomparably
more solid ground when the conditions that had been little
more than embryonic in 1861 grew to maturity. Those participants in the Reform of 1861 who regarded it as nothing
more than a reform* proved to be on more solid ground than
the liberal reformists. The former will forever be remembered
in history as the advanced representatives of their epoch;
whereas the latter will be remembered as people who were
irresolute, weak-willed and impotent in face of the forces
of the old and obsolete.

In their theories, the Narodniks, beginning with 1861
(and their forerunners even prior to 1861), have, throughout more than half a century, always advocated a *different*,
i. e., *non-capitalist*, path for Russia. History has fully

---

* It is probably a printer's error in Russian. According to the
sense, it should read: "as something more than a reform".—*Ed.*

refuted their error. History has fully proved and the events of 1905-07, the action of the various classes of Russian society at that time, have graphically confirmed that Russia is developing along capitalist lines, and that there can be no other path for her development. But he would be a poor Marxist indeed who to this day failed to learn from the history of this half-century the *real* meaning of aspirations expressed in the course of half a century and embodied in an erroneous ideology, in an endeavour to plot a "different" path for the fatherland to travel.

A comparison between 1861 and 1905-07 makes it perfectly clear that the *real* historical meaning of the Narodnik ideology consisted in contrasting *two* paths of *capitalist* development: one path involving the adaptation of the new, capitalist Russia to the old, the subordination of the former to the latter, thus impeding the course of development; the other—the path of supplanting the old by the new, of entirely removing the obsolete that is obstructing the new; of accelerating the course of development. The programmes of the Cadets and the Trudoviks—the former liberal, and the latter democratic—while inconsistent and at times confused and betraying a lack of understanding, represent a vivid expression of the *actual* paths of this development—both *within the framework* of capitalism—which have been steadfastly pursued for more than half a century.

The present period imperatively demands of us that we have a clear understanding of the conditions of these two paths, that we have a clear idea of the two tendencies of 1861 and of their subsequent evolution. We are witnessing a further change in the entire system of the Russian state, *one more* step in its transformation into a bourgeois monarchy. This new step, which is just as hesitant, just as vacillating, just as ill-chosen and just as unsound as the previous one, confronts us with the old problems. History has not yet decided which of the two paths of Russia's capitalist development will finally determine her bourgeois system: the objective forces on which the decision depends are not yet exhausted. We cannot tell beforehand what the decision will be, before we have the experience of all the friction, clashes and conflicts that make up the life of society. We cannot tell beforehand what will be the resultant of the two tendencies that have been making themselves felt ever since 1861. But we can, and must, insist on a clear understanding of both tendencies, insist that Marxists (and this is one of their duties, in their capacity of "leaders", in the period of disintegration, confusion, scepticism and worship of momentary success) should contribute their activity to this resultant—not in a negative form (like liquidationism or, in general, helpless drifting after one decadent mood or another), but in a positive form, in the form of upholding the interests of evolution in its entirety, its fundamental and most essential interests.

The representatives of the democratic tendency, while marching toward their goal, continually waver and are subject to the influence of liberalism. To prevent these waverings and to end this subjection is one of the most important historical tasks of Marxism in Russia.

Mysl, No. 3, February 1911
  Signed: *V. Ilyin*

Published according to
the *Mysl* text

"THE PEASANT REFORM"
AND THE PROLETARIAN-PEASANT REVOLUTION

The celebration of the jubilee, so much feared by the Romanov monarchy, and over which the Russian liberals have gushed so sentimentally, is over. The tsar's government celebrated it by assiduously circulating "among the people" the Black-Hundred jubilee pamphlets issued by the "National Club", by wholesale arrests of all "suspects", by banning meetings at which speeches of even the slightest democratic tinge might be expected, by fining and suppressing newspapers, and by persecuting "subversive" cinemas.

The liberals celebrated the jubilee by weeping buckets of tears about the necessity of "a second February 19" (*Vestnik Yevropy*[79]), by expressing their allegiance (the tsar's picture appearing prominently in *Rech*), and by indulging in talk about their civic despondency, the fragility of the native "Constitution", the devastating "break-up" of the "time-honoured principles of land tenure" by Stolypin's agrarian policy, and so on, and so forth.

In an edict addressed to Stolypin, Nicholas II declared that Stolypin's agrarian policy was the final stage of "the great Reform" of February 19, 1861, i. e., the surrender of peasant land to be plundered by a handful of bloodsuckers, kulaks, and well-to-do peasants, and the surrender of the countryside to the rule of the feudal landowners.

It must be admitted that Nicholas the Bloody, Russia's premier landowner, is nearer to the historical truth than our amiable liberals. The biggest landowner and the chief feudal lord is aware of, or rather has learned from the exhortation of the Council of the United Nobility, the maxim of the class struggle according to which "reforms" that are carried out by feudal lords must of necessity be feudal in every aspect, must of necessity be accompanied by a regime of out and out violence. Our Cadets, and our liberals in general, fear the revolutionary movement of the masses, which alone is capable of wiping the feudal landowners and their unlimited power in the Russian state from the face of the earth; and this fear prevents them from appreciating the truth that so long as the feudal landowners have not been overthrown, every reform—and, particularly, every agrarian reform—is bound to be feudal in its aspect and nature, and in its mode of application. To fear revolution, to dream of reform, and to snivel because in practice "reforms" are applied by the feudal lords in a feudal way, is the height of baseness and stupidity. Nicholas II is much more straightforward and does more to teach the Russian people sense when he clearly "offers" them the plain choice: either feudal "reforms" or the overthrow of the feudal landowners by a people's revolution.

The Reform of February 19, 1861, was a feudal reform which our liberals are able to dress up and represent as a "peaceful" reform only because at that time the revolutionary *movement* in Russia was so weak as to amount to nothing, and, as for a revolutionary *class*, there existed none among the oppressed masses of those days. The decree of November 9, 1906, and the law of June 14, 1910, are feudal reforms with as much bourgeois content as the Reform of 1861; but the liberals *cannot* represent these as "peaceful" reforms, they cannot dress them up so easily (although they are already beginning to do so, as for instance, in *Russkaya Mysl*), for the few isolated revolutionaries of 1861 may be forgotten, but the Revolution of 1905 cannot be forgotten. The year 1905 saw the birth of a revolutionary *class* in Russia, the proletariat, which succeeded in rousing the peasant masses to the revolutionary struggle. And once a revolutionary class has been born in any country it cannot be suppressed by any amount of persecution; it can only perish if the whole country perishes, it can only die, after it has attained victory.

———

Let us call to mind the basic features of the Peasant Reform of 1861. The notorious "emancipation" meant the unscrupulous robbery of the peasants and their subjection to an endless succession of tyrannies and insults. "Emancipation" was seized upon as a pretext to cut off part of the peasants' land. In the black-earth gubernias these cut-off lands amounted to *more* than one-fifth of the total· held by peasants; in some gubernias the land that was cut off, taken away from the peasants, amounted to one-third or even two-fifths of all the peasants' land. As a result of "emancipation" the peasants' land was so divided from the landed estates as to compel the peasants to settle on "bad land", and the landed estates were wedged into the peasants' land to make it easier for the noble lords to enslave the peasants and to lease land to them on usurious terms. As a result of "emancipation", the peasants were forced to "redeem" their own land, moreover, they were forced to pay *double or treble* its real price. The overall result of the whole "epoch of reforms" which marked the 1860s was that the peasants remained poverty-stricken, downtrodden, ignorant, and subject to the feudal landowners in the courts, in the organs of administration, in the schools, and in the Zemstvos.

The "great Reform" was a feudal reform; nor could it be anything else, for it was carried out by the feudal landowners. But what was the force that compelled them to resort to reform? It was the force of economic development which was drawing Russia on to the path of capitalism. The feudal landowners could not prevent the growth of trade between Russia and Europe; they could not bolster up the old, tottering forms of economic life. The Crimean war demonstrated the rottenness and impotence of feudal Russia. The peasant "riots", which had been growing in number and intensity in the decades prior to emancipation, compelled Alexander II, the country's biggest landowner, to admit that it would be better to emancipate *from above* than to wait until he was overthrown *from below*.

"The Peasant Reform" was a bourgeois reform carried out by feudal landowners. It was a step in the transformation of Russia into a bourgeois monarchy. In substance the Peasant Reform was a bourgeois measure. The *less* the amount of land cut off from the peasants' holdings, the *more fully* peasant lands were separated from the landed estates, the *lower* the tribute paid to the feudal landowners

by the peasants (i. e., the lower the "redemption" payments)
and the *greater the extent* the peasants in any locality were able
to escape the influence and pressure of the feudal landowners—the more obvious was the bourgeois essence of the
Reform. *To the extent* that the peasant extricated himself
from the clutches of the feudal landowner, he became a
slave to the power of money, found himself living in the
conditions of commodity production and dependent on rising capitalism. After 1861 capitalism developed in Russia
at such a rapid rate that in a few decades it wrought a transformation that had taken centuries in some of the old countries of Europe.

The celebrated struggle between the feudal landowners
and the liberals, which our liberal and liberal-Narodnik
historians have praised and made so much of, was a struggle
waged *within* the ruling classes, a struggle waged for the
most part *within the ranks of the landowner class*, a struggle
waged *exclusively* over the extent and the forms of the proposed *concessions*. The liberals, like the feudal landowners,
upheld the property rights and rule of the landowners, and
indignantly denounced all revolutionary ideas about *abolishing* those property rights, about *completely overthrowing*
that rule.

Such revolutionary ideas could not but ferment in the
minds of the serf peasants. The peasant masses, however,
were so crushed and stupefied by centuries of slavery that
at the time of the Reform they were incapable of anything
more than scattered, isolated rebellions, or rather "riots",
devoid of any political purpose. Nevertheless, even then
there were revolutionaries in Russia who took the side of
the peasantry, who saw how limited, how poverty-stricken
was the over-advertised "Peasant Reform", and who recognised its true feudal nature. These revolutionaries of whom
there were extremely few at that time were headed by N.G.
Chernyshevsky.

February 19, 1861, heralded the birth of the new, bourgeois, Russia which had been growing out of the era of
serfdom. The liberals of the 1860s, on the one hand, and
Chernyshevsky, on the other, were the representatives of
two historical tendencies, of two historical forces which
to this day have been determining the issue of the struggle

for the new Russia. That is why on the occasion of the fiftieth anniversary of February 19, it is necessary for the class-conscious proletariat to form as clear an idea as possible of the substance and interrelation of these two tendencies.

The liberals wanted to "emancipate" Russia "from above", taking care not to destroy either the monarchy of the tsars, or the property rights and the rule of the landowners, prevailing upon them only to make "concessions" to the spirit of the times. The liberals were, and still are, the ideologists of the bourgeoisie, which cannot reconcile itself to serfdom, but is afraid of revolution, is afraid of the mass movement which would be capable of overthrowing the monarchy and abolishing the rule of the landowners. That is why the liberals confine themselves to a "struggle for reforms", a "struggle for rights", that is to say, a struggle for a division of power between the feudal landowners and the bourgeoisie. As long as that is the relation of forces, there *can be no* "reforms" save those carried out by the feudal landowners, and *no* "rights" save those limited by the tyranny of the feudal landowners.

Chernyshevsky was a utopian socialist, who dreamed of a transition to socialism through the old, semi-feudal peasant village commune.[80] He did not see, nor could he see in the sixties of the past century, that only the development of capitalism and of the proletariat could create the material conditions and the social force for the achievement of socialism. But Chernyshevsky was not only a utopian socialist; he was also a revolutionary democrat, he approached all the political events of his times in a revolutionary spirit and was able to exercise a revolutionary influence by advocating, in spite of all the barriers and obstacles placed in his way by the censorship, the idea of a peasant revolution, the idea of the struggle of the masses for the overthrow of all the old authorities. In speaking of the "Peasant Reform" of 1861, which the liberals at first tried to whitewash and subsequently even glorified, he described it as *vile*, for he clearly saw its feudal nature, he clearly saw that the liberal emancipators were robbing the peasants of their last shirt. Chernyshevsky spoke of the liberals of the sixties as *"windbags, braggarts and fools"*,[81] for he clearly saw their dread of revolution, their spinelessness and their servility before the powers that be.

These two historical tendencies have continued developing in the course of the half-century that has elapsed since February 19, 1861, diverging ever more clearly, definitely and decisively. The forces of the liberal-monarchist bourgeoisie, who preached that "educational" activity was all that was needed, and who fought shy of the revolutionary underground, grew stronger. On the other hand, the forces of democracy and socialism also became stronger, at first merging into one in utopian ideology and in the intellectualist struggles of the Narodnaya Volya and the revolutionary Narodniks. However, since the early nineties, with the transition from the revolutionary struggle of terrorists and individual propagandists to the struggle of the revolutionary classes themselves, these forces diverged.

The decade preceding the Revolution—from 1895 to 1904—was marked by open action of the proletarian masses and by their steady growth, by the growth of the strike struggle, of Social-Democratic working-class propaganda and organisation, and of the Social-Democratic Labour Party. Following the lead of the socialist vanguard of the proletariat, the revolutionary-democratic peasantry has also embarked upon mass struggle, particularly since 1902.

The two tendencies, which in 1861 had just emerged and had begun to appear in literature in bare outline, developed and grew in the Revolution of 1905, and found reflection in the movement of the *masses* and the struggle carried on by *political parties* in the most varied fields of activity, in the press, at mass meetings, in unions, in strikes, in uprisings, and in the State Dumas.

The liberal-monarchist bourgeoisie established the Cadet and Octobrist parties that at first (until the summer of 1905) worked together in one liberal Zemstvo movement, and subsequently split into two separate parties fiercely competing with each other (and still doing so), the one putting forward primarily its liberal, the other primarily its monarchist, *"face"*—but always agreeing on the most essential issues; they both denounce the revolutionaries, disparage the December uprising, and honour as their flag the "constitutional" fig-leaf of absolutism. Both parties have professed and still profess "strictly constitutional" principles, that is to say, they confine themselves to the limited field of activity which the Black-Hundred tsar and the feudal landowners could concede without giving up power, without relinquishing their autocratic rule, without sacrificing a single kopek of revenues, "sanctified" by ages of slave-holding, or parting with the least of their "justly acquired" privileges.

The democratic and the socialist trends separated from the liberal trend, and drew a line of demarcation between themselves. The proletariat organised and acted independently of the peasantry, rallying around its own, working-class, Social-Democratic, party. The organisation of the peasantry in the revolution was incomparably weaker, its actions were infinitely more scattered and feeble, the level of its class-consciousness was much lower, and monarchist illusions (as well as constitutional illusions, which are closely connected with them) often paralysed its energy, made it dependent upon the liberals, and sometimes upon the Black Hundreds and gave rise to empty day-dreams about "God-given land" which prevented it from launching an assault upon the landowning nobility with the object of completely abolishing that class. By and large, the peasantry taken as a mass, nevertheless fought the landowners, acted in a revolutionary spirit, and in all the Dumas—even in the Third Duma which was elected on the basis of representation specifically favouring the feudal landowners—they created Trudovik groups that represented a genuinely democratic movement despite their frequent vacillations. In the mass movement of 1905-07, the Cadets and Trudoviks represented and politically formulated the position and trends of the liberal-monarchist and the revolutionary-democratic bourgeoisie respectively.

The year 1861 begot the year 1905. The feudal character of the first "great" bourgeois reform impeded the course of development, condemned the peasants to a thousand still worse and more bitter torments, but it did not change the course of development, did not avert the bourgeois revolution of 1905. The Reform of 1861 delayed the issue by opening a valve, as it were, by permitting some growth of capitalism; but it did not prevent the inevitable issue, which

in 1905 was fought out in an incomparably wider field, in
the onslaught of the masses upon the tsar's autocracy and
the feudal landowners. The Reform, which the feudal landowners granted at a time when the oppressed masses were
completely undeveloped, begot the revolution by the time
the revolutionary elements among those masses had reached
maturity.

The Third State Duma and Stolypin's agrarian policy
represent the second bourgeois reform carried out by the
feudal landowners. February 19, 1861, was the first step
taken *in the transformation* of the purely feudal autocracy
into a bourgeois monarchy; the period of 1908-10 represents the second step, an even more serious one, *along the
same road.* Nearly four and a half years have elapsed since
the promulgation of the decree of November 9, 1906; more
than three and a half years have elapsed since June 3,
1907[82]; yet today the Cadet bourgeoisie, and to a large
extent the Octobrist bourgeoisie, are becoming convinced
that the "Constitution" of June 3 and the agrarian policy
of June 3 have proved "unsuccessful". "The most Right
among the Cadets", as Mr. Maklakov, that semi-Octobrist,
has been justly dubbed, was fully justified in declaring in
the State Duma on February 25, on behalf both of the
Cadets and of the Octobrists, that "today it is the pivotal elements of the country who are dissatisfied, those who are most
anxious for durable peace, who dread a new rise of the tide
of revolution". There is one common slogan: "It is the general opinion," Mr. Maklakov went on to say, "that if we
continue on the road along which they are taking us they
will lead us to a second revolution".

The common slogan of the Cadet and the Octobrist bourgeoisie in the spring of 1911 confirms that the appraisal
of the state of affairs given by our Party in the resolution
adopted at its conference in December 1908 was correct.
"The principal factors of economic and political life," that
resolution stated, "which gave rise to the Revolution of
1905 continue to operate, and, the economic and political
situation being what it is, a new revolutionary crisis is inevitably maturing."

Menshikov, the paid hack of the tsarist Black-Hundred
government, recently declared in *Novoye Vremya* that the

Reform of February 19 "was a miserable failure", because "the year 1861 failed to prevent 1905". Now the hired lawyers and parliamentarians of the liberal bourgeoisie declare that the "reforms" of November 9, 1906, and of June 3, 1907, are a failure because these "reforms" *lead* to a second revolution.

The two statements, as well as the entire history of the liberal and revolutionary movements in the period 1861-1905, provide extremely interesting material for an elucidation of the very important question of the relation between reform and revolution and the role of reformists and revolutionaries in the social struggle.

The opponents of revolution, some of them with hatred and a gnashing of teeth, others in a spirit of dejection and despondency, admit that the "reforms" of 1861 and of 1907-10 have failed in their purpose, because they do not prevent revolution. Social-Democrats, the representatives of the only consistently revolutionary class of our times, reply: revolutionaries have played an immense historical role in the social struggle and in all social crises *even when* the immediate result of those crises has been half-hearted reforms. Revolutionaries are the leaders of those forces of society that effect all change; reforms are the by-product of the revolutionary struggle.

The revolutionaries of 1861 remained isolated and, on the face of it, suffered complete defeat. Actually, they were the great figures of the day, and the further that day recedes, the more clearly do we see their greatness and the more obvious is the insignificance and paltriness of the liberal reformists of those days.

The revolutionary class of 1905-07, the socialist proletariat, on the face of it, also suffered complete defeat. Both the liberal monarchists and the liquidators among the pseudo-Marxists have been shouting from the house-tops that the proletariat went "too far" and resorted to "excesses", that it succumbed to the attraction of "the spontaneous class struggle", that it let itself be seduced by the pernicious idea of the "hegemony of the proletariat", and so on, and so forth. Actually, the "sin" of the proletariat was that it did not go far enough, but that "sin" is accounted for by the state of its forces at that time and is being atoned for by unremitting activity, even in times of blackest reaction, on the part of revolutionary Social-Democrats, by their steadfast struggle against all manifestations of reformism and opportunism. Actually, everything that has been won from the enemies, and everything that is enduring in these gains, has been won and is maintained only to the extent that the revolutionary struggle is strong and alive in all spheres of proletarian activity. Actually, the proletariat alone has championed consistent democracy to the end, exposing all the instability of the liberals, freeing the peasantry from their influence, and rising with heroic courage in insurrection.

No one is in a position to foretell to what extent really democratic changes will be effected in Russia in the era of her bourgeois revolutions, but there can be no shadow of doubt that *only* the revolutionary struggle of the proletariat will determine the extent and the success of the changes. Between feudal "reforms" in the bourgeois spirit and the democratic revolution led by the proletariat there can only be the vacillations of liberalism and opportunist reformism— impotent, spineless, and devoid of ideals.

When we look at the history of the last half-century in Russia, when we cast a glance at 1861 and 1905, we can only repeat the words of our Party resolution with even greater conviction: "As before, the aim of our struggle is to overthrow tsarism and bring about the conquest of power by the proletariat relying on the revolutionary sections of the peasantry and accomplishing the bourgeois-democratic revolution by means of the convening of a popular constituent assembly and the establishment of a democratic republic".

Sotsial-Demokrat, No. 21-22,   Published according to
March 19 (April 1), 1911   the *Sotsial-Demokrat* text

WRECKERS OF THE PARTY
IN THE ROLE OF "WRECKERS OF LEGENDS"

Exactly a year ago the Central Organ of our Party published the following extremely important letter from the Central Committee Bureau in Russia to the Central Committee Bureau Abroad:

"We [i. e., the Bureau of the C.. C. in Russia] approached Comrades Mikhail, Roman, and Yuri, suggesting that they should start work, but we received a reply which states that, in their opinion, not only are the decisions of the Plenary Meeting harmful, but that the very existence of the Central Committee is harmful. On these grounds, they refuse to attend even a single meeting for co-optation."*

Things could not be clearer. In the persons of Mikhail, Roman, and Yuri we are dealing with open renegades who deem it unnecessary to resort to "diplomacy" and wriggling in the spirit of *Golos*, and who declare *frankly* that they have broken with our Party. Here we have a clash of two "tactics": one, that of Martov, Dan and Co., representing an effort to disintegrate the "old" Party from within, to keep the old Party in a sickly condition until the Stolypin brand of "Social-Democrats", the liquidators, gain a firm foothold; the other, that of Potresov, Levitsky, Mikhail, Roman, Yuri, and Co., proceeds from the fact that the game of sapping the strength of the old Party from within by intrigues is not worth the candle and that it is necessary to effect an open break with the R.S.D.L.P. *at once.*

The publication of the statement by Mikhail, Roman, and Yuri has badly upset the game of their friends and pa-

---

* See present edition, Vol. 16, "*Golos* (Voice) of the Liquidators Against the Party".—*Ed.*

trons of *Golos Sotsial-Demokrata*. But the damage has been done: Dan, Martov and Co. have been obliged to go on covering up their tracks, and while, "on the one hand", they take the part of the three mentioned renegades, "on the other", they make a slight attempt to "disavow" them. Martov even mustered up courage—in the last but one, i. e., in the 23rd, issue of *Golos*, *ten months after* the publication of the fact that his three friends had renounced the Party—to chide the three gentlemen for their "thoughtlessness"....

But now the wheel of "history" (the history of liquidationism) has turned once again. A number of circumstances—primarily the rebuff administered to liquidationism by some Social-Democratic groups engaged in open activities—has caused Potresov, Levitsky, Mikhail, Roman, and Co. to slow down a bit and to get closer to the "wise" and more cautious "tactic" of covering up their tracks *à la* Dan and Martov. This has made it possible for a "rebuttal" of the document quoted above to appear—*a year later*.

Obviously, the "rebuttal" which appeared in *Golos* under the pompous heading "A Wrecked Legend" is *false from beginning to end*. It seems that in "officially" refusing to join the Central Committee or to attend even one meeting for the purpose of co-opting new members the above-mentioned three renegades were actuated by "motives of a personal nature". And only "later, in a *private* [strictly "private", of course] conversation with him [i. e., the representative of the C. C.] we referred to a number of considerations [in this case, of a political nature] which compel us [i. e., Roman, Mikhail, and Yuri] to view with disfavour the proposition made to us".

Hence, Point 1 in the "rebuttal": the statement referred to by the Central Organ was made in "a private conversation" after official uniforms had been laid aside. This extremely "extenuating circumstance" radically alters matters, doesn't it?

But what, *according to their own testimony*, did Mikhail, Roman, and Yuri say in that "private conversation"? They did not say that the decisions of the Central Committee were harmful; all they did, you see, was to take the liberty to observe that *"the road dictated by the Plenary Meeting does not strengthen but weakens the position of the C. C."*;

that the recommendation made by the Central Committee
to the Party about taking advantage of legal opportunities
*"has meant and means the wrecking of the legal workers'
organisations"*; that the very first step taken by the C. C.
along this road (the publication of the resolution dealing
with a conference of the Party) *"has supplied the government
with a pretext"* for wrecking workers' organisations. Well,
don't you think that this is entirely different from what was
stated by the representative of the Central Committee,
according to whom the three liquidators from the candidates
appointed in London "deem the interference of the C. C. in
the spontaneous process of the Social-Democratic forces
grouping themselves in legal organisations, as being tantamount to performing an abortion in the second month of
pregnancy"? And that's what they call a "rebuttal"!

Further it seems that they did not say that the existence of the C. C. is harmful, God forbid! All they did was
to express the opinion, strictly "privately" of course, that
it would be much better if, instead of the C. C., there existed an "organising group" which "would not be requested
to show a mandate" (i. e., a *Party* mandate), just as, in
their time, the *Iskra* and *Zarya* group was never requested
to show one (i. e., a "mandate").* The main accusation has
thus been "rebutted" by Mikhail, Roman, and Yuri almost
as successfully as their colleague Igorev recently "rebutted"
the charges of plotting against the Central Committee and
the Party which the Menshevik pro-Party comrades, Plekhanov and A. Moskovsky, [83] preferred against him.... What
is needed, you see, is not a Central Committee, but an "organising group", such as the *"Iskra* and *Zarya* group". To be
sure, the *Iskra* and *Zarya* group was a revolutionary Social-
Democratic group, whereas Messrs. Mikhail, Roman, and
Yuri need a liquidationist organising group. But that is
not the point at the moment. The point is that *according
to their own testimony*, Martov's and Dan's three allies
proposed to replace the C. C. by a private organising group,
whom nobody could request to show a despised "mandate"
and which could do all the "liquidating" it liked. A fine
"rebuttal" indeed!...

---

* See *Golos*, supplement to No. 24, p. 3.

One of the "pivots" of the "rebuttal" published by Roman, Mikhail, and Yuri is the story that the representative of the C. C., who invited them to attend "at least one meeting" of the collegium, tried to persuade them by saying that he (i. e., the representative of the C. C.) and other "Bolsheviks in Russia" were bent on "freeing themselves from the guiding influence of Lenin's circle". This statement made by a Bolshevik in Russia, *for which we have the evidence of three liquidators*, is particularly relished by the editors of *Golos*, who think they can use it to justify somebody and something. It is obvious, however, that the *Golos* crowd have become entangled in their own snares and speak *against* themselves. Just use your brains, esteemed editors of *Golos*. *Let us assume* that the Bolshevik who approached your friends on behalf of the Central Committee was opposed to what you call "Lenin's circle". *So much the worse for you.* For it was the very same Bolshevik who wrote the letter reporting the repudiation of the Party by your three friends, which we printed in No. 12 of the Central Organ. If that Bolshevik is not a follower of what you call "Lenin's circle", then you must consider his evidence to be all the more unbiased. *Let us assume* that the members of the Central Committee who invited you were opposed to "Lenin's circle"*—from your own standpoint that should only aggravate the guilt of the three liquidators who refused to join the Central Committee even under conditions so favourable for them. What has come over the *Golos* gentlemen? They are generally more clever ... at covering up their tracks. You have made a very clumsy job of it, gentlemen! More stupid even than the "rebuttals" published by Stolypin's "Information Bureau".

---

* Another member of the Central Committee, one of the "Bolsheviks in Russia", is reproached by *Golos* with having, you see, placed "obstacles in the way of co-opting *Golos* people as members of the Central Committee, since he declared that the Bolshevik members of the C.C. ... would permit the co-option only of such candidates as will first sign a statement renouncing 'liquidationism'". The member of the C.C. whom the *Golos* crowd accuse of so terrible a crime is at present *not in a position* to answer the liquidationist gentlemen himself.[84] That is why we shall say on his behalf: *if* what you report of him were true, it would only mean that from the standpoint of the Party he was absolutely right and that he acted fully in the spirit of the decisions of the Plenary Meeting.

You have had ill luck with your "rebuttal", gentlemen of *Golos*, just as you have had ill luck with your recent scurrilous leaflets. You wanted "to prove too much", you wanted to prove that all Social-Democrats are pro-Party—and that's why you have proved nothing. Just reflect a little: one day you publish the leaflet of the fifty-eight[85] (how many of the fifty-eight are hypocrites and how many have been hoodwinked?), in which you represent your opponents ("Lenin's circle") as arch-monsters, as a "gang", etc. And the very next day you (the editors of *Golos*) issue a leaflet containing a "programme of reforms", in which you declare: everything will be perfect if we (the *Golos* group) are allowed representation in all central Party institutions on a basis of equality with these monsters, with people who are guilty of a number of "crimes", etc., etc. Well, when are you acting "for the benefit of the Party", and when are you looking after your own interests, gentlemen—in the first or in the second case? Those fragrant-smelling *Golos* bulletins as well as its supplements, in which "everything has been made use of", including the Geneva otzovists who style themselves an "ideological circle of *Bolsheviks*", would not be worth mentioning, if not for the fact that they shed such glaring light on the entire policy of *Golos*....

Try hard, you "wreckers of legends", do your utmost! There is one legend which you are indeed helping us to wreck —the legend that you still have something in common with revolutionary Social-Democracy.

Sotsial-Demokrat, No. 21-22,
March 19 (April 1), 1911

Published according to
the *Sotsial-Demokrat* text

134

THE CADETS AND THE OCTOBRISTS

The notorious "Cabinet crisis" and the election of a new Chairman of the State Duma[86] have provided additional material on the social nature and political significance of the Cadet and the Octobrist parties. For the hundredth or the thousandth time the Russian liberal (save the mark!) bourgeoisie has shown its true colours. From the daily press and from the preceding issue of *Zvezda*, the reader knows what these colours are. It may not be superfluous, however, to sum up some of the conclusions, in view of the fact that the Cadet press, which is the most widely circulated, willingly "thunders" against the Octobrists, but is very loath to deal with the *results* of the Cadets' own actions.

Let us recall the behaviour of the party of "people's freedom" during the elections of the new Chairman of the State Duma. On March 21, *Rech* hastened to report: "The people's freedom group has decided to vote for M. Alexeyenko if he is nominated for the post of Chairman of the State Duma. If, however, Rodzyanko is nominated, the group will vote against him". The Constitutional-"Democrats" offer their services to the "Left" Octobrists. But that is not all. The leading article in *Rech* of the same date declares that Alexeyenko is "universally respected", and tries to deal with the matter from the standpoint of the *entire* State Duma: if, it says, the Rights support the nominee of the majority of the Octobrists (i. e., Alexeyenko's candidacy), then the State Duma may, perhaps, "regain the unanimity" with which the nomination of Khomyakov was once accepted. "This unanimity would show that the *entire* Duma realises the exceptional gravity of the situation."

Thus wrote *Rech*. "The entire Duma", nothing more nor less. This should be recalled as often as possible during the elections to the Fourth Duma!

The Cadets are perfectly well aware that the Rights, on principle, are for a Duma without rights; that the Nationalists justify and defend Stolypin and the violation of Article 87. And yet, merely for the sake of voting for Alexeyenko, the Cadets are prepared to forget everything and to proclaim the unanimity of "the *entire* Duma", although they too are fully aware that the workers' deputies will *under no circumstances* allow themselves to be duped by the "unanimity" of the Third Duma, any more than they did at the time of Khomyakov's election.

It is obvious that, as far as the Cadets are concerned, the workers' deputies and the Trudoviks do not count. The Third Duma without them, but with the Rights, with Markov the Second and Purishkevich, is "the *entire* Duma". *That is what the statement of* Rech *amounts to.* And this reasoning of *Rech* correctly draws the line which many have so often interpreted wrongly—namely, the line between the feudal landowners and the bourgeoisie (even the most "liberal", i. e., the Cadet variety), on the one hand, and the workers and the peasants, i. e., the forces of democracy, on the other. Without the forces of democracy, but with the Rights, "we", say the Cadets, are "the entire Duma". That means that when they lay claim to the title of democrats the Cadets are deceiving the people. That means that, as far as the Cadets are concerned, "we" implies the feudal landowners and the bourgeoisie; the rest do not count.

The minor question of the election of a new Chairman of the State Duma has served to remind us once again of the essential truth that the Cadets are *not* democrats, but moderate liberal bourgeois, who long for "the unanimity" of "the entire" parliament of diehard reactionaries and Octobrists. *Competition* with the Octobrists—is all that the "struggle" the Cadets are waging against them amounts to. The Cadets are fighting the Octobrists—there is no doubt of that. But they are not fighting them as representatives of a class, as representatives of larger sections of the population, and the aim of their fight is not to remove the old regime to which the Octobrists are adapting themselves; they are fighting them as *competitors* who are anxious to adapt themselves to *the same* regime, to serve the interests of *the same* class, and to protect it from the too exacting demands of the wider sections of the population (the democratic elements in general and of the proletariat in particular). All that the Cadets are after is to adapt themselves to the same regime, but in a slightly different way; that is the substance of their policy, the policy of the liberal bourgeois. And it is this competition with the Octobrists, the struggle to step into *their* shoes, that lends the fight of the Cadets its peculiar "pungency". This explains the *special hostility* of the Rights and the Octobrists towards the Cadets; it is a hostility of a special kind: "those fellows" (the democrats) are out to annihilate them, while "these fellows" (the Cadets) want to force them down one rung of the ladder; the first prospect calls for an irreconcilable struggle as a matter of principle, it calls for a life and death struggle; the second prospect implies a fight *for the top jobs*, a contest in the sphere of intrigue, rivalry as regards the methods of winning the very same landowning and bourgeois majority, or of earning the confidence of the very same old regime.

The picture which the Third Duma presented on the day of the election of the new Chairman clearly showed this difference.

The Cadet recorder of events "in parliamentary circles" continued to sing the praises of Alexeyenko in *Rech* of March 23, describing him as "a man quite independent and with a strong sense of dignity", and so on and so forth. This is said of an Octobrist who delighted in the coup of June 3!

Such is the Cadet gauge for strict legality: not to protest against June 3, but to protest against March 14. It reminds one of the American saying: "If you steal a loaf of bread you'll surely go to jail, but if you steal a railroad you'll be made a senator".

Mr. Litovtsev, who is responsible for the "In Parliamentary Circles" column in *Rech*, on March 23 wrote that the Left Octobrists and the Cadets "spent a good half of the day worrying: what if he decides to accept" (meaning Rodzyanko who pretended that he was declining nomination).

How could the struggle between the Cadets and their opponents help being *sharp* when the matter revolves around a question so close to and so directly affecting the *entire*

Third Duma, namely, "What if Rodzyanko decides to accept?"!

Rodzyanko did decide to accept. What happened at the elections was that the Rights and the Nationalists roared with laughter and applauded for all they were worth; while the "Left" Octobrists and the *Cadets* maintained a stubborn, systematic silence: they were beaten at their own game; they could not rejoice; they *were forced* to maintain silence. "By way of protest", the Cadets cast their vote for the Nationalist Volkonsky. The democrats alone declared loudly, unequivocally, and clearly that they would take no part in the election of the new Chairman of the Third Duma, and that they declined *any* responsibility for "the entire activity of the Third Duma" (Voiloshnikov's words).

On the day of the elections, at the 86th sitting of the Duma, the only ones who *spoke* in the contest between the competitors were Rodzyanko, the head of the Third Duma, Bulat, and Voiloshnikov. The rest were silent.

Voiloshnikov, speaking on behalf of all the members of his group, correctly pointed out that the Cadets, "due to the peculiar nature of their political position, have always placed all their hopes in alliances inside the Duma", and he ridiculed them as gullible liberals.

The Cadets' political position and its peculiar nature are to be explained by the class character of this party. It is an anti-democratic bourgeois-liberal party. That is why they "always place all their hopes in alliances inside the Duma". This is true in two senses: first, in the sense of contrasting what is going on inside the Duma with what is going on outside it; and, secondly, in the sense that it refers to "alliances" among those social elements, those classes, which represent the "entire" Third Duma.

In connection with the election of Rodzyanko, which signified a victory for the Nationalists, only the workers' deputies and the Trudoviks came out with statements which were *not* meant to promote any alliances "inside the Duma"; with statements which explained the attitude of the forces of democracy in general and of the proletarian forces of democracy in particular, toward the *entire* Third Duma, toward the coup of June 3, and toward the Octobrists and the Cadets jointly. These statements represented a proper

notice served on Rodzyanko and the whole of "his" majority, a proper warning to the "responsible" liberal "opposition" (responsible to the Third Duma and to the men of
June 3) by political parties "responsible" to certain other
forces.

Zvezda, No. 16, April 2, 1911
Signed; V. *Ilyin*

Published according to
the *Zvezda* text

IN MEMORY OF THE COMMUNE

Forty years have passed since the proclamation of the Paris Commune. In accordance with tradition, the French workers paid homage to the memory of the men and women of the revolution of March 18, 1871, by meetings and demonstrations. At the end of May they will again place wreaths on the graves of the Communards who were shot, the victims of the terrible "May Week", and over their graves they will once more vow to fight untiringly until their ideas have triumphed and the cause they bequeathed has been fully achieved.

Why does the proletariat, not only in France but throughout the entire world, honour the men and women of the Paris Commune as their predecessors? And what is the heritage of the Commune?

The Commune sprang up spontaneously. No one consciously prepared it in an organised way. The unsuccessful war with Germany, the privations suffered during the siege, the unemployment among the proletariat and the ruin among the lower middle classes; the indignation of the masses against the upper classes and against authorities who had displayed utter incompetence, the vague unrest among the working class, which was discontented with its lot and was striving for a different social system; the reactionary composition of the National Assembly, which roused apprehensions as to the fate of the republic—all this and many other factors combined to drive the population of Paris to revolution on March 18, which unexpectedly placed power in the hands of the National Guard, in the hands of the working class and the petty bourgeoisie which had sided with it.

It was an event unprecedented in history. Up to that time power had, as a rule, been in the hands of landowners and capitalists, i. e., in the hands of their trusted agents who made up the so-called government. After the revolution of March 18, when M. Thiers' government had fled from Paris with its troops, its police and its officials, the people became masters of the situation and power passed into the hands of the proletariat. But in modern society, the proletariat, economically enslaved by capital, cannot dominate politically unless it breaks the chains which fetter it to capital. That is why the movement of the Commune was bound to take on a socialist tinge, i. e., to strive to overthrow the rule of the bourgeoisie, the rule of capital, and to destroy the very *foundations* of the contemporary social order.

At first this movement was extremely indefinite and confused. It was joined by patriots who hoped that the Commune would renew the war with the Germans and bring it to a successful conclusion. It enjoyed the support of the small shopkeepers who were threatened with ruin unless there was a postponement of payments on debts and rent (the government refused to grant this postponement, but they obtained it from the Commune). Finally, it enjoyed, at first, the sympathy of bourgeois republicans who feared that the reactionary National Assembly (the "rustics", the savage landlords) would restore the monarchy. But it was of course the workers (especially the artisans of Paris), among whom active socialist propaganda had been carried on during the last years of the Second Empire and many of whom even belonged to the International, who played the principal part in this movement.

Only the workers remained loyal to the Commune to the end. The bourgeois republicans and the petty bourgeoisie soon broke away from it: the former were frightened off by the revolutionary-socialist, proletarian character of the movement; the latter broke away when they saw that it was doomed to inevitable defeat. Only the French proletarians supported *their* government fearlessly and untiringly, they alone fought and died for it—that is to say, for the cause of the emancipation of the working class, for a better future for all toilers.

Deserted by its former allies and left without support, the Commune was doomed to defeat. The entire bourgeoisie of France, all the landlords, stockbrokers, factory owners, all the robbers, great and small, all the exploiters joined forces against it. This bourgeois coalition, supported by Bismarck (who released a hundred thousand French prisoners of war to help crush revolutionary Paris), succeeded in rousing the ignorant peasants and the petty bourgeoisie of the provinces against the proletariat of Paris, and forming a ring of steel around half of Paris (the other half was besieged by the German army). In some of the larger cities in France (Marseilles, Lyons, St. Étienne, Dijon, etc.) the workers also attempted to seize power, to proclaim the Commune and come to the help of Paris; but these attempts were short-lived. Paris, which had first raised the banner of proletarian revolt, was left to its own resources and doomed to certain destruction.

Two conditions, at least, are necessary for a victorious social revolution—highly developed productive forces and a proletariat adequately prepared for it. But in 1871 both of these conditions were lacking. French capitalism was still poorly developed, and France was at that time mainly a petty-bourgeois country (artisans, peasants, shopkeepers, etc). On the other hand, there was no workers' party; the working class had not gone through a long school of struggle and was unprepared, and for the most part did not even clearly visualise its tasks and the methods of fulfilling them. There was no serious political organisation of the proletariat, nor were there strong trade unions and co-operative societies....

But the chief thing which the Commune lacked was time—an opportunity to take stock of the situation and to embark upon the fulfilment of its programme. It had scarcely had time to start work, when the government entrenched in Versailles and supported by the entire bourgeoisie began hostilities against Paris. The Commune had to concentrate primarily on self-defence. Right up to the very end, May 21-28, it had no time to think seriously of anything else.

However, in spite of these unfavourable conditions, in spite of its brief existence, the Commune managed to promulgate a few measures which sufficiently characterise its real significance and aims. The Commune did away with the standing army, that blind weapon in the hands of the ruling classes, and armed the whole people. It proclaimed the separation of church and state, abolished state payments to religious bodies (i. e., state salaries for priests), made popular education purely secular, and in this way struck a severe blow at the gendarmes in cassocks. In the purely social sphere the Commune accomplished very little, but this little nevertheless clearly reveals its character as a popular, workers' government. Night-work in bakeries was forbidden; the system of fines, which represented legalised robbery of the workers, was abolished. Finally, there was the famous decree that all factories and workshops abandoned or shut down by their owners were to be turned over to associations of workers that were to resume production. And, as if to emphasise its character as a truly democratic, proletarian government, the Commune decreed that the salaries of all administrative and government officials, irrespective of rank, should not exceed the normal wages of a worker, and in no case amount to more than 6,000 francs a year (less than 200 rubles a month).

All these measures showed clearly enough that the Commune was a deadly menace to the old world founded on the enslavement and exploitation of the people. That was why bourgeois society could not feel at ease so long as the Red Flag of the proletariat waved over the *Hôtel de Ville* in Paris. And when the organised forces of the government finally succeeded in gaining the upper hand over the poorly organised forces of the revolution, the Bonapartist generals, who had been beaten by the Germans and who showed courage only in fighting their defeated countrymen, those French Rennenkampfs and Meller-Zakomelskys,[87] organised such a slaughter as Paris had never known. About 30,000 Parisians were shot down by the bestial soldiery, and about 45,000 were arrested, many of whom were afterwards executed, while thousands were transported or exiled. In all, Paris lost about 100,000 of its best people, including some of the finest workers in all trades.

The bourgeoisie were satisfied. "Now we have finished with socialism for a long time," said their leader, the bloodthirsty dwarf, Thiers, after he and his generals had drowned the proletariat of Paris in blood. But these bourgeois crows croaked in vain. Less than six years after the suppression

of the Commune, when many of its champions were still
pining in prison or in exile, a new working-class movement
arose in France. A new socialist generation, enriched by
the experience of their predecessors and no whit discour-
aged by their defeat, picked up the flag which had fallen
from the hands of the fighters in the cause of the Commune
and bore it boldly and confidently forward. Their battle-cry
was: "Long live the social revolution! Long live the Commune!" And in another few years, the new workers' party and
the agitational work launched by it throughout the country
compelled the ruling classes to release Communards who
were still kept in prison by the government.

The memory of the fighters of the Commune is honoured
not only by the workers of France but by the proletariat
of the whole world. For the Commune fought, not for some
local or narrow national aim, but for the emancipation of
all toiling humanity, of all the downtrodden and oppressed.
As a foremost fighter for the social revolution, the Commune
has won sympathy wherever there is a proletariat suffering
and engaged in struggle. The epic of its life and death,
the sight of a workers' government which seized the capital of the world and held it for over two months, the spec-
tacle of the heroic struggle of the proletariat and the torments
it underwent after its defeat—all this raised the spirit of
millions of workers, aroused their hopes and enlisted their
sympathy for the cause of socialism. The thunder of the can-
non in Paris awakened the most backward sections of the
proletariat from their deep slumber, and everywhere gave
impetus to the growth of revolutionary socialist propaganda.
That is why the cause of the Commune is not dead. It lives
to the present day in every one of us.

The cause of the Commune is the cause of the social
revolution, the cause of the complete political and economic
emancipation of the toilers. It is the cause of the proletariat
of the whole world. And in this sense it is immortal.

Rabochaya Gazeta, No. 4-5,
  April 15 (28), 1911

                              Published according to
                              the *Rabochaya Gazeta* text

THE SOCIAL STRUCTURE OF STATE POWER, THE PROSPECTS AND LIQUIDATIONISM

The questions indicated above occupy, from the point of view of their importance, one of the foremost, if not *the* foremost place in the system of views of a Marxist who wishes to understand the realities surrounding him. The period 1908-10 undoubtedly bears a distinctive character. The social structure of society and of state power is characterised by changes, and unless these changes are understood not a single step can be taken in any sphere of social activity. The understanding of these changes determines the prospects for the future, by which we mean, of course, not idle guessing about things unknown, but the basic trends of economic and political development—those trends, the resultant of which determines the immediate future of the country, those trends which determine the tasks, direction and character of the activity of every intelligent public man. And this last question of the tasks, direction and character of activity is most closely connected with the question of liquidationism.

No wonder then that as far back as 1908, as soon as it had become—or was beginning to become—clear that we were confronted with a new, distinctive period in Russian history, the Marxists paid particular attention to the questions of the social structure of state power, prospects for the future, and liquidationism; they pointed to the inseparable connection between these questions and systematically discussed them. Furthermore, they did not confine themselves to mere discussion, for that would have been "literary scribbling" in the worst sense of the word; that would have been possible only in a discussion group of intellectuals not conscious of their responsibility and not troubled by politics. No, they worked out an exact formulation of the results of the discussion, a formulation that could serve as a guide, not only for a member of the given literary circle, not only for a person connected in one way or another with a definite intellectualist category, but for any and every conscious representative of the class who regards the ideology of Marxism as his own. This necessary work was completed by the end of 1908.

I have already pointed out the principal results of this work in No. 2 of our journal. I take the liberty of quoting a few lines in order to make further exposition more intelligible.

"The development of the Russian state system during the past three centuries shows that its class character has been changing in one definite direction. The monarchy of the seventeenth century with the Boyars' Duma did not resemble the bureaucratic-aristocratic monarchy of the eighteenth century. The monarchy of the first half of the nineteenth century was not the same as the monarchy of 1861-1904. In the 1908-10 period a new phase was clearly outlined, marking *one more step* in the same direction, which may be described as the direction leading towards a bourgeois monarchy. The character of the Third Duma and the present agrarian policy are closely connected with this step. The new phase, therefore, is not an accident but represents a specific stage in the capitalist evolution of the country. This new phase does not solve the old problems, nor can it do so; consequently, since *it is unable to eliminate them*, it calls for the use of new methods of approach to old solutions of old problems" (No. 2, p. 43). And a few lines further: "Those who deny (or who do not understand) ... that we are confronted with the old problems and are heading towards the old solution of these problems, are *in fact* deserting Marxism, are *in fact* surrendering to the liberals (as Potresov, Levitsky and others have done)" (p. 44).*

Whatever attitude one may adopt towards the set of ideas expressed in these propositions, it would hardly be possible to deny the very close connection and interrelation existing between the separate parts of this appraisal of the given period. Take, for instance, the decree of November 9,

* See pp. 68-69 of this volume.—*Ed.*

1906 (the law of June 14, 1910). There can be no disputing the fact that each of them bears a clearly expressed bourgeois character which marks a change of principle in the agrarian policy long pursued by the "upper" strata towards the village commune and allotment ownership. But so far, not even the most unprincipled weathercocks such as the Cadets, have ventured to assert that this change of principle has *already* settled the question, has *already* created new foundations of capitalist peasant economy, or has *already* eliminated the old problems. The connection between the law of June 14, 1910, and the system of elections to the Third Duma, as well as the social composition of the latter is obvious; it would have been impossible to carry out this law, to take a series of measures to put it into practice other than by establishing an alliance between the central government and the feudal (let us use this not very exact, general European expression) landowners and the upper strata of the commercial-industrial bourgeoisie. We are thus faced with a distinctive stage in the *entire* process of capitalist evolution of the country. Does this stage do away with the retention of "power and revenue" (speaking in a sociological sense) in the hands of the landowners of the feudal type? No, it does not. The changes that took place in this, as in all the other spheres, do not remove the *fundamental* traits of the old regime, of the old relation of social forces. Hence the fundamental task of a politically conscious public man is clear; he must evaluate these new changes, "make use" of them, grasp them, if we may use that expression, and at the same time, he must not allow himself to drift helplessly with the stream, he must not throw out the old baggage, he must preserve the essentials in the forms of activity and not merely in theory, in the programme, in the principles of policy.

How then did Potresov and Martov, Dan and Axelrod, Levitsky and Martynov, the "ideological leaders" who group themselves round publications of the *Vozrozhdeniye*, *Zhizn*, *Dyelo Zhizni*, *Nasha Zarya*, etc., type, react to this definitely formulated answer to the "vexed questions", to this direct and clear exposition of definite views? The fact is that they did not react like politicians, "ideological leaders", responsible publicists, but like a literary group, like a circle of intellectuals, like free lances of free groups of the writing fraternity. Like men who knew how to appreciate the fashion and the spirit of the times as accepted in liberal parlours, they tittered condescendingly over this antiquated, out-of-date, eccentric striving to formulate answers to vexed questions. Why such exactitude, when one can write wherever one pleases, about anything one pleases, whatever one pleases, and in any way one pleases, when the Milyukovs and Struves furnish excellent examples of all the advantages, conveniences and privileges that follow from the evasion of direct answers, of an exact enunciation of views, of formulated *professions de foi*, etc., when Forgetful Ivans (and especially the Ivans who do not like to recall the exact formulations of the past) are being honoured and respected in the broadest circles of "society"?

Thus, throughout the past three years, we have not observed the slightest attempt on the part of this entire literary fraternity to present *their own* formulated answer to the "vexed questions". There have been many metaphors and idle hypotheses, but not a single straight answer. The distinguishing, characteristic feature of the fraternity under consideration was their love of *amorphism*, i. e., of that symptom which was recognised in the most definite, precise and unequivocal terms to be an integral part of *liquidationism at the very time* the direct reply to the vexed questions was given. To drift aimlessly with the stream, to delight in one's amorphism, to "put paid" to that which is contrasted to the amorphous present—this is one of the main features of liquidationism. Opportunists always and everywhere passively abandon themselves to the stream, rest content with answers "from event to event", from congress (drunks) to congress (factory),[88] they are satisfied to transfer their affiliation from one "association" (albeit the most respectable and useful—trade unions, consumers' societies, cultural societies, temperance societies, etc.) to another, etc. Liquidationism is the sum total of the tendencies that are peculiar to all opportunism in general, and reveal themselves in definite forms in one of our social-political trends in a certain period of Russian history.

History has preserved only two definite opinions of the liquidators on the above "direct answer" (to the vexed ques-

tions). The first opinion: the adjective "bourgeois" ought
to be replaced by the adjective "plutocratic". Such a substitution, however, would be utterly incorrect. The epoch
of 1861-1904 reveals to us the growth of the influence (and
often the preponderating influence) of the plutocracy in
the most varied spheres of life. What we see in the 1908-10
period is no longer plutocracy, but *something different—*
the result of the bourgeoisie having recognised itself as a
class. It is mindful of the lessons received during the preceding three years and is creating an ideology which in principle is hostile to socialism (not to European socialism, not
to socialism in general, but specifically to Russian socialism) and to democracy. Moreover, the bourgeoisie is organised nationally, that is, as a class, a definite section of
which is permanently represented (and in a very influential
way, too) in the Third Duma. Finally, in the agrarian policy of 1908-10, too, there is a system which carries out the
definite plan of a bourgeois agrarian regime. To be sure,
this plan does not "work" yet; but this failure is the failure
of *one* of the bourgeois systems, while the *plutocracy* has
undoubtedly been "successful" in the villages, i. e., the village plutocracy is certainly gaining in consequence of the
agrarian policy of 1908-10, whereas the bourgeois regime,
for which so many sacrifices are made, is still unable to "fit
in". In a word, the proposed term "plutocratic" is inept in
every respect, so much so that the liquidators themselves
apparently prefer to forget this proposal.

Another opinion: the answer outlined above is incorrect
because it is equal to the advice to "shove in where we once
met with ..."[89] bad luck. This brief but energetic opinion is
valuable because it expresses in a striking form the results
of all the literary productions of the liquidators from Potresov's *The Social Movement* down to Mr. Levitsky in
Nasha Zarya. This opinion is a purely negative one; it
confines itself to condemning "shoving" without giving any
positive indication as to *where* one should "shove". Swim,
they seem to say, as best you can, like "everybody else", but
do not consider it worth while to indulge in generalisations
as to where you will or should emerge.

However much the opportunists would like to avoid being
worried by generalisations, to avoid all "unpleasant" talk

about giving a direct answer to the "vexed questions"—this is impossible. Drive Nature out of the door and she will fly in through the window. By the irony of history the very same liquidators who like to pose as "progressives", as alien to "conservatism", and who in 1908 scornfully turned up their noses at the suggestions that there was need for a direct answer, were forced, *almost a year and a half later*, in the summer of 1910, to reckon with these suggestions. And they were forced to do so by events in their own camp. They had almost completely evaded the direct answer demanded in certain contemptible, out-of-date, atrophied, useless, pernicious, "hopeless quarters", when suddenly, a year and a half later, a "trend" arises among the liquidators themselves, which also demands a direct answer and which challengingly gives a direct answer!

As was to be expected, the role of "challenger" was assumed by Y. Larin; but this time he was not alone. Larin, we know, is the *enfant terrible* of opportunism. He is distinguished by a great fault (from the point of view of the opportunists); he takes the trends that appear among them seriously, sincerely and thoughtfully, tries to link them up into a consistent whole, to think them out to the end, to obtain direct answers, to draw practical conclusions. Those who are familiar with Larin's book on a broad workers' party (it appeared three or four years ago) will certainly remember how he crushed in his fervent embraces Axelrod's notorious idea of a labour congress.

In March 1910, Larin began to publish a series of articles in *Vozrozhdeniye* on this very question of the social structure of state power, the prospects for the future, and liquidationism. He was joined by Mr. Piletsky. Both writers tackled these questions, to which they vainly sought a direct answer in their liquidationist camp, with the zeal of neophytes, and they began to hit out right and left: no use talking of serfdom in present-day Russia, the government has *already* evolved into a bourgeois government. "Both the first and the second "elements," says Larin singling out the notorious "third element",[90] "may sleep in peace; October 1905 is not on the order of the day" (*Vozrozhdeniye*, No. 9-10, p. 20). "If the Duma were abolished, it would be restored more rapidly than in post revolutionary Austria, which

abolished the Constitution in 1851 only to recognise it again
in 1860, nine years later, without any revolution, simply
because it was in the interests of the most influential section
of the ruling classes, the section whose economy was run
on capitalist lines. Eventually, the struggle of the various sections of the ruling classes amongst themselves,
after the social system of bourgeois relations has been extended, will force them in our country, as elsewhere, to expand
the framework of the electoral system" (ibid., p. 26). "The
process of bringing Russia into the capitalist world ... is
being completed in the political sphere as well. This means
that at the present stage a *nation-wide* revolutionary movement like that of 1905 is impossible" (p. 27).

"Thus, since power [according to Larin's conclusions]
is not vested 'almost entirely' in the hands of the feudal
landowners, the struggle for power by the 'capitalists of
land and factory' against the feudal landowners cannot be
transformed into a nation-wide struggle against the existing
government" (No. 11, p. 9). "... To base one's tactical line
on the expectation of an approaching 'nation-wide revival'
would mean condemning oneself to fruitless waiting" (ibid.,
p. 11). "One must not sit between two stools. If nothing has
changed in the social nature of the government, then the
tasks and the forms of activity *will necessarily* prove to be
the old ones, and the only thing left to do is 'fight the liquidators'. But if anyone wants to go further, *to build the new*
to replace, to continue and to raise up the old that is in ruins
and has become useless, then let him be consistent and realise what *the conditions for construction* are" (ibid., p. 14).

Well, isn't that Larin naïve? He demands that the opportunists be "consistent", that they should not try "to sit
between two stools".

The editors of *Vozrozhdeniye* were taken aback. In No.
9-10 they announced that they disagreed with Larin and wrote
that while he revealed "freshness of thought", "Y. Larin's
articles failed to convince us". In No. 11, apparently on
behalf of the editors, V. Mirov wrote disagreeing with
Larin, and acknowledged that Larin and Piletsky represented "a definite *trend* which theoretically has not yet been
definitely established, but which speaks in very clear language" (the greatest defect from the standpoint of the oppor-

tunists!). Mr. Mirov wrote: "Larin has touched on another
question of liquidationism incidentally and unexpectedly
[just like that! this restless Larin with his "very clear language" is always causing annoyance to his friends!]. It seems
to us that there is no close connection between the way in
which the Party is to be built up and the nature of the Russian Government, and we reserve to ourselves the right to
deal separately with this matter" (issue of July 7, 1910,
p. 22).

It was L. Martov in *Zhizn*, No. 1, of August 30, 1910,
who "dealt separately" with the matter on behalf of that
"we". He declared (p. 4) that "he could only join" with
V. Mirov and the editors against Larin. Thus the last word
in this entire discussion among the liquidators has been
uttered by L. Martov.

Let us take a close look at this last word of the liquidators.

As usual, Martov tackles the matter in a very lively manner and very ... "dexterously". He begins by saying that
"a careful search was made for the bourgeoisie in power, or
for the ruling bourgeoisie, immediately after the coup d'état
of June 3, 1907". "The June Third regime is that of the
domination of the Russian trading and industrial bourgeoisie.
This conception was accepted equally by the above-mentioned group of Menshevik writers (Larin, Piletsky) and by
their opposites, the orthodox Bolsheviks, who in 1908"
wrote "about the birth of a bourgeois monarchy in Russia".

Isn't this a priceless gem of "dexterity"? Larin reproaches
Martov for trying to sit between two stools and bluntly
admits, without subterfuges and stratagems, that it is
necessary to fight the liquidators if the answer to the vexed
questions given by the "orthodox" is not to be redrafted.

But Martov "dexterously" turns somersaults in mid-air
and attempts to persuade the readers (who in August 1910
had no opportunity whatever of hearing the other side)
that "this scheme" *"was equally acceptable"* to both Larin
and the "orthodox"!!

This dexterity smacks of that of Burenin or Menshikov[91]
for it is impossible to imagine a more shameless ...
deviation from the truth.

Among other things, Martov writes in the same article:
"In literary discussions people usually forget who really

'started it'". True, that happens in discussions *among litera-ry men* in which there is no question of working out an exact, properly formulated answer to vexed questions. But it is *precisely not* a discussion among literary men and *not just a literary "discussion"* with which we are dealing. L. Martov is *fully aware* of the fact but deliberately misleads the read-ers of *Zhizn*. Martov knows perfectly well the nature of the formulated answer given and supported by the "orthodox". Martov knows perfectly well that it is precisely this answer that Larin is fighting, calling it "ossified routine", "build-ing castles in the air", etc. Martov knows perfectly well that *he himself* and all his adherents and colleagues rejected the formulated answer given by the "orthodox". Martov knows perfectly well "who really started it", who began (and finished) the framing of the precise answer, and who confined himself to sniggering and expressing dissent, without giving *any* answer at all.

It is impossible to imagine a more disgusting, a more dishonest trick than the one played by L. Martov! Larin by his straightforwardness and outspokenness painfully hurt the diplomats of liquidationism when he admitted (though only after a year and a half) that it was quite impossible to dispense with a definite answer. They cannot face the truth. And L. Martov tries to deceive the reader by making it appear that Larin accepts a scheme that is identical" with that of the orthodox, although in reality the two schemes are *opposed to each other*; Larin's scheme *implies* the justification of liquidationism, that of the "orthodox" *implies* the condemnation of liquidationism.

In order to cover up his trick, Martov picks out from the "scheme" *one* little word and distorts its connection with the context (a method worked out to perfection by Burenin and Menshikov). Martov asserts that the "orthodox" wrote about the "birth of a bourgeois monarchy in Russia"— and since Larin writes that there can be no talk of feudal-ism in Russia, that the government is already bourgeois— *"ergo"* the schemes of Larin and of the "orthodox" are *"iden-tical"*!! The trick is done; and the reader who believes Mar-tov is fooled.

In reality, however, the "scheme", or, to be more precise, the answer of the orthodox, is that the old power in Russia is *"taking another step in the transformation* into a bourgeois monarchy"; and that the path of capitalist development should be such as would *"preserve* their power and their revenue for *precisely the feudal type* of landowners" and that as a result of this state of affairs "the *basic* factors of economic and political life which called forth" the first crisis in the beginning of the twentieth century *"continue to operate"*.

Larin says that the government is *already* bourgeois, therefore only partisans of "ossified routine" speak of the "preservation of power" by the feudal landowners, therefore the "basic factors" of the former upsurge *no* longer operate, therefore it is necessary to build something new "in place of 'the old that has become useless'".

The "orthodox" say that the government is taking *another* step *along the path* of transformation into a bourgeois (not government in general, but) monarchy, while the real power remains and is preserved in the hands of the feudal landowners, so that the "basic factors" of former tendencies, of the former type of evolution "continue to operate", and therefore those who talk of "the old that has become useless" are liquidators who *in reality* are captives of the liberals.

The contrast between the two schemes, between the two answers is obvious. We have before us two different *complete* answers, which lead to different conclusions.

Martov is juggling *à la* Burenin, alleging that *both* answers *"speak of"* the "birth of a bourgeois monarchy". One might with equal justice refer to the fact that both answers recognise the continuing capitalist development of Russia! *On the basis* of the common recognition (by all Marxists and by all those who wish to be Marxists) of capitalist development, *a dispute is proceeding* as to the degree, forms and conditions of that development. Martov confuses the issue in order to represent what is beyond dispute as the point at issue. It is on the basis of the *common* recognition (by all Marxists and by all those who wish to be Marxists) of the development of the old power *along the path of transformation into a bourgeois monarchy* that the dispute is proceeding as to the degree, forms, conditions and course of this transformation; and Martov confuses the issue (do the former factors continue to operate, is it admissible to renounce the old forms, etc.?) in order to represent what is beyond dispute as the point at issue!

That the government of Russia in the nineteenth and twentieth centuries has been generally evolving "along the path of transformation into a bourgeois monarchy" is not denied by Larin, just as hitherto it has never been denied by *any* sane man wishing to be a Marxist. The proposal to substitute the word "plutocratic" for the adjective "bourgeois" incorrectly appraises the *degree* of this transformation, but it dares not dispute *in principle* the fact that the actual "path", the path of real evolution, *lies* precisely in this transformation. Let him try to assert that the monarchy of 1861-1904 (i. e., undoubtedly a less capitalistic monarchy than the present one) does *not* represent *one* of the steps "in the transformation into a bourgeois monarchy" when it is compared with the period of serfdom under Nicholas I!

Martov does not try to assert this, but on the contrary, "joins" V. Mirov, who, in refutation of Larin, refers to the bourgeois character of the Witte reforms and of the reforms of the sixties! [92]

Now let the reader judge of the "dexterity" of Mirov and Martov. At first, in opposition to Larin, they repeat the arguments which *a year and a half ago* were used by the "orthodox" against the closest friends, adherents and colleagues of Martov and Mirov, and then they assure the reader that the "schemes" of Larin and of the "orthodox" are identical.

This is not only an example of "literary scribbling" versus politics (for politics demands definite and direct answers, whereas literary men often confine themselves to beating about the bush); it is more than that—it is an example of the degradation of literature to the level of Bureninism.

After quoting the above words of Larin that "if nothing has changed", etc., "then ... the only thing to do is to fight the liquidators", Martov replies to him:

"Hitherto we thought that our tasks were determined by the social structure of the society in which we act and that the forms of our activity were determined, in the first place, by these tasks and, in the second place, by *political conditions*. The 'social nature of the government' has, therefore, no *direct* [the italics are Martov's] bearing on the determination of our tasks and forms of activity."

This is not an answer, but an empty, evasive phrase. Martov again attempts to confuse the issue, to shift the dispute to irrelevant ground. The question is not whether the social nature of the government is *directly* or *indirectly* connected with the tasks and forms of activity. Even if this connection is an *indirect* one it will in no way alter things once the close and indissoluble connection is recognised. Martov does not venture to say a *word* against the recognition of this close and indissoluble connection. His reference to "political conditions" is nothing but dust thrown in the eyes of the reader. To draw a contrast between "the social nature of the government" and the "political conditions" is as senseless as if I were to contrast goloshes made by human hands, to overshoes. Overshoes are goloshes. And there are no other goloshes than those made by human hands. The nature of the government corresponds to the "political conditions". And the nature of the government can never be anything but social.

The sum total of all this is that Martov "beat about the bush" and evaded a direct answer to Larin. He evaded an answer because he had no answer to give. Larin is quite right in stating that views on the "social nature of the government" (to be more precise—its economic nature) are closely and inseparably connected with views on the "tasks and forms of activity". Both Larin and the "orthodox" acknowledge and apply this connection. Martov (and his tribe) displays no such consistency in his views. That is why Martov is compelled to wriggle and make shift with "overshoes".

Listen further.

"There flashed more or less clearly in the minds of these Mensheviks [Martov is referring to Kogan, *Obrazovaniye*, 1907, as an *example*] the idea of the gradual, so to speak 'organic', entry of the working class into that 'legal country'* which received the rudim-

---

* Perhaps not all readers will understand this gallicism which to my mind is an extreme misfit. "Legal country" is a literal translation of the French *pays légal* which implies those classes or groups, those strata of the population which are represented in parliament and which, unlike the masses of the people, enjoy constitutional privileges. Incidentally, this is typical and may serve as an appraisal of Martov's vacillations. He does not want to admit that Russia in 1908-10 took "another step in the transformation into a bourgeois monarchy". But he does admit that the "bourgeoisie" (and not the plutocracy) on June 3, 1907, "obtained the rudiments of a constitutional regime". Who can make head or tail of this?

ents of a constitutional regime, of gradual extension of the June Third privileges of the bourgeoisie [not "plutocracy", eh?] to broad democratic circles. If such were really the fundamental principles of contemporary 'liquidationism' in quotation marks, or of contemporary 'legalism', we would be confronted with the actual liquidation of our traditions, with actual legalism elevated to a principle, with a break in principle with all our past. We would have to wage a serious struggle with such liquidationism.... Are we really destined to see the reformists *creeping into* the regime of a renovated Tolmachovism?" Then comes a footnote by Martov: "Of course [!!] I do not suspect Larin of reformist tendencies".

This long quotation was necessary in order to demonstrate Martov's "method" clearly to the reader. He admits that reformism "flashed more or less clearly" in the mind of Kogan (a Menshevik who systematically collaborates in serious "works" with Martov). He admits that *if* reformism were really the fundamental principle of liquidationism it would be a "break with the past". He hurls a ringing, noisy, stinging phrase at the "reformists" who are "creeping into", etc. And he winds up with, what do you think? with an assurance that he, *of course*, "does not suspect" Larin of reformist "tendencies"!

This is exactly what Eduard Bernstein, Jean Jaurès or Ramsay MacDonald say. They all "admit" that in the minds of certain "extremists" there "flashes" something that is bad: reformism, liberalism. They all admit that *if* liberalism were the "fundamental principle" of *their* policy, that would be a "break with the past". They all hurl ringing, noisy, stinging phrases at the "liberals who are cringing", etc. And they all wind up with ... assurances that they "do not suspect" the Larins—I beg pardon—they "do not suspect" their more candid, more "Right" comrades, adherents, friends, colleagues and collaborators, of liberal-bourgeois tendencies.

The crux of the matter is this: in the articles quoted Larin gave an exposition of the "system" of views of the most undoubted, most genuine reformism! To deny this means denying the obvious, robbing the concept reformism of all meaning. And if you "refute" Larin, "condemn" reformism as "a principle", hurl ringing phrases at those who are "creeping into", and at the same time positively assert that you "do not suspect" Larin of reformism, surely you thereby expose yourselves completely! By this you prove to the hilt that your reference to your hostility "on principle" to "reformism as a principle" is the same as the vow of a peddlar who says: "Believe me, upon my oath, I paid more for it".

Believe me, upon my oath: I condemn reformism as a principle, *but* I do not "suspect" Larin of reformism (those *suspicious* orthodox people are really disgusting!), and I am at one with Larin in his liquidationist practice.

Such is the "detailed formula" of present-day Russian opportunism.

Here is an example of the application of this formula by Martov *himself*, whom naïve people (or those unable to understand the depth of the *new* re-grouping) still regard as an "undoubted" non-liquidator:

"The tactics which are to be observed in the activities of the so-called 'liquidators'," writes Martov on pp. 9-10, "are those which place the open workers' movement in the centre, strive to extent it in every possible direction, and seek *within* [the italics are Martov's] this open workers' movement, and only there [note: and only there!], the elements for the revival of the Party."

This is what Martov says. And this is nothing but reformism *creeping into* the regime of a renovated Tolmachovism.[93] The italics "creeping into" I have borrowed from Martov himself, for it is important to note that it is *precisely* "creeping into" that Martov *in fact* preaches in the words just quoted. Irrespective of the extent to which such preachings are accompanied by oaths and imprecations against "reformism as a principle", the *matter* is not changed one iota. In reality, having said "and only there", and "in the centre", Martov specifically pursues a reformist policy (in the particular situation in Russia in 1908-10); and as to the vows, promises, assurances, oaths—let political babes believe them.

"The disputes between Marx and Willich-Schapper in the early fifties of the last century hinged precisely [!!] on the question of the importance of secret societies and the possibility of leading the political struggle *from within them*.... The Blanquist, [in France in the sixties] 'prepared' for these events [the downfall of Bonapartism] by setting up secret societies and bottling up individual workers in them, but the French section of the Marxists ... went into the labour organisations, founded them and 'fought for legality' by every means...."

The cases mentioned are tunes from *quite* a different opera. The dispute between Marx and Willich in the fifties, between the Blanquists[94] and the Marxists in the sixties, *was not one of* whether it was necessary to seek "elements for the revival of the Party" "only" within "peaceful, tolerated organisations" (Martov, *Zhizn*, No. 1, p. 10). Martov knows this perfectly well and is wasting his time trying to mislead his readers. Neither of *these* disputes was conducted over the "revival" of the workers' party; at that time it was impossible to dispute about its revival because it had *never* existed. These two disputes hinged on the question of whether a workers' party—a party based on the *working-class* movement, a *class* party—was necessary at all. That was what Willich denied and the Blanquists of the sixties again denied, as Martov well knows, although he tries to *obscure* matters in dispute *today* by general talk about what is now indisputable. The view that *"only"* in peaceful and tolerated organisations should one seek elements for the revival or for the birth of the Party was *never* shared by Marx, *either* in the fifties or in the sixties; *even at the end of the seventies*, during an immeasurably higher phase of development of capitalism and bourgeois monarchy, Marx and Engels declared *ruthless* war on the German opportunists who had wiped out the recent past of the German party, deplored "extremes", talked of "more civilised" forms of the movement (in the language of the present-day Russian liquidators it is called "Europeanisation"), and advocated the idea that *"only"* in "peaceful and tolerated" organisations should one "seek the elements for the revival", etc.

"To sum up," writes Martov. "The fact that the present regime is an inherently contradictory combination of absolutism and constitutionalism, and that the Russian working class has sufficiently matured to follow the example of the workers of the progressive countries of the West in striking at this regime through the Achilles heel of its contradictions is ample material for the theoretical substantiation and political justification of what the Mensheviks who remain true to Marxism are now doing."

Martov's words ("ample material") are also *ample material* for us to make our summary from. Martov regards as "ample" what is recognised by both the Cadets and a section of the Octobrists. In January 1911 it was none other than

Rech that formulated the question in the way Martov proposed its formulation in August 1910: a contradictory combination of constitutionalism and anti-constitutionalism; two camps—for the constitution and against it. What is *ample* for *Rech* is "ample" for Martov. There is not a *grain* of Marxism in this. Marxism has completely disappeared and has been replaced by liberalism. The fact that we have a "contradictory combination" is *not by any means* "ample" for a Marxist. Marxism only begins with the beginning of the realisation or understanding that this truth is not enough, that it contains within itself a spoonful of truth and a barrel of untruth, that it obscures the depth of the contradictions, that it embellishes reality and rejects the only possible means of finding a way out of the situation.

"The contradictory combination" of the old regime and constitutionalism exists not only in present-day Russia, but also in present-day Germany and even in present-day England (the House of Lords; the Crown's independence of the people's representatives in matters of foreign policy, etc.). What, then, is the position taken up *in reality* (i. e., irrespective of good wishes and pious speeches) by the politician who declares that it is "ample" for a Russian to recognise what is true as regards Germany as well as England? Such a politician is, *in reality*, taking the stand of a *liberal*, of a Cadet. Even a more or less consistent bourgeois democrat in our country cannot, and does not, take such a stand. Martov's *last word*, his concluding *formula* which sums up the entire discussion among the liquidators, is a remarkably exact, a strikingly clear and exhaustively complete expression of *liberal* views smuggled in under a pseudo-Marxist flag.

When the liberals, not only the Cadets, but also a section of the Octobrists, say that it is *ample* for the theoretical substantiation and political justification of our activity to recognise the inherently contradictory combination of the old regime and constitutionalism, the liberals are remaining quite true to themselves. In these words they give a really precise, liberal formula, the formula of the liberal policy of 1908-10 (if not of 1906-10). A Marxist, on the other hand, reveals his Marxism only when and to the extent that he explains the *inadequacy and falsity* of this formula, which eliminates those specific features which radically and in principle distinguish the Russian "contradictions" from those of the English and German. The liberal says: "It is ample to admit that a great many things in our country contradict constitutionalism". The Marxist replies: "Such an admission is altogether inadequate. It must be understood that there is no elementary, fundamental, cardinal, essential, necessary basis *for* 'constitutionalism' *at all*. The fundamental error of liberalism is that it declares that there is such a basis, whereas there is not; and this error accounts for the impotence of liberalism and is itself explained by the impotence of bourgeois altruism".

Translating this political antinomy into the language of economics, we may formulate it as follows. The liberal assumes that the path of economic (capitalist) development is already mapped out, defined, completed, that it is now only a matter of removing obstacles and contradictions from *that* path. The Marxist believes that this particular path of capitalist development has not, so far, provided a way out of the impasse, *despite* such undoubted bourgeois progress in economic evolution as was marked by November 9, 1906 (or June 14, 1910), the Third Duma, etc.; and he believes that there is *another* path which is *also* a path of capitalist development, a path that can lead us on to the high road, a path which must be pointed out, which must be explained, prepared, insisted upon, pursued, in spite of all the vacillation, lack of faith and faint-heartedness of liberalism.

Martov argues with Larin as if he himself were much more to the "Left" than Larin. Many naïve people allow themselves to be deceived by this and say: certainly, Potresov, Levitsky and Larin are liquidators, certainly, they are of the extreme Right, something like Russian Rouanet[95]; but Martov—Martov is certainly no liquidator! In reality, however, Martov's flamboyant phrases against Larin, against the creeping reformists, are only a blind, for in his *conclusion*, in his last word, in his *resumé*, Martov *actually* supports Larin. Martov is not more "Left" than Larin; he is only more diplomatic, more unprincipled than Larin; he hides himself more cunningly beneath the gaudy rags of pseudo-Marxist phrases. Martov's conclusion that recognition of the contradictory combination is "ample", provides just that *corrobo-*

ration of liquidationism (and liberalism) which Larin requires. But Larin wants to justify this conclusion, to prove it, to think it out to the end, to make it a matter of principle. And Martov says to Larin, as Vollmar, Auer and the other "old birds" of opportunism used to say to the young opportunist Eduard Bernstein: "Dear Larin—I mean dear Eddy— you are an ass! Such things are done, but not talked about". "Dear Larin, for you and me, liquidationist practice should be 'ample', the liberal recognition of the contradiction between the old regime and constitutionalism is 'ample'; but, for God's sake, don't go any further, don't 'deepen' the question, don't seek clarity and consistency of principles, don't make any appraisals of the 'present situation', *for that would expose us both.* Let us act and not talk."

Martov teaches Larin how to be an opportunist.

"One must not sit between two stools," says Larin to Martov, demanding an explanation and justification of the liquidator principles so dear to both of them.

"Well, what sort of opportunist are you," replies Martov, "if you don't know how to sit between two stools?" What sort of opportunist are you if you insist on exact, clear and direct justification of the principles of our practice? It is the business of a real opportunist to sit between two stools, he must advocate the "tactics-as-a-process"* (remember Martynov and Krichevsky in the period of 1901), he must drift with the stream, cover up his traces, evade all matters of principle. Take Bernstein, he knows now (after the lessons given him by Vollmar, Auer, etc.) how to be a revisionist *without proposing* any amendments to the *orthodox* Erfurt *profession de foi.* [96] And we two must also know how to act as liquidators *without proposing* any amendments to the *orthodox* formal answer (of 1908) given to the "vexed questions" of the day. [97] In order to be a real opportunist, my dear, dear Larin, one must do the *creeping* in reality, in one's practice, in the way one goes about one's work; but, in words, before the public, in speeches, in the press, one must not only abstain from seeking theories justifying the act of *creeping,* but, on the contrary, one must shout all the more loudly against those who creep, one must all the more

---

* See present edition, Vol. 5, pp. 387-97.—*Ed.*

assiduously vow and protest that we are not of the creeping kind.

Larin was silenced. Probably, in the depths of his heart he could not help admitting that Martov was a more skilful diplomat, a more subtle opportunist.

———

We must examine still another aspect of Martov's concluding formula: it is "ample" to recognise the contradictory nature of the combination of the old regime and constitutionalism. Compare this formula with V. Levitsky's *notorious* formula—"*Not* hegemony, *but* a class party" (*Nasha Zarya*, No. 7). In this formula Levitsky (the Larin of *Nasha Zarya*) expressed, only in a more direct, open, principled manner, what Potresov confused, glossed over, covered up and clothed in pretentious phrases when, under the influence of Plekhanov's ultimatums, he *cleaned up* and revised the article he wrote *against* the hegemony of the proletariat.

Martov's formula and that of Levitsky are two sides of the same medal. The object of the next article will be to explain this circumstance for the benefit of Martov who pretends not to understand the connection between the idea of the hegemony of the proletariat and the question of liquidationism.

P.S. The present article had already been sent to press when we received *Dyelo Zhizni*, No. 2, containing the conclusion of Y. Larin's article "Right Turn and About Turn!" Larin explains reformism, of which L. Martov "of course does not suspect" him, as clearly in the new liquidationist magazine as he explained it previously. For the present, we shall confine ourselves to quoting the *substance* of the reformist programme:

"A state of perplexity and uncertainty, when people simply do not know what to expect of the coming day, what tasks to set themselves—that is what results from indeterminate, temporising moods, from vague hopes of either a repetition of the revolution or of 'we shall wait and see'. The immediate task is, not to wait fruitlessly for something to turn up, but to imbue broad circles with the guiding idea that, in the ensuing historical period of Russian life, the working class must organise itself not 'for revolution', not 'in expectation of a revolution', but simply for the determined and systematic defence of its particular interests in all spheres of life; for the gathering and training of its forces for this many-sided and complex activity; for the training and building-up in this way of socialist consciousness in general; for acquiring the ability to orientate itself [to find its bearings]—and to assert itself—particularly in the complicated relations of the social classes of Russia during the coming constitutional reform of the country after the economically inevitable self-exhaustion of feudal reaction...." (p. 18).

This tirade expresses exactly the entire spirit and meaning of Larin's "programme" and of *all* the liquidationist writings in *Nasha Zarya*, *Vozrozhdeniye*, *Dyelo Zhizni*, and others, including L. Martov's "ample" which we have examined above. It is the purest and most complete reformism. We cannot dwell on it now; we cannot examine it here in the detail it deserves. We shall, therefore, confine ourselves to a brief remark. The Left Cadets, the non-party socialists, the petty-bourgeois democrats (like the "Popular Socialists") and reformists who would like to be Marxists, preach the following programme to the workers: gather your forces, train yourselves, learn, defend your interests *simply* in order to stand up for yourselves during the coming constitutional reform. Such a programme curtails, narrows and emasculates the political tasks of the working class in the period 1908-11 in the same manner as the Economists emasculated these tasks in the period 1896-1901. The old Economists, deluding themselves and others, liked to refer to Belgium (the predominance of reformism among the Belgians was recently brought to light by the excellent writings of de Man and Brouckère; we shall revert to these another time); the Neo-Economists, i. e., the liquidators, like to refer to the peaceful way in which a constitution was obtained in Austria in 1867. Both the old Economists and our liquidators choose instances, cases, episodes in the history of the working-class movement and democracy in Europe that occurred when the workers, for one reason or another, were weak, lacked class-consciousness and were dependent on the bourgeoisie—and they advance such instances as a model for Russia. Both the Economists and the liquidators serve as conductors for bourgeois influence among the proletariat.

Mysl, No. 4, March 1911
Signed: *V. Ilyin*   Published according to
                                                        the *Mysl* text

POLEMICAL NOTES

In an article entitled "The Results of the Artisans' Congress" in *Nasha Zarya*, No. 2, Mr. B. Bogdanov formulates his conclusions as follows:

"The striving to break with the old underground and embark upon really open public and political activity—such is the new feature which also characterises the latest phase of our labour movement." (P. 73.) "At a moment of heightened activity in public life, on the eve of by-elections in Moscow and general elections to the Fourth State Duma, the fact is very keenly felt that the politically organised section of the proletariat exercises no influence. The entire activity of the organised workers during recent years has been directed toward the revival of this independent political force. Consciously or unconsciously, all the participants of this movement are becoming agents of the reviving party of the proletariat. But the task of its organised section is not so much to accelerate this movement, not so much to give it formal shape prematurely, as to contribute to its development and lend it the greatest possible scope by drawing the widest possible masses into it and by resolutely breaking with the inactivity of the underground and its stupefying atmosphere." (Pp. 74-75.)

Only in newspapers of the *Novoye Vremya* type, and possibly also in the writings of embittered renegades to liberalism like Mr. Struve and Co., have we hitherto met with such howls about the "stupefying" atmosphere, and similar hysterical cries and appeals to "break" with it. Hitherto it has been the rule for that political press which is considered in any way decent and honest, not to use a particular platform to attack things that cannot be defended from that same platform. For over a year now, however, the crowd of liquidators, which includes B. Bogdanov, Levitsky, Potresov, and others, has been successfully "overcoming" this antiquated democratic prejudice, systematically choosing for their appeals to "break resolutely", etc., only those platforms which assure them a monopoly in any discussion on the point at issue. It only remains for us to place on record this "well-protected" war waged against the "stupefying atmosphere " and—to pillory the warriors.

The Bogdanovs, Levitskys, and Potresovs juggle with facts when they refer to the workers' urge to act openly and then draw their *own* conclusion that *the workers* are striving to break with the "stupefying atmosphere". They rely for the success of their jugglery on its being impossible for us, the opponents of liquidationism, to make public the facts, known to the Bogdanovs, which testify to the *indignation* of the workers who at various congresses come out openly *against intellectuals* who advocate "breaking" with the underground. At the beginning of 1911, the workers, to their great honour be it said, are striving to engage in open political activity just as energetically as they were, for example, at the beginning of 1905; but neither then nor now have *the workers* ever revolted against the "stupefying atmosphere", nor have they ever wanted "to break" with it. The only ones who may be correctly said to be striving to "break resolutely" are the renegade intellectuals.

Indeed, the reader would do well to reflect on the following fact. A group of writers has been vociferating, particularly since January 1910, about a *"striving to break with the old"*, and to *"embark upon really open political activity"*. During this period alone, this group has published more than twenty issues of its *own* magazines (*Nasha Zarya*, *Vozrozhdeniye, Zhizn, Dyelo Zhizni*), not to mention books, pamphlets, and articles in journals and newspapers that are not specifically liquidationist in character. How then, may it be asked, are we to account for the fact that writers who have been working so energetically in the journalistic field, and who speak with so much conviction of the need "resolutely to break with the old" and to "embark upon really open political activity" have so far *themselves*, in *their own group*, not ventured, not plucked up the courage to "break resolutely" with "the old" and to "embark upon really open political activity" with a programme, platform and tactics that would mark a "resolute break" with the "stupefying atmosphere"?

What kind of a comedy is this? What hypocrisy! They speak of "the revival of this political force", rail at "the stupefying atmosphere", demand a *break* with the old, preach "really open political activity", and at the same time refrain from substituting for it *any* programme, *any* platform, *any* tactics and *any* organisation! Why is it that our legalists, our would-be Marxists, lack even as much political honesty as was displayed by the Peshekhonovs and other publicists contributing to *Russkoye Bogatstvo*[98] who began to speak of the stupefying atmosphere and of the need to "embark upon really open political activity" much earlier (beginning from 1905-06) and who *practised what they preached*, actually "broke resolutely with the old", actually came out with an "open" programme, an "open" platform, "open" tactics and an "open" organisation?

Honesty in politics is the result of strength; hypocrisy is the result of weakness. The Peshekhonovs and Co. are a force among the Narodniks, therefore they come out really "openly". The Bogdanovs, Levitskys, Potresovs and Co. are weak among the Marxists and at every step are repulsed by the class-conscious workers; that is why they play the hypocrite, take cover and do not venture *to come out openly* with a programme and tactics of "really open political activity".

The Peshekhonovs and Co. are so strong among the Narodniks that they carry their wares under their own flag. The Bogdanovs, Levitskys, Potresovs, and Martovs are so weak among the Marxists that they are compelled to smuggle in their goods under a foreign flag. In their petty intellectualist magazine (*Nasha Zarya*) they summon up courage and shout: there is no "hierarchy", we must "resolutely break with the old" and "embark upon really open political activity". But when they face the workers, our liquidators act according to the saying: A lion among the lambs becomes a lamb among the lions.

When facing the workers our heroes, who show such enthusiasm for "open political activity" act *anything but openly* and do not offer *any* open programme, tactics or organisation. Hence the reason for the wise diplomacy of Mr. Bogdanov, who, in summarising "the results" of the artisans' congress, offers the advice "not ... to accelerate" the movement for really open political activity, ".not ... to give it formal shape prematurely". It looks as if Mr. Bogdanov has tried to give *formal shape* to his liquidationist plans, and present them to the workers, but burned his fingers in the attempt. This defecting intellectual met with a rebuff from the workers who, even when they err, act more straightforwardly and demand a straightforward answer ("You want us to break with the old? Well, why not come out openly and honestly with what you propose in its place?"). And Mr. B. Bogdanov, like the fox in Krylov's fable, consoles himself by saying—sour grapes! We must not give the new a formal shape prematurely; while breaking with the old we must keep on waving its flag when we go to the workers—don't hurry with the new.

You may say that this means sitting between two stools. But such is precisely the nature of all opportunism. That is precisely what characterises the bourgeois intellectual of today who *plays* at Marxism. Mr. Struve played at Marxism from 1894 to 1898. The Bogdanovs, Levitskys and Potresovs have been playing at Marxism from 1908 to 1911. The liquidators today, like the Economists of those days, serve as the channel for that same bourgeois influence among the proletariat.

Mysl, No. 4, March 1911

Published according to the *Mysl* text

THE MEANING OF THE CRISIS

The notorious Cabinet and political crisis of which so much has been written in the press, poses more profound questions than the liberals, who are making the most noise about it, think. They say that the crisis confronts us with the problem of violation of the Constitution. Actually what the crisis confronts us with is the Cadets' and the Octobrists' mistaken conception of the Constitution, the profound delusion entertained on that score by the two parties. The more widespread this delusion becomes the more insistently must we explain it. The more the Cadets try to use their accusations against the Octobrists as a means of peddling their wrong ideas about the allegedly "constitutional" character of the crisis, ideas common to the Octobrists and the Cadets, the more important it is to explain this community of ideas now being revealed.

Let us take the recent reflections of *Rech* and *Russkiye Vedomosti* on the slogan for the elections to the Fourth Duma. For or against the Constitution—that, say the two main Cadet publications, is how the question is being and will continue to be presented.

Now take a look at the reasoning of the Octobrists. Here is a typical article by Mr. Gromoboi in *Golos Moskvy* for March 30. It is entitled "A Disturbed Ant-Hill". The Octobrist publicist tries to persuade those, in his opinion, conscientious defenders of Mr. Stolypin who "fear the idea of joining the opposition" by proving to them "that they are taking the wrong steps". "To a constitutionalist," exclaims Mr. Gromoboi, "there can be no graver sin than the violation of the Constitution." What can be said on the essence of the matter? asks Mr. Gromoboi; and answering, says:

"Again the flintlock, nationalism, volitional impulses, state necessity? Alas, we have heard all that before, and we have also heard promises that were not justified."

To the Octobrists (and to the *Vekhi* writers who understood most deeply and expressed most vividly the spirit of Cadetism) Stolypin's policy was an attractive "promise". This "promise", the Octobrists confess, was not justified. What does that mean?

Actually, Stolypin's policy was not a promise, but has been the stark political and economic reality of Russian life in the last four (or even five) years. Both June 3, 1907, and November 9, 1906 (June 14, 1910), were not promises but reality. This reality has been put over and enforced by the representatives of the big landowning nobility and of the élite of the merchant and industrial capitalists, organised on a national scale. When today the spokesman of the Octobrist, Moscow (and, consequently, the all-Russia) capitalists says—"they have not been justified"—that sums up a definite phase of political history, a definite system of attempts to satisfy, through the Third Duma, through Stolypin's agrarian policy, etc., the demands of the epoch, the demands of Russia's capitalist development. The Octobrist capitalists worked conscientiously and assiduously, sparing nothing—not even their pockets—to help these attempts; but now they are obliged to confess that the promise has not justified itself.

Consequently, it is not a matter of broken promises, or of "violation of the Constitution"—for it is ridiculous to dissociate March 14, 1911, from June 3, 1907; the point is that the demands of the epoch cannot be satisfied through what the Octobrists and the Cadets call the "Constitution".

The "Constitution" which gave the majority to the Cadets in the First and Second Dumas could not satisfy the demands of the times, nor can these be satisfied by the "Constitution" which made the Octobrists the decisive party (in the Third Duma). When today the Octobrists say—"they have not been justified", the meaning of this confession, and of the crisis which has extorted it, is that the constitutional illusions both of the Cadets and of the Octobrists have again been shattered, this time finally and completely.

The democratic movement jolted the old out of its groove. The Cadets deprecated the "excesses" of the democratic movement and promised to accomplish the new by peaceful, "constitutional" means. These hopes were not justified. It was Mr. Stolypin who tackled the job of accomplishing the new—but in such a way as to ensure that the changed forms would reinforce the old, that the organisation of the diehard landowners and of the pillars of capital would fortify the old, and that the substitution of private ownership of land for the village commune would create a new stratum of defenders of the old. For years the Octobrists, working hand in glove with Mr. Stolypin, tried to bring this about, "unhampered by the menace" of the democratic movement which for the time being had been suppressed.

These hopes have not been justified.

What has been justified is the words of those who pointed out the futility and harmfulness of constitutional illusions in epochs of rapid and radical changes such as the early twentieth century in Russia.

The three years of the Third, Octobrist Duma, and of its Octobrist "Constitution", of the Octobrists' "life of peace and love" with Stolypin, have not vanished without leaving a trace: the country has made further economic progress, and all and sundry "Right" political parties have developed, grown, shown their worth (and have spent themselves).

The agrarian policy of the Third Duma has shown itself *in operation* in most of the villages and in the most out-of-the-way parts of Russia, where it has stirred up the discontent that had lain dormant for centuries, unceremoniously revealing and accentuating the existing antagonisms, emboldening the kulak and enlightening those at the other end of the scale. The Third Duma has had its effect. And so have the first two Dumas, which produced so many good, well-meaning, innocuous and impotent wishes. The collapse of the constitutional illusions of the years 1906 to 1910, incomparably more pronounced, has been revealed within the shell of the "constitutional" crisis of 1911.

In point of fact, both Cadets and Octobrists alike based their policy on these illusions. They were the illusions of the liberal bourgeoisie, the illusions of the Centre, and there is no essential difference between the "Left" Centre (the

Cadets) and the "Right" Centre (the Octobrists), since, owing to objective conditions, both were doomed to failure. The old has been jolted out of its groove. But neither the Left nor the Right Centre has achieved the new. Who is going to accomplish this inescapable and historically inevitable new, and how, that is a moot question. The "constitutional" crisis is significant because the Octobrists, the masters of the situation, have admitted that this question is *again* an "open" one; they have written "unjustified" across even their apparently most "valid" aspirations, aspirations which are valid from the merchant's point of view, and are commercially sober and modest. The "constitutional" crisis is significant because the experience of the Octobrists has revealed the extreme narrowness, poverty and impotence of the Cadets' catchword—who is for the Constitution, and who is against it.

The democratic movement has shown this slogan to be inadequate. The Octobrist movement has corroborated it by the experience of yet another phase of Russian history. The Cadets will not succeed in dragging Russia back to the former naïve constitutional illusions.

"The orthodox Octobrists," writes Mr. Gromoboi, "are having a fit of nerves; they declare that they will resign from the Bureau, and do not know what to do about their fellow-constitutionalists. Their agitation is unjustified. They should remain calm in the knowledge that truth is on their side, and that this truth is so elementary, so universally recognised, that it does not need a Copernicus or a Galileo to prove it. They should go on calmly doing their duty—declare that unlawful actions are unlawful, and without fail, making no compromises, reject the unlawful law."

That is an illusion, Mr. Gromoboi! You cannot dispense with "a Copernicus and a Galileo". Your own efforts have brought no "justification", you will not manage without them.

"When we contemplate this disturbed, teeming ant-hill— the servile press, servile orators, servile deputies [and, you might add, Mr. Gromoboi: the servile, slavish bourgeoisie]— we can only out of humanity pity them and gently remind them that they can no longer serve P. A. Stolypin; they can only cringe before him."

But P. A. Stolypin is not unique—he is typical; he is not an isolated individual, but is "hand in glove" with the Council of the United Nobility. The Octobrists have tried to live in harmony with him under the new conditions—under the conditions of a Duma, of a "Constitution", of the bourgeois policy of ruining the village commune à la Tolmachov. And if they failed in the attempt, it is by no means Stolypin's fault.

"...After all, the entire strength of people's representatives is derived from their contact with the people; and if they [the Right Octobrists] lose ... their 'identity' by the very fact that they are giving such support [support to Stolypin and his violation of the Constitution], what will they be worth then?"

So this is what we have come to! Octobrists speak of "contact with the people" as the source of "strength of people's representatives"! That is really funny. But no more so than the Cadet speeches in the First and Second Dumas about "contact with the people" alongside their speeches, say, against local land committees. The words which sound funny when uttered by Cadets and Octobrists are by no means funny in themselves; they are significant. For—despite the intentions of those who utter these words today—they express, once more, the collapse of constitutional illusions—which is a useful by-product of the "constitutional" crisis.

Zvezda, No. 18, April 16, 1911
Signed: *V. Ilyin*

Published according to
the *Zvezda* text

CONFERENCE
OF THE BRITISH SOCIAL-DEMOCRATIC PARTY

Many European socialist parties have taken advantage of the Easter holidays (April 16, N. S.) to hold their conferences: the French, Belgian, Dutch (its opportunist section), the British Social-Democratic Party, and the British Independent Labour Party. We propose to draw the attention of our readers to some items discussed at the conferences of the two last-mentioned parties.

The 31st Annual Conference of the British Social-Democratic Party (S.D.P.) was held in Coventry. The most interesting item discussed was that of "armaments and foreign policy". It is well known that Britain and Germany have been arming very intensively during the past few years. Competition between these two countries in the world market is becoming increasingly acute. The danger of a military conflict is approaching more and more formidably. The bourgeois jingoist press of both countries is raining millions upon millions of inflammatory articles upon the masses, inciting them against the "enemy", howling about the inevitable danger of a "German invasion" or of a "British attack" and clamouring for increased armaments. The socialists of Britain and Germany, and also of France (whom Britain would be particularly glad to drag into war in order to have a continental land army against Germany) are devoting much attention to the threatening war, fighting with might and main against bourgeois chauvinism and armaments, and doing all they can to explain to the most backward sections of the proletariat and of the petty bourgeoisie what misfortunes ensue from a war which serves exclusively the interests of the bourgeoisie.

There were sad exceptions to this among the socialists, several of whom were prominent leaders of the British S.D.P., among them Hyndman. The latter allowed himself to be scared by the screams of the British bourgeois press about the "German menace", and went so far as to assert that Britain had to arm for defence, that she had to have a powerful navy, that Wilhelm was the aggressive party.

True, Hyndman encountered opposition, in fact very strong opposition, within the S.D.P. itself. A number of resolutions from the branches were emphatically against him.

The Coventry Congress, or Conference—to use the English term, which does not correspond in meaning to the Russian "konferentsia"—had to settle the issue. A resolution emphatically opposing any kind of jingoist point of view was proposed by the Central Hackney branch (Hackney, a district in North-East London). In its report on the Conference, *Justice*, the central organ of the S.D.P., quotes only the end of what it terms a "lengthy" resolution, calling for a determined struggle against all increases in armaments, and opposing all colonial and financial aggression. Zelda Kahan, in supporting the resolution, emphasised that during the last forty years Britain had been the aggressor, that Germany would not gain by making Britain a German province; and that no such danger existed. "The British Navy," she said, "is kept to maintain the Empire. Never had the S.D.P. made a bigger and more terrible mistake than in identifying the Party with the jingoist warmongers. As a consequence of this mistake," said Kahan, "the British Social-Democrats have placed themselves outside the international movement."

The entire Party Executive Committee, including Harry Quelch—we have to confess with shame—supported Hyndman. The "amendment" they moved declared no more nor less than the following: "This Conference holds that the maintenance of an adequate navy for national defence" is an "immediate object"!... Then, of course, it goes on to repeat all the "good old words"—about combating imperialist policy, about war against capitalism, etc. All this honey, of course, was spoiled by *a spoonful of tar*, by the phrase recognising the need for an "adequate" navy, a phrase that is bourgeois both in its evasiveness and in its pure chauvinism. This is in 1911, a time when the British naval budget clearly reveals a tendency to unlimited growth; this is in a country whose navy "defends and protects the Empire", i. e., India included, with its population of nearly 300,000,000 that is being plundered and outraged by British bureaucrats, where "enlightened" British statesmen, like the liberal and "radical" Morley, sentence natives to *transportation* or inflict *corporal punishment* for political offences!

The miserable sophistry Quelch had to resort to may be seen from the following passage in his speech (as reported in *Justice*, which defends Hyndman)!... "If we believe in national autonomy, we must have national defence and that defence must be adequate, or it is useless. We are opposed to imperialism, whether British or German; the small nationalities under Prussian rule hate her despotism, and the small nations threatened by her regard the British Navy and German Social-Democracy as their only hope...."

How quickly those who step on the slippery slope of opportunism slide to the bottom! The British Navy, which helps to enslave India (not a very "small" nation), is placed *on a par* with German Social-Democracy as a champion of national liberty.... Zelda Kahan was right when she said that never yet had British Social-Democracy so disgraced itself. Its sectarian character, noted and condemned long ago by Engels,[99] had never before been so clearly revealed as it was by the *ease* with which even men like Quelch can *go over* to the chauvinists.

The voting on the resolution was evenly divided: 28 for the Executive Committee and 28 against. In order to win a deplorable victory—Hyndman and Quelch had to demand a branch vote, which secured them 47 votes against 33.

Some members of the Social-Democratic Party have voiced a most emphatic protest against chauvinism in their ranks; there has emerged a very strong minority ready to wage a serious struggle. The situation in the Independent Labour Party is worse: there opportunism is no rarity. There the question of whether socialists and the workers should support armaments is debated quite calmly in "discussion" articles in the official organ of the Party, *The Labour Leader* (No. 16, April 21, 1911).

The London correspondent of *Vorwärts* justly remarked that the best criticism of the position of the S.D.P. was an article in the *extremely jingoist Daily Mail* which *praised* the wisdom of the Social-Democratic leaders. He quotes the beginning of the article in that newspaper as saying: "It is encouraging to learn that, however extravagant some of the fallacies and impossible some of the ideals of the Social-Democratic Party in this country, there is at least one supremely important question on which that Party is guided by reason and common sense."

The really gratifying feature of the Birmingham Conference of the I.L.P. was that from its ranks firm and determined voices were heard protesting against the opportunist policy, the policy of dependence upon the Liberals pursued by this party in general, and by the party leader, Ramsay MacDonald, in particular. In reply to the reproach that the Labour members say little about socialism in the House of Commons, MacDonald said with virginal opportunist innocence that Parliament was hardly the place for "propaganda speeches". "The great function of the House of Commons," he said, "is to translate into legislation the socialism that is preached in the country." The speaker forgot all about the difference between bourgeois social reform and socialism! He was prepared to expect socialism from a bourgeois Parliament....

Leonard Hall pointed out in his speech that the I.L.P. had been formed in 1892 for the purpose of killing the old Labour Electoral Association which was merely a wing of liberalism. They had buried the corpse (after killing the Association), but it seemed to have revived in the Labour Party. He added that the leader of the Party was pursuing this policy in his speeches, letters and books.

Another I.L.P. member, George Lansbury, M. P., sharply criticised the policy of the Parliamentary Labour Party for its dependence upon the Liberals and its fear of "endangering" the Liberal government. Lansbury said that more than once he had been so ashamed of the conduct of the Labour members that he had nearly resigned. He went on to say that all the time the Liberals tried to keep the House busy with minor questions and that Labour members were unable to win independence for themselves. "I have never known a time," said Lansbury, "when both Liberals and Tories had not some great question to hide the poverty question. I am in the House of Commons with the picture before me of those men and women, who night after night toiled in the slums of Bow and Bromley [poor districts in the East End of London] to send me there. They worked for me because they thought I was different from the Liberals and Tories.... They sent me to face the question of poverty, poverty, poverty.... I appeal to you," he said, addressing the Conference, "to keep a solid party in the House of Commons absolutely distinct from the convenience of Liberals and Tories. We must show no more mercy to the Liberals when they do wrong than to the Tories.... The men and women who toil and suffer have nothing to hope for from either Liberals or Tories; their only hope lies in, and salvation can come from, their organised effort...." Let us "make it clear to the men and women of the slums that even in Parliament we are true to what we say outside, namely, that Liberals and Tories are the enemies of the people and socialism their only hope".

Lansbury's speech was interrupted by thunders of applause, and when he finished he received a real ovation. In Germany such speeches are an everyday occurrence. In Britain they are a novelty. And when such speeches are beginning to be delivered, when worker delegates at the Conference of the Independent Labour Party (unfortunately, very frequently independent of socialism, but dependent upon the Liberals) applaud such speeches, then we have the right to conclude that *in Britain*, too, the spirit of proletarian struggle is gaining the upper hand over the diplomacy of opportunist parliamentarians like MacDonald. (Let us add in parenthesis that this MacDonald recently sent the Italian reformists an expression of his complete sympathy with their readiness to join a bourgeois Cabinet, and his dislike for "dry theory".)

The speeches of Hall, Lansbury, and others have not changed the policy of the I.L.P. MacDonald remains at the head of the Party, and its policy will continue to be opportunist. The bourgeois influence upon the proletariat is strong—especially in democratic countries. But these speeches do not pass without leaving a trace, they undermine the influence of the bourgeoisie and of the opportunists. When the British people get a daily newspaper going (and *both* parties are seriously thinking about this), such and only such speeches will reach the minds and hearts of the working class. The Liberals of all countries, Russia included, are rejoicing and laughing now at the sight of the predominance of opportunism in the British labour movement. But "he laughs best who laughs last".

Zvezda, No. 18, April 16, 1911
Signed: V. *Ilyin*

Published according to
the *Zvezda* text

A CONVERSATION BETWEEN A LEGALIST
AND AN OPPONENT OF LIQUIDATIONISM[100]

Legalist: It seems to me that the extreme bitterness of the struggle and controversy with the liquidators in the Social-Democratic press has over-inflamed passions and somewhat obscured the substance of the disagreement.

Anti-liquidator: Isn't it the other way round? Isn't the sharpness of the struggle due to the profundity of the ideological differences? Or you have, perhaps, also joined the camp of the "vacillators"—in other words, the "conciliators"—who are trying to bridge the gulf with hollow phrases and sweeping platitudes?

Legalist: Oh no! I am not at all inclined to "conciliate". On the contrary. The point I want to make is that the liquidators have not enough understanding of what they want and hence are not resolute enough. They are still groping in the dark and developing spontaneously, if one may put it that way. They are still afraid of pursuing their line of thought to its conclusion. That is the reason for that inconsistency, confusion and hesitancy which their opponents mistake for hypocrisy and for fraudulent methods of struggle against the illegal party, etc. The result is a free-for-all and the public at large, for whose benefit the controversy is being conducted, no longer understands what it is all about. Had they had fewer smart diplomats and more confidence in themselves, the liquidators would have proved their case sooner and smashed you to pieces.

Anti-liquidator: That all sounds very nightmarish.... Still, it would be interesting to hear your arguments.

Legalist: In my opinion, the liquidators are right. They ought to adopt the legalist label which has been hurled at them. We shall adopt it and prove that it is the legalists who give the only correct answer—correct from the standpoint of Marxism—to the vexed problems of the working-class movement in Russia today. Do you or do you not admit that the period we are now passing through represents in some ways a distinctive stage in the economic and political evolution of Russia?

Anti-liquidator: I do.

Legalist: You do so only in words, just as your notorious "December" (1908) resolutions do. Seriously considered, an admission of this sort means that the open existence of, let us say, the Social-Democratic group in the Third Duma is not an accident, but an inseparable constituent of "the present moment". The sum total of the present political conditions, the sum total of the conditions obtaining in the working-class movement, is such that it is possible and essential to have an open, *legal* Social-Democratic group in the Duma, and it is possible and essential to have an open, *legal* Social-Democratic workers' party.

Anti-liquidator: Isn't it rather risky—this jump from a Social-Democratic group in the Duma to a Social-Democratic workers' party?

Legalist: Not in the least. The only difference is that the forms in which the Social-Democratic group in the Third Duma exists were determined for us from outside; all we had to do was to accept them, to enter, so to speak, into previously prepared premises, whereas it is up to us to find the forms for the existence of a legal workers' party. Here we must show initiative, we must fight for new forms. Those whom you contemptuously call liquidators have embarked upon this fight, have entered on the new path; but, unfortunately, they have only made the first step. Unfortunately, they are still timid about it, keep looking back and confine themselves to half-measures. This may be inevitable at the beginning of the new road; but the beginning will be followed by further steps. The indecision of the first steps will disappear, and the mistakes will be rectified.

Anti-liquidator: Excellent. Will you be kind enough to explain what these mistakes are and how they will be corrected.

Legalist: With pleasure! We cannot foretell exactly what the legal workers' party of tomorrow will be like, but we can see the general direction in which the working-class movement is developing. Once we grant that this is the direction, I can boldly draw a picture of the legal party, knowing that the actual party may not be exactly like the picture, but it will be *something like it*. And in order to draw this picture for you I don't have to "invent" anything. All I need is to consider the lessons life teaches us, the experience of activity under the new, post-revolutionary conditions. I need only to sum up this experience, disregarding the irrelevant details, and following the main thread. The working class is legally represented in the Duma. There is a legal Social-Democratic group in the Duma. It is hounded, spied on; it is not allowed to hold meetings, it is deprived of experienced people; tomorrow it may perhaps be scattered in prisons and places of exile—a legal party by no means precludes judicial and police persecution, as your short-sighted followers believe. But the legal group in the Duma exists despite the persecutions. There are legal trade unions and clubs, legal Marxist monthly and weekly journals; they are even more hounded, they are being suppressed, bled white by fines, their editors pay perhaps with a month and a half in prison for each month in the editorial office, the unions are constantly being disbanded but still they exist. Think this over. It is one thing when there are no legal trade unions, no legal Marxist press, and no legal Social-Democratic deputies. That was the position up to 1905. It is a different thing when they do exist, *even if* they are hounded all the time, even if they are constantly being suppressed. This has been the state of affairs since 1907. This is the new feature in the situation. It is this "new feature" that we must be able to turn to account, so as to extend, reinforce, and consolidate it.

Anti-liquidator: You started with the promise to be a more courageous and a more consistent legalist than those whom we have heard before, but so far you have done nothing but repeat what all the liquidators said long ago.

Legalist: As I said before, the picture of a consistent and convinced legalism follows logically from close observation of the experience provided by life. Actually all the various elements that go to make up a legal Social-Democratic workers' party already exist. We must speak out loudly and bluntly and call things by their real names. We must fearlessly recognise that these disjointed elements will be, must be, brought together—if not today then tomorrow—and such a party will then emerge. It must be founded, and will be founded. It will be persecuted, but nevertheless it will exist, the years when there was no legal workers' party will be succeeded by years during which a legal workers' party will lead a precarious existence interrupted by numerous persecutions; and these years in their turn will be succeeded by years when Russia will have a legal Social-Democratic party following the purely European pattern. The years for a legal Social-Democratic party have already begun and it is already something more *real* than your underground organisation which is ninety-nine per cent demolished. In order fully to rally the legalists and imbue their activity with more confidence, system, and steadfastness, we must not be afraid of speaking of things as they are, we must not be afraid of calling this reality by its real name, we must not be afraid of issuing the slogan and raising the banner. What if the courts and the police wrench the banner from our hands, what if they wrench it from us scores of times—they *cannot* destroy it, they cannot take it from us for long; for it sums up what actually exists, is growing and is bound to continue growing.

Anti-liquidator: Keep to the point. Or I may have to remind you of the saying: "He sings well, but nobody knows what the end will be". You promised to speak plainly. Well then, make it plain and more concrete: what are you going to inscribe on your banner?

Legalist: That is exactly what I have been leading up to. We establish a legally functioning association to promote the working-class movement. This association is based on the principles of Marxism. Its aim is to bring about a change in the social conditions of life along Marxist lines, to abolish classes, to abolish the anarchy of production, etc. The immediate aim of the legal party, that is to say, of our association, is the complete democratisation of the political and social system, help in solving the agrarian problem along democratic lines, on the basis of Marxist views, and extensive labour legislation. Finally, the means by which the new association carries on its activity are all the legal means of propaganda, agitation, and organisation.

Anti-liquidator: You don't suppose that our government will permit such an association to be officially registered, do you?

Legalist: Don't worry, I am not as naïve as that. Of course, our association will not be registered; but neither will it be right to regard it as illegal—that is the task we set ourselves. In each gubernia, worker after worker will draw up the rules of such an association and submit them to the authorities for endorsement. That will be a consistent and unremitting struggle for legality. The founders and members of such an association will not be liable to prosecution for the "dreadful" clauses of the programme of what is at present our apology for a party; for the R.S.D.L.P. today is nothing but an apology for a party, and the "dreadful" clauses of its programme, such as the demand for a republic and the dictatorship of the proletariat—to say nothing of the "dreadful" clauses in the numerous resolutions about an armed uprising, etc.—frighten no one, are of no significance, and play no role whatever, unless we mean their *"role"* in causing people to be sent to penal servitude, although *in actual fact* they are not guilty of anything illegal. This is the point, this is the tragicomedy of the present situation in the Party. The hand of the dead grips the living. The obsolete "clauses" of various resolutions and of the old Party programme—"clauses" which life itself has repudiated, which have become useless and have actually been relegated to the archives—only serve our enemies, only help them to suppress us, and render no useful purpose, none whatsoever, in promoting the real movement of our days, the *actual* Social-Democratic work now *being carried on* in the Third Duma, in the legally published magazines and newspapers, in the legally existing unions, in the legally held congresses, and so on, and so forth. That is why as far as we legalists are concerned, the *essence* of the question is not the desire to avoid the most dangerous persecutions and penalties (as your followers, who, forgive me for saying so, have been coached to hound the liquidators, would be prepared to conclude), but is, first, the importance *in principle* of an open working-class movement, and, secondly, in taking advantage of the contradictions of the present regime. Yes, yes, Mr. Orthodox, the principles of Marxism can by no means be reduced to a sum of words learned by rote, or to "orthodox" formulas fixed once and for all; no, they consist in helping the broad working-class movement, in promoting the organisation and initiative of the masses. What if some word or other remains *"unspoken"*—I am fully aware that you and your followers make it a point to "voice" what has been left unsaid by the Social-Democratic group in the Duma, by the legally published magazines, etc.; what if some words do remain *"unspoken"*—what of it, the cause will still go on. Larger sections of the workers will be drawn into the movement. A resolute step will be taken towards uniting open actions. Every politically-conscious worker will strike a blow at the regime which oppresses him, he will aim at *the very* contradiction most characteristic of that regime at the moment, the contradiction between the formal recognition of legality and the actual refusal to grant it, between "toleration" of the Social-Democratic group in the Duma and the attempts to suppress the Social-Democratic party, between the recognition of workers' associations in official statements and their persecution in actual fact. To strike a blow at the contradictions of the regime which oppresses the proletariat—that and not dead formulas, is *the living soul* of Marxism. One of the principal—I may even say one of the fundamental—reasons why the German Social-Democratic Party has been successful, is that it has always been willing to sacrifice the *formula* in the interests of the movement. After 1871 it succeeded in creating a party whose programme recognised only "lawful" methods of political activity. It succeeded in building up the strongest Social-Democratic movement in the world by means of a Social-Democratic programme which is much more *"legal"* than ours, for it does not contain and never has contained anything about a republic. You, however, are prepared to show the world an example of a "model-radical" Social-Democratic programme in the model-radical *absence* of a Social-Democratic mass organisation, of a Social-Democratic mass movement.

Anti-liquidator: So far your entire plan reduces itself in practice to a "mass movement" of incoming and outgoing papers in the government offices dealing with the affairs of associations and unions, assuming that in every gubernia every politically-conscious worker copies your draft plan for a legal Marxist "association" and submits them to the authorities for endorsement. Since you, yourself, say that this association will not be permitted, that means that no open movement, not even an "open" association, is going to be launched anywhere, except in your legalist imagination. But before answering you in detail, I should like to ask you one more question: do you conceive of this legal Marxist "association" as existing *in place* of the old, i. e., the present Party, or *alongside* it?

Legalist: That's just it. You have touched upon a very interesting point! This is one of the unfortunate errors committed by the official leaders of liquidationism. They are afraid of taking a big step forward along the obviously correct road; but at the same time they are taking a number of extremely hazardous steps, totally unnecessary for the cause, in a different direction—namely, that of opportunism. For my part, I would say that one can be a legalist, without being a liquidator. One should be a legalist, without being an opportunist. We must accept the legal *forms* of the movement, and we must accept them not halfway, not in words alone, but seriously and in practice, that is to say, we must immediately set up a legal Marxist workers' party; but it would be impermissible opportunism to renounce the revolution. Yet many, if not the majority, of our liquidators do reveal such a tendency. The denial of the hegemony of the working class is opportunism, and I roundly condemn it. There is no need for us to renounce anything, to liquidate anything. The new, legal party must exist together *with the old*, *alongside* of it. They will reinforce one another.

I see you are smiling. But there is nothing funny in this. You may say that it is "double-entry bookkeeping". But, then, let me ask you this: Is not the joint existence of a legal and illegal press something fully analogous to my plan, or rather to the conclusions I draw from all the lessons of present-day experience? Before 1905, émigrés could not contribute to the legal press; in those days periodicals were banned for printing articles written by such émigrés, even under a *nom de plume*, but it is typical of our contradictory era, that well-known émigrés *sign their own names* to articles appearing both in the illegal and *legal* press. Yet you do not object to this instance of "double-entry bookkeeping"! It causes no "confusion" whatever. It is force of habit and nothing else that prevents you from realising that this "double-entry bookkeeping" is dictated by all the conditions of our epoch, that we must turn its contradictions to account and know what action to take in *that* sphere in which the most important events of our times are taking place. In *words* you all subscribe to the "combination of illegal with legal work". Then apply it in practice. Having said A, don't be afraid to say B. Since you have accepted this fundamental thesis for tactics and organisation in general, don't be afraid to accept it for *Party* organisation. Get rid of the absurd anarchist prejudice against legality, can't you, and do it resolutely, seriously and sincerely.

Anti-liquidator: That is just the trouble with you; you are merely playing at "legality", pretending "legality", whereas the Germans relied on a legality which actually existed. The example of the legal and illegal press is a particularly glaring argument against you. When a Social-Democrat who is working illegally uses the legal press to publish what is legally permissible, he is not playing at legality, but is actually taking advantage of a legality that, within certain narrow limits, actually does exist. Your legal workers' party, however, or Marxist association (as well as the "open workers' party" of the liquidators from whom you do not really differ *at bottom*) is just a legalist mirage, nothing more; for you, yourself, admit that it will not be permitted, that *actually* these so-called "legal" associations will have no legal existence. Just as the anarcho-syndicalists indulge mainly in "revolutionary acrobatics", so all you manage to achieve is "legalistic acrobatics". The Cadets have a party that functions legally although it is legally non-existent, not because they have turned the contradictions to account, but because there is nothing revolutionary in the *content* of their work, and it does not imply any democratic organisational activity among the masses. Their work is of a liberal-monarchist nature, and the autocracy can afford to permit and tolerate political activity of this kind. But the autocracy cannot afford to tolerate the activity of Marxists among the working class, and it is naïve to try to promote the cause by a masquerade. Your "legal association", as well as the "open workers' party" of the liquidators, is nothing but a *sham* association, a masquerade, for actually you are counting on the Social-Democrats. The ambiguous and vague formulations which you have chosen to define the aims, platform and tactics of your "association" are but a verbal disguise, flimsy defences, the same sort of legalistic acrobatics. Our Party must speak out in the Duma, found *legally* functioning trade unions and speak at legally held congresses and it would be sheer anarchism or intellectualist nihilism to deny this. It is by recognising *this* kind of activity that we take into account the new conditions of the new epoch. But *legality* for political activity is still out of the question (except for intellectual opportunists), because the conditions for such legality have not yet been won, and it is a futile dream to think that you can "creep into" it. In the case of the Germans, such legality had been fully created by 1871, the transformation of the country on bourgeois lines had been completed and the conditions for a directly revolutionary movement had entirely disappeared. It is these *real* conditions and not the skill of the German Social-Democrats that *made possible* the emergence of a Social-Democratic party that is *really* legal and does not play at legality or indulge in "legalist acrobatics".

It is a naïve dream and a meaningless pastime to try *to copy* some of the legal clauses of the programme of such legal party, some of its resolutions, etc., and transfer this sort of "legality" to Russia, for you cannot *transfer* to Russia the German completion of the bourgeois revolution, the German history of a democracy that had spent itself, the German "revolution from above" of the 1860s,[101] and the *actually* existing German legality. There are some monarchist countries in which republican parties exist. legally; what legality will actually be like in Russia after her bourgeois revolutions have been achieved and we have a bourgeois system similar to that existing in Europe, remains to be seen when the future battles are over; it will be determined by their outcome. The task of the Social-Democratic movement today is to be able to prepare itself and the masses for revolution under the special conditions of the period of the June Third regime.

Under these conditions a legal party of the working class, an open workers' party, is a hollow phrase—it simply conceals the desire for the *legalisation* of ... a group of legalist opportunists. *This* is the kind of legalisation actually enjoyed by the Popular Socialists. *This* legalisation is actually enjoyed by the group of our legal, liquidationist journalists. It is not by chance but of necessity, not due to the "errors" of some liquidators but by virtue of the social composition of all the intellectual-liquidationist groups, that all opportunist elements—all those who nurture the idea of renouncing the revolution and repudiating the hegemony of the proletariat—gravitate and cannot help gravitating toward them. The only way in which the legalist may be distinguished from these people is by his *good intentions*; actually, he is indistinguishable. The real conditions of the present epoch are such that the legalisation of the Popular Socialists and the legalisation of the group of liquidationist writers is possible and inevitable; but the legalisation of a workers' party is mere words.

The illegal party of the working class exists, and even the fact that it has, in our days, been extremely weakened, and that most of its organisations have fallen to pieces, does not militate against its existence. Again and again the revolutionary underground is given fresh impetus by newly-emerging study circles and groups. The question reduces itself to the following: what is the organised force, what is the ideological tradition, what is the party capable of influencing, and which will influence, the open actions of the worker deputies in the Duma, of the workers' trade unions, of the workers' clubs, and of the workers' delegates at various legally held congresses? The revolutionary proletarian party, the Russian Social-Democratic Labour Party, or the opportunist group of liquidationist writers? That is the *real* essence of the "struggle against liquidationism", that is the real background which creates a gulf between the adversaries in this conflict. And this gulf cannot be bridged by any good intentions, by any attempts to draw a verbal distinction between legalism and liquidationism.

Diskussionny Listok, No. 3,
April 29 (May 12), 1911
Signed; *B. V. Kuprianov*

Published according to
the *Diskussionny Listok* text

"REGRET" AND "SHAME"

Every crisis reveals the real nature of phenomena or processes, sweeps away the superficial, the trivial, the external, and demonstrates the more profound fundamentals of what is taking place. Take, for instance, the most common and least complicated of crises in the sphere of economic phenomena, a strike. Nothing serves to reveal more clearly the actual relationships between classes, the real nature of contemporary society, the fact that the vast majority of the population has to submit to the power of *hunger*, and that the propertied minority resorts to organised violence in order to maintain its rule. Take commercial and industrial crises. Nothing refutes so glaringly the various speeches of the champions and apostles of "harmony of interests", nothing reveals so vividly and so fully the entire mechanism of the contemporary, capitalist system, the "anarchy of production", the disunity of the producers and the struggle of each against all and of all against each. Take, lastly, such a crisis as war. All the political and social institutions are tested and verified "by fire and sword". The strength or weakness of the institutions and social system of every nation are determined by the outcome of the war and its consequences. The essential nature of international relations under capitalism—the open robbery of the weaker—is fully and clearly exposed by war.

The significance of our notorious "parliamentary" crisis lies also in its revelation of the *deep-rooted* contradictions of the entire social and political system of Russia. Most of those participating in and acting out this crisis are, unfortunately, not attempting *to explain* it, to indicate its real causes and real significance but are doing their best to obscure it by words, words and more words—some of them are doing so deliberately, others because of their warped judge-ment or in deference to routine and tradition. The "big day" in the Third Duma, April 27, the day of the debate with Stolypin, was a big day of "parliamentary" phrase-monger-ing. But, despite the inordinate torrents of verbiage let loose by Stolypin himself and by his friends and opponents, they were unable *to hide* the essence of the matter. And the more the daily press tries to distract the attention of its readers by harping on liberal phrases, details and juridical formalities, the more appropriate it is to review again the picture of the crisis which was revealed on April 27.

The keynote of Stolypin's speech was defence of the "rights of the Crown" from any "derogation". "The significance of Article 87," said Stolypin, "is that it defines the rights of the Crown, and it cannot be departed from without creating an undesirable precedent." Stolypin objects to the attempts "to discredit the right of the supreme authority to invoke Article 87 in an emergency such as had arisen before the pro-rogation of the Chambers". "This right," he said, "is incon-trovertible; it is based on, and rooted in, the conditions of life itself." "Any other interpretation of this right is inaccepta-ble," he went on to say; "it would violate the meaning and sense of the law, it would reduce to naught the Monarch's right to issue emergency decrees."

All this is very clear, and all this is not mere words. The question is stated in cynically "realistic" terms. The Crown and attempts at its derogation.... If a dispute arises as to who is ultimately to interpret the meaning of the law, then force decides the issue. All this is very clear, and is not mere words.

On the other hand, Maklakov's "ardent, fervent, impas-sioned, and sincere" reproaches were nothing but mere words, juggling, juridical fictions. "It was with a feeling of pro-found regret and great shame" (report in *Rech*, April 28, p. 4) that he had heard certain references to the Crown. Makla-kov, who spoke on behalf of the entire so-called "constitu-tional Centre" (i.e., on behalf of the Cadets and Octobrists), defended the usual fiction of the monarchy being constitu-tional. But the "defence", voiced by the Cadets, or by the Cadets and the Octobrists, consisted of hollow phrase-mongering. What has it to do with regret and shame when it is a question of force? The bourgeoisie, who would like to have a constitution, regret the fact that the Crown refuses to grant a constitution, and is "ashamed" of this. The Crown is "ashamed" to have anyone impose a constitution on it, regards it as "derogation" and "regrets" any and all interpretation of any law that might be intended to "derogate".

Here we have two sides, and two interpretations of the law. Regrets and shame on both sides, with the only difference that one side does nothing else *but* "regret" and be "ashamed"; whereas the other side *says nothing* either about regretting or about being ashamed—it says only that derogation is "unacceptable".

Surely it is obvious that the ones to be "ashamed" of this state of affairs, the ones to be ashamed of their impotence, should be the Maklakovs, should be the whole of our Cadet and Octobrist bourgeoisie. The spokesman of the Council of the United Nobility is cynical about the crisis he cynically engineered, he hurls defiance and draws his sword. And the liberal bourgeoisie, like a street-trader who has been scared out of his wits by a police officer, shrinks back in awe, muttering: I regret, I am ashamed to ... be treated in this manner!

"I say," Maklakov vowed, "that I am a better constitutionalist than the Chairman of the Council of Ministers [I can imagine how Stolypin inwardly, and in the privacy of his home, laughed at these words; the point, my dear sir, is not whether one proclaims oneself a constitutionalist, but *who possesses the power* to determine whether a constitution shall exist, and what kind of constitution it shall be!], but for all that I am no less a monarchist than he. [Stolypin smiles even more contentedly, so that's the kind of a fellow he is—starts off by uttering threats, and winds up by offering regrets! He is a great warrior, this Maklakov!] I consider it lunacy to create a monarchy where it has no roots, but just as much lunacy to renounce it where its historical roots are strong." ...

Having first uttered some threats, and then offered his regrets, he now begins to cite arguments *in favour* of Stolypin. Oh, magnificent parliamentarian of the liberals! Oh, incomparable leader of the "constitutional" (*lucus a non*

lucendo*—"constitutional" though there is no constitution)
Centre, of the Cadet and Octobrist Centre!

"The Chairman of the Council of Ministers," thunders
our tribune of "people's freedom" (read, of the historical
slavery of our people), "may still remain in power; he will
hold on to it both because of fear of the revolution which
is being engineered by his own agents (*shouts from the
benches on the right*: "Shame!", *tumult*) ... and because of
the danger of creating a precedent!"

It is a tale about how Ivan Ivanovich cried "shame"
upon Ivan Nikiforovich, and Ivan Nikiforovich cried
"shame" upon Ivan Ivanovich.[102] "It's a shame not to observe the common standards of constitutional procedure,"
Ivan Ivanovich says to Ivan Nikiforovich. "It's a shame to
threaten a revolution, which you yourself fear, in which you
don't believe, and which you don't help," Ivan Nikiforovich
says to Ivan Ivanovich.

Well, reader, who do you think had the better of that
argument?

The representative of the "constitutional Centre", Lvov
the First, spoke after Gegechkori who had quite correctly
explained that the liberal press *wrongly* represents the crisis
as being of a "constitutional" nature, that the Cadets "have,
through their spokesmen, supported the criminal illusion
about a constitutional Centre", and that a constitution needs
a certain movement, which is still lacking. (Gegechkori
made one awkward slip at the end when he mentioned "anarchy"—that was not the word he should have used.)

To judge by the speech of Lvov the First, it seemed at
one time that even some of the landowners had learned a
thing or two from Gegechkori's explanations. "All that has
happened," said Lvov the First, "goes to show indeed that
we have no Constitution, and we have no parliamentary
system; but neither have we any fundamental laws and, in
general, any organised system [that's a good one! And what
about the existence of the landowners—doesn't that mean
that there is an organised landowners' system? You let your

---

* An untranslatable Latin pun: its meaning is clear from the
context. (Literally "a grove, but not giving light"; *lucus*—a grove,
lucere—to give light.)—*Ed.*

tongues run away with you, gentlemen of the "constitutional Centre"]—there is only arbitrary rule [that is precisely one of the fundamental and most essential features of the organised landowner system] and demagogy."

Judging by the interpretation of the "progressive" landlord Nikolai Nikolayevich Lvov the First, demagogy stands for something highly unpleasant. Listen further:

"And the men who are now in office employ this demagogy in order to enhance their own influence and their own power. But others, too, will make use of this demagogy—those who want to seize power [brr ... what an odious and immoral desire! Far be it from the Russian liberal bourgeois to entertain such a desire. It is only in the decadent West that the immoral bourgeoisie tries to seize power, and has even invented the unnatural doctrine that only the bourgeoisie in power can safeguard a bourgeois constitution. We, the Russian liberals, have been enlightened by the moral and idealist sermons of Struve, Berdayev and Co. and we are, therefore, of the opinion that power must remain in the hands of the Tolmachovs, whereas the Maklakovs ought to be engaged in writing instructions for the truly constitutional application of that power]... those who are more proficient in wielding the instrument of demagogy. Fear this demagogy, for everything will be sacrificed to it: your dignity, your possessions, your honour, and Russia's civic system."

The "progressist" Nikolai Nikolayevich Lvov the First talks sense. He is even fairly clear when he refers to "possessions". For instance, if yesterday a landowner owned 10,000 dessiatines, and today he is left with only 50 dessiatines, it means that 9,950 dessiatines have been "sacrificed" to "demagogy". That is clear. That is not mere words. But matters are not so clear when he refers to "dignity" and "honour". Does our progressist imply that a landlord can be a man of "dignity" and "honour" only when he owns 10,000 dessiatines, and that he is bound to lose both if he loses 9,950 of his dessiatines? Or does Lvov the First imply that dignity and honour stand to be sacrificed if the dessiatines do not fetch a fair price—say, 500 rubles a dessiatine?

On the subject of "Russia's civic system" the "progressist" Lvov the First is somewhat at sea. If it is true, as he said, that we have neither a constitution, nor a parliamentary system, nor fundamental laws, that means that we have no civic system either, and what doesn't exist, cannot be sacrificed. If what Lvov the First said is true this means that our civic system has been sacrificed to our "organised [landowner] system". Wasn't this a slip of the tongue on the part of our "progressist"? Didn't he mean to say that our organised landowner system would be sacrificed to Russia's civic system? Didn't he imply that it would be demagogy if events were to take such a hypothetical course? When he said—"fear this demagogy"—didn't he imply that the majority of the Third Duma ought to fear that hypothetical course of events?

It is a tale about how Ivan Ivanovich accused Ivan Nikiforovich of demagogy, and Ivan Nikiforovich accused Ivan Ivanovich of the same thing: "You are a demagogue," said Ivan Ivanovich to Ivan Nikiforovich, "because you are in office and you are using it to enhance your own influence and your own power, while at the same time pretending to serve the national interests of the population." "No," said Ivan Nikiforovich to Ivan Ivanovich, "you are a demagogue, because you are shouting at the top of your voice and in a public place, that all we have is arbitrary rule, and that we have neither a constitution nor fundamental laws; moreover you are hinting rather impolitely at some sort of sacrifice of our possessions."

We do not know which of them proved, in the long run, that the other was a demagogue. But we do know that when thieves fall out true men come into their own.

Zvezda, No. 21, May 7, 1911
Signed: *V. Ilyin*

Published according to
the *Zvezda* text

THE MEETING OF THE C.C. MEMBERS OF THE R.S.D.L.P.[103]

MAY 28-JUNE 4 (JUNE 10-17), 1911

First published in 1933
in *Lenin Miscellany XXV*

Published according to
the manuscripts

1

LETTER TO THE MEETING OF THE C.C. MEMBERS
OF THE R.S.D.L.P. ABROAD[104]

Igorev's piece of paper dated June 1, 1911, once again shows the disgraceful *game* being played around the convening of the C.C.; that policy of delay and sabotage which the Central Organ of our Party has been exposing for a long time, over a period of several months.

Igorev's assertion that Yudin and Kostrov[105] comprise a temporary Bureau or even a part of it, is out and out lying. *Over a long period of months*, when Makar and Lindov[106] (after Innokenty) *constituted* the Bureau organisation, *selected* agents, *arranged* a number of visits connected with the affairs of the central organisation, organised meetings with agents and candidates for co-option (Makar and Katsap[107] and others, with Milyutin and others), established contact with the general Party centre for Social-Democratic work in the Duma, and with the city Social-Democratic circles at the time of the elections (Moscow), etc., etc., *no such* work was carried out either by Yudin or Kostrov. *Precisely none*, absolutely none of this kind of activity was carried out by either one of them.

Not a single official body of the Party abroad (neither the Central Organ nor the Central Committee Bureau Abroad) received a *single* formal notification of the co-option of Yudin and Kostrov to the Bureau.

For a period of *more than two months* following the arrest of Makar and Lindov, not a single piece of paper, not a single letter was received and no one heard a sound about Yudin or Kostrov regarding their work in the Bureau. Not only were Yudin and Kostrov not recognised by anyone as members of the Bureau (as were, without any argument, Makar and Lindov), but neither did Yudin or Kostrov ask for a kopek, and, unlike Makar and Lindov, they did not inform the Central Committee Bureau Abroad that they comprised the Bureau.

In such a state of affairs we maintain that Igorev's reference to Kostrov and Yudin comprising the "Bureau" is a *mockery* of the Party, is *deception* of the Party. We shall expose this deception.

Further, after the experience of Inok, Makar and others, and following the exposure by Olgin,[108] etc., we regard all attempts to revive the Central Committee in Russia with the old C.C. members, elected in London, *as playing right into Stolypin's hands*. We warn the Party against those who are angling for uninformed people, who send Central Committee members where conditions are *impossible*, who send them on jobs that *cannot be done*, straight *into the hands of the police*.

Finally, as regards the *"plan"* to call a plenary meeting in *a month's time*, announced in Igorev's paper of June 1, 1911, but of which *he said nothing* to the Central Committee Bureau Abroad, we draw the Party's attention to a new *intrigue* of the liquidators in connection with the convening of the Central Committee.

No Central Committee can be convened within a month, but it is possible to *"bring together"* fictitious Central Committee members—that is the kernel of the *Golos* intrigue.

Since the Plenary Meeting, *four* Bolshevik members of the Central Committee (Meshkovsky+Innokenty+Makar+ +Lindov) have been lost *while engaged in the Central Committee work*. The Mensheviks have not lost *one member*, for not one of them has been working!!

And so now, the *Golos* group dare to propose a period of *a month* calculating on bringing in such individuals as *Pyotr*[109] who, for a whole year and a half (since the Plenary Meeting) has not done a *single* stroke of work, who *not once* put in an appearance at the Bureau. The *Golos* group know that within a month it is *not possible* to *"bring together"* Bolsheviks who are in exile either following a trial or by administrative decision.

They sent the Central Committee to Russia *"in order that it might be destroyed there"*!

They lived to see the day when *all* the Bolsheviks had been arrested.

They were able to save all the *fictitious* Menshevik members who had been inactive.

They want to fix a period of one month in which ficticious Central Committee members like Pyotr could be brought there, and Bolsheviks who were working *could not* even be notified!

They are wrong if they think that the *game* the liquidators are playing with the convocation of a plenary meeting will not be disclosed to the Party!

Written between May 19 and 23
  (June 1 and 5), 1911

2

SUMMARY (PLAN) FOR REPORT
BY THREE BOLSHEVIK MEMBERS OF THE C.C.
TO A PRIVATE MEETING
OF NINE MEMBERS OF THE CENTRAL COMMITTEE

1. History of attempts to restore the Central Committee in Russia.

Two periods:

(a) I. 1910-August (or September) 1910.

Two Bolshevik members of the Central Committee arrested following attempts to convene the Committee. Arranged C.C. meetings *many times*. *Not once* did Mikhail+Yuri+Roman, *not a single* Menshevik, put in an appearance.

(b) End of 1910-spring 1911.

New Bureau formed by two Bolshevik members of the Central Committee. *Not a single* Menshevik participated in their *work* (contact with agents, with the Duma group, with the Moscow Social-Democrats in connection with the elections, etc.).

One Menshevik (Kostrov) turned up at the Bureau once or twice in order to "vote"!

Both Bolsheviks arrested.

Conclusion: *all* Bolshevik members of the Committee arrested on account of the Central Committee work and *while engaged in this* work.

Of the Mensheviks, a section (Mikhail+Yuri+Roman) refused to take *any part whatsoever*, one (Pyotr) took *not* the slightest part for a whole year and a half, one (Kostrov) turned up twice at the Bureau in one and a half years (in 1911!), having played absolutely no part whatsoever in the Central Committee work. For two and a half months after the arrests of the Bolsheviks, this Menshevik took *not a single* step, nor did he write a single letter stating that he was re-forming the Committee.

Therefore, we consider it insolent for Igorev to state that this Menshevik+Bundist now comprise the *Bureau* (no formal notification of this having been given the Central Committee Bureau Abroad, and it being recognised by *no one!*).

2. Is it now possible to restore the plenary meeting abroad? Juridically—9 out of 15 members are available. *Formally* they can (a) proclaim themselves the meeting. Beyond question from the formal point of view, such a step is *probably* admissible with a majority of one, that is, by a vote of five out of these nine, against four. *In reality*, the value of such a formally irreproachable step is insignificant; there can be no doubt that it will be *impossible* for the Central Committee to carry out its *role* under such circumstances.

(b) Formally, it is also possible for these nine available members of the C.C. to bring over from Russia people with the rights of alternate members. What is the actual meaning of such a step? The Mensheviks can "bring" either their liquidators (Mikhail+Yuri+Roman, and others), who (after the famous statement of Mikhail+Yuri+Roman) will not be recognised as Central Committee members by a single honest Party member, or two Central Committee members who attended the Plenary Meeting in January 1910 and since then, for one and a half years, have not carried out any Central Committee work. The period required to bring them together is unpredictable.

The Bolsheviks may bring in another two of their alternate members in addition to the three Bolsheviks already available. In order to do this, months and months of work are required to establish contact with exiles, organise escapes, arrange for aid to their families, etc., etc. It is impossible to say how many months would be required for this "work".

For the Party, the real meaning of this protracted work of bringing together "formal" candidates, who at the moment are incapable of providing genuine central leadership in Russia, will not only be nil, the real meaning will be even worse, for the *game* of allocating places in central bodies *hides* from the local Party groups the sad reality in respect of which vigorous action must be taken.

After eighteen months of unsuccessful attempts to restore the Central Committee, to feed the Party with further promises—tomorrow "you" will have a Committee—that would be an affront to the Party. We do not intend to be a party to any such affront.

3. It goes without saying that an attempt to bring together candidates in Russia in order to restore the Central Committee there, can only come from supporters of Stolypin. The police know *all* the candidates and keep them under surveillance as has been shown by the arrests of Innokenty and Makar, twice and three times. That is the first and most important thing to note. And secondly, the real aim of such a gathering—the co-option of people living in Russia—is impossible of achievement now, since there are none available (they were seized with Makar when he was last arrested). It is impossible to achieve the unanimity required by the rules in the co-option of Mensheviks, since not one Bolshevik (as has already been stated by Inok to Sverchkov) will allow in a single liquidator (or *Golos* supporter).

4. At present the *real* position of the Party is such that almost everywhere in the localities there are informal, extremely small and tiny Party workers' groups and nuclei that meet irregularly. Everywhere they are combating liquidator-legalists in the unions, clubs, etc. They are not connected with each other. Very rarely do they see any literature. They enjoy prestige among workers. In these groups Bolsheviks and Plekhanov's supporters unite, and to some extent those *Vperyod* "supporters" who have read *Vperyod* literature or have heard *Vperyod* speakers, but have not yet been dragged into the isolated *Vperyod* faction set up abroad.

This anti-Party faction undoubtedly has some influence, although it is not great, among a section of St. Petersburg workers. There is sufficient proof that it does not hold itself responsible to any Central Committee, and interferes as much as possible with the work of the Social-Democrats (so far it has not given a direct call to the elections to the Fourth Duma, and continues to flirt with the otzovists).

A far more serious anti-Party and anti-Social-Democratic force is the faction of the *independent legalists* (*Nasha Zarya*+ +*Dyelo Zhizni*+*Golos Sotsial-Demokrata*). It has been proved beyond doubt that they recognise no Central Committee and publicly ridicule Central Committee decisions. They *cannot* carry out the Plenary Meeting's decisions (not to "minimise" the role of an illegal party, etc.) because they do not wish to. They cannot help taking the *opposite* line of action.

No honest Social-Democrat can doubt that the "independent legalists" are preparing for the elections to the Fourth Duma, and will conduct their election work *separately from and contrary to* the Party.

The task of Party members is clear: they must no longer permit the slightest delay, nor postpone for even a day a *forthright* declaration against the independent legalists; they must openly and decisively call on Party workers' circles in Russia to prepare for the elections, to work for the election of *only* those Party members who are *fully* loyal and aware of the danger of this tendency, and *during the election campaign* to warn the workers against the "legalist independents" and to struggle against them.

Such is the task of the day for our Party. There must be no deviation from this presentation of an issue with which the existing situation (and the independent legalists) confront us. All evasions, delays, attempts by the legalists to repeat the game of "promises" and "assurances" are fraught with great danger to the Party.

5. Our practical conclusion: the meeting of the nine must absolutely and immediately issue a manifesto to the Party in which the failure to convene the Central Committee in Russia is truthfully and fully described, and which calls upon local Party circles to display initiative and establish regional organising commissions and, following that, a Central *Organising Commission* and to conduct a determined, direct and implacable struggle against the "independent legalists".

A formal vote of the Plenary Meeting of the Central Committee supporting this call should only take place if the overwhelming majority of the nine members of the Central Committee, not merely five, agree to regard themselves as the Plenary Meeting and to take the path of decisive struggle against the group (faction) of legalist independents. It is, of course, understood that such a struggle is incompatible with participation by these legalists in central Party bodies, which they have sabotaged, obstructed, weakened and "kept in a sick condition" for eighteen months.

Written between May 19 and 23
    (June 1 and 5), 1911

3

DRAFT RESOLUTION DEFINING TERMS OF REFERENCE[110]

Placing on record that all members of the Central Committee living abroad have been invited and that all except one are present, this meeting regards itself to be a conference of Central Committee members living abroad and places on its agenda the question of reconstituting the Central Committee in connection with the general situation within theParty.

Written on May 28 (June 10), 1911

THE RESULTS OF THE DUMA SESSION
"WE DID THIS TOGETHER"

During the "historic" sitting of the Duma on April 27 Mr. Teslenko, who took issue with Mr. Stolypin, said in part:

"The Chairman of the Council of Ministers said to the State Duma: Yes, gentlemen, I shall come to your assistance in the very near future. There is the Bill about the Old Believers—you'll probably arrange matters so as to vote it down before the recess, and then it will be put into effect during the recess. I even imagined in this a sort of flippant we-know-each-other-well tone, as if we were told: why, we did this together. And, gentlemen, forgive me if it reminds me of the scene in the *Inspector-General*, in which the Mayor of the town says: 'Ah! So you've come to lodge a complaint against me? Have you forgotten how we did this and that together?' And, I presume, gentlemen, that those among you who, perhaps, once counted on this assistance, or who, perhaps, still count on it, must have felt embarrassed and, perhaps, thought (and you did well if you did think so): 'God preserve us from such friends, we can cope with our enemies ourselves'."

By these words, Mr. Teslenko, according to the Verbatim Report, earned "applause from the Left", apparently from the benches of the people's freedom group. The Cadets regarded it as fitting irony directed against the Octobrists. But in this case, as in many others, they applauded without giving thought to the profound meaning of the words which their speaker let fall. They applauded believing that these words wounded only the Octobrists, that they compromised only their particularly hated rivals. They did not realise that Mr. Teslenko's apt phrase, if its meaning is seriously analysed, represents a truth which stigmatises both the Octobrists and the Cadets. It is worth dwelling on this truth at greater length for it concerns one of the most vital questions of the past five or six years—and what years!—of Russia's political history.

"We did this together"—well put, Mr. Teslenko. But it would, perhaps, be more correct to put it this way: you have excellently *repeated* what has been said time and again at "Left" "meetings" which are usually so disparaged by the Cadet gentlemen. "We did this together"—these words by no means apply only to bills in the Third Duma, they by no means apply only to the notorious so-called "miscellany". They apply to *everything* that the Stolypins and the Russian liberal bourgeoisie (or the bourgeoisie that has pretended to be liberal) "have done together" ever since the end of 1905. As for Mr. Stolypin's "flippant tone", it was not something that the Cadet speaker merely "imagined", it was precisely the tone Stolypin assumes in all his speeches, it is the tone of the whole policy of the Stolypins in dealing with the bourgeoisie (who, in the persons of the Octobrist and Cadet deputies, incidentally, constitute the majority in the Third Duma).

This flippant tone—which at every serious turn of events gives way to gross bullying or even to brute force—is accounted for by the fact that not only the Octobrists but the Cadets as well merely play for effect, exclusively for the sake of winning applause (and the Stolypins know this only too well) when they hurl phrases like: "God preserve us from such friends [i.e., from the Stolypins], we can cope with our enemies [meaning, apparently, the reactionaries on the Right, and—how can we express it in the mildest possible terms?—the "exacting" Left] ourselves".

Had these been more than mere words, Russia would by now have been entirely and irrevocably rid of "such friends". But the point is that the Cadets hurl such phrases only in the heat of "opposition" speeches—opposition speeches cannot be made from the national rostrum unless they are given democratic flavour, even if only a slight one. That is why the Cadets sometimes give vent to democratic statements, which may be usefully compared with the *deeds* of these same Cadets. The historical role of a bourgeoisie playing at democracy (or threatening the enemy on the right with democracy) is such that this "playing" with words sometimes serves a useful purpose for some sections of the popular masses since it awakens sincere and profound democratic thought. "When the fiddle is played upstairs, people downstairs want to dance." There is a Latin proverb that says: *Littera scripta manet*—"what is written is permanent". Nor do spoken words always disappear, even if they are mere words and only spoken for effect.

It does not follow, of course, that hypocritical phrases uttered by the Cadets may be accepted at their face value, and that they may be proclaimed or regarded as an expression of democracy. But it certainly does follow that we ought to make use of every hypocritical phrase uttered by a Cadet so long as it has a democratic ring; that we ought to make use of it, first, to demonstrate the divergence between the words and the deeds of the man uttering them, and, secondly, to show what real, vital and direct significance democracy has for those masses who happen to get an inkling of the flamboyant phrases uttered by the speakers in the Taurida Palace.

The reflections of Mr. Teslenko quoted above are hypocritical, but not because Mr. Teslenko personally was hypocritical in his remarks; he may have been carried away by the torrent of his own oppositionist eloquence. The statement is hypocritical because the *words* of the representative of the Cadet Party are at variance with the *deeds* of that party at all serious moments in modern Russian history.

Recall the events of August 1905. What did Mr. Stolypin's predecessor do at that time? He was setting the stage for the Bulygin Duma[111] and for elections to it. What did Mr. Teslenko and his friends do at that time? Within the limits of their forces and in line with their "speciality" in the sphere of public activity, they were setting the stage for those same elections. Mr. Bulygin (and Mr. Stolypin) would be justified in saying to Mr. Teslenko: "We did this together". And Mr. Teslenko "did this together" for the very reason that he was fearful of being left without those "friends" of his, of whom he now says so magnificently, with the courage of a knight errant: "God preserve us from such friends."...

Recall the events that took place three months after the promulgation of Bulygin's State Duma Act. What did Mr. Stolypin's predecessor do at that time? He resisted, for instance, the movement of the postal and telegraph employees and the numerous ramifications of similar movements. Mr.

Teslenko, or, at any rate, his party as personified by Mr. Struve, Mr. Karaulov, and others, resisted—in its own way—the same movement. Mr. Witte (and Mr. Stolypin) would be justified in saying to the Teslenkos: "We did this together". It was the same in the case of the working-class holiday on May 1, 1906, in the case of the "local land committees" a little later, and in 1907, systematically and invariably, in the attitude to the worker and peasant deputies to the Second Duma, and so on, and so forth.

This policy, which the Cadet Party has been pursuing for many years, was summed up correctly by the well-known Cadet writer Mr. Izgoyev when he declared in *Vekhi*:

"We must at last have the courage to admit that the vast majority of members of our State Dumas, with the exception of thirty or forty Cadets and Octobrists, have not shown themselves to possess the knowledge required to undertake the job of governing and reconstructing Russia."

Mr. Izgoyev's "courageous admission" is courageous because, abandoning all appearances and all diplomacy, he has blurted out some words of *truth*. It is true that in "our State Dumas" the Cadets have indeed been guided by the landowner, bourgeois, liberal-monarchist "knowledge", which could not satisfy "the vast majority of members", particularly those on the left. And it goes without saying, of course, that Stolypin fought these latter members, and in fighting them relied for support on the "knowledge" (or, more correctly: on the interests and point of view) of "thirty or forty Cadets and Octobrists". Mr. Stolypin would be justified in saying to the entire Cadet Party: "We did this together"—together we fought against the clumsiness, inexperience, and ignorance of the workers and peasants.

The principal result of this year's session of the Duma is that the excessively "flippant tone" assumed by Stolypin towards the majority of the Third Duma—and, moreover, towards its bourgeois, Octobrist-Cadet, majority—proved too much even for this majority, which cannot be suspected of lacking in patience. The old regime assumes a flippant attitude towards the bourgeoisie, even though the latter is well aware of its own importance under the new, present day economic conditions, and is longing for independence, even for power. The Article 87 episode brought out this flippant attitude so sharply and, at the same time, affronted some of the mighty of this world so crudely, that even the most patient of people began to grumble. But grumbling is as far as they can go. They are bound hand and foot, and that is why they cannot go any farther. They are bound because at every important juncture of Russian history, in the course of all these last years, they have been afraid of the broad popular movement and turned their backs upon it; they have been hostile to the forces of democracy—to the real, live, active, mass forces of democracy—and have shunned them, attacked them from the rear in the same way as Stolypin has attacked them. And with these facts behind them, the Octobrists and the Cadets now suffer the penalty they deserve; in point of fact, they have *nothing* with which to parry Stolypin when he assumes a flippant tone and tells them: "If I am an enemy of democracy, you, my dear sirs, have proved that you are afraid of democracy—'we did this together'".

Zvezda, No. 28, May 28, 1911
      Signed: *V. Ilyin*

Published according to
the *Zvezda* text

OLD TRUTHS THAT ARE EVER NEW

The incidents that prevented the workers' delegates from attending the second congress of factory doctors in Moscow are known to readers from press reports.[112] We are not in a position to dwell here on the details of those incidents or to comment upon their significance. We shall merely note the instructive reflections that appeared in *Rech* of April 14, i.e., on the day the congress opened, in a leading article which was written on the eve of these events.

"It is to be regretted," wrote the organ of the Constitutional-Democratic Party, "that outside obstacles are placed in the way of such participation [participation by representatives of the workers]. The fate likely to befall some too fiery speakers is all too well known. As a result, the representatives of the workers insist on talking about their difficulties in concentrating on special questions, the impossibility of organising proper representation at the congress, about the obstacles put in the way of their organisations, and many other things of a like nature which are far removed from the programme of the congress and the discussion of which distracts attention from the questions on the agenda and sometimes leads to undesirable consequences. The charged atmosphere explains also the intolerance shown by workers' representatives to 'bourgeois' speakers, to all the measures taken by the government, and to the possibility of collaboration with representatives of other social groups."

This whole tirade is a characteristic example of feeble lamentations whose impotence is explained, not by the chance composition or by any special features of the given liberal party, of the given question, etc., but by causes of a more profound nature—by the actual conditions in which the liberal bourgeoisie in general finds itself in twentieth-century Russia. The liberal bourgeoisie is longing for the kind of "regime" under which it could have dealings with workers not likely "to make too fiery speeches" and who are fairly "tolerant" in their attitude towards the bourgeoisie, towards the idea of *collaboration with the bourgeoisie,* and "*to all* the measures taken by the government". It is longing for a regime under which these unassuming workers "collaborating" with it could "concentrate on the special questions" of social policy and would meekly agree to confine themselves to patching up the threadbare cloak of bourgeois solicitude for "the younger brother". In a word, the Russian liberals are longing for something like the present regime in England or in France, *as distinct* from that of Prussia. In England and France the bourgeoisie holds full sway, and it exercises its rule practically (with few exceptions) by itself, whereas in Prussia it is the feudal landowners, the Junkers, and the monarchist militarists, who are in the ascendancy. In England and France the bourgeoisie makes particularly frequent, free and wide use of the services of men of proletarian origin or traitors to the cause of the proletariat (John Burns, Briand) in the capacity of "collaborators" who "concentrate", undisturbed, "on special questions" and who teach the working class to maintain an attitude of "tolerance" to the rule of capital.

There is not the slightest doubt that the English and French systems are much more democratic than the Prussian; that they are much more favourable for the struggle of the working class, and have to a much greater degree eliminated the medieval institutions which distract the attention of the working class from its principal and real adversary. There is not the slightest doubt, therefore, that support for all aspirations to remodel our country along Anglo-French, rather than Prussian, lines is in the interests of the Russian workers. But we must not confine ourselves to this indisputable conclusion, as is so often done. Only here does the disputed question or questions begin—the dispute is with democrats of various shades.

The aspirations must be given support. To support him who is weak and who wavers, it is necessary to sustain him with something more solid and to dispel the illusions that prevent him from seeing his weakness and understanding its causes. One does not give support to the urge towards bourgeois democracy by strengthening those illusions and by adding one's voice to the feeble lamentations of the weak, inconsistent and wavering adherents of democracy, but, on the contrary, one deprives that urge of its force. The bourgeoisie of England and then of France, in the middle of the seventeenth and the late eighteenth century respectively, did not lament the "intolerance" of the younger brother, and made no wry faces over the "too fiery speakers" among the representatives of that younger brother, but they themselves supplied the *most* fiery speakers (and not only speakers) who inculcated a feeling of contempt for the advocacy of "tolerance", for weak *lamentations*, for vacillation and irresolution. Among those fiery speakers there were men who, in the course of centuries, have served as beacons and guides to humanity, despite historical limitations and often the naïveté of their ideas regarding the means of salvation from every kind of misfortune.

The German bourgeoisie, like the Russian, also lamented the fact that the speakers representing the "younger brother" were "too fiery"—and it left behind it in history a model of abasement, infamy, and flunkeyism for which it was rewarded with kicks administered by the "Junkers". The difference in the attitude of the two bourgeoisies was not due, of course, to the "characteristics" of different "races", but to the different levels of economic and political development which caused one of them to fear the "younger brother", and made it vacillate impotently between deprecating the violence of feudalism and censuring the "intolerance" of the workers.

Those are old truths. But they are ever new, and remain so as long as we are treated, in publications issued by people who profess to be Marxists, to lines like the following:

"The failure of the movement of 1905-06 was not due to the 'excesses' of the Lefts, for those 'excesses' were themselves the consequence of the aggregate of a large number of causes; nor was it due to 'treachery' on the part of the bourgeoisie who, everywhere in the West, had 'betrayed' at the crucial moment; it was due to the fact that there was no clearly defined bourgeois party which could supersede the obsolete bureaucracy at the helm of government, and which would be strong enough economically and sufficiently democratic to enjoy the support of the people." And a few lines further on: "... the weakness of the urban bourgeois democrats who should have become the political centre of attraction for the democratic peasantry..." (*Nasha Zarya*, No. 3, p. 62, article by Mr. V. Levitsky).

Mr. V. Levitsky is more consistent in his renunciation of the idea of "the hegemony of the proletariat" ("the urban bourgeois democrats", and no other group, *should have become* the centre of attraction"!), or he expresses his ideas more boldly, definitely and consistently than Mr. Potresov, who brushed up his article in *The Social Movement* to comply with Plekhanov's ultimatums.

Mr. V. Levitsky argues just like a liberal. He is an inconsistent liberal, despite his use of many Marxist phrases. He has no idea that an entirely different social category, not the urban bourgeois democrats, *should have become* the "centre of attraction for the democratic peasantry". He forgets that this "should" *was* a reality during momentous historical periods in England and in France, as well as in Russia—they were of momentous significance although they were of short duration in the latter country; in the two first-named countries it was for the most part the democratic, ultra-democratic and "too fiery" plebeian sections that united the various elements of the "lower classes".

Mr. V. Levitsky forgets that even in those brief periods of history when these "lower classes" played the role of "centres of attraction for the democratic peasantry", when they succeeded in *wresting* this role from the liberal bourgeoisie, they did exercise a decisive influence in determining *the degree* of democracy the country in question was to enjoy in the succeeding decades of so-called peaceful development. During the brief periods of *their* hegemony, these "lower classes" trained their bourgeoisie and remoulded it to such an extent that subsequently it was anxious to beat a retreat, but *was unable* to go farther in this retrograde movement than, say, an upper chamber in France, or certain departures from the principles of democratic elections, and so on, and so forth.

This idea, confirmed by the historical experience of *all* European countries—the idea that in epochs of bourgeois change (or, more correctly, of bourgeois revolution) the bourgeois democracy of each country is moulded one way or another, assumes one form or another, becomes trained in one tradition or another, and accepts one or another minimum of democracy, depending on the extent to which, in the decisive moments of the history of the nation, *hegemony* passes *not* to the bourgeoisie *but* to the "lower classes", to the "plebeian" elements, as was the case in the eighteenth century, or to the proletariat in the nineteenth and twentieth centuries—this idea is foreign to Mr. V. Levitsky. The idea of the hegemony of the proletariat constitutes one of the fundamental tenets of Marxism; and the liquidators' departure from these tenets (or even their indifference to them) is a profound source of quite a number of their irreconcilable fundamental differences with the opponents of the liquidationist trend.

Every capitalist country passes through an era of bourgeois revolutions which produces a definite degree of democracy, a definite constitutional or parliamentary regime, a definite degree of independence, love of liberty, and initiative among the "lower classes" in general and the proletariat in particular, a definite tradition permeating the entire political and social life of the country. The particular degree of democracy, or the particular tradition, depends on whether, in the *decisive* moments, the hegemony belongs to the bourgeoisie or to those at the other end of the scale; it depends on whether it is the former or the latter which (again in those decisive moments) constitutes the "centre of attraction for the democratic peasantry" and, in general, for all intermediary democratic groups and sections.

Mr. V. Levitsky is a past master at coining brilliant formulations which have the effect of at once revealing the ideological foundations of liquidationism, bringing them out clearly and in bold relief. Such was his famous formula: "*Not* hegemony, but a class party", which—translated into plain language—means: not Marxism, but Brentanoism (social-liberalism). The two formulas noted in the present article—namely: "the urban bourgeois democrats *should have become* the centre of attraction for the democratic peasantry" and "the failure ... was due to the fact that there was no clearly defined bourgeois party"—are, undoubtedly, destined to become just as famous.

Zvezda, No. 25, June 11, 1911
Signed: *V. Ilyin*

Published according to
the *Zvezda* text

RESOLUTION ADOPTED
BY THE SECOND PARIS GROUP OF THE R.S.D.L.P.
ON THE STATE OF AFFAIRS IN THE PARTY[113]

INTRODUCTION

The resolution of the Second Paris Group of the R.S.D.L.P. printed below (this group consists mainly of Bolsheviks with a small number of *Vperyod* supporters and "conciliators") outlines the fundamental propositions of the platform of all the Bolsheviks. At a time when the inner-Party struggle is becoming more acute, it is particularly important to make a *fundamental* statement on the cardinal problems of programme, tactics and organisation. People like Trotsky, with his inflated phrases about the R.S.D.L.P. and his toadying to the liquidators, who have nothing in common with the R.S.D.L.P., today represent "the prevalent disease". They are trying to build up a career for themselves by cheap sermons about "agreement"—agreement with all and sundry, right down to Mr. Potresov and the otzovists —while of necessity maintaining complete silence as to the political conditions of this wonderful supposed "agreement". Actually they preach *surrender* to the liquidators who are building a Stolypin labour party.

The Bolsheviks must now close their ranks more firmly, strengthen their group, define more clearly and precisely its Party line (as distinct from the line of the groups which, in one way or another, conceal their "identity"), rally the scattered forces, and go into battle for an R.S.D.L. Party purged of those who spread bourgeois influence among the proletariat.

N. Lenin

I

The meeting of the Second Paris Group of the R.S.D.L.P. after discussing the state of affairs in the R.S.D.L.P. in general, and the latest manifestations of the struggle that has flared up abroad between the Social-Democrats and those who want to be counted as Social-Democrats, considers it necessary, first of all, to draw attention to the fundamental statement of principles unanimously endorsed by the last (January 1910) Plenary Meeting of the Central Committee, which defines the nature of real Social-Democratic activity. That statement of principles declares that "renunciation of the illegal Social-Democratic Party, the belittling of its role and importance, attempts to curtail the programmatic and tactical tasks and slogans of revolutionary Social-Democracy" are *a manifestation of bourgeois influence over the proletariat*. The only true *Social-Democratic* activity is that which recognises the danger of this deviation and of any ideological and political trend that is otzovist or justifies otzovism, and which *really* overcomes such deviations.

This meeting further places on record that, despite the above-mentioned unanimous resolution of the Plenary Meeting, and despite the solemn promise made by the *Golos* representatives at the last Plenary Meeting *to renounce* liquidationism and to combat it, the editorial board abroad of *Golos Sotsial-Demokrata* and its group of adherents have for more than eighteen months since that Meeting, pursued that very *bourgeois* policy of liquidationism and supported, justified, and defended journals of the Russian legalists that are independent of Social-Democracy and of socialism, such as *Nasha Zarya*, *Vozrozhdeniye*, *Dyelo Zhizni*, etc. Those responsible for these journals, as has been stated repeatedly on behalf of the Party by its Central Organ, and as has also been stated by the pro-Party Mensheviks headed by Comrade Plekhanov, *have nothing in common with the R.S.D.L.P.* Those responsible for these journals not only belittle the role and importance of the illegal Social-Democratic Party, but frankly renounce it, slander the "underground" as renegades would, deny the revolutionary nature of the activity and the revolutionary tasks of the working-class movement

in Russia today, deceive the workers by spreading liberal-
bourgeois ideas about the "constitutional" nature of the
maturing crisis, throw overboard (and not only curtail)
such time-honoured slogans of revolutionary Marxism as
the recognition of the *hegemony* of the working class in the
struggle for socialism and for the democratic revolution.
By preaching and building what they call a legal or "open"
workers' party these people have actually become the build-
ers of a *Stolypin "labour" party* and spread bourgeois influence among the proletariat; in reality, the ideas preached
by these people are bourgeois in content, and an "open"
workers' party under Stolypin amounts to open renegacy on
the part of people who have renounced the tasks of the
revolutionary struggle of the masses against the tsarist autocracy, the Third Duma, and the entire Stolypin regime.

The meeting places on record that the Central Committee
Bureau Abroad, which is supposed to be a technical organ
of the C.C., has come completely under the influence of
the liquidators.*

By its failure to fulfil, in the course of eighteen months,
any one of the commissions given to it by the Central Committee (for instance—to unite the groups abroad on the basis
of the acceptance and implementation of the Plenary Meeting's decisions, to help the organisations in the localities,
or to see to it that *Golos* is discontinued and an end put to
the factional aloofness of the *Vperyod* group), the Bureau
Abroad has been of direct assistance to the enemies of the
Social-Democratic Party, the liquidators.

The majority of the Central Committee Bureau Abroad
showed contempt for the Party by systematically *obstructing*, ever since December 1910, the calling of a plenary meeting (as demanded by the Rules). The first time the Bolsheviks filed their application that the meeting be convened,
the Central Committee Bureau Abroad wasted seven weeks
just "taking a vote" on this question. After those seven
weeks the Central Committee Bureau Abroad acknowledged

---

* Igorev of *Golos* (sufficiently exposed and branded by the
pro-Party Menshevik Plekhanov) and the Bundist Lieber,[114] who is
conducting open propaganda in defence of Mr. Potresov and other
figures of a Stolypin labour party, are the leading lights of this
Central Committee Bureau Abroad.

that the Bolsheviks' demand for a plenary meeting was "legitimate", but at the same time it in practice *obstructed* the calling of a plenary meeting and did the same again at the end of May 1911. Actually, the role of *this* Central Committee Bureau Abroad has been to render assistance from abroad and from within the central Party bodies to leaders of the legalists and active promoters of a Stolypin labour party, such as Mikhail, Yuri, and Roman, who have declared the very existence of the Central Committee to be harmful (see Nos. 12 and 21-22 of *Sotsial-Demokrat*, Central Organ of the Party*). The meeting declares that the holding of Party posts by liquidators is outright *deception* of the Party, for the decisions of the Plenary Meeting clearly and unambiguously state that only *those* Mensheviks should be permitted to hold such posts who *conscientiously* abide by their promise to renounce liquidationism and to combat it. **

The meeting is, therefore, of the opinion that it was absolutely incumbent upon the Bolsheviks to break completely with the Central Committee Bureau Abroad as a body which has placed itself outside Party law and outside the Party, and that the Meeting of members of the Central Committee (see its "Notification"), which represented the vast majority of Social-Democratic Party organisations, groups, and circles actually working in Russia, was absolutely right in declaring that "the Central Committee Bureau Abroad has been pursuing a factional anti-Party policy, thereby violating the clear and precise decisions of the 1910 Plenary Meeting".

The meeting resolves to discontinue all relations with the Central Committee Bureau Abroad, and to support the decisions of the Meeting of members of the Central Committee, which has outlined a number of absolutely necessary measures to be taken in order to paralyse the activity of the liquidators, hampering as it does the entire work of the Party;

---

* See present edition, Vol. 16, "*Golos* (Voice) of the Liquidators Against the Party", and pp. 129-33 of this volume.—*Ed.*

** As regards the methods resorted to by the liquidators abroad in their fight against the R.S.D.L.P., such as political blackmail and the supplying of information to the secret police—which is what Mr. Martov did with the aid of the *Golos* editors—the meeting expresses its scorn for literary efforts of that nature, which can only arouse the disgust of all decent people.

to call a Party conference, and to help Party functionaries in all localities to revive the illegal organisations and
nuclei of the Party. The meeting calls upon all Party comrades in all localities to set to work *at once* (in line with the
decisions of the May-June Meeting) to prepare for a Party
conference and hold elections to it, and, for this purpose,
to establish regular connections with the Organising Commission,[115] the Central Organ and *Rabochaya Gazeta*.

II

The meeting draws the attention of worker Social-Democrats, irrespective of factions, to the fact that the émigré
leaders of the *Vperyod* group, and Trotsky, editor of *Pravda*,
are pursuing a policy of supporting the liquidators and
of an alliance with them against the Party and against
its decisions. This policy must be combated all the more
vigorously since it is profoundly detrimental to the interests of the proletariat and, as such, is completely at variance
with the activity of the *Russian* illegal Social-Democratic
groups which, though connected with *Pravda* or *Vperyod*,
are absolutely loyal in carrying out the decisions of the Party, and are everywhere struggling persistently against the
liquidators to uphold the illegal R.S.D.L.P. and its revolutionary programme.

The meeting particularly warns worker Social-Democrats
against the *deception* systematically practised by the *Golos*
writers, who describe all the comrades active in the legal
movement as opponents of the old Party and adherents
of Potresov's new "open" party. Thus, in the latest bulletin,
published by *Golos* on June 25 (reporting a "conference"
of people active in the legal movement), the *Golos* editors
suppressed the fact that the conference had *voted down*
a motion of the liquidators to boycott a certain legally
published newspaper for its anti-liquidationist policy.[116]
Thus, the editors of *Golos* also *suppressed* the fact that that
same conference *had voted down* the openly legalist and
obviously renegade resolutions which had been proposed by
Golos supporters. Even a Bundist who participated in the
conference had there admitted that the proposals of the "Po-
tresovites" were of an anti-Party nature. A number of those

active in the open movement have *already* embarked upon a resolute struggle against the Stolypin "labour" party. And if all Party members work solidly together, the number of such people will undoubtedly increase.

III

Whenever the struggle between Social-Democrats and those who spread bourgeois influence among the proletariat is intensified, all the unprincipled elements invariably bend their efforts to obscure great questions of principle by cheap sensationalism and scandal-mongering, such as those to which the *Golos* people abroad are assiduously treating audiences avid for contaminated spiritual food at meetings organised by the liquidators.

At a time like this it is more than ever incumbent upon revolutionary Marxists to remind all and sundry of the *old* truths *forgotten* by the liquidators, truths which constitute the foundation of our Social-Democratic activity.

The meeting, therefore, reminds all the members of the R.S.D.L.P. of our Party *programme*, of the programme which, at a time when international opportunism is intensifying and when a decisive struggle is maturing between opportunism and revolutionary Social-Democracy, has given a precise, clear, definite, and unyielding formulation of the revolutionary *ultimate goal* of socialism which can be achieved only by means of the dictatorship of the proletariat, and of the immediate revolutionary aims of the Russian Social-Democratic movement, the overthrow of tsarism and the establishment of a democratic republic. The *entire* propaganda conducted by our legalists and by *Golos* shows that, *in actual fact*, far from adhering to and carrying out our programme, they are frankly defending *reformism* [as the pro-Party Mensheviks have also admitted (see Plekhanov's *The Diary of a Social-Democrat*[117] and the *Discussion Bulletin*, No. 3)] and are plainly renouncing the immediate revolutionary aims of the R.S.D.L.P.

The meeting reminds all members of the R.S.D.L.P. that to be a *real* Party member, it is not enough to *call* oneself such, nor is it enough to carry on propaganda *"in the spirit"* of the programme of the R.S.D.L.P.; one must also carry out the *entire* practical work in conformity with the *tactical* decisions of the Party. In the present period of counter-revolution, at a time of universal renegacy, resignation, and despondency, particularly among the bourgeois intellectuals, only the Party decisions on tactics provide an appraisal of the situation, an appraisal of the practical line of conduct from the viewpoint of the principles of revolutionary Marxism. The real R.S.D.L.P., and not the one which *Golos* writers use as a screen for liquidationism, has *no* Party definition of the tasks of Social-Democracy at the present moment except *the resolutions on tactics adopted in December 1908.*

The liquidators, and to a certain extent the *Vperyod* group, hush up these resolutions or confine themselves to cursory references and outcries *against* them precisely for the reason that they feel that these resolutions call for a *line* of activity which radically repudiates both opportunist and semi-anarchist vacillations; which holds aloft the banner of revolution in spite of all and sundry counter-revolutionary trends; and which *explains* the economic and political characteristics of the present period as a new phase in Russia's bourgeois development, a phase which leads to a revolution destined to achieve the old objectives. A Party member is one who pursues the tactical line of the Party *in practice.* And there is only one tactical line of the R.S.D.L.P., the one stated in the resolutions of December 1908, which combine loyalty to the banner of the revolution with due regard for the new conditions of the present period. The resolutions of *the Plenary Meeting held in January 1910,* which are directed against *those who spread bourgeois influence among the proletariat,* represent a logical and direct corollary to, and are the natural continuation and fulfilment of, the resolutions of December 1908, which condemn liquidationism and categorically demand that Social-Democratic work in the Duma should be recognised and advantage taken of the possibilities offered for legal activity. In our days of confusion and disorganisation, we often come across people who invoke the great principle of the unity of the proletarian army in order to justify their unprincipled or cheap diplomatic attempts to effect "unity" or to "draw closer to" those who *spread bourgeois influence among the prole-*

tariat. The meeting most categorically condemns and repudiates all such attempts, regardless of who is responsible for them, and declares that the great work of uniting and consolidating the fighting army of the revolutionary proletariat cannot be carried out unless a line of demarcation is drawn and a ruthless struggle is waged against those who serve to spread bourgeois influence among the proletariat.

A Party member is one who actually helps *build up* the organisation in conformity with the principles of Social-Democracy. The Party, the R.S.D.L.P., has no other *Party* definition of the nature and tasks of organisational work but the one given in the resolution on the organisational question adopted in December 1908, in the resolution on the same question adopted by the Plenary Meeting of January 1910, and in the letter of the Central Committee published immediately after that Meeting. *Only* all-round help in re-establishing and reinforcing the *illegal* organisation can be regarded as *Party* work; and only the illegal R.S.D.L.P. can and should surround *itself* with a network of legally existing organisations, *make use* of all kinds of legally existing organisations, and *direct* the entire work of such organisations in the spirit of our revolutionary principles. Anyone who does not actually carry on such work, who takes part in the counter-revolutionary crusade in general, and in the liberal crusade in particular, against the "underground", against illegal activity, *deceives* the workers when he speaks of his membership of the R.S.D.L.P.

The elections to the Fourth Duma are drawing near. The more acute the crisis becomes in the top leadership of the Party abroad, the more urgent the need for Social-Democratic functionaries in the localities to show initiative; the more strictly must they insist, and *ensure*, that election activity is *really* carried on in a Party spirit by every group, every nucleus, every workers' circle. Anyone who to this day regards "otzovism" as a "legitimate trend in our Party" takes the name of the R.S.D.L.P. in vain. You *cannot* conduct Party work in the elections to the Fourth Duma unless you most resolutely refuse to have anything to do with such people. He who to this day talks of conducting the Fourth Duma election campaign with the forces and resources of "legally functioning organisations", with the forces and resources of an "open workers' party", and who at the same time refuses to abide by and carry out the decisions of the R.S.D.L.P. on the illegal organisation and the tactics as set forth in the Party's resolutions, takes the name of the R.S.D.L.P. in vain. He who carries on election activity and does not abide by the decisions of the R.S.D.L.P., but follows the line proposed in articles appearing in *Nasha Zarya*, *Golos Sotsial-Demokrata* and *Dyelo Zhizni*, is a builder of a Stolypin "labour" party, and not of the revolutionary Social-Democratic party of the proletariat.

The first aim of our Party at the forthcoming Fourth Duma elections is to educate the masses in socialism and develop mass agitation in favour of a democratic revolution to be accomplished by the forces of the proletariat and revolutionary bourgeois democrats (in the first place the revolutionary peasantry).

In the interests of such propaganda and agitation our Party must organise the *independent* participation of Social-Democrats in the elections and Party candidates must be put forward, not only in the worker curia, but everywhere, in all urban and rural constituencies.

The Party's entire agitational work during the elections must be conducted on two fronts, i.e., against the government and the parties openly supporting it, *as well as* against the Cadet Party, the party of counter-revolutionary liberalism.

Only those people may be Party candidates who really carry out the policy of the R.S.D.L.P. in full, are loyal not only to its programme but also to its resolutions on tactics, and who fight the new Stolypin "labour" party.

As to election agreements, the fundamental principles of the London Party Congress and the Party Conference of July 1907[118] must remain in force.

The Fourth Duma election campaign must be conducted by Party groups of workers, in the spirit of the Party decisions and in strict conformity with them.

Written not later than June 18 (July 1), 1911
Published in July 1911, as a separate leaflet

Published according to the leaflet text and verified with the text of the *Information Bulletin*

INTRODUCTION TO THE PAMPHLET
TWO PARTIES

Kamenev's pamphlet represents a systematised summary of the material on the struggle against the liquidationist trend waged during the period of counter-revolution by the Bolsheviks and, following their lead, by the whole R.S.D.L.P. Quite naturally, Kamenev devotes most of his space to an elucidation of the divergence on questions of principle between Social-Democracy and the liquidationist trend, a subject to which *Proletary*[119] and the Central Organ of the Party, *Sotsial-Demokrat*, also devoted most of their space during the period from 1908 to 1911.

Kamenev has proved conclusively that, *in point of fact*, the liquidationist group represents a separate party, not the R.S.D.L. Party. His evidence sums up the experience primarily of the years 1909-11, which confirmed the resolution of December 1908. That resolution, which was moved and carried by the Bolsheviks on behalf of the R.S.D.L.P., had already declared that the liquidators *were endeavouring to "substitute"* for the R.S.D.L.P. an "amorphous" legally existing federation. That amorphous legally existing federation of Potresov, Larin, Levitsky and Co. (with Mr. Martov and the *Golos* group abroad trailing behind), has now fully revealed itself. It is a group of literary men who have nothing in common with the R.S.D.L.P., and who pursue, not a Social-Democratic, but a liberal labour policy. They are the leading lights of a *Stolypin* "labour" party.

It is a feature specific of Russia at the turn of the century that we often meet with cases of extremely rapid and sometimes very "unexpected" transition from Marxism to liberalism. The Economists and *Credo*—Mr. Struve and Co.—the liquidators, are all rungs of one ladder, stages in a single process of evolution, expressions of the same tendency. The party of the working class in Russia began to form shortly before the Revolution of 1905; now, in the period of counter-revolution, this party is being reconstructed, and to a certain extent built anew, on a more solid foundation. The bourgeois intelligentsia, attracted to the revolution by the knowledge that Russia has not yet passed through the epoch of democratic revolutions, has been joining the proletariat group after group—and group after group has again deserted the proletariat, having found out through experience that they cannot live up to revolutionary Marxism, that their real place is *outside* the ranks of the Social-Democratic Party. Such are our liquidators, too, some of whom are already speaking quite clearly, bluntly, and frankly of a *new* party they are creating.

Otzovism and liquidationism, while similar in the sense that both represent non-Social-Democratic, bourgeois trends, differ materially in respect of the fate that attended their political evolution. Otzovism was nipped in the bud by the Bolsheviks, and it has not gone so far as to attempt to create a party of its own; today it represents an insignificant group abroad, whose activity has been reduced to aiding the liquidators in their intrigues and struggle against the R.S.D.L.P. The liquidationist trend, on the other hand, has its centre (in the first place, political, and then organisational) in Russia; it has created a party *of its own*, even though it is an amorphous one (so far it is amorphous). That is why it has been necessary for Kamenev to dwell at length on the liquidationist tendency and to touch upon otzovism only in passing.

There are not many people among the adherents of the R.S.D.L.P. capable of sincerely defending the liquidationist trend.* Unfortunately, there are still quite a number of

---

* Obviously it would be ridiculous to talk of sincerity on the part of the *Golos* group abroad. They are past masters at blackmail and slander, with gentry like Martov in the lead in this respect. The decision arrived at by Kautsky, Mehring and Zetkin that the disputed funds be turned over, *not* to the Central Committee Bureau Abroad, *but* to the Technical Commission [120] (see *Bulletin* of the Organising Commission, August 1, 1911), means complete vindication of Comrade Alexandrov and all the Bolsheviks (who are *fully* in agreement with Alexandrov) and complete condemnation of the foul

people who are sincerely opposed to liquidationism, *but do not understand* the conditions under which the struggle against it has to be waged. Of course, they say, liquidationism is a bourgeois trend in the Social-Democratic movement; but why not fight it in the ranks of a single party, just as the Germans fight the Bernsteinians? Why not try to come to an "agreement" with the liquidators?

Our champions of "agreement" fail to understand a very important and very simple thing: the liquidators are not only opportunists (like Bernstein and Co.); they are also trying to build a *separate* party of their own, they have issued the slogan that the R.S.D.L.P. *does not exist*; they pay no heed *whatever* to the decisions of the R.S.D.L.P. That is the difference between us and "Europe", and only people who have not given sufficient thought to the question, or who are not acquainted with Russian conditions, can invoke the example of "Europe". In Europe, an opportunist guilty of but one-tenth of what the Potresovs, Igorevs, Bers, Martovs, Dans, and their like have done and are doing against their Party and in defiance of its decisions would not be tolerated in the ranks of the party a single month. In Europe the parties function openly, and it is possible to see at once whether one belongs to an organisation and submits to its decisions.

Our Party is illegal. It is impossible to "see", and it is impermissible (unless one is an agent of the secret police) to talk openly of whether X, Y, or Z belongs to the organisation. But it is a fact that the Potresovs do *not* belong to the organisation, and that they *sneer* at *all* its decisions, just as the *Golos* people do. How can we come to an "agreement" with the Potresovs who have proved that *as far as they are concerned* the Party *does not exist*? Or with the Martovs and Dans who have proved the same thing? *What* can we agree *on* with the liquidators, unless it is the destruction of the R.S.D.L.P.?

Let the advocates of "agreement" try to name the *terms* of agreement with the liquidators, the *means* of exercising

---

slander spread by Martov, Dan, Martynov and Axelrod. We also draw readers' attention to Comrade Victor's[121] letter printed in the Appendix. It shows what vile means Mr. Martov and his abettors stoop to in their fight against political adversaries.

control over the fulfilment of the terms, the *facts* proving
that they would be fulfilled. They can name *none* of these.
And therefore it is beyond any doubt that references to
"agreement" are nothing but idle and puerile talk. This
talk only helps the intrigues of the circles abroad (such as
the *Vperyod* and *Golos* circles, and the Trotskyites), who
have fully demonstrated that they ignore the decisions of
the Party, and that they refuse to give up *an iota* of their
"freedom" to support the liquidators.

In Russia, in the meantime, the illegal workers' circles
have been drawing away from the liquidators, and are dissociating themselves from them to an ever greater extent
with each passing day, at the same time slowly and la-
boriously building up the revolutionary R.S.D.L.P. The task
of the adherents of the *Social-Democratic* Labour Party is
to help these circles, to translate the decisions of the
R.S.D.L.P. into practical work, and to put an end to the
game of agreement with the windbags abroad (the *Golos*
group, the strongest group abroad, are also mere windbags).
Membership of the Party means fighting for the Party.
All talk about "agreement" with the liquidators who are
building a non-Social-Democratic party, is a violation of
the duty deriving from Party membership.

August 2, 1911   *N. Lenin*

P. S. It should be added that the analysis of the "charges"
levelled against the Bolshevik Centre, given in the Appendix,
represents our collective opinion and has been elaborated on the basis of material and documents in the hands of the
Bolshevik Centre, as well as on the basis of information supplied by comrades of the Bolshevik Centre who personally
conducted some of its affairs.

                                                   N. Lenin

Written on July 20 (August 2), 1911   Published according to
      Published in August 1911,   the text of the pamphlet
      in the pamphlet entitled
      Two Parties, Paris, published
      by *Rabochaya Gazeta*

REFORMISM IN THE RUSSIAN SOCIAL-DEMOCRATIC MOVEMENT

The tremendous progress made by capitalism in recent decades and the rapid growth of the working-class movement in all the civilised countries have brought about a big change in the attitude of the bourgeoisie to the proletariat. Instead of waging an open, principled and direct struggle against all the fundamental tenets of socialism in defence of the absolute inviolability of private property and freedom of competition, the bourgeoisie of Europe and America, as represented by their ideologists and political leaders, are coming out increasingly in defence of so-called social reforms as opposed to the idea of social revolution. Not liberalism versus socialism, but reformism versus socialist revolution—is the formula of the modern, "advanced", educated bourgeoisie. And the higher the development of capitalism in a given country, the more unadulterated the rule of the bourgeoisie, and the greater the political liberty, the more extensive is the application of the "most up-to-date" bourgeois slogan: reform *versus* revolution, the partial patching up of the doomed regime with the object of dividing and weakening the working class, and of maintaining the rule of the bourgeoisie, *versus* the revolutionary overthrow of that rule.

From the viewpoint of the universal development of socialism this change must be regarded as a big step forward. At first socialism fought for its existence, and was confronted by a bourgeoisie confident of its strength and boldly and consistently defending liberalism as an integral system of economic and political views. Socialism has grown into a force and, throughout the civilised world, has already upheld its right to existence. It is now fighting *for power* and the bourgeoisie, disintegrating and realising the inevitability of its doom, is exerting every effort to defer that day and to maintain its rule under the new conditions as well, at the cost of partial and spurious concessions.

The intensification of the struggle of reformism against revolutionary Social-Democracy *within* the working-class movement is an absolutely inevitable result of the changes in the entire economic and political situation throughout the civilised world. The growth of the working-class movement necessarily attracts to its ranks a certain number of petty-bourgeois elements, people who are under the spell of bourgeois ideology, who find it difficult to rid themselves of that ideology and continually lapse back into it. We cannot conceive of the social revolution being accomplished by the proletariat without this struggle, without clear demarcation on questions of principle between the socialist Mountain and the socialist Gironde[122] *prior* to this revolution, and without a complete break between the opportunist, petty-bourgeois elements and the proletarian, revolutionary elements of the new historic force *during* this revolution.

In Russia the position is fundamentally the same; only here matters are more complicated, obscured, and modified, because we are lagging behind Europe (and even behind the advanced part of Asia), and we are still passing through the era of bourgeois revolutions. Owing to this, Russian reformism is distinguished by its particular stubbornness; it represents, as it were, a more pernicious malady, and it is much more harmful to the cause of the proletariat and of the revolution. In our country reformism emanates from two sources simultaneously. In the first place, Russia is much more a petty-bourgeois country than the countries of Western Europe. Our country, therefore, more frequently produces individuals, groups and trends distinguished by their contradictory, unstable, vacillating attitude to socialism (an attitude veering between "ardent love" and base treachery) characteristic of the petty bourgeoisie in general. Secondly, the petty-bourgeois masses in our country are more prone to lose heart and to succumb to renegade moods at the failure of any *one* phase of our bourgeois revolution; they are more ready to renounce the aim of a complete democratic revolution which would entirely rid Russia of all survivals of medievalism and serfdom.

We shall not dwell at length on the first source. We need only mention that there is hardly a country in the world in which there has been such a rapid "swing" from sympathy for socialism to sympathy for counter-revolutionary liberalism as that performed by our Struves, Izgoyevs, Karaulovs, etc., etc. Yet these gentlemen are not exceptions, not isolated individuals, but representatives of widespread trends! Sentimentalists, of whom there are many outside the ranks of the Social-Democratic movement, but also a goodly number within it, and who love to preach sermons against "excessive" polemics, against "the passion for drawing lines of demarcation", etc., betray a complete lack of understanding of the historical conditions which, in Russia, give rise to the "excessive" "passion" for swinging over from socialism to liberalism.

Let us turn to the second source of reformism in Russia.

Our bourgeois revolution has not been completed. The autocracy is *trying* to find new ways of solving the problems bequeathed by that revolution and imposed by the entire objective course of economic development; *but it is unable to do so*. Neither the latest step in the transformation of old tsarism into a renovated bourgeois monarchy, nor the organisation of the nobility and the upper crust of the bourgeoisie on a national scale (the Third Dumá), nor yet the bourgeois agrarian policy being enforced by the rural superintendents[123]—none of these "extreme" measures, none of these "latest" efforts of tsarism in the *last* sphere remaining to it, the sphere of adaptation to bourgeois development, prove adequate. It just does not work! Not only is a Russia "renovated" by *such* means unable to catch up with Japan, it is perhaps, even beginning to fall behind China. Because the bourgeois-democratic tasks have been left unfulfilled, a revolutionary crisis is still inevitable. It is ripening again, and we are heading toward it once more, in a new way, *not the same* way as before, not at the same pace, and not only in the old forms—but that we are heading toward it, of that there is no doubt.

The tasks of the proletariat that arise from this situation are fully and unmistakably definite. As the only consistently revolutionary class of contemporary society, it must be the leader in the struggle of the whole people for a fully democratic revolution, in the struggle of *all* the working and exploited people against the oppressors and exploiters. The proletariat is revolutionary only insofar as it is conscious of and gives effect to this idea of the hegemony of the proletariat. The proletarian who is conscious of this task is a slave who has revolted against slavery. The proletarian who is not conscious of the idea that his class must be the leader, or who renounces this idea, is a slave who does not realise his position as a slave; at best he is a slave who fights to improve his condition as a slave, *but not* one who fights to overthrow slavery.

It is, therefore, obvious that the famous formula of one of the young leaders of our reformists, Mr. Levitsky of *Nasha Zarya*, who declared that the Russian Social-Democratic Party must represent "*not* hegemony, but a class party", is a formula of the most consistent reformism. More than that, it is a formula of sheer renegacy. To say, "*not* hegemony, but a class party", means to take the side of the bourgeoisie, the side of the liberal who says to the slave of our age, the wage-earner: "Fight to improve your condition as a slave, but regard the thought of overthrowing slavery as a harmful utopia"! Compare Bernstein's famous formula— "The movement is everything, the final aim is nothing"— with Levitsky's formula, and you will see that they are variations of the same idea. They both recognise *only* reforms, and renounce revolution. Bernstein's formula is broader in scope, for it envisages a socialist revolution (=the final goal of Social-Democracy, as a party of bourgeois society). Levitsky's formula is narrower; for while it renounces revolution in general, it is particularly meant to renounce what the liberals hated most in 1905-07—namely, the fact that the proletariat *wrested* from them the leadership of the masses of the people (particularly of the peasantry) in the struggle for a fully democratic revolution.

To preach to the workers that what they need is "*not* hegemony, but a class party" means to betray the cause of the proletariat to the liberals; it means preaching that *Social-Democratic* labour policy should be replaced by a *liberal* labour policy.

Renunciation of the idea of hegemony, however, is the crudest form of reformism in the Russian Social-Democratic movement, and that is why not all liquidators make bold to express their ideas in such definite terms. Some of them (Mr. Martov, for instance) even try, mocking at the truth, to deny that there is a connection between the renunciation of hegemony and liquidationism.

A more "subtle" attempt to "substantiate" reformist views is the following argument: The bourgeois revolution in Russia is at an end; after 1905 there can be no second bourgeois revolution, no second nation-wide struggle for a democratic revolution; Russia therefore is faced not with a *revolutionary* but with a "constitutional" crisis, and all that remains for the working class is to take care to defend its rights and interests on the basis of that "constitutional crisis". That is how the liquidator Y. Larin argues in *Dyelo Zhizni* (and previously in *Vozrozhdeniye*).

"October 1905 is not on the order of the day," wrote Mr. Larin. "If the Duma were abolished, it would be restored more rapidly than in post-revolutionary Austria, which abolished the Constitution in 1851 only to recognise it again in 1860, nine years later, without any revolution (note this!), simply because it was in the interests of the most influential section of the ruling classes, the section which had reconstructed its economy on capitalist lines." "At the stage we are now in, a nation-wide revolutionary movement like that of 1905 is impossible."

All Mr. Larin's arguments are nothing more than an expanded rehash of what Mr. Dan said at the Conference of the R.S.D.L.P. in December 1908. Arguing against the resolution which stated that the "*fundamental* factors of economic and political life which gave rise to the Revolution of 1905, *continue to operate*", that a new—*revolutionary*, and not "constitutional"—crisis was developing, the editor of the liquidators' *Golos* exclaimed: "They [i.e., the R.S.D.L.P.] want to shove in where they have once been defeated".

To shove again toward revolution, to work tirelessly, in the changed situation, to propagate the idea of revolution and to prepare the forces of the working class for it— that, from the standpoint of the reformists, is the chief crime of the R.S.D.L.P., that is what constitutes the *guilt* of the revolutionary proletariat. Why "shove in where they have once been defeated"—that is the wisdom of renegades and of persons who lose heart after any defeat.

But in countries older and more "experienced" than Russia the revolutionary proletariat showed its ability to "shove in where it has once been defeated" two, three, and four times; in France it accomplished *four* revolutions between 1789 and 1871, rising again and again after the most severe defeats and achieving a republic in which it now faces its *last* enemy—the advanced bourgeoisie; it has achieved a republic, which is the only form of state corresponding to the conditions necessary for the final struggle for the victory of socialism.

Such is the distinction between socialists and liberals, or champions of the bourgeoisie. The socialists teach that revolution is inevitable, and that the proletariat must take advantage of *all* the contradictions in society, of every weakness of its enemies or of the intermediate classes, to prepare for a new revolutionary struggle, to repeat the revolution in a broader arena, with a more developed population. The bourgeoisie and the liberals teach that revolutions are unnecessary and even harmful to the workers, that they must not "shove" toward revolution, but, like good little boys, work modestly for reforms.

That is why, in order to divert the Russian workers *from* socialism, the reformists, who are the captives of bourgeois ideas, *constantly* refer to the example of *Austria* (as well as Prussia) in the 1860s. Why are they so fond of these examples? Y. Larin let the cat out of the bag; because in these countries, after the "unsuccessful" revolution of 1848, the bourgeois transformation was completed *"without any revolution"*.

That is the whole secret! That is what gladdens their hearts, for it seems to indicate that bourgeois change is possible *without* revolution!! And if that is the case, why should we Russians bother our heads about a revolution? Why not leave it to the landlords and factory owners to effect the bourgeois transformation of Russia "without any revolution"!

It was because the proletariat in Austria and Prussia was weak that it was unable to prevent the landed proprietors and the bourgeoisie from effecting the transformation *regardless* of the interests of the workers, in a form *most prejudicial* to the workers, retaining the monarchy, the privileges of the nobility, arbitrary rule in the countryside, and a host of other survivals of medievalism.

In 1905 our proletariat displayed strength unparalleled in any bourgeois revolution in the West, yet today the Russian reformists use examples of the weakness of the working class in other countries, forty or fifty years ago, in order to justify *their own* apostasy, to "substantiate" *their own* renegade propaganda!

The reference to Austria and Prussia of the 1860s, so beloved of our reformists, is the best proof of the theoretical fallacy of their arguments and of their desertion to the bourgeoisie in practical politics.

Indeed, if Austria restored the Constitution which was abolished after the defeat of the Revolution of 1848, and an "era of crisis" was ushered in in Prussia in the 1860s, what does this prove? It proves, primarily, that the bourgeois transformation of these countries had not been completed. To maintain that the system of government in Russia has *already* become bourgeois(as Larin says), and that government power in our country is no longer of a feudal nature (see Larin again), and at the same time to refer to Austria and Prussia as an example, is to refute oneself! Generally speaking it would be ridiculous to deny that the bourgeois transformation of Russia has not been completed: the very policy of the bourgeois parties, the Constitutional-Democrats and the Octobrists, proves this beyond all doubt, and Larin himself (as we shall see further on) surrenders his position. It cannot be denied that the monarchy is taking one more step towards adapting itself to bourgeois development—as we have said before, and as was pointed out in a resolution adopted by the Party (December 1908). But it is still more undeniable that *even* this adaptation, *even* bourgeois reaction, and the Third Duma, and the agrarian law of November 9, 1906 (and June 14, 1910) do *not* solve the problems of Russia's bourgeois transformation.

Let us look a little further. Why were "crises" in Austria and in Prussia in the 1860s *constitutional*, and not revolutionary? Because there were a number of special circumstances which eased the position of the monarchy (the "revolution from above" in Germany, her unification by "blood and iron"); because the proletariat was at that time extremely weak and undeveloped in those countries, and the liberal bourgeoisie was distinguished by base cowardice and treachery, just as the Russian Cadets are in our day.

To show how the German Social-Democrats who themselves took part in the events of those years assess the situation, we quote some opinions expressed by Bebel in his memoirs (*Pages from My Life*), the first part of which was published last year. Bebel states that Bismarck, as has since become known, related that the king at the time of the "constitutional" crisis in Prussia in 1862 had given way to utter despair, lamented his fate, and blubbered in his, Bismarck's, presence that they were both going to die on the scaffold. Bismarck put the coward to shame and persuaded him not to shrink from giving battle.

"These events show," says Bebel, "what the liberals might have achieved had they taken advantage of the situation. But they were already afraid of the workers who backed them. Bismarck's words that if he were driven to extremes he would set Acheron in motion [i.e., stir up a popular movement of the lower classes, the masses], struck fear into their heart."

Half a century after the "constitutional" crisis which "without any revolution" completed the transformation of his country into a bourgeois-Junker monarchy, the leader of the German Social-Democrats refers to the *revolutionary* possibilities of the situation at that time, which the liberals did not take advantage of owing to their fear of the workers. The leaders of the Russian reformists say to the Russian workers: since the German bourgeoisie was so base as to cower before a cowering king, why shouldn't we *too* try to copy those splendid tactics of the German bourgeoisie? Bebel accuses the bourgeoisie of not having "taken advantage" of the "constitutional" crisis to effect a revolution because of their fear, as exploiters, of the popular movement. Larin and Co. accuse the Russian workers of having striven to secure hegemony (i.e., to draw the masses into the revolution in spite of the liberals), and advise them to organise "*not* for revolution", *but* "for the defence of their interests in the forthcoming constitutional reform of Russia". The liquidators offer the Russian workers the rotten views of rotten German liberalism as "Social-Democratic" views! After this, how can one help calling such Social-Democrats "Stolypin Social-Democrats"?

In estimating the "constitutional" crisis of the 1860s in Prussia, Bebel does not confine himself to saying that the bourgeoisie were afraid to fight the monarchy because they were afraid of the workers. He also tells us what was going on among the workers at that time. "The appalling state of political affairs," he says, "of which the workers were becoming ever more keenly aware, naturally affected their mood. Everybody clamoured for change. But since there was no fully class-conscious leadership with a clear vision of the goal and enjoying the confidence of the workers, and since there existed no strong organisation that could rally the forces, the mood petered out [verpuffte]. Never did a movement, so splendid in its essence [in Kern vortreffliche], turn out to be so futile in the end. All the meetings were packed, and the most vehement speakers were hailed as the heroes of the day. This was the prevailing mood, particularly, in the Workers' Educational Society at Leipzig." A mass meeting in Leipzig on May 8, 1866, attended by 5,000 people, unanimously adopted a resolution proposed by Liebknecht and Bebel, which demanded, on the basis of universal, direct, and equal suffrage, with secret ballot, the convening of a Parliament supported by the armed people. The resolution also expressed the "hope that the German people will elect as deputies only persons who repudiate every hereditary central government power". The resolution proposed by Liebknecht and Bebel was thus unmistakably revolutionary and republican in character.

Thus we see that at the time of the "constitutional" crisis *the leader of the German Social-Democrats* advocated resolutions of a republican and revolutionary nature at mass meetings. Half a century later, recalling his youth and telling the new generation of the events of days long gone by, he stresses most of all his regret that at that time there was no leadership sufficiently class-conscious and capable of understanding the revolutionary tasks (*i.e.*, *there was no revolutionary Social-Democratic Party understanding the*

task implied by the hegemony *of the proletariat*); that there
was no strong organisation; that the revolutionary mood
"petered out". Yet the leaders of the Russian reformists,
with the profundity of Simple Simons, refer to the example
of Austria and Prussia in the 1860s as proving that we can
manage "without any revolution"! And these paltry philistines who have succumbed to the intoxication of counter-
revolution, and are the ideological slaves of liberalism, still
dare to dishonour the name of the R.S.D.L.P.!

To be sure, among the reformists who are abandoning
socialism there are people who substitute for Larin's straightforward opportunism the diplomatic tactics of beating
about the bush in respect of the most important and fundamental questions of the working-class movement. They
try to confuse the issue, to muddle the ideological controversies, to defile them, as did Mr. Martov, for instance,
when he asserted in the legally published press (that is to
say, where he is protected by Stolypin from a direct retort
by members of the R.S.D.L.P.) that Larin and "the orthodox
Bolsheviks in the resolutions of 1908" propose an *identical*
"scheme". This is a downright distortion of the facts worthy
of this author of scurrilous effusions. The same Martov
pretending to argue against Larin, declared in print that he,
"of course" did "not suspect Larin of reformist tendencies".
Martov *did not suspect* Larin, who expounded *purely* reformist views, of being a reformist! This is an example of the
tricks to which the diplomats of reformism resort.* The
same Martov, whom some simpletons regard as being more
"Left", and a more reliable revolutionary than Larin,
summed up his "difference" with the latter in the following
words:

"To sum up: the fact that the present regime is an inherently
contradictory combination of absolutism and constitutionalism, and
that the Russian working class has sufficiently matured to follow the
example of the workers of the progressive countries of the West in
striking at this regime through the Achilles heel of its contradictions,
is ample material for the theoretical substantiation and political
justification of what the Mensheviks who remain true to Marxism
are now doing."

---

* Compare the just remarks made by the pro-Party Menshevik
Dnevnitsky in No. 3 of *Diskussionny Listok* (supplement to the Central
Organ of our Party) on Larin's reformism and Martov's evasions.

No matter how hard Martov tried to evade the issue, the result of his very first attempt at a summary was that all his evasions collapsed of themselves. The words quoted above represent a complete renunciation of socialism and its replacement by liberalism. What Martov proclaims as "ample" is ample *only* for the liberals, *only* for the bourgeoisie. A proletarian who considers it "ample" to recognise the contradictory nature of the combination of absolutism and constitutionalism accepts the standpoint of a *liberal labour* policy. He is *no* socialist, he has *not* understood the tasks of his *class*, which demand that the masses of the people, the masses of working and exploited people, be roused against absolutism in all its forms, that they be roused to intervene *independently* in the historic destinies of the country, the vacillations or resistance of the bourgeoisie notwithstanding. But the independent historical action of the masses who are throwing off the hegemony of the bourgeoisie turns a "constitutional" crisis into a *revolution*. The bourgeoisie (particularly since 1905) fears revolution and loathes it; the proletariat, on the other hand, educates the masses of the people in the spirit of devotion to the idea of revolution, explains its tasks, and prepares the masses for new revolutionary battles. Whether, when, and under what circumstances the revolution materialises, does not depend on the will of a particular class; but revolutionary work carried on among the masses is never wasted. This is the only kind of activity which prepares the masses for the victory of socialism. The Larins and Martovs forget these elementary ABC truths of socialism.

Larin, who expresses the views of the group of Russian liquidators who have completely broken with the R.S.D.L.P., does not hesitate to go the whole hog in expounding his reformism. Here is what he writes in *Dyelo Zhizni* (1911, No. 2) —and these words should be remembered by everyone who holds dear the principles of Social-Democracy:

"A state of perplexity and uncertainty, when people simply do not know what to expect of the coming day, what tasks to set themselves—that is what results from indeterminate, temporising moods, from vague hopes of either a repetition of the revolution or of 'we shall wait and see'. The immediate task is, not to wait fruitlessly for something to turn up, but to imbue broad circles with the guiding idea that, in the ensuing historical period of Russian life, the working class must organise itself not 'for revolution', not 'in expectation of a revolution', but simply [note the *but simply*] for the determined and systematic defence of its particular interests in all spheres of life; for the gathering and training of its forces for this many-sided and complex activity; for the training and building-up in this way of socialist consciousness in general; for acquiring the ability to orientate itself [to find its bearings]—and to assert itself—particularly in the complicated relations of the social classes of Russia during the coming constitutional reform of the country after the economically inevitable selfexhaustion of feudal reaction."

This is consummate, frank, smug reformism of the purest water. War against the idea of revolution, against the "hopes" for revolution (in the eyes of the reformist such "hopes" seem *vague*, because he does not understand the depth of the contemporary economic and political contradictions); war against every activity designed to organise the forces and prepare the minds for revolution; war waged in the legal press that Stolypin protects from a direct retort by revolutionary Social-Democrats; war waged on behalf of a group of legalists who have completely broken with the R.S.D.L.P. —this is the programme and tactics of the Stolypin labour party which Potresov, Levitsky, Larin, and their friends are out to create. The real programme and the real tactics of these people are expressed in exact terms in the above quotation—as distinct from their hypocritical official assurances that they are *"also* Social-Democrats", that they "also" belong to the "irreconcilable International". These assurances are only window-dressing. Their deeds, their real social substance, are expressed in this programme, which substitutes a liberal labour policy for socialism.

Just note the ridiculous contradictions in which the reformists become entangled. If, as Larin says, the bourgeois revolution in Russia has been consummated, then the socialist revolution is the next stage of historical development. This is self-evident; it is clear to anyone who does not profess to be a socialist merely for the sake of deceiving the workers by the use of a popular name. *This* is all the more reason why we *must* organise "for revolution" (for socialist revolution), "in expectation" of revolution, for the sake of the "hopes" (not vague "hopes", but the *certainty* based on exact and growing scientific data) *of a socialist* revolution.

But that's the whole point—to the reformist the twaddle about the consummated bourgeois revolution (like Martov's twaddle about the Achilles heel, etc.) is simply a verbal screen to cover up his *renunciation of all revolution*. He renounces the bourgeois-democratic revolution on the pretext that it is complete, or that it is "ample" to recognise the contradiction between absolutism and constitutionalism; and he renounces the socialist revolution on the pretext that "for the time being" we must "simply" organise to take part in the "coming constitutional reform" of Russia!

But if you, esteemed Cadet parading in socialist feathers, recognise the inevitability of Russia's "coming constitutional reform", then you speak against yourself, for thereby you admit that the bourgeois-democratic revolution *has not been completed* in our country. You are betraying your bourgeois nature again and again when you talk about an inevitable "*self-exhaustion* of feudal reaction", and when you sneer at the proletarian idea of *destroying*, not only feudal *reaction*, but *all* survivals of feudalism, by means of a *popular* revolutionary movement.

Despite the liberal sermons of our heroes of the Stolypin labour party, the Russian proletariat will always and invariably put the spirit of devotion to the democratic revolution and to the socialist revolution into *all* that difficult, arduous, everyday, routine and inconspicuous work, to which the era of counter-revolution has condemned it; it will organise and gather its forces for revolution; it will ruthlessly repulse the traitors and renegades; and it will be guided, not by "vague hopes", but by the scientifically grounded conviction that the revolution will come again.

Sotsial-Demokrat, No. 23,
September 14(1), 1911

Published according to
the *Sotsial-Demokrat* text

FROM THE CAMP OF THE STOLYPIN "LABOUR" PARTY

DEDICATED TO OUR "CONCILIATORS" AND ADVOCATES OF "AGREEMENT"

Comrade K.'s[124] letter deserves the profound attention of all to whom our Party is dear. A better exposure of *Golos* policy (and of *Golos* diplomacy), a better refutation of the views and hopes of our "conciliators" and advocates of "agreement" it is hard to imagine.

Is the case cited by Comrade K. an exception? No, it is *typical* of the advocates of a Stolypin labour party, for we know very well that a *number* of writers in *Nasha Zarya*, *Dyelo Zhizni*, etc., have *already* been systematically preaching *these very* liquidationist ideas *for many a year*. These liquidators do not often meet worker members of the Party; the Party very rarely receives such exact information of their disgraceful utterances as that for which we have to thank Comrade K.; but, *always and everywhere*, the preaching of the *group* of independent legalists is conducted precisely in this spirit. It is impossible to doubt this when periodicals of the *Nasha Zarya* and *Dyelo Zhizni* type exist. It is to the advantage of only the most cowardly and most despicable defenders of the liquidators to keep silent about this.

Compare this fact with the methods employed by people like Trotsky, who shout about "agreement" and about their hostility to the liquidators. We know these methods only too well; these people shout at the top of their voices that they are "neither Bolsheviks nor Mensheviks, but revolutionary Social-Democrats"; they zealously vow and swear that they are foes of liquidationism and staunch defenders of the illegal R.S.D.L.P.; they *vociferously abuse those who expose the liquidators, the Potresovs*; they say that the anti-liquidators are "exaggerating" the issue; but *do not say a word* against the definite liquidators, Potresov, Martov, Levitsky, Dan, Larin, and so on.

The real purpose of such methods is obvious. They use *phrase-mongering* to shield the *real* liquidators and do everything to *hamper* the work of the anti-liquidators. This was exactly the policy pursued by *Rabocheye Dyelo*,[125] so notorious in the history of the R.S.D.L.P. for its unprincipled character; it vowed and swore, "We are not Economists, not at all, we are wholly in favour of political struggle"; but in reality it provided a *screen* for *Rabochaya Mysl*[126] and the Economists, directing its whole struggle against those who exposed and refuted the Economists.

Hence it is clear that Trotsky and the "Trotskyites and conciliators" like him are more pernicious than any liquidator; the convinced liquidators state their views bluntly, and it is easy for the workers to detect where they are wrong, whereas the Trotskys *deceive* the workers, *cover up* the evil, and make it impossible to expose the evil and to remedy it. Whoever supports Trotsky's puny group supports a policy of lying and of deceiving the workers, a policy of shielding the liquidators. Full freedom of action for Potresov and Co. in Russia, and the shielding of their deeds by "revolutionary" phrase-mongering abroad—there you have the essence of the policy of "Trotskyism".

Hence it is clear, furthermore, that any "agreement" with the *Golos* group that evades the question of the liquidators' centre in Russia, that is, the leading lights of *Nasha Zarya* and *Dyelo Zhizni*, would be nothing but a continuation of this deception of the workers, this covering up of the evil. Since the Plenary Meeting of January 1910 the *Golos* supporters have made it abundantly clear that they are capable of "subscribing" to any resolution, not allowing any resolution "to hamper the freedom" of their liquidationist activities one iota. Abroad they subscribe to resolutions saying that any disparagement of the importance of the illegal Party is evidence of bourgeois influence among the proletariat, while in Russia they assist the Potresovs, Larins, and Levitskys, who, far from taking part in illegal work, scoff at it and try to destroy the illegal Party.

At present Trotsky, together with Bundists like Mr. Lieber (an extreme liquidator, who publicly defended Mr. Potresov in his lectures and who now, in order to hush up the fact, is stirring up squabbles and conflicts), together with Letts like Schwartz,[127] and so on, is concocting just such an "agreement" with the *Golos* group. Let nobody be deceived on this score: their agreement will be an agreement to shield the liquidators.

P.S. These lines were already set up when reports appeared in the press of an "agreement" between the *Golos* group and Trotsky, the Bundist and the Lett liquidator. Our words have been fully borne out: this is an agreement *to shield* the liquidators in Russia, an agreement between the servants of the Potresovs.

Sotsial-Demokrat, No. 23,   Published according to
September 14 (1), 1911   the *Sotsial-Demokrat* text

COMMENT BY *SOTSIAL-DEMOKRAT* EDITORS ON STATEMENT BY COMMISSION CONVENING PLENARY MEETING OF C.C.[128]

For a long time, ever since December 1910, the Editorial Board of the Central Organ has been warning the Party that the *Golos* group is *sabotaging* the plenary meeting.* We now have the facts of their sabotage of plenary meetings, first in Russia and then abroad.

The meeting in Russia was wrecked by Mikhail, Yuri, and Roman. By their "clever rebuttal" they merely confirmed their having been invited to attend a meeting of the Central Committee, if only to co-opt new members, and that it was not the wicked "factional" "Leninist" Bolsheviks who had invited them, but *conciliators*. Yet the three gentlemen refused to attend the meeting. It was their refusal that sabotaged the work of the Central Committee in Russia, for *all* the Bolshevik members of the Central Committee who went to Russia (and they were *all* of them practical leaders) were "eliminated" before they succeeded in calling a plenary meeting after that trio had refused to attend.

No matter what the *Golos* people say now, no matter what they swear to and what assurances they give, no matter how they try to confuse the issue and wriggle out by resorting to imprecations, feuds, and chicanery, there is no getting away from the facts. And it is a fact that a trio of the *chief* leaders of the legalists—Mikhail+Yuri+Roman, the closest associates of Mr. Potresov and of the other heroes of the Stolypin labour party—*sabotaged* the Central Committee in Russia.

---

* See pp. 23-38 of this volume.—*Ed.*

Now the *Golos* group has sabotaged the Central Committee abroad as well. The Bolsheviks demanded that it be convened in December 1910; but the liquidationist Central Committee Bureau Abroad *refused* to convene it, pleading that that was the business of the Central Committee Bureau in Russia (this was a lie, because a meeting held abroad did *not* preclude one being held in Russia).

The second time, after the arrests in Russia, the Bolsheviks demanded that the meeting be convened abroad *in April or May 1911*. Again the *Central Committee Bureau Abroad refused* on the plea that half the "Russian Bureau" had *survived*.

Four or five months have passed since then, and the falsity of the excuses cited by the Bureau Abroad has been *fully exposed*: *in four months* not a single letter has been received from "that half" of the "Bureau", there has been no news of a single step taken by that half, not a single spark of life shown. The Liebers, Igorevs, and Schwartzes deceived the Party. By referring to the *non-existent* Bureau in Russia, they *refused* to convene the Central Committee abroad. Yet, the Meeting of members of the Central Committee held in June, proved that *nine* members of the Central Committee *were* abroad at the time.

Anyone who is capable of thinking and of keeping a clear head amid the shouts, imprecations, feuds, and chicanery, cannot help seeing that the Central Committee has been definitely wrecked by the *Golos* people.

The *Golos* group has done everything it could to destroy the Party. The Party will do everything it can to destroy them.

Sotsial-Demokrat. No. 23,   Published according to
September 14 (1), 1911   the *Sotsial-Demokrat* text

STOLYPIN AND THE REVOLUTION

The assassination of the arch-hangman Stolypin occurred at a time when a number of symptoms indicated that the first period in the history of the Russian counter-revolution was coming to an end. That is why the event of September 1, quite insignificant in itself, again raises the extremely important question of the content and meaning of the counter-revolution in Russia. One discerns notes of a really serious and principled attitude amid the chorus of reactionaries who are servilely singing the praises of Stolypin, or are rummaging in the history of the intrigues of the Black-Hundred gang which is lording it over Russia, and amid the chorus of the liberals who are shaking their heads over the "wild and insane" shot (it goes without saying that included among the liberals are the former Social-Democrats of *Dyelo Zhizni* who used the hackneyed expression quoted above). Attempts are being made to view "the Stolypin period" of Russian history as a definite entity.

Stolypin was the head of the counter-revolutionary government for about five years, from 1906 to 1911. This was indeed a unique period crowded with instructive events. Externally, it may be described as the period of preparation for and accomplishment of the coup d'état of June 3, 1907. The preparation for this coup, which has already shown its results in all spheres of our social life, began in the summer of 1906, when Stolypin addressed the First Duma in his capacity as Minister of the Interior. The question is, on what social forces did the men who staged the coup rely, or what forces prompted them? What was the social and

economic content of the period ushered in on June 3? Stolypin's personal "career" provides instructive material
and interesting examples bearing on this question.

A landowner and Marshal of the Nobility,[129] he was
appointed governor in 1902, under Plehve, gained "fame"
in the eyes of the tsar and the reactionary court clique
by his brutal reprisals against the peasants and the cruel
punishment he inflicted upon them (in Saratov Gubernia),
organised Black-Hundred gangs and pogroms in 1905 (the
pogrom in Balashov), became Minister of the Interior in
1906 and Chairman of the Council of Ministers after the
dissolution of the First Duma. That, in very brief outline, is Stolypin's political biography. The biography of
the head of the counter-revolutionary government is at the
same time the biography of the class which carried out
the counter-revolution—Stolypin was nothing more than an
agent or clerk in its employ. This class is the Russian landed
nobility with Nicholas Romanov, the first nobleman and
biggest landowner, at their head. It is made up of the thirty
thousand feudal landowners who control seventy million
dessiatines of land in European Russia—that is to say,
as much land as is owned by ten million peasant households. The latifundia owned by this class form a basis for
feudal exaction which, in various forms and under various
names (labour-service, bondage, etc.) still reigns in the traditionally Russian central provinces. The "land hunger" of the
Russian peasant (to use a favourite expression of the liberals and Narodniks) is nothing but the reverse side of the
over-abundance of land in the hands of this class. The
agrarian question, the central issue in our 1905 Revolution,
was one of whether landed proprietorship would remain
intact—in which case the poverty-stricken, wretched, starving, browbeaten and downtrodden peasantry would for
many years to come *inevitably* remain as the bulk of the
population—or whether the bulk of the population would
succeed in winning for themselves more or less human
conditions, conditions even slightly resembling the civil
liberties of the European countries. This, however, *could
not be accomplished* unless landed proprietorship and the
landowner monarchy inseparably bound up with it were
abolished by a revolution.

Stolypin's political biography is the faithful reflection and expression of the conditions facing the tsarist monarchy. Stolypin could only act as he did in the situation in which the revolution placed the monarchy. The monarchy *could not* act in any other way when it became quite clear—became clear in actual practice both *prior* to the Duma, in 1905, and *at the time* of the Duma, in 1906—that the vast, the overwhelming majority of the population had already realised that its interests could not be reconciled with the preservation of the landowning class, and was striving to abolish that class. Nothing could be more superficial and more false than the assertions of the Cadet writers that the attacks upon the monarchy in our country were merely the expression of "intellectual" revolutionism. On the contrary, the objective conditions were such that it was the struggle of the peasants against landed proprietorship that inevitably posed the question of whether our landowning monarchy was to live or die. Tsarism *was compelled* to wage a life-and-death struggle, it *was compelled* to seek other means of defence in addition to the utterly impotent bureaucracy and the army which had been weakened as a result of military defeat and internal disintegration. All that the tsarist monarchy could do under the circumstances was to organise the Black-Hundred elements of the population and to perpetrate pogroms. The high moral indignation with which our liberals speak of the pogroms gives every revolutionary an impression of something abominably wretched and cowardly, particularly as this high moral condemnation of pogroms has proved to be fully compatible with the idea of conducting negotiations and concluding agreements with the pogromists. The monarchy had to defend itself against the revolution, and the semi-Asiatic, feudal *Russian* monarchy of the Romanovs could only defend itself by the most infamous, most disgusting, vile and cruel means. The only honourable way of fighting the pogroms, the only rational way from the point of view of a socialist and a democrat, is not to express high moral condemnation, but to assist the revolution selflessly and in every way, to organise the revolution for the *overthrow* of this monarchy.

Stolypin the pogrom-monger groomed himself for a ministerial post in the only way in which a tsarist governor could:

by torturing the peasants, by organising pogroms and by showing an ability to conceal these Asiatic "practices" behind glib phrases, external appearances, poses and gestures made to look "European".

And the leaders of our liberal bourgeoisie, who are expressing their high moral condemnation of pogroms, carried on negotiations with the pogromists, recognising not only the latters' right to existence, but their leadership in the work of setting up a new Russia and of ruling it! The assassination of Stolypin has occasioned a number of interesting revelations and confessions concerning this question. Witte and Guchkov, for instance, have published letters concerning the former's negotiations with "public figures" (read: with the leaders of the moderate liberal-monarchist bourgeoisie) about forming a Cabinet after October 17,[130] 1905. Among those who took part in the negotiations with Witte—these negotiations must have taken a long time, because Guchkov writes of "the wearisome days of protracted negotiations"—were Shipov, Trubetskoi, Urusov, and M. Stakhovich, i.e., the future leaders of the Cadets, *and* of the Party of Peaceful Renovation,[131] *and* of the Octobrist Party. The negotiations, it turns out, were broken off on account of Durnovo, whom the "liberals" refused to accept as Minister of the Interior, while Witte demanded this in the form of an ultimatum. Urusov, however, a leading light of the Cadet Party in the First Duma, "ardently supported Durnovo's candidacy". When Prince Obolensky suggested Stolypin for the post "some of those present supported the idea, others said that they did not know him". "I remember definitely," writes Guchkov, "that *no one* raised the objection of which Count Witte writes in his letter."

Now the Cadet press, in its desire to emphasise its "democracy" (don't be funny!), particularly, perhaps, in view of the elections in the first curia in St. Petersburg, where a Cadet opposed an Octobrist, is trying to sling mud at Guchkov for those negotiations. "How often," writes *Rech* in its issue of September 28, "the Octobrist fraternity with Guchkov at their head, joined hands with Mr. Durnovo's colleagues in order to please the powers that be. How often, with their eyes riveted on the powers that be, did they turn their backs on public opinion!" The same reproach levelled by the Cadets at the Octobrists is repeated in a number of variations in the leading article of *Russkiye Vedomosti* of the same date.

But, pardon me, gentlemen of the Cadet Party, what right have *you* to reproach the Octobrists, since *your* representatives also took part in those very same negotiations and even defended Durnovo? At that time, in November 1905, were not *all* the Cadets, like Urusov, in the position of people who have "their eyes riveted on the powers that be" and "their backs turned on public opinion"? Yours is a "family quarrel"; not a matter of principle, but rivalry between equally unprincipled parties; that is what we *have* to say apropos of the present reproaches levelled by the Cadets against the Octobrists in connection with the "negotiations" at the end of 1905. An altercation of this sort only serves to obscure the really important and historically undeniable fact that *all* shades of the liberal bourgeoisie, from the Octobrists to the Cadets inclusive, *"had their eyes riveted on the powers that be"* and "turned their backs" on *democracy* from the time our revolution assumed a really popular character, i.e., from the time it became a democratic revolution because of the democratic forces taking an active part in it. The Stolypin period of the Russian counter-revolution is characterised specifically by the fact that the liberal bourgeoisie had been turning its back on democracy, and that Stolypin *was able to turn* for assistance, sympathy, and advice first to one then to another representative of this bourgeoisie. Had it not been for this state of affairs, Stolypin would not have been able to give the Council of the United Nobility dominance over the counter-revolutionary-minded bourgeoisie and obtain the assistance, sympathy, and active or passive support of that bourgeoisie.

This aspect of the matter deserves special attention, precisely because it is lost sight of, or intentionally ignored, by our liberal press, as well as by such organs of liberal labour policy as *Dyelo Zhizni*. Stolypin not only represented the dictatorship of the feudal landlords, and anyone confining himself to this characterisation has understood nothing of the specific nature and meaning of the "Stolypin period". Stolypin was minister during a period when counter-revolutionary sentiments prevailed among the *entire* liberal bourgeoisie, including the Cadets, when the feudal landowners *could*, and did, rely on these sentiments, when they *could*, and did, approach the leaders of this bourgeoisie with "offers" (of hand and heart), when they *could* regard even the most "Left" of these leaders as "His Majesty's Opposition", when they *could*, and did, refer to the fact that the ideological leaders of the liberals were turning towards them, towards the side of reaction, towards those who fought against democracy and denigrated it. Stolypin was minister during the period when the feudal landowners bent all their efforts to inaugurate and put into effect as speedily as possible a *bourgeois* policy in peasant life in the countryside, when they had thrown overboard all romantic illusions and hopes based on the muzhik's "patriarchal" nature, and had begun *to look for* allies among the new, bourgeois elements of Russia in general and of rural Russia in particular. Stolypin tried to pour new wine into old bottles, to reshape the old autocracy into a bourgeois monarchy; and the failure of Stolypin's policy is the failure of tsarism on this last, *the last conceivable*, road for tsarism. The landowner monarchy of Alexander III tried to gain support in the "patriarchal" countryside and in the "patriarchal element" in Russian life in general. *That* policy was completely defeated by the revolution. After the revolution, the landowner monarchy of Nicholas II sought support in the counter-revolutionary sentiments of the bourgeoisie and in a bourgeois agrarian policy put into effect by these very same landowners. The failure of these attempts, which even the Cadets, even the Octobrists can no longer doubt, is the failure of the *last* policy *possible* for tsarism.

Under Stolypin the dictatorship of the feudal landowner was not directed against the whole nation, including the entire "third estate", the entire bourgeoisie. On the contrary, the dictatorship was exercised under conditions most favourable for it when the Octobrist bourgeoisie served it with heart and soul, when the landowners and the bourgeoisie had a representative body in which their bloc was guaranteed a majority, and an opportunity was provided for conducting negotiations and coming to an agreement with the Crown, when Mr. Struve and the other *Vekhi* writers reviled the revolution in a hysterical frenzy and propounded an ideology which gladdened the heart of Anthony, Bishop of Volhynia, and when Mr. Milyukov proclaimed that the Cadet opposition was "His Majesty's Opposition" (His Majesty being a feudal relic). Nevertheless, despite all these favourable conditions for the Romanovs, despite all these conditions being the most favourable that can be conceived from the point of view of the alignment of social forces in twentieth-century capitalist Russia, Stolypin's policy ended in failure. Stolypin has been assassinated at a moment when a new grave-digger of tsarist autocracy—or, rather, the grave-digger who is gathering new strength—is knocking at the door.

*   *
*

Stolypin's attitude to the leaders of the bourgeoisie, and theirs to him, is most fully characterised by the relations that existed at the time of the First Duma. "The period from May to July 1906 was decisive for Stolypin's career," writes *Rech*. What was the centre of gravity during that period?

"The centre of gravity during that period, was not, of course, the speeches in the Duma," states the official organ of the Cadet Party.

That is a valuable admission, isn't it? How many lances were broken at that time in tilts with the Cadets over the question of whether the "speeches in the Duma" could be regarded as the "centre of gravity" during that period! What a torrent of angry abuse and supercilious doctrinaire lecturing was let loose in the Cadet press against the Social-Democrats who, in the spring and summer of 1906, maintained that the centre of gravity during that period was *not* the speeches in the Duma! What reproaches were levelled by *Rech* and *Duma* at the whole of Russian "society" at that time because it dreamed about a "Convention" and was not sufficiently enthusiastic over the Cadet victories in the "parliamentary" arena of the First Duma! Five years have passed since then; it is necessary to make a general estimate of the period of the First Duma, and the Cadets proclaim quite nonchalantly, as if changing a pair of gloves, that, "of course, the centre of gravity during that period was not the speeches in the Duma".

Of course not, gentlemen! But what was the centre of gravity?

"Behind the scenes," we read in *Rech*, "a sharp struggle was going on between the representatives of two trends. One recommended a policy of compromise with the people's representatives, not even shrinking at the formation of a 'Cadet Cabinet'. The other demanded vigorous action, the dissolution of the State Duma and a change in the election law. That was the programme advocated by the Council of the United Nobility which enjoyed the support of powerful influences.... At first Stolypin hesitated. There are indications that on two occasions, with Kryzhanovsky acting as intermediary, he made overtures to Muromtsev, proposing to discuss the possibility of forming a Cadet Cabinet with himself as Minister of the Interior. But at the same time Stolypin undoubtedly maintained contact with the Council of the United Nobility."

That is how history is written by the educated, learned and well-read liberal leaders! It appears that the "centre of gravity" was *not* the speeches, but the struggle of two trends within the Black-Hundred tsarist Court clique! Immediate "attack", without delay, was the policy of the Council of the United Nobility, i.e., the policy not of individual persons, not of Nicholas Romanov, not of "one trend" in *"high places"*, but the policy of *a definite class*. The Cadets clearly and soberly see their rivals *on the right*. But anything *to the left* of the Cadets has disappeared from their field of vision. History was being made by "high places", by the Council of the United Nobility and the Cadets; the common people, *of course*, took no part in the making of history! A definite class (the nobility) was opposed by the party of people's freedom, which stands *above* classes, while the "high places" (i.e., Our Father the Tsar) hesitated.

Is it possible to imagine a higher degree of selfish class blindness, a worse distortion of history and forgetfulness of the elementary truths of historical science, a more wretched muddle and a worse confusion of class, party and individuals?

None are so blind as those who *will not* see democracy and its forces.

Of course, the centre of gravity during the period of the First Duma was not the speeches in the Duma. It was outside the Duma, in the struggle between classes, in the struggle waged by the feudal landowners and *their* monarchy against the masses, against the workers and peasants. It was precisely during that period that the revolutionary movement of the masses was again on the upgrade; the spring and summer of 1906 were marked by a menacing upsurge of the strike wave in general and of political strikes, of peasant riots and of mutinies in the armed forces in particular. *That*, Messrs. Cadet historians, was *why* there was hesitation in "high places". The struggle between the trends within the tsar's gang was over the question whether, bearing in mind the strength of the revolution at the time, they should attempt the coup d'état *at once*, or whether they should *bide their time* and lead the bourgeoisie by the nose a little longer.

The First Duma fully convinced the landowners (Romanov, Stolypin and Co.) that there could be no peace between them and the peasant and working-class masses. This conviction of theirs was in complete accordance with objective reality. All that remained for them to decide was a question of minor importance; when and how to change the election law, at once or gradually? The bourgeoisie wavered; but its entire behaviour, even that of the Cadet bourgeoisie, showed that it feared the revolution a hundred times more than it feared reaction. That was why the landowners deigned to invite the leaders of the bourgeoisie (Muromtsev, Heyden, Guchkov and Co.) to conferences at which they discussed the question of whether they might not *jointly* form a Cabinet. And the *entire* bourgeoisie, including the Cadets, conferred with the tsar, with the pogromists, with the leaders of the Black Hundreds about the means of combating the revolution; but never once since the end of 1905 has the bourgeoisie ever sent representatives of a single one of its parties to confer with the leaders of revolution about *how* to overthrow the autocracy and the monarchy.

That is the principal lesson to be drawn from the "Stolypin period" of Russian history. Tsarism consulted the bourgeoisie when the revolution still seemed to be a force; but it gradually applied its jackboot to kick out *all* the leaders of the bourgeoisie—first Muromtsev and Milyukov, then Heyden and Lvov, and, finally, Guchkov—as soon as the revolutionary pressure from below slackened. The difference between the Milyukovs, the Lvovs, and the Guchkovs is absolutely immaterial—it is merely a matter of the sequence in which these leaders of the bourgeoisie turned their cheeks to receive the ... "kisses" of Romanov-Purishkevich-Stolypin and the sequence in which they did receive these ... "kisses".

Stolypin disappeared from the scene at the very moment when the Black-Hundred monarchy had taken everything that could be of use to it from the counter-revolutionary sentiments of the whole Russian bourgeoisie. Now this bourgeoisie—repudiated, humiliated, and disgraced by its own renunciation of democracy, the struggle of the masses and revolution—stands perplexed and bewildered, seeing the symptoms of a gathering new revolution. Stolypin helped the Russian people to learn a useful lesson: either march to freedom by overthrowing the tsarist monarchy, under the leadership of the proletariat; or sink deeper into slavery and submit to the Purishkeviches, Markovs and Tolmachovs, under the ideological and political leadership of the Milyukovs and Guchkovs.

Sotsial-Demokrat, No. 24, October 18 (31), 1911

Published according to the *Sotsial-Demokrat* text

THE NEW FACTION OF CONCILIATORS, OR THE VIRTUOUS

The *Information Bulletin*[132] of the Technical Commission Abroad (No. 1, August 11, 1911) and the message *To All Members of the R.S.D.L.P.*, signed by "A Group of Pro-Party Bolsheviks", which appeared almost simultaneously in Paris, are attacks identical in substance upon "official Bolshevism" or, according to another expression, upon the "Leninist Bolsheviks". These documents are full of ire; they contain more angry exclamations and declamations than real substance. Nevertheless, it is necessary to deal with them, for they touch upon the most important problems of our Party. It is all the more natural for me to undertake the job of assessing the new faction, first, because it was I who wrote on these very questions in the name of *all* the Bolsheviks *exactly a year and a half ago* (see *Diskussionny Listok*, No. 2*), and, secondly, because I am fully conscious of my responsibility for "official Bolshevism". As regards the expression "Leninist" it is merely a clumsy attempt at sarcasm, intended to insinuate that it is only a question of the supporters of a *single* person! In reality, everybody knows perfectly well that it is not a question of people sharing my personal views on this or that aspect of Bolshevism.

The authors of the message, who sign themselves "pro-Party Bolsheviks", also call themselves "non-factional Bolsheviks", remarking that "here" (in Paris) they are "rather ineptly" called conciliators. Actually, as the reader will see from what follows, this name, which gained currency over fifteen months ago, not only in Paris, not only

---

* See present edition, Vol. 16, "Notes of a Publicist. II".—*Ed.*

abroad, but also in Russia, is the only one that correctly expresses the political essence of the new faction.

Conciliationism is the totality of moods, strivings and views that are *indissolubly* bound up with the very *essence* of the historical task confronting the R.S.D.L.P. during the period of the counter-revolution of 1908-11. That is why, during this period, a number of Social-Democrats, proceeding from essentially different premises, "lapsed" into conciliationism. Trotsky expressed conciliationism more consistently than anyone else. He was probably the only one who attempted to give the trend a theoretical foundation, namely: factions and factionism express the struggle of the intelligentsia "for influence over the immature proletariat". The proletariat is maturing, and factionalism is perishing of itself. The root of the process of fusion of the factions is not the change in the relations between the classes, not the evolution of the fundamental ideas of the two principal factions, but the observance or otherwise of agreements concluded between *all* the "intellectual" factions. For a long time now, Trotsky—who at one moment has wavered more to the side of the Bolsheviks and at another more to that of the Mensheviks—has been persistently carrying on propaganda for an agreement (or compromise) between *all* and sundry factions.

The opposite view (see Nos. 2 and 3 of the *Diskussionny Listok**) is that the origin of the factions is to be traced to the relations between the classes in the Russian revolution. The Bolsheviks and the Mensheviks only formulated the answers to the questions with which the objective realities of 1905-07 confronted the proletariat. Therefore, only the inner evolution of *these* factions, of the "strong" factions, strong because of their deep roots, strong because their ideas correspond to certain aspects of objective reality, only the inner evolution of precisely these factions is capable of securing a *real* fusion of the factions, i.e., the creation of a genuinely and completely united party of proletarian Marxist socialism in Russia. From this follows the practical conclusion that only a rapprochement in practical work between these two strong factions—and only insofar as they

---

* See present edition, Vol. 16, "Notes of a Publicist" and "The Historical Meaning of the Inner-Party Struggle in Russia",—*Ed.*

rid themselves of the non-Social-Democratic tendencies of liquidationism and otzovism—represents a real Party policy, a policy that really brings about unity, not easily, not smoothly, and by no means immediately, but in a way that will produce actual results, as distinguished from the heap of quack promises of an easy, smooth, immediate fusion of "all" factions.

These two views were observed even before the Plenary Meeting, when in my talks I suggested the slogan: "Rapprochement between the two strong factions, and no whining about dissolving factions". This was made public immediately after the Meeting by *Golos Sotsial-Demokrata*. I plainly, definitely, and systematically explained these two views *in May 1910*, i.e., eighteen months ago; moreover, I did this in the "general Party" arena, in *Diskussionny Listok* (No. 2). If the "conciliators", with whom we have been arguing on these subjects since November 1909, have so far not found time to answer that article *even once*, and have not made *even one* attempt to examine this question more or less systematically, to expound their views more or less openly and consistently—it is entirely their own fault. They call their factional statement, which was published on behalf of a separate group, a "public answer". But this public answer of those who *kept silent* for over a year is *not* an answer to the question that was raised long ago, discussed long ago, and answered long ago in two fundamentally different ways; it is a most hopeless muddle, a most incredible confusion of two irreconcilable answers. Every proposition the authors of the message put forward, they immediately refute. In every single proposition, the alleged Bolsheviks (who in reality are *inconsistent* Trotskyites) echo Trotsky's mistakes.

Indeed, look at the main ideas contained in the message. Who are its authors? They say they are Bolsheviks who "do not share the organisational views of official Bolshevism". That looks as if it were an "opposition" *only* on the question of organisation, does it not? Read the next sentence: "... It is precisely the organisational questions, the questions of building and restoring the Party, that are being put in the forefront now, as was the case eighteen months ago." This is quite untrue, and constitutes the very error of principle which Trotsky made, and which I exposed a year and a half ago. At the Plenary Meeting, the organisational question *probably* seemed of paramount importance only because, and only insofar as, the *rejection* of liquidationism by *all* factions *was taken* to be real, because the *Golos* and the *Vperyod* representatives "signed" the resolutions *against* liquidationism and against otzovism to "console" the Party. Trotsky's error was in continuing to pass off the *apparent* for the real *after* February 1910, when *Nasha Zarya* finally unfurled the banner of liquidationism, and the *Vperyod* group—in their notorious school at X^{133}— unfurled the banner of defence of otzovism. At the Plenary Meeting, the acceptance of the apparent for the real *may* have been the result of self-delusion. But after it, ever since the spring of 1910, Trotsky has been *deceiving* the workers in a most unprincipled and shameless manner by assuring them that the obstacles to unity were principally (if not wholly) of an organisational nature. This deceit is being continued in 1911 by the Paris conciliators; for to assert now that the organisational questions occupy the first place is sheer mockery of the truth. In reality, it is by no means the organisational question that is now in the forefront, but the question of the entire programme, the entire tactics and the whole character of the Party, or rather a question of *two* parties— the *Social-Democratic* Labour Party and the *Stolypin* labour party of Potresov, Smirnov, Larin, Levitsky, and their friends. The Paris conciliators seem to have been asleep for the eighteen months that have elapsed since the Plenary Meeting, during which time the *entire* struggle against the liquidators shifted, *both* in our camp and among the pro-Party Mensheviks, from organisational questions to questions of whether *the Party is to be a Social-Democratic*, and not a liberal, labour party. To argue now, let us say, with the gentlemen of *Nasha Zarya* about organisational questions, about the relative importance of the legal and illegal organisations, would be simply putting on an act, for these gentlemen may fully recognise an "illegal" organisation like *Golos*, which is subservient to the liquidators! It has been said long ago that the Cadets are recognising and maintaining an illegal organisation that serves monarchist liberalism. The conciliators call themselves Bolsheviks, in order to repeat, a year and a half later (and specifically stating moreover that this was done in the name of Bolshevism *as a whole!*), Trotsky's errors which the Bolsheviks had exposed. Well, is this not an abuse of established Party titles? Are we not obliged, after this, to let all and sundry know that the conciliators are not Bolsheviks at all, that they have nothing in common with Bolshevism, that they are simply inconsistent Trotskyites?

Read a little further: "One may disagree with the way official Bolshevism and the majority of the editors of the Central Organ understood the task of the struggle against liquidationism...". Is it really possible seriously to assert that the "task of the struggle against liquidationism" is an organisational task? The conciliators themselves declare that they differ from the Bolsheviks *not only* on organisational questions! But on what exactly do they differ? They are silent on this. Their "public answer" continues to remain the answer of people who prefer to keep silent ... or, shall we say, are irresponsible? For a year and a half they did not attempt *even once* to correct "official Bolshevism" or to expound *their own* conception of the task of the struggle against liquidationism! And official Bolshevism has waged this struggle for exactly three years, since August 1908. In comparing these well-known dates we involuntarily seek for an explanation of this strange "silence" of the conciliators, and this quest involuntarily recalls to our mind Trotsky and Ionov,[134] who asserted that they *too* were opposed to the liquidators, but that they understood the task of combating them *differently*. It is ridiculous, comrades—to declare, three years after the struggle began, that you understand the character of this struggle differently! *Such* a difference in understanding amounts to not understanding it at all!

To proceed. In substance the present Party crisis undoubtedly reduces itself to the question whether our Party, the R.S.D.L.P., should completely dissociate itself from the liquidators (including the *Golos* group) or whether it should continue the policy of compromise with them. It is doubtful whether any Social-Democrat at all familiar with the case would deny that this question constitutes the *essence* of the entire Party situation today. How do the conciliators answer this question?

They write in the message: "We are told that thereby [i.e., by supporting the Meeting] we are violating the Party forms and are causing a split. We do not think so [*sic!*]. But even if this were the case, we would not be afraid of it." (Then follows a statement to the effect that the plenary meeting was sabotaged by the Central Committee Bureau Abroad, that the "Central Committee is the object of a gamble", that "Party forms have begun to be filled in with a factional content", etc.)

This answer can truly be called a "classical" specimen of ideological and political helplessness! Think of it: they are being accused, they say, of causing a split. And so the new faction, which claims to be able to show the way the Party should go, declares publicly and in print: "We do not think so" (i.e., you do not think that there is or that there will be a split?), "but" ... but "we would not be afraid of it".

You can be sure no other *such* example of confusion is to be found in the history of political parties. If you "do not think" that there is or that there will be a split, then explain why! Explain *why* it is possible to work with the liquidators! Say outright that it is *possible*, and therefore necessary, to work with them.

Our conciliators not only do not say this; they say the opposite. In the leading article of the *Bulletin*, No. 1 (it is specifically stated in a footnote that this article was opposed by a Bolshevik who was an adherent of the Bolshevik platform, i.e., of the resolution of the Second Paris Group), we read the following:

"It is a fact that joint work with the liquidators in Russia is impossible", while somewhat earlier it is admitted that it is "becoming more and more difficult to draw even the finest line of demarcation" between the *Golos* group and the liquidators.

Who can make head or tail of this? On the one hand, a highly official statement is made on behalf of the Technical Commission (in which the conciliators and the Poles, who now support them, constitute a majority against us Bolsheviks) that *joint work is impossible*. In plain language this means declaring a split. The word split has no other meaning. On the other hand, the same *Bulletin*, No. 1, proclaims that the Technical Commission was set up "not for the purpose of bringing about a split, but for the purpose of averting it"—and the selfsame conciliators write that they "do not think so" (that there is or that there will be a split).

Can one imagine a greater muddle?

If joint work is *impossible*—that can be explained to Social-Democrats and justified in their eyes *either* by an outrageous violation of Party decisions and obligations on the part of a certain group of persons (and then a split with *that* group of persons is inevitable), *or* by a fundamental difference in principle, a difference which causes the *entire* work of a certain trend to be directed *away* from Social-Democracy (and then a split with the whole trend is inevitable). As we know, we have both these things; the Plenary Meeting of 1910 declared it impossible to work with the liquidationist *trend*, while the split with the *Golos* group, which violated all its obligations and definitely went over to the liquidators, is now taking place.

Anyone who consciously says that "joint work is impossible"—anyone who has given any thought to this statement and has grasped its fundamental principles, would inevitably concentrate all his attention and efforts on explaining these principles to the broadest masses so that those masses might be spared as soon and as completely as possible all futile and harmful attempts to maintain *any relations whatsoever* with those with whom it is *impossible* to work. But anyone who makes this statement and at the same time adds "we do not think" there will be a split, "but we would not be afraid of it", reveals by his confused and timid language that *he is afraid of himself*, afraid of the step he has taken, afraid of the situation that has been created! The message of the conciliators produces just such an impression. They are trying to vindicate themselves for something, to appear to be "kind-hearted" in the eyes of someone, to give someone a hint.... Later on we shall learn the meaning of their hints to *Vperyod* and *Pravda*. We must first finish with the question of how the conciliators interpret the "results of the period that has elapsed since the Plenary Meeting", the results summed up by the Meeting of the members of the Central Committee.

It is really necessary to *understand* these results, to understand why they were inevitable, otherwise our participation in events will be spontaneous, helpless, casual. Now see how the conciliators *understand* this. How do they answer the question of why the work and the decisions of the Plenary Meeting, which primarily were meant to bring about unity, resulted in a split between the Central Committee Bureau Abroad (=liquidators) and the anti-liquidators? Our inconsistent Trotskyites have simply copied the answer to this from Trotsky and Ionov, and I am forced to repeat what I said in last May* against those consistent conciliators.

The conciliators answer by saying: it is the fault of factionalism, the factionalism of the Mensheviks, the *Vperyod* group, and of *Pravda* (we enumerate the factional groups in the order in which they appear in the message), and, finally, of the "official representatives of Bolshevism" who "have probably outdone all these groups in their factional efforts". The authors of the message openly and definitely apply the term *non-factional* only to themselves, the Paris conciliators. All are wicked, they are virtuous. The conciliators give no ideological reasons in explanation of the phenomenon in question. They do not point to any of the organisational or other distinguishing features of the groups that gave rise to this phenomenon. They say nothing, not a word, to *explain* matters, except that factionalism is a vice and non-factionalism a virtue. The only difference between Trotsky and the conciliators in Paris is that the latter regard Trotsky as a factionalist and themselves as non-factional, whereas Trotsky holds the opposite view.

I must confess that this formulation of the question, in which political phenomena are explained *only* by the wickedness of some and the virtue of others, always calls to mind those outwardly benevolent faces of which one cannot help thinking, "Probably a rogue".

What do you think of the following comparison? Our conciliators are non-factional, virtuous; we Bolsheviks have outdone all groups in our factional efforts, i.e., we are the most wicked. *Therefore*, the virtuous faction sup-

---

* See present edition, Vol. 16, "Notes of a Publicist. II".—*Ed.*

ported the most wicked, the Bolshevik faction in its fight against the Central Committee Bureau Abroad!! There is something wrong here, comrades! You are confusing matters more and more with every statement you make.

You make yourselves ridiculous when you and Trotsky hurl accusations of factionalism at one another, as if you were playing at ball; you do not take the trouble to *think*: what is a faction? Try to give a definition, and we predict that you will entangle yourselves still more; for you yourselves are a faction—a vacillating, unprincipled faction, one that failed to understand what took place at the Plenary Meeting and after it.

A faction is an organisation within a party, united, not by its place of work, language or other objective conditions, but by a particular platform of views on party questions. The authors of the message are a faction, because the message constitutes their platform (a very bad one; but there are factions with wrong platforms). They are a faction, because like every other organisation they are bound by internal discipline; their group appoints its representative to the Technical Commission and to the Organising Commission by a majority of votes; it was their group that drew up and published the message-programme, *and so on*. Such are the objective facts which show that outcries against factionalism are bound to be *hypocrisy*. Yet Trotsky and the "inconsistent Trotskyites" maintain that they are not a faction *because* ... "the only" object of their uniting (into a faction) is to abolish factions and to advocate their fusion, etc. But all such assurances are merely self-praise and a cowardly game of hide-and-seek, for the simple reason that the *fact* that a faction exists is not affected by any (even the most virtuous) *aim* of the faction. *Every* faction is convinced that *its* platform and *its* policy are the *best* means of abolishing factions, for no one regards the existence of factions as ideal. The only difference is that factions with clear, consistent, integral platforms *openly* defend *their* platforms, while unprincipled factions *hide* behind cheap shouts about their virtue, about their non-factionalism.

What is the reason for the existence of factions in the Russian Social-Democratic Labour Party? They exist as the continuation of the split of 1903-05. They are the result of the weakness of the local organisations which are *powerless* to prevent the transformation of literary groups that express new trends, big and small, into new "factions", i.e., into organisations in which internal discipline takes first place. How can the abolition of factions really be guaranteed? *Only* by completely healing the split, which dates from the time of the revolution (and this will be brought about *only* by ridding the two main factions of liquidationism and otzovism), and by creating a proletarian organisation strong enough to force the minority to submit to the majority. As long as no such organisation exists, the *only thing* that *might* accelerate the process of their disappearance is an agreement by all the factions. Hence, both the ideological merit of the Plenary Meeting and its *conciliationist error* become clear. Its merit was the rejection of the ideas of liquidationism and otzovism; its mistake was the agreement concluded indiscriminately with persons and groups whose deeds are not in accordance with their promises ("they signed the resolution"). The ideological rapprochement on the basis of the fight against liquidationism and otzovism goes ahead—despite all obstacles and difficulties. The conciliationist mistake of the Plenary Meeting* quite inevitably brought about the failure of its conciliatory decisions, i.e., the failure of the *alliance* with the *Golos* group. The rupture between the Bolsheviks (and later also between the Meeting of the members of the Central Committee) and the Central Committee Bureau Abroad *corrected* the conciliationist mistake of the Plenary Meeting. The rapprochement of the factions which are actually *combating* liquidationism and otzovism will now proceed *despite* the forms decided on by the Plenary Meeting, for these forms did not correspond to the content. Conciliationism in general, as well as the conciliationism of the Plenary Meeting, came to grief because the content of the work *separated* the liquidators from the Social-Democrats, and all the forms, diplomacy, and games of the conciliators *could not* overcome this process of separation.

From this, and only this point of view, which I developed in May 1910, *everything* that took place after the Plenary Meeting becomes intelligible, inevitable, resulting

* See *Diskussionny Listok*, No. 2. (See present edition, Vol. 16, "Notes of a Publicist. II".—*Ed.*)

not from the "wickedness" of some and the "virtue" of others, but from the objective course of events, which isolates the liquidationist *trend* and brushes aside all the intermediate major and minor groups.

In order to obscure this undoubted political fact, the complete *failure* of conciliationism, the conciliators are forced to resort to a downright distortion of facts. Just listen to this: "The factional policy of the Leninist Bolsheviks was particularly harmful because they had a majority in all the principal Party institutions, so that their factional policy justified the organisational separatism of other trends and armed those trends against the official Party institutions".

This tirade is nothing but a cowardly and belated *"justification"* of ... liquidationism, for it is precisely the representatives of that tendency who have always justified themselves by references to the "factionalism" of the Bolsheviks. This justification is belated because it was the *duty* of every real Party member (in contrast to persons who use the catchword "pro-Party" for self-advertisement) to act *at the time when* this "factionalism" began, and not a year and a half later! The conciliators, the defenders of liquidationism, *could not* and did not act earlier, because they had *no facts.* They are taking advantage of the present "time of troubles" in order to give prominence to the unfounded arguments of the liquidators. But the facts are explicit and unambiguous; immediately after the Plenary Meeting, in February 1910, Mr. Potresov unfurled the banner of liquidationism. Soon after, in February or March, Messrs. Mikhail, Roman, and Yuri betrayed the Party. Immediately after that, the *Golos* group started a campaign for *Golos* (see Plekhanov's *Diary* the *day following* the Plenary Meeting) and resumed the publication of *Golos.* Immediately after that, the *Vperyod* people began to build up *their own* "school". The *first* factional step of the Bolsheviks, on the other hand, was to found *Rabochaya Gazeta* in *September* 1910, *after* Trotsky's break with the representatives of the Central Committee.

Why did the conciliators resort to such a distortion of well-known facts? In order to give a hint to the liquidators, and curry favour with them. On the one hand, "joint work with the liquidators is impossible". On the other hand—

they are *"justified"* by the factionalism of the Bolsheviks!!
We ask any Social-Democrat not contaminated with émigré
diplomacy, what political confidence can be placed in people
who are themselves entangled in such contradictions? All
they deserve are the bouquets with which *Golos* publicly
rewarded them.

By "factionalism" the conciliators mean the *ruthlessness*
of our polemics (for which they have censured us thousands
of times at general meetings in Paris) and the ruthlessness
of our *exposure* of the liquidators (they were *against* exposing Mikhail, Yuri, and Roman). The conciliators have
been defending and screening the liquidators all the time
but have *never dared* to express their defence openly, either
in the *Diskussionny Listok* or in any printed public appeal.
And now they are using their impotence and cowardice to
put a spoke in the wheel of the Party, which has begun
emphatically to dissociate itself from the liquidators. The
liquidators say, there is no liquidationism, it is an "exaggeration" on the part of the Bolsheviks (see the resolution of
the Caucasian liquidators[135] and Trotsky's speeches). The
conciliators say, it is impossible to work with the liquidators,
but...but the factionalism of the Bolsheviks provides
them with a "justification". Is it not clear that this ridiculous contradiction of subjective opinions has one, and only
one, real meaning: cowardly defence of liquidationism, a desire to trip up the Bolsheviks and lend support to the liquidators?

But this is by no means all. The worst and most malicious distortion of facts is the assertion that we had a "majority" in the *"principal Party institutions"*. This crying
untruth has only one purpose: to cover up the *political*
bankruptcy of conciliationism. For, in reality, the Bolsheviks did *not* have a majority in *any* of the "principal Party
institutions" after the Plenary Meeting. On the contrary,
it was the conciliators who had the majority. We challenge
anyone to attempt to dispute the following facts. *After* the
Plenary Meeting there were only three "principal Party
institutions": (1) the Central Committee Bureau in Russia—
composed chiefly of *conciliators**; (2) the Central Committee

---

* Of course, not all conciliators are alike, and surely not all the
former members of the Russian Bureau could (and would) accept

Bureau Abroad—on which, from January to November 1910, the Bolsheviks were represented by a *conciliator*; since the Bundist and the Latvian *officially* adopted the conciliationist standpoint, the majority, during eleven months following the Plenary Meeting, was *conciliationist*; (3) the Editorial Board of the Central Organ—on which two "Bolshevik factionalists" were opposed by two *Golos* supporters; without the Pole there was *no* majority.

Why did the conciliators have to resort to a deliberate lie? For no other purpose than that of camouflage, to cover up the *political* bankruptcy of conciliationism. Conciliationism predominated at the Plenary Meeting; it had a *majority* in all the principal practical centres of the Party after the Plenary Meeting, and within a year and a half it suffered *complete collapse*. It failed to "reconcile" anyone; it did not create anything anywhere; it vacillated helplessly from side to side, and for that it fully deserved the bouquets of *Golos*.

The conciliators suffered the most complete failure *in Russia*, and the more assiduously and demagogically the Paris conciliators refer to Russia the more important is it to stress this. The *leit-motif* of the conciliators is that Russia is conciliationist in contrast with what we have abroad. Compare these *words* with the *facts*, and you will see that this is just hollow, cheap demagogy. The facts show that for *more than a year* after the Plenary Meeting there were *only* conciliators on the Central Committee Bureau in Russia; they alone made official reports about the Plenary Meeting and officially negotiated with the legalists; they alone appointed agents and sent them to the various institutions; they alone handled all the funds that were sent unquestioningly by the Central Committee Bureau Abroad; they alone negotiated with the "Russian" writers who seemed promising contributors to the muddle (i.e., in respect of conciliationism), etc.

And the result?

The result is nil. Not a single leaflet, not a single pronouncement, not a single organ of the press, not a single "concil-

responsibility for all the pompous stupidities of the Paris conciliators who are merely echoing Trotsky.

iation". As against this the Bolshevik "factionalists" have
put their *Rabochaya Gazeta*, published abroad, on its feet
after two issues (to say nothing of other matters about which
only Mr. Martov speaks openly, thereby helping the secret
police). Conciliationism is nil, words, empty wishes (and
attempts to trip up Bolshevism on the basis of these "conciliatory" wishes); "official" Bolshevism has proved by deeds
that it is absolutely preponderant precisely in Russia.

Is this an accident? The result of arrests? But arrests
"spared" the liquidators, who *did no work* in the Party, while
they mowed down Bolsheviks and conciliators alike.

No, this is not an accident, or the result of the luck or success of *individuals*. It is the result of the bankruptcy of a
political *tendency* which is based on false premises. The very
foundation of conciliationism is false—the wish to base the
unity of the party of the proletariat on an alliance of *all*
factions, including the anti-Social-Democratic, non-proletarian factions; false are its unprincipled "unity" schemes
which lead to nothing; false are its phrases against "factions"
(when *in fact* a new faction is formed)—phrases that are powerless to dissolve the anti-Party factions, but are intended
to weaken the Bolshevik faction which bore nine-tenths
of the brunt of the struggle against liquidationism and
otzovism.

Trotsky provides us with an abundance of instances of
scheming to establish unprincipled "unity". Recall, for
example (I take one of the most recent instances), how he
praised the Paris *Rabochaya Zhizn*,[136] in the management of
which the Paris conciliators and the *Golos* group had an
equal share. How wonderful!—wrote Trotsky—"neither Bolshevik, nor Menshevik, but revolutionary Social-Democrat".
The poor hero of phrase-mongering failed to notice a mere
bagatelle—only that Social-Democrat is revolutionary who
understands how *harmful* anti-revolutionary pseudo-Social-
Democracy can be in a given country at a given time (i.e.,
the harm of liquidationism and otzovism in the Russia of the
1908-11 period), and who *knows how* to fight against such
non-Social-Democratic tendencies. By his praise of *Rabochaya
Zhizn* which had never fought against the *non*-revolutionary
Social-Democrats in Russia, Trotsky was merely *revealing*
the plan of the liquidators whom he serves faithfully—*parity*

on the Central Organ implies the termination of the *struggle* against the liquidators; the liquidators actually enjoy full freedom to fight the Party; and let the Party *be tied* hand and foot by the "parity" of the *Golos* and Party men on the Central Organ (and on the Central Committee). This would assure complete victory for the liquidators and only their lackeys could pursue or defend such a line of action.

Instances of unprincipled "unity" schemes that promise peace and happiness without a long, stubborn, desperate struggle against the liquidators were provided at the Plenary Meeting by Ionov, Innokentiev, and other conciliators. We saw another such instance in the message of our conciliators who justify liquidationism on the grounds of Bolshevik "factionalism". A further example is to be found in their speeches about the Bolsheviks "isolating" themselves *"from other trends [Vperyod, Pravda] which advocate an illegal Social-Democratic party"*.

The italics in this remarkable tirade are ours. Just as a small drop of water reflects the sun, so this tirade reflects the utter lack of principle in conciliationism, which is at the root of its political impotence.

In the first place, do *Pravda* and *Vperyod* represent Social-Democratic trends? No, they do not; for *Vperyod* represents a *non-Social-Democratic* trend (otzovism and Machism) and *Pravda* represents a tiny group, which has *not given* an independent and consistent answer to *any* important fundamental question of the revolution and counter-revolution. We can call a *trend* only a definite sum of political ideas which have become well-defined in regard to *all* the most important questions of *both* the revolution (for we have moved away but little from it and are dependent on it in all respects) *and* the counter-revolution; ideas which, moreover, have proved their right to existence as a trend by being widely disseminated among broad strata of the working class. Both Menshevism and Bolshevism are Social-Democratic trends; this has been proved by the experience of the revolution, by the eight years' history of the working-class movement. As for small groups not representing any *trend*—there have been plenty during this period, just as there were plenty before. To confuse a trend with minor groups means condemning oneself to *intrigue* in Party politics. The emergence of unprincipled tiny groups, their ephemeral existence, their efforts to have "their say", their "relations" with each other as separate powers—all this is the basis of the *intrigues* taking place abroad: and from this there is not nor can there be any salvation, except that of strictly adhering to consistent principles tested by experience in the long history of the working-class movement.

Secondly—and here we at once observe the practical transformation of the conciliators' lack of principle into intrigue —the message of the Parisians is telling a downright and deliberate lie when it declares: "Otzovism no longer finds open adherents and defenders in our Party". This is an untruth, and everybody knows it. This untruth is refuted by documentary evidence in *Vperyod*, No. 3 (*May 1911*) which *openly* states that otzovism is a *"perfectly legitimate trend* within our Party" (p. 78). Or will our very wise conciliators assert that such a declaration is *not a defence* of otzovism?

It is when people cannot justify their close association with this or that group on grounds of principle that they are compelled to resort to a policy of petty lies, petty flattery, nods, hints, i.e., to all those things which add up to the concept "intrigue". *Vperyod* praises the conciliators; the conciliators praise *Vperyod* and falsely reassure the Party with regard to otzovism. As a result there is bargaining and haggling over positions and posts with the *defenders* of otzovism, with the *violators of* all the decisions of the Plenary Meeting. The fate of conciliationism and the substance of its impotent and miserable intriguing, is secretly to assist both the otzovists and the liquidators.

Thirdly—"... joint work with the liquidators in Russia is impossible". Even the conciliators had to admit this truth. The question is—do the *Vperyod* and *Pravda* groups admit this truth? Far from admitting it, they state the very *opposite*, they openly demand "joint work" with the liquidators, and they openly *engage in such work* (see, for example, the report of the Second *Vperyod* School). Is there even a grain of principle *and of honesty* in the proclamation of a policy of rapprochement with groups which give *diametrically opposite* answers to *fundamental* questions?—we ask, because an unambiguous and unanimous resolution of the

Plenary Meeting recognised the question of liquidationism to be a fundamental one. Obviously not; we are confronted with an ideological chasm, and irrespective of the most pious intentions of X or Z all their attempts to span it with a bridge of words, with a bridge of diplomacy, inevitably condemn them to intrigues.

Until it has been shown and proved by reliable facts and a review of the most important questions that *Vperyod* and *Pravda* represent *Social-Democratic trends* (and no one, during the year and a half following the Plenary Meeting has even tried to prove this since it cannot be proved), we shall not tire of explaining to the workers the harmfulness of those unprincipled stratagems, of those underhanded stratagems, which are the substance of rapprochement with *Vperyod* and *Pravda* as preached by the conciliators. It is the *first duty* of revolutionary Social-Democrats to *isolate* these *non*-Social-Democratic and unprincipled groups that are aiding the liquidators. The policy which has been and is being pursued by Bolshevism and which it will pursue to the end despite all obstacles is to appeal to the Russian workers who are connected with *Vperyod* and *Pravda*, over the heads of these groups and against them.

I have said that after a year and a half of *domination* in the Party centres, conciliationism has suffered complete political bankruptcy. The usual answer to this is yes, but that is because you factionalists were hampering us (see the letter of the conciliators—*not* Bolsheviks—Hermann and Arkady[137] in *Pravda*, No. 20).

The *political* bankruptcy of a tendency or a group lies precisely in the fact that *everything* "hampers" it, *everything* turns against it; for it has wrongly estimated this "everything", for it has taken as its basis empty words, sighs, regrets, whimpers.

Whereas in our case, gentlemen, *everything* and *everybody* came to our assistance—and herein lies the guarantee of our success. We were assisted by the Potresovs, Larins, Levitskys—for they *could not* open their mouths without confirming *our* arguments about liquidationism. We were assisted by the Martovs, Dans and others—for they *compelled* everyone to agree with our view that the *Golos* group and the liquidators are one and the same. We were assisted by

Plekhanov *to the very extent* that he exposed the liquidators, pointed out the "loopholes" left open "for the liquidators" (*by the conciliators*) in the resolutions of the Plenary Meeting, and ridiculed the "puffy" and "integralist" passages in these resolutions (*passed by the conciliators against us*). We were assisted by the Russian conciliators whose "invitation", extended to Mikhail, Yuri, and Roman, was accompanied by abusive attacks upon Lenin (see *Golos*), thereby confirming the fact that the refusal of the liquidators was *not* due to the insidiousness of the "factionalists". How is it, my dear conciliators, that, notwithstanding your virtue everybody hampered you, whereas everyone helped us in spite of all our factional wickedness?

It was because the policy of your petty group hinged only on phrase-mongering, often very well-meaning and well-intentioned phrase-mongering, but empty nonetheless. A real approach to unity is created *only* by a rapprochement of *strong* factions, strong in their ideological integrity and an influence over the *masses* that has been tested by the experience of the revolution.

Even now, your outbursts against factionalism remain mere words, because *you yourselves are a faction*, one of the worst, least reliable, unprincipled factions. Your loud, sweeping pronouncement (in the *Information Bulletin*) — "not a centime for the factions" —was mere words. Had you meant it seriously, could you have spent your *"centimes"* on the publication of the message-platform of a new group? Had you meant it seriously, could you have kept quiet at the sight of such *factional* organs as *Rabochaya Gazeta* and *The Diary of a Social-Democrat*? Could you have abstained from publicly demanding that they be closed down?* Had you demanded this, had you seriously stipulated such a condition, you would simply have been ridiculed. However, if, being well aware of this, you confine yourselves to languid sighs, does it not prove over and over again that your conciliationism remains suspended?

---

* In fairness it should be stated that the Paris conciliators, who have now issued their message, were *opposed to* launching of *Rabochaya Gazeta*; they *walked out of the first meeting* to which they were invited by its editors. We regret that they did not help us (to expose the futility of conciliationism) by openly denouncing *Rabochaya Gazeta.*

The disarming of the factions is possible only on the basis of reciprocity—otherwise it is a reactionary slogan, extremely harmful to the cause of the proletariat; it is a demagogical slogan, for it only *facilitates* the uncompromising struggle of the liquidators against the Party. Anyone who advances this slogan now, *after* the attempt of the Plenary Meeting to apply it has failed, *after* the attempt to amalgamate (the factions) has been thwarted by the *Golos* and *Vperyod* factions—anyone who does this without even daring to repeat the condition of reciprocity, without even trying to state it clearly, to determine the methods of control over its *actual* fulfilment, is simply becoming intoxicated by sweet-sounding words.

Bolsheviks, unite—you are the only bulwark of a consistent and decisive struggle against liquidationism and otzovism.

Pursue the policy of rapprochement with *anti*-liquidationist Menshevism, a policy tested by practice, confirmed by experience—such is our slogan. It is a policy that does not promise a land flowing with the milk and honey of "universal peace" which cannot be attained in the period of disorganisation and disintegration, but it is a policy that in the process of work really furthers the rapprochement of *trends* which represent *all* that is strong, sound, and vital in the *proletarian* movement.

The part played by the conciliators during the period of counter-revolution may be described as follows. With immense efforts the Bolsheviks are pulling our Party waggon up a steep slope. The *Golos* liquidators are trying with all their might to drag it downhill again. *In the waggon* sits a conciliator; he is a picture of meekness. He has such an angelic sweet face, like that of Jesus. He looks the very incarnation of virtue. And modestly dropping his eyes and raising his hands he exclaims: "I thank thee, Lord, that I am not as *these* men are"—a nod in the direction of the Bolsheviks and Mensheviks—"insidious factionalists who hinder all progress". But the waggon moves slowly forward and in the waggon sits the conciliator. When the Bolshevik factionalists *smashed* the liquidationist Central Committee Bureau Abroad, thereby clearing the ground for the building of a new house, for a bloc (or at least a temporary alliance) of *Party* factions, the conciliators entered this house and (cursing the Bolshevik factionalists) sprinkled the new abode ... with the holy water of sugary speeches about non-factionalism!

―――

What would have become of the historically memorable work of the old *Iskra*, if, instead of waging a consistent, implacable, principled campaign against Economism and Struveism, it had agreed to some bloc, alliance or "fusion" of *all* groups large and small which were as numerous abroad in those days as they are today?

And yet the differences between our epoch and the epoch of the old *Iskra* considerably increase the harm done by unprincipled and phrase-mongering conciliationism.

The first difference is that we have risen to a far higher level in the development of capitalism and of the bourgeoisie as well as in the clarity of the class struggle in Russia. Certain objective soil already *exists* (for *the first time* in Russia) for the *liberal* labour policy of Potresov, Levitsky, Larin, and their friends. The Stolypin liberalism of the Cadets and the Stolypin labour party are already in process of formation. All the more harmful in practice are conciliationist phrases and intrigues with those groups abroad which support the liquidators.

The second difference is the immeasurably higher level of development of the proletariat, of its class-consciousness and class solidarity. All the more harmful is the *artificial* support given by the conciliators to the ephemeral petty groups abroad (*Vperyod, Pravda, etc.*), which have not created and are unable to create any *trend* in Social-Democracy.

The third difference is that during the *Iskra* period there were illegal organisations of Economists in Russia, which had to be smashed and split up in order to unite the revolutionary Social-Democrats against them. Today, there are *no* parallel illegal organisations; today it is only a question of fighting *legal* groups that have segregated themselves. And this process of segregation (even the conciliators are forced to admit it) is being *hindered* by the political *game* of the conciliators with the factions abroad that are *unwilling* to work and incapable of working for such demarcation.

Bolshevism has "got over" the otzovist sickness, the sickness of revolutionary phrase-mongering, the playing at "Leftism", the swinging from Social-Democracy to the left. The otzovists came out as a faction when it was *no longer* possible to "recall" the Social-Democrats from the Duma.

Bolshevism will also get over the "conciliationist" sickness, the wavering in the direction of liquidationism (for *in reality* the conciliators were always a plaything in the hands of the liquidators). The conciliators are also hopelessly behindhand. They came out as a faction after the *domination* of conciliationism had exhausted itself during the eighteen months following the Plenary Meeting and there was no one left to conciliate.

P.S. The present feuilleton was written more than a month ago. It criticises the "theory" of the conciliators. As for the "practice" of the conciliators, which found expression in the hopeless, absurd, futile, and shameful squabbles which fill the pages of the conciliators' and the Poles' *Bulletin* No. 2, it is not worth wasting a single word on.

Sotsial-Demokrat, No. 24,
October 18 (31), 1911
Signed: *N. Lenin*

Published according to
the *Sotsial-Demokrat* text

THE ELECTION CAMPAIGN
AND THE ELECTION PLATFORM

The elections to the Fourth Duma are due to be held next year. The Social-Democratic Party must launch its election campaign *at once*. In view of these forthcoming elections a "livening-up" of all parties is already noticeable. The first phase of the period of counter-revolution has obviously come to an end. Last year's demonstrations, the student movement, the famine in the countryside, and, last but not least, the strike wave, are all unmistakable symptoms showing that a turn has set in, that we are at the beginning of a new phase of the counter-revolution. Intensified propaganda, agitation, and organisation are on the order of the day, and the forthcoming elections provide a natural, inevitable, topical "pretext" for such work. [It should be noted in parentheses that those who, like the small *Vperyod* group among the Social-Democrats, are still hesitant with regard to these elementary truths which have been fully corroborated by reality, by experience, and by the Party, those who maintain that "otzovism" is a "legitimate shade of opinion" (*Vperyod*, No. 3, *May 1911, p. 78*), thereby forfeit every claim to be regarded in any way as a serious tendency or trend in the Social-Democratic movement.]

To begin with—a few remarks about the organisation and conduct of the election campaign. In order to launch it *at once*, it is necessary for the illegal *nuclei* of the R.S.D.L.P. to start work immediately on their own *initiative* throughout the country, in all and sundry legal and semi-legal organisations, in all the big factories, among all sections and groups of the population. We must look sad reality straight in the face. In most places there are no strictly defined Party organisations at all. There is the working-class vanguard, which is devoted to Social-Democracy. There are isolated individuals, and there are small groups. Therefore the first task of all Social-Democrats is to take the initiative in organising nuclei (a word excellently expressing the idea that the objective conditions call for the formation of small, very flexible groups, circles, and organisations); it is the task of *all* Social-Democrats, even where there are only two or three of them, to gain some "foothold", establish connections of one kind or another, and start work that is systematic even if very modest.

In view of the present situation in our Party, there is nothing more dangerous than the tactics of "waiting" for the time when an influential centre will have been formed in Russia. All Social-Democrats know that the work of forming such a centre *is going on*, that *everything possible* toward this end has been done by those who are primarily responsible for this work; but all Social-Democrats must also be aware of the incredible difficulties created by the police—they must not lose heart at the first, second or third failure!—and all should know that when such a centre has been formed, it will take it a long time to establish reliable connections with all the local organisations, and the centre will have to confine itself to *general* political guidance for some considerable time. There must be no delay in the organisation of local *nuclei* of the R.S.D.L.P., nuclei that will act on their own initiative in a strictly Party spirit, function illegally, start at once on the preparatory work for the elections, and immediately take every possible step to develop propaganda and agitation (illegal printing-presses, leaflets, legally published organs, groups of "legally functioning" Social-Democrats, transport facilities, *etc., etc.*)—any delay would jeopardise the whole work.

The principal question for Social-Democrats who value the elections primarily as a means for the political enlightenment of the people, is, of course, the ideological and political content of all the propaganda and agitation to be carried on in connection with them. That is what is meant by an election platform. To every party at all worthy of the name a platform is something that has existed long before the elections; it is not something specially devised "for the elections", but an inevitable result of the whole *work* of the party, of the way the work is organised, and of its whole trend in the given historical period. And the R.S.D.L.P., too, already has a platform; its platform already exists and has been naturally and inevitably determined by the Party's principles and by the tactics which the Party has *already* adopted, has *already* applied, and is still applying, during the entire period in the political life of the nation which in a certain respect is always "summed up" by elections. The platform of the R.S.D.L.P. is the *sum total* of the work which revolutionary Marxism and the sections of the advanced workers who remained faithful to it have accomplished in the 1908-11 period, the period of the orgy of counter-revolution, the period of the June Third, Stolypin regime.

The three main items that make up this total are: (1) the programme of the Party; (2) its tactics; (3) its appraisal of the dominant ideological and political trends of the given period, or the most widespread of them, or those which are most harmful for democracy and socialism. Without a programme a party cannot be an integral political organism capable of pursuing its line whatever turn events may take. Without a tactical line based on an appraisal of the current political situation and providing explicit answers to the "vexed problems" of our times, we might have a circle of theoreticians, but not a functioning political entity. Without an appraisal of the "active", current or "fashionable" ideological and political trends, the programme and tactics may degenerate into dead "clauses" which can by no stretch of the imagination be put into effect or applied to the thousands of detailed, particular, and highly specific questions of practical activity with the necessary understanding of essentials, with an understanding of "what is what".

As for the ideological and political trends typical of the 1908-11 period and of particular importance for a proper understanding of the tasks of Social-Democracy, the most prominent among them are the *Vekhi* trend, which is the ideology of the *counter-revolutionary liberal* bourgeoisie (an ideology fully in line with the policy of the Constitutional-Democratic Party, no matter what its diplomats say), and *liquidationism*, which is the expression of the same decadent and bourgeois influences in a group which has contact with the working-class movement. Away from democracy, as far away as possible from the movement of the masses, as far away as possible from the revolution, that is the theme of the trends of political thought that hold sway in "society". As far away as possible from the illegal Party, from the tasks of the hegemony of the proletariat in the struggle for liberation, from the tasks of championing the revolution, that is the theme of the *Vekhi* trend among the Marxists, the trend that has built a nest for itself in *Nasha Zarya* and *Dyelo Zhizni*. No matter what is said by narrow-minded practical workers or by people who wearily turn away from the difficult struggle for revolutionary Marxism in our difficult epoch, there is *not a single* question of "practical activity", *not a single* question of the illegal or legal work of the Social-Democratic Party in any sphere of its activity, to which the propagandist or agitator could give a clear and complete answer, unless he understood the full profundity and significance of these "trends of thought" typical of the Stolypin period.

Very often it may be useful, and sometimes even essential, to give the election platform of Social-Democracy a finishing touch by adding a brief general slogan, a watchword for the elections, stating the most cardinal issues of current political practice, and providing a most convenient and most immediate pretext, as well as subject matter, for comprehensive socialist propaganda. In our epoch only the following three points can make up this watchword, this general slogan: (1) a republic, (2) confiscation of all landed estates, and (3) the eight-hour day.

The first point is the quintessence of the demand for political liberty. In expressing our Party's stand on questions of this nature, it would be wrong to confine ourselves to the term political liberty or some other term such as "democratisation", etc., wrong because our propaganda and agitation must consider the experience of the revolution. The dissolution of two Dumas, the organisation of pogroms, support for the Black-Hundred gangs and clemency for the heroes of the Black Hundreds, Lyakhov's exploits in Persia,[138] the coup d'état of June 3, and a number of further "minor coups d'état" which followed it (Article 87, etc.) — is a far from complete record of the deeds of our monarchy as represented by Romanov, Purishkevich, Stolypin and Co. Situations do arise and have arisen in history, when it has been possible for a monarchy to adapt itself to serious democratic reforms, such, for instance, as universal suffrage. Monarchy in general is not uniform and immutable. It is a very flexible institution, capable of adapting itself to the various types of class rule. But it would be playing fast and loose with the requirements of historical criticism and treachery to the cause of democracy if one were to proceed from these indisputable abstract considerations and draw conclusions from them with regard to the actual Russian monarchy of the twentieth century.

The situation in our country and the history of our state power, particularly during the past decade, clearly show us that none other than the tsarist monarchy is the centre of the gang of Black-Hundred landowners (with Romanov at their head) who have made Russia a bogey not only for Europe, but now even for Asia—the gang which has developed tyranny, robbery, venality of officials, systematic acts of violence against the "common herd", the persecution and torture of political opponents, etc., to the inordinate dimensions we know today. Since this is the *real* face, the real economic basis and political physiognomy of *our* monarchy, to make the demand for, say, universal suffrage the central issue in the struggle for political liberty would not be so much opportunism as sheer nonsense. Since it is a question of choosing a central issue to be made the general slogan of the elections, the various democratic demands must be arranged in some sort of likely perspective and proportion. After all, one might only raise laughter among educated persons and create confusion in the minds of the uneducated if one were to demand of Purishkevich that he behave decently toward women and that he should realise the impropriety of using "unprintable" language, or if one were to demand tolerance of Illiodor,[139] altruism and honesty of Gurko and Reinbot, respect for law and order of Tolmachov and Dumbadze, and democratic reforms of Nicholas Romanov!

Consider the question from, so to speak, the general historical standpoint. It is obvious (to all, except Larin and a handful of liquidators) that the bourgeois revolution in Russia has not been consummated. Russia is heading for a *revolutionary* crisis. We must prove that revolution is necessary and preach that it is legitimate and "beneficial". This being the case, we must conduct our propaganda for political liberty so as to pose the question in all its aspects, formulate the goal for a movement that is bent on victory and not one that stops half-way (as was the case in 1905); we must issue a slogan capable of arousing enthusiasm among the masses who can no longer endure life as it is in Russia, who suffer because they are ashamed of being Russians, and are striving for a really free and really renewed Russia. Consider the question from the standpoint of practical propaganda. You cannot help making clear even to the most benighted muzhik that the state must be governed by a Duma which is more freely elected than the First Duma, by a Duma elected by the whole people. But how are we to ensure that the Duma cannot be dispersed? Only the destruction of the tsarist monarchy can guarantee this.

It may be objected that to issue the slogan of a republic as the watchword of the entire election campaign would mean precluding the possibility of conducting it legally, and thereby show that recognition of the importance and necessity of legal work is not seriously intended. Such objections, however, would be sophisms, worthy of the liquidators. We cannot legally advocate a republic (except from the restrum of the Duma, from which republican propaganda can and should be carried on *fully* within the bounds of legality); but we can write and speak in defence of democracy *in such a way* that we do not in the least condone ideas about the compatibility of democracy with the monarchy; *in such a way* as to refute and ridicule the liberal and Narodnik monarchists; *in such a way* as to make sure that the readers and the audiences form a clear idea of the connection between the monarchy, precisely as a monarchy, and the despotism and arbitrary rule reigning in Russia. Russians have gone through a long school of slavery—they have learnt to read between the lines and add what the speaker has left unsaid. "Do not say 'I can't'—say 'I shan't'"—that is the reply we must give Social-Democrats who are working legally, should they plead that it is "impossible" to make the demand for a republic a central point in our propaganda and agitation.

It is hardly necessary to dwell at particular length on the importance of the demand for the confiscation of all landed estates. At a time when the Russian villages never cease groaning under the burden of the Stolypin "reform", when an extremely fierce struggle is going on between the mass of the population on the one hand and the "new landowners" and the rural police on the other, and when, according to the testimony of extremely conservative people hostile to the revolution, bitterness such as has never before been seen is making itself felt ever more strongly—at such a time the demand must be made a *central* plank of the whole democratic election platform. We shall only point out that this is the very demand that will draw a clear line of demarcation between consistent proletarian democracy and not only the landlord liberalism of the Cadets, but also the intellectual-bureaucratic talk about "standards", "consumption standards", "production standards", "equalitarian distribution", and similar nonsense, of which the Narodniks are so fond, and at which every sensible peasant laughs. For us it is not a question of "how much land does the muzhik need"; the Russian people need to confiscate the *entire* land of the landowners, so as to throw off the yoke of feudal oppression in the *entire* economic and political life of the country. Unless this measure is carried out, Russia will never be free, and the Russian peasant will never eat anything like his fill, nor will he ever be truly literate.

The third point—the eight-hour day—stands even less in need of comment. The counter-revolutionary forces are frantically robbing the workers of the gains of 1905; and all the more intense, therefore, is the struggle of the workers for better working and living conditions, chief among which is the introduction of the eight-hour day.

To sum up, the substance and mainspring of the Social-Democratic election platform can be expressed in three words: *for the revolution*! Shortly before his death Lev Tolstoi said—in a tone of regret typical of the worst aspects of "Tolstoi-ism"—that the Russian people had "learned how to make a revolution" all too quickly. We regret only the fact that the Russian people have not learned this science *thoroughly enough*, for without it they may remain the slaves of the Purishkeviches for many centuries to come. It is true, however, that the Russian proletariat, in its striving to achieve the complete transformation of society on socialist lines, has given the Russian people in general, and the Russian peasants in particular, indispensable *lessons* in this science. Neither the gallows erected by Stolypin, nor the efforts of *Vekhi*, can make them forget these lessons. The lesson has been given, it is being assimilated, it will be repeated.

The basis of our election platform is the programme of the R.S.D.L.P., our old programme of revolutionary Social-Democracy. Our programme gives a precise formulation of our socialist aims, of the ultimate goal of socialism; and it is a formulation, moreover, which is particularly emphatic in its opposition to opportunism and reformism. At a time when in many countries, including our own, reformism is raising its head and when, on the other hand, there is a growing number of indications that in the most advanced countries the period of so-called "peaceful parliamentarianism" is drawing to a close and a period of revolutionary unrest among the masses is setting in—at such a time our old programme assumes even greater significance (if that is possible). With regard to Russia the programme of the R.S.D.L.P. sets the Party the immediate aim of "overthrowing the autocratic tsar and establishing a democratic republic". The special sections of our programme dealing with the questions of government, finances, and labour legislation, and with the agrarian question, provide exact and definite material to guide the *entire* work of every propagandist and agitator, in all its many aspects; they should enable him to particularise on our election platform in speaking before any audience, on any occasion, and on any subject.

The tactics of the R.S.D.L.P. during the period of 1908-11 have been determined by *the resolutions adopted in December 1908*. Endorsed by the Plenary Meeting held in January 1910, and tested by *the experience* of the whole "Stolypin period", these resolutions provide an exact appraisal of the situation and of the tasks dictated by that situation. Just as before, the old autocracy is still the main enemy; just as before, a revolutionary crisis is inevitable, and Russia is again heading for such a crisis. But the situation is not the same as before; autocracy has taken "a step in the transformation into a bourgeois monarchy"; it is trying to strengthen

feudal landed proprietorship by a new, bourgeois agrarian
policy; it is trying to arrange alliances between the feudal-
minded landowners and the bourgeoisie in the reactionary
and servile Duma; it is making use of widespread counter-
revolutionary (*Vekhi*) sentiments among the liberal bourgeoisie. Capitalism has advanced a few steps, class contradictions have sharpened, the split between the democratic elements and the *Vekhi* type liberalism of the Cadets has become
more pronounced, and the activity of the Social-Democrats has extended to new spheres (the Duma and "legal
opportunities"), which enables them to broaden the scope
of their propaganda and agitation despite the counter-revolution and even though the illegal organisations have been
badly "battered". The old revolutionary tasks and the old,
tested methods of revolutionary mass struggle, that is what
our Party champions in this period of disorganisation and
disintegration, when it is often necessary "to start from the
beginning", when, in view of the changed circumstances,
it is necessary to resort not only to old methods, but also
to conduct the work of preparation and gather forces for
the impending period of new battles in a new way, and by
new methods.

Sotsial-Demokrat, No. 24,   Published according to
   October 18 (31),1911   the *Sotsial-Demokrat* text

FROM THE CAMP OF THE STOLYPIN "LABOUR" PARTY

Nos. 6, 7, and 8 of *Nasha Zarya* are in the main devoted to the election campaign and the election platform. In the articles dealing with these subjects the essence of the liquidators' views is concealed behind an extraordinary number of inordinately inflated, laboured, high-sounding phrases about "the fighting mobilisation of the proletariat", "the widespread and open mobilisation of the masses", "political mass organisations of independent active workers", "self-governing groups", "class-conscious workers", etc., etc. Yuri Chatsky even went so far as to declare that the platform must be a "product" not only of "deep thought" but also of "keen feeling".... These phrases, which, doubtlessly, arouse the enthusiasm of high-school boys and girls, are intended to stun the readers, to "produce a smoke-screen", so as to make it easier for the writers to smuggle in their contraband.

Mr. Yuri Chatsky, for instance, extols the significance of a platform and the importance of having a single platform. "We attach the greatest importance," he writes, "to the sanction [of the platform] by the Social-Democratic group in the Duma; but at the same time we absolutely insist on the condition that the latter does not follow the line of least resistance by sanctioning a platform imposed upon it by circles abroad."

These are the words as they appear in print. Nor are they printed in a Black-Hundred publication which specialises in Jew and émigré baiting, but in a "Social-Democratic" magazine! How low these gentlemen must have fallen if, instead of explaining the difference in principle between *their* platform and the platform of "circles abroad", they raise a howl against those abroad!

Yuri Chatsky goes about it so clumsily that he betrays the name of the circle on whose behalf he is pursuing his liquidationist line. "The element of possible centralisation," he writes, "is the group of Social-Democratic [?] functionaries who are closely connected with the open workers' movement [you mean, through *Nasha Zarya*, don't you?] and are acquiring ever greater stability... [and an ever more pronounced liberal appearance].... We refer particularly to St. Petersburg."...

Why not speak out more plainly, gentlemen! It is unbecoming and foolish to play here at blind-man's-buff; when you speak of "the element of centralisation", or simply the centre (of liquidationism), you mean, and properly so, the group of contributors to the St. Petersburg *Nasha Zarya*. The truth will out.

L. Martov is trying to hide the truth by paraphrasing those postulates of the Social-Democratic programme that are legal and offering them as the basis for an election platform. Nor does he spare fine words to the effect that we need not "renounce" or "curtail" anything. He says this on page 48 of No. 7-8. But on page 54, in the concluding paragraph of his article, we read:

"We [? apparently *Nasha Zarya* and *Dyelo Zhizni*] must conduct the entire election campaign under the banner [*sic!*] of the struggle of the proletariat for the freedom of its political self-determination, of the struggle for its right to have a class party of its own and to develop its activities freely, for the right to take part in political life as an independent organised force. This principle must govern both the content and tactics of the election campaign and the methods to be used for organisational work."

What a splendid exposition of a *liberal* labour platform! A worker Social-Democrat will "conduct the campaign under the banner" of the struggle for the freedom of the *whole people*, for a democratic republic. A worker who is a liberal is fighting "for the right to have a class party [in the Brentano, social-liberal sense] of its own". To make this the governing principle means betraying the democratic cause. The liberal bourgeois and the astute agents of the government desire nothing better than that the workers should fight for the freedom of their "political self-determination", but not for the freedom of the whole country. Martov has merely paraphrased Levitsky's formula: *"Not* the hegemony of the proletariat, but a class party"! Martov has formulated a slogan of pure "Neo-Economism". The Economists said that the workers should confine themselves to the economic struggle, leaving the political struggle to the liberals. The Neo-Economists, the liquidators, say that the whole content of the election campaign should be subordinated to the principle: the struggle of the workers for the right to have a class party of their own.

Is Martov aware of the import of these words of his? Does he realise that they imply the renunciation of the revolution by the proletariat? —"liberal gentlemen, in 1905 we opposed you and roused the masses in general, and the peasants in particular, to revolution, we fought for the freedom of the people in spite of liberal efforts to halt the movement, to confine it to the achievement of semi-freedom. From now on we will no longer allow ourselves to be 'carried away'; we will fight for the freedom of the workers to have a class party of their own". That is actually all the *Vekhi*-type, counter-revolutionary liberals (cf. particularly the writings of Izgoyev) demand of the workers. The liberals do not deny the workers' right to have a class party of their own. What they do deny is the "right" of the proletariat, which is the only consistently revolutionary class, to rouse the *masses* of the people to the struggle in spite of and even against the liberals.

Vowing not to "renounce" and not to "curtail", Martov has so *curtailed* the Social-Democratic platform as to fully satisfy Larin, Potresov, Prokopovich, and Izgoyev.

See how Martov criticises the resolution of the Party on tactics (adopted in December 1908). With regard to the phrase —"a step in the transformation into a bourgeois monarchy" —he says that it is "an unfortunate formula", for "it fails to account for the actual step *back* toward division of power between the protagonists of absolutism and the landowning nobility", and "it takes no account of the decisive collision between classes" —meaning, apparently, between the bourgeois liberals and the feudal-minded landowners! Martov forgets that in 1905-07 the liberal bourgeois *feared* a "decisive collision" with the feudal landowners, preferring a "decisive collision" with the workers and peasants (just as the liberals forget about this and accuse the workers of "excesses"). Martov sees the "step back" of autocracy toward the feudal-minded landowners. (This step is *explicitly* mentioned in the resolution of the Party in the words: "... to preserve the power and revenue of the feudalminded landowners".) But Martov *fails* to see the "step back" taken by the liberal bourgeois *from* democracy to "law and order", to the monarchy, to a rapprochement with the landowners. Martov fails to see the *connection* between the "step towards a bourgeois monarchy" *and* the counterrevolutionary character of the liberal bourgeoisie with its *Vekhi* mentality. He fails to see it because he is himself "a *Vekhi* advocate among Marxists". Like a liberal who dreams of a "decisive collision" between the liberal bourgeois and the feudal-minded landowners, he throws overboard the historic reality of the *revolutionary* collision between the workers and peasants on the one hand and the feudal-minded landowners on the other, *notwithstanding* the vacillations of the liberals, notwithstanding even their desertion to the party of law and order.

Here, too, we get the same result: Martov rejects the resolution of the Party from the viewpoint of a *liberal* labour policy, but, unfortunately, he does not oppose it by any resolution *of his own* on tactics (although he is compelled to admit that tactics must be based on an appraisal of "the historical meaning of the June Third period"!).

It is therefore quite obvious why Martov writes: "The workers' party should strive ... to prevail upon the propertied classes to take one step or another toward the democratisation of legislation and an extension of constitutional guarantees...". Every liberal concedes that it is quite legitimate for the workers to strive "to prevail upon *the propertied classes*" to take one step or another; all that the liberal stipulates is that the workers should not dare to prevail upon *the non-propertied* to take "steps" which are *not* to the liberals' *liking*. The entire policy of the British liberals, who have so profoundly corrupted the British workers, is to allow the workers to try "to prevail upon the propertied classes", but *not to allow the workers* to win for themselves the leadership of a movement of the whole people.

Similarly it is quite obvious why Chatsky, Martov, and Dan hate the tactics of a "Left bloc". They see in it not just a "Left bloc" for the elections, but the general tactics established by the London Congress —*to wrest* the peasants (and the petty bourgeois in general) away from the influence of the Cadets and *compel* the Narodnik groups *to choose* between the Constitutional-Democrats and the Social-Democrats. To reject these tactics is tantamount to *renouncing democracy.* Only Stolypinite Social-Democrats could fail to see this *today*, after the "Stolypin period", after the exploits of the "Stolypin liberalism of the Cadets" (Milyukov's London slogan—"His Majesty's Opposition"!), *after* the publication of *Vekhi*.

There should be no illusions —we have *two* election platforms, that is a fact. It is a fact that cannot be argued away by phrase-mongering, lamentations, wishes. One is the platform explained above, based on the decisions of the Party. The other is the Potresov-Larin platform, developed and supplemented by Levitsky, Yuri Chatsky and Co., and touched up by Martov. The latter platform, which *claims to be Social-Democratic* is actually *the platform of a liberal labour policy.*

Anyone who fails to understand the difference, the irreconcilable difference, between these *two* platforms of working-class policy cannot conduct the election campaign *intelligently.* He is sure to be haunted at every step by disappointments, "misunderstandings"; and comic or tragic mistakes.

Sotsial-Demokrat, No. 24.
  October 18 (31), 1911

Published according to
the *Sotsial-Demokrat* text

THE GRAND TOTAL

The controversy between Witte and Guchkov was eagerly seized upon by both *Rech* and *Russkiye Vedomosti*, who made use of it in their election campaign. The nature of the controversy is evident from the following tirade in *Rech*:

"How often the Octobrist fraternity, with Guchkov at their head, joined hands with Mr. Durnovo's colleagues in order to please the powers that be. How often, with their eyes riveted on the powers that be, did they turn their backs on public opinion!"

This is written because in October and November 1905 Witte conferred with Messrs. Urusov, Trubetskoi, Guchkov, and M. Stakhovich regarding the formation of a Cabinet, and the three last-mentioned were categorically opposed to Durnovo's candidature for the post of Minister of the Interior.

While reproaching the Octobrists, the Cadet gentlemen, however, reveal an amazingly poor memory about their own past. The Octobrists "joined hands with Mr. Durnovo's colleagues". That is true. And it goes to prove, beyond any doubt, that it would be ridiculous to talk about the democratic nature of the Octobrists. The Octobrists lay no claim to democracy. But the Cadets call themselves "Constitutional-Democrats". Were not these "democrats" who, in the person of Mr. Urusov, supported Durnovo's candidature at the conferences with Witte, among those who "joined hands with Mr. Durnovo's colleagues"? Weren't the Cadets, as a party, in the First and Second Dumas among those who, "with their eyes riveted on the powers that be, turned their backs on public opinion"?

How can one forget or try to distort facts that are generally known? Recall the discussion in the First Duma on the organisation of local land committees. It was *precisely* "to please the powers that be" that the Cadets opposed this. On this issue (one of the most important political issues in the period of the First Duma) the Cadets were definitely among those who, "with their eyes riveted on the powers that be, turned their backs on public opinion". For the Trudoviks and the worker deputies, who represented nine-tenths of Russia's population, were at that time *in favour* of local land committees. A similar division of the parties in the First and Second Dumas was observed on scores of other occasions as well.

It is hard to imagine how the Cadets could dispute these facts. Can they really assert that they did not disagree with the Trudoviks and the worker deputies in the First and Second Dumas, or that in all those cases they did not go hand in hand with the Heydens, the Octobrists, and the powers that be? Or that the Trudoviks and the worker deputies, because of the existing electoral system, did not represent the vast majority of the population? Or by public opinion do our "democrats" mean the opinion of the "educated public" (educated in the sense of possessing official diplomas), but not the opinion of the majority of the population?

An historical appraisal of the period during which Stolypin held the post of Prime Minister, i.e., the five years from 1906 to 1911, provides incontrovertible proof that *neither* the Octobrists *nor* the Cadets were democrats. And since only the Cadets claim this title, it is precisely their self-deception, and their deception of "public opinion", of the opinion of the masses on this score, that is particularly obnoxious and harmful.

We do not mean to imply, of course, that the Octobrists and the Cadets represent "one reactionary mass", or that the Octobrists are not less liberal than the Cadets. What we do mean to tell them is that liberalism and democracy are two different things. It is natural for liberals to regard as "public opinion" the opinion of the bourgeoisie, but not that of the workers and peasants. A democrat cannot accept that point of view, and whatever illusions he may at times entertain regarding the interests and aspirations of the masses, the democrat has *faith* in the masses, in the *action* of the masses, in the legitimacy of their sentiments and the expediency of their methods of struggle.

The greater the abuse of the name of democrat, the more insistently must this difference between liberalism and democracy be borne in mind. In all bourgeois countries elections serve as a means of gaining publicity for the bourgeois parties. From the working-class point of view, elections and the election campaign must serve the aim of political enlightenment, of bringing out the *true* nature of the various parties. Political parties cannot be judged by their names, declarations or programmes; they must be judged by their *deeds*.

The controversy between Witte and Guchkov, which touched upon the question of how Stolypin was started on his ministerial career (incidentally, Guchkov testifies that *in the autumn of 1905 none* of the "public figures" objected to Stolypin's candidature), raises a number of other, much more important and pertinent, questions.

The first time Stolypin was mentioned as candidate for the post of Minister of the Interior (in the autumn of 1905) was at a conference Witte held with representatives of the liberal bourgeoisie. Even during the period of the First Duma, Stolypin, in his capacity of Minister of the Interior, "on two occasions, with Kryzhanovsky acting as intermediary, ... made overtures to Muromtsev, proposing to discuss the possibility of forming a Cadet Cabinet". That is what *Rech* wrote in an editorial on September 6, prefacing this statement with the cautious and evasive reservation that "there are indications" that Stolypin did act in that way. It is sufficient to recall that the Cadets had previously either maintained silence on this score, or met any such "indications" with abuse. Now they themselves refer to these indications, thereby obviously confirming their accuracy.

Let us go further in this matter. After the dissolution of the First Duma, when Stolypin became Prime Minister, direct offers to join the Cabinet were made to Heyden, Lvov, and M. Stakhovich. After the failure of this "combination", "P. A. Stolypin, during the first interim between two Dumas, established intimate political connections with Guchkov", and, as we know, these connections were maintained up to 1911.

What is the sum total of all this? Stolypin's candidature for the post of Minister was discussed with the representatives of the bourgeoisie; then, during his entire ministerial career, from 1906 to 1911, Stolypin made "overtures" to one set of representatives of the bourgeoisie after another, initiating, or trying to initiate, political relations first with the Cadets, then with the Party of Peaceful Renovation, and, finally, with the Octobrists. First Stolypin, as candidate for the post of Minister, was "proposed" to the "public figures", i.e., to the leaders of the bourgeoisie; then Stolypin — *during the whole of his career* in his capacity as Minister — made "overtures" to the Muromtsevs, Heydens, and Guchkovs. Stolypin's career came to an end (it is a well-known fact that Stolypin's resignation was imminent) when he had *exhausted* the whole list of bourgeois parties and groups to whom he could make "overtures".

The conclusion to be drawn from these facts is clear. If the Cadets and the Octobrists are now wrangling over the question as to who was more sycophantic in the negotiations about ministers or with ministers—Urusov or Guchkov, Muromtsev or Heyden, Milyukov or Stakhovich and so on and so forth—it is nothing but a petty squabble which only serves to distract the attention of the public from a vital political question. This vital question is obviously the necessity to understand the conditions and meaning of that particular epoch in the history of the Russian political regime, when ministers were compelled systematically to make "overtures" to the leaders of the bourgeoisie, when ministers *could* find at least some common ground with those leaders, a common ground for frequently conducting negotiations. What is important is not the question as to who was more sycophantic during those negotiations—X or Z—but, first, the fact that the old landowning class could no longer rule without making "overtures" to the leaders of the bourgeoisie; and, secondly, that the diehard landowner and the bourgeois found a *common ground* for negotiations, and that common ground was their *counter-revolutionism*.

Stolypin was not merely a minister of the landowners who had experienced the year 1905; no, he was also a minister during the period of counter-revolutionary sentiments among the bourgeoisie, when the landowners had to make overtures to them, and could make them because of their common hatred for "nineteen-five". These sentiments of the

bourgeoisie—even if we take only the Cadets, the most Left
of the "liberal" parties—were expressed in the sermons of
Vekhi, which showered abuse on democracy and the movement of the masses, and in Milyukov's "London" slogan,
in the numerous unctuous speeches by Karaulov, in the
speech of Berezovsky the First on the agrarian question, etc.

It is this particular aspect of the matter that all our
liberals, the entire liberal press, and the liberal labour politicians tend to forget. Yet this aspect of the matter is the
most important; it explains the historical distinction between the conditions under which landowners were made
governors and ministers in the nineteenth century or in the
beginning of the twentieth century, and those obtaining
after 1905. In its altercation with Guchkov, the Cadet
Rech writes (September 30): "Russian society well remembers
Octobrism's record of service".

Of course they do! The liberal public well remember the
petty squabble "between friends"—between the Urusovs
and Milyukovs on the one hand and the Heydens, Lvovs,
and Guchkovs on the other. But Russian democracy in general, and working-class democracy in particular, *remember
very well* the "record" of the *entire* liberal bourgeoisie, the
Cadets included; they remember very well that the great
upheaval of 1905 drove the landowners and the landowners'
bureaucracy to seek the support of the bourgeoisie, and that
the bourgeoisie took advantage of its position in a remarkably fitting manner: it fully agreed with the landowners
that local land committees are unnecessary—nay, harmful; and it differed from them on an exceptionally vital
question, truly a question of principle—namely: Durnovo
or Stolypin!

Zvezda, No. 26, October 23, 1911
        Signed: *V. F.*

                                              Published according to
                                                  the *Zvezda* text

TWO CENTRES

The opening of the last session of the Third Duma immediately raised the question as to the results of the work of that body. One of the principal results may be formulated in the words of *Rech*, which recently stated in a leading article:

"A number of votes recently taken in the Duma actually reflect the domination of a 'Left Centre' in that body.... The real activity of the Duma, that concerns the vital interests and demands of life, from the very beginning of the session has invariably and systematically proceeded along the lines of a Left Centre (non-existent, of course)."

And, as if to catch out the Prime Minister himself, *Rech* exclaims in a transport of rejoicing: "Mr. Kokovtsov did not hesitate [in his first speech] to declare three times that he was fully in agreement with the arguments of [the Cadet] Stepanov".

It is an indisputable fact that a "Left Centre" actually does exist. Only, it is open to question whether this fact is a symptom of "life" or of stagnation.

From the very beginning there have been two possible majorities in the Third Duma. As far back as the end of 1907, before this Duma began its "activities", the Marxist estimate of the situation and of the Third Duma centred around the recognition of the existence of these "two possible majorities" and their characterisation.

One majority is the Black-Hundred and Right-Octobrist combination, the other—that of the Octobrists and Cadets. The Third Duma was elected on the basis of a law so devised as to produce these two possible majorities. Our liberals pretend in vain that they do not see this.

It was neither accident nor the cunning calculation of individuals, but the entire course of the class struggle in the 1905-07 period, that forced the government to take this path, and no other. Events had shown that it was impossible to bank on the mass of the population. Previously, before the "events", it had been possible to maintain the illusion of an official "popular policy", but that illusion had been shattered by the events. It had become necessary to bank openly and cynically on one ruling class—the class of the Purishkeviches and Markovs—and on the sympathy or the fright of the bourgeoisie. The dominating tendency among some sections of the bourgeoisie was an eager desire to render systematic support (the Octobrists); among other sections it was sympathy for so-called "law and order" or fright (the Cadets)—the difference was of no material importance.

The change referred to in the *entire* political system of Russia was already indicated by the conversations which Witte, Trepov, and Stolypin had conducted since the end of 1905 with Urusov, Trubetskoi, Guchkov, Muromtsev, and Milyukov. This change became fully defined and assumed a state-constitutional form in the Third Duma with its two possible majorities.

There is no need to dwell upon the reason why the present political regime is in need of the first majority. But people are wont to forget that it stands in just as much need of the second—that of the Octobrists and the Cadets. Without the "bourgeois plaintiff" the government could not be what it is. Unless it comes to terms with the bourgeoisie it cannot exist. Without attempts to reconcile the Purishkeviches and Markovs with a bourgeois system and with the bourgeois development of Russia, neither the Ministry of Finance nor all the ministries combined can survive.

And if today the "Left Centre", despite its unassuming character, proves to be dissatisfied, it testifies, of course, to the growing conviction among the bourgeoisie *as a whole* that its sacrifices on the altar of the Purishkeviches have been made in vain.

But "the vital interests and demands of life" cannot be satisfied by these lamentations and complaints of the "Left Centre"; they can only be satisfied if all the forces of democracy are aware of the causes of the impotence and wretched position of the Centre. This is because the entire Centre, including the Left, is counter-revolutionary: the Purishkeviches make them groan but the Centre *will not and cannot* dispense with them. That is why theirs is such a bitter lot, that is why the Left Centre cannot boast a single victory, not even a shred of a victory.

The "Left Centre" of which *Rech* speaks, represents death and not life —at decisive moments of Russian history, all those belonging to it became scared of democracy and turned their backs on it. But the cause of democracy is a live cause, the most vital in Russia.

The vital interests and demands of life are asserting themselves in spheres that are far removed from the "Left Centre" which occupies the whole attention of the Cadets. On reading, for instance, the reports on the Duma debate on the secret political police, the thoughtful reader naturally could not help noticing that the presentation of the question in the speeches of Pokrovsky the Second and, particularly, of Gegechkori, was vastly different from that of Rodichev and his colleagues, as different as earth and sky, as life and death.

Zvezda, No. 28,
November 5, 1911

Published according to
the *Zvezda* text

OLD AND NEW

NOTES OF A NEWSPAPER READER

You take up a batch of newspapers and at once you are completely surrounded by the atmosphere of "old" Russia. You read of a trial held in connection with a pogrom in Armavir: people beaten up with the knowledge and complicity of the authorities; a trap set by the authorities; "a massacre of the Russian intelligentsia in the broad sense of the term suggested and ordered by someone" (the words of the plaintiff in the civil suit). The old but ever new picture of Russian life, a bitter ridicule of the "constitutional" illusions.

Bitter, yet useful ridicule! For it is clear, and the young generation in Russia realises it ever more clearly, that condemnations and resolutions are of no avail. It is a question of the political system as a whole. Historical truth is paving a way for itself through the haze of deceptive dreams that it is possible to pour new wine into the old bottles.

Famine.... People selling cattle, selling girls; throngs of beggars, typhus, death from starvation. "The population have but one privilege—to die quietly and unobtrusively," writes one correspondent.

"The Zemstvo authorities, to put it bluntly, are scared that they may find themselves, with their estates, surrounded by starved and embittered people who have lost all hope of any improvement." (A report from Kazan Gubernia.)

There can hardly be anything more docile than the present-day Zemstvos; yet even they are wrangling with the government over the amount of credit appropriations. They asked for 6,000,000 rubles (in Kazan Gubernia) and the government gave them 1,000,000. They asked for 600,000 rubles (Samara) and received 25,000!

Everything as of old!

At a Zemstvo meeting in Kholm Uyezd,* Pskóv Guberñia, even rural superintendents opposed Zemstvo agronomical aid intended only for farmers who had left the village commune! In the Kuban area, at a gathering of Cossack village elders all present unanimously opposed the Third Duma plan to make the peasants' land allotments their private property.

In Tsaritsyn, the Uyezd Assembly resolved not to prosecute an elder who had tortured a woman ("with the object of ascertaining the whereabouts of a criminal"). The gubernia court rescinded that decision.

In the neighbourhood of St. Petersburg, workers caught the manager of Mr. Yakovlev's factory, threw a sack over his head and dragged him towards the Neva. The police dispersed the workers. Eighteen of them were arrested.

Small wonder therefore that, faced with such pictures of real life, even *Rech* is obliged to speak of the "great humiliation of the public". And Mr. Kendurushkin, in his letters from Samara on the famine,** complains: "Russian society seems to me as yielding as rubber, or dough. It can be kneaded and pressed by word or deed. But as soon as it is let alone, it resumes its shape as of old".

"He, this Russian average citizen and intellectual, rich or poor, is unperturbed. But when people begin to 'swell' from hunger, he will then exult, and rejoice with tears in his eyes. When he sets out to render aid he will absolutely insist on doing so with tears in his eyes and 'noble' feelings in his breast. He will not miss the splendid opportunity to do something for the salvation of his soul. Without feelings and tears, work is not real work, nor is aid real aid. Unless there is an opportunity for him to shed tears, he will not think the cause worthy of his attention and will not lift a finger. No, he must first excite his emotions, make himself cry and blow his nose into a clean handkerchief. But stern calculation, a sound and sober realisation of *state necessity*—that is tedious, there is no soft moodiness in that."

To be sure, it is very much worth while preaching "sternness" in a world of "dough" and "rubber". Only our liberal does not notice *from what aspect* he is doing his preaching;

---

* See footnote to p. 88.—*Ed.*
** In the throes of "the melancholy of the universal Russian bleakness".

"a sound and sober realisation of state necessity"—didn't you copy that from Menshikov, Mr. Kondurushkin? Is not such talk about state necessity possible only where there is "dough" and "rubber", only where there is a soft and lachrymose moodiness? It is just because there are dough-like people that the heralds of "sound and sober state necessity" feel so confident.

"Russian society is as yielding as rubber," says Mr. Kondurushkin *as of old*. There are different kinds of society. There was a time when the word "society" included everything and covered everything, when it implied the heterogeneous elements of the population that were waking to conscious activity, and it was also taken to mean only the so-called "educated" people.

But it is in this very respect that things in Russia are no longer what they used to be. At the time when we could speak of society in general, the finest representatives of that society advocated stern struggle, not "sound and sober realisation of state necessity".

But today we can no longer speak of "society" in general. A variety of new forces have revealed themselves in old Russia. The old disasters, like famine, etc., which, as of old, are again looming up in Russia, accentuating the old questions, demand that we take stock of how these new forces have manifested themselves during the first decade of the twentieth century.

"Society" is soft and lachrymose because of the impotence and irresolution of the class towards which it gravitates, and to which nine-tenths of it belong. The preaching of "stern calculation, a sound and sober realisation of state necessity" serves but to justify the domination of the "authorities" over this flabby society.

The last decade, however, has brought forward elements of the population who do not belong to "society" and are not distinguished by softness and lachrymosity....

Everything in Russia is "as of old"—at the top. But there is also something new—at the bottom. He whom "the melancholy of the universal Russian bleakness" helps to discern, find, and ascertain this hard new element which is neither lachrymose nor dough-like, will be able to discover the road that leads to deliverance from the old.

But he who intersperses his lamentations about this melancholy with talk about "sound and sober realisation of state necessity", will surely remain forever a component part of the "dough" that permits itself to be "kneaded and pressed". Such people are "kneaded and pressed" for the sake of that very "sound and sober state necessity"—and it serves them right.

If, out of a hundred persons who are subjected to that operation, one member of "society" grows hard, that will be a useful result. There will be nothing good without demarcation.

Zvezda. No. 28. November 5. 1911
Signed: *V.F.*

Published according to
the *Zvezda* text

SPEECH DELIVERED IN THE NAME OF THE R.S.D.L.P. AT THE FUNERAL OF PAUL AND LAURA LAFARGUE NOVEMBER 20 (DECEMBER 3), 1911

Comrades, on behalf of the Russian Social-Democratic Labour Party I wish to convey our feelings of deep sorrow on the death of Paul and Laura Lafargue. Even in the period of preparation for the Russian revolution, the class-conscious workers and all Social-Democrats of Russia learned profound respect for Lafargue as one of the most gifted and profound disseminators of the ideas of Marxism, ideas that were so brilliantly confirmed by the class struggle during the Russian revolution and counter-revolution. United under the banner of those ideas, the vanguard of the Russian workers waged an organised mass struggle and dealt a blow to absolutism, it upheld, as it continues to uphold, the cause of socialism, the cause of the revolution, the cause of democracy despite the treachery, vacillation, and irresolution of the liberal bourgeoisie.

For the Russian worker Social-Democrats Lafargue symbolised two eras: the era in which the revolutionary youth of France, animated by republican ideas, marched shoulder to shoulder with the French workers to attack the Empire, and the era in which the French proletariat, under Marxist leadership, waged a sustained class struggle against the entire bourgeois system and prepared for the final battle against the bourgeoisie to win socialism.

We, Russian Social-Democrats, who have experienced all the oppression of an absolutism impregnated with Asiatic barbarity, and who have had the good fortune, through the writings of Lafargue and his friends, directly to draw on the revolutionary experience and revolutionary thought of the European workers—we can now see with particular clarity how rapidly we are nearing the triumph of the cause to which Lafargue devoted all his life. The Russian revolution ushered in an era of democratic revolutions throughout Asia, and 800 million people are now joining in the democratic movement of the whole of the civilised world. In Europe, too, there are increasing signs that the era of so-called peaceful bourgeois parliamentarianism is drawing to an end, to give place to an era of revolutionary battles by a proletariat that has been organised and educated in the spirit of Marxist ideas, and that will overthrow bourgeois rule and establish a communist system.

Sotsial-Demokrat, No. 25,   Published according to
   December 8 (21), 1911   the *Sotsial-Demokrat* text

HYNDMAN ON MARX

The voluminous memoirs of one of the founders and leaders of the British Social-Democratic Party, Henry Mayers Hyndman, have recently been published. The book of nearly five hundred pages is entitled *The Record of an Adventurous Life** and represents the reminiscences, written in lively fashion, of the author's political activity and of the "celebrities" he knew. Hyndman's book provides a great deal of interesting material for the characterisation of British socialism and for an appraisal of certain important problems affecting the entire international working-class movement.

We therefore think it timely to devote a few articles to Hyndman's book, particularly in view of the fact that the Right-wing Cadet *Russkiye Vedomosti* published (on October 14) an article by the liberal Dioneo, which provides an admirable example of how the liberals throw light, or rather darkness, on these problems.

Let us start with Hyndman's reminiscences of Marx. Hyndman made his acquaintance only in 1880, when he apparently knew very little about Marx's teachings and about socialism in general. It is characteristic of British relationships that, born in 1842, Hyndman, until the moment we are speaking of, was a "democrat" of an indefinite hue who had contacts and sympathies with the Conservative Party (Tories). Hyndman turned to socialism after reading *Capital* (in the French translation) during one of his numerous voyages to America between 1874 and 1880.

---

* *The Record of an Adventurous Life*, by Henry Mayers Hyndman, London (Macmillan & Co.), 1911.

Accompanied by Karl Hirsch, Hyndman, on his way to visit Marx, mentally compared him to—Mazzini!

The level at which Hyndman makes this comparison can be judged from the fact that he describes Mazzini's influence on those around him as "personal and individually ethical", and considered Marx's influence to be "almost wholly intellectual and scientific". Hyndman went to Marx as to a "supreme analytical genius" and was eager to learn from him; what attracted him in Mazzini was his character and his "elevation of thought and conduct". But that Marx "was far the more powerful mind cannot be disputed". Nor can it be disputed that Hyndman very poorly understood in 1880 (and does not quite understand even now—but of that later) the difference between a bourgeois democrat and a socialist.

"The first impression of Marx as I saw him," writes Hyndman, "was that of a powerful, shaggy, untamed old man, ready, not to say eager, to enter into conflict, and rather suspicious himself of immediate attack. Yet his greeting to us was cordial and his first remarks to me, after I had told him what a great pleasure and honour I felt it to be to shake hands with the author of *Capital*, were agreeable enough; for he told me that he had read my articles on India* with pleasure and had commented on them favourably in his newspaper correspondence.

"When speaking with fierce indignation of the policy of the Liberal Party, especially in regard to Ireland, the old warrior's small deep-sunk eyes lighted up, his heavy brows wrinkled, the broad, strong nose and face were obviously moved by passion, and he poured out a stream of vigorous denunciation, which displayed alike the heat of his temperament and the marvellous command he possessed over our language. The contrast between his manner and utterance when thus deeply stirred by anger and his attitude when giving his views on the economic events of the period was very marked. He turned from the role of prophet and vehement denunciator to that of the calm philosopher without any apparent effort, and I felt from the first that on this latter ground many a long year might pass before I ceased to be a student in the presence of a master.

---

* Until he recently turned to jingoism, Hyndman was a determined enemy of British imperialism, and from 1878 carried on a noble campaign of exposure against the shameful acts of violence, outrage, plunder, and indignity (including the flogging of political "criminals") for which Britishers of all parties in India, including the "educated" and "radical" author, John Morley, have long made themselves famous.

"I had been surprised in reading *Capital*, and still more when perusing his smaller works, such as his pronouncement on the Commune of Paris, and his *Eighteenth Brumaire*, how he combined the ablest and coolest examination of economic causes and social effects with the most bitter hatred of classes and even of individual men such as Napoleon III or M. Thiers, who, according to his own theories, were little more than flies upon the wheels of the great Juggernaut car of capitalist development. Marx, or course, was a Jew, and to me it seemed that he combined in his own person and nature, with his commanding forehead and great overhanging brow, his fierce glittering eyes, broad sensitive nose and mobile mouth, all surrounded by a setting of untrimmed hair and beard, the righteous fury of the great seers of his race, with the cold analytical powers of Spinoza and the Jewish doctors. It was an extraordinary combination of qualities, the like of which I have known in no other man.

"As I went out with Hirsch, deeply impressed by the great personality we had left, Hirsch asked me what I thought of Marx. 'Well,' I replied, 'I think he is the Aristotle of the nineteenth century.' And yet as I said it, I knew that this did not cover the ground. For one thing it was quite impossible to think of Marx as acting the courtier to Alexander (of Macedonia) while carrying on the profound studies which have so deeply influenced later generations, and besides he never so wholly segregated himself from immediate human interests—notwithstanding much that has been said to the contrary—as to be able to consider facts and their surroundings in the cold hard light of the greatest philosopher of antiquity. There can be no doubt whatever that his hatred of the system of exploitation and wage slavery by which he was surrounded was not only intellectual and philosophic but bitterly personal.

"I remember saying to him once that as I grew older, I thought I became more tolerant. 'Do you,' he said, '*do* you?' It was quite certain he didn't. It has been, I think, Marx's deep animosity to the existing order of things and his scathing criticism of his opponents which has prevented many of the educated well-to-do class from appreciating his masterly life-work at its full value and has rendered third-rate sciolists and logomachers like Böhm-Bawerk, such heroes in their eyes, merely because they have misrepresented and attempted to 'refute' him. Accustomed as we are nowadays, especially in England, to fence always with big soft buttons on the point of our rapiers, Marx's terrible onslaughts with naked steel upon his adversaries appeared so improper that it was impossible for our gentlemanly sham fighters and mental gymnasium men to believe that this unsparing controversialist and furious assailant of capital and capitalists was really the deepest thinker of modern times."

In 1880 Marx was practically unknown to the British public. His health was then failing. His strenuous exertions (sixteen hours a day and more of mental labour!) had sapped his constitution. He was now forbidden by his doctors to do any work in the evenings and, Hyndman relates, "at the close of 1880 and the beginning of 1881, I had the advantage of very frequent conversations with the Doctor".

"Our method of talking was peculiar. Marx had a habit when at all interested in the discussion of walking actively up and down the room as if he were pacing the deck of a schooner for exercise. I had acquired on my long voyages (to America, Australia, etc.) the same tendency of pacing to and fro when my mind was much occupied. Consequently, master and student could have been seen walking up and down on opposite sides of the table for two or three hours in succession, engaged in discussing the affairs of the past and the present."

Hyndman does not give anything like a detailed account of the position Marx took *on even a single one of the questions* he discussed with him. From what is quoted above it can be seen that Hyndman concentrated mostly, almost exclusively, indeed, on the *anecdotal* side; this is in line with the rest of his book. Hyndman's autobiography is the life story of a British bourgeois philistine who, being the pick of his class, finally makes his way to socialism, but never completely throws off bourgeois traditions, bourgeois views and prejudices.

While repeating the philistine reproaches against Marx and Engels that they were "autocrats" in "what was supposed to be a democratic" International, that they did not understand practical affairs, did not know people, etc., Hyndman never makes an attempt to test a single one of these reproaches on the basis of an exact, concrete analysis of the circumstances at the periods concerned.

The result is anecdote and not Marxist historical analysis. Marx and Engels fought against the unification of German Social-Democracy (with the Lassalleans[140]), whereas this unity was necessary! That is all that Hyndman says. He does not say a word about Marx and Engels having been a thousand times right in principle in their opposition to Lassalle and the Lassalleans. He does not even raise the question. He does not even ask himself whether "democracy" (organisational) in the period of the International was not a screen for bourgeois sects engaged in disrupting the work of building up proletarian Social-Democracy.

As a result, the story of Hyndman's rupture with Marx is told in such a way that we get absolutely nothing but gossip (in the spirit of the Dioneos). Engels, you see, was "exacting, suspicious, jealous"; Marx's wife is alleged to have told Hyndman's wife that Engels was Marx's "evil genius" (!); Engels, whom Hyndman never even met (despite what Mr. Dioneo has written in *Russkiye Vedomosti*), was "not disinclined to give full weight to the exchange value of his ready cash in his relations with those whom he helped" (with money; Engels was very rich, Marx very poor). Engels is said to have caused a quarrel between Marx and Hyndman, out of fear that Hyndman, a wealthy man at that time, would take Engels's place as Marx's rich friend!

Of course, the liberals derive pleasure from rehashing such inexpressible vulgarities. And of course it is not at all in the interests of the liberal hacks at least to acquaint themselves with the letters (of Marx and Engels[141]) to Sorge, referred to by Hyndman himself, and *to try and understand* the point at issue. They do not take the trouble to do that! And yet a reference to these letters and a comparison between them and Hyndman's "memoirs" would immediately settle the matter.

In 1881 Hyndman published a pamphlet entitled *England for All* in which he adopts socialism but remains a very, very confused bourgeois democrat. The pamphlet was written for the Democratic Federation (not socialist) which had then been founded and to which a large number of anti-socialist elements belonged. Hyndman paraphrases and copies from *Capital* in two chapters of this pamphlet, *but does not mention Marx*; however, in the preface he speaks vaguely of a certain "great thinker" and "original writer" to whom he is greatly indebted, etc. Hyndman tells us that it was over this that Engels caused a "breach" between him and Marx, and at the same time quotes a letter Marx had written to him (dated December 8, 1880), in which Marx says that, according to Hyndman, he, Hyndman, "does not share the views of my [Marx's] party for England".

It is clear what the difference was—a difference not understood, noticed, or appreciated by Hyndman. It was that Hyndman at that time (as Marx plainly wrote to Sorge on December 15, 1881) was a "well-meaning, petty-bourgeois writer", "half-bourgeois, half-proletarian". Obviously if a man who makes the acquaintance of Marx, becomes intimate with him, calls himself a student of his, later forms a "democratic" federation and writes a pamphlet for it in which he misrepresents Marxism and does not mention Marx, the latter could not let it pass without making a "furious" protest. Evidently the protest was made, for Marx in the same letter to Sorge quotes extracts from letters of apology in which Hyndman excuses himself on the ground that "the English don't like to be taught by foreigners" and that "my [Marx's] name was so much detested" (!), etc. (Hyndman himself states that he destroyed nearly all of Marx's letters to him, so that the discovery of the truth from this side is not to be expected.)

Fine apologies, are they not! Well, at a time when the question of the then existing differences between Hyndman and Marx has been cleared up quite definitely, and when even the whole of Hyndman's present book shows that there is much of the philistine and bourgeois in his views (for example, the arguments with which Hyndman defends capital punishment for criminals!), what is offered as the explanation of his rupture with Marx is the "intrigues" of Engels, who for forty years, followed a common line of principle with Marx. Even if all the rest of Hyndman's book were a barrel of honey, this one spoonful of tar would be enough to spoil it!

The differences between Marx and Hyndman at that time are most characteristically revealed by what Hyndman tells us about Marx's opinion of Henry George. Marx's appraisal of Henry George is known from his letter to Sorge dated June 20, 1881. Talking with Marx, Hyndman defended Henry George using the following argument: "George will teach more by inculcating error than other men can impart by complete exposition of the truth".

"Marx," writes Hyndman, "would not hear of this as a sound contention. The promulgation of error could never be of any good to the people, that was his view. 'To leave error unrefuted is to encourage intellectual immorality. For ten who go farther, a hundred may very easily stop with George, and the danger of this is too great to run!'" That was what Marx said!

Yet Hyndman tells us that, on the one hand, he still holds to his previous opinion of Henry George, and that, on the other hand, George was a boy with a bright farthing dip fooling around within the radius of a man using an electric searchlight.

An excellent comparison, only ... only it was risky for Hyndman to make this excellent comparison side by side with his miserable gossip about Engels.

Zvezda, No. 31, November 26, 1911
Signed: *Vl. Ilyin*

Published according to
the *Zvezda* text

A LIBERAL LABOUR PARTY MANIFESTO

I

The above would be a fit title for N. R-kov's article in *Nasha Zarya*, No. 9-10.[142]

Painful though it is for Marxists to lose in the person of N. R-kov, a man who, in the years when the movement was on the upgrade served the workers' party faithfully and energetically, the cause must take precedence over all personal or factional considerations, and over all recollections, however "pleasant". The interests of the cause compel us to admit that thanks to the straightforwardness, clarity, and completeness of its views, the manifesto of this new liquidator serves a very useful purpose. N. R-kov enables and compels us to pose the extremely important and cardinal question of "two parties" *irrespective* of any material relating to the "conflict" and to do so on a purely ideological basis, largely outside even the division into Bolsheviks and Mensheviks. After R-kov's article, liquidationism can no longer be discussed *as formerly* for he has definitely raised the question to a higher plane. Furthermore, after N. R-kov's article, liquidationism cannot be *merely discussed*; for what we have before us is the most comprehensive plan imaginable of immediate practical action.

N. R-kov begins with an exposition of the "principal objective task in Russia"; he then passes on to an appraisal of the revolution, after which he analyses the present situation and in this connection discusses every class in clear and precise terms, and winds up with a quite explicit description of the entire nature of the new "open political workers' association", which, he says, must be formed and "actually put into effect" without delay. In short, R-kov

begins at the very beginning and by consecutive stages
arrives at the very end, as is to be expected of anyone who
has any realisation of the serious political responsibility
he bears for his words and deeds. And it must be said in
fairness to R-kov that from beginning to end he most consistently substitutes liberalism for Marxism.

Take the starting-point of his arguments. He regards
it as "absolutely beyond doubt or dispute" that "the principal objective task in Russia at present is the completion
of the change from grossly predatory semi-feudal economic
practices to civilised capitalism". In his opinion it is debat-
able whether Russia has reached a position in which, "although the possibility of social upheavals is not excluded,
these upheavals are not indispensable or inevitable in the
near future".

We consider it to be absolutely beyond doubt or dispute
that this is a purely liberal way of presenting the question.
The liberals confine themselves to the question of whether
we are going to have a "civilised capitalism" or not, whether
there are going to be "upheavals" or not. The Marxist refuses
to confine himself to this. He demands an analysis that
will show *which classes, or strata of classes* in the bourgeois
society that is emancipating itself, are pursuing this or
that definite line in this emancipation —what, for example,
are the political forms of the so-called "civilised capitalism"
which they are creating. Both in times of "upheaval" and
during their undoubted absence, Marxists pursue a line different in principle from liberalism —that of creating truly
democratic ways of life, not just "civilised" ways in general.
We are all striving for "civilised capitalism", say the liberals, posing as a party that stands above classes. We Marxists, however, must tell the workers and democrats that
our understanding of the term "civilisation" differs from that
of the liberals.

R-kov presents us with an even more vivid and typically
"professorial" distortion of Marxism when he criticises the
"superficial observers" who "think that our revolution has
failed". "The weak-nerved intelligentsia as a whole," says
R-kov, "has always and everywhere indulged in snivelling
and whining, followed by moral prostration, renegacy, and
mysticism." The "thoughtful observer", on the other hand,

knows that "the raging of reaction often expresses profound social change", that "new social groups and forces take shape and mature in the epoch of reaction".

Thus reasons R-kov. In presenting the question of "renegacy" he has managed to display so much philistinism (even though accompanied by learned verbiage) that no trace is left of the connection between the counter-revolutionary sentiments in Russia and the position and interests of *definite* classes. Not a single *Vekhi* contributor, i.e., the most rabid counter-revolutionary liberal, will dispute the fact that new forces are maturing in the period of reaction; not a single contributor to the liquidationist five-volume publication, which the best of the Mensheviks turned away from,[143] will refuse to subscribe to this. The actual face and the class character of our counter-revolution have vanished from the arguments of our historian, and only hackneyed and hollow phrases remain about some intellectuals being weak-nerved while others are thoughtful observers. R-kov failed to take notice of a question of the utmost importance to a Marxist—namely, how our revolution demonstrated the various methods of action and the various aspirations of the different classes, and why this has given rise to a "renegade" attitude towards the struggle for "civilisation" on the part of other bourgeois classes.

Let us turn to the main issue—R-kov's appraisal of the present situation based on an estimate of the position of all the classes. He begins with the "representatives of our big landowning class", of whom he says: "Not so long ago the bulk of them were [were!] real feudal landowners, typical landed aristocrats. At present only a few of these last Mohicans have survived. This small handful is still grouped around Purishkevich and Markov the Second, and are impotently [!] spluttering the venom of despair.... The majority of our big landowners, noblemen and commoners, who are represented in the Duma by the Nationalists and the Right Octobrists, are gradually and steadily being converted into an agricultural bourgeoisie."

Such is R-kov's "appraisal of the situation". It is obvious that this appraisal is a mockery of reality. In actual fact, the "handful ... grouped around Purishkevich and Markov the Second" are not powerless, but all-powerful. It is pre-

cisely their power and their revenue that the present social
and political institutions of Russia protect; it is their will
that prevails in the last analysis; it is they who constitute
the element determining the entire line of activity and the
entire character of the so-called bureaucracy from top to
bottom. All this is so generally known, the actual domination in Russia by this very handful is so striking and common,
mon, that it requires a truly boundless liberal self-delusion
to forget it. R-kov's error is, first, in ridiculously exaggerating the "conversion" of feudal economy into bourgeois economy, and, secondly, in forgetting a "trifle"—just the sort of
"trifle" that distinguishes a Marxist from a liberal—namely,
the intricacy and spasmodic nature of the process of
adaptation of the political superstructure to economic
transformation. To explain these two errors of R-kov's
it is sufficient to cite the example of Prussia where to this
day, despite the considerably higher level of development
of capitalism in general, and of the conversion of the old
landowning economy into bourgeois economy in particular, the Oldenburgs and the Heidebrands are still omni-
potent and control state power, their social substance permeating, as it were, the entire Prussian monarchy, the
entire Prussian bureaucracy! To this day, sixty-three years
after 1848, and despite the unprecedentedly rapid development of capitalism, the law governing the Landtag elections in Prussia is still so framed as to ensure the domination of the Prussian Purishkeviches. Yet for Russia, six
years after 1905, R-kov paints an Arcadian idyll of the
"powerlessness" of the Purishkeviches!

The point is that painting an Arcadian idyll about the
"steady" conversion of the Purishkeviches and the "triumph
of a quite moderate bourgeois progressism" is the main
theme of *all* of R-kov's reflections. Take his ideas on present-day agrarian policy. "There is no more striking and
widespread illustration" of the conversion (of feudal economy into bourgeois economy) than this policy, declares
R-kov. The system of splitting farms into strips isolated
from each other is being abolished, and "the elimination
of land hunger in twenty agricultural gubernias in the black-
earth belt presents no difficulties to speak of, it constitutes
one of the urgent tasks of the day, and apparently it will

be settled by a compromise among various groups of the bourgeoisie".

"This anticipated inevitable compromise on the agrarian question already has a number of precedents."

Here you have a complete sample of R-kov's method of political reasoning. He begins by eliminating the extremes, without any supporting data, merely because of his liberal complacency. Then he goes on to declare that a compromise among the various groups of the bourgeoisie is not difficult, and is likely. Then he winds up by saying that such a compromise is "inevitable". By this method one could prove that "upheavals" were neither likely nor indispensable in France in 1788 and in China in 1910. To be sure, a compromise among the various groups of the bourgeoisie presents no difficulties, *if we assume* that Markov the Second has been eliminated not only in R-kov's complacent imagination. But to assume this would mean adopting the standpoint of the liberal who is afraid to dispense with the Markovs and who thinks that everybody will always share his fear.

To be sure, a compromise would be "inevitable" if (the first "if") there were no Markovs; and if (the second "if") we assume that the workers and the peasants who are being ruined are politically sound asleep. But then, again, would not such an assumption (the assumption of the second condition) mean accepting the liberals' wish as reality?

II

Since we are not inclined to accept the liberal wishes or liberal conjectures as reality, we have reached a different conclusion. Without doubt the present agrarian policy is bourgeois in character. But since it is the Purishkeviches who are directing this bourgeois policy, who remain masters of the situation, the result is such a tremendous accentuation of the contradictions that, for the immediate future, at any rate, the likelihood of a compromise must be considered entirely out of the question.

Another important social process, says R-kov in continuing his analysis, is the process of the consolidation of the big industrial and commercial bourgeoisie. Correctly indicating the "mutual concessions" of the Constitutional-Democrats and the Octobrists, the author draws the conclusion: "We must not cherish any illusions—what we see in the offing is the triumph of a quite moderate bourgeois 'progressism'".

Trumph?—Where? Over whom? Is it at the elections to the Fourth Duma of which R-kov has just spoken? If that is what he means, then it will be a "triumph" within the narrow confines of the election law of June 3, 1907. Hence one of two conclusions is inevitable: either the "triumph" will not set up a wave and thus the actual domination of the Purishkeviches will in no way be changed; or this "triumph" will indirectly be the expression of a democratic revival which is bound to come into sharp conflict with the above-mentioned "narrow confines" and with the domination of the Purishkeviches.

In either case the triumph of moderation at elections conducted within moderate bounds will not bring about the least triumph of moderation in real life. The point is, however, that R-kov has already lapsed into a state of "parliamentary cretinism", which enables him to confuse elections conducted on the basis of the June Third law with reality! To demonstrate this incredible fact to the reader we must quote R-kov in full:

"And this triumph is all the more probable since the mass of the urban petty bourgeoisie which, in its philistine way, is dejectedly contemplating its shattered illusions, will helplessly gravitate towards moderate progressism, and the peasantry will be all too weak at the elections because the peculiar features of our electoral system enable the landowners who predominate in the gubernia panels of electors to elect 'Rights' to represent the peasants. Such is the picture of the social changes that are taking place in Russia at present, if, for the time being, we leave out the working class out of consideration. It is by no means a picture of stagnation or of regression. New, bourgeois, Russia is undoubtedly gaining in strength and is advancing. The State Duma, based on the electoral system established on June 3, 1907, will provide the political sanction for the coming domination of the moderately progressive industrial and commercial bourgeoisie that will share power with the conservative rural bourgeoisie. (England, pure and simple! We omit the comparison with France and Prussia, on which we shall dwell below.) Thus, in summing up everything that has just been said, we must admit that there exist all the prerequisites for a slow, extremely painful for the masses, but nevertheless certain advance of the bourgeois social and political system in Russia. The possibility of storms and upheavals is, naturally, not out of the question, but they will not become something indispensable and inevitable, as was the case before the revolution."

An intricate philosophy, that one cannot deny. If we leave the peasantry out of account, because it is "weak at the elections", and if "for the time being, we leave the working class out of consideration", then, of course, there is absolutely no possibility of upheavals! But what it amounts to is that one who examines Russia from a liberal viewpoint can see nothing but liberal "progressism". Remove your liberal blinkers and the picture becomes an entirely different one. Since the part played by the peasantry in life is quite different from the part it plays in the June Third electoral system, the fact that it is "weak at the elections" — far from opening the gates to a "moderate progressism" — accentuates the antagonism between the peasantry as a whole and the entire system. Since the working class *cannot* be left "out of consideration" either in a capitalist country in general, or in Russia after the experience of the first ten years of the twentieth century in particular, R-kov's argumentation is entirely useless. Since the dominating factor in Russia (both in the Third Duma and above it) is Purishkevichism, occasionally moderated by the grumbling of the Guchkovs and Milyukovs, the talk about the "impending domination" of the moderately progressive bourgeoisie is just a liberal lullaby. Since the Guchkovs and Milyukovs by virtue of their class position can oppose the domination of the Purishkeviches with nothing but their grumbling, a conflict between the new, bourgeois Russia and the Purishkeviches is inevitable, and its motive forces will be those whom R-kov, following the example of the liberals, leaves "out of consideration". Just because the Milyukovs and Guchkovs are making "mutual concessions" in cringing before the Purishkeviches, it is all the more necessary for the workers to draw the line between democracy and liberalism. N. R-kov sees neither the conditions giving rise to upheavals in Russia nor the task just indicated, which is obligatory even in the definite absence of an upheaval.

A vulgar democrat may reduce the whole matter to the question whether there is an upheaval or not. The Marxist is primarily concerned with the line of political demarcation between the classes, which is the *same* during an upheaval and in its absence. R-kov's statement that "the workers must assume the task of exercising political hegemony in the struggle for a democratic regime", is extraordinary after all he has written in his manifesto. What it means is that R-kov gets a guarantee from the bourgeoisie to recognise the hegemony of the workers, while he himself gives the bourgeoisie a guarantee to the effect that the workers renounce the tasks which constitute the substance of hegemony! After he has removed this substance, leaving no trace whatsoever, R-kov naïvely goes on to repeat a hollow phrase. First he gives an appraisal of the situation from which it is evident that, as far as he is concerned, the hegemony of the liberals is an accomplished, irrevocable, and inescapable fact, and then he tries to assure us that he recognises the hegemony of the working class!

The "real" significance of the Duma, argues R-kov, "is no less than that of the French Legislative Corps during the last years of the Second Empire, or that of the proportional mean between the German Reichstag and the Prussian Landtag that was characteristic of Prussia in the eighties of the past century".

This kind of comparison is so frivolous that it is mere playing at historical parallels. In France in the sixties the epoch of bourgeois revolutions had long since come to an end, a direct clash between the proletariat and the bourgeoisie was already knocking at the door, and Bonapartism was the expression of the government's manoeuvring between these two classes. It is ridiculous to compare that situation with contemporary Russia. The Third Duma is more reminiscent of the *Chambre introuvable*[144] of 1815! In Prussia, the eighties also marked the epoch of the consummation of the bourgeois revolution, which had completed its work by 1870. The entire bourgeoisie, which included both the urban and rural petty bourgeoisie, was contented and reactionary.

Perhaps R-kov fancied he saw a comparison between the role of the democratic and the proletarian deputies in the Legislative Corps and in the Reichstag, and the role of the deputies of the same classes in the Third Duma? That would be a legitimate comparison; but, then, it would not prove his point, for the conduct of Gegechkori and, to a certain extent, also of Petrov the Third, testifies to such strength, self-confidence, and readiness for battle on the part of the classes which they represent that a "compromise" with the Purishkeviches is not only unlikely but appears to be absolutely out of the question.

III

It was necessary to dwell at particular length on R-kov's appraisal of the role of the various classes, because here we have the ideological roots of our unqualified disagreement. The practical conclusions which R-kov draws, with rare fearlessness and straightforwardness, it must be said in all fairness to him, are interesting primarily because they reduce the author's "theory" to an absurdity. R-kov is a thousand times right, of course, when he connects the question of the possibility of an open political organisation of the workers with an appraisal of the situation, with an estimate of fundamental alterations in the political system. But the trouble is that instead of pointing out such alterations *in real life*, he is only able to present us with amiable professorial syllogisms: the transition to "civilised capitalism" "presupposes" the necessity for an open political organisation of the workers. It is easy to put this on paper, but in real life the Russian political regime will not become a whit more "civilised" because of it.

"Progressism, even if of the most moderate variety, will undoubtedly have to extend the all too narrow confines existing at present." To this we answer: the progressism of the Cadets in the Fourth Duma will not have to, and cannot "extend" anything so long as elements far removed from the Cadets do not bestir themselves in a manner very dissimilar to that customary in the Duma.

"Unless such an organisation exists," says R-kov, referring to an open and broad political organisation of the workers, "the struggle is bound to assume an anarchistic character harmful, not only to the working class, but to the civilised bourgeoisie as well."

We shall not dwell on the last part of the phrase, comment will only spoil this "gem". As for the first part, it is historically wrong. There was no anarchism in Germany in 1878-90, although there was no "open and broad" political organisation in existence.

Further, R-kov is a thousand times right when he puts forward a concrete plan for an open political workers' "organisation" and suggests that it be inaugurated by the founding of a "political association for the protection of the interests of the working class". He is right in the sense that only empty phrase-mongers can prattle for months and years about the possibility of an *"open"* party, without taking the first simple and natural step to launch it. R-kov is not a phrase-monger; he is a man of deeds and, as such, starts at the beginning and goes the whole hog.

But the point is that his "deeds" are *liberal* deeds, and the "banner" which he is "unfurling" (see p. 35 of the article we are quoting) is the banner of a liberal labour policy. It is immaterial that the programme of the association which R-kov wants to found provides for "the establishment of a new society based on the public ownership of the means of production", etc. Actually, the recognition of this great principle did not prevent a section of the German Social-Democrats in the sixties from pursuing a "royal-Prussian labour policy", nor does it prevent Ramsay MacDonald (leader of the British "Independent Labour Party"—meaning independent of socialism) from pursuing a liberal labour policy. When R-kov speaks of the political tasks of the immediate period, of our present period, it is a system of liberal principles that he propounds. The "banner" which R-kov is "unfurling" was unfurled by Prokopovich, Potresov, Larin, etc., long ago, and the more this banner is "unfurled" the clearer does it become to one and all that what we have before us is a dirty liberal rag worn to shreds.

"There is not a grain of utopia in all this," R-kov tries to persuade us. We must needs reply with a paraphrase of a well-known saying: "You are a great utopian, but your utopia is tiny". Indeed, it would be rather frivolous perhaps to reply to an obviously frivolous statement other than with a joke. How is it possible to regard as other than utopian the suggested foundation of an open workers' association at a time when absolutely peaceful, tame, non-political trade unions are being suppressed? How can one write about the role of the various classes in a way that is liberal from A to Z and yet assure the readers that this does not mean creeping into a regime of renovated Tolmachovism? The good R-kov goes out of his way to declare: "There is no advocacy of any violence in this; there is not a word, not a thought about a violent revolution being necessary, because in reality, too, no such necessity may ever arise. If anyone, blinded by reactionary frenzy, took it into his head to accuse the members of such an 'association' of striving for violent revolution, the whole burden of an absurd, unfounded and juridically flimsy accusation of this sort would fall upon the head of the accuser"!

N. R-kov has an eloquent pen, just like Mr. P. B. Struve who, in 1901, hurled similar terrifying thunderbolts "upon the heads" of those who persecuted the Zemstvo.[145] What a picture—N. R-kov trying to prove to the accusing Dumbadzes that, since he now harbours no "thoughts", the burden of the juridically flimsy accusations will fall upon the Dumbadzes' own heads! Yes, indeed, we have no parliament as yet, but we have parliamentary cretinism galore. Apparently such members of the new association as the Marxist Gegechkori or even the non-Marxist but honest democrat Petrov the Third would be summarily expelled at the very first meeting of the new association—provided the assembled members are not dispatched, by mistake, to various chilly places before the meeting opens.

The *Nasha Zarya* "liquidators" are rejoicing because R-kov has joined their ranks. But the enthusiastic liquidators do not realise how ardent is the embrace which the newly-won liquidator R-kov brings to them. It is so ardent and so powerful that this much can be vouched for—liquidationism will be smothered by R-kov's ardent embrace just as the labour congress was smothered by Y. Larin's ardent embrace. Y. Larin perpetrated that bloodless murder by the simple device of writing a pamphlet, after which people, primarily out of fear of the embarrassment involved, began to be wary of defending the idea of a labour congress. After the new "manifesto" of liquidationism published by R-kov in *Nasha Zarya*, people, primarily out of fear of the embarrassment involved, will begin to be wary of defending the idea of an open liquidationist party.

And, since we must find at least one point on which to agree with R-kov, that idea does contain a "grain" of non-utopianism. Remove your professorial blinkers, my dear sir, and you will then see that the "association" which you intend to "actually put into effect" (after the burden of your admonitions has fallen "upon the heads" of the Mymre-tsovs[146]) already *exists*—that it has been in existence *for two years.* And you yourself already belong to it! The magazine *Nasha Zarya* (not as a collection of so much printed matter, but as an ideological group) is just such an "association for the protection of the interests of the working class". An open and broad organisation of workers is a utopia; but "open" and frank magazines of opportunist intellectuals are not a utopia—not by any means. In their own way they are undoubtedly protecting the interests of the working class; but to anyone who has not ceased to be a Marxist it is obvious that theirs is an "association" for protecting, in a liberal manner, the interests of the working class as conceived by the liberals.

Zvezda, No. 32, December 3, 1911
   Signed: *Vl. Ilyin*

                                        Printed according to
                                        the *Zvezda* text, verified
                                     with the text of the symposium
                                     Marxism and Liquidationism, 1914

THE SOCIAL-DEMOCRATIC GROUP
IN THE SECOND DUMA[147]

AN ACCOUNT OF THE WHOLE AFFAIR

Four years have passed since all the members of the Social-Democratic group in the Second Duma, victims of an infamous plot by our government, were put on trial and sent to penal servitude like the worst of criminals. The Russian proletariat fully understood that the charges against its representatives were based on a forgery, but this was the period of unbridled reaction and in addition, sentence was passed behind closed doors so that sufficient evidence of the crime committed by tsarism was not available. Only quite recently the convincing facts contained in the confession of Brodsky, an agent of the secret political police, have thrown full light on the revolting intrigues of our authorities.

This is what actually happened.

Despite the very limited franchise, the Russian proletariat returned 55 Social-Democrats to the Second Duma.

This Social-Democratic group was not only numerically large, but outstandingly sound ideologically. It bore the hallmark of the revolution from which it sprang. Its pronouncements, in which there could still be heard the echoes of the great struggle that had involved the whole country, levelled deep and well-founded criticism, not only at the bills submitted to the Duma, but also at the whole tsarist and capitalist system of government in general.

Armed with the invincible weapon of contemporary socialism this Social-Democratic group was, of all the Left groups, the most revolutionary, the most consistent, and the most deeply imbued with class-consciousness. It drew the others in its wake and set its revolutionary seal on the Duma. Our rulers considered the group to be the last stronghold of the revolution, its last symbol, the living proof of the powerful influence of Social-Democracy on the proletarian masses and, consequently, a constant threat to reaction, the last obstacle to its triumphant march. Therefore, the government considered it essential not only to rid itself of this too revolutionary Duma, but also to restrict the electoral rights of the proletariat and of the democratically-inclined peasantry to the minimum, thus preventing any possibility of the election of a similar Duma in the future. The best method for the realisation of such a coup d'état was to get rid of the socialist Duma group, to compromise it in the eyes of the country—to cut off the head in order to destroy the body.

However, some pretext had to be found for this,—for instance, the possibility of accusing the group of some serious political crime. The inventiveness of the police and the secret political police soon found such an excuse. It was decided to compromise the parliamentary socialist group, accusing it of close ties with the Social-Democratic combat organisation and with the Social-Democratic military organisation. With this aim in view, General Gerasimov, the chief of the secret political police, suggested to his agent Brodsky that he enter these organisations. (All these facts are taken from *L'Avenir*,[148] No. 1 [*The Future*], issued under the editorship of Burtsev in Paris, 50, Boulevard St. Jacques.) Brodsky succeeded in doing so as a rank-and-file member, and later became a secretary. Several members of the military organisation had the idea of sending a delegation of soldiers to the socialist parliamentary group. The secret police decided to use this for its own ends, and Brodsky, having won the confidence of the military organisation, undertook to execute this plan. Several soldiers were elected; a list of soldiers' demands was drawn up and a day was appointed for the delegation to visit the Duma group at its headquarters, without the group even having been warned. As the soldiers were not allowed to go there in army uniform they were obliged to change their clothes. This was actually carried out at the home of one of the agents of the secret police, where they changed into clothes bought and prepared for them by the secret police. According to this vile plan of Gerasimov's, Brodsky was to have arrived at the premises of the socialist group at the same time as the soldiers, bringing with him revolutionary documents which would implicate our delegates even more. Further, it was agreed that Brodsky would be arrested together with the others, and then, aided by the secret police who would enable him to effect a sham escape, he would be at liberty. But Brodsky arrived too late, and when he reached the premises of the group with the compromising documents, the search had already commenced, and he was not allowed to enter.

Such was the setting prepared most thoroughly by the secret police which allowed reaction, not only to condemn and send to penal servitude the representatives of the proletariat, but, apart from this, to dissolve the Second Duma and to carry out its coup d'état of June 3 (16), 1907. Actually, on that date the government announced in its manifesto (which, like all tsarist manifestos, astounds one with its shameless hypocrisy) that it was compelled to dissolve the Duma, for, instead of supporting and aiding the government in its desire to re-establish peace in the country, the Duma, on the contrary, had acted against all the proposals and intentions of the government and, incidentally, did not wish to append its signature to repressive measures against the revolutionary elements of the country. Furthermore (and I give the text word for word), "acts hitherto unheard of in the annals of history were committed. The judiciary discovered a plot by a whole section of the State Duma against the state and the power of the tsar. When our government demanded the temporary removal of the 55 members of the Duma accused of the crime until the conclusion of the trial, and the imprisonment of those most guilty, the State Duma did not immediately carry out the lawful demands of the authorities which brooked no delay".

Incidentally, the proofs of the tsar's crime were known not only to the government and its closest friends. Our dear Constitutional-Democrats, who never tire of babbling about legality, justice, truth, and so on, who embellish their Party with such a high-sounding title as "party of people's freedom", have for the past four years also known all the vile details of this dirty affair which had been kept so secret. They looked on passively for four long years while our deputies were tried in defiance of all law, while they suffered penal servitude, while some died and others lost their reason, and ... they remained cautiously silent. Yet they could have spoken for they had deputies in the Duma and had many daily newspapers at their disposal. Caught between reaction and revolution—they feared the revolution more. For this reason they flirted with the government and by their silence shielded it for four long years and so became its accomplices in crime. It is only recently (the sitting of the Duma of the 17th October, 1911) that during debates on the secret police, one of them, Deputy Teslenko, at last decided to let the cat out of the bag. Here is part of his speech (word for word according to the Verbatim Report): "When it was proposed that proceedings be taken against 53 members[149] of the Second State Duma, a commission was set up by the Duma. This Commission was given all the documents that were to provide evidence that 53 members of the State Duma had organised a plot to set up a republic in Russia by means of an armed uprising. The Commission of the Second State Duma (I made the report on its behalf) came to the conclusion, a unanimous conclusion, that what was being discussed was not a plot hatched against the state by the Social-Democrats, but a plot hatched by the St. Petersburg department of the secret police against the Second State Duma. When the Commission's report, based on documents, was ready, on the eve of the day when all these facts were to be made public from this rostrum, the Second State Duma was dissolved and it was not possible to state (from this rostrum) what had been brought to light. When the trial of the accused commenced, these 53 members of the State Duma demanded that it be heard in public, and that the public should be told that it was not they who were the criminals but the St. Petersburg department of the secret police—the doors were closed and the public was never told the truth."

Such are the facts. For four years our deputies have been languishing in chains in terrible Russian prisons, the severity and savagery of which you are, of course, aware. Many have already died there. One of the deputies has lost his reason, the health of many others, as a result of unendurable living conditions, has been impaired and they may die any day. The Russian proletariat can no longer calmly look on while its representatives, whose only crime is that they waged an unremitting struggle in its interests, perish in tsarist prisons. It is even more impossible for it to look on calmly, since from the legal point of view Brodsky's admissions provide complete justification for demanding a fresh trial. A campaign for the release of the deputies has already commenced in Russia.

The workers' paper *Zvezda*, appearing in St. Petersburg devoted a considerable part of its issue dated October 29, 1911 to the question. It appeals to the press, to liberal and Left deputies, to associations and trade unions, but mostly to the proletariat. "There is not, and cannot be," exclaims the paper, "calmness and peace of mind while every hour and every minute all can hear the clanging of the chains fettering those who have been immured, deprived of freedom and every political and civil right only because they had the courage to carry out before the whole country their duty as men and citizens. The public conscience cannot and should not remain calm after the exposure of the horrifying truth. No matter what the difficulties may be they must be overcome and a retrial of the deputies to the Second State Duma demanded! But in the first instance the proletariat must make its powerful voice heard, for it was its representatives who were falsely tried, and who at the present moment languish in penal servitude."

In commencing this struggle, the Russian proletariat appeals to socialists of all countries to give it support, and together with it to proclaim loudly to the whole world their indignation at the savagery and infamy of our present ruling autocracy which, screening itself with a mask of pitiful hypocrisy, surpasses even the barbarism and uncivilised behaviour of the Asiatic governments.

In France, Comrade Charles Dumas has already started the campaign and in an article printed in the newspaper *L'Avenir* has called for energetic support to be given to the Russian proletariat at this difficult moment. Let socialists of all countries follow this example, let them everywhere, in parliament, in their press, at their public meetings, express their indignation and demand a review of the case of the Social-Democratic group in the Second Duma.

Written after November 6 (19), 1911
Printed in the German,
French, and English languages
in December 1911
in *Bulletin périodique du Bureau
socialiste international*, No. 8
Signed: *N. Lenin*
First printed in Russian
in 1940, in *Proletarskaya
Revolutsia*, No. 4

Published according to
the *Bulletin* text

THE SLOGANS AND ORGANISATION OF SOCIAL-DEMOCRATIC WORK INSIDE AND OUTSIDE THE DUMA

The question put by the Social-Democratic group in the Third Duma concerning the dastardly frame-up staged by the secret police that led to the criminal proceedings being instituted against the Social-Democrat members of the Second Duma,[150] apparently marks a certain turn in our entire Party activity, as well as in the position of democracy in general and in the mood of the working masses.

It is probably the first time that such a resolute protest, revolutionary in tone and content, against the "masters of June Third" has been heard from the rostrum of the Third Duma, a protest supported by the entire opposition, including the extremely moderate, liberal-monarchist, *Vekhi* variety of "His Majesty's Opposition", i.e., the Cadet Party, and including even the Progressists. It is probably the first time since the period of gloom set in (i.e., since 1908), that the country sees, feels, and is tangibly aware that in connection with the revolutionary protest voiced by the deputies of the revolutionary proletariat in the reactionary Duma, the masses of workers are stirring, that there is a rising spirit of unrest in the working-class districts of the capital, that workers are holding meetings (meetings again!) at which revolutionary speeches are delivered by Social-Democrats (the meetings at the Putilov Works, the Cable Works, and other plants), and that there is talk and rumour of a political mass strike (see report from St. Petersburg in the Octobrist *Golos Moskvy* of November 19).

To be sure, revolutionary speeches were made by Social-Democrat deputies in the Third Duma on more than one occasion in the past, too. On more than one occasion our comrades of the Social-Democratic group in the Third Duma did their duty splendidly and from the platform of the reactionary and servile Purishkevich "parliament" they spoke plainly, clearly and sharply of the bankruptcy of the monarchy, of a republic, of a second revolution. These services rendered by the Social-Democrat members of the Third Duma must be emphasised all the more strongly, the more often we hear the contemptible opportunist talk of the sham Social-Democrats of *Golos Sotsial-Demokrata* or *Dyelo Zhizni* who frown upon such speeches.

But never before has there been such a combination of political symptoms indicating a turn—the entire opposition backing the Social-Democrats; the liberal-monarchist, "loyal", "responsible", and cowardly *Rech* stating that the situation is fraught with conflict; the masses showing unrest in connection with the question in the Duma; and the censored press reporting the existence of "alarming sentiments" in the rural districts. Following as it does upon the "Muromtsev" and "Tolstoi" demonstrations of last year, the strikes in 1910 and 1911, and last year's students' "affair", the present instance undoubtedly serves to confirm us in our conviction that the first period of the Russian counter-revolution—the period of absolute stagnation, of dead calm, hangings and suicides, of the orgy of reaction and the orgy of renegacy of every brand, particularly the liberal brand— that this period *has come to an end.* The second period in the history of the counter-revolution has set in: the state of utter dejection and often of "savage" fright is waning; among the broadest and most varied sections of the population there is a noticeably growing political consciousness— or, if not consciousness exactly, at least a feeling that "things cannot go on as before", and that a "change" is required, is necessary, is inevitable; and we see the beginning of an inclination, half instinctive, often still undefined, to lend support to protests and struggle.

It would, naturally, be imprudent to exaggerate the significance of these symptoms and to imagine that the revival is already under way. That is not yet so. The features that characterise the counter-revolution at present are *not the same* as those distinguishing its first period; but the counter-revolution still reigns supreme and imagines itself to be invincible. To quote the December 1908 resolution of the R.S.D.L.P., the "protracted task of training, educating, and organising" the proletariat[151] is still, as before, on the order of the day. However, the fact that a turn has set in, compels us to pay particular attention to the attitude of the Social-Democratic Party to other parties, and to the immediate tasks of the working-class movement.

"His Majesty's Opposition", including the Cadets and the Progressists, appeared to recognise for a moment the leading role of the Social-Democrats and, following the lead of the workers' deputies, walked out of the Duma of landowners and Octobrists, the Duma founded by the Black-Hundred and pogrom-making monarchy of Nicholas Romanov; they walked out and stayed away during the base trickery of the majority who were afraid that the story of the frame-up would be made public.

What does this mean? Have the Cadets ceased to be a counter-revolutionary party or have they never been one, as is asserted by the opportunist Social-Democrats? Ought we to make it our task to "support" the Cadets and to think of some slogan calling for a "general national opposition"?

The enemies of revolutionary Social-Democracy have from time immemorial, it may be said, resorted to the method of reducing its views to an absurdity and have, for the convenience of their polemics, drawn a caricature of Marxism. Thus, in the second half of the nineties of the last century, when Social-Democracy was just springing up in Russia as a mass movement, the Narodniks drew a caricature of Marxism which they labelled "strike-ism". And, such was the irony of history that there were Marxists whom that caricature fitted. They were the Economists. It was possible to save the honour and good name of Social-Democracy only by a ruthless struggle against Economism. And after the Revolution of 1905, when Bolshevism, as the adaptation of revolutionary Marxism to the particular conditions of the epoch, scored a great victory in the working-class movement, a victory which now even its enemies concede, our adversaries drew a caricature of Bolshevism, which they labelled "boycottism", "combatism", etc. And, again, such was the irony of history that there were Bolsheviks whom that caricature fitted. They were the *Vperyod* group.

These lessons of history should serve as a warning against attempts to distort the views of revolutionary Social-Democrats concerning the attitude towards the Constitutional-Democrats (see, for instance, *Vperyod*, No. 2). The Cadets are unquestionably a counter-revolutionary party. Only absolutely ignorant or unscrupulous persons can deny this; and it is the bounden duty of Social-Democrats to make this fact known far and wide, including the rostrum of the Duma. But the Cadets are a party of counter-revolutionary *liberals*, and their liberal nature, as has been emphasised in the resolution on non-proletarian parties adopted at the London Congress of the R.S.D.L.P. (in 1907), makes it our duty to "take advantage" of the peculiar situation and the particular conflicts or cases of friction arising from this situation, to take advantage, for instance, of their sham democracy to advocate true, consistent, and selfless democracy.

Since counter-revolutionary liberalism has sprung up in the country, the forces of democracy in general, and of proletarian democracy in particular, must do everything to separate themselves from it; not for a moment must they forget the dividing line between it and them. But it does not in the least follow from this that it is permissible to confuse counter-revolutionary liberalism with, say, counter-revolutionary feudalism, or that it is permissible to ignore the conflicts between them, to hold aloof from these conflicts or brush them aside. Counter-revolutionary liberalism, for the very reason that it is counter-revolutionary, will *never* be able to assume the role of leader in a victorious revolution; but, for the very reason that it is liberalism, it will *inevitably* keep coming into "conflict" with the Crown, with feudalism, with non-liberal bourgeoisie, and by its behaviour it will sometimes indirectly reflect the "Left", democratic sentiments of the country, or the beginning of a revival, etc.

Let us recall the history of France. At the time of the revolution, bourgeois liberalism had already shown its counter-revolutionary nature—this subject is dealt with, for instance, in Cunow's fine book on revolutionary newspaper literature in France. Yet, not only after the great bourgeois revolution, but even after the revolution of 1848, when the counter-revolutionary nature of the liberals had brought matters to such a pass that workers were being shot down by republicans—in 1868-70, the last years of the Second Empire—these liberals by their opposition expressed the change of sentiment in the country and the beginning of the democratic, revolutionary, republican revival.

If the Cadets are now playing at "eyes left", as the Octobrists taunt them, that is one of the symptoms and one of the results of the country moving "leftward"; it shows that revolutionary democracy is stirring in the womb of its mother, preparing to come into God's world again. The womb of Russia under the rule of the Purishkeviches and Romanovs is such that it must give birth to revolutionary democracy!

What is the practical conclusion to be drawn from this? The conclusion is that we must watch the growth of this new revolutionary democracy with the greatest attention. Just because it is new, because it is coming into the world after 1905 and after the counter-revolution, and not before it, it is sure to grow *in a new way*; and in order to be able properly to approach this "new", to be able to influence it and help it grow successfully, we must not confine ourselves to the old methods, but must search for new methods as well—we must mingle with the crowds, feel the pulse of real life, and sometimes make our way not only into the thick of the crowd, but also into the liberal salon.

Mr. Burtsev's sheet *L'Avenir*, for instance, is very reminiscent of a liberal salon. There the stupid, liberal, Octobrist-Cadet slogan calling for "a revision of the Statutes of June 3" is defended in a liberal manner; there they prattle eagerly about stool-pigeons, police, *agents provocateurs*, Burtsev, bombs. Nevertheless, when Mr. Martov was in a hurry to get into that salon, he might have been accused only of tactless haste, but not of a fundamental falsehood, *if* ... *if* he had not behaved there like a liberal. We may justify, and sometimes even praise, a Social-Democrat who makes his appearance in a liberal salon as long as he behaves like a Social-Democrat. But in the liberal salon Mr. Martov came out with the liberal balderdash about "solidarity in the struggle for the very freedom of elections and election propaganda", which is supposed to be maintained "for the period of the elections"!! (*L'Avenir*, No. 5).

A new democracy is growing up—under new conditions, and in a new way. We must learn to approach it properly—that is beyond doubt. We must not approach it for the purpose of lisping like liberals, but in order to uphold and advocate the slogans of true democracy. Social-Democrats must advocate *three* slogans to the new democracy, slogans which are alone worthy of our great cause and which alone correspond to the *real* conditions for the attainment of *freedom* in Russia. These slogans are: a republic; the eight-hour day; and the confiscation of all landed estates.

This is the one correct nation-wide programme of struggle for a free Russia. Anyone who doubts this programme is not yet a democrat. Anyone who denies this programme while calling himself a democrat, has understood all too well how necessary it is for him to hoodwink the people in order to achieve his anti-democratic (i.e., counter-revolutionary) aims.

Why is the struggle for the eight-hour working day a natural condition for the attainment of freedom in Russia? Because experience has shown that freedom cannot be achieved without a selfless struggle on the part of the proletariat, and such a struggle is inseparably bound up with the struggle to improve the workers' conditions. The eight-hour day is an example of such improvements and is the banner of struggle for them.

Why is the struggle for the confiscation of all landed estates a natural condition for the attainment of freedom in Russia? Because, without radical measures to help the millions of peasants who have been reduced by the Purishkeviches, Romanovs, and Markovs to unheard of ruin, suffering, and death from starvation, all talk of democracy and of "people's freedom" is absurd and utterly hypocritical. And unless the landed estates are confiscated for the benefit of the peasants, there can be no question of any *serious* measures to help the muzhik, there can be no question of any serious determination to put an end to muzhik Russia, i.e., to feudal Russia, and to build up a Russia of free tillers of the soil, a democratic bourgeois Russia.

Why is the struggle for a republic a natural condition

for the attainment of freedom in Russia? Because experience, the great and unforgettable experience of one of the greatest decades in the history of Russia—the first decade of the twentieth century—has shown clearly, conclusively, and incontestably that our monarchy is *incompatible* with even the most elementary guarantees of political freedom. The result of Russia's historical development and centuries of tsardom is that at the beginning of the twentieth century there is no other monarchy in Russia, *nor can there be any other*, than *a Black-Hundred and pogrom-making monarchy*. With social conditions and class relations what they are, all the Russian monarchy can do is to organise gangs of murderers to shoot our liberal and democratic deputies from behind, or set fire to buildings in which meetings are held by democrats. The only answer the Russian monarchy can give to the demonstrations of the people demanding freedom is to let loose gangs of men who seize hold of Jewish children by their legs and smash their heads against stones, who rape Jewish and Georgian women and rip open the bellies of old men.

The liberal innocents prattle about the example of a constitutional monarchy like that of England. But if in a civilised country like England, a country which has never known anything like the Mongolian yoke or the tyranny of a bureaucracy, or a military clique riding roughshod over it, if it was necessary in that country to chop off the head of one crowned robber in order to impress upon the kings that they must be "constitutional" monarchs, in a country like Russia we should have to chop off the heads of at least a hundred Romanovs in order to wean their successors from the habit of organising Black-Hundred murders and anti-Jewish pogroms.

If Social-Democracy has learned anything at all from the first Russian revolution, it must insist that in all our speeches and leaflets we discard the slogan "Down with the autocracy", which has proved to be vague and worthless, and that we advance *only* the slogan: "Down with the tsarist *monarchy*, long live a republic".

And let no one try to tell us that the slogan calling for a republic does not apply to the present stage of the political development of the workers and peasants. About ten or twelve years ago there were not only some Narodniks who would not dare even to think of the slogan, "Down with the autocracy", but even certain Social-Democrats, the so-called Economists, opposed that slogan as being inopportune. Yet by 1903-04 the slogan, "Down with the autocracy", had become a "household word"! There cannot be even a shadow of doubt that systematic and persistent republican propaganda is now bound to find very fertile soil in Russia; for there can be no doubt that the broadest masses, particularly the peasant masses, are thinking grim, profound thoughts about the meaning of the dispersal of two Dumas and the connection between the tsarist government and the landowner-ridden Third Duma, between the tsarist government and the ruin of the countryside by the Markovs. Nobody today can tell how quickly the seed of republican propaganda will sprout—but that is beside the point; the main thing is that the sowing should be done properly, really democratically.

Since we are discussing the question of the slogans for the forthcoming elections to the Fourth Duma and those for all our work outside the Duma, we cannot refrain from mentioning a very important and very incorrect speech made by the Social-Democrat Kuznetsov in the Third Duma. On October 17, 1911, the sixth anniversary of the first victory of the Russian revolution, Kuznetsov spoke in the debate on the workers' Insurance Bill. It must be said in fairness to him, that, in general, he spoke very well. He vigorously championed the interests of the proletariat and made no bones about telling the truth directly, not only to the majority of the reactionary Duma, but to the Cadets as well. But, while fully granting this service rendered by Kuznetsov, we must likewise make no bones about pointing out the mistake he committed.

"I think," said Kuznetsov, "that the workers who have followed attentively the general debate on these questions, as well as the debate on individual clauses of the Bill under discussion, will come to the conclusion that their immediate slogan at present must be: 'Down with the June Third Duma, long live universal suffrage!' Why? Because, I say, the interests of the working class can be properly taken care of only if and when that class will, through universal suffrage, send into the legislative body a sufficient number of its deputies; they alone will be able to provide a proper solution to the problem of insurance for the working class."

It was here that Kuznetsov came a cropper in a way he probably never suspected, but which we foretold long ago — he came a cropper because the mistakes of the liquidators coincide with those of the otzovists.

While launching, from the rostrum of the Duma, a slogan inspired by the liquidationist magazines *Nasha Zarya* and *Dyelo Zhizni*, Kuznetsov did not notice that the first (and most essential) part of this slogan ("Down with the Third Duma") *fully* reproduces the slogan which the otzovists openly advanced three years ago, and which since then only *Vperyod*, that is to say, the cowardly otzovists, have defended stealthily and covertly.

Three years ago *Proletary*, No. 38, of November 1 (14), 1908, wrote the following in regard to this slogan advanced at the time by the otzovists:

"Under what conditions could a slogan like 'down with the Duma' acquire meaning? Let us assume that we are faced with a liberal, reform-seeking, compromising Duma in a period of the sharpest revolutionary crisis, which had developed to the point of direct civil war. It is quite possible that at such a moment our slogan might be 'down with the Duma', i.e., down with peaceable negotiations with the tsar, down with the deceptive institution of 'peace', let's call for a direct attack. Now let us assume, on the contrary, that we are faced with an arch-reactionary Duma, elected under an obsolete electoral law, and the absence of any acutely revolutionary crisis in the country. In that case the slogan 'down with the Duma' might become the slogan of a struggle for electoral reform. We see nothing of either of these contingencies at the present time."[*]

The supplement to *Proletary*, No. 44 (of April 4 [17], 1909) printed the resolution of the St. Petersburg otzovists

---

[*] *Proletary* then went on to defend the slogan, "Down with the autocracy". This slogan, as we have already pointed out, must now give way to the slogan: "Down with the tsarist monarchy, long live a republic". (See present edition, Vol. 15, "The Assessment of the Present Situation".—*Ed.*)

which demanded outright that "*Widespread* agitation *should
be started* among the masses in favour of the slogan 'Down
with the Third Duma'". In the same issue *Proletary* came
out against this resolution and pointed out: "This slogan,
which for a time appealed to some anti-otzovist workers,
is *wrong*. It is either a Cadet slogan, calling for franchise
reform under the autocracy [it so happens that, although
this was written at the beginning of 1909, it is a perfectly
fitting argument against the way Kuznetsov presents the
question at the end of 1911!], or a repetition of words
learned by rote during the period when the liberal Dumas
were a screen for counter-revolutionary tsarism designed to
prevent the people from seeing clearly who their real
enemy was."*

Hence the nature of Kuznetsov's mistake is clear. His
generalised slogan is the Cadet slogan for an electoral reform, which is absolutely meaningless if all the other charms
of the Romanov monarchy—the Council of State, the omnipotence of bureaucrats, the Black-Hundred pogrom organisations of the tsar's clique, etc., are left intact. What
Kuznetsov should have said, assuming that the question
is approached in the same way as he approached it, and
assuming that nothing is changed in the general tone of
his speech, is approximately the following:

"The workers' Insurance Bill provides the very example
which again proves to the workers that neither the immediate interests of their class nor the rights and needs of the
people as a whole can be defended without such changes
as the introduction of universal suffrage, full freedom
of association, of the press, etc. Is it not obvious, however,
that it is useless to expect the realisation of such changes
so long as the present political system of Russia remains
intact, so long as any decisions of any Duma can be over-
ruled, and so long as even a single non-elective govern-
mental institution is left in the state?"

We know perfectly well that Social-Democrat deputies
succeeded—and that is to their credit—in making even
much plainer and clearer republican statements from the

---

* See present edition, Vol. 15, "A Caricature of Bolshevism".
—*Ed.*

rostrum of the Third Duma. The members of the Duma have an opportunity to conduct republican propaganda legally from the floor of the Duma, and it is their duty to avail themselves of this opportunity. Our example of how Kuznetsov's speech could be corrected is merely intended to illustrate how he could have avoided the mistake, while preserving the general tone of the speech, and pointing to and emphasising the tremendous importance of such unquestionably indispensable changes as the introduction of universal suffrage, freedom of association, etc.

Wherever a Social-Democrat makes a political speech, it is his duty always to speak of a republic. But one must know how to speak of a republic. One cannot speak about it in the same terms when addressing a meeting in a factory and one in a Cossack village, when speaking at a meeting of students or in a peasant cottage, when it is dealt with from the rostrum of the Third Duma or in the columns of a publication issued abroad. The art of any propagandist and agitator consists in his ability to find the best means of influencing any given audience, by presenting a definite truth in such a way as to make it most convincing, most easy to digest, most graphic, and most strongly impressive.

Never for a moment must we forget the main thing: a new democracy is awakening to a new life and a new struggle in Russia. It is the duty of class-conscious workers, the vanguard of the Russian revolution and leaders of the popular masses in the struggle for freedom, to explain the tasks of consistent democracy: a republic, the eight-hour day, and the confiscation of all landed estates.

Sotsial-Demokrat, No. 25.
December 8 (21), 1911

Published according to
the *Sotsial-Demokrat* text

AGENCY OF THE LIBERAL BOURGEOISIE

This issue was almost complete when we received *L'Avenir*, No. 9. We have called this paper a liberal salon. It appears that sometimes agents of the Russian liberal bourgeoisie take the floor in this salon in order to gain control over the revolutionaries. An agent of this kind wrote the leader in No. 9 *welcoming* the decision of the Cadets to form a bloc with the Octobrists! "We could wish," write the liberals with bombs, "that all Left parties, including the socialist and revolutionary parties, would express themselves *in the same spirit* and be guided by *similar principles.*"

Of course, why shouldn't the counter-revolutionary liberal want this to happen! Only it is necessary for the public to know what it is all about; when the leader in *L'Avenir* says "we socialists", "we revolutionaries", it must be read as meaning "we liberals".

We have just received the papers with the news that Voiloshnikov has been barred from fifteen sessions of the Duma.[152] The Cadets were *in favour of* his exclusion from *five* sessions! Long live the Cadet-Octobrist bloc—for the exclusion of democrats and Social-Democrats from ten sessions!!

Sotsial-Demokrat, No. 25,
December 8 (21), 1911

Published according to
the *Sotsial-Demokrat* text

THE CLIMAX OF THE PARTY CRISIS

Two years ago one could find statements in the Social-Democratic press about a "unity crisis" in the Party.* The disorganisation and disintegration of the period of counter-revolution caused new re-groupings and splits, a new intensification of the struggle abroad, and many who lacked faith or who were weak-nerved lost heart in face of the difficult situation within the Social-Democratic Labour Party. Now, with the formation of the Russian Organising Commission (R.O.C.),[153] we are obviously approaching, if not the end of the crisis, then at any rate a new and decisive turn for the better in the development of the Party. The moment is, therefore, opportune to attempt a general review of the past period of inner Party evolution and of the prospects for the immediate future.

After the revolution the R.S.D.L.P. consisted of three separate, autonomous, national, Social-Democratic organisations, and two factions that were Russian in the narrow sense of the word. The experience of the years 1905, 1906, and 1907, which were unprecedented for their wealth of events, demonstrated that these factions had deep roots in the trends governing the development of the proletariat, in its general way of life during this period of the bourgeois revolution. The counter-revolution again threw us from the heights to which we had already climbed, down into the valley. The proletariat had to re-group its ranks and gather its forces anew surrounded by Stolypin's gallows and the jeremiads of *Vekhi*.

The new situation gave rise to a new grouping of tendencies in the Social-Democratic Party. In both the new factions—under the severe pressure of the adverse times—a process of segregation commenced, the segregation of the

---

* See present edition, Vol. 16, "Notes of a Publicist. II".—*Ed.*

least stable Social-Democratic elements, of the various
bourgeois fellow-travellers of the proletariat. Two currents
strikingly expressed this *departure* from Social-Democracy
—liquidationism and otzovism. And it was these that inevitably gave rise to the tendency to closer relations between
the main cores of both the factions which had remained
true to Marxism. Such was the state of affairs which led
to the Plenary Meeting of January 1910—the source of
both positive and negative results, of the steps forward
and of the steps back in the subsequent development of
the Social-Democratic Party.

To this very day, many people have failed to understand
properly the undeniable ideological merit of the work performed by the Meeting, and the great "conciliationist"
mistake it committed. But unless this is understood it is
impossible to understand anything at all in the present
Party situation. We must therefore pause again and again
to explain the source of the present crisis.

The following quotation from an article by a conciliator, written just before the Plenary Meeting and published
immediately after it, may help to make this clearer than
long discussions or quotations from more direct and more
numerous "documents". One of the leaders of the conciliationism which dominated the Meeting—Comrade Ionov, a
Bundist—wrote the following in an article "Is Party Unity
Possible?", published in *Discussionny Listok*, No. 1 (March
19, 1910; on page 6 we read the editors' note: "the article
was written before the Plenary Meeting"):

"However harmful otzovism and liquidationism, as such, may be
to the Party, their beneficial effect on the factions seems to be beyond
doubt. Pathology recognises two kinds of abscess—harmful and harmless. The harmless type is a disease beneficial to the organism. As it
grows, it draws various injurious substances from the entire organism
and thus helps improve the health of that organism. I believe that a
similar role was played by liquidationism in respect of Menshevism
and by otzovism-ultimatumism in respect of Bolshevism."

Such is the assessment of the case made by a "conciliator" at the time of the Plenary Meeting; it describes *exactly*
the psychology and the ideas of the conciliationism that
triumphed there. In the above quotation the main idea
is correct, a thousand times correct; and just because it

is correct the Bolsheviks (who even before the Meeting had fully developed the struggle against both liquidationism and otzovism) *could not* break with the conciliators at the Meeting. They could not, because there was agreement on the main idea; it was only on the question of the form in which it should be applied that there were differences. The form will become subordinated to the content — thought the Bolsheviks, and they proved to be right, though this "adaptation of form to content" has cost the Party *two years*, which have been almost "wasted", owing to the mistake committed by the conciliators.

What was this mistake? It was that the conciliators recognised all and sundry tendencies on their mere promise to heal themselves, instead of recognising only those tendencies that were healing (and only insofar as they were healing) their "abscesses". The *Vperyod* and *Golos* groups and Trotsky all "signed" the resolution against otzovism and liquidationism—that is, they promised to "heal their abscesses"—and that was the end of it! The conciliators "believed" the promise and entangled the Party with *non-*Party groups that were, as they themselves admitted, "abscesses". From the point of view of practical politics this was infantile, while from a deeper point of view it lacked an ideological basis, was unprincipled and full of intrigue. Indeed, those who were seriously convinced that liquidationism and otzovism-ultimatumism were abscesses, must have realised that as the abscesses grew they were certain *to draw out* and drain injurious substances from the organism; and they would not contribute to the poisoning of the organism by attempts to drive inside the poisons gathered in the "abscesses".

The first year after the Plenary Meeting was a practical revelation of the ideological poverty of the conciliators. As a matter of fact, all Party work (healing "abscesses") during the whole of that year was done by the Bolsheviks and Plekhanov's group. Both *Sotsial-Demokrat* and *Rabochaya Gazeta* (after Trotsky had expelled the Central Committee's representative) prove that fact. Some of the generally known, legally issued publications of 1910[154] also bear out that fact. These are not words but facts proving joint work in the leading bodies of the Party.

During that year (1910), the *Golos* and *Vperyod* groups and Trotsky, all in fact, moved away from the Party precisely in the direction of liquidationism and otzovism-ultimatumism. The "harmless abscesses" behaved harmfully, since they did not drain away the "injurious substances" from the organism of the Party, but continued to contaminate that organism, keeping it in a diseased condition and rendering it incapable of doing Party work. This Party work (in literature, which was accessible to all) was conducted by the Bolsheviks and the Plekhanovites *in spite of* the "conciliatory" resolutions and the collegiums set up by the Plenary Meeting, not in conjunction with the *Golos* and *Vperyod* groups, but *against* them (because it was impossible to work in conjunction with the liquidators and otzovists-ultimatumists).

And what about the work in Russia? Not a single meeting of the Central Committee was held during the whole year! Why? Because the members of the Central Committee in Russia (conciliators who well deserved the kisses of *Golos Likvidatorov**) kept on "inviting" the liquidators for twelve, for fifteen months but never got them to "accept the invitation". At the Plenary Meeting, our good conciliators unfortunately did not provide for the institution of "escorts" to bring people to the Central Committee. As a result the Party found itself in the absurd and shameful position, predicted by the Bolsheviks at the Meeting when they fought the credulity and naïveté of the conciliators—work in Russia is at a standstill, the Party's hands are tied, while a disgusting stream of liberal and anarchistic attacks on the Party is pouring forth from the pages of *Nasha Zarya* and *Vperyod*. Mikhail, Roman, and Yuri, on the one hand, the otzovists and the "god-builders" on the other, are doing their utmost to *ruin* Social-Democratic work, while the conciliationist members of the Central Committee are "inviting" the liquidators and are "waiting" for them!

By their "application" of December 5, 1910, the Bolsheviks stated openly and formally that they cancelled the agreement with all the other factions. The violation of the

---

* *Voice of the Liquidators*, punning on *Golos Sotsial-Demokrata* (Voice of a Social-Democrat).—*Tr*

"peace" made at the Plenary Meeting, its violation by *Golos*, *Vperyod*, and Trotsky, had become a fully recognised fact.

About six months were spent (until June 1911) in attempts to convene a plenary meeting abroad, which under the agreement was to be convened within three months. The liquidators (*Golos*-ists—Bundists—Schwartz) likewise prevented the convening of this meeting. Thereupon the bloc of three groups—the Bolsheviks, the Poles, and the "conciliators"—made a final attempt to save the situation: to call a conference and to form a Russian Organising Commission. As before, the Bolsheviks were in a minority: from January 1910 to June 1911, the liquidators were predominant (in the Central Committee Bureau Abroad they were the *Golos*-ists—a Bundist—Schwartz; in Russia—those "conciliators" who had been continually "inviting" the liquidators): from June 1911 to November 1, 1911 (the time-limit fixed by the trustees),[155] the conciliators, who were joined by the Poles, were predominant.

This was the state of affairs: both money and the dispatch of agents were in the hands of Tyszka and Mark (the leader of the Paris conciliators)[156]; the only assurance the Bolsheviks received was agreement that they too would be sent on work. The differences arising out of the Plenary Meeting reduced themselves to the last point which it was impossible to evade: whether to work with all one's energy, without "waiting" for anyone, without "inviting" anyone (anyone who wishes and is able to work in a Social-Democratic fashion needs no invitations!), or whether to continue bargaining and haggling with Trotsky, *Vperyod*, etc. The Bolsheviks chose the first path, a fact which they had already openly and directly declared at the Paris Meeting of Central Committee members. Tyszka and Co. chose (and foisted on both the Technical Commission and the Organising Commission Abroad) the second path, which, as was shown in detail in the article of *Sotsial-Demokrat*, No. 24,* was objectively nothing but empty and miserable intrigue.

The result is now clear to all. By November 1, the *Russian Organising Commission* was formed. In reality, it was created by the Bolsheviks and by the pro-Party Mensheviks in

---

* See pp. 257-77 of this volume.—*Ed.*

Russia. "The alliance of the two strong factions" (strong in their ideological solidity and in their work of healing "abscesses"), which so enraged the weak-minded people at the Plenary Meeting and after it (see *Golos, Vperyod, Otkliki Bunda*,[157] *Pravda*, etc.), became a fact. In such model and outstanding Social-Democratic organisations as the Baku and the Kiev[158] organisations were in the Russia of 1910 and 1911, this alliance, to the great joy of the Bolsheviks, became almost complete fusion, a single indissoluble organism of pro-Party Social-Democrats.

After the test of two years' experience, the snivelling for the dissolution of "all" factions proved to be but a miserable phrase used by empty-headed people who had been fooled by the Potresovs and the otzovists. "The alliance of the two strong factions" performed its work, and in the above-mentioned model organisations it reached a stage where a complete merging into a single party could be effected. The waverings of the pro-Party Mensheviks abroad can no longer alter this accomplished fact.

The two years following the Plenary Meeting, which to many sceptics or dilettantes in Social-Democracy who do not wish to understand the devilish difficulty of the task, seem to be years of useless, hopeless, senseless squabbles, of disorganisation and ruin, were in reality years in which the Social-Democratic Party was led out of the marsh of liquidationist and otzovist waverings on to the high road. The year 1910 was a year of joint work by Bolsheviks and pro-Party Mensheviks in *all* the leading (both official and unofficial, legal and illegal) bodies of the Party; this was the first step of the "alliance of the two strong factions" towards ideological preparation, the gathering of the forces under a single banner, that of anti-liquidationism and anti-otzovism. The year 1911 has witnessed the second step — the creation of the Russian Organising Commission. The fact that a pro-Party Menshevik presided at its first meeting is significant: the second step, the creation of an actually functioning centre in Russia, has now been taken. The locomotive has been raised and placed on the rails.

For the first time following *four* years of ruin and disorganisation, a Social-Democratic centre has met together in Russia — in spite of incredible persecution by the police and the unheard-of intrigues of *Golos*, *Vperyod*, the conciliators, the Poles, and *tutti quanti*. For the first time a leaflet has appeared in Russia addressed to the Party by that centre.[159] For the first time the work of re-establishing the local underground organisations has systematically and thoroughly covered both capital cities, the Volga Region, the Urals, the Caucasus, Kiev, Ekaterinoslav, Rostov, Nikolayev. All this has taken place in about three months, from July to October 1911, for the Russian Organising Commission met only *after* all these places had been visited. Its first meeting took place *simultaneously* with the restoration of the St. Petersburg Party Committee and with a series of workers' meetings arranged by it, and with the passing of resolutions by the Moscow city district organisations in favour of the Party, etc.

Of course it would be unpardonable naïveté to indulge in light-hearted optimism; we are still confronted with enormous difficulties; police persecution has increased tenfold since the first leaflet by the Social-Democratic centre was published in Russia; one may anticipate long and hard months of work, new arrests and new interruptions. But the main thing has been accomplished. The banner has been raised, workers' circles all over Russia are being drawn to it, and no counter-revolutionary attack can possibly haul it down.

How did the conciliators abroad, and Tyszka and Leder, respond to this gigantic stride forward in the work in Russia? By a final flare-up of miserable intrigue. The "growth of the abscess", which was so prophetically foretold by Ionov on the eve of the Plenary Meeting, is unpleasant, no doubt. But anyone who does not understand that this unsightly process makes Social-Democracy *healthier* should not apply himself to revolutionary work! The Technical Commission and the Organising Commission Abroad refuse to submit to the Russian Organising Commission. The Bolsheviks, of course, turn their backs upon those intriguing abroad with contempt. Then vacillations set in. At the beginning of November, a report on the calling together of the Russian Organising Commission was delivered to the remnants of the

Organising Commission Abroad (two Poles and one concilia-tor). The report presented such a comprehensive survey of the work that the opponents of the Bolsheviks, the con-ciliators whom *Golos* praised, *were forced* to recognise the Russian Organising Commission. The Organising Commission Abroad resolved on November 13, 1911, "to be guided by the decisions of the Russian Organising Commission". Four-fifths of the money in possession of the Organising Commis-sion Abroad is transferred to the Russian Organising Com-mission, which indicates that the Poles and conciliators themselves are *not* able to cast a shadow of doubt on the seriousness of the whole undertaking.

Nevertheless, a few days later, both the Technical Com-mission and the Organising Commission Abroad again refused to submit to the Russian Organising Commission!! What is the meaning of this game?

The editors of the Central Organ are in possession of a document[160] which will be submitted to the conference and which reveals that Tyszka is agitating for non-participa-tion in the Russian Organising Commission and for non-participation in the conference.

Is it possible to imagine more vile intrigue than this? In the Technical Commission and in the Organising Commis-sion Abroad they undertook to help convene the conference and to form the Russian Organising Commission. They boast-ed that they would invite "all", but invited no one (though, being in the majority, they had the right to do so and to stipulate any conditions). They could find no one to do the work except the Bolsheviks and the pro-Party Mensheviks. They suffered utter defeat in the field they themselves had chosen. They sank so low as to attempt to "trip up" the Russian Organising Commission, to which, as the au-thorised body, they had voluntarily handed over four-fifths of their funds for convening the conference!

Yes, an abscess is an unpleasant affair, especially when it is in the process of growth. In No. 24 of the Central Organ it has already been shown why the theoreticians of an alli-ance of all and sundry groups abroad can only engage in intrigues. Now the Russian worker Social-Democrats will make their choice without any difficulty: whether to defend their Russian Organising Commission and their conference, or to allow Tyszka, Leder and Co. to sabotage their conference by intrigues. The intriguers have condemned themselves—that is a fact; Tyszka and Leder have already passed convicted into the history of the R.S.D.L.P., but they will never succeed in hindering the conference or in undermining the Russian Organising Commission.

What about the liquidators? For eighteen months, from January 1910 to June 1911, when they had a majority in the Central Committee Bureau Abroad and faithful "friends" in the persons of the conciliators in the Central Committee Bureau in Russia, they did nothing, absolutely nothing, to further the work in Russia! When they were in the majority—work was at a standstill. But when the Bolsheviks broke up the liquidationist Central Committee Bureau Abroad and proceeded to convene the conference, the liquidators began to bestir themselves. The form in which that "stir" expressed itself is very characteristic. The Bundists, who have always very faithfully served the liquidators, recently wanted to take advantage of the present "time of troubles" (among the Latvians, for instance, the issue of the struggle between the two tendencies—liquidationist and Party—has not yet been decided); they got hold of a Caucasian somewhere and the whole company went to the city of Z[161] to grab signatures for the resolutions drafted by Trotsky and Dan in Café Bubenberg (in Berne, August 1911). But they failed to find the leading Latvian organisation; they failed to get the signatures, and no document with the high-sounding heading "Organising Commission of the Three Strongest Organisations" was prepared. Such are the facts.*

Let the Russian workers learn about the way the Bundists are trying to break up the Russian Organising Commission in Russia! Just think: at a time when the comrades preparing the conference were touring the Urals, the Volga

---

* In addition to the never-lose-heart Bundists, the *Vperyod* people also galloped off to snatch resolutions. From that tiny group—by no means otzovist, heaven forbid!—there galloped off a well-known otzovist[162]; he "galloped" through Kiev, Moscow, Nizhni-Novgorod, "reconciled himself" with the conciliators, and went away without achieving anything anywhere. It is said that the *Vperyod* group blames the unsatisfactory god devised by Lunacharsky for its failure and that it passed a unanimous resolution to devise a better god.

Region, St. Petersburg, Moscow, Kiev, Ekaterinoslav, Rostov, Tiflis, Baku—the Bundists "got hold of" a "Caucasian" (probably one of those committee men who were in possession of the "seal" of the Regional Caucasian Committee and who, in December 1908, sent Dan and Axelrod as representatives to the conference of the R.S.D.L.P.) and took a journey in order to "grab signatures" from the Latvians. Not much more was needed to cause this gang of intriguers, who serve the liquidators and who are absolutely alien to all work in Russia, to come out as the "Organising Commission" of "three organisations" (including the two "strongest" possessors of the seal!). Or perhaps the Bundist gentlemen and the Caucasian will please inform the Party what Russian organisations they visited, when exactly they made these journeys, where they restored the work, and where they made reports? Do try and tell us, dear fellows!

And the past masters of diplomacy abroad with the serious mien of experts, pass judgement: "one must not isolate oneself", "it is necessary to talk things over with the Bund and with the Regional Caucasian Committee".

What comedians!

Let those who are wavering now, who regret the "isolation" of the Bolsheviks, learn and ponder over the significance of the history of the Party during these past two years. *This* isolation makes us feel better than we have ever felt before now that we have cut off the bunch of intriguing nonentities abroad, and have helped to consolidate the ranks of the Russian worker Social-Democrats of St. Petersburg, Moscow, the Urals, the Volga Region, the Caucasus, and the South!

Anyone who complains about isolation understands absolutely nothing of the great ideological work accomplished by the Plenary Meeting or of its conciliationist mistake. For a year and a half after the Meeting there was a semblance of unity abroad and complete stagnation of Social-Democratic work in Russia. For the first time in four or six months of 1911 the seemingly extreme isolation of the Bolsheviks served as an impetus to Social-Democratic work in Russia, and restored the Social-Democratic centre in Russia.

Those who have not yet understood the ideological danger of such "abscesses" as liquidationism and otzovism will now understand it from the history of the impotent squabbles and miserable intrigue to which the wretched *Golos* and *Vperyod* groups have sunk, dragging with them, in their fall, all those who attempted to defend them.

To work, comrades, Party Social-Democrats! Shake off the last remnants of your contacts with non-Social-Democratic tendencies and the groups that foster them in spite of the decisions of the Party. Rally round the Russian Organising Commission, help it convene a conference and strengthen local work. The R.S.D.L.P. has gone through a serious illness; the crisis is passing.

Long live the united, illegal, revolutionary Russian Social-Democratic Labour Party!

Sotsial-Demokrat, No. 25,
December *8* (21). 1911

Published according to
the *Sotsial-Demokrat* text

FROM THE CAMP OF THE STOLYPIN "LABOUR" PARTY

An outstanding event in this camp is the article by N. R-kov published in No. 9-10 of the liquidationist *Nasha Zarya*. This article is a real *Credo* or manifesto of a liberal labour party. From the very beginning, from his assessment of the revolution and the role of all the classes involved, and proceeding with remarkable consistency to the end, to the scheme for a legal workers' (?) party, in all his arguments, R-kov substitutes liberalism for Marxism.

What is the real task facing Russia? The complete replacement of semi-feudal economy by "civilised capitalism".

That is not Marxism, however, but Struveism or liberalism, for a Marxist distinguishes between classes with their Octobrist, Cadet, Trudovik, or proletarian ideas as to what constitutes "civilised" capitalism.

What is the crux of the problem of appraising of the revolution? R-kov condemns the whining and renegacy of those who shout that the revolution has "failed" and against them puts forward ... the great professorial maxim that during periods of "reaction" too, new social forces are maturing. It is evident that R-kov's answer disguises the *essence* of the matter to the advantage of the counter-revolutionary liberals who fully acknowledge the maxim newly-discovered by R-kov. The essence of the question is: which of the classes that took part in the revolution showed that they were capable of waging a direct, mass revolutionary struggle, which classes betrayed the revolution and directly or indirectly joined the counter-revolution? R-kov concealed this essence and was thus able to ignore the difference between revolutionary democracy and the liberal-monarchist "progressive" opposition.

As regards the role of the landlord class, R-kov managed without further ado to say something absurd. Not so long ago, he says, the representatives of that class "were" real serf-owners; now "a small handful are still grouped around Messrs. Purishkevich and Markov the Second, and are helplessly [!] spluttering the venom of despair". The majority of the landed nobility, he goes on to say, "are gradually and steadily being converted into an agricultural bourgeoisie".

In actual fact, as everybody knows, the Markovs and the Purishkeviches have *full* power in the Duma, still more in the Council of State, and even more in the tsar's Black-Hundred clique, and yet more in the administration of Russia. It is precisely "their power and their revenue" (resolution of the December 1908 conference) that are guaranteed by a step in *this kind* of transformation of tsarism into a bourgeois monarchy. The conversion of serf economy into bourgeois economy by no means does away immediately with the political power of these Black-Hundred-type landowners. This is obvious from the viewpoint of elementary Marxism, and it also follows from the experience, say, of Prussia after sixty years of "conversion" (since 1848). According to R-kov there is no absolutism and no monarchy in Russia! R-kov applies a liberal school method: the benign elimination (on paper) of social extremes serves as "proof" that a "compromise is inevitable".

Present-day agrarian policy, according to R-kov, indicates an "imminent and inevitable [!] compromise"—between whom?—"between the different groups of the bourgeoisie". But, we ask our "Marxist", what social force will compel the Purishkeviches, who wield all the power, to agree to a compromise? R-kov does not answer this question. But since he goes on to refer to the process of the consolidation of the big commercial and industrial bourgeoisie, and "the impending domination of the moderately progressive" bourgeoisie, there is only one conclusion to be drawn— R-kov expects that the moderately progressive bourgeoisie will peacefully take over power from the Purishkeviches and Romanovs.

Incredible as this is, it is a fact. It is precisely this most puerile of liberal utopias that forms the basis of R-kov's conception, although he boasts that "there is not a grain of utopia" in what he says. There is no actual difference between N. R-kov and the extreme liquidators, all of whom—from Larin to Cherevanin, Dan, and Martov—set forth, in slightly different forms and phrases, *the very same fundamental idea* of a peaceful assumption of power by the bourgeoisie (with, at most, *pressure* exerted from "below").

But in real life not in a liberal utopia, we see the domination of Purishkevichism moderated by the grumbling of the Guchkovs and Milyukovs. The "moderately progressive" Octobrists and Cadets, far from undermining this domination, are perpetuating it. The contradiction between this domination and the unquestionably advancing bourgeois development of Russia is becoming ever sharper (and not weaker, as the theorists of "inevitable compromise" think). The motive force in the solution of this contradiction can only be the masses, i.e., the proletariat with the peasantry following its lead.

This former Bolshevik, who has now become a liquidator, dismisses these masses so readily, that it is as if the Stolypin gallows and the torrent of filth let loose by *Vekhi* had eliminated them, not only from the arena of open politics, not only from the pages of liberal publications, but also from real life. The peasantry, says our liberal in his "analysis", are weak at the elections; and as for the working class, he provisionally leaves it "out of consideration"!!

R-kov undertook to prove that a revolution ("upheaval") in Russia, though possible, is not essential. Once the working class and the peasantry are "left out of consideration", even if only provisionally, if only "for the time being", if only because of their "weakness at the elections", a revolution is not, of course, possible, to say nothing of its being essential. But liberal benevolence cannot conjure away either the unrestricted power of Purishkevich and Romanov, or the revolutionary resistance which is growing stronger both among the maturing proletariat and the starving and tormented peasantry. The trouble with R-kov is that he has abandoned the Marxist *line*, the line followed by revolutionary Social-Democrats, who always, under all circumstances and in every possible form, in speeches at mass meetings, from the rostrum of the Third Duma, at meetings of Soviets of Workers' Deputies, or in the most peaceable and legally functioning workers' associations, insist that this resistance must be given support, that it must be strengthened, developed, and properly directed toward the achievement of complete victory. In all his arguments N. R-kov has substituted for this line that of the liberal who refuses to see the force that has been driven underground, who refuses to see anything but the Purishkeviches who are being "converted" into "civilised Junkers", or the "moderately progressive" Milyukovs.

That is the specific kind of blindness which is characteristic of the whole of *Nasha Zarya* and of the whole Stolypin labour party. Closely connected with this conception—one due to the blindness caused by liberal blinkers— is the extraordinarily strong emphasis on the legalisation of the workers' party. Since "a compromise is inevitable", there is no point in fighting the inevitable, and all that remains for the working class to do is to follow the example of the other classes of the fully established bourgeois system and feather for itself a humble little philistine nest in a nook of this system. That is the real meaning of the legalists' propaganda, no matter how much Martov, given that role by the Potresovs, Yuri Chatskys, Larins, Dans, and others, may hide it behind "revolutionary" phraseology.

This *real* meaning of a legal "association for the protection of the interests of the working class" is very clearly revealed in R-kov's article. It is obvious that the "powers that be" will never permit such an association, even if it is dominated by the Prokopoviches. It is obvious that they will never agree to let it be "put into effect". Only blind liberals can fail to see this. But an *association* of intellectuals who, under the guise of socialism, are spreading *liberal* propaganda among the working masses is something that has already been put into effect. This "association" consists of the contributors to *Nasha Zarya* and *Dyelo Zhizni*. And it is their "banner", the ideological banner of liberalism, that R-kov "unfurls" when he asserts that, unless there exists an open organisation the struggle will inevitably (!) assume an anarchist character; that the old slogans have become dead letters; that tactics must not be reduced to a "scuffle"; that the new "association" harbours *"no thought* [!] of the need for a forcible revolution", etc. This liberal, renegade propaganda of intellectuals is a reality, whereas the talk of an open working-class association is mere eyewash. An association for the liberal protection of the interests of the working class as understood by the liberals is a reality; *Nasha Zarya* is this "association", and the "open and broad political organisation" of workers in present-day Russia, is an innocuous, empty, misleading liberal dream.

It is a useful thing to organise legally functioning trade unions, as long as we are aware that under present conditions they cannot become either broad, or "political", or stable. But it is an empty and harmful occupation to preach liberal concepts of a political workers' association that *exclude* any idea of the use of force.

In conclusion, here are two amusing bits. The first: "If anyone," writes R-kov, "blinded by reactionary frenzy, took it into his head to accuse the members of such an association of striving for violent revolution, the whole burden of such an absurd, unfounded, and juridically flimsy accusation would fall upon the head of the accuser." We can just visualise the picture of the burden of juridically flimsy accusations falling upon the heads of Shcheglovitov and Co. — and it is not Rodichev but N. R-kov who crushes them under that "burden".

The second: "The workers," writes R-kov, "must assume the task of political hegemony in the struggle for a democratic system." R-kov is in favour of hegemony after he has deprived it of its entire *meaning*. "Workers," says R-kov in effect, "you must not fight against the 'inevitable' compromise, but you must call yourselves leaders." But the very thing a leader has to do is to expose the fiction about a compromise being "inevitable" and to work to organise proletarian and proletarian-peasant resistance to undemocratic bourgeois compromises.

N. R-kov will be as useful in the struggle against liquidationism, as Y. Larin was in the struggle against the false idea of a labour congress. N. R-kov and Y. Larin have had the courage to appear ... naked. R-kov is an honest liquidator. By his fearlessness he will compel people *to think* about the ideological roots of liquidationism. He will provide ever more corroboration of the correctness of the December 1908 resolutions of the R.S.D.L.P., for he regularly poses (and invariably gives wrong answers to) the very problems which those resolutions analysed and answered correctly. R-kov will help the workers to obtain a particularly clear idea of the wretchedness of those liquidationist diplomats who, like the editors of *Nasha Zarya* (or of *Golos*), twist and turn, piling up reservation upon reservation, and disclaiming responsibility for "certain passages" in R-kov's article, or for the "detailed exposition" of his plan. As if it were a question of separate passages, and not of a uniform, integral, and consistent line —the line of a liberal labour policy!

Sotsial-Demokrat. No. 25,
    December 8 (21), 1911

Published according to
the *Sotsial-Demokrat* text

TROTSKY'S DIPLOMACY
AND A CERTAIN PARTY PLATFORM

Trotsky's *Pravda*, No. 22, which appeared recently after a long interval in which no issue was published, vividly illustrates the decay of the petty groups abroad that attempted to base their existence on their diplomatic game with the non-Social-Democratic trends of liquidationism and otzovism.

The publication appeared on November 29, New Style, nearly a month after the announcement issued by the Russian Organising Commission. *Trotsky makes no mention of this whatsoever*!

As far as Trotsky is concerned, the Russian Organising Commission does not exist. Trotsky calls himself a Party man on the strength of the fact that to him the Russian Party centre, formed by the overwhelming majority of the Social-Democratic organisations in Russia, means nothing. Or, perhaps it is the other way round, comrades? Perhaps Trotsky, with his small group abroad, is just nothing so far as the Social-Democratic organisations in Russia are concerned?

Trotsky uses the boldest type for his assertions—it's a wonder he never tires of making solemn vows—that his paper is "not a factional but a Party organ". You need only pay some little attention to the contents of No. 22 to see at once the obvious mechanics of the game with the *non*-Party *Vperyod* and liquidator factions.

Take the report from St. Petersburg, signed S. V., which advertises the *Vperyod* group. S. V. reproaches Trotsky for not having published the resolution of the St. Petersburg *Vperyod* group against the petition campaign,[163] sent to him some time ago. Trotsky, accused by the *Vperyod* group of "narrow factionalism" (what black ingratitude!), twists and turns, pleading lack of funds and the fact that his paper does not appear often enough. The game is too obvious: We will do you a good turn, and you do the same for us—we (Trotsky) will keep silent about the fight of the Party people against the otzovists and, again, we (Trotsky) will help advertise *Vperyod*, and you (S. V.) give in to the liquidators on the question of the "petition campaign". Diplomatic defence of both non-Party factions—isn't that the sign of a true Party spirit?

Or take the florid editorial grandly entitled "Onward!". "Class-conscious workers!" we read in that editorial. "At the present moment there is no more important [*sic*!] and comprehensive slogan [the poor fellow has let his tongue run away with him] than freedom of association, assembly, and strikes." "The Social-Democrats," we read further, "call upon the proletariat to fight for a republic. But if the fight for a republic is not to be merely the bare [!!] slogan of a select few, it is necessary that you class-conscious workers should teach the masses to realise from experience the need for freedom of association and to fight for this most vital class demand."

This revolutionary phraseology merely serves to disguise and justify the falsity of liquidationism, and thereby to befuddle the minds of the workers. Why is the slogan calling for a republic the *bare* slogan of a *select few* when the existence of a republic means that it would be impossible to disperse the Duma, means freedom of association and of the press, means freeing the peasants from violence and plunder by the Markovs, Romanovs, and Purishkeviches? Is it not clear that it is just the opposite—that it is the slogan of "freedom of association" as a "comprehensive" slogan, used *independently* of the slogan of a republic, that is "bare" and senseless?

It is absurd to demand "freedom of association" from the tsarist monarchy, without explaining to the masses that such freedom cannot be expected from tsarism and that to obtain it there must be a republic. The introduction of bills into the Duma on freedom of association, and questions and speeches on such subjects, ought to serve us Social-Democrats as an occasion and material for our agitation in favour of a republic.

The "class-conscious workers should teach the masses to realise from experience the need for freedom of association"! This is the old song of old Russian opportunism, the opportunism long ago preached to death by the Economists. The *experience* of the masses is that the ministers are closing down their unions, that the governors and police officers are daily perpetrating deeds of violence against them—this is real *experience of the masses.* But extolling the slogan of "freedom of association" as opposed to a republic is merely phrase-mongering by an opportunist intellectual who is alien to the masses. It is the phrase-mongering of an intellectual who imagines that the "experience" of a "petition" (with 1,300 signatures) or a pigeon-holed bill is something that educates the "masses". Actually, it is not paper experience, but something different, the experience of life that educates them; what enlightens them is the agitation of the class-conscious workers for a republic —which is the sole comprehensive slogan from the standpoint of political democracy.

Trotsky knows perfectly well that liquidators writing in legal publications *combine* this very slogan of "freedom of association" with the slogan "down with the underground party, down with the struggle for a republic". Trotsky's particular task is to conceal liquidationism by throwing dust in the eyes of the workers.

It is impossible to argue with Trotsky on the merits of the issue, because Trotsky holds no views whatever. We can and should argue with confirmed liquidators and otzovists; but it is no use arguing with a man whose game is to hide the errors of both these trends; in his case the thing to do is to expose him as a diplomat of the smallest calibre.

It is necessary, however, to argue with the authors of the theses of the platform that got into No. 22 of *Pravda.* The error they are committing is due either to their not being familiar with the December 1908 resolutions of the R.S.D.L.P., or to their not having rid themselves completely of some liquidationist and *Vperyod* waverings of thought.

The first thesis says that the regime established on June 3, 1907, represents, "in fact, the unrestricted domination of the feudal-type landed nobility". It goes on to point out that they are "disguising the autocratic and bureaucratic nature of their domination with the pseudo-constitutional mask of a State Duma that actually possesses no rights".

If the landowners' Duma "actually possesses no rights" —and that is true—how, then, can the domination of the landowners be "unrestricted"?

The authors forget that the class character of the tsarist monarchy in no way militates against the vast independence and self-sufficiency of the tsarist authorities and of the "bureaucracy", from Nicholas II down to the last police officer. The same mistake, that of forgetting the autocracy and the monarchy, of reducing it *directly* to the "pure" domination of the upper classes, was committed by the ot-zovists in 1908-09 (see *Proletary*, supplement to No. 44),[164] by Larin in 1910, it is now being committed by some individual writers (for instance, M. Alexandrov[165]), and also by N. R-kov who has gone over to the liquidators.

The analysis of the domination of the feudal landowners assisted by the bourgeoisie, given in the December (1908) resolutions, strikes at the roots of this error.

The second thesis refers to the minimum programme of the R.S.D.L.P., and in this connection "a particularly prominent place" is given to many demands, such as the demand for freedom of association and for the confiscation of the landed estates, but no mention is made of a republic. In our opinion, this is wrong. While we fully admit that it is absolutely necessary to agitate for freedom of association, we consider that the slogan calling for a republic must be given the greatest prominence.

The third thesis: "The necessity of new revolutionary action on the part of the masses", without which our demands cannot be achieved.

This last statement is absolutely true, but it is only half the truth. Marxists cannot confine themselves to a reference to the "necessity" of new action on the part of the masses; they must first show the causes that give rise (if they do give rise) to a new revolutionary crisis. Unless there is such a crisis, "action"—which, indeed, is always "necessary"—is impossible.

The authors are actuated by the best of revolutionary

intentions, but there is some defect in their method of thought. The December (1908) resolutions deduce the "necessity" of new action by a process of reasoning that is not so simple, but that is, however, more correct.

The fourth thesis: "The possibility of such new revolutionary action on the part of the masses in the more or less immediate future, and relentless criticism ... of the counter-revolutionary role of the bourgeoisie", etc.

Criticism is always necessary, *irrespective* of "the possibility of action", even at a time when action on the part of the masses is definitely impossible. To tie up the possibility of action with criticism means confusing the Marxist *line*, which is *always* obligatory, with *one* of the forms of the struggle (a particularly high form). That is the first error. And the second error may be described by the saying: "Don't halloo until you are out of the wood". It is pointless to talk of the possibility of action, this must be proved by deeds. In a platform it is sufficient to note that a revival has set in, and to emphasise the importance of carrying on agitation and paving the way for the action of the masses. Events will show whether the action of the masses will become a fact in the near or not so distant future.

The fifth thesis is splendid, for it stresses the immense importance of the State Duma as a platform from which to carry on agitation.

We do not know who the authors of the platform are. But if (judging by certain indications) they are Russian *Vperyod*-ists they should be warmly congratulated on having got rid of one error of the *Vperyod* group. They are *Vperyod*-ists with the conscience of Party people, for they give a straightforward and clear answer to one of the "vexed" questions. The *Vperyod* group, however, is deceiving the Party in the most unscrupulous manner; for it is defending and screening otzovism, and to this day, December 1911, it has not given a straight answer to the question of participation in the Fourth Duma. To treat such a group as Social-Democratic is a mockery of Social-Democracy.

Sotsial-Demokrat, No, 25, December 8 (21), 1911

Published according to the *Sotsial-Demokrat* text

THE RESULTS OF THE ARBITRATION OF THE "TRUSTEES"

At the Plenary Meeting of the Central Committee in January 1910, the representatives of the Bolshevik faction (recognised as the representatives of that faction by all participants in the Meeting) concluded, as is well known, an agreement with all the other factions of our Party. This agreement was published in No. 11 of the Central Organ, and its purport was that the Bolsheviks agreed to dissolve their faction and transfer its property to the Central Committee, *on condition* that all the other factions did the same and followed the Party line, that is to say, an anti-liquidationist and anti-otzovist line. The agreement, which was endorsed by the Central Committee, definitely provided that in the event of violation of these conditions the funds were to be returned to the Bolsheviks (see the resolution, published in No. 11 of the Central Organ).

The generally known facts of the violation of that agreement by the other factions compelled the Bolsheviks, a year ago, on December 5, 1910, to file an application, i.e., to declare that the agreement was null and void, and to demand the return of their funds.

This demand had to be submitted to the "trustees" — Kautsky, Mehring, and Zetkin—for arbitration. The court of arbitration ruled that, provisionally, up to November 1, 1911, part of the funds were to be turned over for accountable expenditure to the Technical Commission and the Organising Commission Abroad composed of representatives of the Bolsheviks, conciliators, and the Poles.

In October 1911, two of the arbitrators, Mehring and Kautsky, resigned their posts. After this the third arbitrator had not the right to exercise authority alone, and after some hesitation also resigned.

Thus it turned out that after November 2, 1911, the Bolshevik faction, which had, on December 5, 1910, annulled the agreement with the other factions, was no longer bound by any contractual relations with the former trustees. Therefore it took possession of its printing-plant and is now taking possession of its other property.

Naturally, having freed itself from the "ties" with the liquidationist, otzovist, and simply intrigue-mongering groups abroad, the Bolshevik faction will devote all its energy, as has already been proved by the efforts of its members in forming the Russian Organising Commission, to rallying all the pro-Party elements around the Russian Organising Commission and the general Party conference which it is convening.

The representatives of the Bolshevik faction, who concluded the agreement at the Plenary Meeting in January 1910.[166]

P. S. The above statement had already been submitted to the Editorial Board of the Central Organ, when we read the leaflet of the so-called Central Committee Bureau Abroad containing a letter from two of the former arbitrators, dated November 18, 1911. Whom are Igorev and Lieber trying to deceive by posing as the Central Committee Bureau Abroad, when the Letts and *even* Tyszka have resigned from it? Why are they silent about this resignation? Why do they say nothing about the fact that by November 18, two and a half weeks had elapsed since the court of arbitration had ceased to exist, and that therefore the letter of November 18, 1911, has no significance whatever, nor can it have any? Or, are we, perhaps, to conclude that *prior* to November 1, 1911, Igorev and Martov did *not* recognise the court of arbitration? Then say so, gentlemen, and prove it! Perhaps you recognise the court of arbitration *after* November 1, 1911? Prior to November 1, 1911, *you stood condemned* by the universally recognised court of arbitration; for, despite all your entreaties, demands, and "protests", it refused to give a centime to either you or Trotsky. Now the gentlemen who were condemned by the legitimate, universally recognised court of arbitration, are trying to shelter behind the private opinion of former members of the court which is no longer binding on anyone. Since the *First* of November, 1911, no court of arbitration has existed, and in this respect we have all gone back to the situation which existed prior to the Plenary Meeting. If the former trustees now attempted to hold up the Bolshevik funds, that would be an unlawful act.

But the point is that all that Igorev and Lieber are after is to create a "sensation"; they are afraid, however, to set forth the history of the arbitration on the basis of exact documents. Unless you cheat you won't sell—that is their motto.

Sotsial-Demokrat, No. 25,
   December 8 (21), 1911

                              Published according to
                              the *Sotsial-Demokrat* text

THE CAMPAIGN FOR THE ELECTIONS TO THE FOURTH DUMA

1. FUNDAMENTAL QUESTIONS OF PRINCIPLE

The Cadet Party, which, of all the so-called opposition parties is most favourably situated because of its legal status, has just taken an extremely important step by defining its policy in the election campaign. To judge by the evidence of sources sympathising with the Cadets and most accessible to us, its policy has been defined as follows:

1. The Cadets will put up their own candidates wherever they are sure of being elected.

2. Wherever a Cadet candidate cannot expect an absolute majority, the Cadets will support the *progressive* candidate likely to obtain the highest vote, irrespective of his party affiliation.

3. Where an opposition candidate has no chance at all, and there is the danger of the election of a Black-Hundred candidate, support may be given to the Octobrist candidate but only on condition that he is a genuine constitutionalist which, strange as it may seem, they occasionally are.

4. The Cadets will not enter into any election agreements with the Right Octobrists or with the Nationalists and monarchists. In general, while not forgetting the interests of the Party, they will not sacrifice to the latter the supreme interests of the opposition, in the broad sense of the term.

Such is Cadet policy. Working-class democracy must examine this policy with the greatest attention, analysing its true class substance and its real meaning, which are veiled in the usual conventional phrases. These phrases about "the higher interests of the opposition", etc., are the first to strike the eye when we read the Cadet resolutions. The fact of the matter, however, is that the policy of the Cadets has been fully and finally defined as the policy of a *Cadet-Octobrist* bloc. This fact must be understood, it is the grain that must be separated from the chaff of official liberal catchwords.

(1) Not a word about a bloc with the Lefts, with the democrats. (2) Only blocs with Right Octobrists are forbidden—with the Gololobov group,[167] who are an insignificant minority among the Octobrists. (3) In practice the phrase about "the higher interests of the opposition in the broad sense of the term" can *only* mean one thing: that as a general rule blocs with the Octobrists are actually permitted (and recommended!).

These three conclusions regarding the *real* policy of the Constitutional-Democratic Party must be firmly borne in mind.

What do they mean? They mean that the "Left Centre" of the bourgeois liberals has defined its policy as that of a bloc with the Right Centre of the bourgeois so-called liberals—speaking openly of its hostility to the Black Hundreds, and expressing its hostility to the Lefts, to the forces of democracy, by omitting any reference to any blocs with the Trudoviks, non-party Lefts, and workers' candidates.

What we said in *Zvezda*, No. 28, in the article "Two Centres", has been fully confirmed.*

There are three *basic* political forces in Russia, and, consequently, three political lines—the Black Hundreds (representing the class interests of the feudal landowners) and, alongside of and above them, the "bureaucracy"; then, the liberal-monarchist bourgeoisie, the Left (Cadet) and Right (Octobrist) "Centre"; finally, the bourgeois democrats (the Trudoviks, Narodniks, non-party Lefts) and proletarian democracy. That this, and only this is the case, is confirmed by the entire experience of the first decade of the twentieth century, which was an extremely important and eventful decade.

It goes without saying that all boundaries in nature and in society are dynamic; they are not static, but, to a certain

---

* See pp. 297-99 of this volume.—*Ed.*

extent, conditional and changing. Among the parties and groups standing *"on the boundary line"* of the main divisions, transitional forms and fluctuations are inevitable; but the substance of the matter, resulting from the relations of the class forces in Russia at the beginning of the twentieth century, is undoubtedly determined by none other than the indicated "triple" division. The lumping of the bourgeois liberals (headed by the Cadets) with the bourgeois democrats has caused considerable harm to the Russian liberation movement, and we must bend every effort to ensure that the experience of the great decade (1900-10) helps the democratic movement as a whole to become finally aware that it is a fatal mistake to lump things together in this fashion. Working-class democracy in our epoch is, therefore, faced by two inseparably connected tasks: first, to secure the independent political organisation of the class of wage-earners, independent of all bosses, big and little, even the most democratic, and pledging allegiance to the entire international movement of that class; and, second, to develop and strengthen the forces of Russian democracy (inevitably headed by the workers, just as the bourgeois liberals are inevitably headed by social elements of the Cadet type). The latter task cannot be fulfilled unless we persistently explain to the broadest masses the class roots and the political significance of the difference between bourgeois liberalism (the Cadets) and bourgeois democracy (the Trudoviks, etc.).

The liberal bourgeoisie does not want to and cannot dispense with the Markovs and Purishkeviches, whose domination it only strives to moderate. Bourgeois democracy and the workers can only strive, more or less consistently and consciously, to destroy all the economic and political foundations of that domination.

That, from the standpoint of working-class democracy, is the main content of the campaign in connection with the elections to the Fourth Duma. It is this content that must be primarily emphasised to counteract the Cadet policy of deliberately confusing all the cardinal questions of principle by means of stock phrases about "progressism" and "opposition".

The Cadet-Octobrist bloc is nothing new. It was foreseen by Marxists long ago. They pointed out the inherent class affinity of the two component parts of this bloc as far back as 1905-07. Two possible majorities became defined as soon as the Third Duma was convened, and by the end of 1907 the Marxists had made this conclusion the cornerstone of their policy. The five years' existence of the Third Duma has confirmed this conclusion. In general outline, the composition of the Third Duma is as follows:*

Rights	160 ⎫	⎫ 284 — First majority
Octobrists	124 ⎭	
Liberals	127	⎭ 251 — Second majority
Democrats	29	

Total . . . 440

Throughout its existence the Third Duma relied on these two majorities, which represent the necessary component parts of the entire system inaugurated on June 3, 1907. The first majority signifies that the "old" is to be preserved in power entirely intact; the second majority signifies "a step toward" a bourgeois monarchy. The first is needed by the June Third system to preserve the "power and revenue" of the Markovs, Purishkeviches and Co.; the second is needed to moderate this domination and to advance in the bourgeois manner (according to the formula: one step forward, two steps back). Experience has now clearly shown that this kind of advance is equal to stagnation, and that no progress is being made in "moderating" Purishkevichism.

Quite a number of votes taken in the Third Duma were decided by the "second majority". Recently, *Rech* definitely admitted this, stating that "a number of votes" at the beginning of the last session "actually reproduce the domination of a Left Centre" (read of the Cadet-Octobrist bloc) in the Duma. Such votes are possible only because the second majority *too*, like the first, is a bulwark of counter-revolution; to illustrate this we need only recall *Vekhi*, or Karaulov's pious speeches, or the "London" slogans.

---

* The calculation is based on the figures supplied by the official *Handbook* for 1910 (Issue II). The Rights include: Rights proper—51, Nationalists—89, Right Octobrists—11, and 50 per cent of the independents—9. The liberals include: Progressists—39, Cadets—52, all the nationality groups—27, and 50 per cent of the independents —9. The democrats include 14 Trudoviks and 15 Social-Democrats.

Where are the results of these "victories" of the second majority? Where is the proof of the truly marvellous discovery of the Cadet Party that there are "genuine constitutionalists" among the Octobrists? Doesn't this discovery rather show how paltry is the Cadets' conception of "genuine constitutionalism"?

The first and fundamental question of the election campaign is its political content, the ideological line it expresses. The resolution of the Cadet Party proves once more its anti-democratic nature, for the content of the Cadets' election campaign reduces itself to further lowering the concept "constitutionalism" in the eyes of the masses. Instil into the minds of the people the idea that there are genuine constitutionalists among the "Left" Octobrists; that is what the Cadet Party is bent on, that is the meaning of its election policy.

The task of the democrats is a different one; not to belittle the idea of constitutionalism, but to explain that as long as power and revenue remain in the hands of the Markovs and their like it is nothing but a fiction. The content of the election campaign of the working-class democrats is determined by the task of bringing out the difference between liberalism and democracy, of rallying the forces of the latter, and of closing the ranks of the wage-workers throughout the world.

The resolutions of their conference imply that the Cadets are departing still further from democracy. Our task is to rally the forces of democracy to counter every sort of medievalism, and to counter the Cadet-Octobrist blocs.

II. THE ROLE OF WORKER ELECTORS IN THE ELECTION CAMPAIGN

The campaign for the elections to the Fourth Duma has opened. It was launched by the government sending out circular instructions on assistance to the "national" party, and by taking "measures" to provide for the qualifications of the government candidates, and to eliminate opposition candidates in general, and democratic candidates in particular.

The opposition press has also entered the election campaign. So has the Cadet Party, and its first step was the adoption of resolutions providing for a bloc with the "Left" Octobrists.

Therefore, working-class democracy must immediately pay the utmost attention to the elections, and promptly, without a single week's delay discuss its tactics in all their details, preparing all supporters of democracy in advance for the important and responsible role they are to perform.

In this article we propose to dwell on the role of worker electors. It is clear that in this case too, as always, we must stress the content of the work, that is to say, the ideological-political line of the campaign. Educate and organise the working class, unite it in an independent party that maintains solidarity with the West-European parties, explain to the working class its historical aims in changing the basic conditions of commodity economy and capitalism, segregate its party from *all* bourgeois democratic trends, even those that are "Left", Narodnik, etc.—such is the basic task.

This fundamental task is the same for working-class democracy in all countries. And for this very reason its application in the present epoch in one country, in Russia, requires that the special and concrete tasks of our times be taken into consideration *for the sake* of this general common task. At the present moment two of these specific tasks of Russian working-class democracy are indissolubly connected and, because of objective conditions, require the greatest attention. The first of these two tasks is to understand clearly the connection between the liquidationist trend (represented, as we know, by the magazines *Nasha Zarya* and *Dyelo Zhizni*) and the widespread bourgeois counter-revolutionary *Vekhi* trend. It is necessary to be clearly aware of the harm of bourgeois influence upon the proletariat in order to overcome it and to achieve the immediate aims affecting the very *existence* of working-class democracy, which the liquidators *are denying*. The second is the task of organising the Left democrats, clearly bearing in mind the necessity to draw a line between democracy (bourgeois democracy) and bourgeois liberalism. This is imperative if working-class democracy is to exercise that leadership which is one of the indispensable conditions for any step forward by the general movement for freedom.

The lumping of the liberals (the Constitutional-Democratic Party) with the democrats (the Trudoviks, "Narodniks" of the Left persuasion) is fundamentally wrong in principle, and, in practice, leads to the betrayal of the interests of democracy. Upon the worker electors devolves the duty of upholding the correct interpretation of the liberation movement and explaining the class essence of the various parties (without allowing themselves to be taken in by "labels", fine words and fancy names); they must draw a clear line between the *Rights* (from the Black Hundreds to the Octobrists), the bourgeois *liberals* (the Cadets and their kind), and the *democrats* (the Trudoviks and kindred trends are bourgeois democrats; the Marxists represent proletarian democracy).

In accordance with the electoral system instituted by the law of June 3, 1907, the worker electors play a particular role in the gubernia electoral assemblies. Therefore the immediate practical task is to ensure that *all* these electors are staunch and loyal representatives of working-class democracy.

As we know, the election of one of the worker electors to the State Duma is guaranteed in each of the following six gubernias: St. Petersburg, Moscow, Vladimir, Ekaterinoslav, Kostroma, and Kharkov. But the deputies are elected by the *entire* electoral assembly of each gubernia, which means, as a rule, by the *Right* electors, landowners and big bourgeoisie, Octobrists. To secure the election to the Duma of working-class democrats we must see to it that all the worker electors, without a single exception, are true working-class democrats and firmly support one definite candidate from their midst. Even if only one worker elector turns out to be a deserter, a liberal, a Right, the Octobrists will be sure to elect him, against the will of the majority of the worker electors!

But the enumerated six gubernias are not the only ones having worker electors in their electoral assemblies. Altogether the law provides for a total of 112 worker electors in 44 gubernias (out of 53).

What should be the role of these electors? To begin with, they must always pursue a principled line, endeavouring to organise the forces of democracy (particularly, the peasantry) and to help them cast off the influence of the liberals. This is an extremely important field of activity. Secondly, the worker electors are in a position (and should strive) to take advantage of the vote being split between the Rights and the liberals to elect their own candidates to the Duma.

Here is an example to illustrate the last-named task. Two members of the Third Duma from Vyatka Gubernia are Social-Democrats—Astrakhantsev and Putyatin. Yet the law does not provide for a deputy from the worker curia in Vyatka Gubernia. The gubernia electoral assembly in Vyatka is made up of 109 electors, of whom four are elected by the workers. How, then, did *four* workers (out of 109 electors) manage to send *two* deputies to the Duma? Most likely, the votes in the gubernia electoral assembly were equally divided, and the liberals could not gain the upper hand over the Rights without the support of the workers. Compelled to form a bloc with the workers, the liberals had to share seats in the Duma with them, and thus they elected two Social-Democrats to the Duma. The representation from Vyatka in the Duma was constituted as follows: 1 Progressist, 3 Cadets, 2 Trudoviks, and 2 Social-Democrats, or 4 liberals and 4 democrats. In that gubernia the workers might have gained three seats had they succeeded in driving a wedge between the democratic electors and the liberals, provided the former had had a majority over the latter. Suppose that, out of 109 electors, 54 are Rights (50 out of the 53 electors chosen by the landowners and 4 out of the 17 electors from the first assembly of urban voters). Let us suppose, further, that out of the other 55 electors, 20 are liberals (three from the landowner curia, 13 from the first urban curia, and four from the second urban curia), 35 are democrats (23 peasant electors, 8 electors from the second urban curia and 4 from the worker curia). Under these circumstances the democrats would have been bound to obtain 5 seats out of 8, and the workers could have obtained 3 of these seats, provided they enjoyed the confidence of the peasant democrats.

In Ufa Gubernia *all* the seats were captured by the liberals (including Moslems). Not a single representative of the democrats was elected. Yet, considering that there were 30 peasant electors, the three worker electors could undoubtedly have captured seats both for themselves and the Trudoviks had they shown greater skill in organising the democratic forces.

Perm Gubernia is represented in the Third Duma by 6 liberals and 3 democrats, of whom only one is a Social-Democrat. Yet the situation in Perm was as follows: there were 26 peasant electors, and out of them the *liberals*, who had a majority in the gubernia electoral assembly, elected a Trudovik, which means that the peasant curia was a hundred per cent Trudovik (and if, among the peasants, there had been a single deserter from the camp of democracy to the liberals, the latter would have elected the deserter!). The same applies to the second urban curia (13 electors), because from that curia, too, a Trudovik was elected by the votes of the *liberals*. Hence the number of democrats among the electors may be placed at $26+13+5$ workers$=44$, out of a total of 120 electors, including 59 from the landowner curia and 17 from the first urban curia. Even assuming that, with the exception of the democrats, all the electors were liberals, their number was 76, i.e., less than two-thirds. It is more likely, however, that some of the electors were Rights. Consequently, the liberals, although comprising less than two-thirds in the electoral assembly, captured two-thirds of the Perm seats in the Duma. The inevitable conclusion to be drawn from this is that, had the democrats been more class-conscious and better organised (and it is above all the workers who must see to this!), they would not have let the liberals put anything over on them. The Social-Democrat Yegorov was elected in Perm Gubernia at the general assembly of the electors, i.e., by the liberals—which means that the liberals *needed* the support of the workers. And it was plainly a mistake on the part of the workers, a direct infringement of the interests of democracy, to give this support *without* securing a *proportionate* share of the seats in the Duma for democracy.

In making these calculations we wish to emphasise that they are merely meant as examples, to illustrate our idea, for we are not in possession of any exact data regarding the party affiliations of the electors in general or of the electors in each separate curia. Actually, matters are more complicated and represent a more motley picture than might be assumed from our examples. But it is necessary for the workers to understand the *basic* relation of forces in the "intricate mechanism" of elections based on the June Third law. Once they have assimilated the fundamentals, they will be able to understand the details as well.

The two most democratic curias (after the worker curia, of course, which can and should be completely Marxist, completely anti-liquidationist) are the peasant curia and the second urban curia. Of these, the first is more democratic than the second, despite the infinitely greater lack of freedom at the elections in the rural districts and the infinitely worse conditions for agitation and organisation among the peasants, as compared with townspeople.

Indeed, deputies specially elected at the second assembly of urban voters to the Third Duma represented 28 gubernias. Among those thus elected were 16 Rights, 10 liberals, and 2 democrats (Rozanov from Saratov and Petrov the Third from Perm). Deputies specially elected from the peasant curia were sent to the Third Duma from all the 53 gubernias. They included 23 Rights, 17 liberals, 5 democrats and 8 independents. If we divide the independents equally between the Rights and the opposition, we obtain the following comparative data:

Members of the Third Duma	From the Second Urban Curia	From the Peasant Curia
Rights	16	27
Opposition parties	12=43 per cent	26=49 per cent

Opposition deputies thus comprised 43 per cent of the deputies elected by the second urban curia and 49 per cent of the deputies elected by the peasant curia. Considering that, as we know, the peasant deputies in the Third Duma introduced an agrarian bill which was in substance more *democratic* than the bill introduced by the Cadets, and that the bill bore the signatures also of independent and *Right* peasant deputies, it is obvious that the democracy of the peasant curia surpasses the democracy of the second urban curia *to an even greater extent* than would appear from our data.

Consequently, the workers in general and the worker electors in particular must devote most of their attention to the peasant curia and the peasant electors. As the organisers of the forces of democracy the workers must carry on their activities in the first place among the peasants, and then among the electors from the second urban curia. In both these curias the intermingling of the liberals and democrats is particularly pronounced, is particularly frequent, and is particularly cultivated by the Cadets, who are taking advantage of their experience in "parliamentary deals" and their "democratic" name ("Constitutional-*Democrats*", the "party of *people's freedom*"), which disguises their *anti-democratic*, *Vekhi*, counter-revolutionary substance, in order brazenly to deceive politically undeveloped people.

The ideological and political task of the workers at the present stage of the Russian liberation movement is to organise the forces of democracy. The technical work of the election campaign must be subordinated to this task. Hence the necessity to devote special attention to the peasant curia and then to the second urban curia. In the gubernia electoral assembly, the first duty of the worker elector is to unite all the democrats. In order to get himself nominated, the worker elector needs three votes—he must find two peasant democrats or, if the worst comes to the worst, persuade two liberals, who would not risk anything by nominating a worker. The democratic members of the gubernia electoral assemblies should form blocs with the liberals against the Rights. If it proves impossible to form such a bloc immediately (and most likely this is what is going to happen in the majority of cases, because the electors will not be acquainted with each other), the tactics of the democrats should be to unite first with the liberals to defeat the Rights, and then *with the Rights to defeat the liberals*, so that neither are able to secure the election of their candidates (provided that neither the Rights nor the liberals command an absolute majority by themselves, for if they do the democrats cannot hope to get into the Duma). In accordance with Article 119 of the

Regulations governing the elections, the assembly adjourns. Then the democrats, guided by the exact figures of the votes cast, form a bloc with the liberals, demanding a proportionate share of the seats. *In such cases it is essential that the liberals elect the democrat first and not the other way round*, for history and the entire experience of Europe show that the liberals have often cheated the democrats, whereas the democrats have never cheated the liberals.

If they know which curias send democratic electors, and learn to drive a wedge between the democrats and the liberals, the worker electors *in 44 gubernias* can play an *enormous* role both in organising the forces of democracy in general and in securing the election of a larger number of worker democrats and bourgeois democrats (Trudoviks) to the Duma. In the present Duma there are fifteen of the former and fourteen of the latter. If the workers pursue correct tactics they can, under favourable conditions, secure the election of double that number. The liberals are sure to have a strong group—about a hundred or more deputies—in the Fourth Duma. They will constitute the "responsible opposition" (of the London type) capable of forming a bloc with the Octobrists. We must work to elect a group of several dozen deputies who will constitute a really democratic opposition, not an opposition of the *Vekhi* brand. And this can be achieved.

The law gives the workers the right to choose electors in 44 gubernias. Class-conscious workers in each factory must at once familiarise themselves with the law, take careful note of their duties and their position, and ensure that the electors they send are genuine working-class democrats, not liquidators.

If, as a result of class-conscious, careful and systematic work one hundred and twelve worker electors are elected, they can render very great service both in rallying the working class, which everywhere in Europe aspires to achieve lofty aims of world-wide significance, and also in organising the forces of democracy in Russia.

Time is short. Every class-conscious worker must shoulder this difficult, but doubly worth-while task.

III. THE PEASANTRY AND THE PEASANT ELECTORS
IN THE ELECTION CAMPAIGN

In the preceding article (*Zvezda*, No. 34) we discussed the role of the worker electors in the election campaign. The long and the short of our reflections was that working-class democrats are faced by a vital twofold task—to unite the class of wage-workers, developing their class-consciousness, their understanding of the great historical objectives of their class, and then to organise the forces of democracy.*

Let us now examine the question of non-proletarian, i.e., bourgeois, democracy. What is its principal class basis in Russia? What are its specific features, its immediate tasks? What is its role in the elections?

The principal class support for Russian bourgeois democracy is the peasantry. The condition of the great bulk of the peasantry is so burdensome, the oppression of the landowners so heavy, the economic conditions so desperately bad, and its lack of civil rights so extraordinarily great, that democratic feelings and desires are springing up among them with an elusive spontaneous inevitability. The way out of the situation which the bourgeois liberals (with the Cadet Party at their head) picture to themselves—the sharing of power with the Purishkeviches, the joint rule of the Purishkeviches and the Guchkovs (or the Milyukovs) over the masses—*cannot* satisfy the peasant millions. That is why the class position of the peasantry, on the one hand, and of the big bourgeoisie, on the other, inevitably creates a wide gulf between democrats and liberals.

As a rule, neither of the two political trends is clearly defined, neither is a fully conscious one, but it is a fact that the peasants *gravitate* towards democracy, the bourgeoisie towards monarchist liberalism; this was proved to the hilt during the extremely eventful first decade of the twentieth century in Russia. Not only did the peasant masses display their democracy in the liberation movement of 1905, and in the First and Second Dumas, but even in the nobility-dominated Third Duma; *forty-three* peasant deputies, including Rights and independents, introduced an agrarian bill

---

* See p. 372 of this volume.—*Ed.*

which was more democratic than that introduced by the Cadets.

In general, the land problem is the main problem of the Russian peasantry today. Less than 30, 000 landowners in European Russia possess 70 million dessiatines of land, and practically the same amount is held by 10 million poor peasant households. On the one hand, an average of 2,300 dessiatines per farm; on the other, an average of seven dessiatines. At the present level of Russia's historical development, this could lead to but one economic result—the most widespread practice of all sorts of "labour-service" economy, that is to say, of survivals of the old corvée system. Peasants held in bondage, poverty such as has not been seen in Europe for many years, and periodic famines reminiscent of the Middle Ages, are consequences of this state of affairs.

The Cadet bourgeoisie seeks to settle the agrarian problem in a liberal fashion, so as to preserve the landed estates, selling part of the land to the peasantry at "a fair price", and giving the landowners the upper hand over the peasants in the bodies effecting the "reform". Naturally, the peasants would certainly prefer a democratic solution of the agrarian problem. This democratic solution, even if all the land is transferred to the peasants without compensation, does not and cannot in the least encroach on the foundations of capitalist society—the power of money, commodity production, and the domination of the market. The peasants, for the most part, have a rather hazy idea of the matter and the Narodniks have created a complete ideology, a whole doctrine, which gave that haze something of a "socialist" hue, although there is nothing socialist even in the most radical agrarian revolution.

But, in practice, as the peasant movement grows in volume and in strength, the influence of this hazy conception diminishes, and the real, democratic, substance of the agrarian wishes and demands of the peasants becomes more pronounced. In this sphere, and even more so in the sphere of political questions, of paramount importance is the role played by working-class democracy and its struggle to prevent the submission of the peasants to liberal leadership. It will be no exaggeration to say that there is a very close connection between the successes of Russian democracy as a whole, those of the past and those yet to come, and the transfer of the political leadership of the peasantry from the liberals to working-class democracy. Unless this leadership passes to the working class, Russian democracy cannot hope to attain any more or less serious successes.

The electoral law of June 3, 1907, as we know, made the greatest "inroads" upon the suffrage of the peasants. We need only remind the readers that that law provided for an increase from 1,952 to 2,594, or 32.9 per cent in the number of electors sent by the landowners, while the number of electors from the peasants and Cossacks was reduced to less than a half, from 2,659 to 1,168, or by 56.1 per cent. In addition, the law of June 3, 1907, provides that the deputies to the Duma from the peasant curia (officially designated: "from conventions of delegates from volosts*") are not to be chosen by the peasant electors alone, as was the case previously, but by the entire electoral assembly of each gubernia, that is to say, by bodies in which landowners and big capitalists predominate.

This being the procedure, the peasant democrats (Trudoviks) can secure seats in the Duma only if *all* the peasant electors, without a single exception, are Trudoviks. In that case the Right landowners will be compelled to elect Trudoviks from the peasant curia, just as they have been compelled to elect Social-Democrats from the worker curia. However, solidarity, organisation, and class-consciousness are naturally much less developed among the peasants than among the workers. Thus there still remains an almost untapped field of serious and rewarding work of political education. And it is this sphere of activity that should command the main attention of all democrats and all Marxists who "go among all classes of the population",** and not that of making advances to and flirting with the counter-revolutionary liberals (the Cadets), a sphere that has become a favourite one with the liquidators on *Nasha Zarya*, etc.

We pointed out in the preceding article that in the elections to the Third Duma the peasant curia proved to be the most democratic of the non-proletarian curias. Out of

---

* See footnote to p. 88.—*Ed.*
** See present edition, Vol. 5, p. 468.—*Ed.*

53 deputies elected to the Third Duma from the peasant curia, 26, or 49 per cent, were members of the opposition; whereas in the case of the second urban curia (the second assembly of urban voters), only 12 out of 28, or 43 per cent, were members of the opposition. The number of democrats elected to the Third Duma from the peasant curia was 5 out of 53, or 10 per cent; whereas in the case of the second urban curia, their number was 2 out of 28, or 7 per cent.

It is worth while examining which gubernias elected representatives of the opposition from the peasant curia and what was the composition of all the deputies elected by each of them to the Third Duma. Of the 53 gubernias, in each of which the law provides for the election of one deputy from the peasant curia, 23 sent *Rights* (including Octobrists) as representatives of the peasant curia, 17 sent *liberals* (Cadets, Progressists, and Moslems), and only five sent *democrats* (Trudoviks). In eight gubernias independent peasants were elected.

On closer examination we see that *not a single one* of the gubernias which elected a majority of Right deputies to the Third Duma sent a democrat to represent the peasant curia. Democrats (Trudoviks) were elected only in those gubernias where no Right deputies were returned. These five gubernias—Archangel, Vyatka, Perm, Stavropol, and Tomsk—are represented in the Third Duma by 15 liberals, 8 Trudoviks, and 3 Social-Democrats. There is hardly any room for doubt that, had the peasants and the workers in these gubernias been more class-conscious and better organised, it would have been possible to increase, at the expense of the liberals, the proportion of democrats elected.

It may not be perhaps amiss to point out here that altogether 24 gubernias sent a majority of opposition deputies to the Third Duma. In 18 of these 24 only opposition deputies were elected. In all, these 24 gubernias are represented in the Duma by 9 Right deputies, 2 independents, 55 liberals, 14 Trudoviks, and 8 Social-Democrats. The reader will thus readily see that there is a fairly widespread opportunity to increase the proportion of democratic deputies at the expense of the liberals and, in general, to win the petty bourgeoisie and the peasantry away from their influence.

It is interesting to note further that in 10 gubernias out of the 17 which elected liberals from the peasant curia, the Rights gained more seats than the opposition. We must therefore assume that, as a rule, *there were no Rights at all* among the peasant electors in these gubernias, for if there had been, the Right majorities in the gubernia electoral assemblies would surely have elected them....

The duty of the working-class democrats with regard to the peasants in the elections is perfectly clear. They must carry their purely class propaganda to a peasantry that is becoming proletarianised. They must help the peasants to unite their forces in the elections to enable them, even on the basis of the June Third electoral law, to send to the Fourth Duma their *own* representatives in as large numbers as possible despite the obstacles put in their way both by the supporters of the old regime and by the liberals. They must strive to consolidate the leadership of working-class democrats and explain the great harm caused by the vacillation of the peasant democrats toward the liberals.

IV. CONCLUSIONS BASED ON THE EXPERIENCE OF THE ELECTIONS TO THE THIRD DUMA

For the purpose of providing a concrete definition of the duties of working-class democrats in the election campaign, it would be useful, we believe, to examine, in as great detail as possible, the data relating to the elections to the Third Duma in a few individual gubernias. In the first place, such an examination will help us to understand more clearly and to become more thoroughly familiar with the intricate and involved electoral system provided by the law of June 3, 1907; and, secondly, it will give all those active in the election campaign a very real idea of their position as democrats, of the "circumstances" under which they will have to carry on their work. If the democrats in the various localities study the data relating to their respective gubernias, that will add to our data, help to correct errors, and immediately arouse the interest of everyone who is aware of his duty to participate in the elections with a view to the political enlightenment of the wage-workers and the organisation of the forces of democracy.

Take, for example, Kazan Gubernia. It is represented in the Third Duma by ten deputies, equally divided between the Rights and the opposition—five Rights (four Octobrists and one Nationalist) and five liberals (one Progressist, two Cadets, and two Moslems). There are neither Trudoviks nor Social-Democrats.

And yet, judging by the data on Kazan Gubernia, it must be admitted that the democrats had a fairly good chance there. Of the Rights, one (Sazonov) was elected by the assembly of landowners, three Octobrists were elected by the first and second assemblies of urban voters (including Mr. Kapustin, an inveterate counter-revolutionary, who was elected at the second assembly of urban voters), and *one* Octobrist at the general assembly of electors. Of the liberals, one was elected by the assembly of landowners, one from the peasants (the Cadet Lunin) and *three* at the general assembly of electors.

Since the general assembly of electors elected three liberals and one Right, it is obvious that the liberals had a majority in the gubernia electoral assembly, but it was a precarious majority, otherwise not a single Right would have been elected by the general assembly. The precariousness of the liberal majority is also evident from the fact that the landowners elected one Progressist and one Right; had the liberals had a stable majority they would have prevented the latter's election.

Altogether Kazan Gubernia is allowed 117 electors who are divided among the several curias as follows: peasants 33, landowners 50, first urban curia 18, second urban curia 14, and workers 2. Consequently, the landowners together with the first urban curia represent the majority $(50+18=68$ out of 117). As we know, the law of June 3, 1907, is so framed as to *guarantee* in all gubernias such a majority or an even more "reliable" one, i.e., a majority made up of landowners alone (the landowner curia alone to have an absolute majority in the gubernia electoral assembly).

The liberals won half the seats in the Duma because they were apparently well represented among the landowners. On the other hand, it seems that the urban electors were practically all Rights. Unless we assume this to have been the case, it is hard to explain how it happened that the deputies elected from the two urban assemblies were Rights when the liberals had a majority in the gubernia electoral assembly. The Cadets were compelled to vote for Rights. Given the precarious majority of the liberals among the electors, mentioned above, the working-class democrats would have a convenient field for action; they could take advantage of the dissensions among the landowners and capitalists to organise the forces of democracy as a whole and to get Social-Democrats and, in particular, Trudoviks elected to the Duma.

If, for instance, there were 57 Rights and as many liberals among the electors and only three democrats (two worker Social-Democrats, and one peasant Trudovik), that alone would enable the three democrats to elect one Social-Democrat to the Duma—not to mention the rewarding task of rallying the democratic forces which these three could tackle, considering that there would be 33 peasant electors. We have assumed that there might be three democrats, because three is the minimum required by the law (Article 125 of the Regulations governing the elections), to nominate candidates by ballot—a candidate who fails to obtain three nomination ballots, cannot stand for election. Obviously, the three required by the law could be made up by two liberals joining a democrat, provided the liberals do not "progress" (in the *Vekhi* direction) to the point where even in the gubernia electoral assembly they prefer an Octobrist to a Social-Democrat.

In the case of a tie between the Rights and the liberals even one democrat, by voting now with the Rights against the liberals, now with the liberals against the Rights, could prevent the election of any candidate to the Duma and thus (in accordance with Article 119 of the Regulations governing the elections) bring about an adjournment the duration of which, according to the same article, is set by the assembly itself, but may not exceed twelve hours, and arrange for an understanding between the liberals and the democrats on condition that the latter obtain seats in the Duma.

The example of Kazan may serve as an illustration of two possible lines for the workers' policy in the elections to the Fourth Duma (and, consequently, lines for the workers' policy *in general*, since the policy pursued in the elections is but the application of the general policy to a specific case). One line is to vote, as a general rule, for the more progressive candidates, without going into any further definitions. The other line is to take advantage of the antagonism between the Rights and the liberals to organise the democrats. The ideological implication of the first line is passive subordination to the hegemony of the Cadets; the practical result of this line in case of success would be an increase in the Octobrist-Cadet majority in the Fourth Duma at the expense of the Right-Octobrist majority (with a possible *decrease* in the democratic minority). The ideological implication of the second line is the waging of a struggle against the leadership of the Cadets over the peasants and over bourgeois democracy in general; its practical result in case of success would be the increase and consolidation, the strengthening of the group of democrats in the Fourth Duma.

In practice the first line would amount to a liberal labour policy. The second line represents the Marxist working-class policy. As for a more detailed explanation of the meaning of these two policies, we shall have many occasions to revert to that in the future.

Zvezda, Nos. 33, 34, 36, and 1 (37),
   December 10, 17, 31, 1911,
   and January 6, 1912
   Signed: *William Frey*
   and *W. Frey*

Published according to
the *Zvezda* text

OLD AND NEW

Nik. Nikolin's article in *Zvezda*, No. 29, characteristically entitled "The New in the Old", raises a number of extremely interesting and important questions. A discussion on these questions is undoubtedly desirable in order to lay down an exact, clear, and definite line of conduct for adherents to the Russian working-class democratic movement.

The chief shortcoming of Nik. Nikolin's article is that many of his propositions are extremely vague. The author says, without explaining why, that "on many points" he would "perhaps disagree" with me. I, for my part, must say that none of Nikolin's propositions call for disagreement, since he never makes outspoken statements.

Thus, for instance, Nikolin comes out dead against people who believe that "our present situation ... is approximately what it was at the beginning of the twentieth century". According to his interpretation, people holding such an opinion deny that there is something *new* in the old. Of course, they are wrong if they deny that. And, of course, Nikolin is a thousand times right when he says that there is something new in the old which it is necessary to take into consideration and make use of. But Nikolin says nothing as to what the new consists of, as to how exactly it is to be taken into consideration, etc. On the other hand, it is not clear from the passages he quotes what exactly his opponents mean by the word "approximately". If the new in the old is to be taken into consideration in the same way as the Russian Marxists did exactly three years ago in their appraisal of the political situation created after the three years of storm and stress (i.e., after 1905-07), then, in my opinion, it would not be wrong to say: "our present situation is *approximately* what it was at the beginning of the twentieth century". If, however, people put forward a proposition of this kind without, at first, giving a precise, clear, and definite appraisal of the situation and the problems involved, then, of course, it is wrong.

The old problems, the old methods of solving them, and new ways of preparing for the solution—that, it seems to me, is how, approximately, the answer given three years ago could be formulated. From the standpoint of this answer, participation in the Third Duma, which Nik. Nikolin advocates so warmly and so correctly, appears to be *absolutely* indispensable. The "trend" which repudiates this participation or which hesitates to come out, openly, clearly, and without beating about the bush, in favour of participating in the Third Duma, is taking the name of working-class democracy in vain. Actually this is a trend outside working-class democracy, for it represents a "legitimate shade" of anarchist ideas but by no means of Marxist ideas.

Take the question of the "superstructure". "Formerly," writes Nik. Nikolin, "it may have seemed that the bureaucracy was the sole and chief enemy of 'all Russia'; today nobody thinks so any longer.... We are sufficiently well aware that the Markovs, Krestovnikovs, Volkonskys, Purishkeviches, Guchkovs, Khomyakovs, Avdakovs, and their like, are all representatives of that particular social milieu from which the bureaucracy draws its strength and obtains the motives for its activity."

Nik. Nikolin's emphasis on the connection of the "bureaucracy" with the upper ranks of the commercial and industrial bourgeoisie is quite correct and extremely valuable. Only people who have never given a thought to the new brought by the first decade of the twentieth century, who understand nothing about the interdependence between the economic and the political relations in Russia and about the significance of the Third Duma can deny that this connection exists, deny that the present agrarian policy is bourgeois in character, deny in general that "a step" has been taken "towards the transformation into a bourgeois monarchy".

But it is not enough to concede that the connection exists, it is necessary to point out what exactly is the actual nature of this connection. The step taken toward the transformation into something new by no means eliminates the old, say, "bureaucratic" regime with its vast self-sufficiency and independence, with its "peculiar nature" which the methods of Tolmachov and Reinbot (etc., et al.) lend it, and with its uncontrolled finances. While "drawing strength" from the support of the upper ranks of the bourgeoisie the bureaucracy is *not* recruited from the bourgeoisie, but from the old, very old, not only pre-revolutionary (before 1905), but even pre-Reform (before 1861), landed and office-holding nobility. While it "obtains the motives for its activity" largely from the upper ranks of the bourgeoisie the bureaucracy lends its bourgeois activity *a tendency and a form* that is purely and solely feudal. For, if there is a difference between the bourgeois character of the Prussian Junker and the American farmer (although both of them are unquestionably bourgeois), there is a no less evident and equally great difference between the bourgeois character of the Prussian Junker and the "bourgeois character" of Markov and Purishkevich. Compared with the latter, the Prussian Junker is quite a "European"!

The principal, cardinal, and fatal mistake which, for instance, M. Alexandrov commits in his well-known pamphlet is that he forgets about the vast self-sufficiency and independence of the "bureaucracy"; and N. R-kov, in No. 9-10 of the liquidationist *Nasha Zarya*, indulges in this mistake to a point where it is reduced to an absurdity. Only the above-mentioned answer given three years ago contains an exact definition of the extent to which the old persists in the so-called "bureaucratic" regime, and of the changes, or, rather, modifications, that have been introduced by the "new".

I am by no means opposed to the "exploration of other ways and means", and I attach vast importance to constant and repeated discussion of the direct answers to the vexed questions, but I cannot refrain, however, from voicing my protest against the contraband that the liquidators, for example, are smuggling in under the flag of "exploration". It is obvious that the differences of opinion between the "exploring" R-kov and the "exploring" Potresovs, Yezhovs, and Chatskys concern only *details* of their liberal labour policy. The stand taken by all these "explorers" is that of a liberal, not a Marxist, labour policy! It is one thing to "explore ways" and discuss them from a Marxist standpoint in books, magazines, etc.; and it is a different thing to come out with definite answers in publications giving practical guidance.

Take the question of "romanticism". Nik Nikolin condemns romanticism as a hopelessly obsolete feature of the "old" and cites the following example: "The liberal thought that he was performing the part of champion of all the oppressed, while the socialist believed that he was backed by all 'thinking' and 'labouring' Russia". The example refers to the failure to understand the class struggle, and Nikolin would have been perfectly right, of course, had he said that such a "socialist"—obviously a Narodnik—was really no socialist at all but a *democrat* who cloaked his democracy with pseudo-socialist phrases. But in speaking of romanticism, one must not overlook the *Vekhi*, i.e., counter-revolutionary, interpretation of that term which is current in the most widely circulated, namely, the liberal press. We cannot help protesting against such an interpretation. We cannot help noting the "new" feature, namely, that liberalism in Russia has given rise to the liberal trend of the *Vekhi* type, the policy which the Milyukovs actually pursue although in words they renounce it for purely diplomatic reasons.

Hence the following practical conclusion of major importance: on the basis of the "new" experience of the first ten years of the twentieth century, the line of demarcation between liberalism and democracy must be drawn more sharply. It is, of course, absurd to "lump the liberal opposition with reaction", but this conclusion alone (which Nikolin draws), without the one I have just indicated, is decidedly insufficient.

In general, it must be said that it is in his conclusion that Nik. Nikolin commits his chief sin—that of being vague and leaving things unsaid. Take the first part of his conclusion: "Both the unreasonable infatuation with the old methods of action and the emphatically negative attitude to those methods are equally harmful". In my opinion this is not a dialectical, but an eclectic, conclusion. The unreasonable is unreasonable, and therefore it is always and absolutely harmful—that goes without saying. In order to lend this part of the conclusion a vital, dialectical significance, it would have to be couched in approximately the following terms: an attempt to justify the refusal to take part in the Third or in the Fourth Duma by references to the old methods of action would be an extremely grave mistake, a hollow phrase, a meaningless cry, in spite of the fact, or — more correctly — because of the fact, that we must have an emphatically positive attitude to those methods.

It is just in passing, since it is impossible for me to dwell on this question in greater detail, that I have thus indicated how, in my opinion, the second part of the quoted conclusion ought to be corrected.

Zvezda, No. 33, December 10, 1911   Published according to
         Signed: V. *Ilyin*   the *Zvezda* text

MEETING OF THE BOLSHEVIK GROUPS ABROAD[168]

DECEMBER 14-17 (27-30), 1911

1

DRAFT RESOLUTION ON THE REPORT "STATE OF AFFAIRS IN THE PARTY"

Organisation of the Social-Democratic Party Forces Abroad and the Tasks of the Bolsheviks

The present state of Social-Democratic organisations abroad is abnormal in the extreme.

From 1908 onwards, when Social-Democratic publishing had begun to shift more and more abroad, and prior to the Plenary Meeting, there was a complete organisational split in all important centres abroad, owing to the complete secession of the Menshevik groups from the Party.

The Plenary Meeting (January 1910) attempted to create unity on the basis of its unanimous approval of an anti-liquidationist and anti-otzovist line, and made a particularly energetic call for the establishment of complete unity abroad.

After the Plenary Meeting, however, in view of the non-fulfilment of its terms by the liquidators and otzovists, no unity of the groups abroad was achieved. On the contrary, there was greater disintegration, as in fact the *Vperyod* group broke away from the Bolsheviks, and Plekhanov's followers from the Mensheviks. The parallel—"first" and "second" or Menshevik and Bolshevik—groups continued to exist traditionally, but actually in no way united any sound elements capable of carrying out joint Social-Democratic work.

At the present moment Bolshevik, "conciliator", *Vperyod*, *Golos*, and Plekhanov's groups exist abroad in factional isolation, linked together purely formally, and often not at

all, completely independent of each other, following different ideological lines and having their own individual ties
with various Social-Democratic elements in Russia.

The formation of the Russian Organising Commission
(R.O.C.) in Russia by the forces of the Bolsheviks and pro-
Party Mensheviks and the energetic start made by this
R.O.C. Collegium to call a general Party conference of the
R.S.D.L.P. make for a decisive turn in the history of the
Party and show the only possible way, demanded by re-
ality, out of the condition of disruption and collapse.

Since the Plenary Meeting, real Social-Democratic work
has been carried out only by the Bolsheviks and the pro-
Party Mensheviks; it was particularly harmonious in 1910.
The *Golos* group represents nothing but a section abroad
of the Russian liquidator group *Dyelo Zhizni* and *Nasha
Zarya*, which has placed itself outside the Party; and the
Vperyod group abroad, which continues to cover up otzo-
vism and through its leader Lunacharsky to carry out reli-
gious propaganda, conducts work which is not Social-
Democratic.

At the present moment, the R.O.C., created by the Bolsheviks and the pro-Party Mensheviks and supported by
nearly all the local Social-Democratic organisations in Russia, is, in fact, the only absolutely competent centre of
Social-Democratic Party work.

Uniting the Bolsheviks in one Social-Democratic organisation abroad, the Meeting places the responsibility for
the continuing split abroad on those groups who do not
wish to support the Russian centre, the R.O.C., or on those
who, cut off from Russia, continue "to play at agreeing",
thus supporting *non*-Social-Democratic groups that are isolated from Russian work.

The Bolshevik organisation abroad will, as hitherto,
use all its strength to attract, irrespective of trends, all
Social-Democrats prepared to support the R.O.C. and to
carry out the Party line, that is, the anti-liquidationist
and anti-otzovist (and equally anti-god-seeker) line, in
order that they join forces and merge into one Party organisation.

The practical task of the Party organisation abroad is
to struggle against the liquidationist and otzovist trends,

against the disintegration of the groups abroad having no ideological basis, assisting the unification of all real Social-Democratic Party members and pro-Party Mensheviks in particular, and assisting the R.O.C. We consider that the organs which should be supported by Party members are the Central Organ and *Rabochaya Gazeta*, as the isolation of the pro-Party Mensheviks (abroad) can in no manner be justified, and no change of the *line* confirmed by Party decisions can be found in the above-mentioned journals.

Written early in December 1911

First published in 1933
in *Lenin Miscellany XXV*

Published according to
the manuscript

2

RESOLUTION ON THE RUSSIAN ORGANISING COMMISSION
FOR THE CONVENING OF A CONFERENCE[169]

This Meeting confirms that for a long time, for two years
at least, the Party has recognised the urgent need to call
a Party conference. At the present time, despite all obstacles
a decisive step has been taken to bring this about. An
R.O.C. has been formed in Russia, supported by all local
organisations (Kiev, Baku, Tiflis, Ekaterinoslav, Ekaterinburg, St. Petersburg, Moscow, Nikolayev, Saratov, Kazan,
Wilno, Dvinsk, Nizhni-Novgorod, Sormovo, Samara, Tyumen, Rostov, and others).

This Meeting welcomes the formation of the R.O.C.,
and declares it to be the duty of every Party member to
render it every support.

Written early in December 1911   Published according to
                                                       the text of the *Notification*
Published on January 12, 1912,
   in the *Notification* of the
Committee of the Organisation Abroad

FUNDAMENTAL PROBLEMS OF THE ELECTION CAMPAIGN

I

The elections to the Fourth Duma are close at hand, and naturally, the question of the election campaign is on the order of the day. It is clear that any wavering as to the advisability, from the point of view of Marxism, of our participation in the elections, is impermissible. It is not within the bounds of Marxism and the working-class party, but only *outside* them, that views, hostile or indefinite, or even merely indifferent to our participation in the elections, can be regarded as "legitimate" shades of opinion. It may even seem somewhat embarrassing to repeat this elementary truth, proved and corroborated by experience many years ago (beginning with the end of 1907), but we nevertheless have to repeat it, for the worst evil we have to contend with now, is confusion and disintegration. And it is not only those who give vague or evasive answers to elementary questions that contribute to this confusion and disintegration, but also those who, for reasons of diplomacy or through lack of principles, etc., defend vagueness and evasion.

The elections to the State Duma naturally impose upon all Marxists, upon all members of the working-class movement, the duty to bend all their efforts to develop the most energetic, persistent activity and initiative in every field of that movement. The answers to the questions on the principles and the programmatic, political and organisational content and line of this activity which were elaborated during recent years, must now be directly applied in practice to the special sphere of "election" activity.

We deliberately speak of answers already formulated. It would be ridiculous indeed to suppose that now, several months, or, for that matter, even a year before the elections, you could manage to "find" the answers, if they had not yet been found, if they had not been thought out and tested by the practical experience of several years. After all, it is a matter of providing answers to *all* the "vexed questions" relating to our world outlook in general, to our appraisal of the previous, extremely eventful period of Russian history, to our estimate of the present period (which, in its main features, became defined as far back as 1908), and to the political and organisational problems which had to be solved, one way or another, by everyone who took part in the working-class movement during the last, say, four years. At present it can only be a matter of applying formulated answers and methods of work to the present particular field of activity, the elections to the Fourth Duma. To say that "in the course of the election campaign", i.e., of one branch of activity, we can work out the answers to the questions relating to *all* branches of activity, relating not only to 1912, but also to "the entire period beginning with 1908", would mean comforting ourselves with illusions, or concealing, justifying the reigning confusion and disintegration.

We are concerned, in the first place, with answers to programme questions. What have developments in the past four years in Russia given us in this respect? It must be admitted by each and all that during these four years no attempts have been made to revise, or amend, or further elaborate the old programme of the Marxists as far as its principles are concerned. Characteristic of the "current period", or more correctly in many respects it could be called the "stagnation" or "rotten" period, is the scornful attitude to the programme, and the desire to abridge and reduce it *without* the least attempt at definite and downright revision. In our epoch "revisionism", in its specific role of bourgeois emasculation of Marxist truths, is not of the militant variety which raises "the banner of revolt" (as, for instance, Bernstein's in Germany some ten years ago, Struve's in Russia some fifteen years ago, or Prokopovich's somewhat later); it is merely a cowardly and furtive renunciation, often defended on the ground of "practical", mainly only allegedly practical, considerations. The successors and continuers of the "cause" of Struve and Prokopovich—people like Potresov, Maslov, Levitsky and Co.—"took part" in the reigning disorder and contributed to it (as also did Yushkevich, Bogdanov, Lunacharsky, etc.), mostly by means of timid and unsystematic attempts to throw the "old" Marxism overboard and to replace it by a "new", bourgeois doctrine. It was no mere chance, nor was it due to the caprice of "groups", that questions of theory have attracted so much attention during the past four years. Such questions have been treated as "trivialities", even if only in part, by those who timidly renounce the old Marxism, and by them alone. If we speak today of the defence of the Marxist programme and the Marxist world outlook in connection with and in the course of the election campaign—if we speak of them not merely as an official duty or with the intention of saying nothing, we must take into account the *experience* of the past four years and not mere words, promises, or assurances. These four years have actually brought to light quite a number of "unreliable fellow-travellers" of Marxism among our intellectuals (who often desire to be Marxists), they have taught us to distrust such fellow-travellers, they have served to *enhance* in the minds of thinking workers the importance of Marxist theory and of the Marxist programme in its uncurtailed form.

There is a range of questions in which the programme comes close to or actually merges with tactics. Naturally, these problems assume a considerably greater immediate and practical significance during the election campaign. It is in respect of these problems that the spirit of renunciation and confusion has expressed itself in by far the sharpest form. Some said that the old tasks were no longer valid, because the system of government in Russia had, in essence, already become bourgeois. Others maintained that from now on Russia's development could proceed, like that of Germany or Austria after 1848, without any "leaps". Others again insisted that the idea of the hegemony of the working class had outlived its day, and that Marxists must aspire "*not* to hegemony, but to a class party", etc.

It goes without saying that, literally, not a single problem of tactics can be solved or explained to any extent completely, fully, and coherently, without an analysis of these ideas, justly described as "liquidationist", and which form an inseparable part of the broad stream of bourgeois public opinion which is turning back and away from democracy. Anyone who has kept his eyes open to what is going on in practical life knows that confusion in these problems is a hundred times more pronounced than might be judged from what has been written on this subject. Nor, of course, could it be otherwise in the years following the events at the end of 1905 and of 1906-07. But the more "natural" this disintegration (in a bourgeois environment), the more urgent and vital is the Marxists' task of waging a comprehensive and unremitting fight against it.

Periods of renunciation and disintegration similar to those of the past four years in Russia have been known to all countries. There were cases when not even groups remained, but only isolated individuals who in similar circumstances managed for ten or more years to "keep the banner flying", to keep the ideas of continuity alive, and subsequently to apply these ideas in a materially changed social and political situation. In Russia matters are not so bad as that; for our "heritage" includes both a programme which has remained intact, and *formulated* answers to the fundamental tactical and organisational problems of the "moment". The liquidationist trend, which has renounced this answer, cannot replace it by anything resembling an explicit and clear answer of its own.

An election campaign implies the application of a definite solution of political problems to complicated propaganda, agitational, organisational, etc., activity. You cannot embark upon such a campaign without a definite answer to the problems. And the answer which the Marxists formulated in 1908 has been fully corroborated by the experience of the past four years. The new, bourgeois content of the government's agrarian policy; the organisation of the landowners and the bourgeoisie in the Third Duma; the behaviour of even the most "Left" bourgeois party, the Cadets, so vividly illustrated by the trip to London, and not only by that trip; the ideological currents of the *Vekhi* type, which enjoyed such immense success among "educated" society—all these facts clearly indicate that the old problems have not been solved but have to be tackled now under new conditions, in a more bourgeois atmosphere, when the bourgeoisie is systematically turning *away from* democracy and *assuming the role* of a responsible, party, "loyal", etc., "opposition". A new situation and new methods of preparing for the old solution of the old problems, a more evident split between democracy and the anti-democratic liberal bourgeoisie, such are the main features of the answer formulated by the Marxists to the fundamental political questions of the present period.

The answer to the problems of organisation is inseparably connected with the entire world outlook of the Marxists, with their estimate of the political meaning and significance of the June Third period. In the main the old methods are to be preserved and adapted to the new circumstances with their so-called "opportunities" of all sorts, such as open associations, unions, etc. Nuclei, and a network of organisations around them, connected with them, and directed by them, are to be formed. The "nuclei" are to show greater flexibility, using more adaptable methods of work which do not in every particular resemble the old forms. It is also obligatory to take advantage, not only of the platform provided by the Duma, but of all sorts of similar "opportunities". It is an answer that does not in the least tie our hands by any uniform standards or obligatory forms of work; it leaves vast scope for working out the most suitable ways and means of combining various forms of activity. But it is a "firm" answer, based on unshakable principles, and as such it counters the prevailing disorder, spirit of renunciation, and confusion, not only by a verbal proclamation of loyalty to the old, but also by setting up a fundamental organisational principle, which enables us to secure ideological stability in real life. Those who have "accumulated a reserve", even if they are few in number, are uniting and systematically upholding the "hierarchy"— its spirit, its teachings, its principles and traditions, but not, of course, its forms.

The liquidationist trend, on the other hand, *succumbs* to the prevailing amorphousness (prevailing *not only* among us, by no means only in the working class, but to an even greater extent among other classes and parties); it abandons the work for the old, and uses the quest for "something new" as an excuse for justifying confusion. The liquidationist trend among the Marxists is but one rivulet joining the broad ideological stream of bourgeois society, the stream directed against democracy in general, against the mass movement in particular, and especially against the recent forms of the organisation and leadership of the movement.

Such are the general propositions of Marxism, its attitude to the tasks and problems of the present period, an attitude, we repeat, of long standing, which ought now to be translated into an "election campaign" with an integral ideological, programmatic, tactical, and organisational content.

II

Let us now examine the stand taken on the question of the election campaign by *Nasha Zarya*, leading organ of the liquidationist trend.

There is nothing more repugnant to the spirit of Marxism than phrase-mongering. And the most unpleasant feature that strikes one in Nos. 6 and 7-8 of *Nasha Zarya* is the incredible orgy of phrase-mongering that might truly be that of a Tartarin. The Tartarins of our liquidationist trend have converted an election campaign, something customary for Marxists in all lands, and which even in Russia has already been conducted *twice* on a large scale, into something wrapped up in so many pompous words, words and words, that it is simply unendurable.

Mr. Yuri Chatsky, in his article "Time to Begin", *begins* an exposition of the views of the liquidators, and, to all intents and purposes, *finishes* the exposition of these views and does so as the mastermind, leaving it to L. Martov to provide the trimmings, the gloss, the literary ornamentation.

Here is a sample of the writings of Yuri-Tartarin:

"It is hardly possible to expect with any certainty that the election campaign will be conducted, organisationally, in an absolutely centralised manner, although we must strive for this by all those ways we have spoken of ... by organisationally consolidating the results of the political amalgamation of the worker Social-Democrats in the course of the political campaign...."

For mercy's sake, dear man—why compete with Trotsky? Why try to stun the readers in general, and the workers in particular, with all that verbiage about the results of political amalgamation in the course of the political campaign? Or about consolidating those results? After all, it is nothing but words, merely giving yourself airs by the ponderous repetition of a simple idea. Organisational "consolidation" is always essential, before, as well as after, elections. You call the elections a political campaign, then—"to add weight" —you speak of a "series [!] of all-Russian [!] political campaigns", and by all this din and clatter of words you *obscure* the really urgent, vital, and practical question: *how* to organise. Do we need "nuclei" and a network of more or less open, if unstable, unions around them? Yes or no? If we do need them, we need them both before and after the elections—since the elections are but one of our jobs, one of many. If no systematic work has been carried on *for a long time*, you will not succeed in "consolidating" *anything* in the course of the election campaign. Any practical worker will tell you it is nonsense. High-sounding phrases are used only to cover up the absence of an explicit answer to the *fundamental* question, viz., how to organise for every form of activity, and not just for the election campaign.

To speak, apropos of the elections, about "*the fighting mobilisation of the proletariat*" (*sic*! see p. 49), or about a "broad and open mobilisation of the worker masses" (p. 54), and so on and so forth, means not only to lack any sense of proportion, but plainly to harm the modest, necessarily modest, work by fostering phrase-mongering *of exactly the same quality* as that of the "otzovists", "ultimatumists", etc. According to the latter, a boycott is needed as a means of especially stressing that the "spirit" is not dead (but the "spirit" of the work must permeate all spheres of activity, including the elections); the barkers of liquidationism, on the other hand, maintain that the elections will solve everything—"the fighting mobilisation" (one merely wonders how this Russian quasi-"Marxist" can unblushingly put down such things on paper!) and "organisational consolidation of the results of the political amalgamation in the course of a political campaign"! We all know perfectly well that the elections of 1912 (unless conditions arise which will radically change the situation that existed in 1908 and exists in 1911) will not, and cannot, bring about *either* a "broad" *or* an "open" "mobilisation of the masses". All they will give is a modest opportunity for activity that is not very broad and not very open, and this opportunity should be made use of. But there is no point in imitating Trotsky's inflated phrases.

The cry about "open" organisations in connection with the elections is just a bit of plain stupidity. What we say is: better let us do the work *not quite so* openly, fellow-workers, that will be safer, more proper, saner, and *more useful* as a means of influencing *wider sections* of the population than the twaddle about existing "openly". In times such as ours, only utterly stupid or utterly frivolous people can shout and brag: "We can do everything openly".

"A party (a class party) will appear only as a product of the organised creative efforts of the independently active vanguard of the workers" (p. 41).

Phew! Have mercy on us! Don't you know that in all countries it took the advanced workers and real Marxist "intellectuals", who whole-heartedly threw in their lot with the workers, decades to form and train their parties? *Nor can it be different* in our country, and there is no point in this attempt to scare away the Russian working-class reader by that pompous bunk about "creative efforts" (when it is a question of teaching the ABC and of carrying small ordinary stones to lay the foundation), about the "independently active" vanguard, etc. Under the spell of Chatsky-Tartarin, Mr. Martov also lets his tongue run away with him, and he speaks of "independently conscious elements of the working class" (No. 7-8, p. 42), who are coming forward to replace the old personnel now going through a process of "self-liquidation" (ibid.).

They are laying it on thick: "independently active", "independently conscious", "creative", "fighting mobilisation", "the broadest", "most open".... One wonders how it is these gentlemen are not nauseated by all this "verbal incontinence", to use Shchedrin's expression.

The whole point is that they *have* to resort to florid, laboured phrases which are meant to stun and stupefy the workers (and still more so the intellectual, because workers laugh at a style like Yuri Chatsky's, and it is mostly high-school boys who "*fall*" for it), because they have no plain, direct, and clear answer to the plain, clear, and immediate questions. The question of the election platform enables us to give a particularly vivid illustration of the truth regarding the conversion of *vague* thoughts into vague, bombastic, and pompous phrases.

III

In referring to the importance of an election platform, Mr. Yuri Chatsky again speaks with great eloquence. The question of a platform is "one of the most cardinal questions". Splendid! "To the worker Social-Democrats it [the platform] must be a product of feeling [!], of deep thought; they must consider it *their own*." (Yuri Chatsky's italics.)

It is true that the workers ought to give *deep thought* to the platform. Nor would it be at all amiss for intellectuals writing in near-Marxist magazines to give the platform some thought. But the statement that the platform must be "a product of feeling" is more than we can understand. Perhaps Nevedomsky and Lunacharsky will treat us in the next issue of *Nasha Zarya* to "feeling" articles on how the independently active vanguard of the independently conscious masses that are being mobilised is to "feel" an election platform.

And here, if you please, is a gem from an article by Mr. F. Dan: "... the sense and the political content of election tactics change completely depending on who creates and applies these tactics: a self-governing collective of the Social-Democratic working-class vanguard, with all its proletarian and intellectual forces, or various petty groups of intellectuals, be they even 'Social-Democrats', but not backed up by such a collective, not acting under its control and pressure... ". Who, indeed, can doubt that Potresov and Dan are by no means a "petty group of intellectuals", *but* men "backed up by the self-governing collective of the vanguard" and "acting under its control"! O, these Tartarins of the liquidationist trend!

Have Yuri Chatsky, L. Martov, and F. Dan given any thought to the platform? "It's a shame to admit and a sin to conceal," writes Yuri Chatsky, "but it has also happened that for some of us the platform was one thing, and other things were said in election speeches and articles, everyone pulling his own way."

The truth cannot be denied. "For some of us" such things have indeed often happened.

For instance, Yuri Chatsky, after indulging in words full of feeling about a platform which is a product of feeling, begins to talk at extremely great length, and in words no less full of feeling, about the importance and the indispensability of a *single* platform. The words full of feeling are deliberately used to obscure the simple question as to whether there can be a *single* platform where there is no unity of political opinion. If there is among us unity of opinion, why waste words and go to the trouble of breaking down an open door when a platform represents an exposition of opinion!

Yuri Chatsky, however, after a lot of beating about the bush apropos of a "single" platform, very clumsily gives away his own "secret". "We attach the greatest importance," he writes, "to the sanction [of the platform] by the Social-Democratic group in the Duma; but at the same time we absolutely insist on the condition that the latter does not follow the line of least resistance by sanctioning a platform imposed upon it by circles abroad." (P. 50.)

This is described thus: *Der König absolut, wenn er unseren Willen tut*—the king is absolute ruler so long as he does *our* bidding. It is desirable to have a single platform—provided it is not a platform "imposed by circles abroad". Surely this means that *actually there are* two platforms? One is the platform which you are abusing as being "imposed from abroad" (truly a language worthy of Purishkevich. Just think of it: Yuri Chatsky, working hand in glove with Martov and Dan, writes in Potresov's magazine about something being imposed from abroad! How low one must have fallen to resort to such methods of inciting ignorant people against "abroad"!). The other platform, apparently, does not come from abroad, but from the self-governing collective of the broad and open organisations of the mobilised masses. In plainer words and without any flourishes: "the other element of possible centralisation is the group of Social-Democratic [?] functionaries who are closely connected with the open workers' movement and are acquiring ever greater stability and prestige in the process of conducting political campaigns. We refer particularly to St. Petersburg and its leading role in the political campaigns of the past year". That is what Yuri Chatsky writes.

It is all quite simple: the "group" of St. Petersburg liquidators, well known for their work in Mr. Potresov's magazine—that is the "element of centralisation". Clear, very clear, indeed, friend Yuri Chatsky!

There must be a single platform, *but* ... it must not be one "imposed by circles abroad", and it must satisfy the "group" of St. Petersburg liquidators.... What an ardent advocate of "unity" he is—this Yuri Chatsky!

IV

Let us now take a look at L. Martov's "fundamental platform propositions".... As the basis of the platform he takes the programme—and that is as it should be, of course. Martov gives a paraphrase of sections of the programme. Only it is not clear whether Martov is advocating *that* programme which he outlined in No. 7-8 of *Nasha Zarya*. *That* particle of the old programme is acceptable even to Larin and Levitsky, and, probably, to Prokopovich. Or, does Martov subscribe to the *whole* of the *old* programme?

In fairness it must be noted that there is one passage in Martov's article which indicates the latter to be the case. It is the passage on p. 48 in which he states that sometimes they are compelled to "refrain from speaking out in clear terms" (that is true), but, they must not *renounce*. Nobody can make them *reduce* the content of their demands, he says. These are very fine words. Unfortunately, the *deeds* do not correspond to these words, for we know perfectly well, for instance, that Larin, whom Martov does "not suspect of reformism", *does reduce* and *renounce*. We shall very soon have occasion to see that Martov, too, in that very same article, while promising not to "reduce", and not to "renounce", actually does both.

Consequently, the actual situation is that, on the question of using the programme as a component part and basis of a platform, we have not one but two platforms: *without* reduction and renunciation, and *with* reduction and renunciation, the purport of which is clearly indicated by the nature of the sermons preached by Larin, Levitsky, and Potresov.

Then comes the question of tactics. We must assess the historical meaning of the June Third period, and this assessment ought to serve as the basis of *all* the definitions of our tasks, of *all* the opinions we "express" on any general and particular problems of current politics. Martov himself is obliged to admit—despite the liquidators' characteristic habit of sneering at "assessments of current events"—that this is a cardinal question. And so, this is what Martov declares with regard to the "old", formulated answer to that question:

"Attempts were made to define the historical meaning of the 'June Third' period by an inept formula, inept because it is liable to lead to misconceptions, which referred to 'a step toward the transformation ["in the transformation" would be the exact quotation] into a bourgeois monarchy',"...

An "inept" formula.... How mild that sounds! Yet it is only recently that Martov's colleagues saw in this formula a complete negation in principle of the viewpoint which seems to them to be the only salvation. It is only recently that F. Dan spoke of those who "want to shove in where they have once been defeated". Why, then, this change of tone? Is there a fundamental divergence on the question of the historical meaning of the June Third period, or not? Listen further:

"This formula fails to account for the actual step *back* toward division of power between the protagonists of absolutism and the landed nobility. It follows from the above that after the events of 1905 the forms in which alone it was possible for this division to be effected created favourable conditions for the mobilisation and organisation of the social forces whose historical mission it is to work for the creation of a 'bourgeois monarchy'."...

According to Martov, these social forces are represented by the bourgeoisie that was "given the right to act as a legal or tolerated opposition" by the June Third period.

Now, examine Martov's reasoning. *On the face of it*, he reproaches the "inept formula" only of overlooking the step back taken by the *government*. But, in the first place, this is factually incorrect. Martov has amazingly bad luck with the "formula" of 1908: whenever he sets out to speak of it he immediately reveals a strange inability (or reluctance?) to give an exact reproduction of the "formula" which is so well known to him. The "formula" speaks plainly and explicitly about the preservation of the "power and revenue" of the *feudal* landowners (and not of bourgeois landowners, as Larin would have us say)! Consequently, if this sort of division of power is to be regarded as a "step back", then this step back, far from being overlooked in our formula, is referred to in the most explicit terms. And, secondly, and *this is the main point*, while speaking of the step back taken by the government, Martov obscures, glosses over, the *step back* taken by the *liberal bourgeoisie*. There's the rub! That is the essence of the arguments, which Martov obscures.

The step back taken by the liberal bourgeoisie consists in the *Vekhi* sentiments of this bourgeoisie, its renunciation of democracy, its *drawing closer* to the "parties of law and order", its support (direct and indirect, ideological and political) for the attempts of the old regime to maintain itself at the cost of minimum "steps in the transformation into a bourgeois monarchy". Without the counter-revolutionary (*Vekhi* type) liberal bourgeoisie, it is not only impossible for the bourgeois monarchy to take shape, it cannot even begin to take shape. Martov "forgets" this primarily and mainly for the simple reason that he himself is a *Vekhi* man among Marxists.

In evaluating the June Third period, the liberal is entirely concerned with the fact that the government took a "step back" towards the Purishkeviches. Had the same government, with the same fundamental features of the regime (and of its policy of suppression with regard to *democracy*) left intact, taken a "step" towards him, towards the liberal, that would have been all he required. What the liberal says, in effect, is the following: I have proved by *Vekhi* and its policy (Milyukov's "London") that I, the liberal, am a sincere, serious, implacable enemy of democracy—of the democracy that is "anti-state", apostate, infantile, criminal, "thievish", immoral, godless, and what not, as stated in *Vekhi*. Yet, notwithstanding all this, power is shared not with me but with Purishkevich! That is the *meaning* of the policy of the liberals after June 3, 1907, that is the meaning of the "Stolypin liberalism" of Struve, Milyukov, and their like. I offer you my very soul, says the liberal lifting up his eyes to the government, yet you prefer Purishkevich!

On the other hand, the standpoint of proletarian democracy in regard to the June Third period, is fundamentally and radically different. The government took its "step back" to the Purishkeviches at a different, considerably higher, stage of development than before. A "step back" to the nobility was taken in the eighties too. But that was a step back taken in post-Reform Russia, in a Russia a long way advanced beyond the era of Nicholas I, when the noble landowner had ruled in the absence of a "plutocracy", in the absence of railways, and in the absence of a growing third element. And so today, the "step back" to the Purishkeviches is combined with a bourgeois agrarian policy and with the bourgeoisie organised and firmly entrenched in the representative institutions. It is Purishkevich's hegemony in the common (both Purishkevich's and Milyukov's) turn *against* democracy, against the movement of the masses, against so-called "excesses", against the so-called "high-brow [*Vekhi*] revolution", etc.

The liberal's job is to "threaten" Purishkevich so as to get him to "move over" a bit, to make more room for the liberals, but making sure at the same time that this does not obliterate from the face of the earth all the economic and political foundations of Purishkevichism. The task of a democrat in general, and of a Marxist, a representative of proletarian democracy, in particular, is to take advantage of any sharp conflict to bring the masses into the arena for the very purpose of effecting this obliteration. From the point of view of the task of the general transformation of Russia, the historical meaning of the June Third period, is precisely that the new step in the transformation into a bourgeois monarchy is a step towards a greater separation of the classes in every respect and, especially, towards a greater separation of the liberals (the "responsible" opposition to the Purishkeviches) from the democrats (working for the elimination of all the foundations of Purishkevichism).

Hence it is obvious that Martov, while apparently criticising only the "inept formula", *actually* puts forward the platform of a *liberal labour policy*. He sees the "step back" taken by the old regime towards the Purishkeviches, but he refuses to see the step back taken by the liberal bourgeoisie towards the old regime. He sees that the events of 1905 created favourable conditions "for the mobilisation and organisation" of the liberal bourgeoisie against the Purishkeviches and alongside the Purishkeviches, but he *refuses* to see that those events created "favourable conditions" for the mobilisation and organisation of the *Vekhi*-type, counter-revolutionary liberal bourgeoisie against democracy, against the movement of the masses. From the passage quoted from Martov's article it, therefore, follows inevitably that the workers ought to "support" the liberals in the *latter*'s struggle against the Purishkeviches, that they ought to leave the *hegemony* to the liberals; but it does not by any means follow that, *in spite* of the *Vekhi* sentiments of the liberals, *in spite* of the aspirations of the Milyukovs to get a seat next to the Purishkeviches, the workers ought to rouse the masses to the job of doing away entirely with the deepest roots (and the loftiest pinnacles) of Purishkevichism.

Hence it is obvious, further, why Martov can and should agree with Larin on the basic points, differing from him only in details, only in the manner of formulating the tasks of a liberal labour policy. We already have a bourgeois monarchy in Russia, says Larin, our landowners are no longer "feudal lords" but agrarians, i.e., bourgeois entrepreneurs in the countryside. Therefore, we are not facing any historical "leaps", and what we need is *"not* hegemony, but a class party" (Levitsky), our task is to support the liberal constitutionalists, while preserving our own independence.* So far we still have no bourgeois mon-

---

* As Larin wrote: "to stand up for itself ... during the coming constitutional reform".

archy, objects Martov, but it is "ample" for us to know that the combination of absolutism and constitutionalism is contradictory, and therefore it is necessary for us to strike at the old regime "through the Achilles heel of its contradictions". Neither of the two disputants sees the connection between the bourgeois monarchy that has been born or is being born and the counter-revolutionary nature of the liberal bourgeoisie; both of them fail to take account of the activity of the "leader" in determining not only the extent but also the type of bourgeois transformation in Russia; according to both of them, whether they say so or not, the "arrangements are made" for the working class in the new, bourgeois Russia, but the workers do not *do the arranging* and secure for themselves a democratic following capable of repudiating all the foundations of Purishkevichism.

V

It is interesting to note that Martov's further arguments defeat him even more glaringly.

"Thus," Martov continues, "the Bourbons who were restored to power in 1815 did not create a bourgeois monarchy, but were compelled to cloak their rule, and the rule of the nobility that backed them, in political forms which hastened the organisation of the bourgeoisie and enabled it to grow into the force that was capable of creating the bourgeois monarchy of 1830."

Splendid. Prior to the Bourbons of 1815 and prior to 1789, France had a feudal, patriarchal monarchy. After 1830 France had a bourgeois monarchy. But what kind of monarchy did Martov set out to discuss (to his own discomfiture), i.e., the monarchy of 1815-30? It is obvious that it was "a step toward the transformation into a bourgeois monarchy". The example cited by Martov is a splendid refutation of his arguments! Further, the French liberal bourgeoisie already began to reveal its hostility to consistent democracy during the movement of 1789-93. As Martov knows perfectly well, democracy did not by any means set itself the task of creating a bourgeois *monarchy*. *In the face* of the vacillations, betrayals, and counter-revolutionary sentiments of the liberal bourgeoisie, France's democrats, with the working class at their head, created, after a long series of trying "campaigns", the political system which became consolidated after 1871. At the beginning of the era of bourgeois revolutions, the French liberal bourgeoisie was monarchist in outlook; at the end of a long period of bourgeois revolutions, and to the extent to which the actions of the proletariat and of the bourgeois-democratic elements (the "Left bloc" elements, in spite of all that L. Martov may say to the contrary!) became increasingly determined and independent, the French bourgeoisie in its entirety was *recast* into a republican bourgeoisie, retrained, re-educated, reborn. In Prussia, and in Germany in general, the landowner never relinquished his hegemony during the whole period of bourgeois revolutions and he "educated" the bourgeoisie in his own image, after his own likeness. In France, during all the eighty years of bourgeois revolutions, the proletariat, in various combinations with the "Left bloc" elements of the petty bourgeoisie, won for itself hegemony at least four times, and as a result the bourgeoisie had to create a political system more acceptable to its opposite.

Bourgeoisies differ. Bourgeois revolutions provide a vast variety of combinations of different groups, sections, and elements both of the bourgeoisie itself and of the working class. To "deduce" an answer to the concrete problems of the Russian bourgeois revolution of the first decade of the twentieth century from "the general concept" of bourgeois revolution in the narrowest sense of the term is to debase Marxism to liberalism.

"Thus," Martov continues, "after it suppressed the Revolution of 1848, the Prussian government found itself compelled to introduce a constitution and a legislative representative body, organised in the interests of the landowners; these paltry rudiments of a constitutional-parliamentary system served as the basis for the political organisation of the bourgeoisie, which, however, to this day has not succeeded in transforming the state into a 'bourgeois monarchy'.

"Hence the above-mentioned formulation errs in making no mention of the decisive collision between the classes, without which the objective tendency revealed in acts of the June Third type cannot be translated into reality!"

That is truly magnificent, isn't it? Martov is positively a virtuoso when it comes to disguising reformist arguments, theories, and platforms with catchwords which create the impression of being Marxist and revolutionary! Apropos of the same "formula" which Martov is criticising, F. Dan poured scorn on people who want "to shove in where they have once been defeated". Y. Larin wrote that the working class must organise, not "in expectation of a revolution", but simply for the purpose of "firmly and systematically defending its special interests". Now Martov makes the discovery that the formula errs because *it makes no mention of the decisive collision between the classes*. Simply charming!

But Martov's phrase is not merely comical, it has another feature to it. Martov expressed himself with consummate evasiveness. He did not say to *which* classes he was referring. In the preceding sentences he spoke of the landowners and the bourgeoisie. It might be conjectured that Martov here refers to a decisive collision *only* between the landowners and the bourgeoisie. Only on *this* assumption may Martov's words be "taken seriously". But if *this* assumption is correct, then that shows him up with particular clarity as an advocate or defender of a liberal labour policy.

Our formula "makes no mention of the decisive collision" between the classes of the landowners and the bourgeoisie! But, hold! Our formula speaks plainly, definitely and explicitly of *"petty dissensions"* between these classes. From our viewpoint the dissensions between these classes are *petty*. Great importance attaches to the collision, *not* between these classes, but between other classes, of which the "formula" speaks further on in just as plain and unmistakable terms.

Consequently the question is as follows. No one who shares the Marxist viewpoint can expect Russia's salvation from the "June Third period" to come from anything other than a "decisive collision between the classes". We must be clear on the historical meaning of the "June Third period" if we want to know *which* classes in contemporary Russia can and must (in the sense of objective necessity, not of a subjective "must") come into decisive collision. Martov, apparently, thinks, as do all the liquidators, that in Russia a decisive collision is bound to take place between the landed nobility and the liberal bourgeoisie. (Be it noted in parenthesis that the liquidators will render the working-class movement a real service if they *openly* set forth this view in the draft platform of *Nasha Zarya* and *Dyelo Zhizni*, because they will thereby explain the matter to the workers; if, however, the platform of these publications does *not* openly express this view, it will be shown that the purpose of their platform is to conceal their real views, that the platform is at variance with the real ideological content of the propaganda carried on by these two magazines.)

We think, and this is plainly stated in our "formula", that *no* decisive collision is to be expected between the old type of landed nobility and the liberal bourgeoisie in Russia. Clashes between these two classes are inevitable, but they will be mere "petty dissensions" which *will* "*not decide*" *anything* in Russia's destiny and cannot bring about any decisive, real change for the better.*

A really decisive collision is still to come between *other* classes—a collision on the basis and within the framework of bourgeois society, i.e., of commodity production and capitalism.

What ground is there for this opinion? It is justified both by theoretical considerations and by the experience of 1905-07. In these three years Russia experienced a sharp collision of classes that ranks as one of the greatest class collisions in world history. Nevertheless, even in those three years, in a bourgeois society which lacked even the most

---

* Naturally, it does not follow from this that the liberal bourgeoisie, together with the landed nobility, represents "one reactionary mass", that the conflicts between these two are of no political significance, that they cannot give rise to a democratic movement, or that it is permissible to ignore these conflicts. To draw such conclusions would be tantamount to reducing a correct proposition to an absurdity, it would betray a lack of understanding of the limits within which this proposition is correct. For it is a well-known fact that "the greatest justice", if reduced to an absurdity because of a failure to understand the limits and conditions of the just and unjust, becomes "the greatest injustice": *summum jus—summa injuria*. We should remember the following fact in the history of Russian Marxism. The appraisal of the liberal-bourgeois parties in Russia (with the Cadet Party at their head) given at the well-known London Congress was exactly the same as that outlined in the present article; but that did not prevent the Congress from recognising the necessity "to make use of the activity of these parties to further the political education of the people".

elementary conditions and guarantees of bourgeois liberty, the collision between the landed nobility and the liberal bourgeoisie, between the latter and the old regime, was neither sharp nor decisive. On the other hand, the sharp and decisive collisions, collisions that could in any way be described as sharp and decisive, were those between the peasants and the landowners, between the workers and the capitalists.

How is this phenomenon to be explained? In the first place, by the fact that the liberal bourgeoisie is so closely linked with the landed nobility economically, their mutual interests are so closely intertwined, that from the standpoint of the former the safest and most desirable course is to reform the latter, but by no means to abolish it. The slowest, even imperceptibly slow, reform is better than abolition, that is how the overwhelming majority of the liberal bourgeois reason, and with Russia's economic and political situation *as it is at present* this class *cannot* reason otherwise.

Further, if we take for instance the strike movement, we find that in Russia, during the three years referred to, it developed to a point never achieved in any of the most advanced and most developed capitalist countries in the world. That is why it was *inevitable* for the liberal bourgeoisie to reason that the slowest, the most imperceptibly slow, reform of the antiquated conditions of labour was better than a resolute breach with the old, that it was better to preserve the old than to make a decisive break with it. On the other hand, the economic condition of the workers and peasants made it *impossible* for them to reason along those lines; here the economic conditions gave rise to really sharp and really decisive collisions. It is wrong to think, as the Narodniks think with regard to the peasantry, and Trotsky with regard to the workers, that those collisions went beyond the limits of bourgeois society. But there can be no shadow of doubt that it is by *such*, and *only by such*, collisions (provided they lead to a definite outcome) that *all* the old, the threadbare, the pre-bourgeois can be fully eradicated, can be abolished without leaving a trace.

The Russian landlords, from Purishkevich to Dolgorukov, have trained our liberal bourgeoisie in a spirit of servility, inertia, and fear of change unparalleled in history.

The Russian peasants, under the economic and political conditions *at present obtaining* in Russia, represent that *bourgeois* stratum of the population out of which the era of "collisions", the era of bourgeois revolutions (in the historico-methodological meaning of the term), with the workers taking a leading part, *is educating* a bourgeoisie that is free of the above-mentioned pleasant qualities. But will it complete this education? This question can only be answered when the era of bourgeois revolutions in Russia is at an end. Until that time all the progressive trends of political thought in Russia will inevitably be divided into two main types, depending on whether they are gravitating to the hegemony of the liberals who are striving to remake and renovate Russia in a manner that will not be injurious to the Purishkeviches, or to the hegemony of the working class with the best elements of the peasantry as its following.

I said "are gravitating", because we cannot expect all the progressive trends to be conscious of, i.e., to understand, the class roots of the various policies. But Marxists would not be worthy of the name if they failed to delve down to those roots, and if they failed to understand that both the defence of the special interests of the working class and the training of the working class for its future role in bourgeois Russia will inevitably, owing to the objective interrelation of the social forces, follow the same two main channels: it will either trail along *behind* the liberals (who are marching behind the Purishkeviches or alongside of them), or lead the democratic elements forward *in spite* of the vacillations, desertions, and *Vekhi* sentiments of the liberals.

VI

We have now come face to face with the question of the celebrated "Left bloc" policy. Yuri Chatsky and F. Dan, it may be said without exaggeration, rave and fulminate against a Left bloc. This is all the more natural to the second of these two politicians since he must somehow cover up his betrayal of the workers' cause and his part in the split of the St. Petersburg workers' organisation, for the sake of a bloc with the Cadets, in the spring of 1907! But the question of a Left bloc is an interesting and important question of principle, not only, and even not so much, from the

standpoint of election agreements (under the existing electoral law the "Left bloc" has seldom been realised in practice), but from the point of view of the general character and
content of election propaganda and agitation. To "compel"
the most numerous democratic masses in the country (the
peasants and sections of the non-agricultural petty bourgeoisie akin to them) "to choose between the Cadets and the
Marxists", and to pursue a line of "joint action" of the
workers and the peasant democrats both against the old
regime and against the vacillating counter-revolutionary
liberal bourgeoisie, is the basis and substance of the tactics
of a "Left bloc". These tactics were sanctioned by the
course of events in 1905 (the working-class and peasant
movement), by the votes of the "Trudovik" and workers' groups
in the First and the Second Dumas, by the attitude of the
press of the different parties to the cardinal questions of
democracy, and even by the stand on the agrarian question
taken by the "peasant group" in the *Third* Duma (considering that there are many Right elements in that group!).
It is a well-known fact that the agrarian bill introduced
by forty-three peasant members of the *Third* Duma[170] is
far more democratic than the liberal bill of the Cadets, a
fact the Cadets themselves admit!

There is no doubt that it is precisely in this sense, on
general principles, that the liquidators repudiate the "Left
bloc" policy. And there is just as little doubt that their repudiation of the Left bloc policy constitutes treason to the
cause of democracy. *Not a single* bourgeois-liberation movement the world over has ever failed to provide examples
and instances of "Left bloc" tactics, and wherever these
movements triumphed, in *all* such cases, it was *always* as a
result of these tactics, a result of the struggle being directed
along these lines in spite of the vacillations and treachery
of the liberals. It was the "Left bloc" tactics—the alliance
between the urban "plebs" (=the modern proletariat) and
the democratic peasantry that lent sweep and force to the
English revolution in the seventeenth century and the
French revolution in the eighteenth century. Marx and
Engels drew attention to this fact on many occasions, not
only in 1848, but much later as well. In order to avoid quoting frequently quoted passages, we shall merely mention

the correspondence between Marx and Lassalle in 1859. Apropos of Lassalle's tragedy *Franz von Sickingen*, Marx wrote that the intended collision in the drama was "not simply tragic, but really the tragic collision that spelled the doom, and properly so, of the revolutionary party of 1848-49". And Marx, indicating in general terms the *entire* line of the future differences between the Lassalleans and the Eisenachers,[171] reproached Lassalle for making the mistake of "placing the *Lutheran-knightly* opposition above the *plebeian-Muncerian* opposition".[172]

We are not here concerned with the question whether Marx was right or wrong in making that reproach; we think he was right even though Lassalle defended himself vigorously against this reproach. The important point is that Marx and Engels considered it an obvious mistake to place the "Lutheran-knightly" opposition (the opposition of the liberals and landowners in Russia at the beginning of the twentieth century) *above* the "plebeian-Muncerian" opposition (proletarian and peasant, in that same Russia); that both of them considered this absolutely impermissible for a Social-Democrat!

In heaping abuse upon Left bloc tactics, the liquidators try by their words to drown the inescapable fundamental issue of the principle that a "Left bloc" policy is obligatory for every workers' party in every bourgeois-democratic movement. Since they are unable to deal with the question in terms of principle they get into curious contradictions and defeat their own case. Here is an instance. The very same Martov, who dreads a "Left bloc" like the plague, writes in formulating the agrarian programme in his "Fundamental Theses of a Platform" that "as before, the surest, most painless and most advantageous path of cultural development is ... to take the landed estates from their present owners and transfer them to the people". Involuntarily he thus went so far as to advocate, oh horror! nationalisation! That in the first place. Secondly, in expressing this correct idea, Martov (despite his colleague Cherevanin— see the latter's *Vekhi*-type book on *The Present Situation* in 1908) expressed a *Left bloc* idea; his agrarian programme is a programme of *Left bloc* action both against the old regime and *against the liberal parties of the Cadet type*!

"Drive Nature out of the door, and she will fly in through the window"!

The agrarian programme formulated by L. Martov is one on which the workers and the peasant Trudoviks together with their ideological leaders, the Narodniks, are making common cause (actually making common cause, i.e., working together *regardless* of any "agreements"). On the other hand, this programme *separates* both the workers and the peasant Trudoviks, taken together, *from* the Cadets (and from the bourgeois liberals in general). If in addition to this absolutely indisputable political conclusion, you will bear in mind that the agrarian question (the question of democratic agrarian change) is a key question of our liberation movement, then it is obvious that Martov was *compelled* to formulate "Left bloc" tactics in regard to the *central* issue of our epoch!

How and why did this misfortune befall our opponent of the "Left bloc" policy? Very simply. It was necessary for him either to *break* with the old programme openly and unequivocally, which he could not make up his mind to do; he had not yet "caught up" with the courageous (in their renegacy) Cherevanin and Larin. Or else it was necessary to reproduce, at least more or less correctly, the old programme—from which the "Left bloc" policy follows as an inescapable conclusion. Such is the bitter lot of our liquidators.

VII

It remains for us to point out two more important passages in Martov's article. "In each case," he writes, "of such a conflict arising within the June Third system [he is speaking of conflicts and friction which disintegrate and sap this system] the workers' party should strive to prevail upon the propertied classes to take one step or another toward the democratisation of legislation and an extension of constitutional guarantees, and, what is of the greatest independent value to us, toward an extension of the sphere of the unrestricted organisation of the popular forces" (*Nasha Zarya*, No. 7-8, p. 50).

Martov's formulation is very apt, only it is a formulation of the tasks and the line of a liberal labour policy.

"To prevail upon the propertied classes to take a step", to "extend the sphere of the unrestricted organisation of labour"—these.phrases of Martov's are exactly those repeated throughout the world by *all* more or less educated liberal bourgeois, all liberal bourgeois imbued to any extent with the "European" spirit. The distinction between a liberal labour policy and a Marxist labour policy begins *only* when and where it is explained to the workers that the above-quoted liberal formulation is inadequate, unsatisfactory, and a deception. To prevail upon the non-propertied classes to take a step toward changing *the very* "sphere" which the liberals are promising to "extend", and to substitute for it a *fundamentally* different "sphere"—that (approximately) is how the tasks and aspirations of the workers' party should be defined, if there is no desire to build up a liberal labour party.

It should be remarked, as a curiosity, that in a note to the quoted passage L. Martov makes the following observation: "As a matter of course, this formulation is sure to give rise to charges of opportunism and 'legalism at all costs'". And how do you think he refutes these charges? By referring to an article by N. Rozhkov printed in the *Obskaya Zhizn*,[173] No. 171. From that article Martov quotes five lines of extremely inept and unintelligible statements about "open political associations". We have not read that article. But, assuming that Rozhkov advocates an "open party", what is this supposed to prove when we are dealing with *Martov*'s formulation of a *liberal* labour *policy*? Since when has it become customary for anyone to justify *one* mistake of his own by pointing to *another* mistake committed by *another* writer?

But the entire *spirit* of Martov's article is best and most vividly conveyed by the following tirade in the concluding section of the last paragraph:

"We must conduct the entire election campaign under the banner of the struggle of the proletariat for the freedom of its political self-determination, of the struggle for its right to have a class party of its own and to develop its activities freely, for the right to take part in political life as an independent organised force. This principle [mark this!] must govern both the content and tactics of the election campaign and the methods to be used for organisational work."

Those are words that *correctly* express the "principle" which determines the "content" of the entire election agitation (and of the entire policy) of the liquidators! As for the fine words about "reducing nothing and renouncing nothing", with which Martov tried to console the Marxist readers, they are nothing but words, hollow words, so long as *this* is how the "principle" is formulated. For the crux of the matter is that the principle itself turns out to be that of a liberal labour policy.

The liberal bourgeois tells the workers: you are justified in fighting, indeed, you must fight, for the freedom of *your own* political self-determination, for the right to have a class party of *your own*, for the right freely to develop your activities, for *the right to take part* in political life as an independent organised force. It is these principles of the liberal, educated, radical, to use the English or French term, bourgeoisie that Martov is offering the workers in the guise of Marxism.

The Marxist tells the workers: in order really and successfully to fight for the freedom of your "own" political self-determination, you must fight for the free political self-determination of the entire people, you must show the people what the successive democratic forms of its political existence should be, and win the masses and the undeveloped sections of the working people away from the influence of the liberals. If your party is really to attain a full understanding of the tasks of the class, and if its activity is actually to be of a class nature and not of a guild nature, it is necessary for it not only to take part in political life, but, in spite of all the vacillations of the liberals, to direct the political life and initiative of the broad strata on to a greater arena than that indicated by the liberals, toward more substantial and more radical aims. He who confines the class to an "independent" corner of "activity" in an arena, the bounds, form, and shape of which are determined or permitted by the liberals, does not understand the tasks of the class. Only he understands the tasks of the class who directs its attention (and consciousness, and practical activity, etc.) to the need for so reconstructing this very arena, its entire form, its entire shape, as to extend it beyond the limits allowed by the liberals.

Wherein lies the difference between the two formulations? In the very fact, *among other things*, that the first *excludes* the idea of the "hegemony" of the working class, whereas the second deliberately defines this very idea; the first is the modern, latest variation of old Economism ("the workers should confine themselves to the economic struggle, leaving the political struggle to the liberals"), whereas the second strives to leave no room in the minds of the workers either for the old Economism or for its new variety.

Now it remains but to answer the concluding question: In what way does Levitsky differ from Martov? The former is one of the younger liquidators, one of the new generation, unaffected by the traditions and memories of the past. He does not beat about the bush, but says plainly, with the eagerness and straightforwardness of youth: "*not* hegemony, but a class party"! Martov, however, is "a man of the world", he once belonged to the old *Iskra* group, he represents a mixture of the old traditions, which have not yet completely vanished,* and of the new liquidationism which has not yet mustered a sufficient amount of courage. That is why he first swears and vows to — "reduce nothing, renounce nothing" — and then, after long and devious circumlocutions, blurts out that the "principle" of the entire election campaign must be a liquidationist one.

But, then, it is precisely the "principle" of the election campaign that constitutes the whole crux of the matter.

Prosveshcheniye, Nos. 1 and 2,
December 1911 and January 1912
Signed: *K. Tulin*

Published according to
the *Prosveshcheniye* text

---

* It would be more correct to say: The substance of these traditions, their ideological core, has completely vanished as far as Martov is concerned, but the *words* have remained, the habit of carrying the "decent label" of an "unswerving internationalist" still makes itself felt.

FIRST EXPOSURE OF CADET NEGOTIATIONS WITH THE CABINET

Those who, six or five and a half years ago, sounded the alarm about the negotiations which the Constitutional-Democrats were, in general, conducting with Cabinet ministers, especially on the subject of ministerial portfolios, cannot help entertaining a feeling of profound satisfaction today. Historical truth is bound to out—it is sometimes divulged in quarters from which truth is least expected. The first revelations have now been made, and, despite all the efforts of "interested" persons (and parties) to hush them up, they will not end here. It may be said with absolute certainty that these exposures will fully corroborate the accusations we levelled against the Cadets at that time.

Witte started them in his controversy with Guchkov. Witte's object and the nature of his revelations are of the basest; it is an intrigue of the worst kind, a desire to trip somebody up, a bid for a portfolio. But it is a well-known fact that when two thieves fall out honest men always come into their own; and when three thieves have fallen out, the gain is likely to be the greater.

What matters most in Witte's letter is that willy-nilly he had to establish certain *facts*—thus providing an opportunity (and making it indispensable) to verify these facts by questioning all those involved in the affair. The basic facts to be gleaned from Witte's letter are the following:

(1) The conference called by Witte was attended by Shipov, Guchkov, Urusov, Y. Trubetskoi, and M. Stakhovich, that is to say, leading figures of the Cadet, Peaceful Renovation, and Octobrist parties.

(2) "At the first session of the conference between Count Witte [we are quoting his letter] and the above-mentioned prominent persons, agreement in principle was reached on all the main questions, except the question of the appointment of the Minister of the Interior."

(3) "Count Witte insisted on Durnovo's appointment, while the prominent persons, with the exception of Prince Urusov, were opposed to it. As for Prince Urusov, he tried to persuade his colleagues at the conference to agree to Durnovo's appointment in view of the gravity of the situation and the impossibility of delaying the matter, and, for his own part, he declared that, in order to set an example, he was prepared to accept the post of Vice-Minister under Durnovo.... At the next session Shipov, Guchkov, and Prince Trubetskoi declared that they could not join a Cabinet that would include Durnovo...."

(4) Stolypin's candidature was mentioned, but it failed to receive unanimous approval. Some were in favour, others were opposed to it.

What amendments has Guchkov introduced to this statement of the facts? He has confirmed that "Durnovo's candidature had the warm support of Prince Urusov, subsequently a member of the First Duma." Witte, according to Guchkov, hesitated, and there was a moment when he was prepared to give up Durnovo because it was known that the press was about to come out with revelations and bitter articles against him. "The whole incident," adds Guchkov, "took place immediately after the Manifesto of October 17, when there reigned the fullest, the most unbridled, I should say, freedom of the press."

The negotiations were prolonged. Guchkov writes of "wearisome days of protracted negotiations". In respect of Stolypin, he says that "nobody expressed the unfavourable opinion mentioned by Cound Witte. In describing the general situation obtaining at that time, Guchkov says: "Many 'saviours' of the country have now appeared on the scene.... But where were they in those days? ... At that time many of them had not yet made up their minds on which side of the barricades they were going to stand".

Those are the essential points in Witte's and Guchkov's revelations. The minor details we naturally leave out of consideration. The historical truth is now quite definitely established: (1) *At that extremely grave moment in the history of Russia there were no serious differences of opinion between the Cadets and the Octobrists*; (2) "At that time many [of the bourgeois leaders and, as Guchkov "subtly" hints, perhaps even of the ministers] had not yet made up their minds on which side of the barricades they were going to stand". But the fact is that those who attended the conference, and did so more than once, were men who all stood *on one definite "side of the barricades"*. During those conferences the ministers, and the Octobrists, and the Cadets all stood on the same side of the barricade. Historical truth permits of no doubt or misinterpretation: these were conferences at which the government conducted negotiations with the counter-revolutionary, liberal bourgeoisie.

Now look at the behaviour of the Cadets. Ever since the publication of Witte's and Guchkov's revelations (their letters were printed in St. Petersburg on September 26, and in Moscow on September 27, Old Style), the Cadets *have been maintaining complete silence about their* part in the affair, confining themselves to attempts to "twit" Guchkov. That is exactly what *Rech* did in its issue of September 28, and *Russkiye Vedomosti* in its issue of the same date, where they "twitted" Guchkov with having subsequently joined Durnovo's colleagues, but *they have never printed any corrections or denials that affect the historical facts*. The third thief hopes that, thanks to the controversy between Witte and Guchkov, he will go unnoticed!

Then the Octobrists begin to "revenge" themselves on both Witte and the Cadets. On *October 14* (after two weeks of reconnoitring by the Octobrists and of cowardly and mean silence on the part of the Cadets) *Golos Moskvy* carried a "statement of facts" headed "Count Witte and P. N. Durnovo in Alliance with the Cadets". The new revelations bring out the following points: (1) Prince Trubetskoi was a member of the Constitutional-Democratic Party at the time. (2) "Since he did not want to create any misconceptions in Count Witte's mind, Prince Trubetskoi considered it his duty to warn him that he, Prince Trubetskoi, would inform the bureau of his party, which met every day in Professor Petrazhitsky's apartment to discuss current affairs, about all of Witte's negotiations with men prominent in public life" (it is obvious that neither the Octobrists nor the Cadets regard the worker and peasant democrats as "prominent in public life"; apparently, in October 1905 the workers and peasants were *outside* "public life"!). (3) Mr. Petrunkevich was particularly vehement in his objections to Stolypin's candidature. He said that, "if the worst came to the worst [*sic!*], it was necessary to advise Count Witte to appoint Durnovo, rather than Stolypin, to the post of Minister of the Interior. The other leaders of the Constitutional-Democratic Party fully shared Petrunkevich's opinion, and Prince Trubetskoi was instructed to convey to Count Witte the opinion of the prominent public men who met in Petrazhitsky's apartment". The next morning Trubetskoi visited Count Witte and conveyed to him the exact opinion of the bureau of the Constitutional-Democratic Party about both candidates.

Has Trubetskoi corroborated the reference to his part in the affair? He fully corroborated it when he told both the correspondent of *Novoye Vremya* (see issue of October 15) and the *correspondent* of *Rech* (see issue of October 19) that the information printed in *Golos Moskvy* was *"quite exact"*. "The word 'bureau'," said Trubetskoi, "is *perhaps out of place*, it would have been more correct to say 'leaders of the Party'" (meaning the Cadets). Trubetskoi made another, just as immaterial, "correction", stating that he had visited Witte "not the next morning, perhaps, but two or three days later". Finally, in the interview he gave to the *Rech* correspondent, Trubetskoi said:

"Exception must be taken to one statement made by Guchkov. He says that the prominent people refused to join the Cabinet only because of Durnovo. That is not quite so [not quite so!] as far as I am concerned and, if I am not mistaken, the same applies to Shipov and I expressed our willingness to join the Cabinet, but on condition that its programme was drafted beforehand. Witte, however, tried to persuade us to join the Cabinet without insisting on that condition. That was the difference between us and Guchkov, who, as far as I can remember, stipulated no such condition." Trubetskoi is very cautious in his choice of expressions on this point: "not quite so", "as far as I can remember"!

Mr. Petrunkevich deals with the subject in *Rech* of October 19—*three weeks* after the first revelations were published! Now, see *how* he does it.

He begins with a long-winded argument (27 lines) about the inadvisability of relying on people's memories, and points out that Shipov was the only one who kept a diary.

What is the purport of this argument? Do you want to have the truth published, at once and in full? Then nothing could be easier than to *name all* those who took part in the conferences and to question them about it. If, however, you do not want to have the truth about *your own* party published, then do not play at hide-and-seek and do not refer to Shipov.

Then follow *27 lines* of argument about the propensity of the Octobrists for "canards". But what is the point of this argument, once *Golos Moskvy* mentioned *the person* who corroborated its information? Mr. Petrunkevich is obviously at pains to obscure a plain and clear question by heaping up literary and diplomatic rubbish around it. That is a *dishonest* method.

Further follow *20 lines* of jibes at Trubetskoi: that he indulges in "personal reminiscences"—as though reminiscences could be anything but personal!—and that the Prince *"never mentioned the matter to anyone"*—the emphasis being Petrunkevich's, who obviously intends this as a rebuke for Trubetskoi's indiscretion. Instead of giving a plain answer to the question, the Cadets have begun to rebuke one another for being indiscreet. What *can* this kind of method mean, except that the Cadets are *chagrined* by the revelations? It betrays their efforts *to hush up* the matter (what they say, in effect, is: don't be indiscreet in the future, Prince).

The 74 lines of introduction are followed, at last, by the denial proper on the following points: (1) The bureau of the Constitutional-Democratic Party was in Moscow and, therefore, could not meet in Petrazhitsky's apartment. (2) "At that time" Petrazhitsky "was not one of the group of persons who directed the affairs of the Party". (3) "The few members [of the bureau of the Constitutional-Democratic Party] who were living in St. Petersburg were not authorised to enter into any negotiations, and still less alliances, with Count Witte, Mr. Durnovo, or any other persons."

(4) "Personally, I [Petrunkevich] visited Petrazhitsky *once* [Mr. Petrunkevich's emphasis], and it is true that on that one occasion there was some talk about the possibility of Prince Trubetskoi being offered the post of Minister of Education, and all those present expressed their conviction that the Prince could accept the offer only on condition that the entire Cabinet adopted a clear and definite programme fully conforming to the conditions of the political situation. Moreover, the Cabinet was to be one that could command the confidence of 'society' [bear in mind *what all* the disputants mean by the word "society": the workers and peasants are *not* "society"]. It is quite possible that at the same time the personal and political qualities of the various candidates, among them Durnovo and Stolypin, were discussed. But neither my memory, nor the memory of others whom I consulted on the subject, has retained any recollection of a warm speech which, presumably, convinced all those present."

That is all there is to the relevant part of Mr. Petrunkevich's "denial", to which he adds a further 48 lines of jibes at Trubetskoi, to the effect that the latter's memory has failed him, that the Constitutional-Democratic Party concluded no alliance with Durnovo and that it "prevented one of its members, Prince Trubetskoi, from joining a Cabinet which the Party could not support".

Trubetskoi's and Petrunkevich's letters in the *Rech* of October 27 add nothing new. The former insists that it was no other than Petrunkevich who "advised that Durnovo be preferred to Stolypin". Petrunkevich denies this.

Now, what does this all boil down to?

Mr. Petrunkevich declares that the few members of the bureau who were living in St. Petersburg *were not authorised to enter into any negotiations*, but he cannot help confirming the *fact* that negotiations were conducted! He himself states (*Rech*, October 27): "At the conference in Petrazhitsky's apartment we discussed Prince Trubetskoi's candidature".

This then means that *negotiations were conducted*. If, as Mr. Petrunkevich says, the Party "prevented" Prince Trubetskoi, *this means* that the negotiations *were conducted on behalf of the Party*!

Mr. Petrunkevich has an amazing knack of contradicting himself. There were no negotiations, but ... but there was "a conference on the candidature". The bureau of the Party held no meetings, but ... but the Party took a decision. Such pitiful evasions are characteristic of people who are trying in vain *to conceal* something. What, indeed, could be simpler than to name *all* those who took part in the conference, or to cite the exact decision of the "bureau", or of the Party, or of the leaders, or to set forth the allegedly clear and allegedly definite programme which (allegedly) the Cadets demanded of Witte's Cabinet? But the trouble with our liberals is that they *cannot afford* to tell the truth, they are *afraid* of it, the truth is their *ruin*.

And so they resort to petty and shabby subterfuges, equivocations and evasions, the purpose of which is to prevent the reader (at least the inattentive one) from getting a clear idea of a historical question of great importance, namely, the question of the attitude of the liberals to the government in October 1905.

Why is the truth the ruin of the Cadets? Because the fact that negotiations were conducted, and the circumstances and conditions under which they were conducted, explode the fable that the Cadets are democrats and prove the counter-revolutionary nature of their liberalism.

Could a really democratic party even think of entering into negotiations with a man like Witte at a time like October 1905? Certainly not; for such negotiations necessarily implied that both parties stood, to a certain extent, on common ground, namely the common ground of counter-revolutionary aspirations, sentiments, and proclivities.* There was nothing to negotiate with Witte, except ways and means of putting an end to the democratic mass movement.

Further, assuming for a moment that the Cadets, in entering into negotiations, did have *some* democratic purposes in

---

* See the excellent explanation of *this* common ground, on the basis of articles written by Mr. Milyukov *himself* (*A Year of Struggle*), in Y. K.'s article, "From the History of Russian Liberalism", in the almanac *Summer Lightnings*, St. Petersburg, 1907. "Count Witte's resignation means the loss of the last opportunity to come to terms," wrote Mr. Milyukov on April 18, 1906, thus admitting quite clearly and definitely that there had been *negotiations* for *deals* and that there had been *opportunities*, that there was some sense in *repeating* the attempts to negotiate a deal.

mind, could a democratic party have failed to inform the people of those negotiations when they were broken off? It could not. This is exactly where we see the difference between counter-revolutionary liberalism and democracy, undeserving of the epithet counter-revolutionary. The liberal *desires* an extension of liberty, but *in such a way* as not to lend strength to democracy; he wants the negotiations and the rapprochement with the old government to continue, to gain in force, to be put on a firm basis. That is why the liberal *could not afford* to inform the public of the negotiations after they had been broken off, for that would have made it difficult to resume the negotiations, he would thereby "have shown his hand" to democracy and broken with the authorities—but that is precisely something a liberal cannot bring himself to do. A democrat, on the other hand, who happened to be in the position of someone conducting negotiations with Witte and who saw the hopelessness of the negotiations, would immediately make them public, and thereby put the Wittes to shame, expose their game, and bring about a further advance of the democratic movement.

Consider also the question of the programme of the Cabinet and of its composition. All those involved in the affair speak of the latter and say quite clearly and explicitly, such and such portfolios were offered to such and such individuals. But *not a single* clear and explicit word is said about the *former*, i.e., about the programme! Both Trubetskoi and Petrunkevich remember the candidates for portfolios perfectly well, and name them. But *none* of them *says anything* about what the "programme" was! Is it just an accident? Of course not. It results from (and is also positive proof of) the "programmes" having been the last thing the liberal gentlemen thought of, simply meaningless window-dressing, hollow "literature"—actually, Witte could have had no other programme than that of strengthening the government and weakening the democratic movement, and no matter what assurances he gave, and what promises and statements he made, that would be the only policy he would have *pursued*. The "vital" business that they were primarily concerned with was that of the distribution of portfolios. For this reason only, Witte, for instance, could forget *all* about the programme (according to Witte, there was even complete agreement on principles!), but the controversy over the question as to who was better (or worse?), Durnovo or Stolypin, that is something they all remember, of which they all talk, and in connection with which they all refer to the speeches and arguments made by one person or another.

Murder will out. Even in the deliberately touched up stories of three or four persons the historical truth stands out in fairly bold relief.

Immediately after October 17, the entire liberal bourgeoisie of Russia—from Guchkov to Milyukov, who is undoubtedly politically responsible for Trubetskoi—turned away *from* democracy and drew closer to Witte. Nor was this an accident or the treachery of individuals—it was the *class* that went over to the counter-revolutionary position that corresponds to its economic interests. Only when they had assumed that position could the Cadets conduct negotiations with Witte through Trubetskoi in 1905, with Trepov through Muromtsev in 1906, etc. Unless we understand the distinction between counter-revolutionary liberalism and democracy, we cannot understand anything either about the history of the latter or about its tasks.

Prosveshcheniye, No. 1,   Published according to
    December 1911   the *Prosveshcheniye* text
    Signed: *P.*

433

THREE QUESTIONS

The verbatim reports of the State Duma, even of the Third Duma, represent extremely interesting and instructive political material. It will not be an exaggeration to say that the supplement to the rag called *Rossiya* is worth more than all the liberal newspapers. For the liberal newspapers make it their business to whitewash the liberals, and to gloss over the presentation of essential problems, by the Rights on the one hand, and by the representatives of the real masses of the population on the other; they invariably introduce an element of falsehood into the appraisal of the *real nature* of our "home policy". Yet it is precisely the *way* in which the various questions are *presented*, and the appraisal of the *real nature* of the issues involved, that is of prime importance in dealing with all the socio-economic and political problems of the present period.

We shall try to illustrate the above, as far as possible, by the debate in connection with three questions: on the secret political police, the famine, and the "temporary" Regulations of 1881.[174]

The first meeting of the current session of the Duma opened with a speech dedicated to Stolypin by the Chairman, an Octobrist. An interesting feature of the speech was the statement made by the leader of the Octobrists that "his [Stolypin's] constant concern was to ensure steady, even if cautious and circumspect, progress along the path of political and social development in Russia". Well put, isn't it? Stolypin in the capacity of a "progressist"! Many a democrat who read Rodzyanko's speech must have paused to ask why, under the present system of government, under the present political regime, and as long as there exists the class whose policy Stolypin put into effect, there can be no *other* kind of "progress" except the kind that we are witnessing at present, a kind of "progress" which fails to satisfy even the Octobrists. What a pity that none of the members of the Duma who were present during that speech*—those of them who pose as representatives of democracy—displayed any desire to dwell on the *class* roots of the Stolypin brand of "progress".

Yet the debate on the secret political police was a suitable occasion for going into that matter.

Stolypin "trusted the honourable A. I. Guchkov", thundered Markov the Second, "and his no less honourable friends in the Duma Centre. And he paid with his life for his trustfulness. The tranquillity which we experienced is the tranquillity of the grave. There is no other tranquillity. (Voices from the benches on the left: Hear, hear!) There is a revival of revolution.... There is no tranquillity, revolution is imminent. Revolution must be fought, we must fight it tooth and nail, we must give no quarter (laughter on the Left), we must hang all those rascals, fanatics, and scoundrels. That is all I have to say in opposition to the motion that this question be recognised as urgent[175]".

That was how the representative of the landowners presented the question.

Markov the Second was followed by Rodichev, who spoke on the real substance of the question. As usual, he spoke eloquently. But this eloquent liberal presented the question in an incredibly crude way. Liberal words and words—nothing more. "When their [the Octobrists'] Central Committee," exclaimed Mr. Rodichev, "declares with reference to the opposition that it is bent on assassinating its political antagonists, that is a shameful lie. But I am ready to for-

---

* We learn from the speech of Markov the Second that the workers' deputies were not in the hall at the time. "You," said Markov the Second, addressing the workers' deputies, "... frankly expressed your attitude ... when your benches were vacated a little while ago.... You withdrew.... Even if I don't respect you for that, I can understand you." Markov the Second very often behaves in the Duma like a common rowdy. But the words quoted above, as well as very many statements of his colleagues, show clearly that the question is presented from the standpoint of a definite class. This outspokenness is, as a rule, a hundred times more useful for the development of the political consciousness of the masses than the hackneyed phrases of the liberals who claim to be "above classes".

give you this lie if you vow to put an end to the serpent that has acquired power over the Russian government, to put an end to the spyocracy." (See page 23 of the Verbatim Report in *Rossiya*, and also page 24, again with a "vow".)

Impressive language—terribly impressive! Rodichev is prepared to forgive the Octobrists if they "vow" to put an end! But isn't it all bluff, Mr. Windbag? Not only the Octobrists, but *you*, Cadets, as well—no matter how much you "vow"—cannot *put an end* to any serious evil. Your talk about "vows" in connection with so grave a question only serves *to obscure* the political consciousness of the masses instead of enlightening them; you *muddle* peoples' minds by the din of words, instead of calmly, plainly and clearly explaining *why* the "serpent" has acquired power in the present instance, why it was able to and had to acquire power.

Since Mr. Rodichev does not explain this, since he is afraid of looking simply and directly at the root and the essence of the question, the thing that distinguishes him from the Octobrists is not the way he presents the question, nor his principles, but only the sweep of his eloquence. We need but pay just a little attention to his speech, we need only to ponder over it a little to see that, in substance, Mr. Rodichev shares the standpoint of the Octobrists; it is *only* for this reason that he can promise them "forgiveness" if they "vow". All these offers of forgiveness and all these vows are nothing but a farce played by liberals afraid of more or less consistent democracy. Hence the approach to the question which we see in Rodichev's words about "proportion", in his defence of Lopukhin, etc. At bottom there is *no* distinction between the stand taken by the Octobrists and that taken by the liberals.

On the other hand, consider the speech of Pokrovsky the Second. He began by pointing out that the question put by him and his colleagues "is entirely different in substance" from that put by the Octobrists. And, notwithstanding the fact that there were a few somewhat inept passages in the question put by Pokrovsky the Second and his colleagues, this distinction *in substance* was correctly noted. "We are not worried," said Pokrovsky the Second, "by what seems to worry you—that the political police may spell ruin for the government; what worries us is that the political police, which the government is cultivating with your assistance, spells ruin for the country.".....

And Pokrovsky the Second tried *to explain*—not declaim but explain—why the government needs the political police, and what are the class roots of that institution (class roots are not affected by "vows" and offers of "forgiveness"). "The government," said Pokrovsky the Second, "had become completely alien to society, it had no support whatever in society, because it was the enemy of democracy and in itself consisted only of the paltry remnants of the extinct class of the nobility; therefore it *was obliged* [our emphasis] to entrench itself, to separate and isolate itself from society— and so it created the political police.... Thus we see that as the broad social movement grows and ever larger sections of democracy are swept into this movement, the significance and the influence of the political police also grows."

Pokrovsky the Second apparently felt that the word "society" used here was not explicit in that context, and so he began to use the *correct* word "democracy" instead. At any rate he tried—and that was the great service he rendered—to *explain* the essence of the political police, to throw light on its class roots, and on its connection with the *entire* system of government.

Even if we overlook Mr. Rodichev's unrestrained and vulgar phrase-mongering, is it not obvious that the presentation of the question by Pokrovsky the Second and Gegechkori was as different as earth and sky from the presentation of the question by the Rodichevs? Yet the essential feature distinguishing the presentation of the question by the workers' deputies was their consistent application of democratic principles, only of democratic principles. It is one of our most important tasks in the Third Duma in general, after the period 1906-11 in particular, and especially on the eve of the elections to the Fourth Duma, to explain the profound difference between genuine democracy and the liberalism of the Cadets (the liberalism of "society") who take the name of democracy in vain.

Let us now turn to the second question, that of the famine. The first to speak was Mr. Dzyubinsky, and he spoke very badly. Not that there was anything wrong with his facts, he had certainly marshalled the proper facts and presented them simply, clearly, and truthfully. He showed no lack of sympathy for the famine-stricken people, he certainly sympathised with the sufferers and was not remiss in his criticism of the government—he criticised it all the time. But his speech was not that of a democrat but of a liberal official; this was its principal defect, and this is also the principal defect of the entire attitude of the "intellectual" members of the Trudovik group, a defect which is even more clearly shown in the verbatim reports of the proceedings in the First and Second Dumas. The only distinction between Dzyubinsky and the Cadets was that the former's speech was free of the counter-revolutionary notes which no attentive person could fail to distinguish in all the speeches of the Cadets. Judging by the presentation of the question, however, Dzyubinsky did not go far beyond the liberal official's point of view. That is why his speech was so infinitely weak, so murderously tedious, so wishy-washy, particularly as compared with the speech made by his colleague, another member of his party, the peasant Petrov the Third, in whom, as in almost all the *peasant* members of the Trudovik group in the First and Second Dumas, one feels a genuine democrat to the marrow of his bones, a democrat "rooted in the soil".

Observe how Mr. Dzyubinsky starts his speech. In speaking of the famine he lays the main stress, of all things, on the relief clauses of the Relief Regulations of June 12, 1900! You feel at once that this man, this political leader, received his most vivid impressions of the famine, not from personal experience, not from his own observations of the life of the masses, not from any clear ideas of that life, but from a textbook on police law. To be sure, he used the most up-to-date and best textbook written by a most liberal professor, one who is as liberal as they make them.

Mr. Dzyubinsky criticised the Regulations of June 12, 1900. Now see *how* he criticises: "Practically from the very moment the Regulations of June 12, 1900, were issued, both the government itself and society recognised that they were unsatisfactory".... The government itself has recognised that they are unsatisfactory, hence, the task of the democrats is to amend the Regulations of June 12,

1900, so that the government itself may consider them "satisfactory"! You can plainly visualise the atmosphere of a Russian provincial government institution. The air is stale, it reeks of a government office. The company is made up of the governor, the prosecutor, the colonel of the gendarmerie, the permanent member and two liberal members of the Zemstvo. One of the liberal members argues that it is necessary to present a petition for amendments to the Regulations of June 12, 1900, since "the government itself has recognised that they are unsatisfactory".... Have a heart, Mr. Dzyubinsky! Why, indeed, do we democrats need the Duma, if we are going to carry *into it* too the language and manners, the way of "political" thinking and the presentation of questions which were pardonable (if they were pardonable) thirty years ago in a provincial government office, or in a snug philistine "nest"—the private office of a liberal engineer, lawyer, professor, or Zemstvo member? A Duma is not needed for that!

There is a proverb: "You can tell a man by the company he keeps". When you read the Duma verbatim reports you feel like paraphrasing that proverb in regard to some of the deputies as follows: "Show me *whom* you are addressing when speaking from the rostrum of the State Duma, and I'll tell you who you are".

Mr. Rodichev, for instance, like all the Cadets, always addresses his words to the government and the Octobrists. Mr. Rodichev, like all the Cadets, calls upon them to take a "vow" and, on that condition, is willing to "forgive" them. In substance, this brilliant phrase uttered by Rodichev (who involuntarily let his eloquence betray him into telling the truth) perfectly expresses the entire spirit of the political stand generally taken by the Cadets in *all* the Dumas, in all the important pronouncements of the Constitutional-Democratic Party in parliament, in the press, and in the ante-rooms of ministers. "I am ready to forgive you this lie if you vow to put an end to the serpent that has acquired power over the Russian government"—these words should be chiselled on the monument which it is high time to erect to Mr. Rodichev.

But Mr. Dzyubinsky is not a Cadet, nor is he one of those political illiterates who regard the Cadets as a democratic party. He calls himself a Trudovik, a Narodnik. But he lacks democratic sense to such an extent that when he rises to speak from the rostrum of the State Duma he continues to address officials. He lacks the proper democratic sonse to such an extent that he does not address his words to the millions of famine-stricken peasants—and in Russia it is possible to address them from the rostrum of the Duma, and so far, in fact, only from the rostrum of the Duma—but to the few hundred officials who know about the Regulations of June 12, 1900.

"The Regulations of June 12," said Mr. Dzyubinsky, "were intended to serve a purely political purpose; their purpose was to eliminate the Zemstvo-run public organisations and concentrate the relief work among the population entirely in the hands of the government."

"The Regulations of June 12 were intended to serve a purely political purpose." What sort of language is this? How it reeks of hoary antiquity! Twenty-five or thirty years ago, in the cursed eighties of the past century, that was precisely the language *Russkiye Vedomosti* used in criticising the government from the Zemstvo point of view. Wake up, Mr. Dzyubinsky! You have slept all through the first decade of the twentieth century. While you were asleep old Russia died and a new Russia came into being. In this new Russia you *cannot* use the language you do — reproaching the government for intending its regulations to serve a "purely political" purpose. With all the good intentions, manners, and benevolence of your language it is more reactionary than that of the reactionaries in the Third Duma. It is the language of people—or of provincial officials who fight shy of all politics—who regard "politics" as something in the nature of sorcery, and dream of a relief campaign "without politics". The only way to speak to the Russia of today is to appeal for a change from one kind of politics to another, from the politics of one class to the politics of another class or other classes, from one political system to another. This is the ABC not only of democracy, but even of the most narrow liberalism—if we take the meaning of these political terms seriously.

The whole of Dzyubinsky's speech was pervaded with the same spirit. He spoke of the circular instructions regarding the collection of taxes, of the tax spiral, of reduced railway fares for harvestmen and peasant delegates, he spoke about seed being received too late for the sowing, of cows demanded as security for credits advanced —because the government is more interested in feeding cattle than in feeding people—and about the fact that peasants would rather borrow 75,000 rubles at 12 per cent interest from a private bank than go through the *red tape* of borrowing 70,000 rubles interest free from the treasury. He wound up by citing informative letters from the localities that describe appalling distress. But in the whole of this very well-intentioned speech there was not a spark of democratic feeling, not a trace of appreciation of the tasks of democratic *"politics"*. What undoubtedly does follow from his speech—and this was what the well-intentioned Mr. Dzyubinsky wanted to prove—is that our regime is rotten; but the trouble is that the speaker did not even notice that at the same time there "followed" from his speech the rotten morals of a rotten liberal official.

The next speaker but one after Dzyubinsky was Count Tolstoi, deputy from Ufa Gubernia. He is very far removed from Trudovik views, but he spoke exactly like Dzyubinsky: "Guided by some sort of political considerations, the government is systematically preventing the Zemstvos from taking part in relief work, with the result that a vast section of the common people are suffering".... Dzyubinsky's and Count Tolstoi's speeches could have been made twenty and fifty years ago. In these speeches there still lingers the spirit of the old, now fortunately dead, Russia, in which there were no classes that were aware, or beginning to be aware, of the difference between the "politics" of the various sections of the population, and that had learned, or had begun to learn, to fight openly and directly for their conflicting interests—the Russia of "common people" at the bottom and liberal Zemstvos and for the most part non-liberal officials on the top. At that time both "the common people" and the liberal Zemstvos were most of all afraid of "some sort of political considerations".

Turn over a few more pages of the Verbatim Report. There you come across speeches which, on the whole, could not have been made in Russia either fifty or twenty years ago, nor for that matter, seven years ago. There is an altercation between Markov the Second and Petrov the Third— men with numbers to their names,[176] as if deliberately to show that we have before us typical representatives of the various classes, that there are many like them. Markov the Second is attacking in the old way; Petrov the Third, on the other hand, is defending himself and is passing from defence to attack *not* in the old way.

Markov the Second: "The wordy and completely irrelevant attacks are to be explained, of course ... by the fact that, no matter what the Russian Government does, there will always be those who raise the people to revolt...". "In the Western gubernias ... people are toiling on the land and doing things which your people on the Volga refuse to do [it is not quite clear whom the speaker means by the words "your people on the Volga" for the only speaker who preceded him was the Trudovik Kropotov from Vyatka Gubernia; apparently, "your people on the Volga" did *not* refer to any member of the Duma, *nor* to anything that was or might have been said in the Duma, but to something else], for there are too many loafers on the Volga, and this must be borne in mind.... We know that there are many among your famine-stricken people who actually ought to be made to starve, so as to compel them to work instead of loafing."

Petrov the Third, although he is not from the Volga but from Perm Gubernia, replies: "Let me remind you again, gentlemen, that if Markov the Second is not a loafer he ought to recall the years 1905 and 1906 after which the landed gentry received millions in subsidies from the state treasury. What does that mean? This is what you should have remembered first; you had no right to cast a slur on the peasants."

Markov the Second (from his seat): "Easier there, you!"

These "Seconds" and "Thirds" behave very rudely, don't they?

What lack of restraint compared with the well-mannered, respectable, official language which the Dzyubinskys used to prove to the Marshals of the Nobility that the relief regulations of 1850 ... of 1900 I mean ... are not perfect! It is as if we had just emerged from the respectable private office of a respectable "public figure" into the crush and

jam of some city square or busy street. What lack of deco-
rum, what disorder! But we shall see later how "order" was
introduced—not by the Chairman, as you might think, oh
no!—but introduced by a respectable public figure, Mr.
Shingaryov, member of the Constitutional-Democratic Party. However, let us finish with this picture of contemporary
manners.

Petrov the Third: "It is said that if funds are allocated
for relief, the people will spend the money on drink. That
is not true, gentlemen. Whose duty is it to prevent this?
The fact is that in many gubernias the people have requested
that the taverns be closed down, but nothing is being done
about it. It is possible, yes, that the population spends part
of the money on liquor; but how about yourselves, Markov
the Second and you other gentlemen, how much do you spend
on liquor? Perhaps, if we divide the total per head, it will
turn out that you spend much more on drink than the peasants do.... As long as the land, which ought to belong to
the peasants, is in the hands of such Markovs, Purishkeviches, and their fraternity, famines will most certainly
keep recurring. But these gentlemen will say that the peasants are to blame for the famine because they are loafers."

Markov the Second (from his seat): "Our peasants are
not starving".

Petrov the Third: "I think, gentlemen, that the cardinal point of the question of how to put an end to all starvation is that the land must be taken from those who do
not cultivate it, from the 'non-loafing' gentlemen, and
transferred to those who do. So long as you do not transfer the land, and I know for certain that you will not, the
peasant population will starve. It is thus obvious that strife
similar to that which took place in 1905 is again inevitable,
and you yourselves are inviting that strife, for a hungry
man is like a beast and you, therefore, are provoking the
population to make a revolution and to wrest by force
what belongs to it by right."

If Muromtsev had been Chairman of the Third Duma he
would have surely stopped the speaker—in the First Duma
he always stopped speakers for such inappropriate statements. In Muromtsev's absence, Shingaryov, who spoke
next, took it upon himself to restore "order". He immedi-

ately took Markov the Second to task for "speaking in a tone worthy of a cheap show", and then he went on to lecture Petrov the Third on *how* to argue with the Markovs. Markov's party colleague Vishnevsky, said Mr. Shingaryov, "spoke sincerely" and came out in favour of supporting the question. He, Shingaryov, expressed the "hope that the government will show more wisdom than Deputy Markov had shown in his speech.... It is the duty of a representative of the Russian people to say to gentlemen: Shame on you".

Rodichev and Shingaryov thus put Markov utterly to shame and, on top of that, Shingaryov, by the model manner in which he polemised with Markov, utterly confounded "the Third".

———

The last of the questions which form the subject of these notes concerned the "temporary" Regulations of August 14, 1881, i.e., the notorious Regulations for the protection of the state, which have been systematically reaffirmed in the course of thirty years and which represent the actual constitution of Russia. The main speakers on this question were Teslenko and Milyukov, and the episode that provided the finishing touch was the "expulsion of Jellinek", i.e., the expulsion of Teslenko for fifteen sittings for quoting a passage from Jellinek,[177] *despite* Teslenko's statement that his words had "nothing in common with the construction which is now, apparently, being put on them by those who want to vote" in favour of expulsion.

Without going into greater detail in respect of this interesting episode, we shall merely note that even in the presentation of this, politically so plain and clear, question of the Regulations of August 14, 1881, Mr. Milyukov, the leader of the Constitutional-Democratic Party, managed to provide a "brilliant" illustration of specific Cadet narrow-mindedness and hypocrisy. "Gentlemen," exclaimed Milyukov, "there is no question more urgent than the one we have raised, for it represents the principal and fundamental contradiction of Russian life [can the contradiction between a scrap of paper and Russian life be called the contradiction of Russian life?]; it is the contradiction between the existing system of government and the methods of administration."

That is not true, Mr. Milyukov. The very Regulations of August 14, 1881, their thirtieth anniversary, and their "peculiar" "juridical nature" prove that there is *perfect* harmony between the "existing system of government" and the methods of administration, that there is no "contradiction" at all. Considering, as he does, that there is a contradiction between the two, and trying, as he does, to make it appear that a gulf lies between the "system of government" and the "methods of administration", Mr. Milyukov *thereby* descends in his criticism of the evil from the plane of the democratic struggle to that of liberal good wishes. By the very fact that he is creating the fiction of a gulf between things that are *indissolubly* connected in real life, Milyukov is lending support to juridical and state-law fictions that are intended *to facilitate* the justification of the evil, to obscure its real roots. Milyukov thereby takes an *Octobrist stand*; for the Octobrists, too, do not deny the existence of the evil, but try to remove the *formal* contradictions while leaving intact the *real* omnipotence of the bureaucracy from top to bottom and from bottom to top.

Like the genuine Cadet that he is, Milyukov—far from even noticing that, for a "democrat", he has hopelessly muddled things, and that he is arguing like an Octobrist—is even *proud* of his "statesmanlike" presentation of the question. Immediately after the words quoted above we read:

"This contradiction, gentlemen, is so obvious that even in your midst [Mr. Milyukov is, of course, addressing the "leading party of the Third Duma"—the Octobrists] it has been pointed out quite frequently; but very seldom did you reach the substance, the root, the primary cause, which we are discussing today. As a rule, what did you make of this problem of the contradiction between the system and the methods of government? You pleaded that the customs of administration cannot be rooted out at one stroke ... [the reference is correct so long ... so long as the entire "administration" is not removed, and this is something the Cadets themselves do not countenance] ... you referred to the local administrative bodies not obeying central instructions, instructions issued by the central authorities; the most that you dared, was to accuse the central authorities of not giving proper instructions. To you this has always been a question of facts, to us it is a question of right."

You refute yourself splendidly, Mr. Milyukov! The Octobrists are *right*, a hundred per cent right, when they refer to the close and indissoluble connection, to the closest and most indissoluble connection, between the central and local authorities. From this fact a democratic conclusion must be drawn, for it would be ridiculous to deny this connection after all that Russia knows about Tolmachov, Dumbadze, Reinbot, Illiodor, the murderers of Herzenstein, etc. You, however, are drawing the conclusion, naïve in its half-heartedness, that it is a "question of right". But who is going to determine the extent of this right? How will you reach an "agreement" on this point? What is political right, if not the formulation, the registration, of the relationships of might? You have copied your definitions of right from West-European textbooks which *record* what has come into being as a result of a long period of battles in the West, as a result of the established (until disestablished by fundamentally different movements of the working class) balance of forces among the various elements of the West-European bourgeoisie, the West-European peasants, the West-European feudal landowners, government authorities, etc. In Russia this period has just begun, here the question *is presented*—such is the current historical situation—precisely as a question of "facts"; you, however, shrink back from this plain and clear presentation of the question, hiding your head, covering it with a magic cap of invisibility woven from the fictions of "right". Yours is the standpoint of a liberal official, not of a democrat.

Prosveshcheniye, No. 1,
December 1911
Signed: *Peterburzhets*

Published according to
the *Prosveshcheniye* text

THE FAMINE AND THE REACTIONARY DUMA

Not so long ago, under the influence of last year's harvest, the hack journalists confidently held forth on the beneficial results of "the new agrarian policy", and, taking their cue from them, some naïve persons proclaimed that there had been a turn in our agriculture and that it was on the upgrade throughout Russia.

Now, as if timed to coincide with the fifth anniversary of the decree of November 9, 1906, the famine and crop failure which have gripped nearly half of Russia have shown most graphically and incontrovertibly how much wanton lying or childish simplicity there was behind the hopes placed in Stolypin's agrarian policy.

Even according to government calculations, the authenticity and "modesty" of which were demonstrated during preceding spells of famine, the crop failure has affected twenty gubernias; twenty million people "are entitled to receive relief", in other words, they are bloated from hunger and their farms are being ruined.

Kokovtsov would not be Minister of Finance and the head of the counter-revolutionary government if he did not make "encouraging" statements—there is really no crop failure, you see, but merely "a poor harvest"; hunger "does not cause disease", but, on the contrary, "sometimes cures" diseases; the stories about the sufferings of the famine-stricken are all newspaper inventions—as is eloquently testified to by the governors; on the contrary, "the economic conditions of the localities affected by the poor harvest are not so bad at all"; "the idea of giving free food to the population is pernicious", and, finally, the measures taken by the government are "sufficient and timely".

The head of the constitutional government forgot to mention his brilliant invention designed to combat the famine, namely, that police agents should be given authority to organise "famine relief".

"Public aid" even from legal liberal societies has now been abolished and a Saratov police agent, as the only champion of the starving, has been able to spend freely in taverns the funds entrusted to him to aid the famine-stricken.

Naturally, the feudal landowners on the Right were enthusiastic about "the detailed and, so to speak, all-embracing speech of the Chairman of the Council of Ministers" (Deputy Vishnevsky on November 9); naturally, the grovelling Octobrists promptly stated in their motion to pass to next business that "the government has taken timely measures to combat the effects of the crop failure"; and one of their leaders (by no means an ordinary mortal!) indulged in a profound discourse on "unrestricted circulation of canned fish as a means of providing the population with desirable food".

Hunger-typhus, scurvy, people eating carrion for which they fight dogs, or bread mixed with ashes and manure such as was demonstrated in the State Duma—all these things do not exist as far as the Octobrists are concerned. To them the word of the Minister is law.

And the Cadets? Even on this issue they refrained from voicing a straightforward opinion on the infamous behaviour of the government and found nothing better than, through the medium of Kutler, one of their speakers, to "draw reassuring conclusions from the comprehensive speech of the Chairman of the Council of Ministers" (sitting of November 9); and in formulating their motion to pass to next business, they gently described the activity of the government as being merely "insufficiently [!] systematic, inadequate, and not always [!] timely".

The question of relief and of its organisation is but one aspect of the matter, as the Social-Democrat deputy, Comrade Belousov, correctly pointed out in his speech. No less important is the fundamental question which arises each time the discussion turns on the famine—the question of the *causes* of famine and of the measures to combat crop failures.

The feudal landowners on the Right have a "very simple" solution: the "loafing" muzhik must be made to work still harder and then "he'll deliver the goods". Markov the

Second, the diehard from Kursk, thinks that it is "horrible" that "out of 365 days in the year the muzhik works only 55-70 days, doing nothing for three hundred days", merely warming his back on the stove and "demanding a ration from the government".

The semi-feudal landowners among the Nationalists and Octobrists take a "deeper" view of the matter. In line with their duty to sing the praises of the authorities, they are still trying to persuade people that "the question of famine will be radically solved when the land passes from the hands of the feeble and the drunkards into the hands of the strong and the sober", "when the reform inaugurated by the late P. A. Stolypin is fully implemented, when the stake on the strong is won". (Kelepovsky's speech at the sitting of the Duma on November 9.)

However, the more far-sighted among the recent defenders of the decree of November 9 are already beginning to sense that the breath of death is hovering over this "great reform". N. Lvov, a deputy from Saratov, who was and, as he declared, still is "in favour of the law of November 9", shared with the Duma the following impressions he had gained "from contact with reality": "All those things you are saying here in the State Duma somehow seem terribly removed from the actual suffering which one sees with one's own eyes". "It is necessary to exercise great caution, and it is necessary to spare that section of the population whom some people are inclined to ignore. As a result of the law of November 9, many newcomers have appeared in some gubernias, including Saratov, land prices have risen and the condition of the poor population has become extremely difficult.... Terrible hatred and condemnation are welling up among the peasant poor—and some measures ought to be taken against this state of affairs.... For relying on the strong by no means implies that the poorer peasants ought to be hastened to their doom and left to perish in poverty", and so on and so forth.

In brief, the impressions "gained from contact with reality" are beginning to open the eyes of this landowner who was "in favour of the law of November 9".

The seeds of immeasurably more profound doubt as to the salutary effect of Stolypin's "agrarian reform" have been planted by this year's famine in the minds of the Right-wing peasants. The motion put forward by Andreichuk, a Right-wing peasant, "that the government shall, at an early date, introduce into the State Duma a bill to limit the amount of land in the hands of big landowners"—a motion supported by all the Right-wing peasants and even by rural priests—shows more than anything else along what lines the peasants, even the Rights among them, think the "struggle against the famine" should be conducted.

The demand voiced by Andreichuk, the demand that comes direct from the peasant world, provides additional proof (recall the statement of the Right- and Left-wing peasant deputies suggesting the compulsory alienation of landed estates in order to provide allotments for those who possess little land, recall the speeches of the peasant deputies in the debate on the decree of November 9, etc.), showing how deeply the need for an agrarian revolution is penetrating into the minds even of the Right-wing peasants, to what great extent even they regard the struggle against famine as *inseparable from the struggle "for land"*.

A real struggle against famine is inconceivable without the appeasement of the peasants' land hunger, without the relief from the crushing pressure of taxes, without an improvement in their cultural standard, without a decisive change in their legal status, without the confiscation of the landed estates—*without a revolution*.

In this sense this year's crop failure is a new reminder of the doom that awaits the entire existing political system, the June Third monarchy.

Rabochaya Gazeta, No. 7,   Published according to
   December 22, 1911   the *Rabochaya Gazeta* text
   (January 4, 1912)

THE SIXTH (PRAGUE) ALL-RUSSIA CONFERENCE OF THE R.S.D.L.P. [178]

JANUARY 5-17 (18-30), 1912

1

DRAFT RESOLUTION ON
THE CONSTITUTION OF THE CONFERENCE[179]

RESOLUTION ON THE CONSTITUTION

Whereas:

1. The disintegration and collapse of most Party organisations caused by the broad stream of counter-revolutionary feeling and ferocious persecution on the part of tsarism, as well as the prolonged absence of a practical Party centre, a Central Committee, have all been factors responsible for the extremely serious position of the Russian S.D.L. Party;

2. At the present moment, due to the revival of the working-class movement, progressive workers everywhere show an intense desire to re-establish the illegal organisations of the Party, and in this connection most local organisations of the R.S.D.L.P. have displayed tremendous and successful initiative in re-establishing the Party and convening a general Party conference;

3. The extremely urgent practical tasks of the working-class movement and of the revolutionary struggle against tsarism (leadership in the economic struggle, political agitation, and proletarian meetings; elections to the Fourth Duma, etc.) make it imperative that prompt and most energetic measures be taken to re-establish a competent practical Party centre, closely linked with the local organisations;

4. After an interval of more than three years since the last conference of the R.S.D.L.P., and after many attempts during more than two years to convene a meeting of representatives of all Party organisations, we have now succeeded in uniting twenty organisations in Russia around the Russian Organising Commission which called the present Conference and which several months ago notified all Social-

Democrats of its convocation and invited to the Conference all, without a single exception, organisations of our Party; furthermore, all organisations were given an opportunity to take part in our Conference;

5. Despite the delay and a number of arrests all the Party organisations functioning in Russia, with very few exceptions, are represented at the present Conference;

It is therefore resolved:

The Conference constitutes itself the general Party Conference of the R.S.D.L.P. which is the supreme Party authority and is pledged to establish competent central bodies.

Written not later than
January 5 (18), 1912

First published on January 18, 1937,
in *Pravda*, No. 18

Published according to
the manuscript

2

DRAFT RESOLUTION ON THE TASKS OF THE PARTY IN THE PRESENT SITUATION

This Conference endorses, first and foremost, the resolution adopted at the Party Conference in December 1908 on "The Tasks of the Party in the Present Situation". This Conference points to the extreme importance of that resolution, whose provisions relating to the historical meaning and class essence of the entire June Third regime on the one hand, and the growing revolutionary crisis on the other, have been fully confirmed by the events of the past three years.

Of these events the Conference particularly notes the following:

(a) The agrarian policy of tsarism, with which both the government parties of the landowners and big bourgeoisie and the counter-revolutionary liberals have bound up their counter-revolutionary interests, has not led to the creation of anything like stable bourgeois relations in the village, nor has it relieved the peasantry of mass hunger, which reflects the extreme worsening of the condition of the population and an enormous loss of productive forces.

(b) In view of its impotence in the face of the world competition of the modern capitalist states and being pushed more and more into the background in Europe, the tsarist autocracy in alliance with the reactionary nobility and the growing industrial bourgeoisie, is now endeavouring to satisfy its predatory interests by means of crude "nationalist" politics, directed against the more cultured regions (Finland, Poland, North-Western Area), and, through colonial conquest, against the peoples of Asia (Persia and Mongolia) who are waging a revolutionary struggle for freedom.

(c) The developing economic advance is largely offset by the complete disruption of peasant economy, by the rapacious budgetary policy of the autocracy and the absolute corruption in the bureaucratic apparatus; on the other hand, the increasing cost of living intensifies the poverty of the working class and the broad masses of the population.

(d) In view of this the broad masses of the population have become convinced, during the five-year existence of the Third Duma, that it is unwilling, unable, and powerless to do anything to improve their conditions, and that the parties predominating in the Duma are anti-popular in character.

(e) The onset of a political revival is to be noted among broad democratic circles, chiefly among the proletariat. The workers' strikes of 1910-11, the beginning of demonstrations and proletarian meetings, the start of a movement among urban bourgeois democrats (the student strikes), etc., all these are signs of the growing revolutionary feelings of the masses against the June Third regime.

This Conference, proceeding from all these facts, confirms the tasks confronting the Party as outlined in detail in the resolution of the December 1908 Conference, and draws the particular attention of comrades to:

(1) The fact that, as heretofore, the first task on the order of the day is the continued work of the socialist education, organisation, and unification of the politically-conscious masses of the proletariat;

(2) The necessity for intensive work to re-establish the illegal organisation of the R.S.D.L.P., which more than ever before takes advantage of all and every legal possibility, which is capable of leading the economic struggles of the proletariat, and which is the only party able to take the lead in political actions by the proletariat that are growing more frequent;

(3) The necessity to organise and extend systematic political agitation and to give wholehearted support to the incipient mass movement and secure its development under the banner of full implementation of the Party slogans.

Propaganda for a republic, and against the policy of the tsarist monarchy, must be given special prominence to counteract, among other things, the widespread propaganda in favour of curtailed slogans and adaptation to existing "legality".

Written early in January 1912

First published in 1941
in *Proletarskaya Revolutsia*, No. 1

Published according to
the manuscript

3

DRAFT RESOLUTION ON THE TASKS
OF SOCIAL-DEMOCRATS
IN THE STRUGGLE AGAINST THE FAMINE [180]

Whereas:

(1) The famine affecting 20 million peasants in Russia once again shows the absolutely unbearable conditions of the peasant masses, crushed and oppressed by tsarism and the class of feudal landowners, conditions unimaginable in any civilised country of the world;

(2) The present famine once again confirms the failure of the government's agrarian policy and the impossibility of ensuring anything like normal bourgeois development in Russia so long as its policy in general, and its agrarian policy in particular, are directed by the class of feudal landowners who, through the parties of the Right, dominate the Third Duma, the Council of State, and circles at the Court of Nicholas II;

(3) The Black-Hundred parties (with the Markovs and similar people at the head), by their statements in the Duma and their attempts to lay the blame on the "loafing peasants" have so flaunted the shamelessness of the tsarist-landowner gang that is plundering Russia that the eyes of even the most ignorant are being opened, and indignation of even the most indifferent is being aroused;

(4) The actions of the government in hindering relief for the famine-stricken, the police interference with the Zemstvos, with the collectors of funds and the organisers of kitchen committees, etc., give rise to widespread dissatisfaction even among the bourgeoisie, and voices of protest are raised even among such backward and counter-revolutionary bourgeoisie as the Octobrists;

(5) The liberal-monarchist bourgeoisie, while helping in its press to inform the public of the famine and of the

behaviour of the government, nevertheless, in the person of the Constitutional-Democrat Kutler in the Third Duma, adopted such a moderate-oppositional position that can, under no circumstances, satisfy democrats, any more than it is possible to accept the presentation of the question of relief for the famine-stricken as philanthropy, which is the way the majority of the liberals present it;

(6) Among the working class, despite the worsening of its economic position arising from the increasing numbers of starving and unemployed, a spontaneous desire is to be observed to collect funds to aid the starving and to help them in other ways. This desire natural to every democrat, to say nothing of a socialist, must be supported and furthered by all Social-Democrats in the spirit of class struggle;

The Conference resolves that it is essential:

(a) To bend all efforts to extending propaganda and agitation among the broad masses of the population, and in particular among the peasantry, explaining the connection between the famine and tsarism and its entire policy; to distribute in the villages for agitational purposes the Duma speeches, not only of the Social-Democrats and Trudoviks, but even of such friends of the tsar as Markov the Second, and to popularise the political demands of Social-Democracy —in the first instance the overthrow of tsarist monarchy and the establishment of a democratic republic, followed by the confiscation of landed estates;

(b) To support the desire of the workers to aid the famine-stricken as far as possible, advising them to send their donations only to the Social-Democratic group in the Duma, to the workers' press, or to workers' cultural-educational and other associations, etc., and forming special nuclei of Social-Democrats and democrats upon their joining groups, committees or commissions for aid to the famine-stricken;

(c) To endeavour to give expression to the anger of the democratic masses aroused by the famine in demonstrations, mass meetings, and other forms that constitute the beginning of a revolutionary mass struggle against tsarism.

Written early in January 1912   Published according to
                                                  the manuscript
First published on January 18, 1937,
    in *Pravda*, No. 18

4

DRAFT RESOLUTION ON LIQUIDATIONISM AND THE GROUP OF LIQUIDATORS

LIQUIDATIONISM AND THE GROUP OF LIQUIDATORS

Whereas:

(1) The Russian Social-Democratic Labour Party for nearly four years has been waging a determined fight against the liquidationist trend, which was characterised at the conference of the Party in December 1908 as

"an attempt on the part of a group of Party intellectuals to liquidate the existing organisation of the R.S.D.L.P. and to replace it at all costs, even at the price of downright renunciation of the programme, tactics, and traditions of the Party, by a loose association functioning legally";

(2) The Plenary Meeting of the Central Committee held in January 1910, continuing the fight against this trend, unanimously declared it to be "a manifestation of bourgeois influence upon the proletariat" and demanded, as a condition for real Party unity and for the fusion of the former Bolshevik and Menshevik groups, a complete rupture with liquidationism and the utter rout of this bourgeois deviation from socialism;

(3) In spite of all Party decisions, and in spite of the obligation assumed by the representatives of Menshevism at the Plenary Meeting held in January 1910, a section of the Mensheviks, grouped around the magazines *Nasha Zarya* and *Dyelo Zhizni*, refused to help restore the Central Committee (the refusal of Mikhail, Yuri, and Roman, in the spring of 1910, not only to join the Central Committee but even to attend a single meeting to co-opt new members);

(4) It was precisely after the Plenary Meeting of 1910 that the above-mentioned publications definitely turned to liquidationism all along the line, not only "belittling [contrary to the decision of the Plenary Meeting] the importance of the illegal Party", but openly renouncing it, declaring that the Party was already liquidated, that the idea of reviving the illegal Party was "a reactionary utopia", using the columns of censored magazines to heap ridicule and abuse on it, calling upon the workers to regard the nuclei of the Party and its hierarchy as "dead", etc.;

(5) The few local groups of liquidators, consisting mainly of representatives of the intelligentsia, continuing their work of destroying the Party, not only refused to listen to the call, repeated in 1911, to help revive the illegal Party and convene a Party conference, but, banded together in entirely independent small groups, they openly began to agitate among the workers against the illegal Party and launched an open fight against reviving it—even in those places where the pro-Party Mensheviks predominated (for example, in Ekaterinoslav, Baku, Kiev, etc.);

The Conference declares that by its conduct the above-mentioned group has definitely placed itself outside the Party.

The Conference calls upon all Party members, irrespective of tendencies and shades of opinion, to combat liquidationism, explain its great harmfulness to the cause of the emancipation of the working class, and bend all their efforts to revive and strengthen the illegal Russian Social-Democratic Labour Party.

Written early in January 1912

First published in
1929-30, in 2nd and 3rd
editions of *Collected Works*
of V. I. Lenin, Vol. XV

Published according to
the manuscript

5

RESOLUTIONS OF THE CONFERENCE

THE RUSSIAN ORGANISING COMMISSION
FOR CONVENING THE CONFERENCE

Having heard and discussed the report of the representative of the Russian Organising Commission on its activity in connection with the convening of a general Party conference:

The Conference deems it its duty to stress the enormous importance of the work accomplished by the Russian Organising Commission in rallying all the Party organisations in Russia irrespective of factional affiliation, and in re-establishing our Party as an all-Russian organisation.

The activity of the Russian Organising Commission, in which Bolsheviks and pro-Party Mensheviks in Russia worked in harmony, is to be all the more commended since it was carried out under incredibly trying conditions due to police persecution and in face of numerous obstacles and difficulties arising out of the situation within the Party.

THE CONSTITUTION OF THE CONFERENCE

Whereas:

(1) The disintegration and collapse of most Party organisations, caused by the broad stream of counter-revolutionary feelings and ferocious persecution on the part of tsarism, as well as the prolonged absence of a practical Party centre, a Central Committee, have all been factors responsible for the extremely serious position in which the R.S.D.L.P. found itself in the period 1908-11;

(2) At the present moment, due to the revival of the working-class movement, progressive workers everywhere

show an intense desire to re-establish the illegal organisations of the Party and inaugurate systematic legal and illegal Social-Democratic activity, and in this connection most local organisations of the R.S.D.L.P. have displayed tremendous and vigorous initiative in re-establishing the Party and convening a general Party conference;

(3) The extremely urgent practical tasks of the working-class movement and of the revolutionary struggle against tsarism (leadership in the economic struggle, general political agitation, proletarian meetings, the campaign in connection with the elections to the Fourth Duma, etc.) make it imperative that prompt and most energetic measures be taken to re-establish a competent practical Party centre, closely linked with the local organisations;

(4) After an interval of more than three years since the last conference of the R.S.D.L.P., and after many attempts during more than two years to convene a meeting of representatives of all Party organisations, we have now succeeded in uniting more than twenty organisations in Russia (St. Petersburg, Moscow, Saratov, Kazan, Samara, Nizhni-Novgorod, Sormovo, Rostov, Ekaterinoslav, Kiev, Nikolayev, Lugansk, Baku, the Tiflis group, the Wilno group, the Dvinsk group, Ekaterinburg, Ufa, Tyumen, a number of places in the Central Region, and others) around the Russian Organising Commission which called the present Conference, and which several months ago notified all Social-Democrats of its convocation and invited to the Conference all, without a single exception, organisations of our Party; furthermore, all organisations were given an opportunity to take part in the Conference;

(5) Despite a number of arrests made by the police, all the Party organisations functioning in Russia, with very few exceptions, are represented at the present Conference;

(6) Groups of Social-Democrats active in the legal working-class movement in some of the big centres of Russia (St. Petersburg, Moscow, the Caucasus) were invited to attend the Conference and have given it their endorsement;

It is therefore resolved:

The Conference constitutes itself the general Party Conference of the R.S.D.L.P., which is the supreme Party authority.

THE ABSENCE OF DELEGATES FROM THE NON-RUSSIAN NATIONAL
CENTRES FROM THE GENERAL PARTY CONFERENCE

Recognising that it is extremely important to strengthen
the unity of the Social-Democratic workers of all the nationalities of Russia, and considering it absolutely imperative
to establish unity with the non-Russians in the localities
and to strengthen the ties between the national organisations and the all-Russia centre, the Conference at the
same time is compelled to place on record that:

(1) Experience has conclusively proved that in the Party
we cannot tolerate a situation where non-Russians working
in total isolation from Russian organisations have chosen
to set up a federation of the worst type and—frequently
regardless of whether they wanted to or not—placed key
Russian organisations in such a position that without non-
Russian national centres, which for all practical purposes do
not concern themselves with Russian affairs, the R.S.D.L.P.
was unable to effect very essential and important Party work.

(2) During the past year one of the non-Russian national
centres (that of the Bund) openly co-operated with the
liquidators and tried to bring about a split in the R.S.D.L.P.;
others (the central bodies of the Latvians and the Polish
S.D.) at the decisive moment kept aloof from the fight
against the liquidators who are trying to destroy the Party.

(3) The pro-Party elements in the non-Russian organisations, in the first place all the worker members of the Party,
knowing what is going on in the *Russian* organisations, are
coming out resolutely *in favour* of unity with the Russian
illegal Social-Democratic organisations, *in favour* of supporting the Russian Organising Commission, and *in favour*
of fighting the liquidationist trend.

(4) The Central Committees of the three national organisations were invited three times (by the Organising Commission Abroad, the Russian Organising Commission, and
the delegates to the Conference) to attend the Party Conference, and every facility has been provided for them to
send their delegates.

In view of all this, and considering it inexpedient to sus-
pend the activity of the R.S.D.L.P. because of the reluctance of the non-Russian national centres to send delegates
to the general Party Conference, the Conference places the

entire responsibility for the failure of the non-Russians to attend on their central bodies. At the same time the Conference instructs the Central Committee of the R.S.D.L.P. to work unremittingly for unity and the establishment of normal relations with the non-Russian national organisations affiliated to the R.S.D.L.P.

The Conference is confident that, in spite of all obstacles, worker Social-Democrats of all the nationalities of Russia will work in harmony and fight shoulder to shoulder for the cause of the proletariat and against all the enemies of the working class.

ON THE REPORTS OF THE LOCAL ORGANISATIONS

Having heard the reports of the local organisations the Conference places on record that:

(1) Energetic work is being conducted everywhere among worker Social-Democrats with the object of strengthening the local illegal Social-Democratic organisations and groups;

(2) It has been recognised everywhere that it is necessary to combine illegal with legal Social-Democratic work; it has been recognised everywhere by Social-Democrats that our illegal Party organisations should use the legally existing working-class associations of every kind as bases for carrying on work among the masses. Nevertheless, not enough has so far been done to promote practical Social-Democratic work in trade unions, co-operative societies, clubs, etc.; not enough has so far been done to disseminate Marxist literature, to make use of the speeches of Social-Democrat deputies in the Duma, etc. In this field it is absolutely imperative for the illegal Social-Democratic groups to show greater energy;

(3) Everywhere in the localities, without a single exception, Party work is being conducted jointly and harmoniously mainly by the Bolsheviks and the pro-Party Mensheviks, as well as by *Vperyod* supporters in Russia wherever there are any, and by all other Social-Democrats who recognise the need for an illegal R.S.D.L.P. The entire work is, furthermore, conducted in the spirit of the defence of Party principles and the struggle against liquidationism.

The Conference is confident that, in connection with the revival of the working-class movement, energetic efforts will be continued to strengthen the old and create new, sufficiently flexible, organisational forms which will help the Social-Democratic Party to carry on its struggle for the *old* revolutionary aims and revolutionary methods of achieving them in *new* circumstances.

THE TASKS OF THE PARTY IN THE PRESENT SITUATION

This Conference endorses, first and foremost, the resolution on the June Third regime and the tasks of the Party, adopted at the Party Conference in December 1908. This Conference points to the extreme importance of that resolution, whose provisions relating to the historical meaning and class essence of the entire June Third regime on the one hand, and the growing revolutionary crisis on the other, have been fully borne out by the events of the past three years.

Of these events the Conference particularly notes the following:

(a) The agrarian policy of tsarism, with which both the government parties of the landowners and big bourgeoisie and, actually, the counter-revolutionary liberals have bound up their counter-revolutionary interests, has not led to the creation of anything like stable bourgeois relations in the village, nor has it relieved the peasantry of mass hunger, which reflects the extreme worsening of the condition of the population and an enormous loss of the productive forces of the country.

(b) In view of its impotence in the face of the world competition of the modern capitalist states and being pushed more and more into the background in Europe, tsarism in alliance with the reactionary nobility and the growing industrial bourgeoisie, is now endeavouring to satisfy its predatory interests by means of crude "nationalist" politics, directed against the inhabitants of the border regions, against all oppressed nationalities, against the more cultured regions in particular (Finland, Poland, North-Western Area) and, through colonial conquest, against the peoples of Asia (Persia and China) who are waging a revolutionary struggle for freedom.

(c) The developing economic advance is largely offset by the complete disruption of peasant economy, by the rapacious budgetary policy of the autocracy and corruption in the bureaucratic apparatus; on the other hand, the increasing cost of living intensifies the poverty of the working class and the broad masses of the population.

(d) In view of this the broad masses of the population have become convinced, during the five-year existence of the Third Duma, that it is unwilling, unable, and powerless to do anything to improve their conditions, and that the parties predominating in the Duma are anti-popular in character.

(e) The onset of a political revival is to be noted among broad democratic circles, chiefly among the proletariat. The workers' strikes of 1910-11, the beginning of demonstrations and proletarian meetings, the start of a movement among urban bourgeois democrats (the student strikes), etc., all these are signs of the growing revolutionary feelings of the masses against the June Third regime.

This Conference, proceeding from all these facts, confirms the tasks confronting the Party, as outlined in detail in the resolution of the December 1908 Conference, particularly pointing out that the task of winning power by the proletariat, carrying with it the peasantry, remains as before, the task of the democratic revolution in Russia. This Conference draws the particular attention of comrades to:

(1) The fact that, as heretofore, the first task on the order of the day is the continued work of the socialist education, organisation, and unification of the politically-conscious masses of the proletariat;

(2) The necessity for intensive work to re-establish the illegal organisation of the R.S.D.L.P., which more than ever before takes advantage of every legal possibility, which is capable of leading the economic struggles of the proletariat, and which is the only party able to take the lead in political actions by the proletariat that are growing more frequent;

(3) The necessity to organise and extend systematic political agitation and to give wholehearted support to the incipient mass movement and secure its development

under the banner of full implementation of the Party slogans.

Propaganda for a republic, and against the policy of the tsarist monarchy, must be given special prominence to counteract, among other things, the widespread propaganda in favour of curtailed slogans and of confining activity to the existing "legality".

ELECTIONS TO THE FOURTH DUMA

I

This Conference recognises the undoubted necessity for participation by the R.S.D.L. Party in the forthcoming election campaign to the Fourth State Duma, the nomination of independent candidates of our Party and the formation in the Fourth Duma of a Social-Democratic group, which as a section of the Party is subordinated to the Party as a whole.

The main tasks of our Party in the elections, and equally of the future Social-Democratic group in the Duma itself—a task to which all else must be subordinated—is socialist, class propaganda and the organisation of the working class.

The main election slogans of our Party in the forthcoming elections must be:

(1) *A democratic republic.*
(2) *The eight-hour working day.*
(3) *Confiscation of all landed estates.*

In all our election agitation it is essential to give the clearest possible explanation of these demands, based on the experience of the Third Duma and all the activities of the government in the sphere of central as well as local administration.

All propaganda on the remaining demands of the Social-Democratic minimum programme, namely: universal franchise, freedom of association, election of judges and officials by the people, state insurance for workers, replacement of the standing army by the arming of the people, and so on, must be inseparably linked with the above-mentioned three demands.

II

The general tactical line of the R.S.D.L.P. in the elections should be the following: the Party must conduct a merciless struggle against the tsarist monarchy and the parties of landowners and capitalists supporting it, at the same time steadfastly exposing the counter-revolutionary views of the bourgeois liberals (headed by the Cadet Party) and their sham democracy.

Particular attention in the election campaign must be paid to dissociating the position of the proletarian party from that of *all* non-proletarian parties and explaining the petty-bourgeois essence of the sham socialism of the democratic (chiefly Trudovik, Narodnik and Socialist-Revolutionary) groups, as well as the harm done to democracy by their waverings on the question of consistent and mass revolutionary struggle.

As far as electoral agreements are concerned, the Party, adhering to the decisions of the London Congress, must:

(1) Put forward its candidates in all worker curias and forbid *any* agreement *whatsoever* with other parties or groups (liquidators);

(2) In view of the great agitational significance of the mere fact of nomination of independent Social-Democratic candidates, it is necessary to ensure that in the second assemblies of urban voters, and as far as possible in the peasant curias, the Party puts forward its own candidates;

(3) In cases of a second ballot (Article 106 of the Election Regulations) in the election of electors at the second assemblies of urban voters it is permissible to conclude agreements with bourgeois democrats against the liberals, and then with the liberals against all the government parties. One form of agreement can be the compilation of a general list of electors for one or several towns in proportion to the number of votes registered at the first elections;

(4) In those five cities (St. Petersburg, Moscow, Riga, Odessa, Kiev) where there are direct elections with a second ballot, it is essential in the first elections to put forward independent Social-Democratic candidates for the second urban curia voters. In the event of a second ballot here, and since there is obviously no danger from the Black

Hundreds, it is permissible to come to an agreement only with the democratic groups against the liberals;

(5) There can be no electoral agreements providing for a common platform, and Social-Democratic candidates must not be bound by any kind of political commitment, nor must Social-Democrats be prevented from resolutely criticising the counter-revolutionary nature of the liberals and the half-heartedness and inconsistency of the bourgeois democrats;

(6) At the second stage of the elections (in the uyezd assemblies of delegates, in the gubernia assemblies of voters, etc.), wherever it proves essential to ensure the defeat of an Octobrist-Black Hundred or a government list in general, an agreement must be concluded to share the seats, primarily with bourgeois democrats (Trudoviks, Popular Socialists, etc.), and then with the liberals (Cadets), independents, Progressists, etc.

III

All Social-Democrats must *immediately* commence preparation for the election campaign, and should pay special attention to the following:

(1) It is urgently necessary everywhere to form illegal Social-Democratic nuclei in order that they may without delay prepare for the Social-Democratic election campaign;

(2) To pay the necessary attention to the strengthening and broadening of the legally existing workers' press;

(3) The entire election campaign must be carried out in close alliance with workers' trades unions and all other associations of workers, and the form in which these societies participate must be chosen with due consideration paid to their legal status;

(4) Special attention must be paid to the organisational and agitation preparation of the elections in the worker curias of those six gubernias in which the election of deputies to the Duma from the worker curias is guaranteed (St. Petersburg, Moscow, Vladimir, Kostroma, Kharkov and Ekaterinoslav). Every single worker elector—here and in the other gubernias—must be a Social-Democratic Party member;

(5) Assemblies of workers' delegates, guided by the decision of the illegal Party organisations, must decide *who precisely* is to be elected to the Duma from the workers, and bind all electors, under threat of boycott and being branded as traitors, to withdraw their candidature in favour of the Party candidate;

(6) In view of persecution by the government, the arrest of Social-Democrat candidates, etc., it is necessary to carry out particularly restrained, systematic and careful work, using every means to react quickly to all police tactics and nullify all the tricks and coercion of the tsarist government, and to elect Social-Democrats to the Fourth State Duma, and then in general to strengthen the group of democratic deputies in the Duma;

(7) The candidates of the Social-Democratic Party are endorsed, and instructions concerning the elections are given by the local illegal organisations and groups of the Party, under the general supervision and guidance of the Central Committee of the Party;

(8) If, despite all efforts, it proves impossible to convene a Party congress or a new conference before the elections to the Fourth Duma, the Conference empowers the Central Committee, or an institution appointed for the purpose by the latter, to issue concrete instructions on questions concerning the conduct of the election campaign in the various localities, or to meet special circumstances arising, etc.

THE SOCIAL-DEMOCRATIC GROUP IN THE DUMA

This Conference recognises that the Social-Democratic group in the Duma made use of the Duma platform in accordance with the line defined by the December (1908) Party Conference, which must remain the guide for the direction of Party work in the Duma.

The Conference, in particular, regards as consistent with the tasks of the proletariat that aspect of the group's activities that it has energetically defended the interests of the workers and all measures for improving their lot (for instance, the labour bills) and in so doing has endeavoured to show all the partial tasks in their relation to the general aims of the liberation movement led by the proletariat, and points to the mass movement as the only way to rid Russia of the sufferings and shame to which she has been brought by tsarism.

The Conference welcomes the beginning of open actions by the workers in connection with the praiseworthy behaviour of the Social-Democratic group in the Duma, which in the reactionary Duma raised the banner of the Social-Democratic deputies to the Second Duma and exposed to the workers of the entire world all the provocative filth of the Black-Hundred tsarist gang that organised the government coup d'état of 1907. The Conference calls on all class-conscious workers in Russia to give wholehearted support to the speeches of the Social-Democrats in the Third Duma, and the campaign of proletarian meetings commenced by the St. Petersburg workers.

The Conference recognises that in view of the forthcoming election campaign to the Fourth Duma, the Social-Democratic Duma group must devote still more attention to explaining to the people the class essence of the non-proletarian parties (and in particular to exposing the counter-revolutionary and treacherous nature of the Cadet Party) being guided by the resolution of the London (1907) Congress, which in all its significant sections has been confirmed by the experience of the period of counter-revolution. Furthermore, the central slogans, which must be common to all statements made by members of the Social-Democratic group, must determine the nature of its work and concentrate all its partial demands and reforms on the main points, should be the following three slogans: (1) a democratic republic, (2) the eight-hour day, (3) confiscation of all landed estates and their transfer to the peasantry.

THE CHARACTER AND ORGANISATIONAL FORMS OF PARTY WORK

Recognising that the experience of the past three years has undoubtedly confirmed the main provisions of the resolution on the problem of organisation carried by the December (1908) Conference, and assuming that the new upswing of the working-class movement makes possible the further development of organisational forms of Party work along the lines indicated therein, i.e., by the formation of illegal Social-Democratic nuclei surrounded by as wide a network as possible of every kind of legal workers' associations,

The Conference considers that:

(1) It is essential for illegal Party organisations to participate actively in the leadership of the *economic struggle* (strikes, strike committees, etc.), and to ensure co-operation in this sphere between the illegal Party nuclei and the trade unions, in particular with the S.D. nuclei in the trade unions, and also with various leaders of the trade union movement;

(2) It is desirable that S.D. nuclei in unions organised on an *industrial* basis should, whenever local conditions permit, function in conjuction with Party branches organised on a *territorial* basis;

(3) It is essential for the maximum possible initiative to be shown in the organisation of S.D. work in legally existing associations—unions, reading rooms, libraries, various types of workers' entertainment societies, the circulation of the trade union journals and the guidance of the trade union press in the spirit of Marxism; the use of the Duma speeches of the S.D. members, the training of workers to become legal lecturers, the creation (in connection with the elections to the Fourth Duma) of workers' and other voters' committees for each district, each street, etc., and the organisation of Social-Democratic campaigns in connection with the elections to municipal bodies, etc.;

(4) It is essential to make special efforts to strengthen and increase the number of illegal Party nuclei, and to seek for new organisational forms for them of the greatest possible flexibility, to establish and strengthen leading illegal Party organisations in every town and to propagate such forms of mass illegal organisations as "exchanges", factory Party meetings, and so on;

(5) It is desirable to draw the study circles into everyday *practical* work—the distribution of illegal Social-Democratic and legal Marxist literature, and so on;

(6) It is essential to bear in mind that systematic agitation through S.D. literature and particularly the regular distribution of the illegal Party paper, issued frequently and regularly can have a tremendous significance for the

establishment of organisational links, both between the illegal nuclei, and between the S.D. nuclei in legally existing workers' associations.

THE TASKS OF SOCIAL-DEMOCRACY IN THE STRUGGLE AGAINST THE FAMINE

(1) The famine affecting 20 million peasants in Russia once again shows the absolutely unbearable conditions of the impoverished peasant masses, crushed and oppressed by tsarism and the class of feudal landowners, conditions unimaginable in any civilised country of the world;

(2) The present famine once again confirms the failure of the government's agrarian policy, and the impossibility of ensuring anything like normal bourgeois development in Russia so long as its policy in general, and its agrarian policy in particular, are directed by the class of feudal landowners who, through the parties of the Right, dominate the June Third Duma, the Council of State, and circles at the Court of Nicholas II;

(3) The Black-Hundred parties (with the Markovs and similar people at the head), by their statements in the Duma and their attempts to lay the blame on the "loafing peasants", have so flaunted the shamelessness of the tsarist-landowner gang that is plundering Russia that the eyes of even the most ignorant are being opened, and the indignation of even the most indifferent is being aroused;

(4) The actions of the government in hindering relief for the famine-stricken, the police interference with the Zemstvos, with the collectors of funds and the organisers of kitchen committees, etc., give rise to widespread dissatisfaction even among the Zemstvos and the urban bourgeoisie;

(5) The liberal-monarchist bourgeoisie, while helping in its press to inform the public of the famine and of the behaviour of the government, nevertheless, through the Constitutional-Democratic group in the Third Duma acted as such a moderate opposition that under no circumstances can its conduct satisfy democrats, any more than it is possible to accept the presentation of the question of relief to the famine-stricken as philanthropy, which is the way the majority of the liberals present it;

(6) Among the working class, despite the worsening of its economic position arising from the increasing numbers of starving and unemployed, a spontaneous desire is to be observed to collect funds to aid the starving and to help them in other ways. This desire natural to every democrat, to say nothing of a socialist, must be supported and furthered by all Social-Democrats in the spirit of class struggle.

Having considered all these points,

The Conference resolves that it is essential:

(a) To enlist all Social-Democratic forces to extend propaganda and agitation among the broad masses of the population, and in particular among the peasantry, explaining the connection between the famine and tsarism and its entire policy; to distribute in the villages for agitational purposes the Duma speeches, not only of the Social-Democrats and Trudoviks, but even of such friends of the tsar as Markov the Second, and to popularise the political demands of Social-Democracy—the overthrow of the tsarist monarchy, the establishment of a democratic republic and the confiscation of landed estates;

(b) To support the desire of the workers to aid the famine-stricken as far as possible, advising them to send their donations only to the Social-Democratic group in the Duma, to the workers' press, or to workers' cultural-educational and other associations, etc., and forming special nuclei of Social-Democrats and democrats upon their joining groups, committees or commissions for aid to the famine-stricken;

(c) To endeavour to give expression to the anger of the democratic masses aroused by the famine in demonstrations, mass meetings, and other forms of mass struggle against tsarism.

THE PARTY'S ATTITUDE TO THE WORKERS' STATE INSURANCE DUMA BILL

I

1. The share of the wealth produced by the wage-worker which he receives in the form of wages is so insignificant that it is scarcely sufficient to provide for his most essential requirements; the proletarian is therefore deprived of any

opportunity to lay aside any part of his earnings to provide for himself in case of inability to work as a result of accident, illness, old age or permanent disablement, as well as in case of unemployment which is inseparably linked up with the capitalist mode of production. The insurance of workers in all the aforementioned cases is therefore a reform imperatively dictated by the entire course of capitalist development.

2. The best form of workers' insurance is *state* insurance based on the following principles: (a) it should provide for the workers in *all* cases of incapacity (accidents, illness, old age, permanent disablement; extra provisions for working women during pregnancy and childbirth; benefits for widows and orphans upon the death of the bread-winner) or in case of loss of earnings due to unemployment; (b) insurance must include *all* wage-earners and their families; (c) all insured persons should receive compensations equal to their *full* earnings, and *all* expenditures on insurance must be borne by the employers and the state; (d) all forms of insurance should be handled by *uniform* insurance organisations of the *territorial* type and based on the principle of *full* management by the insured persons themselves.

3. The government Bill, passed by the State Duma, is in radical contradiction to all these fundamental requirements of a rational insurance scheme; for (a) it provides for only *two* kinds of insurance, cases of accident and cases of illness; (b) it extends to only a small part (according to the most liberal calculations, to one-sixth) of the Russian proletariat, since it excludes from insurance whole regions (Siberia and, in the government's version, also the Caucasus) and whole categories of workers who particularly need insurance (farm labourers, building workers, railway workers, post and telegraph workers, shop assistants, etc.); (c) it provides for beggarly rates of compensation (the maximum compensation in case of *total* disablement resulting from accidents is set at two-thirds of the earnings, the latter, moreover, calculated on the basis of standards lower than the actual earnings) and at the same time makes the workers pay the lion's share of the expenditure on insurance —for the plan is to make the workers cover the expendi-

tures not only on insurance against illness but also on insurance against "minor" injuries, which in practice are the most numerous. This new procedure is a change for the worse even compared with the present law, according to which compensation for injuries is paid entirely by the employers; (d) it deprives the insurance bodies of every vestige of independence, placing them under the combined surveillance of civil servants (from the courts and the "Council for Insurance Affairs"), the gendarmerie, the police (who, besides exercising general surveillance, are invested with the right to direct the practical activities of the insurance bodies, influence the selection of their personnel, etc.), and the employers (the accident insurance societies under the exclusive control of employers; sick benefit societies run by the factories; society rules guaranteeing the influence of the employers, etc.).

4. This law, which rides roughshod over the most vital interests of the workers, is the only one possible in this present period of frenzied reaction, this period of the domination of counter-revolution, and is the result of many years of preliminary negotiations and agreement between the government and the representatives of capital. An insurance reform really corresponding to the interests of the workers can only be accomplished after the final overthrow of tsarism and the achievement of conditions indispensable for the free class struggle of the proletariat.

II

In view of the aforementioned, the Conference resolves that:

(1) It is the urgent task both of the illegal Party organisations and of the comrades active in the legally existing organisations (trade unions, clubs, co-operative societies, etc.) to develop the most extensive agitation against the Duma Insurance Bill, which affects the interests of the entire Russian proletariat as a class, since it grossly violates them.

(2) The Conference considers it necessary to emphasise that all Social-Democratic agitation concerning the Insurance Bill should be presented in relation to the class posi-

tion of the proletariat in modern capitalist society, and should criticise the bourgeois illusions being spread by the social-reformists; this agitation must, in general, be linked up with our fundamental socialist tasks; on the other hand, it is necessary in this agitation to show the connection between the character of the Duma "reform" and the current political situation and, in general, its connection with our revolutionary-democratic tasks and slogans.

(3) Fully approving of the vote of the Social-Democratic group in the Duma against the Bill, the Conference draws the attention of the comrades to the extensive and valuable material clarifying the attitude of the various classes to labour reforms furnished by the debate in the Duma on this question; the Conference particularly stresses the fact that the debate vividly brought out the aspirations of the Octobrist representatives of backward capital openly hostile to the workers, as well as the attitude of the Constitutional-Democratic Party masked, in the hypocritical speeches of its representatives, by social-reformist phrases about "social peace"; in point of fact, the Cadets came out in the Duma against the independent activity of the working class and virulently contested the principal amendments to the Bill proposed by the Social-Democratic group in the Duma.

(4) The Conference most earnestly warns the workers against all attempts to curtail or completely distort Social-Democratic agitation by confining it to what is legally permissible in the present period of the domination of the counter-revolution; on the other hand, the Conference emphasises that the main point of this agitation should be to explain to the proletarian masses that no real improvement in the worker's conditions is possible unless there is a new revolutionary upsurge, that whoever wishes to achieve a genuine labour reform must above all fight for a new, victorious revolution.

(5) Should the Duma Bill become law in spite of the protest of the class-conscious proletariat, the Conference summons the comrades to make use of the new organisational forms which it provides (workers' sick benefit societies) to carry on energetic propaganda for Social-Democratic ideas in these organisational units and thus turn the new law, devised as a means of putting new chains and a new

yoke upon the proletariat, into a means of developing its class-consciousness, strengthening its organisation and intensifying its struggle for full political liberty and for socialism.

THE "PETITION CAMPAIGN"

1. The counter-revolution, as represented by the government and the Third Duma, regards the working-class movement as its chief enemy and persecutes it in all its forms, systematically infringing upon even those "legal opportunities" remaining to the working class as a result of the revolution.

2. This regime constantly confronts the masses of workers with the fact that they cannot achieve even their most elementary rights (above all, the freedom of association) without the complete overthrow of the tsarist monarchy.

3. The petition circulated in the winter of 1910 by a group of St. Petersburg liquidators, and the agitation which accompanied this petition campaign, isolated the demand for freedom of association from the sum total of all the revolutionary demands of the working class. Instead of explaining to the workers that to win full freedom of association in Russia it is indispensable for the masses to wage a revolutionary struggle for fundamental democratic demands, the liquidators actually preached the so-called "fight for right", that is to say, a liberal fight for the "renovation" of the June Third regime by partial improvements.

4. In view of the specific conditions obtaining in Russian political life and the condition of the masses of the workers, the above-mentioned campaign has inevitably degenerated into the purely formal and meaningless signing of papers and has met with no response and aroused no political interest among the masses.

5. The fate of this petition campaign clearly confirmed the incorrectness of the entire undertaking and its isolation from the working-class masses: altogether 1,300 signatures were collected, the petition campaign having met with absolutely no response in any of the Party organisations *regardless of factions and trends*; nor did our Social-Democratic group in the Duma deem it possible to have anything to do with it.

6. The workers' mass meetings in connection with the fate of the deputies to the Second Duma and the workers' demonstrations held in various cities on January 9, 1912, show that the independent activity of the workers by no means runs in such channels as a petition campaign, nor is it conducted under the banner of "partial rights".

In view of the aforementioned, the Conference

(1) calls upon all Social-Democrats to explain to the workers the paramount importance to the proletariat of freedom of association; this demand must always be closely linked up with our general political demands and our revolutionary agitation among the masses;

(2) while recognising that under certain conditions a mass petition of workers could prove a very effective means of protest, is of the opinion that in the present period in Russia a petition is one of the least effective methods of Social-Democratic agitation.

LIQUIDATIONISM AND THE GROUP OF LIQUIDATORS

Whereas:

(1) The R.S.D.L.P. for nearly four years has been waging a determined fight against the liquidationist trend, which was characterised at the conference of the Party in December 1908 as

"an attempt on the part of a group of Party intellectuals to liquidate the existing organisation of the R.S.D.L.P. and to replace it at all costs, even at the price of downright renunciation of the programme, tactics, and traditions of the Party, by a loose association functioning legally";

(2) The Plenary Meeting of the Central Committee held in January 1910, continuing the fight against this trend, unanimously declared it to be a manifestation of bourgeois influence upon the proletariat and demanded, as a condition for real Party unity and for the fusion of the former Bolshevik and Menshevik groups, a complete rupture with liquidationism and the utter rout of this bourgeois deviation from socialism;

(3) In spite of all Party decisions, and in spite of the obligation assumed by the representatives of all the factions

at the Plenary Meeting held in January 1910, a section of Social-Democrats, grouped around the magazines *Nasha Zarya* and *Dyelo Zhizni*, began to defend openly the trend which the entire Party has recognised as being the product of bourgeois influence on the proletariat;

(4) The former members of the Central Committee, Mikhail, Yuri, and Roman, refused not only to join the Central Committee in the spring of 1910, but even to attend a single meeting to co-opt new members, and bluntly declared that they considered the very existence of the Party Central Committee to be "harmful";

(5) It was precisely after the Plenary Meeting of 1910 that the above-mentioned chief publications of the liquidators, *Nasha Zarya* and *Dyelo Zhizni*, definitely turned to liquidationism all along the line, not only "belittling [contrary to the decisions of the Plenary Meeting] the importance of the illegal Party", but openly renouncing it, declaring that the Party was "extinct", that the Party was already liquidated, that the idea of reviving the illegal Party was "a reactionary utopia", using the columns of legally published magazines to heap slander and abuse on the illegal Party, calling upon the workers to regard the nuclei of the Party and its hierarchy as "dead", etc.;

(6) At a time when throughout Russia the members of the Party, irrespective of factions, united to promote the immediate task of convening a Party conference, the liquidators, banded together in entirely independent small groups, split away from the local organisations even where the pro-Party Mensheviks predominated (Ekaterinoslav, Kiev) and definitely refused to maintain any Party relations with the local organisations of the R.S.D.L.P.;

The Conference declares that by its conduct the *Nasha Zaryà* and *Dyelo Zhizni* group has *definitely placed itself outside the Party*.

The Conference calls upon all Party members, irrespective of tendencies and shades of opinion, to combat liquidationism, explain its great harmfulness to the cause of the emancipation of the working class, and bend all their efforts to revive and strengthen the illegal R.S.D.L.P.

THE CENTRAL ORGAN

Having heard and discussed the report of the representative of the Central Organ, the Conference approves of the Central Organ's line in principle and expresses the wish that more space be devoted to articles of a propagandist nature, and that the articles be written in a more popular style, so as to make them more, intelligible to the workers.

RABOCHAYA GAZETA

Whereas:

Rabochaya Gazeta has resolutely and consistently championed the Party and its principles, and enjoys the full sympathy of Party functionaries in local Party branches, irrespective of factional affiliation,

The Conference:

(1) calls upon all comrades in the localities to support *Rabochaya Gazeta* in every way;

(2) recognises *Rabochaya Gazeta* as an official organ of the Central Committee of the Party.

NEWSPAPER *PRAVDA* [181]

The Conference annuls the agreement with the editors of *Pravda* concluded by the Plenary Meeting of the Central Committee in January 1910.

CHANGES IN THE ORGANISATIONAL RULES OF THE PARTY

The following is to be added to Clause 2:

"Co-option is considered permissible—in accordance with the decisions of the December (1908) Conference."

Clause 8 is to be deleted and replaced by the following:

"The Central Committee shall convene conferences of representatives of all the Party organisations as frequently as possible."

Clause 9, third paragraph, dealing with representation at congresses, is amended to read:

"The basis of representation at Party congresses shall be fixed by the Central Committee after preliminary communication with local organisations."

PROPERTY IN THE HANDS OF THE FORMER TRUSTEE, AND FINANCIAL REPORTS

The Conference notes the statement of the authorised representatives of the Bolsheviks, with whom the Plenary Meeting of the Central Committee concluded an agreement in January 1910, providing for the conditional transfer by the Bolsheviks of the property of their group to the Central Committee, and resolves that

(1) in view of the fact that the liquidators violated the agreement, and that the trustees have refused to act as arbitrators, the Bolshevik representatives have every formal right to dispose both of the property in their own hands and of the property now in the hands of Comrade Zetkin, former trustee;

(2) following the application made by the representatives of the Bolsheviks, the Conference regards the funds now in Comrade Zetkin's keeping as unquestionably belonging to the Party through the Central Committee elected by the Conference, and

(3) instructs the Central Committee to take all measures immediately to obtain the property of the Party from Comrade Zetkin.

*   *
*

The Auditing Committee, having examined the financial reports and the receipts submitted by *Rabochaya Gazeta*, now endorsed by the Conference as an organ of the Central Committee, and also the receipts presented by the group of Bolsheviks to whom funds were advanced by the Plenary Meeting of the Central Committee for the purpose of publishing Social-Democratic literature, has found the accounts to be in order and moves that they be accepted by the Conference.

THE RED CROSS

The Conference instructs all the comrades in the localities to make every effort to revive the Red Cross organisation, which is so urgently needed for aid to imprisoned and exiled comrades.

THE PARTY ORGANISATION ABROAD

The Conference recognises the absolute necessity for a single Party organisation abroad that carries on its work of assisting the Party under the control and guidance of the Central Committee.

The Conference approves the Committee of the Organisation Abroad [182] as one of the Party organisations functioning abroad, and summons all Party elements, irrespective of factions and trends, who support the illegal Party and are waging an implacable fight against the anti-Party trends (liquidationism), to rally around the Central Committee in order to assist in the work of the Party in Russia and in creating a single organisation abroad.

All groups abroad, without any exception, may communicate with Russian organisations only through the Central Committee.

The Conference declares that the groups abroad which refuse to submit to the Russian centre of Social-Democratic activity, i.e., to the Central Committee, and which cause disorganisation by communicating with Russia independently and ignoring the Central Committee, have no right to use the name of the R.S.D.L.P

THE RUSSIAN GOVERNMENT'S ATTACK ON PERSIA

The Russian Social-Democratic Labour Party protests against the rapacious policy of the tsarist gang which is bent on suppressing the freedom of the Persian people and, in pursuing this policy, does not shrink from carrying out the most barbarous and infamous acts.

The Conference places on record that the alliance between the Russian and British governments which the Russian liberals are widely advertising and supporting in every way, is directed primarily against the revolutionary movement of the democratic forces in Asia, and that, by virtue of this alliance, the Liberal government of Britain is a party to the bloody atrocities perpetrated by the tsarist government.

The Conference expresses its unqualified sympathy for the struggle waged by the Persian people and, particularly, by the Persian Social-Democratic Party, which has lost so many of its members in the fight against the tsarist butchers.

THE CHINESE REVOLUTION

In view of the campaign of propaganda conducted by the government and liberal newspapers (*Rech*) in favour of taking advantage of the revolutionary movement in China in order to annex, in the interests of Russian capitalists, the Chinese provinces bordering on Russia, the Conference recognises the world-wide importance of the revolutionary struggle of the Chinese people, which is bringing emancipation to Asia and is undermining the rule of the European bourgeoisie. The Conference hails the revolutionary republicans of China, testifies to the profound enthusiasm and complete sympathy with which the proletariat of Russia is following the successes of the revolutionary people of China, and condemns the behaviour of the Russian liberals who are supporting tsarism's policy of conquest.

THE POLICY OF THE TSARIST GOVERNMENT IN FINLAND

The Conference of the R.S.D.L.P., the first to be convened since Russian tsarism and the counter-revolutionary Duma passed laws abolishing the rights and liberties of the Finnish people, expresses its complete solidarity with the fraternal Social-Democratic Party of Finland, emphasises that the workers of Finland and Russia have a common task in the struggle against the Russian counter-revolutionary government and counter-revolutionary bourgeoisie who are trampling on the rights of the people, and expresses its firm conviction that only as a result of the joint efforts of the workers of Russia and of Finland will tsarism be overthrown and the Russian and Finnish people attain freedom.

THE ELECTION PLATFORM OF THE R.S.D.L.P.[189]

Worker comrades, and all citizens of Russia!

The elections to the Fourth Duma are to be held in the very near future. Various political parties and the government itself are already energetically preparing for the elections. The Russian Social-Democratic Labour Party, the party of the class-conscious proletariat, that by its glorious struggle in 1905 dealt the first serious blow to tsarism and forced it to concede representative institutions, calls on each and every one of you who enjoy electoral rights, as well as the great majority deprived of rights, to play a most energetic part in the elections. All those who strive for the liberation of the working class from wage slavery, all those who hold the cause of Russia's freedom dear, must start work at once so that at the elections to the Fourth Duma, the landowners' Duma, they may unite and strengthen the fighters for freedom, and advance the class-consciousness and organisation of Russian democrats.

It' is five years since the government coup of June 3, 1907, when Nicholas the Bloody, the Khodynka Tsar,[190] "the victor and destroyer" of the First and Second Dumas, threw aside his pledges, promises, and manifestos, so that, together with the Black-Hundred landowners and the Octobrist merchants, he could take vengeance on the working class and all the revolutionary elements in Russia, in other words, on the vast majority of the people, for 1905.

Vengeance for the revolution is the hallmark of the entire period of the Third Duma. Never before has Russia known such raging persecution on the part of tsarism. The gallows erected during these five years beat all records of three centuries of Russian history. The places of exile, penal establishments and prisons overflow with political

GREETINGS TO THE GERMAN SOCIAL-DEMOCRATIC PARTY

The following telegram was sent on behalf of the Conference to the Central Organ of the German Social-Democratic Party:

The Russian Social-Democratic Labour Party, as represented by the Russian Organising Commission and the Central Organ of the Party, sends its ardent greetings to the fraternal German Social-Democratic Party on the occasion of the brilliant victory over all the forces of the bourgeois world it won at the recent elections.[183]

Long live international Social-Democracy; long live the German Social-Democratic Party!

Written in January 1912

Published in February 1912
in a pamphlet *All-Russian
Conference of the R.S.D.L.P.*
Central Committee
Publishing House, Paris

Published according to
the pamphlet text

AN ORGAN OF A LIBERAL LABOUR POLICY

Before me lie three issues of the St. Petersburg weekly newspaper *Zhivoye Dyelo*[184] which began publication in January last.

I invite readers to look closely at the sermons which it preaches.

The main political question of the day is the elections to the Fourth Duma. Martov's article in No. 2 is devoted to this subject. The slogan he puts forward reads: "We must endeavour to dislodge reaction from its positions in the Duma." And in No. 3 Dan repeats this idea—"The best way to weaken its pernicious influence [that of the Council of State] is to wrest the Duma from the hands of the reactionaries."

The slogan is clear, and every class-conscious worker will have no difficulty, of course, in seeing that it is not a Marxist, not a proletarian, not even a democratic, but a *liberal* slogan. It is the slogan of a liberal labour policy.

Here is Martov's defence of this slogan: "Is this task *feasible* under the existing electoral law? Unquestionably, it is. True, this electoral law guarantees beforehand a majority of electors from the landowners and the first urban [capitalist] curia in a considerable [?] number of gubernia assemblies...".

In his attempt to defend a bad cause Martov was at once forced to make a flagrantly wrong assertion. The electors from the landowners plus the first urban curia comprise an absolute majority, not "in a considerable number" of gubernia assemblies, but *positively in all of them* (in European Russia). And this is not all. In 28 out of 53 gubernias, the electors sent by the landowners *alone* comprise an *absolute majority* in the gubernia assemblies. And these 28 gubernias send 255 deputies to the Duma—out of a total of 442, i.e., again an absolute majority.

In order to defend the liberal slogan about "dislodging reaction from its positions in the Duma" Martov had to begin by whitewashing the Russian landowners so as to make them look like liberals. Not a bad beginning!

"However," Martov continues, "the last elections showed that among the landowners and the big urban bourgeoisie too, there are elements hostile to the Black-Hundred, nationalist and Octobrist reactionaries."

True. Even some of the electors delegated by the landowners are members of the opposition, Cadets. What conclusion is to be drawn from this? Only that the Duma majority elected on the basis of the law of June 3, 1907, cannot be shifted *farther than a landowners'* "liberal" opposition. The landowner has the last say. This fact remains true, and Martov tries to evade it. Consequently, only if the landowner joins the opposition can the "opposition" (*of the landowners*) gain the upper hand. But that is precisely the crux of the whole question; can one say, without turning into a liberal, that the (*landowners'*) "liberal opposition will be capable of dislodging reaction from its positions in the Duma"?

In the first place, we must not gloss over the fact that our electoral law favours the landowners. Secondly, we must not forget that the landowners' "opposition" has all the distinguishing features of so-called *"Left Octobrism"* (with which the Cadets are permitted by their last conference to form blocs!—something that it is no use Martov keeping quiet about). Only comical liberal politicians can talk about a possible victory of "Left Octobrists", and of "wresting the Duma from the hands of the reactionaries" or of "dislodging reaction from its positions in the Duma".

The task of worker democrats is to *take advantage* of the conflicts between the liberals and the present majority in the Duma *for the purpose* of strengthening the democratic forces in the Duma, and by no means to support liberal illusions about the possibility of "wresting the Duma from the hands of the reactionaries".

Our author lands into an even worse mess when he turns to a question of *principle*, to the question as to what *significance* should be attached to the eventuality of "the *entire* opposition breaking down the Black-Hundred Octobrist majority in the Duma".

"It is to the interest of the workers," argues Martov, "that power in a class state should be transferred from the hands of the savage landowner into the hands of the more civilised bourgeoisie."

A wonderful argument. Only a minor detail has been forgotten—a mere trifle—that *"it is to the interest"* of the Russian "more civilised bourgeoisie", the liberals, the Cadets, *not to undermine* the power of the savage landowner. "It is to the interest" of the liberals to share power with him, taking care not to undermine this power and not to place a single weapon in the hands of democracy.

That is the crux of the matter! And it is to no purpose that you try to evade a serious question and, with an air of importance, chew the cud of trivial commonplaces.

"By strengthening their representation in the Duma," says Martov, "the Cadets and the Progressists will still not be able to assume power, but it will facilitate their advance towards power." Well, well. If that is the case, why is it that, since 1848, the German Cadets and Progressists have "strengthened their representation" in Parliament time and again, but, for all that, they have so far "not come to power"? Why is it that during sixty-four years, *and to this very day*, they have *left* power in the hands of the Junkers? Why is it that the Russian Cadets, although they "increased their representation" in the First and Second Dumas, did not "facilitate their advance towards power"?

Martov accepts Marxism only insofar as it is *acceptable* to *any* educated liberal. It is to the interest of the workers that power should be transferred from the hands of the landowner into the hands of the more civilised bourgeois—every liberal in the world will subscribe to this "conception" of the *"interest of the workers"*. But that is still not Marxism. Marxism goes further and says: (1) it is to the interest of the liberals not to undermine the power of the landowner, but to take a place next to him; (2) it is to the interest of the liberals to share power with the landowners in such a way as to leave absolutely nothing to the worker or to democracy; (3) power *actually* does "fall out" of the hands of the landowners and "passes into the hands" of the liberals *only when* democracy triumphs *in spite* of the liberals. You want proof? Take the entire history of France and the latest events in China. In the latter country the liberal Yüan Shih-kai would never have come to power even provisionally, even conditionally, if Chinese democracy had not scored a victory *in spite* of Yüan Shih-kai.

If the commonplace maxim that a liberal is better than a member of the Black Hundreds is *all* that Struve, Izgoyev and Co. accept in the way of Marxism, the dialectics of the class struggle is a sealed book both to the liberal as well as to Martov.

To sum up: precisely in order that power in Russia may actually "pass" from the hands of the landowners *into* the hands of the bourgeoisie, democracy in general, and the workers in particular, must not be deceived and enfeebled by the *false* slogan of "wresting the Duma from the hands of the reactionaries". The practical task that faces us at the elections is by no means to "dislodge reaction from its positions in the Duma", but to strengthen the forces of democracy in general and of working-class democracy in particular. This task may sometimes clash with the "task" of increasing the number of liberals, but five additional democrats are more important to us, and more useful to the proletariat, than fifty additional liberals.

Hence the following conclusion which Martov refuses to draw, even though he does pretend to agree that the Cadets are *not* democrats, but liberals: (1) in the five big cities,[185] in the event of a second ballot, agreements are permissible *only* with the democrats against the liberals; (2) at *all* the ballots and in *all* the agreements at the second stage, *precedence* should be given to agreements with the democrats against the liberals, and only subsequently may agreements be concluded with the liberals against the Rights.

Zvezda, No. 11 (47), February 19, 1912
    Signed: *F. L-ko*

Published according to
the *Zvezda* text

AGAINST UNITY—WITH THE LIQUIDATORS

No. 7 of the liquidationist newspaper *Zhivoye Dyelo* carries an editorial entitled "For Unity—Against a Split". The article deals with a question that is undoubtedly extremely interesting and important and is exercising the mind of every thinking worker. We consider it our duty to express our opinion—even if in part and in brief, on the obviously and definitely incorrect information offered readers by *Zhivoye Dyelo*.

On the basis of reports in the newspapers *Golos Zemli*, *Russkoye Slovo* and *Kievskaya Mysl*[186] which "agree with the information received by *Zhivoye Dyelo*", the latter establishes the fact that a general Party conference was held abroad, and that this conference has "imposed upon all Marxists in Russia definite tactics to be pursued in the election campaign", and, among other things, placed the *Nasha Zarya* and *Dyelo Zhizni* group *outside the Party* (italics of the *Zhivoye Dyelo*). In this connection, *Zhivoye Dyelo* (which intersperses its article with the usual slander and insinuations against the anti-liquidators) is, first, trying its utmost to discredit the conference, and, second, takes *Nasha Zarya* and Co. under its wing, declaring that they cannot be placed "outside", that the "writers" of that trend "contemptuously shrug their shoulders at this resolution", etc.

We note, to begin with, that the entire content of the article in *Zhivoye Dyelo*, its hysterical tone and its vociferous shouting "for unity" clearly testify to the fact that the liquidators have been touched to the quick and are trying, unsuccessfully, to obscure *the substance of the matter*. It is with this *substance* that we shall now deal.

Naturally, we can neither defend the conference nor supplement or correct the information printed in the above-mentioned newspapers (to which *Golos Moskvy* should now be added). For that matter this is not what we have set out to do. And, for that matter, too, it is sufficient to reproduce *word for word* just one sentence from the article in *Zhivoye Dyelo*: "We ask," the liquidators exclaim, "who elected them [the delegates to the conference], who authorised them to speak and decide on behalf of the Moscow, St. Petersburg, etc., Marxists?" It would be quite natural for Mr. Purish-kevich or Mr. Zamyslovsky, for example, openly to "ask" such a question. But it is the liquidators who *ask* this question of the public in the columns of *Zhivoye Dyelo* and this question in itself so splendidly reveals their liquidationist nature, so magnificently exposes them, that it only remains for us to point to these methods of the liquidators and to leave it at that.

We repeat that we are dealing with the questions touched upon in this article only insofar as it is our duty to comment on statements in the press and to note all that is related to the workers' election campaign. The readers must know the truth. When the liquidators say—"For unity—against a split"—it is our duty to reveal the falsehood contained in this statement. First, why play at hide-and-seek and speak of "unity" in general, when as a matter of fact, it is a question *only of unity with the liquidators*? Why does *Zhivoye Dyelo* obscure the real issue? Why doesn't it say openly whether or not it is in agreement with the point of view expressed by *Nasha Zarya* and *Dyelo Zhizni*? Secondly, it is premature to speak of a *split* so long as we are not confronted by two organised, integral political collectives functioning in the same milieu.

This is the *substance of the matter* that *Zhivoye Dyelo* should speak about—its shouting and abuse will lead it nowhere.

Unity with the liquidators is not a new, but rather an old, issue. More than two years ago, in January 1910, a most determined attempt was made to establish such unity; it was formulated in an agreement and sealed by a unanimous resolution. The attempt failed, that is admitted by *all*, the liquidators included (see *Nasha Zarya* for 1911,

No. 11, p. 130). Why did it fail? People who are really interested in the question ought to find the answer themselves, by examining the *documents*. We shall cite here only a few of the documents, but the most decisive.

One of the "uniters" or "conciliators", Mr. Ionov, who is well known for his part in the attempt to establish unity with the liquidators, wrote *at the very time* that attempt was made:

"However harmful otzovism and liquidationism, as such, may be to the Party, their beneficial effect on the factions [the Menshevik and the Bolshevik factions] seems to be beyond doubt. Pathology recognises two kinds of abscess—harmful and harmless. The harmless type is a disease beneficial to the organism. As it grows, it draws various injurious substances from the entire organism and thus helps improve the health of that organism. I believe that a similar role was played by liquidationism in respect of Menshevism and by otzovism-ultimatumism in respect of Bolshevism."

Here is one documented confirmation of the fact that the declared condition for unity with the liquidators was that they should completely renounce liquidationism. That was in January 1910. In February 1910, Mr. *Potresov* wrote the following in *Nasha Zarya*, No. 2:

"I ask the reader," wrote Mr. Potresov, "whether it is possible that there can exist, in this year of 1909, as something that is actually real and not a figment of a diseased imagination, a liquidationist tendency, a tendency to liquidate what is already beyond liquidation and actually no longer exists as an organised whole". (*Nasha Zarya*, 1910, No. 2, p. 61.)

All practical workers know that the liquidators *acted* exactly as directed by Mr. Potresov. *Vozrozhdeniye*, another well-known organ of the liquidators, to which the same Martov, Larin, Levitsky and Co. contributed, quoted these words of Mr. Potresov's in its issue of March 30, 1910, and added approvingly on its own behalf: "There is nothing to liquidate—and for ourselves we [i.e., the editors of *Vozrozhdeniye*] may add, the dream of resuscitating that hierarchy, in its old, underground shape is nothing but a harmful, reactionary utopia." (*Vozrozhdeniye*, 1910, No. 5, p. 51).

Were there any other persons and trends, besides ours, who interpreted these statements as a *breach* on the part of the liquidators with the old, previously existing political collective? There certainly were. The proof: (1) An article by Mr. Izgoyev in *Russkaya Mysl*, 1910, No. 8— "A *Vekhi* Writer Among Marxists". Mr. Izgoyev always assesses the events taking place among the Marxists from a consistently *Vekhi* viewpoint. "The answer [given by Mr. Potresov to the questions of the working-class movement] *fully accords,*" wrote Mr. Izgoyev, "with what was written in *Vekhi*, which he reviles, and what the publicists of *Russkaya Mysl* are saying" (*Russkaya Mysl*, 1910, No. 8, p. 67). (2) The Menshevik Plekhanov wrote in May 1910 apropos of Mr. Potresov's words quoted above: "There is no doubt, however, that *a man for whom our Party does not exist, does not himself exist for our Party.* [Plekhanov's italics.] Now all the members of the Party will have to say that Mr. Potresov is no comrade of theirs, and some of them, will, perhaps, stop accusing me on the score that I have long since ceased to regard him as such."

The fact is established, and no subterfuges and evasions can alter matters. The liquidators broke with the previously existing political collective as far back as 1910. No historian of Russian political life can evade this fact unless he wants to depart from the truth. In 1911, Levitsky, Martov, Dan, Larin, Chatsky and Co. repeatedly made statements fully in line with Potresov's. We have only to recall how Larin, in *Dyelo Zhizni* (for 1911, No. 6, p. 15), preached to the workers that it is not difficult "to form circles ... of several hundred people ... in each town", but that it would be just a "masquerade"!

It is our profound conviction that the inevitable conclusion to be drawn from this, from more than two years' experience, is that unity *with the liquidators* is an impossibility. Nor is an agreement with them possible. Agreements in this case are *inconceivable* because it is a question of the existence or non-existence of what the liquidators have contemptuously dubbed "the hierarchy". And no abuse from *Zhivoye Dyelo*—an organ of the *very same* liquidators of the *very same* trend—can change anything. The liquidators are *outside....* That is an irrevocable fact.

It may be objected, perhaps, that this fact implies a split. It does not. A split means the formation of *two* political collectives instead of one. At the present time, however, in March 1912, an observer of our political life, one equipped with the finest telescope and looking from the vantage point of St. Petersburg, Moscow, Kiev, New York or elsewhere— will be able to discern *only one* organised, integral political collective, and the only result of the liquidators' abuse is that this collective is gaining strength among the workers.

The trouble with the liquidators is that they have indeed *liquidated* their relations with the old, but they have *created nothing* new. When they do create something, we shall see what it is and, in our capacity of political observers, inform readers about it. But so far the fact remains that there is no other integrated political collective, consequently, there is no split.

The liquidators have long since given notice that they are going to form an "open" political association. But that has nothing to do with the facts. Mr. Levitsky *"himself"*, Potresov's and Martov's closest colleague, expressed, in a leading article in *Nasha Zarya*, No. 11 (1911), his *regret* that "we do not see a single, more or less serious, attempt to organise a legally existing *political* [Mr. Levitsky's italics] association". Mr. Levitsky thinks that both the "masses" and the "leaders" are to blame for this. But it is not now a question of who is to blame, but of establishing a fact. *If* Mr. Levitsky and his friends form a legally existing political association, *if* it actually pursues a Marxist (and not a liberal) labour policy, then ... then we shall see. Only you had better make haste, gentlemen, not much time remains to the elections, and Herculean efforts are needed to do in months what has not been done in *years* (or to *do it* in a way diametrically *opposed* to the way it was done before).

The liquidators have decapitated themselves. And it is no use weeping for the hair when the head is gone.

An observer of Russian political life may discover only one political collective in the sphere which interests us. Around it he will find individuals and unorganised small groups which offer no complete answer even to the *most urgent* political problems. In other words, there is disintegration everywhere. As in every case of disintegration there are some who vacillate and some who hope (in vain, alas!) to prevail upon the liquidators *actually* to break with liquidationism. But only hopeless politicians can try to feed themselves on hopes a mere six months before the elections.

Take, for instance, the question of slogans for the election campaign, of tactics, of agreements. There is only one formulated, clear, explicit, and complete answer, and this answer is already known to all the leading workers throughout Russia. *There is no other answer.* Once more, Messrs. Liquidators: It's no use weeping for the hair when the head is gone.

P.S. Trotsky, apparently, classes himself among those who "hope" that the liquidators may mend their ways; for, writing in *Zhivoye Dyelo* he gives a simplified paraphrase of the introductory section of the December 1908 resolutions on the essence of the June Third regime. We shall be very glad if Trotsky succeeds in convincing Larin and Martov, for instance, not to mention others, that they all ought to agree on one definite, explicit, and clear answer to the question of what the substance of our present "Constitution" is. They are shouting about the usefulness of "unity", about the harm of "the circle outlook", and yet they cannot elaborate a united opinion even of their "own" circle, either on questions of principle, or on practical questions of our entire activity! But, to compensate for this, there is phrase-mongering galore! "Social-Democracy," writes Trotsky, "is able to inscribe its great tasks on the inner surface of the cranium, not only as a formula...." What an elegant writer Trotsky is—as elegant as Potresov and Nevedomsky.

Prosveshcheniye, No. 3-4,   Published according to
  February-March 1912   the *Prosveshcheniye* text
    Signed: *M. B.*

POLITICAL PARTIES IN THE FIVE YEARS
OF THE THIRD DUMA

I

In the *Rech Year Book for 1912* —that miniature political encyclopaedia of liberalism —we find an article by Mr Milyukov: "Political Parties *in the State Duma* in the Past Five Years". Written by the acknowledged leader of the liberals, and an outstanding historian at that, this article deserves our special attention, all the more so since it deals with what may be termed the *most important pre-election subject*. The political results of the activity of the parties, the question of their role, scientific generalisations regarding the alignment of social forces, the slogans of the forth-coming election campaign simply ask to be written about, and Mr. Milyukov *had* to touch on all these points, once he had tackled the subject, no matter how much he tried to confine himself to a plain relation of the facts concerning the "external history" of the Duma.

The result is an interesting picture, illustrating the old, but ever new, subject: how is Russian political life reflected in the mind of a liberal?

"The party of people's freedom," writes Mr. Milyukov, "which in the First Duma predominated numerically and in the Second Duma morally, was represented in the Third Duma by only 56-53 deputies. After holding the position of a leading majority it became an opposition party, retaining, however, its dominant position in the ranks of the opposition, both numerically and qualitatively and by the strict group discipline which characterised the speeches and voting of its representatives."

The leader of a party, writing about political parties, declares that his party "retained ... its domination ... qualitatively". Not bad—only this self-advertisement might have been somewhat more subtle.... And, then, is it true that the Cadets dominated in respect of strict group discipline? This is not true, for we all remember the numerous speeches of Mr. Maklakov, for example, who isolated himself from the Cadet group and took up a position to the right of it. Mr. Milyukov made an incautious statement: for, while it is safe to advertise the "qualities" of one's party, because such an appraisal is entirely subjective, the facts at once refute the advertisement of party discipline. It is characteristic that the Right wing of the Cadets—both in the Duma, in the person of Maklakov, and in the press, in the person of Messrs. Struve and Co. in *Russkaya Mysl*—took their own line and, far from adhering to strict discipline, they destroyed all discipline in the Cadet Party.

"To its left," continues Mr. Milyukov, "the people's freedom group had only 14 Trudoviks and 15 Social-Democrats. The Trudovik group retained but a shadow of the importance it had formerly had in the First and the Second Dumas. The somewhat better organised Social-Democratic group came out from time to time with sharp invectives regarding 'class contradictions', but, in essence, it could not pursue any tactics other than those also pursued by the 'bourgeois' opposition."

This is all, literally all, that the distinguished historian has to say about the parties to the left of the Cadets in the twenty pages of his article. But the article is supposed to be devoted to an examination of the political parties in the State Duma—it goes into the minutest details of every shift in the ranks of the landowners, dealing at length with the sundry "moderate-Right" or "Right-Octobrist groups" and with every step taken by those groups. Why, then, are the Trudoviks and the Social-Democrats practically ignored? For to describe them as Mr. Milyukov *does* is tantamount to ignoring them.

The only possible answer is: because Mr. Milyukov has a particular dislike for these parties, and even a plain statement of generally known facts regarding these parties would run counter to the *interests* of the liberals. In fact,

Mr. Milyukov is perfectly well aware of the reshuffling effected in the composition of the electors which reduced the Trudoviks to "a shadow of the former importance they had had" in the Dumas. This reshuffling, which was effected by Mr. Kryzhanovsky and other heroes of June 3, 1907, undermined the Cadet majority. But can this justify the ignoring and, even worse, the distortion of data relating to the importance of parties having very small representation in the landowners' Duma? The Trudoviks are very poorly represented in the Third Duma, but they have played a very great role during these five years, for they represent millions of peasants. The interests of the landowners especially demanded the reduction of peasant representation. But, we should like to ask, what interests prompt the liberals to brush aside the Trudoviks?

Or take Mr. Milyukov's ill-tempered sally against the Social-Democrats. Is it possible for him not to know that the "tactics" of the latter are distinguished from that of the Cadets not only because there is a difference between a proletarian and a bourgeois opposition, but also because democracy differs from liberalism? Of course, Mr. Milyukov knows this perfectly well, and he could quote examples from the modern history of all European countries to illustrate the difference between democrats and liberals. The point is that when it concerns Russia the Russian liberal *refuses* to see the distinction between himself and the Russian democrats. It is *to the advantage* of the Russian liberal to pose before the Russian readers as a representative of the whole "democratic opposition" in general. But this advantage has nothing in common with the truth.

Actually, it is common knowledge that the Social-Democrats in the Third Duma pursued tactics *absolutely* different from those of the bourgeois opposition in general and of the Cadet (liberal) opposition in particular. It may be safely asserted that, had Mr. Milyukov tried to deal with any one specific political issue, he would not have found *a single one* on which the Social-Democrats did not pursue fundamentally *different* tactics. Having chosen as his subject a survey of the political parties in the Third Duma, Mr. Milyukov distorted the principal and cardinal point: that there were three main groups of political parties, which

pursued three different kinds of tactics —namely, the government parties (from Purishkevich to Guchkov), the liberal
parties (Cadets, Nationalists and Progressists), and the
democratic parties (the Trudoviks representing bourgeois
democracy, and working-class democrats). The first two
generalisations are clear to Mr. Milyukov, he sees perfectly
well the essence of the affinity between Purishkevich and
Guchkov on the one hand, and all the liberals on the other.
But he.does not see the distinction between the latter and
the democrats, because *he will not* see it.

II

This is repeated when he deals with the class basis of
the various parties. To the right of him Mr. Milyukov sees
this basis and reveals it; but he grows blind the moment he
turns to the left. "The very law of June 3," he writes, "was
dictated by the united nobility. It was the Right wing
of the Duma majority that undertook to defend the interests of the nobility. To this the Left wing of the majority
added the defence of the interests of the big urban bourgeoisie". How edifying, isn't it? When the Cadet looks to the
right he draws distinct lines of "class contradictions": here
the nobility, there the big bourgeoisie. But the moment the
liberal turns his glance to the left he puts the words "class
contradictions" in ironical quotation marks. The class dis-
tinctions disappear: the liberals, in the capacity of a general
"democratic opposition", are supposed to represent the peasants, the workers, and the urban democrats!

No, gentlemen, this is not scientific history, nor is it
serious politics —it is cheap politics and self-advertisement.

The liberals represent neither the peasants nor the workers.
They merely represent a section of the bourgeoisie —urban,
landowning, etc.

The history of the Third Duma is so generally known
that even Mr. Milyukov cannot help admitting that on frequent occasions the liberals voted together with the Octobrists —not only *against* (the government), but also *in favour*
of certain positive measures. These facts, in view of the common history of Octobrism and Cadetism (which in 1904-05,
up to October 17, 1905, were one), *prove* to everyone to whom

historical reality means anything at all that the Octobrists and the Cadets are the two flanks of *one class*, the two flanks of the bourgeois *Centre*, which vacillates between the government and the landowners, on the one hand, and democracy (the workers and the peasants), on the other. Mr. Milyukov fails to draw this *fundamental* conclusion from the history of "the political parties in the Third Duma" only because it is not to his interest to do so.

In a new way and under new circumstances, the Third Duma has *confirmed* the fundamental division of Russian political forces and Russian political parties of which there were definite signs in the middle of the nineteenth century, and which acquired a growingly distinct shape in the period 1861-1904, rose to the surface and became fixed in the open arena of the struggle of the masses in 1905-07, remaining unchanged in the 1908-12 period. Why is this division valid to this day? Because the objective problems of Russia's historical development—problems which have always and everywhere, from France in 1789 to China in 1911, formed the content of democratic change and democratic revolutions—have as yet not been solved.

This is grounds for the inevitably stubborn resistance of the "bureaucracy" and the landowners, as well as for the vacillations of the bourgeoisie, for whom changes are essential but who are afraid that the changes may be made use of by democracy in general and by the workers in particular. In the sphere of Duma politics this fear was particularly apparent among the Cadets in the First and the Second Dumas, and among the Octobrists in the Third Duma, i.e., when those parties represented the "leading" majority. Although the Cadets contend with the Octobrists, they take the same stand on questions of principle and it is really more a matter of rivalry than of a fight. They share with them a cosy place near the government, *alongside* the landowners; hence the apparent keenness of the conflict between the powers that be and the Cadets, their closest rivals.

While ignoring the distinction between the democrats and the liberals, Mr. Milyukov goes into extraordinary detail and examines at great length, with gusto, one might say, the shifts in the ranks of the landowners: Rights, moderate-Rights, Nationalists in general, independent Na-

tionalists, Right Octobrists, plain Octobrists, Left Octobrists. No serious significance can be attached to the divisions and shifts within these limits. At most they are connected with the substitution of a Tverdoonto for an Ugryum-Burcheyev[187] in an administrative post, with the
change of persons, with the victories of circles or coteries. In
everything essential, their political lines are absolutely
identical.

"Two camps will contend [in the elections to the Fourth
Duma]", insists Mr. Milyukov, in the same way as the entire
Cadet press never tires of insisting. That is not true, gentlemen. There are *three* principal camps that *are contending*
and will contend: the government camp, the liberals, and
working-class democracy as the centre towards which all
the forces of democracy in general gravitate. The division
into two camps is a trick of liberal politics, which, unfortunately, does occasionally succeed in misleading some supporters of the working class. Only when it realises the
inevitability of a division into three main camps, will the
working class be able actually to pursue, not a liberal labour policy, but a policy of its *own, taking advantage* of
the conflicts between the first camp and the second, but not
allowing itself to be deceived even for a moment by the
sham democratic phrases of the liberals. The workers must
not allow themselves to be deceived, nor must they allow
the peasants, the mainstay of bourgeois *democracy*, to be
deceived. That is the conclusion to be drawn from the history
of the political parties in the Third Duma.

Zvezda, No. 14 (50), March 4, 1912   Published according to
        Signed: *K. T.*   the *Zvezda* text

REPORT TO THE INTERNATIONAL
SOCIALIST BUREAU
ON THE ALL-RUSSIA CONFERENCE
OF THE R.S.D.L.P.[188]

The last few years have been years of indecision and dis-organisation for the R.S.D.L.P. For three years the Party could not convene either a conference or a congress, and during the last two years the Central Committee has been unable to develop any activity. True enough, the Party has continued to exist, but only in the form of isolated groups in all the larger cities and, in view of the absence of a Central Committee, each of these groups has led a life of its own, somewhat isolated from the others.

Not so long ago, under the influence of the new awakening of the Russian proletariat, the Party again began to gain in strength, and quite recently we were able, at last, to con-vene a conference (something that had been impossible ever since 1908), at which the organisations of St. Petersburg and Moscow, of the North-West and the South, the Caucasus and the central industrial region were represented. In all, twenty organisations established close ties with the Organ-ising Commission convening this conference; that is to say, practically all the organisations, both Menshevik and Bol-shevik, active in Russia at the present time.

During its twenty-three sessions the Conference, which assumed the rights and duties of the supreme authority of the Party, discussed all the questions on the agenda, among which were a number that were extremely important. The Conference made a comprehensive evaluation of the present political situation and of Party policy, this evaluation fully corresponding to the resolutions of the Conference held in

1908 and to the decisions of the Plenary Meeting of the Central Committee in 1910. The Conference devoted special attention to the Duma elections which are to be held in a few months' time, and adopted a resolution in three sections which gives a very explicit and detailed explanation of the intricate and involved election law, analyses the question of election agreements with other parties, and thoroughly elucidates the position and tactics of the Party in the forthcoming election campaign. The Conference also discussed and adopted resolutions on the questions of combating the famine, of workers' insurance, of trade unions, of strikes, etc.

Further, the Conference considered the question of the "liquidators". This trend denies the existence of the illegal Party, declares that the Party is already liquidated and that the attempts to revive the illegal Party are a reactionary utopia, and maintains that the Party can be revived only as a legally existing organisation. Nevertheless, this trend, which has broken with the illegal Party, has so far been unable to found a legally existing party. The Conference placed on record that for four years the Party had been waging a fight against this trend, that the Conference held in 1908 and the Plenary Meeting of the Central Committee in 1910 had both declared against the liquidators, and that in spite of all the attempts made by the Party, this trend continued to maintain its factional independence and to carry on a struggle against the Party in the columns of publications appearing legally. The Conference, therefore, declared that the liquidators, grouped around the magazines *Nasha Zarya* and *Dyelo Zhizni* (to which *Zhivoye Dyelo* should now be added), had placed themselves outside the ranks of the R.S.D.L.P.

Finally, the Conference elected a Central Committee and an editorial board for *Sotsial-Demokrat*, the Party's Central Organ. In addition, the Conference specially noted the fact that many groups abroad more or less adhering to socialism are, in any case, entirely divorced from the Russian proletariat and its socialist activity; consequently, these groups are absolutely irresponsible, and under no circumstances can they represent the R.S.D.L.P. or speak in its name; that the Party does not hold itself in any way responsible or answerable for these groups, and that all relations with the R.S.D.L.P. must be carried on solely through the Central Committee, whose address abroad is: Vladimir Ulyanov, 4, Rue Marie Rose, Paris XIV (for the Central Committee).

Written early in March 1912

Published on March 18, 1912,
  in Circular No. 4 of the
International Socialist Bureau

Published according to
  the Circular text
Translated from the German

prisoners in unheard-of numbers, and never before has there been such torture and torment of the vanquished as under Nicholas II. Never before has there been such a wave of embezzlement, such tyranny and violence on the part of officials, who are forgiven everything because of their zeal in the struggle against "sedition"; never before have the ordinary people, and the peasants in particular, been so humiliated by any representative of authority. Never before has there been such avid, ferocious, reckless persecution of the Jews, and after them of other peoples, not belonging to the dominant nation.

Anti-Semitism and the most crude nationalism became the only political platform of the government parties, and Purishkevich became the one complete, undiluted, and perfect personification of all the methods of rule by the present tsarist monarchy.

And what have these frenzied acts of the counter-revolutionaries led to?

The consciousness that it is impossible to continue living in this way is penetrating into the minds of even the "higher", exploiting, classes of society. The Octobrists themselves, the dominant party in the Third Duma, the party of landowners and merchants, terrified of the revolution and cringing before authority, are more and more expressing the conviction in their own press that the tsar and the nobility, which they have served so faithfully and truly, have led Russia into an impasse.

There was a time when the tsarist monarchy was the gendarme of Europe, protecting reaction in Russia and assisting in forcibly suppressing all movements for freedom in Europe. Nicholas II has brought things to such a pass, that he is now not only a European, but an Asiatic gendarme who, with the help of intrigues, money and the most brutal violence, tries to suppress all movements for freedom in Turkey, Persia, and China.

But no tsarist atrocities can halt Russia's progress. No matter how these feudal survivals, the Purishkeviches, Romanovs and Markovs, disfigure and cripple Russia, she is still advancing. With each step of Russia's development the demand for political freedom is becoming ever more insistent. In the twentieth century Russia cannot live without political freedom any more than any other country can. Is it possible to expect political reforms from the tsarist monarchy, when the tsar himself dissolved the first two Dumas and rode roughshod over his own Manifesto of October 17, 1905? Is it possible to conceive of political reforms in modern Russia, when the gang of officials mocks at all laws, knowing that in doing so, they have the protection of the tsar and his associates? Do we not see how, taking advantage of the tsar's protection, or that of his relatives, Illiodor yesterday, Rasputin today, Tolmachov yesterday, Khvostov today, Stolypin yesterday, Makarov today, trample underfoot all and every law? Do we not see that even the tiny, ludicrously pathetic "reforms" of the landowners' Duma, reforms directed towards refurbishing and strengthening tsarist rule, are repudiated and distorted by the Council of State or the personal decrees of Nicholas the Bloody? Do we not know that the Black-Hundred gang of murderers who shoot at the backs of the deputies whom the rulers want out of the way, who sent to penal servitude the Social-Democratic deputies to the Second Duma, who are always organising pogroms, who insolently rob the treasury on all sides—do we not know that that gang enjoys the special blessings of the tsar and receives his poorly-disguised aid, direction and guidance? Look at the fate, under Nicholas Romanov, of the main political demands of the Russian people for the sake of which the best representatives of the people have been waging a heroic struggle for more than three-quarters of a century, for the sake of which millions rose up in 1905. Is universal, equal and direct suffrage compatible with the Romanov monarchy, when even the non-universal, unequal and indirect suffrage of the elections to the First and Second Dumas was trampled underfoot by tsarism. Is freedom of unions, associations, strikes, compatible with the tsarist monarchy, when even the reactionary, ugly law of March 4, 1906[191] has been brought to nought by the governors and the ministers? Do not the words of the Manifesto of October 17, 1905 about the "immutable principle of freedom of citizens", about the "real inviolability of the individual", about "freedom of conscience, speech, assembly, and unions", sound like mockery? Every subject of the tsar witnesses this mockery daily.

Enough of liberal lies! As if a union between freedom and the old rule were possible, as if political reforms were conceivable under a tsarist monarchy. The Russian people have paid for their childish illusions with the hard lessons of the counter-revolution. Anyone seriously and sincerely desiring political freedom, will raise the banner of *a republic* proudly and bravely, and *all* the live forces of Russian democracy will certainly be drawn to that banner by the politics of the tsarist-landowner gang.

Time was, and not so long ago, when the slogan "Down with the autocracy" seemed too advanced for Russia Nevertheless, the R.S.D.L. Party issued this slogan, the advanced workers caught it up and spread it throughout the country; and in two or three years this slogan became a popular saying. To work then, worker comrades and all citizens of Russia, all those who do not want to see our country sink finally into stagnation, barbarity, lack of rights and the appalling poverty of tens of millions. The Russian Social-Democrats, the Russian workers will succeed in making "Down with the tsarist monarchy, long live the Russian Democratic Republic!" a nation-wide slogan.

Workers, remember 1905. Millions of toilers then were given new life, raised to class-consciousness, to freedom, through the strike movement. Tens of years of tsarist reforms did not and could not give you a tenth part of those improvements in your lives which you then achieved by mass struggle. The fate of the Bill on workers' insurance, made unrecognisable by the landowners' Duma with the aid of the Cadets, has once again shown what you can expect "from above".

The counter-revolution has taken away almost all our gains, but it has not taken and cannot take away the strength, courage and belief in their cause of the young workers, nor of the all-Russian proletariat that is growing and becoming stronger.

Long live the new struggle to improve the lot of workers who do not wish to remain slaves doomed to toil in workshops and factories! *Long live the 8-hour working day!* He who desires freedom in Russia must help the class which dug a grave for the tsarist monarchy in 1905, and which will throw the mortal enemy of all the peoples of Russia into that grave during the forthcoming Russian revolution.

Peasants! You sent your deputies, the Trudoviks, to the First and Second Dumas, believing in the tsar, hoping by peaceful means to win his agreement to the transfer of landed estates to the people. You have now been able to convince yourselves that the tsar, the biggest landowner in Russia, will stop at nothing in defence of the landowners and officials; at neither perjury nor lawlessness, oppression or bloodshed. Are you going to tolerate the yoke of the former serf-owners, silently bear the affronts and insults of the officials, and die in hundreds of thousands, nay millions, from the agonies of starvation, from disease caused by hunger and extreme poverty, or will you die in the fight against the tsarist monarchy and tsarist-landowner Duma, in order to win for our children a more or less decent life, fit for a human being.

This is the question which the Russian peasants will have to decide. The working-class Social-Democratic Party calls on the peasants to struggle for complete freedom, for the transfer of all land from the landowners to the peasantry, without any compensation whatsoever. Sops thrown to the peasants cannot remedy their poverty or relieve their hunger. The peasants are not asking for charity, but for the land which has been drenched in their blood and sweat for centuries. The peasants do not need the tutelage of the authorities and the tsar, but freedom from officials and the tsar, freedom to arrange their own affairs.

Let the elections to the Fourth Duma sharpen the political consciousness of the masses and draw them again into decisive battles. Three main parties are contesting at the elections: (1) the Black Hundreds, (2) the liberals, and (3) the Social-Democrats.

The Rights, Nationalists, and Octobrists belong to the Black Hundreds. They all support the government; this means that any differences which may exist between them are of no serious significance whatsoever. Merciless struggle against all these Black-Hundred parties—this must be our slogan!

The liberals are the Cadet Party (the "Constitutional-Democrats" or "people's freedom" party). This is the party of the liberal bourgeoisie, which seeks to share power with the tsar and the feudal landowners in such a way, that their power is not basically destroyed, and does not pass to the people. While the liberals detest the government which prevents them from taking power, while they help to expose it, and introduce vacillation and disintegration into its ranks, their hatred of the revolution and fear of mass struggles is even greater than their hatred of the government, and their attitude towards the popular liberation movement is even more wavering and irresolute, so that in decisive moments they treacherously go over to the side of the monarchy. During the counter-revolution, the liberals, echoing the "Slavonic dreams" of tsarism, posing as a "responsible opposition", grovelling before the tsar as "His Majesty's Opposition", and pouring dirt on the revolutionaries and the revolutionary struggle of the masses, have turned away more and more from the struggle for freedom.

The Russian Social-Democratic Labour Party was able to raise the revolutionary banner even in the reactionary Third Duma, it has succeeded even there in helping the organisation and revolutionary enlightenment of the masses, and the peasants' struggle against the landowners. The party of the proletariat is the only party of the advanced class, the class capable of winning freedom for Russia. Today, our Party goes into the Duma, not in order to play at "reforms", not in order to "defend the Constitution", "convince" the Octobrists or "to dislodge reaction" from the Duma, as the liberals who are deceiving the people say they will, but in order to call the masses to the struggle from the Duma rostrum, to explain the teachings of socialism, to expose every government and liberal deception, to expose the monarchist prejudices of the backward sections of the people, and the class roots of the bourgeois parties, —in other words in order to prepare an army of class-conscious fighters for a new Russian revolution.

The tsarist government and the Black-Hundred landowners have recognised to the full the tremendous revolutionary force represented by the Social-Democratic group in the Duma. Hence, all the efforts of the police and Ministry of the Interior are directed towards preventing the Social-Democrats from entering the Fourth Duma. Unite then,

workers and citizens! Rally around the R.S.D.L.P. which
at its recent conference, recovering from the breakdown
during the evil years, again gathered its forces and raised
aloft its banner. Let each and every one take part in the
elections and the election campaign, and the efforts of the
government will be defeated, the red banner of revolutionary Social-Democracy will be hoisted from the rostrum
of the Duma in police-ridden, oppressed, blood-drenched,
down-trodden and starving Russia!

Long live the Russian Democratic Republic!

Long live the 8-hour day!

Long live the confiscation of all landed estates!

Workers and citizens! Support the election campaign of
the R S.D.L.P.! Elect the candidates of the R.S.D.L.P.!

*Central Committee of the Russian
Social-Democratic Labour Party*

Written early in March 1912

Printed as a leaflet
in March 1912

Published according to
the text of the leaflet
and verified with
a handwritten copy corrected
by V. ·I. Lenin

TO THE EDITORIAL BOARD OF *ZVEZDA*

P.S. TO "THE ELECTION PLATFORM OF THE R.S.D.L.P."[192]

This platform* is being sent only for the *information of all*, particularly the *compilers* of platforms. It is time to *cease writing* platforms when there already *exists* one confirmed and published by the Central Committee. (Leaflets *have already been issued* about this in Russia, but as we *only* possess *one* of them, we cannot send it, but are sending you a handwritten copy.) It would be particularly stupid to draw up a *legal* platform. *Each* and *every* article about the platform and "its principles" must be printed with the signature of the author and with the *subheading*: An Essay in Comment.

Incidentally, I would *very strongly* advise the editors, known to you, *not* to approve *any* platform. For the platform to be confirmed by anyone except the C.C. is a liquidationist trick. Besides, in essence, no good will be done by the editors approving a platform. Let the editors agree with the existing platform or remain silent.

Written on March 13 (26), 1912

Sent from Paris to
St. Petersburg

Published for the first
time in the Fourth Edition
of the *Collected Works*,
from the manuscript

---

* See p. 506 of this volume.—*Ed.*

PUT YOUR CARDS ON THE TABLE[193]

Our nobility, ministers, members of the Council of State, etc., are well acquainted with the language of the Duchy of Monaco.[194] It is well known who introduced this language to our Council of State! That is why we were somewhat surprised when we came across the expression which heads this article, in *Zhivoye Dyelo*, No. 8.

But the important thing is not the mode of expression. The prestige among the liquidators of the writer using this expression (L. Martov), the importance of the subject touched on ("put your cards on the table" in relation to the election campaign, its principles, tactics, etc.), all this compels us to take up this slogan, irrespective of how it has been expressed.

"Put your cards on the table" is an excellent slogan. And in the first place, we should like to see it applied to the paper *Zhivoye Dyelo*. Put your cards on the table, gentlemen!

People who are experienced in literary affairs can immediately gauge the character of a publication by its contributors, even by isolated expressions which indicate the *trend* of the publication if that trend belongs to those in any degree established and well-known. Such people only need to take one glance at *Zhivoye Dyelo* to realise its adherence to the liquidationist trend.

But it is not so easy for the general public to understand the trend followed by newspapers, particularly when the subjects in question are not theoretical principles, but current politics. It is here that it is very important and appropriate to remember the extremely apt slogan put forward by L. Martov — "Put your cards on the table". For it so happens that in *Zhivoye Dyelo* the cards are under the table!

Karty na stol

Язык княжества Монако есть язык, хорошо знакомый нашей экаде, господам министрам, членам Гос. Совета и т. д. Удивительно, что ввел в употребление этот язык в нашем Гос. Совете! Поэтому мы несколько удивились, встретив в газете "Живое Дело", № 8, то выражение, которое появилось в заголовке статьи.

Но дело не в способе выражения. Авторитетность — среди ликвидаторов — лица, употребившего его (Л. Мартов), важность затронутой темы ("карты на столе" в вопросе об избирательной кампании, её принципах, её задачах и т. д.), всё это заставило нас подвергнуть вопрос, независимо от того, как он выражен.

"Карты на стол", это — превосходный вопрос. И нам прежде всего хочется за,

Those ideas which *Zhivoye Dyelo* is beginning to propound have been worked out at all systematically and consistently *only* in the course of the past two years in *Nasha Zarya*, *Zhizn*, *Vozrozhdeniye*, and *Dyelo Zhizni*. A considerable amount of material has accumulated in this period. What is lacking are *summaries*, particularly those produced by the people who for two years have been engaged in the elaboration of those ideas. What is lacking is an *open* exposition, by those holding liquidationist views, of the conclusions they have drawn from two years of "work" by *Nasha Zarya*.

It is precisely at this point that the lovers of talks about an *"open* workers' party" turn out to be lovers of a game with *hidden* cards. You read, for instance, in the leader appearing in No. 8, that "the path of the struggle for the general, for general improvement and *basic* change in working and living conditions" lies *through* "the defence of *partial* [author's italics] rights". You read in the same issue about some "Petersburg leaders of the open labour movement", that they *"as previously"* will ... "popularise among Social-Democrats those methods for the revival and creation of a proletarian Social-Democratic party which they have hitherto defended".

Put your cards on the table! What is this theory of the defence of partial rights? This theory has not been stated in any properly formulated, official, *openly* announced postulates, recognised by groups, or representatives of groups of workers. Is it, for instance, the theory propounded to us by V. Levitsky in *Nasha Zarya*, No. 11 for 1911? And then, how can the paper's readers know *what* methods were advocated by some unnamed leaders of the open movement, for the "revival and *creation* of the party", which apparently has not been created, i.e., does not exist? Why not name those leaders, if they are indeed leaders of an "open" movement, if these words are not merely a *conventional* phrase?

The question of "methods of revival and *creation* of the party" is not some incidental question, which can be touched on and resolved in passing among other political questions of interest to any newspaper. On the contrary, this is a basic question. It is impossible to talk about a Party election campaign, about the election tactics of the Party, about Party candidates, until this question has been resolved; and resolved it must be, in the most unambiguous, positive manner, for apart from a clear-cut theoretical answer, a *practical* decision is required.

The arguments which we frequently meet with to the effect that during an election campaign the elements of revival and creation of the Party, etc., etc., will emerge or rally, are sophistry, and sophistry of the worst kind. It is sophistry because a party is something *organised*! There is not and cannot be an election campaign for the working *class*, without decisions, *tactics*, a platform, and candidates *common to* the whole class, or at any rate to its advanced section.

Sophistry of this kind, obscure statements made in the name of anonymous, unknown, and —*for the proletariat*— elusive open leaders (who does not call himself a "leader of the open labour movement"? How many bourgeois shelter behind this name?) —all this represents a great danger which the worker must be warned against. The danger is that all this talk about "open action" is meant *merely as a blind* while in reality, the worst form of *hidden* dictatorship of a group results.

They inveigh against the "underground" although it is there we see open decisions which have now become pretty well known thanks to the bourgeois press (*Golos Zemli, Kievskaya Mysl, Russkoye Slovo, Golos Moskvy, Novoye Vremya*—how many *hundreds of thousands* of readers have now been *openly* informed of quite definite decisions, which mean genuine unity in the election campaign). It is those who cry out *against* the underground or *for* "open political activity" who provide an example of people leaving one shore and not landing on the other. The "old" has been abandoned, but there is only talk of the "new".

We know, and all *openly* know, that "the methods of revival and creation" spoken of by *Zhivoye Dyelo* are merely those which have been developed and defended in *Nasha Zarya*. We know of no others, either stated openly or in any other form. There has been no attempt whatsoever to discuss these methods, openly or otherwise, by representatives of the groups, nor has *any* formal and properly formulated, official *exposition* of these methods been made. They use the *words* "open", "openly" in a hundred ways to cover what is really something completely closed in the full meaning of the word, something emanating from a circle, from a coterie of writers.

We know some writers, who are responsible to no one, and are indistinguishable from the free-lances of the bourgeois press. We know *their* speeches about "methods", about the liquidation of the "old".

We know nothing more, and nobody knows anything more about *open* political activity. Here you have a paradox— it seems to be a paradox, but in reality it is a direct and natural product of *all* the conditions of Russian life—that through the above-mentioned series of the most widespread bourgeois papers, the masses were informed more accurately, swiftly and directly about "underground" political activities, decisions, slogans, tactics, etc., than about the *non-existent* decisions of "the leaders of the open movement"!

Or maybe someone will assert that an election campaign can be carried out without formulated decisions? That it is possible for tens and hundreds of thousands of voters scattered all over the country to determine tactics, platform, agreements and candidacies without formulated decisions?

In speaking of "putting cards on the table" Martov touched the liquidators' raw spot, and it is impossible to overestimate the effort that must be made to warn the workers. The masses are offered ... the thoughts and projects of "leaders of the open movement", who are *not openly named*, that is, the Potresovs, Levitskys, Chatskys, Yezhovs, and Larins, without formulated decisions, without any definite replies to practical questions, without the participation of at least tens or hundreds of advanced workers in the discussion of every sentence, every word of the important decisions.

They keep their cards hidden because any attempt to turn them face up would reveal quite clearly to the workers that all this has nothing to do with a working-class party or a working-class policy, that it is preaching by *liberal* publicists who take a liberal's attitude to the workers, who liquidate the old and are powerless to provide anything new to replace it.

The danger is great. Under cover of phrases about the "open" tomorrow, the workers are left *not only* without an "open" decision, but *without any* decision *at all* on the urgent practical problems of the present election campaign, of present-day Party life.

Let class-conscious workers give some thought to this dangerous situation.

———

P. S. (1) Please send immediately books on the electoral law of June 3, 1907, or another copy of the handbook of 1910.[195] Also the electoral *law* with the comments of a *lawyer*. Consult "your people" and send them promptly. Unless I get them I cannot work on the voter's handbook.[196] (2) I am again receiving *Zvezda* irregularly. Speak about it again in your dispatch department. Give my (old) address. It mustn't be sent so irregularly. (3) The article "Fundamentals of a Platform" *does not* require the approval of the Editorial Board; publish it with the signature and with the subheading "An Essay in Comment"; the Board must *not* approve *any* platform; remember, one clumsy step and a squabble is unavoidable. Let the Board refrain and keep silent. The approval of the platform is the job of quite another body. (4) Send me newspapers, journals, books. It is impossible to work without them. (5) Write and tell me exactly when a daily newspaper is likely to come out, its size, etc. (6) Fight against *Zhivoye Dyelo* more energetically —then victory is guaranteed. Otherwise things will be bad. Don't be afraid of polemics. Two or three polemical articles a week are imperative.

Written on March 12 or 13
(25 or 26), 1912

First published on January 21,   Published according to
1935 in *Pravda*, No. 21   the manuscript

DEPUTY T. O. BELOUSOV'S WITHDRAWAL
FROM THE SOCIAL-DEMOCRATIC GROUP
IN THE DUMA

We were greatly surprised to find in No. 7 of *Zhivoye Dyelo* a reprint from *Rech* of Mr. Belousov's acrimonious statement.[197] There is nothing surprising in the fact that *Rech* opened its columns to this statement of the latest turncoat. It is natural for *Rech* to print the outcries of a former Social-Democrat who alleges that the appraisal of his defection given by the Social-Democratic group in the Duma was prompted by "feelings of revenge". But why does *Zhivoye Dyelo* reprint this? And is it not strange that the same *Zhivoye Dyelo* carries an article, "The Withdrawal of Deputy Belousov", with bitter-sweet statements to the effect that "we must not be upset by the cases of desertion which have occurred."

Zhivoye Dyelo does "not deem it proper to go into an appraisal of Belousov's step so long as the motives by which he was guided have not been made public". Nevertheless, it does attempt it ... but stops half-way and merely pulls faces at "this kind of desertion"!

Why this game? Surely it is time for the press to do its duty by openly discussing facts of political importance.

The Social-Democratic group in the Duma gave a its *unanimous* opinion that the proper procedure for Mr. Belousov would be *immediately to resign his office as deputy*, since he was elected by the votes of Social-Democrats and had been a member of the Social-Democratic group in the Duma for four and a half years.

Mr. Belousov's answer, printed in *Rech*, entirely *evades* this issue. But the voice of class-conscious workers *must not permit* this question to be passed over in silence. Mr. Belousov may prefer to keep silent, but we have no right to. What would be the use of the working-class press if it refrained from discussing facts which are of importance to working-class representation in the Duma?

Is it permissible, from the standpoint of the obligations of any democrat, for a deputy who was elected *as* a Social-Democrat and for four and a half years had belonged to the Social-Democratic group in the Duma to withdraw from the group a few months before the elections, *without at the same time resigning from the Duma*? This is a question of general interest. No democrat who is aware of his obligations to his constituents—not in the sense of being a "solicitor" on behalf of local interests, but of the obligations of a *politician* who in the elections paraded *before all the people* under a *definite* banner—not a single democrat will deny that this is an extremely important question of principle.

Let all workers who read the working-class press and who are interested in the question of workers' representation in the State Duma pay the closest attention to Mr. Belousov's withdrawal, let them ponder over and discuss this question. *They must not keep silent.* It would be unworthy of a class-conscious worker to keep silent on an occasion like this. The workers must learn to stand by *their rights*, by the right of all voters to insist that deputies elected by them remain true to their banner, their right to show these deputies that they *dare not* desert, that they cannot do so with impunity.

Is the Social-Democratic group in the Duma right in insisting that a deputy who has belonged to it for four and a half years, and who was elected to the State Duma by Social-Democratic votes, is *in duty bound, now* that he has withdrawn from the group, to resign from the Duma as well? Yes, it is absolutely right! If we are for unity, solidarity, integrity and loyalty to principles on the part of working-class representatives, not only in words, but *in fact*, then we must voice our opinion, we must, each and every one of us, individually and collectively, write to

Zvezda and to the Duma group (also sending copies of the letters to the local press) stating that we emphatically and irrevocably condemn Mr. Belousov's conduct, that not only every supporter of the working class, but every *democrat* as well, must condemn conduct of this kind. What, indeed, will our *"popular* representation" be like, if deputies who were elected under a definite banner and who during nine-tenths of the Duma sessions professed allegiance to that banner, declare *on the eve of new elections:* "I withdraw from the group, *but* I retain my mandate, I desire to remain a representative of the 'people' "!

Not so fast, Mr. Turncoat! What *people* do you now represent? Surely *not* the people that elected you as a Social-Democrat! *Not* the people who, for nine-tenths of the Duma sessions, saw you in the ranks of the Social-Democratic group in the Duma! You are not a representative of the people but a deceiver of the people; for during the time left to the elections it is *impossible*, physically impossible, for the people (even if they enjoyed complete political liberty) to study from the facts, on the basis of your conduct, *who* you are, *what* you have become, *where* you have landed, *who or what* is attracting you. You are in duty bound to quit the Duma, otherwise everyone will have a right to treat you as a political adventurer and a fraud!

There may be many reasons for a withdrawal. There may be a change of views so obvious, definite, open, and motivated by universally known facts, as to prompt a withdrawal which raises no doubts, in which there is nothing reprehensible or dishonourable. But, surely, it is not an accident that at present, and *only* at present, *only* in this case, has the Duma group published a protest in the press! The Social-Democratic group states openly that Mr. Belousov "expressed the desire that the fact of his withdrawal from the group should not be made public". In his answer, reprinted by *Zhivoye Dyelo*, Mr. Belousov is abusive, but he does not deny the fact. We ask: what must every worker think of a man who, while leaving the group, expresses the desire to conceal his withdrawal? If this is not deception, what is?

The Social-Democratic group states in plain words that it "is quite unable to gauge the limits of the further evolution of its former member". Let the reader give some thought to these highly significant words! The Social-Democratic group in the Duma made no such grave statements in the case of others who have left it. In the present case it is, therefore, a vote of complete non-confidence. More than that, it is a warning to all the voters, to the whole people that no confidence whatsoever may be placed in this deputy. The Social-Democratic group has issued this unanimous warning to all. It is now up to every class-conscious worker to reply that he has heard the warning, has understood it and agrees with it, that he will not tolerate in silence the creation in Russia, among people professing to be democrats, of such parliamentary morals (or, rather, parliamentary immorality) which allow deputies to grab mandates for personal gain, for the purpose of "freely" manipulating these spoils. This has been the case in all bourgeois parliaments, and everywhere the workers who are aware of their historic role are fighting these practices and, *in the process of the struggle*, are training their own working-class members of parliament, men who are not out for mandates, not out to profit by parliamentary manipulations, but are the trusted envoys of the working class.

The workers should not allow themselves to be hoodwinked by sophistry. One such piece of sophistry is the statement of *Zhivoye Dyelo*: "we do not deem it proper to go into an appraisal of T. O. Belousov's step so long as the motives by which he was guided have not been made public".

To begin with, we read in the statement of the Social-Democratic group in the Duma: "In justifying his withdrawal, Mr. Belousov explained that as much as two years ago the group had become utterly alien to him." Is not this making a motive public? Is this not plain language? If *Zhivoye Dyelo* does not believe the statement of the group, let it say so outright—let it not twist and squirm, let it not tell us that it does "not deem it proper to go into", when, as a matter of fact, the group has *already* gone into and made public the motives, or the motive, which it considers to be the most important.

Secondly, we read in Mr. Belousov's reply printed in the Cadet *Rech* and the liquidationist *Zhivoye Dyelo*: "I declare that in its statement the group said absolutely nothing [?!] about the real motives of my rupture with it. I know that circumstances beyond its control do not permit the group to make public my differences with it, which I have set forth both in my oral and written statements".

Now, see how it all works out. The group officially makes public what Mr. Belousov represented as his motive. Mr. Belousov fulminates ("insinuations, innuendoes", etc.), but does not deny that this was what he said; he declares that circumstances beyond the control of the group *do not permit* the latter to "make public" something else. (If it is true that circumstances do not permit it to be *made public*, why do you, sir, *make a public* hint at what cannot be made public? Does not your method smack of insinuation?) Yet *Zhivoye Dyelo* reprints Mr. Belousov's flagrant and crying untruth and adds, on its own behalf: "We do not deem it proper to go into ... *so long* as the motives ... have not been made public"—the very motives which cannot be made public because circumstances beyond control "do not permit" it! In other words, *Zhivoye Dyelo* will withhold its opinion of Mr. Belousov's withdrawal until the publication of things which (according to the statement of Mr. Belousov himself) cannot be made public.

Is it not obvious that, instead of exposing the falsehood of Mr. Belousov's statement reprinted in its pages, *Zhivoye Dyelo* covers up the falsehood?

There is little more that we can add. One who pleads the non-publication of things which cannot be made public, thereby gives his own game away. But it is indispensable and obligatory for everybody who holds dear working-class representation in the Duma to appraise those things which have already been made public and are already known. Mr. Belousov asserts: "My withdrawal from the group has not altered the tendency of my political and public activity one iota". These are hollow words. This is what all renegades say. These words contradict the statement made by the group. We believe the Social-Democratic group, and not the turncoat. As regards Mr. Belousov's "tendency", we, as well as most other Marxists, know one thing—that it has been a sharply *liquidationist* tendency. Mr. Belousov has gone to such lengths of liquidationism that the group

No Social-Democratic Party in the world was ever formed—
particularly in the period of bourgeois revolutions—without a hard struggle and a number of splits with the bourgeois
fellow-travellers of the proletariat. The same is true of
the Russian Social-Democratic Labour Party, which ever
since 1898 has been taking shape, growing, gaining in
strength and becoming tempered, despite all obstacles, in
the hard struggle against such fellow-travellers.

has finally "liquidated" his connections with the Social-Democratic movement. All the better for the movement, for the workers, for the cause of the workers.

And not only the workers but all democrats must demand Mr. Belousov's resignation from the Duma.

Zvezda, No. 17 (53), March 13, 1912
Signed: *T*.

Published according to
the *Zvezda* text

FAMINE

Again famine —as in the past, in the old, pre-1905, Russia. Crops may fail anywhere, but *only* in Russia do they lead to such grave calamities, to the starvation of millions of peasants. The present disaster, as even the supporters of the government and the landowners are compelled to admit, surpasses in extent the famine of 1891.

Thirty million people have been reduced to the direst straits. Peasants are selling their allotments, their livestock, everything saleable, for next to nothing. They are selling their girls —a reversion to the worst conditions of slavery. The national calamity reveals at a glance the true essence of our allegedly "civilised" social order. In different forms, in a different setting, and with a different "civilisation", this system is the *old slavery*, it is the slavery of millions of toilers for the sake of the wealth, luxury and parasitism of the "upper" ten thousand. On the one hand there is hard labour, always the lot of slaves, and on the other the absolute indifference of the rich to the fate of the slaves. In the past, slaves were openly starved to death, women were openly taken into the seraglios of the masters, slaves were openly tortured. In our day, the peasants have been robbed —by means of all the tricks and achievements, all the progress of civilisation—robbed to such an extent that they are starving, eating goosefoot, eating lumps of dirt in lieu of bread, suffering from scurvy, and dying in agony. At the same time the Russian landlords, with Nicholas II at their head, and the Russian capitalists are raking in money wholesale—the proprietors of places of amusement in the capital say that business has never been so good. Such barefaced, unbridled luxury as that now flaunted in the big cities has not been seen for many years.

Why is it that in Russia alone, of all countries, we still witness these medieval spells of famine alongside of the progress of modern civilisation? Because in the conditions under which the new vampire, capital, is stealing upon the Russian peasants the latter are bound hand and foot by the feudal landowners, by the feudal, landowning, tsarist autocracy. Robbed by the landowner, crushed by the tyranny of officials, entangled in the net of police restrictions, harassed and persecuted, and placed under the surveillance of village policemen, priests, and rural superintendents, the peasants are just as defenceless in the face of the elements and of capital, as the savages of Africa. Nowadays it is only in savage countries that one meets with cases of people dying from hunger in huge numbers as they do in twentieth-century Russia.

But famine in present-day Russia, after so many boastful speeches by the tsarist government on the benefits of the new agrarian policy, on the progress of the farms that have left the village commune, etc., is sure to *teach* the peasants a great deal. The famine will destroy millions of lives, but it will also destroy the last remnants of the savage, barbarian, slavish faith in the tsar, which has prevented the peasants from seeing that there must inevitably be a revolutionary fight against the tsarist monarchy and the landowners. The peasants can find a way out of their condition only by abolishing the landed estates. Only the overthrow of the tsarist monarchy, that bulwark of the landlords, can lead to a life more or less worthy of human beings, to deliverance from starvation and hopeless poverty.

It is the duty of every class-conscious worker and every class-conscious peasant to make this clear. This is our main task in connection with the famine. The organisation, wherever possible, of collections among the workers for the starving peasants and the forwarding of such funds through the Social-Democratic members of the Duma—that, of course, is also one of the necessary jobs.

Rabochaya Gazeta, No. 8,   Published according to
March 17 (30), 1912   the *Rabochaya Gazeta* text

THE PEASANTRY AND THE ELECTIONS TO THE FOURTH DUMA

The tsarist government has already begun to "prepare" for the elections to the Fourth Duma. The rural superintendents, prodded by the circulars of the governors and the minister, are trying to do their bit, the police and the Black Hundreds are showing their zeal, the "holy fathers", who have been ordered to do their level best for the "Right" parties, are not letting the grass grow under their feet. It is high time the peasants also began to think of the elections.

The elections are of particular importance for the peasants, but their position in the elections is a very difficult one. The peasants are the least politically organised—both as compared with the workers and as compared with the liberal, Cadet Party. Without political organisation, the peasants, who, owing to the conditions under which they live, are the most disunited section of the population, will be absolutely unable to offer resistance to the landowners and officials who are now persecuting and ill-treating them worse than ever before. A group of peasant deputies to the Fourth Duma, really devoted to the cause of the peasantry, politically-conscious and capable of defending all its interests, politically organised and working steadily to extend and strengthen their ties with the peasants in the villages—such a group could be of immense service in helping to unite the peasant masses in their struggle for freedom and for life.

Can such a group be formed in the Fourth Duma? In the Third Duma, there was a group of 14 *Trudoviks*, who championed the democratic interests of peasants; unfortunately, they all too often became dependent on the liberals, the Cadets, who are leading the peasants by the nose, deceiving them with the illusion of "peace" between peasants and landowners, between the peasants and the landowning tsarist monarchy. Besides, it is a known fact that even the *"Right"* peasants in the Third Duma took a more democratic stand than the Cadets on the question of land. The agrarian bill introduced by forty-three peasant deputies in the Third Duma proves this incontrovertibly; and the recent "sally" of Purishkevich against the Right peasant deputies shows that the Black Hundreds have, in general, every reason to be dissatisfied with these "Right" peasant deputies.

Thus the mood of the peasantry, which during the period of the Third Duma has been taught the cruel *lessons* of the new agrarian policy, of the "land misregulation" and of that most terrible calamity—the famine—warrants the belief that it is fully capable of sending *democratic* representatives to the Fourth Duma. The main drawback is the electoral law! Framed by the landowners for their benefit, and endorsed by the landowners' tsar, it provides that the deputies who are to represent the peasants in the Duma shall be elected *not by the peasant electors but by the landowners.* The landowners can choose which peasant electors they like to represent the peasants in the Duma! It is obvious that the landowners will always choose peasants who follow the Black Hundreds.

Hence, if the peasants are to elect their *own* deputies to the Duma, if they are to elect truly reliable and staunch champions of their interests, *they have only one means.* That is to follow the example of the workers and choose as electors only Party members, class-conscious and reliable men thoroughly devoted to the peasantry, and no others.

The working-class Social-Democratic Party resolved at its conference that already at the meetings of the *delegates* (who elect the electors) the workers must decide *who* is to be elected to represent them in the Duma. All the other electors must stand down in their favour, *on pain of being boycotted and branded as traitors.*

Let the peasants do the same. Preparations for the elections must be started at once, and in this connection it is necessary to make their condition clear to the peasants and wherever possible form village groups, even if only small ones, of politically-conscious peasants, to conduct the election campaign. At the meetings of their *delegates,* before electing the electors, the peasants must decide *who* is to be elected to the Duma from the peasants, and all the other peasant electors must be requested, on pain of being boycotted and branded as traitors, to turn down any offers made them by the landowners, and categorically to *decline* their nomination in favour of the candidate decided on *by the peasants.*

All class-conscious workers, all Social-Democrats, and all true democrats in general, must lend the peasantry a helping hand in the elections to the Fourth Duma. May the severe lessons of the famine and of the plunder of the peasants' land not have been in vain. May there be a stronger and more solid group of peasant deputies in the Fourth Duma, a group of real democrats loyal to the peasantry.

Rabochaya Gazeta, No. 8,
March 17 (30), 1912

Published according to
the *Rabochaya Gazeta* text

THE ANONYMOUS WRITER IN *VORWÄRTS* AND THE STATE OF AFFAIRS IN THE R.S.D.L.P.[198]

Written in March 1912

First published as a separate
pamphlet in German, Paris, 1912
Signed: *Editorial Board of* Sotsial-
Demokrat,
Central Organ of the R.S.D.L.P.

Published according to
the pamphlet text
Translated from the German

PREFACE

Vorwärts of March 26 carried an official statement on the Conference of the Russian Social-Democratic Labour Party and an anonymous article whose author, in line with a resolution adopted by Russian Social-Democratic groups abroad,[199] heaps abuse on the Conference. The Conference was the culmination of the four years' struggle of the R.S.D.L.P. against the liquidators, and it was held in spite of all the intrigues of the liquidators who endeavoured at all costs to hinder the rebuilding of the Party. The Conference placed the liquidators outside the Party. It is therefore quite natural that the liquidators and their supporters should now attack the Conference.

Since *Vorwärts* refuses to print our reply to the infamous lying article of the anonymous writer and continues its campaign in favour of the liquidators, we are publishing this reply as a separate pamphlet for the information of the German comrades. It is devoted, mainly, to a brief statement of the significance, course and results of the fight against the liquidators.

Editorial Board of Sotsial-Demokrat,
Central Organ of the R.S.D.L.P.

P.S. Our pamphlet had already been sent to the printer when we received Plekhanov's *Diary of a Social-Democrat* No. 16 (April 1912). This issue provides the best proof that *Vorwärts* was deceived by the anonymous writer and, in its turn, misled the German workers.

Plekhanov, while definitely stating that he is still no supporter of the Conference held in January 1912, says in so many words that what the Bund is convening is not a conference of *existing* Party organisations but a *"constituent"* conference, i.e., one which is expected to found a new party; that the organisers of the conference follow a *"typical anarchist principle"*; that they adopted a "liquidationist resolution"; that this new conference "is being convened by liquidators".

Some German comrades displayed an amazing naïveté in taking seriously all those dreadful words like "usurpation", "coup d'état", etc., which tiny groups of Russian Social-Democrats abroad like to use in their attacks on the Conference of the Russian organisations of the R.S.D.L.P. Still, we must not forget the saying that a man who has been condemned to death may abuse his judges for 24 hours.

The article in the March 26 issue of *Vorwärts* entitled "Russian Party Life" reproduces the official statement of the Conference, which says that the liquidators have been expelled from the Party. It is a perfectly clear statement: the Russian organisations of the R.S.D.L.P. have taken the viewpoint that it is impossible to work jointly with the liquidators. One may, of course, have a different point of view on this matter, but in that case the author should have dealt in greater detail with the motives leading to the decision and with the entire history of the four years' fight against the liquidationist trend! The anonymous author of the article in *Vorwärts*, however, has not a single word to say on the merits of *this fundamental issue*. It is, indeed, a sign of a very low opinion of the readers when an author completely ignores the substance of the matter but unburdens himself with melodramatic outpourings. How helpless, then, is our anonymous author if his reply to the fact that the Party has broken with the liquidationist trend contains nothing but abuse.

It is only necessary to quote at random several curious passages from the article of the unknown author. He says that the "trends" or "groups" represented by *Vperyod, Pravda, Golos Sotsial-Demokrata*, etc., did not take part in the Conference. We should like to ask, what would you say of a German Social-Democrat who lamented the fact that the "group" or "trend" of Friedberg or of the *Sozialistische Monatshefte* was not represented at a Party congress? We, in our Party, also adhere to the custom that organisations functioning in Russia are entitled to take part in Party conferences, but not all sorts of "trends" or "groups" abroad. If such "groups" are at variance with the Russian organisations, that alone constitutes their severest condemnation, their death sentence which they have justly deserved. The history of the Russian political exiles, like that of exiles from all other countries, abounds in cases of such "trends" or "groups" having become divorced from the activity of the Social-Democratic workers in Russia and dying a natural death.

Don't the cries of our author sound absurd when he alleges that the pro-Party (i.e., anti-liquidationist) Mensheviks who took part in the Conference have been disavowed even by Plekhanov? The Kiev organisation could, of course, disavow the foreign "Plekhanovites" (i.e., Plekhanov's followers); but no writer abroad, no matter who he is, can "disavow" the Kiev organisation. The organisations of St. Petersburg, Moscow, Moscow District, Kazan, Saratov, Tiflis, Baku, Nikolayev, Kiev, Ekaterinoslav, Wilno, and Dvinsk have "disavowed" all groups abroad which assisted the liquidators or flirted with them. The outcries and abuse of the "disavowed" are hardly likely to change anything in this respect.

Further, surely it is strange for the author to declare in so many words that the "national" Social-Democratic organisations in Russia (the Polish, Latvian, and the Bund) and the Transcaucasian Regional Committee represent "the oldest and strongest organisations of our Russian Party, those which, to all intents and purposes, constitute the backbone of the movement"? The problematical existence of the Transcaucasian Regional Committee is something generally known and was proved by the character of its representation at the conference in 1908. The Polish and Latvian organisations, during the first nine years of the R.S.D.L.P. (1898-1907), led an existence entirely apart, and, in fact, remained isolated from it in the 1907-11 period as well. The Bund seceded from the Party in 1903 and remained outside it until 1906 (or, to be more exact, 1907). Nor have its local branches fully rejoined the Party to this day, as was officially established at the conference of the R.S.D.L.P.

in 1908.[200] Within the Latvian organisation and the Bund at one time the liquidationist, at another the anti-liquidationist elements gained the upper hand. As for the Poles, they sided with the Mensheviks in 1903, with the Bolsheviks in 1905, and in 1912 made an unsuccessful attempt at a "reconciliation" with the liquidators.

This latter failure the author diffidently tries to cover up with the following phrase: "At the beginning a representative of the Social-Democrats of Poland and Lithuania also attended this Conference". Why only *at the beginning?* We find the explanation of this diffident silence in the official communiqué of the Bund about this Conference. There it says in black and white that the representative of the Poles withdrew from the Conference and submitted a written statement, which said that it had become impossible for him to collaborate with the Conference because it revealed a spirit of bias and a partiality for the *liquidators!*

To be sure, it is much easier to heap up hollow and meaningless phrases about "unity" (with the liquidators?), as the author is fond of doing, than to study the real essence of the trend of the liquidators, their refusal to help rebuild the Party, and their work of disrupting the Central Committee of the Party. And it is all the more easy to indulge in phrase-mongering if at the same time silence is maintained regarding the fact that the representative of the Poles refused to work jointly (because such work would be fruitless), not with the Bolsheviks or Leninists, God forbid, but with the Bundists and Latvians.

But what, really, is the origin of liquidationism, and why was it necessary for the Conference of 1912 to constitute itself the supreme Party authority and to expel the liquidators?

The counter-revolution in Russia gave rise to a very pronounced process of disintegration in the ranks of our Party. Persecutions of unparalleled fury rained down upon the proletariat. Defection assumed wide proportions in the ranks of the bourgeoisie. The bourgeois fellow-travellers, who had naturally joined the proletariat as the leader of our bourgeois revolution in 1905, began to turn their backs on the Social-Democratic Party. This defection took two forms — that of *liquidationism* and of *otzovism*. The nucleus of the former was made up of the majority of Menshevik writers

(Potresov, Levitsky, Larin, Martov, Dan, Martynov, etc.). They declared that the illegal Party had already been liquidated and that any attempt to revive it was a reactionary utopia. Their slogan was: an open labour party. Obviously, under the political conditions prevailing in Russia, where even the party of the liberals, the Cadets, has no legal status, the formation of an open Social-Democratic working-class party can only remain wishful thinking. The liquidators repudiated the illegal party, but did not fulfil their obligation to found a legal party. In the long run, all they did was to write articles in the legal press in which they ridiculed the "underground", declared, in unison with the liberals, that it was dead, and extolled the virtues of a liberal labour policy. Plekhanov was absolutely right when he compared the liquidationist *Nasha Zarya* to the German *Sozialistische Monatshefte*. The Menshevik Plekhanov (to say nothing of the Bolsheviks) declared ruthless war on the liquidationist trend, refused to contribute to any of their publications and broke off relations with Martov and Axelrod. "A man for whom our Party does not exist," wrote Plekhanov in the Central Organ about Potresov, "does not himself exist for our Party." As far back as December 1908, a Party conference emphatically condemned liquidationism, which it described as "an attempt on the part of a group of Party intellectuals to liquidate the existing organisation of the R.S.D.L.P. and to replace it [note this well!] by a loose association that is *legal, no matter what it costs*". It is obvious that, far from denying that it is essential to make use of all legal opportunities, the R.S.D.L.P. has stressed this point in no unmistakable terms. However, an open legal *party* in Russia is out of the question, and only opportunist intellectuals can speak about such a party. The type of our Party organisation may to a certain extent, of course, be compared to the German type of Party organisation at the time the Anti-Socialist Law was in operation: a legally functioning group in Parliament, all sorts of legally existing workers' associations, as an indispensable condition, but with the *illegal Party organisation* as the foundation.

The "otzovists" wanted to recall the Social-Democratic group from the Third Duma, and issued the slogan calling for a boycott of that Duma. The otzovists were joined by a section of the Bolsheviks, on whom Lenin and others declared implacable war. The otzovists and their defenders formed the *Vperyod* group, and the writers collaborating in the magazine of that name (Maximov, Lunacharsky, Bogdanov, Alexinsky) have been preaching various forms of the idealistic philosophy, which they describe by the grand name of "proletarian philosophy", and the amalgamation of *religion* with socialism. This group has never exerted any perceptible influence, and it led some sort of existence only by pursuing a policy of compromise with various impotent groups abroad which had lost all contact with Russia. Such groups, inevitable in every split, vacillate now to one side, now to the other; they engage in cheap politics, but represent no definite trend and their activity expresses itself mainly in petty intrigue. One of these groups is represented by Trotsky's *Pravda*.

It is clear, of course, to every Marxist that both liquidationism and otzovism are petty-bourgeois tendencies which attract the bourgeois fellow-travellers of the Social-Democratic Party. "Peace" or "conciliation" with these *tendencies* is something excluded *a priori*. The alternative facing the Social-Democratic Party was either to perish or to rid itself entirely of these tendencies.

That this theoretical conclusion is correct was proved by the attempt at conciliation made in January 1910, when the last Plenary Meeting of the Central Committee declared *unanimously*, *with the liquidators and otzovists concurring*, that *neither* of these tendencies is *Social-Democratic*. But things did not go further than pious wishes. True, both the liquidators and the otzovists "signed" the appropriate resolution, but they continued with all their might to conduct their anti-Party propaganda, and maintained their own organisations. All through 1910 the fight against both tendencies was *steadily growing sharper*. Plekhanov's words quoted above are dated May 1910, and in May 1910 Lenin declared on behalf of the Bolsheviks that, since the liquidators had violated the January resolution there could be no question of conciliation with them.*

---

* See V. I. Lenin, *Collected Works*, Vol. 16, "Notes of a Publicist, II".—*Ed.*

The attempt to revive the Central Committee in Russia failed because the liquidators refused their assistance. A last means of saving the cause of "unity" was to convene a meeting of the Central Committee abroad. This attempt was made in May 1911. Of the fifteen members of the Central Committee, nine were abroad. *Eight* came to the meeting, but *two liquidators*—Igorev, adherent of *Golos*, and a Bundist (Ber)—immediately withdrew and thus finally wrecked the Central Committee of the Party.

The refusal of the liquidators to participate in the Central Committee meant their complete secession and the dissolution of the Central Committee. Only one central body still remained abroad at the time—the so-called Central Committee Bureau Abroad. The Bolsheviks withdrew from it when the Central Committee ceased to exist. Only the Poles, Latvians, Bundists and members of the *Golos* group (the liquidators abroad) remained. The reader who is familiar with the article in *Vorwärts* can thus see for himself that it was the same outfit as that of the notorious conference called by the Bund; for the Transcaucasian Regional Committee had commissioned *Golos* supporters to represent it as far back as 1908. Now, let us see what these "oldest and strongest Russian organisations"—to use the words in which our anonymous author describes this latest discovery of his — have done? They *could not agree,and even dissolved the Bureau Abroad themselves*! Already in the autumn of 1911 the Central Committee Bureau Abroad published a statement in which it announced its own dissolution, and Plekhanov, in his *Diary*, commented on this in the following lines: "*Requiescat in pace!* This Party institution, which became a weapon in the hands of gentry who strove to liquidate the Party and therefore exposed the Russian Social-Democratic movement to grave peril, could render the revolutionary proletariat only *one* service: to die in good time". (*The Diary of a Social-Democrat*, Part 2. Supplement to No. 15, p. 1.) This opinion, voiced by Plekhanov, of whom nobody can say that he is a supporter of the Conference, shows with sufficient cogency how ridiculous is the pretence of those who shout about "usurpation" and similar things!

One more course remained open to bring about the unity of the Party, viz., to call a conference of *Russian* organisations. The national organisations of the Poles, the Latvians and the Bundists, utterly divorced as they were from the work in Russia, could do absolutely nothing for such a conference.

On November 26, 1910, Trotsky issued an appeal calling for a conference. He had the support (in words) of the *Vperyod* and *Golos* groups (the liquidators abroad). But as might have been foreseen, all the efforts of these groups, owing to their impotence, were fruitless.

In June 1911 an appeal signed by the Bolsheviks, "conciliators" (otherwise known as "pro-Party Bolsheviks") and the Poles was issued. The first step in the work was to invite the strongest organisation at the time, namely, the *Kiev* organisation. October 1911 saw the inauguration of the Russian (i. e., working in Russia, set up by the Russian organisations) Organising Commission for the convening of a conference. This Commission was formed by the Kiev, Ekaterinoslav, Tiflis, Baku and Ekaterinburg organisations, which were soon joined by twenty more organisations. The enlistment of representatives of the *Russian* organisations revealed *at once* the absolute preponderance of the Bolsheviks (so-called "Leninists") and the pro-Party Mensheviks. *Inde ira** of the groups abroad which found themselves "disavowed", because they had no followers in Russia.

In January 1912 the Russian Organising Commission at last convened the Conference, which *all* the Russian organisations, without exception, had been invited to attend. Neither the liquidators, nor the "non-Russians" (the Poles, the Latvians, and the Bund), nor the vacillating groups abroad sent delegates. When the Conference was convinced that the *Russian* organisations were represented as fully as possible considering the unprecedentedly difficult conditions under which the Party worked, when it established that without a central body in Russia the Party was doomed, that the split abroad was continuing and that the forthcoming elections to the Fourth Duma demanded the rebuilding of the Party without any further delay, it *had to* constitute itself the *supreme authority of the Party*, elect a Central Committee and place the liquidators outside the Party.

---

* Hence the ire.—*Ed.*

Such was the course and the outcome of the protracted fight. The future will show whether the liquidators will succeed in creating an "open" party, or whether they will concoct some kind of fiction of a party on the basis of a rotten compromise.

Are there any clear and easily verifiable data on the strength of the liquidators and the pro-Party people, the followers of the Conference, in Russia *itself*? Yes, there are. There exist *two*—and only two—all-Russia political organs in Russia, to which Marxist writers and members of the Social-Democratic group in the Duma contribute. These organs represent *trends*—not like the sheets abroad, which are full of abuse, but in the form of open and serious literary work carried on over a number of years. To be sure, they are not Party organs; they are strictly legal and keep within the bounds fixed by the regime now existing in Russia. However, *all* the most important shades of theoretical thought in the ranks of the Social-Democratic movement find in these organs, on the whole, an unquestionably correct expression. Only *two* "trends" — liquidationism and anti-liquidationism (the followers of the Conference) — are represented; for *no* other more or less serious "trends" *exist*. All those tiny groups, such as the *Pravda*, *Vperyod*, "pro-Party Bolsheviks" (or "conciliators", inclining to conciliatory sentiments), etc., count for nothing. The views of the liquidators find expression in Russia in the monthly *Nasha Zarya* (founded in 1910) and in the weekly *Zhivoye Dyelo* (last issue No. 8). The views of the Party people (Bolsheviks and pro-Party Mensheviks) find expression in the monthly *Prosveshcheniye*[201] (founded in 1911 — previously appeared under the name of *Mysl*) and in the newspaper *Zvezda* (last issue No. 53). There is nothing more erroneous than the view that the pro-Party Social-Democrats repudiate "legal" activity. The very opposite is the truth, since *in this activity too* they are stronger than the liquidators. The sole undisputed all-Russia open organisation of legally functioning Social-Democrats is the Social-Democratic group in the Duma. It is strictly legal and is not directly connected with the Party. But all its members are known, and it is also known which trend each of them represents.

The liquidationist *Zhivoye Dyelo* counts among its permanent contributors *two* members of the group in the Duma—Astrakhantsev and Kuznetsov.* In the anti-liquidationist *Zvezda* there are eight members of the group—Voronin, Voiloshnikov, Yegorov, Zakharov, Pokrovsky, Predkaln, Poletayev, and Surkov. Two members of the Duma, Chkheidze and Gegechkori, contribute to neither of these organs. One (Shurkanov) contributes to both.

The ratio is 2 to 8! These are indeed indisputable, easily verifiable and clear data enabling us to judge of the relation of forces between the liquidators and the anti-liquidators.

This being so it is unnecessary to waste words on the unknown author's tall talk to the effect that the overwhelming majority follows the liquidators, etc. These phrases à la Tartarin de Tarascon are all too reminiscent of Trotsky, ** so that it is not worth while discussing them seriously.

The struggle within the R.S.D.L.P. at times assumes very bitter forms. Nothing else could be expected under the conditions of life in exile; nothing else could ever be expected in any other country whose lot it was to endure counter-revolution and exile.

It is nothing but frivolous on the part of anyone to "condemn" these forms of the struggle in high-sounding phrases, to brush them aside and merely indulge in philistine and unctuous reflections on the "merits of unity". Anyone who seriously intends to study the history of the R.S.D.L.P. in the trying period 1908-11 will find at his disposal plenty of illegal and even more of legal literature. This literature contains highly instructive material on the nature of the trends, the fundamental significance of the differences, the roots of the fight, the circumstances and conditions of its development, etc.

---

* Until recently there was also Belousov. Now this extreme liquidator—a Russian Bissolati—has resigned from the group in the Duma. The latter has publicly warned all the voters of this, and has demanded his resignation from the Duma. A minor example showing to what lengths consistent liquidationism goes at times!

** At the time of the Copenhagen Congress Trotsky published in *Vorwärts* an anonymous article full of such vile attacks upon the R.S.D.L.P. that not only Lenin, but Plekhanov and Warski as well, both members of the Russian delegation, felt obliged to send a written protest to the Executive Committee.

A LETTER TO HUYSMANS, SECRETARY
OF THE INTERNATIONAL SOCIALIST BUREAU[202]

Dear Comrade,

In connection with the resolution adopted by a number of groups abroad and also by the editors of two periodicals published abroad, who claim to belong to the R.S.D.L.P., I, as representative of the Central Committee of the R.S.D.L.P., state the following:

(1) While for several years it was impossible to convene a conference of the Russian organisations, or to form a Central Committee, or revive the previously elected Central Committee which might have united those organisations, the recently held Party Conference succeeded in bringing together twenty-three Party organisations active in Russia.

All the reports on this Conference, already delivered to most of the Russian Party organisations, were received with warm sympathy everywhere, and all these organisations declared that they would support the Central Committee elected by the Conference. In the issue of *Rabochaya Gazeta* (organ of the Central Committee of the Party) of March 30, 1912, we were already able to publish a number of resolutions adopted by the organisations in St. Petersburg (Vasilyevsky Ostrov District), Moscow, Kiev, Samara and Nikolayev expressing warm sympathy with the Conference and promising to support it and the Central Committee. (Since the publication of that issue, we have received a similar resolution from Tiflis.) Thus we cannot attach the least significance to the protests of small groups abroad which are not backed by any Party organisations in Russia.

(2) The Conference of Party members active in Russia, which has aroused the protest of all the small groups abroad,

dealt especially with the disorganising activities of the groups abroad and with the disrupting effect which these groups often have upon the Party work in Russia. These groups, which are not connected with any organisation functioning in Russia, taking advantage of the fact that they are not responsible to anybody, permit themselves to speak in the name of the Party. This malady, which has gnawed at our Party for a long time, is a result of Russia's political regime, which, on the one hand, condemns our Party to an underground existence and, on the other, compels a great number of Party functionaries to live abroad in exile.

The Conference severely condemned the disorganising activities of these groups, all of them existing abroad and absolutely irresponsible. As far as the Party is concerned, there is nothing unexpected in the attacks by which these groups are trying to discredit the Conference that condemned their conduct.

(3) Among those who signed the resolution we see the *Golos Sotsial-Demokrata* group. This signature speaks volumes, for it explains the true meaning of the hostile campaign launched against the Conference by the liquidationist press, as well as by the bourgeois press, in Russia, and even by some foreign newspapers.

The point is that in its resolution summarising the results of the fight among the various trends in our Party in the past four years, the Conference came out emphatically against the trend represented by *Golos Sotsial-Demokrata*. In order that you may be quite clear on this question, I consider it worth while to quote the resolution in question. Here it is in full.

"Whereas:

"(1) The Russian Social-Democratic Labour Party for nearly four years has been waging a determined fight against the liquidationist trend, which was characterised at the conference of the Party in December 1908 as

"'an attempt on the part of a group of Party intellectuals to liquidate the existing organisation of the R.S.D.L.P. and to replace it at all costs, even at the price of downright renunciation of the programme, tactics, and traditions of the Party, by a loose association functioning legally';

"(2) The Plenary Meeting of the Central Committee held in January 1910, continuing the fight against this trend, unanimously declared it to be a manifestation of bourgeois influence upon the proletariat and demanded, as a condition for real Party unity and for the fusion of the former Bolshevik and Menshevik groups, a complete rupture with liquidationism and the utter rout of this bourgeois deviation from socialism;

"(3) In spite of all Party decisions and in spite of the obligation assumed by the representatives of all the factions at the Plenary Meeting held in January 1910, a section of Social-Democrats, grouped around the magazines *Nasha Zarya* and *Dyelo Zhizni*, began to defend openly the trend which the entire Party has recognised as being the product of bourgeois influence on the proletariat;

"(4) The former members of the Central Committee—M-l, Yuri, and Roman, refused not only to join the Central Committee in the spring of 1910, but even to attend a single meeting to co-opt new members, and bluntly declared that they considered the very existence of the Party Central Committee to be 'harmful';

"(5) It was precisely after the Plenary Meeting of 1910 that the above-mentioned chief publications of the liquidators, *Nasha Zarya* and *Dyelo Zhizni*, definitely turned to liquidationism all along the line, not only 'belittling [contrary to the decision of the Plenary Meeting] the importance of the illegal Party', but openly renouncing it, declaring that the Party was 'extinct', that the Party was already liquidated, that the idea of reviving the illegal Party was 'a reactionary utopia', using the columns of legally published magazines to heap slander and abuse on the illegal Party, calling upon the workers to regard the nuclei of the Party and its hierarchy as 'dead', etc.;

"(6) At a time when throughout Russia the members of the Party, irrespective of factions, united to promote the immediate task of convening a Party conference, the liquidators, banded together in entirely independent small groups, split away from local Party organisations even in those places where the pro-Party Mensheviks predominated (in Ekaterinoslav, Kiev) and finally renounced all Party connections with the local R.S.D.L.P. organisations;

"The Conference declares that by its conduct the *Nasha Zarya* and *Dyelo Zhizni* group has *definitely placed itself outside the Party.*

"The Conference calls upon all Party members, irrespective of tendencies and shades of opinion, to combat liquidationism, explain its great harmfulness to the cause of the emancipation of the working class, and bend all their efforts to revive and strengthen the illegal Russian Social-Democratic Labour Party."

(4) In view of all this, it is quite obvious that it is not a question of "usurpation", or a "split", etc., and that this is not the cause of the liquidators' anger. The Conference of the R.S.D.L.P. declared against the trend which in practice had long kept aloof from every kind of Party work, which had done its utmost to prevent the re-establishment of the Central Committee and had turned the last remaining Party institution (the Central Committee Bureau Abroad) into "a weapon in the hands of gentlemen who strove to liquidate the Party" (the words of Comrade Plekhanov, who is not a supporter of the Conference).

(5) As regards Social-Democratic organisations of the national minorities, I must put it on record that the R.S.D.L.P. existed as the R.S.D.L.P. up to 1906 (or, more correctly, up to 1907), before the national minority organisations joined our Party (the Bund withdrew from the Party in 1903 and remained outside it until 1906, or, rather, 1907). Hence, in view of their absence from the Conference, it is the duty of the Central Committee to start negotiations with these organisations for the purpose of resuming normal relations with them.

Written late in March 1912

Printed on April 12, 1912
in Circular No. 7 of the
International Socialist Bureau
Signed: *N. Lenin*

Published according to
the Circular text
Translated from the French

THE BLOC OF THE CADETS WITH
THE PROGRESSISTS AND ITS SIGNIFICANCE

Several days ago the newspapers carried the story of a conference of "independent Progressists" on the one hand, and Cadets on the other, held in Moscow on March 18.

A semi-official editorial in the semi-official Cadet *Rech* (of March 21) confirms that the conference was held and gives it its appraisal. Even a superficial study of this appraisal is sufficient to enable one to grasp the carefully concealed nature of the matter and to realise the disguise which serves to keep up appearances.

The point is that both the Progressists and the Cadets are opposition groups, and "belong to that section of the opposition which is described as 'responsible'". This is what *Rech* says. Hence, the Cadets cannot help admitting that there are two "sections" within the opposition: one which deserves the title "responsible", and another which does not. This admission of the Cadets brings us at once to the main point.

By referring to themselves as the "responsible" opposition, which is even more often and better described by Milyukov's celebrated "London" slogans about an opposition in the possessive case,[203] the Cadets set themselves and similar groups apart from the democratic movement, i. e., from the Trudoviks and the workers. Actually, the term "responsible opposition" is used to describe the liberal-monarchist bourgeois Centre, which stands midway between democracy on the one hand and autocracy with the feudal landowners on the other. This bourgeois liberal-monarchist Centre, which dreads consistent democracy even more than so-called "reaction", appeared in the Russian political arena long ago. It has such a long and instructive history behind it that we must not allow ourselves to be deceived with regard to its true nature and still less to keep silent or plead ignorance about it.

This Centre became quite clearly indicated in the epoch of the decline of serfdom. During the interval of almost half a century separating that epoch from 1905, the influence of the liberal-monarchist bourgeoisie in the Zemstvos, in the municipalities, in the schools, and in the press, grew and developed to a considerable degree. The crisis of the old regime in 1905 and the open action of all the classes in Russia gave final form to the liberal-monarchist bourgeois Centre and embodied it in parties representing its right flank (the Octobrists) and its left flank (the Cadets). The separation of this Centre from democracy was extremely pronounced and existed in all fields of public activity and at all "sharp turns" in 1905-07; however, not all the democrats and even not all working-class democrats have grasped the essence and the meaning of this separation.

The Russian bourgeoisie is tied by thousands of economic threads to the old landowning nobility and to the old bureaucracy. In addition to this, the working class of Russia has shown that it is quite independent and capable of taking care of itself; more, it has shown itself capable of leading democracy in spite of the liberals. That is why our bourgeoisie has turned liberal-monarchist and anti-democratic, anti-popular, in fact. That is why it dreads democracy more than reaction. That is why it is constantly vacillating, manoeuvring, betraying the former in favour of the latter. That is why it turned counter-revolutionary after 1905 and obtained a "nook" for itself in the June Third system. The Octobrists (with the permission and under the supervision of the Purishkeviches) have become a government party, while the Cadets have assumed the role of a *tolerated* opposition.

The decision of the Cadet conference to permit blocs with the "Left" (don't laugh!) Octobrists, and the present "informal" amalgamation of the Cadets with the "independent Progressists" are links in a single long chain, stages in the development of the liberal-monarchist bourgeois Centre,

But on the eve of the elections the opposition has to cloak itself in "democratic" attire. The Cadet who is out to catch not only the votes of the big and middle bourgeoisie, but also those of the democratic petty bourgeoisie, shop assistants, etc., must stress that he is a member of the "people's freedom party", a "Constitutional-*Democrat*", no less! On the eve of the elections, and for the sake of the elections, the Cadet Party, actually representing a moderate brand of monarchist liberalism, dresses itself in democratic finery and throws a veil over its rapprochement with the "independent Progressists" and "Left" Octobrists.

This explains the numerous contortions and diplomatic subterfuges we find in *Rech*, its high-flown statements that "the people's freedom party will not adapt itself to circumstances", and so on and so forth. Of course, all this is merely funny. For the entire history of the Cadet Party is nothing but a mockery of its programme, nothing but "adaptation" to circumstances in the worst sense of the term. "Given different political conditions," writes *Rech*, "under which the people's freedom party would be in a position to voice in the legislative body its entire programme, the so-called 'Progressists' would, of course, be its antagonists, just as they were at the more acute occasions in the recent past."

That the period of the Second Duma was a more acute occasion—that is something the Cadet gentlemen will hardly venture to dispute. However, not only the Progressists, but even elements more to the right, far from opposing the Cadets, were their allies *against* the democrats. Furthermore, in the Third Duma the democrats made statements that went far beyond any clause in the programme of the Cadets, hence, the Cadet Party was fully *"in a position to voice... its entire programme"* even in a *"legislative body"* like the Third Duma! If the Constitutional-Democratic Party refrained from doing so, it is by no means the "political conditions" that are to blame (don't say, "I can't", say "I shan't!"), but the utter alienation of the Cadets from democracy. The Cadets *could have* voiced their entire programme, but it was their *own* estrangement from democracy, *their own turn to the right* that prevented them from doing so.

The arguments of the *Rech* editorial on the bloc with the Progressists is one of the numerous examples of the

ease with which the leaders of the Cadet Party, Milyukov and others, can lead the few "Left" Cadets by the nose.
They feed the Left Cadets fine words, use flashy catchwords
about "democracy" to appease the Kolyubakins, and at the
same time actually conduct their policy in a purely anti-
democratic spirit, in the spirit of a rapprochement, of
merging with the Progressists and Left Octobrists. The Cadet
Party has introduced exactly the same kind of "division
of labour" we see among all the West-European bourgeois
parliamentarians: the Kolyubakins and other "Left Cadets"
speak of "liberty" to the people, while in parliament, in its
practical policies, the Cadet Party is entirely at one with
the most moderate liberals.

"The new group," write the liquidators referring to the
Progressists, "only seals and aggravates the political amorphism, the political confusion of the bourgeois voters, *which
is at the root of the political helplessness of the Russian bourgeoisie.*"

The political helplessness of the Russian bourgeoisie
is by no means caused by the "amorphism" of the "bourgeois
voters"—only Left-Cadet illusion-mongers can think so;
it is caused by economic conditions, owing to which the bourgeoisie is an enemy of the workers and a slave of the Purishkeviches, a slave who never goes further than grumbling
and expressing pious wishes.

The Left-Cadet parliamentarians, whether actuated by
an idealist theory of politics or by a vulgar fear of losing
the votes of the Left-inclined voters embittered by the Purishkeviches, may conduct their struggle against the official Cadet Party by arguments to the effect that it is high
time to listen to reason, recall the programme, take up the
cudgels against amorphism, philistinism, unprincipledness,
and so on and so forth, in line with the usual bourgeois-
democratic phrases.

The Marxists are waging a fight against Cadets of all
shades, basing themselves on the materialist theory of
politics, explaining the class interests of the bourgeoisie as
a whole, which impel it towards a liberal-monarchist
programme, towards a rapprochement with the Progressists and "Left" Octobrists. Our response, therefore,
will not be to appeal to Cadet "reason", to Cadet "memory",

or to Cadet "principles", but to explain to the people *why* the liberals are becoming counter-revolutionaries and are breaking with democrats. We shall not exclaim: Will the Cadets listen to reason at last, will they recall their programme? We shall say: Will the democrats realise, at last, what a deep gulf separates them from the counter-revolutionary liberals—the Cadets? Will those whose economic interests do not fetter them to the landowning nobility, or to the soft jobs and revenues of the bureaucracy, the bar, etc., realise that, if the people's freedom is really dear to them, they must join the working-class democratic movement against the Rights and against the Constitutional-Democratic Party?

Zvezda, No. 23 (59), March 29, 1912
Signed: *B. K.*

Published according to
the *Zvezda* text

A POOR DEFENCE OF A LIBERAL LABOUR POLICY

In No. 8 of *Zhivoye Dyelo* Martov replies to my article, "An Organ of a Liberal Labour Policy", published in No. 11 of *Zvezda*.* The question under discussion concerns the fundamental line to be followed by the workers in the election campaign and, therefore, merits special attention.

I described *Zhivoye Dyelo* as a publication with a *liberal* labour policy on the following grounds: (1) The slogan issued by Martov and Dan about dislodging reaction from its positions *in the Duma,* about wresting the *Duma* from the hands of the reactionaries, is not a democratic, but a liberal, slogan. The struggle against "reaction" in Russia, far from being confined to the wresting of the Duma from the hands of the reactionaries, is *not* even *focussed* on this. (2) In speaking of the possibility of achieving this aim, Martov started by embellishing our electoral law. He declared that "a majority of electors from the landowners and the first urban curia" is guaranteed "in a considerable number of gubernia assemblies". I reminded him of the facts: that this majority is guaranteed in *all* gubernia assemblies, that in 28 out of 53 gubernias a majority (in the assemblies) is guaranteed to the landowners *alone,* and that these gubernias send 255 out of a total of some 440 deputies to the Duma. (3) In speaking of dislodging reaction from its positions in the Duma, Martov forgot that the Duma *cannot* become anything more than a *landowners'* liberal opposition. The slogan issued by Martov and Dan implies wresting the *landowner* from the grip of reaction. (4) In saying that it is to the interest of the workers that power should be transferred to the "civilised bourgeoisie", Martov "forgot" to mention one thing, namely, that it is to the interest of the liberals to

---

* See pp. 487-90 of this volume.—*Ed.*

share power with Purishkevich so as to prevent democracy from possessing "a single weapon"! (5) In saying that, by growing stronger in the Duma, the Cadets "are facilitating their advance towards power", Martov forgot the experience of 1905-06 in Russia, of 1789 and subsequent years in France and of 1911 in China. This experience tells us that power is transferred to the liberals (or further to the left) only when democracy triumphs *in spite* of the liberals. (6) Consequently, Martov accepts Marxism only insofar as it is acceptable to any educated liberal.

What does Martov reply to these six points? Nothing. He maintains absolute silence. Why then start a controversy if you have decided to say nothing?

While passing over in silence *all* my arguments, Martov tries to "catch" me in the following passage from my article:

"The practical task that faces us at the elections is by no means 'to dislodge reaction from its positions in the Duma', but to strengthen the forces of democracy in general and of working-class democracy in particular. This task may sometimes clash with the 'task' of increasing the number of liberals, but five additional* democrats are more important to us, and more useful to the proletariat, than fifty additional liberals."

Quoting this passage, Martov (pretending that he has caught "an adherent of reaction"!) gleefully exclaims: "I suggest that the readers ponder over this phrase". I heartily support this proposal.

Martov begins to ponder and in so doing arrives at the following syllogism: The law now provides for a second ballot everywhere. Consequently, *"there may be only one instance"* when, by repulsing fifty liberals, we can elect five democrats. Such an "instance" involves *selling* the democratic vote to the Black Hundreds in exchange for seats in the Duma.

And Martov rejoices and prances for a full fifty lines, pretending that he has smitten an abettor of the Black Hundreds and that in smiting F. L-ko he has also "hit" W. Frey[204] who "is steering the same course".

---

* There was a misprint in the article: "strong" instead of "additional". Martov might have easily noticed that it was absurd to juxtapose "strong" democrats to "additional" liberals. But that is not the point at issue.

Martov must think his readers are very naïve. And how careless it was of him to suggest to readers that they should *ponder*, while he himself writes *without thinking*.

The passage in my article to which Martov took such strong exception poses *two* questions for thinking people to answer: (1) Is it true that five democrats in the Duma are of greater use to the workers than fifty liberals? (2) Is it possible for these tasks to "clash" in actual practice?

The pondering Martov evaded the first question *altogether*. That's a pity. You, Messrs. Liquidators, evade questions of politics in order to accuse us of partiality for arithmetic. Fifty liberals in the Duma will give the people a pile of *sham democratic* speeches, thereby corrupting the people, and a *few* "reforms" which, to begin with, will be confined to wash-basins, and, secondly, will be held up in the Council of State and so *forth*. Five democrats, on the other hand, will use the Duma rostrum to explain to the people a number of truths of *democracy* (and workers will use the rostrum also to explain some of the truths of socialism). Which is more useful to the proletariat?

The second question. Is Martov right when he says that the task of electing five democrats ("additional", i. e., in addition to those we have at present) *may clash* with the task of electing fifty liberals *only* in the case which he mentions? For after inviting the readers to ponder, Martov declares without further ado: "There may be only one such instance."

If Martov is right, the reader ought to accuse me, F. L-ko, either of discussing an impossible case, or of a secret desire to sell the votes of the democrats to the Black Hundreds in exchange for seats in the Duma (a secret and *stupid* desire, I may add confidentially. Imagine Purishkevich purchasing the votes of the friends of Petrov the Third and Voiloshnikov *in exchange for* electing Voiloshnikov to the Fourth Duma—that is the sort of probability in which the "pondering" Martov indulges).

If there can be another instance of these two tasks clashing, then Martov is wrong.

Thus, is another instance of such a clash possible? *There could be, without any doubt*, if at the *second ballot* the democrats, without entering into an agreement with the liberals, were to fight both the Rights and the liberals.

That is all there is to it.*

The pondering Martov, like all the liquidators, is a prisoner of the idea of two camps, and fails to notice the fight waged by a third camp both against the first and against the second!

Immediately following the passage which fills Martov with indignation, it says in my article:

"Hence the following conclusion ["hence", dear Martov!] which Martov refuses to draw, even though he does pretend to agree that the Cadets are *not* democrats, but liberals: (1) in the five big cities, in the event of a second ballot, agreements are permissible *only* with the democrats against the liberals; (2) at *all* the ballots and in *all* the agreements at the second stage, *precedence* should be given to agreements with the democrats against the liberals, and only subsequently may agreements be concluded with the liberals against the Rights".

Martov mentioned *only* the second point, and declared that I was not telling the truth, because Martov agrees with that point (it remains to be seen whether *all* the liquidators agree!), *but he maintained silence on the first point*!

Once again: either you keep silent or you argue the issue.

In the event of a second ballot being taken in the five cities, the general line should be: with the democrats *against* the liberals. Agreements with the liberals to be *prohibited* (for experience has shown that on the *whole* there is no danger of a Black-Hundred victory in any of these cities).

Are you *for* or *against* this sort of prohibition? Give a straight answer.

Further, what *can* be the practical result of this second ballot? The votes may be divided *nearly* equally among the three camps. The issue is then decided by the relative majority. Take the simplest example: out of a total of 100 votes, the Rights command 33, the liberals 33, and the democrats 34 votes. The democratic candidate is elected. One vote

---

* The following "terrible" suspicion occurs to me: is it possible that Martov's whole article is to be explained by his *not knowing* that, according to the law, the second ballot represents new elections and not a contest between two candidates? If this is the case, it will be necessary, before "fighting reaction" in the elections, to fight ignorance of the electoral law!

less for the Social-Democrat and one vote more for the reactionary may decide the issue in favour of the Black Hundreds!

There are two lines of working-class policy: the *liberal*
line—fear above all the election of a reactionary, therefore
surrender the leadership to the liberal without a fight!
The *Marxist* line—do not be dismayed by the liberal cries
about the danger of a Black-Hundred victory, but *boldly*
plunge into a "three-cornered" contest (to use the English expression). As a general rule there is no danger of the Black
Hundreds gaining a victory. And if in exceptional cases
a Black-Hundred candidate is elected, this will be compen-
sated for by the fact that *here and there democrats will be
elected!*...

You cannot learn to swim unless you go into the water.
There can be no contest in which all the chances are known
beforehand. If the workers allow themselves to be frightened by the liberal cries about the danger of a Black-Hundred
victory, they will *never* learn to fight in a "three-cornered"
contest. Everywhere in the world the camp of reaction and
the liberal camp rallied their forces earlier and were better
organised (with the aid of reactionary laws, of course)
than the workers. Everywhere in the world the liberals tell
the workers the very same things that Martov is repeating.

Now, for one more, and final, step to show the "pondering"
Martov what it means to ponder over matters.

At the second ballot in the five cities, agreements with
the liberals are prohibited. In other cases of a second ballot
such agreements are not prohibited. Does this mean that
they will be concluded *as a rule*? It seems not, doesn't it?

If there is *no* agreement, may it not happen that in *each*
case of a second ballot the votes will be divided nearly
equally among the three camps?

Apparently it may be, if one really "ponders" over it.

From this follows the conclusion that there are two lines
of working-class policy.

The liberal labour policy: there is a swing to the left in
the country; "therefore" ... fear above all the danger of a
Black-Hundred victory; the slogan is to dislodge reaction
from its positions in the Duma; but only the liberals can dislodge it from its positions in the Duma; threfore, you must

not "threaten" the liberals, or "extort" seats from them —
surely it is unbecoming for "cultured" workers to extort anything from such nice people as the liberals! —but be prepared
to make every kind of concession in concluding agreements
with the liberals, and steer clear of a "three-cornered" contest.

The Marxist working-class policy: there is a swing to the
left in the country; therefore, do not believe the liberal fables
about the danger of a Black-Hundred victory; when entering
into agreements with the liberals, you must by all means
threaten them and extort from them seats in the Duma; and in
order to lend weight to your threats, worker comrades, don't
fear a "three-cornered" contest; boldly engage in such a fight,
and expose the counter-revolutionary liberals to the people;
to be sure, wherever there is a fight, there is a possibility
of defeat, here and there a reactionary may be elected, but,
on the other hand, *here and there democrats will be elected*;
it is better for five additional democrats to get into the Duma
than for fifty additional liberals; as a general rule, the Black
Hundreds will not win in the elections, for the Purishkeviches are too well known, and the liberals are *purposely*
trying to scare the people by magnifying the danger of a
Black-Hundred victory in order to secure the leadership
for themselves (although the Maklakovs are almost as black
as the Black Hundreds) and ward off the danger threatening
them from the "left".

To sum up: he made no reply to a single point of the
six I brought up in dealing with the liberal labour policy.
He ignored the question of prohibiting blocs with the liberals in the five cities. He gave no thought to three-cornered
election fights *at* the second ballot, although he had promised to "ponder". On the other hand, there are two things
he did accomplish: (1) he defended the liberals from "threats",
and (2) accused Voiloshnikov's friends of plotting with Purishkevich to sell votes to him on condition that Purishkevich, *in exchange*, should help elect Voiloshnikovs to the
Fourth Duma!!

Zvezda, No. 24 (60), April 1, 1912
Signed; *F. L-ko*

Published according to
the *Zvezda* text

THE SECOND BALLOT IN RUSSIA
AND THE TASKS OF THE WORKING CLASS

More and more frequently we come across examples showing how widespread is the wrong idea people have of the second ballot under our electoral law. Dan, writing in No. 1-2 of *Nasha Zarya*, said that our tactics at the second ballot must be the same as in Western Europe. Martov, writing in No. 8 of *Zhivoye Dyelo*, directly pointed to the "German workers" as an example for the Russian workers to follow in their tactics at the second ballot. A special article dealing with the second ballot, recently published by Trotsky, is based on the same error.

The error is repeated so frequently, that we cannot help wondering whether the "general leaning" in certain quarters to the same error of fact is not due to the *unwillingness* to appreciate the tasks of working-class democracy in the fight against the Cadets.

In Russia, the law of June 3, 1907 does *not* provide for a second ballot of the German type; in fact, it does *not* provide for any "second ballot" at all in the strict sense of the term; it only provides for supplementary or new elections. The second ballot in Germany is a choice between two candidates only, those who have received the highest number of votes in the first elections. In the case of the Germans, the second ballot decides solely which of the two candidates receiving the highest number of votes is to be elected.

There is nothing of the sort in Russia. According to our law, any number of any candidates may run for election in the second ballot. Strictly speaking, it is not a second ballot, but new or supplementary elections. Therefore, all references to the German example are quite wrong!

The main article of the law dealing with the second ballot is Article 106 of the Regulations governing the elections. Here we read: "Delegates of the preliminary assemblies and, likewise, electors elected at the assemblies of voters, are recognised as such if they have received more than half the votes cast at the assembly".

Here we have the clearly expressed requirement of an absolute majority in the first round of the elections. Further, the same article states that in cases where no absolute majority has been obtained, "supplementary elections are to be held for the remaining vacancies" (that is to say, for all the electors except those who have been elected by an absolute majority).

Who is regarded as elected at the "supplementary elections"? "Those who obtained a relative majority of the votes," it is stated at the end of this article, "are to be regarded as elected."

The same is stipulated in the law of June 3, 1907 with regard to the second ballot in the case of *direct* elections, i.e., in the cities of St. Petersburg, Moscow, Odessa, Kiev, and Riga. Only instead of using the expression "a relative majority of the votes", Article 140 speaks of "the greatest number of votes". Finally, provision is also made for the second ballot at the elections of members of the Duma by gubernia electoral assemblies—in case none of the candidates received "more than half of the votes cast", i.e., an absolute majority. When a second ballot is taken "those who have received a relative majority of the votes cast are regarded as elected". (Article 350.)

Consequently, our electoral law does not provide for anything like the second ballot in Germany. In this connection there can be nothing more erroneous than to refer to the example and conduct of the German workers. In the official edition of the Regulations Governing the Elections to the State Duma, issued by the Ministry of the Interior, St. Petersburg, 1912, it says in Clause 14 of the interpretations of Article 106: "Persons who took no part in the first round of the elections may also be permitted to participate in the supplementary elections". It is obvious that this refers not only to new voters, but also to new candidates. The law permits the nomination for the second ballot of a candidate who did not stand in the first elections.

The question is, what political conclusions for our election tactics should be drawn from this feature of the June Third election regulations.

The first, fundamental, and most general conclusion is the, following: our law, unlike the German law, provides a *wider* field for election agreements at the second ballot. In Germany it can be only a question of choosing *the lesser evil*: those defeated at the first elections (and they are all those excluded from the second ballot) can have no other aim. In Russia, if on the one hand in the primary elections there were no victors, on the other hand there would, strictly speaking, be no defeated contestants, for *each* may try his luck a second time, in a new contest, by concluding agreements of various kinds with one ally or another.

In Germany, for one thing, the working-class candidate cannot derive any benefit *for himself*, i.e., any direct benefit, from the fight between the Right parties and the bourgeois opposition parties. He may support the liberal opposition against the Rights if both are of practically equal strength; but he cannot take advantage of a tie between his liberal and reactionary opponent to win the victory *himself*. In Russia the latter is possible.

Hence the second conclusion. The Russian electoral law, unlike the German law, provides working-class democracy with a *wider field* for fighting the *liberals* at the second ballot. In Russia, as in most West-European countries, two wings (or two groups of parties) of the ruling propertied classes predominate in the elections: "conservatives" and liberals, the Black Hundreds and the "opposition". The workers are fighting *both* groups of parties. The backward sections of the people, who at first awaken to the struggle against feudalism and absolutism, do not immediately realise their tasks in the struggle against capital, and usually follow the liberals for rather a long time. That is why the working-class parties, when their influence is growing, as a rule win over more followers from the liberals than from the Rights. Hence the usual hypocritical wailings of the "Cadets" of *all* countries about the working-class parties allegedly playing into the hands of the reactionaries, weakening the "general forces of progress", and so on and so forth.

In Germany, the working-class candidate can measure strength with a liberal at the second ballot only in instances when the Rights have been defeated in the first round of the elections, and are excluded from the second ballot. In Russia a working-class candidate can, and therefore should, compete in the second ballot against a liberal *whenever* the Right has obtained a smaller number of votes than the liberal in the first elections. In other words: when a second ballot is taken in Germany, the working-class candidate can meet the liberal only "in single combat"; in Russia, however, it is possible for the second ballot also to be a "three-cornered contest", i. e., one in which Right, liberal, and working-class candidates participate. In cases of a second ballot in Russia, therefore, there may occur *more* instances when the mass of the workers will be interested in securing the election of their own candidate.

We have now come to the third conclusion. In Russia, bearing in mind the present political divisions, a particularly wide field is open at the second ballot for the so-called *Left bloc* in all the curias and at all stages where the liberals are stronger than the reactionaries (the latter including, of course, all the Rights, the Nationalists, and the Octobrists, i. e., all the government parties without exception). Wherever the liberals at the first elections prove stronger than the reactionaries, and the working-class candidates weaker than the liberals, it is the *duty* of the workers, both from the viewpoint of the political task of organising the forces of democracy in general, and from the viewpoint of electing working-class candidates to the Duma, to make common cause with bourgeois democracy (Narodniks, Trudoviks, etc.) *against* the liberals.

Are such instances likely to occur often?

Not very often in the gubernia electoral assemblies; here, in most cases, the liberals will be weaker than the reactionaries, and it will, therefore, be necessary to form a bloc of all the opposition forces in order to defeat the reactionaries.

In the peasant curia, the political divisions are less definite and distinct; here the tyranny of the police is felt more

acutely than anywhere else; here delegates, electors, and
even candidates for election to the Duma, are most keenly
aware of the necessity to "conceal" their true "face"; there
are very few worker candidates so far as party affiliation is
concerned. The political task to be performed in this curia
is, unquestionably, to organise the forces of democracy and
combat the influence and prejudices of the liberal-monarchist bourgeoisie. As for the second ballot, it is difficult to
draw any definite conclusions regarding the frequency of
one contingency or another, or even regarding the number of
actual cases of a second ballot.

In the landowner and the first urban curias the role
of democrats in general and of working-class democrats in particular is too insignificant to be dwelt on
at all.

There remains the second urban curia. Here there are
quite a few workers and voters close to the workers: shop
assistants, worker tenants, pensioners, etc. Here there is
at least something resembling a political press and something in the nature of meetings. In brief, this is the principal field for a second ballot, with the voters directly participating. Now, how do matters in this curia stand with
regard to the party alignment of the voters?

A fairly exact, even if indirect, answer to this question is
provided by data on the party allegiance of the electors of
the second urban curia in the elections to the Third State
Duma. According to the returns published in the Cadet *Rech*
(1907, No. 241) for 4,897 electors out of a total of 5,161 in 51
gubernias of European Russia, the 533 electors in the second
urban curia were divided by parties as follows: opposition
parties 405 (100 "Lefts", 209 Cadets, and 96 Progressists),
Right parties 101 (17 moderates, 19 Octobrists and 65
Rights), 21 independents and 6 whose party affiliation was
unknown. The three main groups of parties contending in the
present elections are clearly indicated here: 100 democrats,
305 liberals, 101 Rights.

The liberals are thus more than three times as strong
as the Rights, whose strength is practically equal to that
of the democrats. *As a rule*, therefore, there can obviously
be no question here of any danger of a Black-Hundred victory. It is further obvious that the *main* task of working-

class democrats in this curia is to fight the liberals. At the present juncture particularly, when, as even the liberals, Octobrists and Purishkeviches admit, there is undoubtedly a general swing to the left in the country, this fight must be put in the forefront. Obviously, in the first stage of the elections the working-class candidates must wage an absolutely independent struggle, putting forward a hundred per cent working-class election lists. In the second stage, at the second ballot, it will *in the majority of cases* be a question of a fight of democrats against liberals.

In order to conduct *that* struggle it will be necessary for the Marxists at the second ballot to make common cause with *all* democrats (i.e., also with the bourgeois democrats, Narodniks, Trudoviks, etc.) *against* the liberals. The entire behaviour of the notorious "responsible opposition", the Cadets, in the Third Duma, the entire policy and tactics of the liberal-monarchist bourgeoisie, on the one hand, and on the other, the present movement among the shop assistants, provide a particularly favourable ground for this fight by the democrats, organised by the workers, against the liberals, i.e., against the Cadet Party. Inasmuch as the second urban curia is the one in which there will be the greatest number of cases of a second ballot, the *principal* line to be pursued by the workers at the second ballot is precisely this: with the democrats *against* the Rights and *against* the liberals.

In the final analysis, we come to the conclusion that the liquidators and their defenders are committing both a "technical" and a political mistake on the question of the second ballot. "Technically", they are committing a mistake by confusing the German second ballot with the Russian "supplementary" or new elections. Politically, they are committing a mistake by sinking down to a liberal labour policy, by confining themselves to general phrases about supporting the opposition against the Rights. Actually, the general task of the Marxists in present-day Russia, the task of organising the workers as the vanguard of democracy against *both* the Rights *and* the counter-revolutionary liberals, as well as our special position in the principal "second ballot" curia, demand a different slogan. In cases of a second ballot, primarily in the second urban curia, common cause is

to be made more often with all democrats against the liberals and against the Rights; and only subsequently it may
be necessary at the second ballot to join the general opposition bloc against the reactionaries.

Zvezda, No. 25 (61), April 3, 1912   Published according to
          Signed; *M. Sh.*   the *Zvezda* text

LIBERALISM AND DEMOCRACY

I

The Trudovik conference of which we have already spoken and which was reported in several newspapers (among others, in *Rech* of March 28), is of special importance from the standpoint of making clear party alignments in the elections to the Fourth Duma. After the bloc of moderate liberals (the Cadets and "independent Progressists") and after the resolutions of the working-class democrats about their tactics in the elections, it only remained for the Trudoviks to "define themselves" in order to complete the picture.

By now *all* classes of Russian society, as represented by all political parties of any importance and worthy of attention, have defined their position in the election campaign. For the bourgeois parties, particularly those that have found a "permanent" place for themselves under the June Third regime, the elections are primarily an occasion for an intensified publicity drive, but for working-class democrats, for Marxists, the main task in the election campaign is to *explain* to the people the *nature* of the various political parties, *what* views are advocated and *who* advocates them, what are the real and vital interests behind each party, which *classes* of society shelter behind each party label.

From this point of view we shall have to deal with the conference of the Trudoviks *repeatedly*, and in the interests of the working class, our special attention must be devoted to the fundamental question indicated above. The Black Hundreds, the Right parties, and the *liberals* (the Cadets) all ignore this question, or else they misinterpret its presentation and solution in a thousand ways, not because of any lack of understanding or because of the malice of individuals, but because the *class* interests of the land-owners and the bourgeoisie *compel* them to misrepresent the essence of the peasants' and workers' parties.

On the other hand, the Trudoviks, a mainly peasant party, do not try to evade the question, say, of what distinguishes liberalism from democracy, but their answer to it is a wrong one. Nor is it possible to give a proper answer to the question when approached from the peasant point of view, i.e., that of the small proprietor. It is only from the point of view of the wage-earner that the question is *settled* —this is borne out not only by theory and science, but also by the *experience* of all European countries, by the entire economic and political history of the European parties, particularly in the nineteenth century.

Observe, for one thing, what the liberals say of the Trudoviks and what the Trudoviks say of themselves. The liberal *Rech*, chief organ of the Cadet Party, says that the Trudoviks suffered most from the change in the electoral law effected on June 3, 1907, and that their tactics "cannot in any way differ perceptibly" from the tactics of the Cadets; for the Cadets, if you please, can "repeat" and do repeat practically everything said by the Trudoviks. "Lastly," writes *Rech*, "election agreements with the Trudoviks may perhaps turn out to be necessary in isolated places only, and in few such places at that."

Consider this statement, and you will see that it is the statement of a liberal bourgeois, whom the law of June 3 deprived of his leading position (which he enjoyed under the law of December 11, 1905[205]), but at the same time gave him a by no means insignificant place in the opposition, *segregated* from democracy. You don't matter much, Messrs. Trudoviks, and we are not taking you seriously—that is what the *Rech* statement really amounts to. Why do they not matter? Because the law of June 3 has made them powerless in the elections.

From the standpoint of any democrat, and particularly from the standpoint of any worker, the parties that matter are not those that enjoy a monopoly or privileges under the given electoral law, but those that represent the large masses of the population, especially of the toiling and exploited population. As it happens, however, it is precisely from these masses that the law of June 3 *protects* the liberal bourgeois —and that is why they do not matter to him. The liberal lawyers and journalists want seats in the Duma, the liberal bourgeois want to share power with the Purishkeviches, that is what they really want. As for the development of the independent political thought of the peasant masses, the development of their initiative as a class, this is something the liberal does not want; more, it constitutes an outright danger to him. The liberals need voters, they need a crowd that would trust and follow them (in order to compel the Purishkeviches to make room), but they fear the political independence of the crowd.

Why, then, are they not afraid of the Trudoviks who, as an "independent" party particularly close to the peasantry, i.e., to the vast majority of the population, are *not* liberals but representatives of bourgeois democracy? For the very reason that the Trudoviks are democrats *insufficiently* independent in their relations with the liberals, *lacking the ability* to fight the liberals for influence over the masses! We must not tire of dwelling hundreds of times on this most important problem of contemporary politics in Russia if we take these politics seriously, conscientiously, as a matter of principle, and not in the fraudulent (or liberal) sense of chasing after Duma seats. As long as Russia's political transformation along democratic lines remains the historical task of the present epoch, the *entire crux* of the problem of this transformation will inevitably consist in the necessity for *very* broad, the broadest possible, masses of the population to become conscious democrats, i.e., emphatic, consistent and determined opponents of liberal narrow-mindedness, half-heartedness and cowardice. And no worker can claim to be a class-conscious worker if he has not realised that he cannot be a consistent fighter for the abolition of wage slavery, *unless* he is fully aware of and works for this political task of our times.

When the liberals, the Cadets, say that their "tactics" do not in any way "differ perceptibly" from Trudovik tactics, it is a case of unmitigated ignorance or shameless lying. The political history of Russia for the past decade teems with hundreds and thousands of refutations of this lie. Russia's most recent history provides proof based on our

Russian *experience* showing that the difference between the liberals and the peasant democrats is immeasurably deeper than any question of "tactics"; this difference has always and invariably come to the surface during the past, say, eight years, despite the fact that the course of events has often given rise to the most drastic changes in "tactics"; this difference goes much deeper than any "programmes", for a programme expresses simply what the advanced representatives of a given class *think* of the tasks and position of their class. Not the opinions of advanced individuals, but the actions of the millions, have shown us the root difference between the *present-day* economic and political condition of the liberal bourgeoisie on the one hand, and the bourgeois-democratic peasantry on the other. Hence the fundamental difference between their class *interests* in regard to the "forces in control" of Russia today. Hence the fundamental difference between them on all points of departure and in the entire scope of political activity.

Both the liberal and the Trudovik may be under the illusion that they hold the same political opinions, for both are "against Purishkevich". But probe just a little below these *opinions* of political leaders, down to the *class position* of the masses, and you will find that in *real life* the liberal bourgeoisie shares political privileges with the Purishkeviches, and their controversy is *only* over the question whether the Purishkeviches are to hold two-thirds of these privileges and the Milyukovs one third, or the other way round. Take "real life", take the economic position of the present-day Russian peasantry as a stratum of small proprietors in agriculture, and you are sure to find that it is by no means a question of dividing political privileges, by no means a question of political privileges at all, but that even the word "*life*" must be written in inverted commas, for the very existence of the Purishkeviches means *death from starvation* for millions of such petty proprietors.

Modern Russia has two bourgeoisies. One is the very narrow stratum of ripe and overripe capitalists who, in the person of the Octobrists and Cadets, are *actually* concerned with sharing the present political power, the present political privileges, with the Purishkeviches. The word "present" in this case must be given a rather broad meaning, so as to include, for instance, the privileges which the law of June 3, 1907, safeguards today, and the privileges which the law of December 11, 1905, safeguarded yesterday.

The other bourgeoisie is the very wide stratum of petty and in part medium proprietors, who have not yet matured but are energetically endeavouring to do so. They are mostly peasants who in the present era of Russian history are by no means *actually* confronted with the question of privileges, but with the question of how not to starve to death *because of* the Purishkeviches. This is a question that concerns the very foundations of the power of the Purishkeviches in general, the sources of all power held by the Purishkeviches.

The entire history of Russia's political emancipation centres around the struggle between these two bourgeois tendencies. Behind all the thousands upon thousands of fine words about liberty and equality, about "equalitarian" distribution of the land and "Narodism", is the struggle between these bourgeois tendencies. The result of the struggle will inevitably be a Russia that is completely bourgeois and painted entirely or predominantly in one of these two "colours". It is clear that this struggle is by no means without significance for the wage-worker; quite the contrary, if he is a class-conscious wage-worker he most vigorously interferes in this fight, doing his utmost to get the peasant to follow him and not follow the liberal.

This also underlies the problems which the Trudovik conference could not help touching upon. We shall deal with those in greater detail in later articles. For the time being, we shall confine ourselves to a brief summary of what has been said. The question of the Trudoviks and the Cadets is one of the most important questions of Russia's political emancipation. There is nothing more banal than to reduce this question to one of the "strength" of this or that party in the June Third system or of the "advantage" to be derived from different agreements in elections based on this system. On the contrary, the particular questions of agreements, second ballots, etc., can, from the standpoint of the wage-worker, be settled correctly only if the *class* roots of both parties, the bourgeois democrats (Trudoviks) and the bourgeois liberals (Cadets, "Progressists", etc.), have been understood.

II

The conference of the Trudoviks raised a number of highly interesting and instructive political questions. We
are now in possession of a splendid commentary on its
decisions—Mr. V. Vodovozov's article on "The Election
Programme of the Trudovik Group" in No. 13 of the St.
Petersburg weekly *Zaprosy Zhizni*,[206] whose closest contributors include Messrs. Kovalevsky and Blank. Mr. Vodovozov's commentary is "splendid", not from our point of
view, of course, but because it correctly represents the views
and aspirations of the Trudoviks. Everyone interested in the
role of the democratic social forces in Russia must pay due
attention to Mr. Vodovozov's article.

"The Trudovik group," he writes, "proceeds from the belief that
at the present historical moment the interests of the peasantry, the
working class and the working intelligentsia, far from contradicting
each other, are practically identical; therefore, one party could fully
take care of the interests of these three classes of society. But, owing
to the force of historical conditions, the working class found its
representation in the Social-Democratic Party, and that is why the
Trudovik group necessarily had to become primarily the political
representative of the peasantry. And such it has been."

Here we see at a glance the fundamental mistake shared
by all the Narodniks, including those who are the most
"left". They proceed from a "belief" which contradicts all
the maxims of economic science and the entire experience
of countries which have gone through epochs resembling the
present epoch in Russia. They cling to these "beliefs" even
when the experience of Russian history compels them to
admit that in our country, too, these beliefs are refuted by
the course of events.

The Trudoviks' second phrase contradicts their first. If
one party could have taken care of the interests both of the
working class and the peasantry, what could have given rise
to a separate party of the working class? Since such a party
was created and became consolidated during a particularly
important and particularly crucial period of Russian history (1905), and since even the Trudoviks have to admit
that the working class "found" its party "owing to the force
of historical conditions", this, consequently, means that

the "beliefs" of the Trudoviks have been *refuted* by "the force of historical conditions".

If the Trudoviks *have turned out* to be a party of the peasantry, although, according to their own beliefs, they ought not to be a party only of the peasantry, their beliefs must be wrong, must be an illusion. And it is the same sort of illusion as the one entertained by *all* bourgeois-democratic parties of Europe in the period of the struggle against feudalism and absolutism. In one form or another, the idea of a "non-class party" dominated, but the "force of historical conditions" invariably refuted this idea and shattered this illusion. The attempts or efforts to include different classes in "one party" have always been characteristic of bourgeois democracy at the time when it had to look for its main enemy in the past, not in the future—when it saw its enemy in the feudal lords, not in the proletariat.

The claim to "encompass" various classes makes the Trudoviks akin to the Cadets. The latter, too, want to be a party standing *above classes*, they also insist that the interests of the working class, the peasantry and the working intelligentsia are "practically identical". And when they speak of the working intelligentsia, they include the Maklakovs too! The class-conscious workers will always combat the various concepts of parties that stand above classes, against every attempt to gloss over the gulf between the class of wage-workers and the class of the petty proprietors.

The Trudoviks resemble the Cadets in sharing bourgeois illusions as to the possibility of fusing the different classes. The difference between them lies in *the class* to which the particular party will be drawn under the influence of events, against the wishes of that party and sometimes in spite of the ideas entertained by some of its members. The Trudoviks have been taught by history to keep closer to the truth, to call themselves a peasant party. The Cadets continue to call themselves democrats, although in actual fact they are counter-revolutionary liberals.

Unfortunately, the Trudoviks are far from being aware of the latter truth—so much so that in the official decisions of their conference they *failed* to give any characterisation of the Cadets. All we read in the official resolutions is that agreements should be concluded *"in the first place*

with the Social-Democrats, *and subsequently* with the Constitutional-Democrats". This is insufficient. The question of
election agreements can be settled correctly, consistently,
and in a principled manner, *only* if there exists complete
clarity as to the class nature of the parties concluding
the agreement, as to what constitutes their fundamental
divergence, and on what points their interests temporarily
coincide.

These matters are dealt with only in Mr. Vodovozov's
commentary. *Rech*, which noted and discussed that article,
took care to leave its readers entirely *in the dark* with regard to *these very points*. In our opinion, these points ought
to be dwelt on with all due attention.

"The Trudovik group," writes Mr. Vodovozov, "is fully
aware that the present regime in Russia is a regime of absolutism and arbitrary rule; that is why it has emphatically
disapproved of all the actions and steps taken by the Constitutional-Democratic Party to proclaim *urbi et orbi** that in
Russia we have a constitutional regime, and why it has
assumed a negative attitude to the solemn receptions given
to the representatives of the British and French Parliaments
as a demonstration of Russian constitutionalism. The Trudovik group has never doubted that only a radical and profound revolution in the entire political and social system can
lead Russia on to the highroad of proper and sound development; that is why it has been in sympathy with all expressions of such convictions in our public life. It is this conviction that has implied the existence of a deep gulf between
it and the Constitutional-Democratic Party...." Further on
the author repeats the same idea about "the peaceful evolutionism of the Cadets and Cadet tactics produced by this
evolutionism", "owing to which the Trudoviks have always
been farther removed from the Constitutional-Democrats
than from the Social-Democrats".

It is obvious why the Cadet *Rech* was obliged to take care
to withhold these reflections from its readers. For these
reflections represent a clearly expressed desire to draw a
line between democratism and liberalism. The line is unquestionably there, but Mr. Vodovozov, although he speaks

---

* Far and wide   *Ed.*

of a "deep gulf", has a very shallow conception of this line. According to him, the difference, at bottom, is one of tactics and of the appraisal of the situation: the Trudoviks are in favour of a radical revolution, while the Cadets are peaceful evolutionists; according to the Trudoviks the regime in Russia is one of absolutism, according to the Cadets we have, thank God, a constitution. Such differences may exist between the Right and the Left wings of the same class.

Are these all the differences there are between the Trudoviks and the Cadets? Has not Mr. Vodovozov himself admitted that the Trudoviks are a party of the peasantry? If we take the *class position* of the peasantry in relation, say, to Purishkevich and Purishkevichism, are there no features that distinguish this position from that of the liberal bourgeoisie?

If there are no such distinguishing features, then there is no profound difference between the Trudoviks and the Cadets even in their attitude to feudalism and absolutism. If there are such distinguishing features, then it is the difference of *class interests*, and not the difference of "opinion" on absolutism and the Constitution or on peaceful evolution, that must be stressed.

The Trudoviks want to be more radical than the Cadets. That is very good. But their radicalism would be more consistent and profound if they had a clear idea of the class essence of the liberal-monarchist bourgeoisie, if they plainly referred in their platform to the counter-revolutionary liberalism of the Cadets.

It is therefore in vain that Mr. Vodovozov tries to "justify" himself by pleading external obstacles owing to which, he claims, the Trudoviks "were obliged to draft a resolution in which the most essential points were concealed behind a reference, one not very intelligible to most readers, to the 'platform of the Trudovik group', which is hardly accessible to them". But, to begin with, the Trudoviks were not obliged to confine themselves to the arena fenced off by such obstacles; by confining themselves to this arena, they, just like our liquidators, are betraying how little they differ from the Cadets. Secondly, it was always possible, no matter what the arena, to formulate the class essence of the Cadet liberalism and its counter-revolutionary nature.

Thus we see that the vacillations of the Trudoviks between the Cadets and the Social-Democrats are not fortuitous, but the result of very profound and fundamental conditions, those under which the peasantry has to live. The intermediary position of aloofness from the direct fight between the bourgeois and the proletarian nourishes illusions about a party that stands outside or above classes. What brings the Trudoviks and the Cadets close to one another are the common bourgeois prejudices characteristic both of the big and the small proprietor. Hence, as bourgeois democrats, the Trudoviks lack consistency even in their struggle against the foundations of the power of the Purishkeviches.

The task of the class-conscious workers is to help rally the forces of the peasant democracy, those who are least dependent on the liberals and least liable to yield to their influence, those who are most consistent and determined. Such is the condition of the vast mass of the peasantry that the striving for "a radical and profound revolution", as formulated by Mr. Vodovozov, has extremely strong, widely ramified and deep-seated roots.

Zvezda, Nos. 27 (63) and 32 (68),
   April 8, and April 19, 1912
          Signed: *P.P.*

Published according to
the *Zvezda* text

NOTES

[1] *The Russian Collegium of the Central Committee* ("narrow circle of the C.C.", "the acting C.C. in Russia"), confirmed by the Plenary Meeting of the C.C. of the R.S.D.L.P. in August 1908, existed until 1910. It consisted originally of one representative each from the Bolsheviks, Mensheviks, Polish Social-Democrats, Latvian Social-Democrats and the Bund.

According to the C.C. Rules adopted at the Plenary Meeting in January 1910, the composition of the Russian Collegium of the C.C. was to be enlarged to seven to include the four members of the C.C. elected at the Fifth (London) Congress and three representatives of national (non-Russian) organisations. However, owing to the refusal of the Menshevik-liquidators to co-operate, it was impossible to organise the work of the Russian Collegium of the C.C. after the January Plenary Meeting. Lenin suggested bringing into the Russian Collegium pro-Party Mensheviks to replace the liquidators, but the conciliator members of the C.C. (Nogin, Goldenberg, Leiteisen, and others) did not carry this out.

In the course of 1910 and early in 1911 all Bolshevik members of the C.C. working in Russia were arrested.

This letter is published according to a copy found in the files of the Police Department. The heading to the document has been provided by the Institute of Marxism-Leninism of the Central Committee of the C.P.S.U   p. 17

[2] *Golos Sotsial-Demokrata* (*Voice of the Social-Democrat*)—a Menshevik-liquidator organ published in Geneva, and later in Paris, from February 1908 to December 1911.

For Lenin's appraisal of *Golos Sotsial-Demokrata* see his article "*Golos* (Voice) of the Liquidators Against the Party" (see present edition, Vol. 16).   p. 17

[3] *The Plenary Meeting of the C.C. of the R.S.D.L.P.*, commonly known as the "Unity" Meeting, was held from January 2 to 23 (January 15-February 5), 1910, in Paris. The Meeting was convened despite Lenin's wishes with the assistance of Trotsky's secret allies, Zinovyev, Kamenev, and Rykov. In addition to the Bolsheviks, representatives of all the factions and factional groups and representatives of the non-Russian Social-Democratic organisations were present. Lenin's plan for closer relations with the pro-Party Mensheviks (Plekhanov's group) in the struggle against the

liquidators was opposed by the conciliators, who were secret Trotskyites. They demanded the disbandment of all factions, and the amalgamation of the Bolsheviks with the liquidators and Trotskyites. The conciliators were in the majority at the Meeting. The Bolsheviks were in the minority. It was only due to Lenin's insistence that the Plenary Meeting adopted a resolution condemning liquidationism and otzovism. Notwithstanding Lenin's attitude, the Meeting adopted decisions to abolish the Bolshevik organ *Proletary*, disband the Bolshevik Centre and hand over its property to the C.C., and the available funds to the representatives of the international Social-Democratic movement (the "trustees") Franz Mehring, Clara Zetkin, and Karl Kautsky. Lenin succeeded in getting conditions for the simultaneous liquidation of the *Golos* and *Vperyod* factional centres included in the resolution of the Plenary Meeting. The Meeting carried a resolution to the effect that financial assistance be given to Trotsky's Vienna *Pravda*, which his agents, Zinovyev and Kamenev, tried to convert into the organ of the Central Committee.

Despite Lenin's protest, Menshevik-liquidators were elected to the central bodies. For Lenin's struggle at the Plenary Meeting against the liquidators, Trotskyites and conciliators see his article "Notes of a Publicist" (see present edition, Vol. 16).

p. 17

[4] *Mikhail* (I. A. Isuv), *Roman* (K. M. Yermolayev) and *Yuri* (P. A. Bronstein)—Menshevik-liquidators, candidate members of the Central Committee of the R.S.D.L.P., elected at the Fifth (London) Congress of the Russian Social-Democratic Labour Party.

p. 17

[5] *Vperyod* (*Forward*) group—an anti-Party group of otzovists, ultimatumists, god-builders (see Note 56), and empirio-monists (supporters of the reactionary, idealistic philosophy of Mach and Avenarius). The group was formed in December 1909 on the initiative of A. Bogdanov and G. Alexinsky. It had its own organ called *Vperyod*. In 1912 the *Vperyod* group, together with the Menshevik-liquidators, united in a general anti-Party bloc (the August bloc) organised by Trotsky against the Bolsheviks.

Since it had no support among the workers the group actually began to disintegrate as early as 1913, and its final, formal dissolution took place in 1917, after the February Revolution.   p. 17

[6] *Central Organ of the R.S.D.L.P.—Sotsial-Demokrat (The Social-Democrat)*—an illegal newspaper published from February 1908 to January 1917; in all there were 58 issues. The first number was published in Russia, later it was published abroad, first in Paris, then in Geneva. In accordance with the decision of the Central Committee of the R.S.D.L.P., the Editorial Board of the Central Organ was made up of representatives of the Bolsheviks, Mensheviks, and Polish Social-Democrats. More than 80 articles and notes by Lenin appeared in *Sotsial-Demokrat*. Within the Editorial Board Lenin campaigned for a consistent Bolshevik

line. Some of the editors (Kamenev and Zinovyev) adopted a conciliatory attitude towards the liquidators, and tried to prevent the implementation of the Leninist line. The Menshevik members, Martov and Dan, sabotaged the work of the Editorial Board of the paper and at the same time openly defended liquidationism in *Golos Sotsial-Demokrata*. Lenin's uncompromising struggle against the liquidators led to Martov and Dan leaving the Editorial Board of *Sotsial-Demokrat* in June 1911. From December 1911 it was edited by Lenin.   p. 18

⁷ *Liquidationism*—an opportunist trend that spread among the Menshevik Social-Democrats after the defeat of the 1905-07 Revolution.

The liquidators demanded the dissolution of the illegal party of the working class. Summoning the workers to give up the struggle against tsarism, they intended calling a non-Party "labour congress" to establish an opportunist "broad" labour party which, abandoning revolutionary slogans, would engage only in the legal activity permitted by the tsarist government. Lenin and other Bolsheviks ceaselessly exposed this betrayal of the revolution by the liquidators. The policy of the liquidators was not supported by the workers. The Prague Conference of the R.S.D.L.P. which took place in January 1912 expelled them from the Party.

Otzovism (from the Russian word *otozvat*—to recall)—an opportunist trend represented by a small section of the Bolsheviks which arose after the defeat of the 1905-07 Revolution.

The otzovists demanded the recall of the Social-Democratic deputies from the State Duma, and the rejection of work in the trade unions and other mass legal and semi-legal organisations. Under cover of "revolutionary" phrases, the otzovists would actually have deprived the Party of the possibility of employing legal methods of struggle, isolated it from the workers and placed it in danger of attacks by the reactionary forces. Lenin sharply criticised the otzovists and called them "liquidators of a new type" and "Mensheviks turned inside-out".   p. 18

⁸ Lenin is referring to the conditions ("agreement") of the Bolsheviks which were signed and made known at the "Unity" Plenary Meeting of the Central Committee of the R.S.D.L.P. in January 1910 (see pp. 365-67 of this volume).   p. 18

⁹ *Igor* (Igorev, Gorev)—the Menshevik-liquidator B. I. Goldman.
                                                              p. 18

¹⁰ *The Central Committee Bureau Abroad* was set up by the Plenary Meeting of the C.C., R.S.D.L.P. in August 1908 as a general Party representative body abroad, subordinate and responsible to the Russian Collegium of the C.C. Shortly after the January Plenary Meeting of the C.C. in 1910, the liquidators were in the majority, and the Bureau Abroad became the centre of the anti-Party forces. Its liquidationist tactics compelled the Leninist

Bolsheviks to recall their representative Alexandrov (N. A. Semashko) in May 1911. Some time later the Polish and Latvian Social-Democrat representatives were also recalled. In January 1912 the Bureau Abroad was disbanded.   p. 18

[11] This refers to the representatives of the Polish Social-Democrats in the Central Committee Bureau Abroad.

The Social-Democratic Party of the Kingdom of Poland and Lithuania—a revolutionary party of the Polish working class, arose in 1893, first as the Social-Democratic Party of the Kingdom of Poland, and from August 1900, after the Congress of the Social-Democratic organisations of the Kingdom of Poland and Lithuania at which the Polish and part of the Lithuanian Social-Democratic parties merged, it began to call itself the Social-Democratic Party of the Kingdom of Poland and Lithuania (S.D.P.P. & L.). Its merit was in guiding the Polish working class towards unity with the Russian working-class movement and in fighting against nationalism.

During the 1905-07 Revolution, the S.D.P.P. & L. conducted its struggle under slogans very similar to those of the Bolshevik Party, and adopted an uncompromising attitude towards the liberal bourgeoisie. At the same time the S.D.P.P. & L. committed a number of errors; it did not understand Lenin's theory of socialist revolution, did not appreciate the leading role of the Party in the democratic revolution, underestimated the role of the peasantry as an ally of the working class, and the significance of the national-liberation movement. Lenin criticised the mistaken views of the S.D.P.P. & L. but at the same time drew attention to its services to the revolutionary movement in Poland. He noted that the Polish Social-Democrats "for the first time formed a purely proletarian party in Poland, and proclaimed the vitally important principle of the closest alliance between Polish and Russian workers in their class struggle" (see present edition, Vol. 20, "The Right of Nations to Self-Determination"). At the Fourth (Unity) Congress of the R.S.D.L.P. in 1906 the S.D.P.P. & L. was accepted into the R.S.D.L.P. as a territorial organisation.

The S.D.P.P. & L. welcomed the Great October Socialist Revolution and launched a struggle for the victory of the proletarian revolution in Poland. In December 1918, at the Unity Congress of the S.D.P.P. & L. and the Left wing of the P.P.S., these parties united and formed the Communist Workers' Party of Poland.
                                                                    p. 19

[12] This refers to the representatives of the Social-Democratic Party of the Latvian Region and the Bund.

The Social-Democratic Party of the Latvian Region (until 1906 the Latvian Social-Democratic Workers' Party) was formed in June 1904 at the First Congress of the Party, and its programme was adopted at its Second Congress in June 1905. In 1905-07 the Latvian Social-Democratic Workers' Party (L.S.D.W.P.) led the revolutionary action of the workers. Lenin pointed out that "during the Revolution the Latvian proletariat and Latvian Social-

Democratic Party occupied one of the first and most important places in the struggle against the autocracy and all the forces of the old order" (see present edition, Vol. 16, "The Jubilee Number of *Zihna*").

The L.S.D.W.P. joined the R.S.D.L.P. at the Fourth (Unity) Congress as a territorial organisation and became known as the Social-Democratic Party of the Latvian Region.

The Bund—the General Jewish Workers' Union of Lithuania, Poland, and Russia, was organised in 1897 at an inaugural Congress of Jewish Social Democratic groups in Wilno; it united in the main the semi-proletarian elements, Jewish artisans, in the Western regions of Russia. At the First Congress of the R.S.D.L.P. (1898) the Bund joined it "as an autonomous organisation, independent only in regard to questions specially concerning the Jewish proletariat".

The Bund was the vehicle of nationalism and separatism in the Russian working-class movement. The Fourth Congress of the Bund, held in April 1901, voted to change the organisational relations with the R.S.D.L.P. which had been established by the First Congress of the R.S.D.L.P. In its resolution the Congress stated that it regarded the R.S.D.L.P. as a federated association of national organisations which the Bund joins as a federal unit.

After the Second Congress of the R.S.D.L.P. had rejected its demand to be recognised as the sole representative of the Jewish proletariat, the Bund left the Party. It rejoined in 1906 on the basis of a decision of the Fourth (Unity) Congress of the R.S.D.L.P.

Within the R.S.D.L.P. the Bundists constantly supported the opportunist wing (Economists, Mensheviks, liquidators) and waged a struggle against the Bolsheviks and Bolshevism. They opposed the Bolshevik programmatic demand for the right of nations to self-determination and called for national cultural autonomy. During the years of Stolypin reaction the Bund adopted a liquidationist position and played an active part in forming the anti-Party August bloc. During the First World War, the Bundists took a social-chauvinistic stand. In 1917 the Bund supported the bourgeois Provisional Government, and fought on the side of the enemies of the October Socialist Revolution. During the years of foreign military intervention and civil war, the Bund leadership joined the forces of counter-revolution. At the same time there was evidence of a change among the rank-and-file members of the Bund in favour of co-operation with Soviet power. In March 1921 the Bund dissolved itself, and part of its members were accepted into the Russian Communist Party (Bolsheviks) on the conditions as laid down in the Rules.   p. 19

[13] This refers to the pro-Party Mensheviks who, led by G. V. Plekhanov, opposed the liquidators during the years of reaction. In December 1908, Plekhanov left the Editorial Board of the liquidationist newspaper *Golos Sotsial-Demokrata* and in 1909 resumed publication of *The Diary of a Social-Democrat* in order to struggle against the liquidators. While maintaining a Menshevik position, Ple-

khanov's group stood at the same time for the preservation and strengthening of the illegal Party organisation, and with this aim in view supported a bloc with the Bolsheviks. In 1909 groups of pro-Party Mensheviks were formed in Paris, Geneva, San Remo, Nice and other towns. In St. Petersburg, Moscow, Ekaterinoslav, Kharkov, Kiev, and Baku, many pro-Party Mensheviks opposed the liquidators and supported the revival of the illegal R.S.D.L.P.

Lenin, calling on the Bolsheviks to draw closer to the pro-Party Mensheviks, showed that agreement with them was possible on the basis of a struggle for the Party, against liquidationism, "without any ideological compromises, without any glossing over of tactical and other differences of opinion within the *limits* of the Party line" (see present edition, Vol. 16, "Methods of the Liquidators and Party Tasks of the Bolsheviks"). The pro-Party Mensheviks and the Bolsheviks worked together in the local Party committees, contributed to the Bolshevik publications *Rabochaya Gazeta*, *Zvezda*, and the Central Organ of the Party, *Sotsial-Demokrat*. Lenin's tactics of collaboration with Plekhanov's group, which was supported by the majority of the worker Mensheviks in Russia, assisted the extension of Bolshevik influence in the legal workers' organisations, and the ousting of the liquidators from them.

At the end of 1911 Plekhanov dissolved the bloc with the Bolsheviks. Under the guise of struggle against "factionalism" and against the split in the R.S.D.L.P. he tried to reconcile the Bolsheviks and the opportunists. In 1912, Plekhanov's group, together with the Trotskyites, Bundists and liquidators, opposed the decisions of the Prague Conference of the R.S.D.L.P.   p. 19

[14] *Rabochaya Gazeta* (*Workers' Gazette*)—the popular organ of the Bolsheviks, to which the pro-Party Mensheviks also contributed, published in Paris from October 30 (November 12), 1910, to July 30 (August 12), 1912. In all, nine issues appeared. Lenin was the founder and leading editor of *Rabochaya Gazeta*, and it published about a dozen of his articles.

The Prague Conference of the R.S.D.L.P. (January 1912) noted that *Rabochaya Gazeta* was a determined and consistent defender of the Party and Party principles and pronounced it the official organ of the Central Committee of the R.S.D.L.P. (Bolsheviks).
                                                              p. 19

[15] *Factional school abroad*—the factional centre of the otzovists, ultimatumists and god-builders, who united for struggle against the Bolsheviks. It was organised in 1909 by A. Bogdanov (Maximov), G. Alexinsky and A. Lunacharsky on the Isle of Capri with the participation of Maxim Gorky. Using the Party as a screen Bogdanov's supporters persuaded a number of local Social-Democratic organisations to send thirteen students to the school, which lasted nearly four months (August-December 1909). A split took place amongst the students in November and a group headed by the worker N. Y. Vilonov definitely dissociated themselves from Bogdanov's group. The Leninist students sent a protest to the Editorial Board of the newspaper *Proletary* against the anti-Party behav-

iour of the lecturers and, as a result, were expelled from the school. At the end of November 1909 at Lenin's invitation they went to Paris and attended a course of lectures including his lectures on "The Present Situation and Our Tasks" and the "Agrarian Policy of Stolypin". Those students who remained at Capri together with the lecturers formed the anti-Party *Vperyod* group in December 1909.

A meeting of the enlarged Editorial Board of *Proletary* condemned the Capri school as a "new centre of the faction breaking away from the Bolsheviks". p. 19

[16] Lenin is referring to the joint work of the Bolsheviks with G. V. Plekhanov in the R.S.D.L.P. delegation to the International Socialist Congress in Copenhagen which was held from August 28 to September 3 (N. S.), 1910. During the Congress, V. I. Lenin and G. V. Plekhanov sent a protest to the Executive Committee of the German Social-Democratic Party against the publication, in *Vorwärts*, the central organ of German Social-Democrats, of an anonymous, scurrilous article by Trotsky on the internal situation in the Russian Social-Democratic Party. p. 20

[17] *Pravda* (Vienna)—a Menshevik-liquidator newspaper, Trotsky's factional organ, published during 1908-12 in Vienna. Posing as "non-factional", the newspaper adopted a liquidationist position on all basic questions, and also supported the otzovists and ultimatumists. In 1912 Trotsky with the help of his paper organised the anti-Party August bloc. p. 20

[18] *The letter of the sixteen*—an open letter of the Menshevik-liquidators, their reply to G. V. Plekhanov's statement in No. 9 of *The Diary of a Social-Democrat* (August 1909) against the liquidators and their leader, A. N. Potresov.

Lenin called the letter of the sixteen a "document, which ... will have the ill-fame attaching to the name of Herostratus" (see the article *"Golos* (Voice) of the Liquidators Against the Party" in the present edition, Vol. 16). p. 24

[19] *Vekhi* group—contributors to a Cadet symposium entitled *Vekhi* (*Landmarks*), published in Moscow in the spring of 1909, containing articles by N. Berdyaev, S. Bulgakov, P. Struve, M. Herschensohn, and other representatives of the counter-revolutionary liberal bourgeoisie. In articles on the Russian intelligentsia these writers tried to discredit the revolutionary-democratic traditions of the best representatives of the Russian people, including V. G. Belinsky and N. G. Chernyshevsky. They vilified the revolutionary movement of 1905, and thanked the tsarist government for having "with its bayonets and jails" saved the bourgeoisie from "the fury of the people". They urged the intelligentsia to serve the autocracy. Lenin compared the philosophy and politics of *Vekhi* with that of the Black-Hundred newspaper *Moskovskiye Vedomosti* (*Moscow Recorder*), and called the symposium an *"encyclopaedia of liberal renegacy"*, "nothing but a flood of reactionary mud poured on democracy". p. 25

[20] *Black Hundreds*—monarchist bands, set up by the tsarist police to fight the revolutionary movement. They murdered revolutionaries, assaulted progressive intellectuals, and organised anti-Jewish pogroms. p. 25

[21] *Rossiya (Russia)*—a daily newspaper of a reactionary Black-Hundred type published in St. Petersburg from November 1905 to April 1914. From 1906 it was the organ of the Ministry of the Interior. The newspaper was subsidised from the secret government fund put at the disposal of the Ministry of the Interior. Lenin called *Rossiya* a "venal police newspaper". p. 25

[22] *Cadets*—members of the Constitutional-Democratic Party, the leading party of the liberal-monarchist bourgeoisie in Russia. Founded in October 1905, its membership was made up of representatives of the bourgeoisie, Zemstvo leaders of the landowning class, and bourgeois intellectuals. Its leading members were: P. N. Milyukov, S. A. Muromtsev, V. A. Maklakov, A. I. Shingaryov, P. B. Struve, F. I. Rodichev, and others. In order to hoodwink the working people, the Cadets hypocritically called themselves "the party of people's freedom", while in actual fact they did not go beyond the demand for a constitutional monarchy. They considered a struggle against the revolutionary movement to be their primary task; they hoped to share power with the tsar and the feudal landlords. During the First World War they actively supported the tsarist government's predatory foreign policy, and did their best to save the monarchy during the bourgeois-democratic revolution of February 1917. Holding leading posts in the bourgeois Provisional Government they carried out a counter-revolutionary policy opposed to the interests of the people, but approved by U.S., British and French imperialists. After the victory of the Great October Socialist Revolution the Cadets became irreconcilable enemies of Soviet power and actively participated in all armed counter-revolutionary acts and campaigns of the interventionists. They continued their anti-Soviet counter-revolutionary activities when they fled abroad after the rout of the interventionists and whiteguards. p. 36

[23] *Rech (Speech)*—a daily newspaper, the central organ of the Cadet Party, published in St. Petersburg from February 1906. It was closed down by the Military Revolutionary Committee of the Petrograd Soviet on October 26 (November 8), 1917. p. 36

[24] *Zvezda (The Star)*, in which this article appeared, was a Bolshevik legal newspaper, the forerunner of *Pravda*, published in St. Petersburg from December 16 (29), 1910 to April 22 (May 5), 1912 (at first weekly, then from January 1912 twice and from March, three times a week). On February 26 (March 10), 1912, No. 1 of *Nevskaya Zvezda (Neva Star)* was published at the same time as *Zvezda*, and, after the latter was closed down, continued its work. The last, the 27th issue of *Nevskaya Zvezda* was published on October 5(18), 1912.

Contributors to *Zvezda* were N. N. Baturin, K. S. Yeremeyev, N. G. Poletayev, M. S. Olminsky, and others, including Maxim Gorky, whom Lenin enlisted as a contributor. The pro-Party Mensheviks (Plekhanov's group) contributed to *Zvezda* until the autumn of 1911. Lenin gave the paper ideological leadership from abroad, and together *Zvezda* and *Nevskaya Zvezda* published nearly fifty of his articles.

Under Lenin's guidance the legal newspaper *Zvezda* became the militant paper of the Bolsheviks which defended the programme of the illegal Party. *Zvezda* established workers' correspondence on a broad scale, maintaining strong and regular contact with the workers. Some of its issues achieved a circulation of 50,000-60,000 copies.

The newspaper was the constant target of government repression; out of 96 issues of *Zvezda* and *Nevskaya Zvezda*, 39 were confiscated and 10 were subject to fines. *Zvezda* paved the way for the publication of the daily Bolshevik newspaper *Pravda* and on the very day it was closed down by the government the first issue of *Pravda* appeared.   p. 39

[25] The "diehards" was the name given by Russian political literature to the extreme Right-wing representatives of the reactionary landlord class.   p. 41

[26] *Nasha Zarya (Our Dawn)*—a legal journal published monthly by the Menshevik-liquidators in St. Petersburg from 1910 to 1914. It became the rallying centre of the liquidators in Russia.   p. 45

[27] *Vorwärts (Forward)*—the central organ of German Social-Democrats which began publication in 1876. Wilhelm Liebknecht was one of its editors. Frederick Engels waged a struggle in its columns against all opportunist manifestations. In the mid-nineties, after the death of Engels, *Vorwärts* regularly published articles by the opportunists who dominated German Social-Democracy and the Second International.   p. 45

[28] The *School Commission* (or *School Committee*) was appointed by the January Plenary Meeting of the C.C. of the R.S.D.L.P., 1910, to organise a Party school abroad. It was composed of nine people: two Bolsheviks, two Mensheviks, two members of the *Vperyod* group and one representative from each of the national organisations—the Bund and the Latvian and Polish Social-Democratic organisations.   p. 45

[29] *Socialist-Revolutionary Party*—a petty-bourgeois party in Russia, which arose at the end of 1901 and beginning of 1902 as a result of the union of various Narodnik groups and circles. The newspaper *Revolutsionnaya Rossiya (Revolutionary Russia)* (1900-05) and the magazine *Vestnik Russkoi Revolutsii (Herald of the Russian Revolution)* (1901-05) became its official organs. The Socialist-Revolutionaries did not recognise the class differences between the proletariat and petty proprietors, glossed over the class differentiation

and contradictions within the peasantry and rejected the leading role of the proletariat in the revolution. The views of the Socialist-Revolutionaries were an eclectic mixture of the ideas of Narodism and revisionism, and they tried, as Lenin expressed it, to patch up "the rents in the Narodnik ideas with bits of fashionable opportunist 'criticism' of Marxism." (see present edition, Vol. 9, p. 310). The tactics of individual terrorism advocated by the Socialist-Revolutionaries as the main form of struggle against the autocracy, did great harm to the revolutionary movement and hampered the organisation of the masses for revolutionary struggle.

The agrarian programme of the Socialist-Revolutionaries envisaged the abolition of private ownership of the land and its transfer to the village communes on the basis of the "labour principle" and equalitarian land tenure (i.e., as much land to be given to each peasant household as it could farm without employing hired labour), and also the development of co-operatives. This programme, which the Socialist-Revolutionaries called the "socialisation of the land", in reality bore no resemblance whatsoever to socialism. In analysing the programme of the Socialist-Revolutionaries, Lenin showed that the preservation of commodity production and private farming on commonly-owned land does not eliminate the domination of capital, does not relieve the working peasants of exploitation and ruin. Co-operatives cannot be the means of salvation for the small peasants under capitalist conditions since they serve to enrich the village bourgeoisie. At the same time, Lenin pointed out that the demand for equalitarian land tenure, although not socialist, was of an historically progressive revolutionary-democratic character, inasmuch as it was directed against reactionary landed proprietorship.

The Bolshevik Party exposed the attempts of the Socialist-Revolutionaries to masquerade as socialists, carried out a determined struggle against the Socialist-Revolutionaries for influence over the peasantry, and showed the danger to the working-class movement of their tactics of individual terrorism. At the same time the Bolsheviks were prepared, on definite conditions, to enter into temporary agreements with the Socialist-Revolutionaries in the struggle against tsarism.

The fact that the peasantry is not a homogeneous class determined the political and ideological instability and organisational disunity of the Socialist-Revolutionaries and their constant waverings between the liberal bourgeoisie and the proletariat. As early as the first Russian revolution the Right wing of the Socialist-Revolutionary Party broke away and formed the legal Popular Socialist Party, whose outlook was close to that of the Cadets, and the Left wing formed the semi-anarchist league of Maximalists. During the Stolypin reaction the Socialist-Revolutionary Party experienced a complete ideological and organisational breakdown. The majority of its members adopted a social-chauvinist position during the First World War.

After the victory of the February bourgeois-democratic revolution in 1917, the Socialist-Revolutionaries together with the Mensheviks and Cadets were the mainstay of the counter-revolutionary bourgeois-landlord Provisional Government of which the Party leaders (Kerensky, Avksentyev, Chernov) were members. The Socialist-Revolutionaries refused to support the demands of the peasants for the abolition of landlordism, supporting its preservation, and the Socialist-Revolutionary ministers of the Provisional Government sent punitive detachments against those peasants who had seized the landlords' estates.

At the end of November 1917, Left-wing Socialist-Revolutionaries founded the independent party of Left Socialist-Revolutionaries. Striving to preserve their influence over the peasant masses, the Left Socialist-Revolutionaries formally recognised Soviet power and entered into an agreement with the Bolsheviks, but very soon began to struggle against Soviet power.

During the years of foreign military intervention and civil war, the Socialist-Revolutionaries engaged in counter-revolutionary subversive activities, actively supported the interventionists and the whiteguard elements, took part in counter-revolutionary plots, organised terrorist acts against leaders of the Soviet state and the Communist Party. After the civil war, the Socialist-Revolutionaries continued their hostile activities against the Soviet state both within the country and abroad among whiteguard émigrés. p. 46

[30] *L'Humanité*—a daily newspaper founded in 1904 by Jean Jaurès as the organ of the French Socialist Party. Soon after the split in the Socialist Party at the Tours Congress (December 1920) and the formation of the Communist Party, the paper became the latter's organ. It is now published in Paris as the central organ of the French Communist Party. p. 46

[31] *Narodnaya Volya* (People's Will)—the secret political organisation of Narodnik-terrorists, formed in August 1879 following the split in the Narodnik organisation *Zemlya i Volya* (*Land and Freedom*). *Narodnaya Volya* was headed by an Executive Committee which included A. I. Zhelyabov, A. A. Kvyatkovsky, A. D. Mikhailov, N. A. Morozov, Sophia Perovskaya, Vera Figner, M. F. Frolenko, and others. While still adhering to Narodnik utopian-socialist ideas, Narodnaya Volya took up the political struggle, regarding the overthrow of the autocracy and the achievement of political freedom as a major aim. Its programme envisaged a "permanent popular representative body" elected by universal suffrage, the proclamation of democratic liberties, the transfer of the land to the people, and measures to put the factories in the hands of the workers. "The Narodnaya Volya members," wrote Lenin, "made a step forward when they took up the political struggle, but they failed to connect it with socialism" (see present edition, Vol. 8, p. 72).

Narodnaya Volya fought heroically against the tsarist autocracy; guided by their erroneous theory of "active" heroes and a "passive" mass, they planned to remould society without the participation of the people, by their own efforts, through individual terrorism that would intimidate and disorganise the government. After the assassination of Alexander II on March 1, 1881, the government was able, by savage reprisals, death sentences, and acts of provocation, to crush it out of existence. Repeated attempts to revive the organisation during the eighties ended in failure. Thus, in 1886 a group in the Narodnaya Volya tradition was formed by A. I. Ulyanov (elder brother of Lenin) and P. Y. Shevyryov; but after an unsuccessful attempt to assassinate Alexander III in 1887, the group was uncovered and its active members executed.

While criticising Narodnaya Volya's erroneous utopian programme, Lenin expressed great respect for its members' selfless struggle against tsarism and valued highly the technique of its underground activities and strictly centralised organisation. p. 46

[32] *Vestnik Narodnoi Voli* (*Messenger of the People's Will*) was published in Geneva from 1883 to 1886, as the organ of the Narodnaya Volya Party. It was edited by P. L. Lavrov and L. A. Tikhomirov; in all there were five issues.   p. 46

[33] *Birzheviye Vedomosti* or *Birzhevka* (*Stock-Exchange Recorder*)— a daily bourgeois newspaper published in St. Petersburg from 1880. The name *Birzhevka* was commonly used to indicate the lack of principle and corruption of the bourgeois press. The newspaper was closed down at the end of October 1917.   p. 46

[34] *Narodniks*—followers of a petty-bourgeois trend, Narodism, in the Russian revolutionary movement, which arose in the sixties and seventies of the nineteenth century. The Narodniks stood for the abolition of the autocracy and the transfer of the landlords' lands to the peasantry. At the same time, they believed capitalism in Russia to be a temporary phenomenon with no prospect of development and they therefore considered the peasantry, not the proletariat, to be the main revolutionary force in Russia. They regarded the village commune as the embryo of socialism. With the object of rousing the peasantry to struggle against the autocracy, the Narodniks "went among the people", to the village, but found no support there.

In the eighties and nineties the Narodniks adopted a policy of conciliation to tsarism, expressed the interests of the kulak class, and waged a bitter fight against Marxism.   p. 50

[35] Here and elsewhere, in this article, Lenin refers to *The Communist Manifesto* (see Marx and Engels, *Selected Works*, Vol. I, Moscow, 1958, pp. 21-64).   p. 52

[36] This article was published in No. 3 of *Sovremennaya Zhizn* (*Contemporary Life*), a Bolshevik legal weekly socio-political magazine published in Baku from March 26 (April 8) to April 22 (May 5), 1911, under the editorship of S. G. Shahumyan. Three issues ap-

peared, but after the confiscation of the third issue, the magazine
was closed down by the government.   p. 54

[37] *Vozrozhdeniye (Regeneration)*—a legal Menshevik-liquidator magazine, published in Moscow from December 1908 to July 1910;
it was replaced by the magazines *Zhizn (Life)* in 1910 and *Dyelo
Zhizni (Life's Cause)* in 1911.   p. 55

[38] *Dyelo Zhizni (Life's Cause)*—a legal magazine of the Menshevik-
liquidators, published in St. Petersburg from January to October
1911.   p. 57

[39] This refers to the thesis of Eduard Bernstein, an outspoken expo-
nent of revisionist ideas, founder of Bernsteinism, the anti-Marxist,
opportunist trend in international Social-Democracy, which arose
at the end of the nineteenth century in Germany.   p. 57

[40] The reference is to the thesis of the Economists developed in their
programme *Credo*, written in 1899 by Y. D. Kuskova.
     Economism was an opportunist trend in Russian Social-Democ-
racy at the turn of the century, a Russian variety of international opportunism. The newspaper *Rabochaya Mysl (Workers'
Thought)* (1897-1902) and the magazine *Rabocheye Dyelo (The
Workers' Cause)* (1899-1902) were organs of the Economists.
     The Economists limited the tasks of the working-class move-
ment to the economic struggle for higher wages, better working
conditions, etc., asserting that the political struggle was the affair
of the liberal bourgeoisie. They denied the leading role of the
party of the working class, considering that it should merely
observe the spontaneous development of the movement and record
events. Deferring to the "spontaneity" of the working-class movement, they belittled the importance of revolutionary theory and
class-consciousness, and claimed that socialist ideology could
develop from the spontaneous working-class movement; they
denied the necessity for bringing socialist consciousness into the
working-class movement from without, by the Marxist party, and
thus, they actually cleared the way for bourgeois ideology. They
championed the existing scattered, isolated study circles with their
parochial amateurish approach, encouraged disunity in the Social-
Democratic ranks, and opposed the creation of a centralised working-class party. Economism threatened to turn the working class
away from the path of class, revolutionary struggle, and to convert it into a political appendage of the bourgeoisie.
     Comprehensive criticisms by Lenin of the Economist standpoint
are to be found in a number of his articles. They include "A Protest by Russian Social-Democrats" (directed against the *Credo*;
written in 1899, while Lenin was in Siberian exile, and signed by
17 other exiled Marxists), "A Retrograde Trend in Russian Social-
Democracy", "Apropos of the *Profession de foi*" and "A Talk with
Defenders of Economism" (see present edition, Vol. 4, pp.167-82,
255-85, 286-96, and Vol. 5, pp. 313-20). Lenin's *What Is To Be Done?*

brought about the ideological rout of Economism (see present edition, Vol. 5, pp. 347-529). A major part in the struggle against
the Economists was also played by the newspaper *Iskra*.   p. 57

[41] *Lujo Brentano* (1844-1931)—the German bourgeois economist,
the author of a variety of bourgeois distortion of Marxism known
as Brentanoism. Brentáno advocated "social peace" in capitalist
society, the possibility of overcoming the social contradictions of
capitalism without resorting to the class struggle, maintaining
that the solution of the working-class problem lay in the organisation of reformist trade unions and the introduction of factory
legislation and that the interests of workers and capitalists could
be reconciled.

A theory analogous to that of Brentanoism was propounded in
Russia by the chief representative of "legal Marxism", P. B. Struve, in an attempt to use Marxism in the interests of the bourgeoisie. Lenin pointed out that "Struveism" takes "from Marxism all
that is acceptable to the liberal bourgeoisie" and rejects its "living
soul", its revolutionary nature. Struve was in complete agreement
with the vulgar political economy preached abroad, and ascribed
to capitalism aims which were foreign to it, namely the fullest
satisfaction of man's needs; he invited people to "learn from
capitalism", and openly advocated Malthusian ideas. According to Lenin, Struve was the "great master of renegacy, who,
starting with opportunism, with 'criticism of Marx', ended in
the ranks of counter-revolutionary bourgeois national-liberalism".

Among Struve's followers was the bourgeois publicist A. S. Izgoyev whom Lenin called, as he did Struve, a "hack writer for the
landlords and capitalists".   p. 57

[42] *Mayevsky*—the Menshevik V. A. Gutovsky.   p. 58

[43] Lenin is referring to Cherevanin's pamphlet *The London Congress
of the R.S.D.L.P. in 1907*, at the end of which the author criticised the decision of the Congress on the question of the labour
congress and non-Party workers' organisations from the liquidationist standpoint.   p. 58

[44] The article *"Those Who Would Liquidate Us"* appeared in the magazine *Mysl (Thought)*, a Bolshevik legal monthly philosophical
and socio-economic magazine published in Moscow from December
1910. The magazine was started and guided by Lenin from abroad,
in order to counter the journals of the liquidators and struggle
against them.

Lenin published six articles in the first four issues of *Mysl*,
including the major work *Strike Statistics in Russia*. Closely
connected with the work of the magazine were V.V. Vorovsky,
M. S. Olminsky, I. I. Skvortsov-Stepanov; G. V. Plekhanov and
other pro-Party Mensheviks also collaborated. The magazine was
published until April 1911. In all, five issues appeared, the last
being confiscated.   p. 60

[45] *Osvobozhdeniye (Emancipation)*—a fortnightly bourgeois-liberal magazine, published abroad from 1902 to 1905 under the editorship of P. B. Struve. From January 1904 it became the organ of the liberal-monarchist *Osvobozhdeniye* League. Later, the *Osvobozhdeniye* group made up the core of the Cadet Party, the chief bourgeois party in Russia.   p. 61

[46] Lenin refers to his article *"The Victory of the Cadets and the Tasks of the Workers' Party"*, written in March 1906, and published as a pamphlet in April of that year (see present edition, Vol 10, pp. 199-276).   p. 62

[47] *Octobrists*—members of the Union of October Seventeenth, founded in November 1905, as a counter-revolutionary party representing the big industrial and commercial capitalists and the landlords who farmed their land on capitalist lines. The Octobrists claimed to accept the Manifesto of October 17, but fully supported the domestic and foreign policy of the tsarist government. The leaders of the Octobrists were K. Guchkov, a big industrialist, and M. Rodzyanko, who owned huge landed estates.   p. 62

[48] *The law of November 9 (22), 1906* on "Additions to Certain Regulations of the Existing Law on Peasant Land Ownership and Land Tenure", and the law of June 14 (27), 1910 on "Amendments and Addenda to Certain Regulations on Peasant Land Ownership" defined the regulations for the withdrawal of the peasants from the village communes, and for obtaining the title to their allotments.
                                                      p. 66

[49] *Platform of the 104*—the Land Reform Bill of the Trudovik deputies to the First and Second Dumas was based on Narodnik principles of equalitarian land tenure: the creation of a national fund from state, crown and monastery lands, and also privately-owned lands if the estates exceeded the established "labour standard" (i.e., the amount of land that can be tilled by a peasant family without the help of hired labour). Provision was also made for compensation in respect of alienated land. The implementation of the land reform was to be the responsibility of local land committees. (For information on the Platform of the 104 see present edition, Vol. 12, pp. 201-03 and Vol. 13, pp. 267-72.)   p. 66

[50] *Trudoviks* (Trudovik group)—a group of petty-bourgeois democrats in the Dumas composed of peasants and intellectuals with Narodnik leanings. The Trudovik group was formed in April 1906 from peasant deputies to the First Duma.
    The Trudoviks demanded the abolition of all social-estate and national restrictions, the democratisation of urban and rural local government, and universal suffrage in elections to the State Duma. Their agrarian programme was that outlined in Note 49. Owing to the class nature of the small landowning peasantry the Trudo-

viks in the State Duma wavered between the Cadets and the Social-Democrats. Since the Trudoviks to some extent represented
the peasantry, the Bolsheviks in the Duma collaborated with them
on certain questions relating to the general struggle against tsarism
and against the Cadets. In 1917 the Trudovik group merged with
the Popular Socialist Party and actively supported the bourgeois
Provisional Government. After the October Socialist Revolution
the Trudoviks supported the bourgeois counter-revolution.   p. 67

⁵¹ *Zhizn (Life)*—a magazine published in Moscow by the Menshevik-
liquidators. There were two issues, in August and September 1910.
                                                                p. 71

⁵² *Russkaya Mysl (Russian Thought)*—a monthly magazine of the
liberal bourgeoisie published in Moscow from 1880. After the 1905
Revolution it became the organ of the Right wing of the Cadet
Party. During the period of its existence Lenin called it "Black-
Hundred Thought". The magazine was closed down in the middle
of 1918.   p. 71

⁵³ Lenin quotes N. A. Nekrasov's lyrical comedy *The Bear Hunt*.
                                                                p. 72

⁵⁴ Lenin quotes the words of Bazarov from Turgenev's *Fathers and
Sons*.   p. 72

⁵⁵ *N. Beltov*—G. V. Plekhanov's pseudonym under which his book
The Development of the Monist View of History was published in
1895.   p. 74

⁵⁶ *God-builders*—a religious-philosophical trend hostile to Marxism,
which arose during the period of Stolypin reaction among a section
of the Party intellectuals who had broken with Marxism after the
defeat of the 1905-07 Revolution. The "god-builders" (A. V. Lunacharsky, V. Bazarov, and others) advocated the creation of a new
"socialist" religion, attempting to reconcile Marxism with religion.
At one time Maxim Gorky was associated with them.
    A meeting of the enlarged Editorial Board of *Proletary*, held
on June 8-17 (21-30), 1909, condemned the "god-building" trend
and in a special resolution declared that the Bolshevik faction had
nothing in common with such distortion of scientific socialism.
    The reactionary character of god-building was exposed by Lenin
in his *Materialism and Empirio-Criticism*, and in letters to Gorky
during February-April 1908 and November-December 1913. p. 77

⁵⁷ *The Social Movement in Russia at the Beginning of the Twentieth
Century*—a five-volume Menshevik publication (four volumes were
published) under the editorship of L. Martov, P. Maslov, A. N.
Potresov. Plekhanov, who was a member of the original editorial
board, left it at the end of 1908 because he disagreed with the
inclusion of a liquidationist article by A. N. Potresov in the first
volume.   p. 78

58 *Russkiye Vedomosti (Russian Recorder)*—a daily newspaper published in Moscow from 1863 by liberal professors of the Moscow University and Zemstvo personalities; it expressed the views of the liberal landlords and bourgeoisie. From 1905 it was an organ of the Right Cadets, and was closed down after the 1917 October Revolution. p. 82

59 *Progressists*—chiefly representatives of the urban petty bourgeoisie, and to some extent of the peasantry, who stood for election to the Second and Third Dumas. p. 83

60 *Council of the United Nobility*—a counter-revolutionary landlord organisation formed in May 1906, which exercised great influence on government policy. During the period of the Third State Duma a considerable number of its members were in the Council of State and leading centres of the Black-Hundred organisations. p. 85

61 *"Kolupayev"* capitalism. Kolupayev is the name of a kulak in M. Y. Saltykov-Shchedrin's *The Mon Repos Retreat*. Lenin described this type of capitalism in "The Agrarian Programme of Social-Democracy in the First Russian Revolution, 1905-07" (see present edition, Vol. 13, p. 422). p. 86

62 *Tolmachov, I. N.*—Governor of Odessa, an extreme reactionary. p. 86

63 *Zemstvos*—local government bodies introduced in the central gubernias of tsarist Russia in 1864. Nobility played the leading part in them. Their functions were limited to purely local economic problems (hospitals and road-building, statistics, insurance, etc.). Their activities were controlled by the gubernia governors and the Minister of the Interior, who could overrule any of their decisions disapproved by the government. p. 87

64 The war between Russia and the coalition of England, France, Turkey, and Sardinia in 1853-56. p. 88

65 *The Anti-Socialist Law (Exceptional Law Against the Socialists)* was promulgated in Germany in 1878. Under this law all organisations of the Social-Democratic Party and all workers' mass organisations were forbidden; the working-class press was proscribed and socialist literature forbidden; repressions against Social-Democrats began. The law was annulled in 1890 under pressure of the working-class movement. p. 93

66 *The "young"*—the petty-bourgeois semi-anarchist opposition in the German Social-Democratic Party; emerged in 1890. Its central group consisted of young writers and students (hence the name) who claimed the role of theoreticians and leaders in the party. This opposition did not understand the changes that took place

after the rescinding of the Anti-Socialist Law (1878-90) and denied the need for making use of legal forms of struggle; they opposed the participation of Social-Democrats in Parliament and accused the party of defending the interests of the petty bourgeoisie and of opportunism. Engels engaged in struggle against the "young".
p. 94

[67] *Gromoboi*—contributor to *Golos Moskvy* (*Voice of Moscow*).
Izgoyev—a Cadet publicist, contributor to *Vekhi* (*Landmarks*) and *Rech* (*Speech*) collaborator.   p. 96

[68] The statement made by 66 representatives of Moscow commercial and industrial capital, was printed in *Russkiye Vedomosti*, No. 33, February 11 (24), 1911. While recognising the need to combat the students' strikes, the authors of the statement also condemned the government action on the grounds that its measures against the participants in student disturbances jeopardised the existence of the higher school.   p. 96

[69] *Golos Moskvy* (*Voice of Moscow*)—a daily newspaper, organ of the Octobrists, the counter-revolutionary party of the big industrial bourgeoisie and the landlords; published in Moscow from December 1906 to June 1915.   p. 97

[70] *Zemshchina* (*Land Affairs*)—a daily Black-Hundred newspaper, published in St. Petersburg from July 1909 to February 1917; organ of the extreme Right deputies to the State Duma. p. 100

[71] *Council of State*—one of the highest state bodies in tsarist Russia. Formed in 1810, according to M. M. Speransky's plan, as a legislative-consultative body whose members were appointed and confirmed by the tsar. It was a reactionary body which voted down even the most moderate bills adopted by the State Duma. p. 105

[72] *Meshkovsky* (I. P. Goldenberg)—member of the Central Committee of the R.S.D.L.P., a Bolshevik-conciliator.   p. 106

[73] *Innokenty* (Innokentiev, Inok)—I. F. Dubrovinsky, member of the Central Committee of the R.S.D.L.P., a Bolshevik; in 1910-11 he became a conciliator.   p. 107

[74] *Olgin*—V. P. Fomin, a pro-Party Menshevik.   p. 108

[75] Lenin's signature and those of two other members of the Central Committee follow.   p. 109

[76] *V. V.* (pseudonym of V. P. Vorontsov) and *N —on*, or *Nikolai —on* (pseudonym of N. F. Danielson)—ideologists of liberal Narodism in the 1880s and 1890s.   p. 110

[77] *Regulations of February 19, 1861*—the law abolishing serfdom in Russia.   p. 110

[78] *Novoye Vremya (New Times)*—a daily newspaper appearing in St. Petersburg from 1868 to October 1917. At first it was moderately liberal, but towards the end of the 1870s it became an organ of reactionary circles among the aristocracy and bureaucracy. It conducted a struggle, not only against the revolutionary, but also against the liberal-bourgeois movement. From 1905 it became an organ of the Black Hundreds. Lenin called *Novoye Vremya* a typical example of the venal press.   p. 115

[79] *Vestnik Yevropy (European Messenger)*—a monthly historico-political and literary magazine, of bourgeois-liberal trend, published in St. Petersburg from 1866 to 1918. The magazine printed articles directed against the revolutionary Marxists. Until 1908 its editor and publisher was M. M. Stasyulevich.   p. 119

[30] The *village* (land) *commune* (Russ. *obshchina* or *mir*)—the communal form of peasant use of the land characterised by compulsory crop rotation and undivided woods and pastures. Its principal features were collective liability (the compulsory collective responsibility of the peasants for timely and full payments, and the fulfilment of all kinds of services to the state and the landlords) and the periodical redistribution of the land, with no right to refuse the allotment given. The sale of the allotment was also forbidden.

The landlords and the tsarist government used the village commune to intensify feudal oppression and to squeeze land redemption payments and taxes out of the people.   p. 123

[81] These are the words of Volgin, the hero of N.G. Chernyshevsky's novel *Prologue*.   p. 123

[82] This refers to *the government coup of June 3 (16), 1907*, reactionary coup, whereby the Second Duma was dissolved and the law on Duma elections changed. The new law greatly increased landlord and commercial-industrial bourgeois representation, and greatly reduced the already small representation of peasants and workers. A large proportion of the population of Asiatic Russia was denied electoral rights, and the representation from Poland and the Caucasus was reduced by half. The composition of the 1907 Third Duma was, therefore, representative of the Black Hundreds and Cadets.   p. 126

[83] *A. Moskovsky*—Menshevik G. I. Khundadze.   p. 131

[84] *The Bolshevik member of the C.C.* was I. F. Dubrovinsky who was arrested in June 1910 (see Note 73).   p. 132

[85] *Leaflet of the fifty-eight*—a leaflet published in Paris in 1911 under the title "To All Members of the Party from the Meeting of Mensheviks in Paris".   p. 133

[86] In March 1911 the Council of State turned down the Bill on the establishment of Zemstvos in the Western Gubernias, which had been introduced by the Chairman of the Council of Ministers, P. A. Stolypin.

As a result of this attitude, Stolypin handed in his resignation which Nicholas II refused to accept. Stolypin then succeeded in having the State Duma and the Council of State prorogued for three days (from March 12 to 14 [25 to 27]) and passed the law on Zemstvos in the Western Gubernias by invoking Article 87 which empowered the government to adopt laws by-passing the legislative organs when they were not functioning "if extraordinary circumstances make such action essential".

This invoking of Article 87 to by-pass the legislative organs led to the demonstrative resignation of A. I. Guchkov, Chairman of the State Duma, and the election of a new Chairman, the Right Octobrist M. V. Rodzyanko.   p. 134

[87] *Rennenkampf* and *Meller-Zakomelsky*—tsarist generals, notorious for their brutal punitive actions during the 1905-07 Revolution.

p. 142

[88] Lenin refers here to the first all-Russia temperance congress, held in St. Petersburg on December 28, 1909-January 6, 1910 (January 10-19, 1910), and the first all-Russia congress of factory doctors and representatives of industry, which took place in Moscow on April 1-6 (14-19), 1909.   p. 147

[89] Lenin is quoting from the speech of the Menshevik-liquidator Dan, at the Fifth (All-Russia) Conference of the R.S.D.L.P. in 1908, in the discussion on "The Present Moment and the Tasks of the Party".   p. 148

[90] The expression "third element" was first used by the Vice-Governor of Samara, V. G. Kondoidi, in his speech at the opening of the Samara Gubernia Zemstvo meeting in 1900, to describe persons representing neither the administration nor the social estates—employees of the Zemstvo, doctors, statisticians, teachers, agronomists, etc. The expression "third element" found its way into literature to describe the democratically-minded intellectuals of the Zemstvos.   p. 149

[91] *The dexterity of Burenin or Menshikov*—a dishonest method of conducting polemics, characteristic of Burenin and Menshikov, contributors to the Black-Hundred monarchist paper *Novoye Vremya* (*New Times*). Lenin used these names as synonyms for dishonest methods of controversy.   p. 151

[92] *Witte reforms*—reforms in the sphere of finance, customs policy, railroad construction, factory legislation, carried out by S. Y. Witte between 1892 and 1906, while Minister of Communications

and later Minister of Finance and Chairman of the Council of Ministers.

Reforms of the sixties—bourgeois reforms carried out by the tsarist government: the Peasant Reform (1861), financial reforms (1860-64), abolition of corporal punishment (1863), reforms in the sphere of public education (1862-64), Zemstvo reform (1864), legal reform (1864), reform of press and censorship (1865), municipal reform (1870), military reform (1874).   p. 154

[93] See Note 62.   p. 157

[94] *Blanquists*—supporters of a trend in the French socialist movement headed by the outstanding revolutionary and prominent representative of French utopian communism—Louis-Auguste Blanqui (1805-1881). The Blanquists expected "that mankind will be emancipated from wage slavery, not by the proletarian class struggle, but through a conspiracy hatched by a small minority of intellectuals" (see present edition, Vol. 10, p. 392). Substituting the actions of a small group of conspirators for those of a revolutionary party, they took no account of the real situation necessary for a victorious uprising and disregarded the question of ties with the masses.   p. 158

[95] *Rouanet, Gaston*—a French journalist, member of the Socialist Party; belonged to the Right wing of the Party.   p. 160

[96] *The Erfurt profession de foi*—programme of the German Social-Democratic Party adopted at the Erfurt Congress in 1891.   p. 161

[97] Lenin refers to the section of the resolution "The Present Moment and the Tasks of the Party" adopted at the Fifth All-Russia Conference of the R.S.D.L.P. in 1908, in which it was decided to combat liquidationism.   p. 161

[98] *Russkoye Bogatstvo (Russian Wealth)*—a monthly magazine published in St. Petersburg from 1876 to the middle of 1918. From the early 1890s it was the organ of the liberal Narodniks. From 1906 *Russkoye Bogatstvo* became factually the organ of the semi-Cadet Popular Socialist Party.   p. 166

[99] Engels frequently referred to the sectarian nature of British Social-Democracy in letters to F. A. Sorge (see, for example, Engels's letters to Sorge on June 10, 1891, on March 18, 1893, on May 21, 1894 and November 10, 1894; an English translation of the last letter is to be found in: Marx and Engels, *Selected Correspondence*, Moscow, p. 556).   p. 175

[100] This article was written following an article by N. A. Rozhkov "An Essential Beginning" sent to the editors of *Sotsial-Demokrat.*

In this article Rozhkov developed his liquidationist plan for the creation of a legal labour party under the Stolypin regime. Lenin attempted to convince Rozhkov of the incorrectness of his views. "... I earnestly implore you to delay, give up, think over, correspond..." he wrote to Rozhkov on February 23 (March 8), 1911 (*Lenin Miscellany XXV*, p. 66). When it became clear that Rozhkov insisted on the publication of this article, Lenin published his reply in *Diskussionny Listok* (*Discussion Bulletin*), No. 3, a supplement to *Sotsial-Demokrat*, on April 29 (May 12), under the above heading.   p. 179

101 After the defeat of the 1848-49 Revolution, whose main aim had been the reunification of Germany into a single democratic republic, reactionary Prussian Junkers led by Bismarck carried out a policy of uniting Germany "by blood and iron". Its aim was the formation of a single monarchist state with a Prussian king as monarch. The Prussian Junkers relied on the support of the big German bourgeoisie for the fulfilment of this "revolution from above".   p. 187

102 *Ivan Ivanovich* and *Ivan Nikiforovich*—characters in Gogol's *Tale of How Ivan Ivanovich Quarrelled with Ivan Nikiforovich*.   p. 192

103 *The Meeting of the C.C. members of the R.S.D.L.P. living abroad*, organised on Lenin's initiative, was held in Paris on May 28-June 4 (June 10-17), 1911.

The purpose of this Meeting was to work out measures for the calling of a plenary meeting of the C.C. of the R.S.D.L.P. and an all-Party conference at an early date. By this time, all the Bolshevik members of the Central Committee working in Russia had been arrested, and the Central Committee Bureau Abroad, which consisted of liquidators, refused to convene the plenary meeting abroad. Invitations to the Paris Meeting were sent on May 14 (27), 1911 by the Bolsheviks and representatives of the Polish Social-Democrats.

Three Bolsheviks, two representatives of the Polish and Lithuanian Social-Democrats, and one representative of the Latvian S.D.W.P. attended the Meeting. A Menshevik *Golos*-ist (who left the Meeting after the resolution on defining terms of reference had been adopted), and a representative of the Bund (who left the Meeting on the second day) were also present.

The agenda of the Meeting included the following items: (1) the convening of a plenary meeting of the C.C.; (2) the holding of a meeting on the forthcoming elections to the Fourth Duma; (3) the convening of a Party conference; (4) the Central Committee Bureau Abroad; (5) the organisation of a Technical Commission.

The Meeting adopted a resolution to convene a plenary meeting of the C.C. abroad; to set up an Organising Commission for calling an all-Russia conference and a Technical Commission Abroad (the T.C.A.) to cater to the needs of the Party press, to provide transport facilities, etc.

The Meeting condemned the anti-Party behaviour of the Central Committee Bureau Abroad and placed the question of its further existence before the Plenary Meeting. Notification about the Meeting was published in a separate leaflet which called on Party organisations to contact the Organising Commission, and to "immediately start practical work for the calling of the conference, which is the only means whereby the Party can be assisted to unite its ranks and prepare itself for the forthcoming struggle". The local Party organisations welcomed the decisions of the Meeting. By September 1 (14), 1911, nearly ten of the more important Party organisations had expressed their confidence in the C.C. Meeting abroad and had started the practical work of preparation for the conference.　　　　　　　　　　　　　　　　　　　　　　p. 195

[104] The manuscript had no heading. The heading has been provided by the Institute of Marxism-Leninism of the Central Committee of the C.P.S.U.　　　　　　　　　　　　　　　　　　p. 197

[105] *Yudin* (I. L. Eisenstadt), *Kostrov* (N. N. Zhordaniya)—members of the Central Committee of the R.S.D.L.P., Menshevik-liquidators.　　　　　　　　　　　　　　　　　　　　　　　　p. 197

[106] *Makar* (V. P. Nogin), *Lindov* (G. D. Leiteisen)—members of the C.C., R.S.D.L.P., Bolshevik-conciliators, arrested at the end of March 1911.　　　　　　　　　　　　　　　　　　p. 197

[107] *Katsap*—A. Polyakov.　　　　　　　　　　　　　　　p. 197

[108] For *the exposure by Olgin* (pro-Party Menshevik, V. P. Fomin) see p. 108 of this volume.　　　　　　　　　　　　p. 198

[109] *Pyotr* (N. V. Ramishvili)—member of the Central Committee of the R.S.D.L.P., one of the leaders of the Georgian Menshevik-liquidators.　　　　　　　　　　　　　　　　　　　p. 198

[110] The manuscript had no heading. The heading has been provided by the Institute of Marxism-Leninism of the Central Committee of the C.P.S.U.　　　　　　　　　　　　　　　　　　p. 205

[111] *The Bulygin Duma*—the "advisory representative assembly" which the tsarist government promised to convene in 1905. The Act for its convocation and the regulations governing the elections were drafted by a commission presided over by Minister of the Interior Bulygin, and published on August 6 (19), 1905. The Bolsheviks proclaimed an active boycott of the Bulygin Duma, and its convocation was prevented by the forces of the revolution.　p. 208

[112] The workers' delegates to the second all-Russia congress of factory doctors and representatives of industry were arrested on April 13 (26), 1911, on the eve of the congress.　　　　　　　p. 211

¹¹³ *The meeting of the Second Paris Group of the R.S.D.L.P.* took place on June 18 (July 1), 1911.   p. 216

¹¹⁴ *Lieber, Ber* (M. I. Goldman)—a liquidator, one of the leaders of the Bund.   p. 218

¹¹⁵ *Organising Commission* (Organising Commission Abroad, O.C.A.) was set up at the Meeting of members of the Central Committee, R.S.D.L.P. in June 1911 in order to prepare for a conference of the R.S.D.L.P. The O.C.A. consisted of Bolsheviks, conciliators and representatives of the Polish Social-Democrats. Other factions (pro-Party Mensheviks, *Vperyod* group, etc.) did not appoint any representatives to the O.C.A.

The O.C.A. issued a "Notification" about the June Meeting of the members of the Central Committee, and a leaflet "To All Social-Democratic Party Organisations, Groups and Circles" on the calling of a conference and also sent three representatives with full powers to Russia, including G. K. Orjonikidze, who were to carry out the preparatory work for the calling of the conference, and to set up the Russian Organising Commission.

From its inception, the conciliators, supported by the representatives of the Polish Social-Democrats, were in the majority in the O.C.A. In November 1911 it refused to submit to the decisions of the Russian Organising Commission, after which the Bolshevik members of the O.C.A. declined responsibility for its actions and withdrew from it. Subsequently, the conciliator majority of the O.C.A. openly campaigned against the Russian Organising Commission.

In his "Letter to the Editorial Board", published in December 1911 in No. 25 of *Sotsial-Demokrat*, G. K. Orjonikidze exposed the anti-Party activities of the O.C.A.   p. 220

¹¹⁶ The reference is to the legal Bolshevik newspaper *Zvezda* (see Note 24).   p. 220

¹¹⁷ *The Diary of a Social-Democrat* was published by G. V. Plekhanov, and issued irregularly in Geneva at long intervals from March 1905 to April 1912; 16 numbers appeared. Publication of *The Diary* was recommenced in 1916 in Petrograd but only one number appeared.   p. 221

¹¹⁸ *The Fifth* (London) *Congress of the R.S.D.L.P.* (April 30-May 19 [May 13-June 1], 1907) in its resolution on "Attitude to Non-proletarian Parties" recognised that any united activity with the Narodnik parties must exclude any deviation from the programme and tactics of Social-Democracy, and should serve only the aims of a general attack both against reaction and the treacherous tactics of the liberal bourgeoisie.

The Third (Second All-Russia) *Conference of the R.S.D.L.P.* (July 21-23 [August 3-5], 1907) in a resolution on the question of participation in elections to the State Duma resolved that in the election campaign and in the Duma itself, Social-Democrats must spread and inculcate in the mass of the people the ideas of socialism and revolutionary slogans, and carry out a determined struggle both against reaction and the leadership of the Cadets in the liberation movement in general, and in the Duma in particular.

p. 224

[119] *Proletary*—an illegal newspaper founded by the Bolsheviks after the Fourth (Unity) Congress of the Party. Published from August 21 (September 3), 1906 to November 28 (December 11), 1909 under Lenin's editorship. The organ of the Moscow and St. Petersburg Party Committees, and for a time also of the Moscow District, Perm, Kursk and Kazan Committees, *Proletary* was actually the Bolshevik Central Organ. Altogether fifty issues appeared (the first twenty in Vyborg, Finland). From February 13 (26) to December 11 (14), 1908, *Proletary* was published in Geneva, and from January 8 (21) to November 28 (December 11), 1909, in Paris.

Proletary carried over one hundred articles and shorter items by Lenin. During the Stolypin reaction it played an outstanding part in preserving and strengthening the Bolshevik organisations.

p. 225

[120] *The Technical Commission* (the Technical Commission Abroad, T.C.A.) was set up at the Meeting of C.C. members in June 1911 to deal with technical matters (publishing, transport, etc.). It was an *ad hoc* Commission designed to function until the convening of the plenary meeting of the C.C., and subordinate to a group of C.C. members who took part in the Meeting of June 1911. It consisted of one representative each, from the Bolsheviks, conciliators, and Polish Social-Democrats respectively. The conciliators were in the majority and sabotaged the organisational work of the Bolsheviks; refused to abide by the decisions of the Russian Organising Commission and stopped allocating funds for the publication of the Party's Central Organ—*Sotsial-Demokrat*. They also attacked Lenin and the Bolsheviks in the press (publishing leaflets and the *Information Bulletin*).

M. F. Vladimirsky, the Bolshevik representative on the Commission, withdrew from it on October 19 (November 1), 1911, and the Bolsheviks severed all connections with it.

p. 226

[121] A letter "To the Party" from the Bolshevik V. K. Taratuta was written because of rumours spread in 1906 about his alleged provocative actions. The investigating committee appointed by the January Plenary Meeting of the Central Committee of the R.S.D.L.P. in 1910 went into this matter and unanimously decided that in view of the absence of any incriminating facts, the matter be considered closed and that Taratuta be reinstated with full Party rights.

p. 227

[22] *Mountain and Gironde*—the two political groups of the bourgeoisie during the French bourgeois revolution at the close of the eighteenth century. Montagnards (representatives of the Mountain), or Jacobins, was the name given to the more resolute represent-

atives of the bourgeoisie, the revolutionary class of the time; they stood for the abolition of the autocracy and the feudal system. The Girondists, as distinct from Jacobins, vacillated between revolution and counter-revolution, and their policy was one of compromise with the monarchy.

Lenin called the opportunist trend in Social-Democracy the "socialist Gironde" and the revolutionary Social-Democrats "proletarian Jacobins". After the R.S.D.L.P. split into Bolsheviks and Mensheviks, Lenin frequently stressed that the Mensheviks represented the Girondist trend in the working-class movement.   p. 230

[123] *Rural superintendent*—the administrative post introduced in 1889 by the tsarist government in order to increase the power of the landlords over the peasants. The rural superintendents were selected from among the local landed nobility, and were given enormous administrative and judicial powers over the peasantry including the right to have the peasants arrested and flogged. p. 231

[124] In this letter, published in *Sotsial-Democrat*, No. 23, September 1 (14), 1911, it was reported that a prominent St. Petersburg liquidator, addressing a meeting of worker members of the Party in Vyborg District, proposed that instead of reviving the Party organisation they should set up "organising groups" for legal educational work. This proposal was met with a unanimous rebuff, no one voting in its favour.   p. 242

[125] *Rabocheye Dyelo* (*Workers' Cause*)—a magazine of the Economists, organ of the Union of Russian Social-Democrats Abroad. It was published at irregular intervals in Geneva from 1899 to 1902. Lenin criticised the views expressed by the *Rabocheye Dyelo* group in a number of articles published in *Iskra* and in his book *What Is To Be Done?*   p. 243

[126] *Rabochaya Mysl* (*Workers' Thought*)—the Economist newspaper published from 1897 to 1902. Lenin's criticisms of the views of *Rabochaya Mysl* as a Russian variety of international opportunism appeared in articles published in *Iskra* and in his book *What Is To Be Done?*   p. 243

[127] *Schwartz* (U. Elias)—a Latvian Social-Democrat, liquidator. p.244

[128] Lenin wrote this comment to the statement made by the commission appointed by the Meeting of Central Committee members in June 1911 to prepare for a plenary meeting of the Central Committee. The statement cited facts of sabotage on the part of the liquidators to prevent preparations for a plenary meeting of the Central Committee in Russia and abroad.   p. 245

[129] *Marshal of the Nobility*—the representative of the nobility of a gubernia or uyezd in tsarist Russia, elected by the local nobility for each uyezd and gubernia. The Marshal of the Nobility was in

charge of all the affairs of the nobility, held an influential post in the administration and took the chair at the Zemstvo meetings.
p. 248

[130] In the Manifesto of October 17, 1905, the tsar, terrified by the revolution, promised the people civil liberties and a constitution.
p. 250

[131] *The Party of Peaceful Renovation*—a party of big commercial and industrial capitalists and big landowners; it was formed in 1906 and united the Left Octobrists and the Right Cadets.
p. 250

[132] The *Information Bulletin* of the Technical Commission Abroad was published in Paris, two issues appearing (in August and October 1911). The conciliators made it their factional organ, in which they conducted an unscrupulous struggle against Bolshevism.
p. 257

[133] This school was held in Capri, in 1909, and was the factional centre of the otzovists; it was organised by A. A. Bogdanov. See Note 15.
p. 260

[134] *Ionov* (F. M. Koigen)—one of the Bund leaders.
p. 261

[135] Lenin is referring to the resolution "On Liquidationism" adopted by the "Conference of Transcaucasian Social-Democratic Organisations", which was really a conference of Caucasian liquidators. The anti-Party nature of the "conference" was exposed in correspondence published in No. 24 of *Sotsial-Demokrat* of October 18 (31), 1911.
p. 268

[136] *Rabochaya Zhizn (Workers' Life)*—a monthly newspaper, organ of the Menshevik *Golos* group and the conciliators. It was published in Paris from February 21 (March 6) to April 18 (May 1), 1911. Three issues appeared.
p. 270

[137] *Hermann*—K. K. Danishevsky, *Arkady*—F. I. Kalinin. p. 273

[138] *Lyakhov, V. P.*—colonel in the tsarist army, was in command of the Russian troops that suppressed the revolutionary movement in Persia in 1908.
p. 281

[139] *Monk Illiodor* (S. M. Trufanov, born 1889)—one of the leaders of the Black Hundreds.
p. 282

[140] *Lassalleans*—supporters of the German petty-bourgeois socialist Ferdinand Lassalle (1825-1864), members of the General Association of German Workers founded in 1863 at the Congress of Workers' Organisations, held in Leipzig, to counterbalance the bourgeois progressists who were endeavouring to gain influence over the working class. The first Chairman of the Association was Lassalle, who formulated its programme and tactics. The Asso-

ciation's political programme was the struggle for universal suffrage, and its economic programme, the struggle for the workers' production associations, subsidised by the state. In their practical activities, Lassalle and his followers adapted themselves to the hegemony of Prussia and supported the Great-Power policy of Bismarck. "Objectively", wrote Engels to Marx on January 27, 1865, "this was a base action and a betrayal of the whole working-class movement to the Prussians". Marx and Engels frequently and sharply criticised the theory, tactics, and organisational principles of the Lassalleans as an opportunist trend in the German working-class movement.   p. 309

141 This refers to the letters, quoted below by Lenin, of Marx to Sorge of June 20 and December 15, 1881.   p. 310

142 The reference is to N. Rozhkov's article "The Present Situation in Russia and the Main Task of the Working-Class Movement at the Present Moment". Another article by Lenin, "From the Camp of the Stolypin 'Labour' Party", is also a criticism of Rozhkov (see pp. 354-59 of this volume).   p. 313

143 This refers to *The Social Movement in Russia*; see Note 57. p. 315

144 *Chambre introuvable*—the name given by Louis XVIII to the French counter-revolutionary Chamber of Deputies, elected after the restoration of the Bourbons in August 1815. Its composition was so reactionary that Louis XVIII, fearing a new revolutionary outbreak, was forced to dissolve it.   p. 320

145 Lenin is referring to the preface to S. Y. Witte's "The Autocracy and the Zemstvo" written by P. B. Struve (signed: R.N.S.) which he criticised in "The Persecutors of the Zemstvo and the Hannibals of Liberalism" (see present edition, Vol. 5, pp. 31-80).   p. 323

146 *Mymretsov*—a character from G. I. Uspensky's *Budka* (*The Centry Box*) a coarse and boorish type of policeman from an out-of-the-way small town of tsarist Russia.   p. 324

147 This report was published by the Executive Committee of the International Socialist Bureau as a supplement to Circular No. 21. The article and material relating to the affair of the Social-Democratic deputies to the Second Duma were published in German, French, and English in the *Bulletin périodique du Bureau Socialiste International*, No. 8. After the publication of Lenin's report the campaign abroad for the release of the Social-Democratic deputies was intensified. In an editorial appearing in No. 8 of the Bolshevik newspaper *Rabochaya Gazeta* it was stated that "following the call of the International Socialist Bureau, which sent all parties the report on this matter by Comrade Lenin, our Party representative on the I.S.B., the campaign was consider-

ably intensified by Social-Democratic parties abroad. All Social-Democratic deputies in Germany, France, Belgium, Sweden, Finland, Austria, etc., made public protests."

The heading to the document has been provided by the Institute of Marxism-Leninism of the Central Committee of the C.P.S.U. p. 325

148 *L'Avenir* (*The Future*)—a liberal-bourgeois Russian newspaper which was published in Paris from October 22, 1911 to January 4, 1914 (N.S.) and edited by V. L. Burtsev (some items were published in French). Mensheviks and Socialist-Revolutionaries also contributed to its columns. p. 326

149 Fifty-five members of the Social-Democratic group in the Second Duma were tried, and two of them died shortly after, during imprisonment. It was for this reason that 53 deputies were referred to at the sitting of the Duma held on October 17 (30), 1911. p. 328

150 The question put by the Social-Democratic group was discussed on November 15 (28), 1911 and it was again discussed on three occasions behind closed doors; the question was then handed over to a commission by which it was rejected. p. 331

151 This quotation is from the resolution of the Fifth (All-Russia) Conference of the R.S.D.L.P. in 1908 "The Present Moment and the Tasks of the Party". p. 333

152 A. A. Voiloshnikov, member of the Social-Democratic group in the Third Duma, spoke on December 2 (15), 1911 at the 35th sitting of the Duma during the discussion of the Bill on Amendments to the Regulations on Military Service. He described the tsarist army as a police army, and urged the arming of the people in place of the standing army. The Chairman of the Duma thereupon recommended that he be barred from five Duma sittings. After a second statement by A. A. Voiloshnikov at the same sitting, the number of exclusions from sittings was raised to 15. The Cadets voted for the first proposal of the Chairman. p. 342

153 *Russian Organising Commission* (R.O.C.) for the convening of a Party conference was formed at the end of September 1911 at a meeting of representatives of local Party organisations. The meeting opened in Baku and was guided by G. K. Orjonikidze who had been delegated to call the conference by the Organising Commission Abroad. Representatives of the Baku, Tiflis, Ekaterinburg, Kiev, and Ekaterinoslav organisations took part. Among the delegates were S. G. Shahumyan and S. S. Spandaryan. In view of police persecution and the danger of those participating in the meeting being arrested it was transferred to Tiflis. The Meeting discussed reports from local organisations, the constitution of the R.O.C., relations with the Organising Commission Abroad, elections to the conference, representation from legal organisations, and elections from the non-Russian organisations. A report

of the meeting of the Russian Organising Commission was published by G. K. Orjonikidze in No. 25 of *Sotsial-Demokrat*, December 8 (21), 1911. The meeting drew up an appeal to the local organisations, and issued it in leaflet form together with the resolutions of the meeting. p. 343

[154] Lenin is referring to the Bolshevik organs, the newspaper *Zvezda* and the magazine *Mysl*, to which pro-Party Mensheviks also contributed. p. 345

[155] For more information see Lenin's article "The Results of the Arbitration of the 'Trustees'" (see pp. 365-67 of this volume). p. 347

[156] *Mark*—pseudonym of A. I. Lyubimov. p. 347

[157] *Otkliki Bunda* (*Echoes of the Bund*)—an organ of the Bund committee abroad which appeared at irregular intervals in Geneva from March 1909 to February 1911. There were five issues. p. 348

[158] *The Baku Social-Democratic Party organisation* was one of the most active local bodies during the period of reaction and the years of the new revolutionary upsurge. At the beginning of 1911 the Baku Bolshevik Committee and the "leading Menshevik group members" (pro-Party Mensheviks) united for struggle against otzovism and liquidationism, and for the revival of the illegal R.S.D.L.P.; they formed the United Baku Committee of the R.S.D.L.P. The Baku Committee supported the decision of the 1911 June Meeting of members of the Central Committee to convene an all-Russia Party conference and actively participated in setting up the Russian Organising Commission.

The Kiev Social-Democratic Party organisation worked almost uninterruptedly during the years of reaction. In 1910-11, the Bolsheviks worked with the pro-Party Mensheviks. The Kiev organisation was the first to support the June Meeting of the Central Committee members and the idea of forming the Russian Organising Commission to convene a Party conference, appointing one of its Committee members to assist the representative of the Organising Commission Abroad. p. 348

[159] This refers to the leaflet issued by the Russian Organising Commission in the autumn of 1911. p. 349

[160] Lenin is referring to G. K. Orjonikidze's letter to the Editorial Board of *Sotsial-Demokrat*, published in No. 25 of December 8 (21), 1911, under the signature of N. p. 350

[161] *The city of Z* refers to Brussels, where the Social-Democratic Party of the Latvian Region had its committee abroad. p. 351

[162] This refers to the otzovist Stanislav Volsky (the pseudonym of A. V. Sokolov). p. 351

163 *The petition campaign* refers to a fuss created by the liquidators and Trotsky for agitational purposes around a petition drawn up by the St. Petersburg liquidators in December 1910. The petition, which demanded freedom to organise unions, to hold meetings, and to strike, was to be sent to the Third Duma in the name of the workers. However, the petition campaign was not a success among the workers, only 1,300 signatures having been collected. The Bolsheviks exposed the "liquidationist" character of the petition campaign, and the Resolution of the Sixth (Prague) All-Russia Conference of the R.S.D.L.P. "The 'Petition Campaign'" defined the attitude of the Bolsheviks (see pp. 479-80 of this volume).   p. 360

164 Lenin is referring to the resolution put forward by the St. Petersburg otzovists at the extended meeting of the St. Petersburg Committee prior to the December All-Party Conference, 1908 (the Fifth Conference of the R.S.D.L.P.). The resolution was published in the supplement to No. 44 of *Proletary*, on April 4 (17), 1909. A critical analysis of this document made by Lenin appears in the same supplement, in an article entitled "A Caricature of Bolshevism" (see present edition, Vol. 15).   p. 363

165 *M. Alexandrov*—the Bolshevik M. S. Olminsky. Here and elsewhere, Lenin is referring to his pamphlet *The State, Bureaucracy and Absolutism in the History of Russia*. St. Petersburg, 1910.
                                                        p. 363

166 The signatures of Lenin and others follow.   p. 366

167 *The Gololobov group*—supporters of Y. G. Gololobov, one of the extreme Right-wing members of the Union of October Seventeenth (Octobrists) in the Third Duma.   p. 369

168 *The Meeting of the Bolshevik Groups Abroad* took place in Paris on December 14-17 (27-30), 1911. It was called on the initiative of the Paris Group supporting the Bolshevik newspaper *Rabochaya Gazeta*. The aim of the Meeting was to unify the Bolshevik organisations abroad and support the convening of an all-Russia Party conference. Eleven delegates with full voting rights participated from Bolshevik groups in Paris, Nancy, Zurich, Davos, Geneva, Liége, Berne, Bremen, and Berlin. Lenin reported on the state of affairs in the Party, and the draft resolution on this question, drawn up by Lenin, served as a basis for the general resolution, adopted by the Meeting. The "Notification" and resolution of the Meeting were published by the Committee of the R.S.D.L.P. Organisation Abroad in a leaflet on January 12, 1912 (N.S.).
    The heading to the document has been provided by the Institute of Marxism-Leninism of the Central Committee of the C.P.S.U.   p. 393

[169] The resolution was adopted on December 17 (30), 1911, at the last session of the Meeting of the Bolshevik groups abroad. The resolution was published in the "Notification" of the Committee of the R.S.D.L.P. Organisation Abroad, with the following explanation: "A special resolution of the Meeting drew the attention of all Party comrades to the need to give energetic support to the Russian Organising Commission and the conference which it is convening".

The heading to the document has been provided by the Institute of Marxism-Leninism of the Central Committee of the C.P.S.U.
p. 396

[170] This refers to the agrarian bill of the independent and Right peasant deputies, introduced into the Third Duma on May 10 (23), 1908. The bill envisaged the compulsory alienation with compensation at average market prices of the landed estates not being exploited by their owners. It was proposed to implement the land reform through local land committees elected by a general vote. For Lenin's appraisal of this bill see his articles "The New Agrarian Policy" and "The Agrarian Debates in the Third Duma" in Vol. 13 and Vol. 15 of the present edition respectively. p. 418

[171] *Eisenachers*—members of the Social-Democratic Workers' Party of Germany, founded in 1869 at the Eisenach Congress. The leaders of the Eisenachers were August Bebel and Wilhelm Liebknecht, who were under the ideological influence of Marx and Engels. The Eisenach programme stated that the Social-Democratic Workers' Party of Germany considered itself "a section of the International Working Men's Association and shared its aspirations". Thanks to the regular advice and criticism of Marx and Engels, the Eisenachers pursued a more consistent revolutionary policy than did Lassalle's General Association of German Workers; in particular, on the question of German unification, they followed "the democratic and proletarian path and struggled against any concessions to Prussianism, Bismarckism or nationalism" (see present edition, Vol. 19, "August Bebel"). p. 419

[172] Lenin is quoting from a letter written by Marx to Lassalle on April 19, 1859. When Lenin wrote this article, Marx's letter had not yet been published, and he availed himself of extracts from it which Lassalle had quoted in his reply to Marx and Engels dated May 27, 1859 (see Marx and Engels, *Selected Correspondence*, Moscow, 1955, pp. 138-40). p. 419

[173] *Obskaya Zhizn* (*Ob Life*)—daily newspaper of a liberal-bourgeois trend, published in Novonikolayevsk (Novosibirsk) from 1909 to 1912.
p. 421

[174] The questions were discussed at the sessions of the Third Duma held on October 15 and 17 (28 and 30), 1911. . p. 433

175 *Urgent question.* In Russia's Duma procedure questions were not usually put directly to a minister or submitted for debate without having first been examined by a commission. The Duma itself, however, could decide that a question was "urgent" and should be the subject of an immediate debate. As the reader can see from this article, the debate on whether a question was sufficiently urgent for a debate could obstruct any real discussion of it and ensure its relegation to a commission. From this it follows that no question raised by a small minority in the Duma could ever be voted "urgent" and discussion on it permitted. p. 434

176 *Men with numbers to their names*—ordinal numbers were added when several members of the Duma had the same name (e.g., Markov the First, Markov the Second). p. 441

177 *Jellinek, Georg*—a German bourgeois lawyer. p. 443

178 *The Sixth (Prague) All-Russia Conference of the R.S.D.L.P.* worked from January 5 to January 17 (18-30), 1912 in Prague, and actually assumed the character of a Party congress. More than 20 Party organisations were represented at the Conference, as well as representatives of the editorial boards of the Central Organ *Sotsial-Demokrat* and of *Rabochaya Gazeta*, of the Committee of the R.S.D.L.P. Organisation Abroad, and the group of the C.C. of the R.S.D.L.P. arranging underground transport and travel facilities and known as "the transport group". Apart from two pro-Party Mensheviks, the delegates were all Bolsheviks. Among the delegates were G. K. Orjonikidze, representing the Tiflis organisation, S. S. Spandaryan from Baku, Y. P. Onufriyev from St. Petersburg, F. I. Goloshchokin from Moscow. The Committee of the Organisation Abroad was represented by N. A. Semashko, and the transport group of the C.C. by I. A. Pyatnitsky.

V. I. Lenin represented the Editorial Board of the Central Organ.

Lenin was the leading figure at the Conference. Opening the Conference, he defined the terms of reference, spoke on the current situation and the tasks of the Party, the work of the International Socialist Bureau, made some informative reports and took part in the discussions on the work of the Central Organ, on the tasks of Social-Democracy in the struggle against the famine, on the organisational question, on the work of the Party Organisation Abroad, and on a number of other questions. It was Lenin who drafted the resolutions on the major questions on the conference agenda.

Lenin's speech and the conference resolution on "The Tasks of the Party in the Present Situation" contained a profound analysis of the political situation within the country, reflected the growing revolutionary mood of the people. The Conference emphasised that, as before, the conquest of power by the proletariat, acting as the leader of the peasantry, still remained the chief task of the democratic revolution in Russia.

One of the cardinal problems confronting the Conference was that of ridding the Party of the opportunists. The resolutions adopted on "Liquidationism and the Group of Liquidators", on "The Party Organisation Abroad" were of tremendous theoretical and practical significance. The liquidators were grouped around two legal magazines, *Nasha Zarya* and *Dyelo Zhizni*. The Conference declared "that by its conduct the *Nasha Zarya* and *Dyelo Zhizni* group had definitely placed itself outside the Party". The liquidators were expelled from the R.S.D.L.P. The Conference condemned the activities of the anti-Party groups abroad—the Menshevik *Golos* group, the *Vperyod* and Trotsky groups, and recognised the absolute necessity for a single Party organisation abroad, conducting its work under the supervision and guidance of the C.C., and pointed out that Party groups abroad "which refuse to submit to the Russian centre of Social-Democratic activity, i.e., to the Central Committee, and which cause disorganisation by communicating with Russia independently and ignoring the Central Committee, have no right to use the name of the R.S.D.L.P." These resolutions considerably strengthened the unity of the Marxist party in Russia.

A major part of the Conference deliberations was taken up with the question of participation in the election campaign to the Fourth Duma. The Conference stressed that the main Party task in the elections, and of the Social-Democratic group in the Duma itself, was socialist class propaganda and the organisation of the working class. The main election slogans put forward by the Conference were the basic demands of the Party's minimum programme: a democratic republic, the eight-hour day, confiscation of all landed estates.

The Conference adopted a resolution on "The Character and Organisational Forms of Party Work", adopted Lenin's draft on changes in the organisational Rules of the Party, approved the newspaper *Sotsial-Demokrat* as the Party Central Organ, elected a Party Central Committee and set up the Bureau of the C.C. in Russia.

The Prague Conference of the R.S.D.L.P. played an outstanding role in building the Bolshevik Party, a party of a new type. It summed up a whole historical period of struggle by the Bolsheviks against the Mensheviks, and consolidated the victory of the Bolsheviks. The Menshevik-liquidators were driven out of the Party. Local Party organisations rallied still closer round the Party on the basis of conference decisions. The Conference strengthened the Party as an all-Russia organisation and defined its political line and tactics in the conditions of a new revolutionary upsurge. Free of opportunists, the Bolshevik Party led the new powerful upsurge of the revolutionary struggle of the masses. The Prague Conference was of great international significance. It showed the revolutionary elements of the parties of the Second International how to conduct a decisive struggle against opportunism by carrying the struggle to a complete organisational break with the opportunists.

p. 451

179 The heading to the document has been provided by the Institute of Marxism-Leninism of the Central Committee of the C.P.S.U.
p. 453

180 The heading to the document has been provided by the Institute of Marxism-Leninism of the Central Committee of the C.P.S.U.
p. 458

181 This refers to the Vienna *Pravda*—Trotsky's factional Menshevik-liquidator paper.
p. 482

182 *The Committee of the Organisation Abroad* was set up in December 1911 at a meeting of the Bolshevik groups abroad. The tasks of this Committee were dealt with in the general resolution adopted by this meeting.
p. 484

183 The January 1912 German elections to the Reichstag resulted in a great victory for the Social-Democrats, 110 of their candidates being elected, receiving a total of 4,500,000 votes.
Vorwärts published the message of greetings sent by the R.S.D.L.P. in its issue No. 22 of January 27, 1912.
p. 486

184 *Zhivoye Dyelo* (*Vital Cause*)—the weekly legal newspaper of the Menshevik-liquidators, published in St. Petersburg from January 20 (February 2) to April 28 (May 11), 1912. Sixteen issues appeared.
p. 487

185 The five big cities where, according to the electoral law, there were direct elections with second ballots were St. Petersburg, Moscow, Riga, Kiev and Odessa.
p. 490

186 *Golos Zemli* (*Voice of the Land*)—a liberal-bourgeois newspaper, published in St. Petersburg in 1912.
Russkoye Slovo (*Russian Word*)—a daily liberal-bourgeois newspaper, published in Moscow from 1895 until it was banned in 1917.
Kievskaya Mysl (*Kiev Thought*)—a daily liberal-bourgeois newspaper, published in Kiev from 1906 to 1918. Menshevik-liquidators were among its most active contributors.
p. 491

187 Characters from the works by M. Y. Saltykov-Shchedrin.
Tverdoonto—a retired administrator travelling abroad, from the series of essays *Abroad*.
Ugryum-Burcheyev—a satirical portrait of a mayor, drawn by Saltykov-Shchedrin in his *History of a Town*, who came to be recognised as a typical example of reactionary, stupid and narrow-minded officials.
p. 502

188 *The International Socialist Bureau* (I.S.B.)—the permanent Executive-Information Bureau of the Second International. The decision to set up this Bureau representing the various socialist par-

ties existing at the time was taken at the Paris Congress of the International (September 1900). The Russian representatives elected to the Bureau were G. V. Plekhanov and B. N. Krichevsky; V. I. Lenin became a member of the Bureau in 1905, as the representative of the R.S.D.L.P. In 1912 the Sixth (Prague) All-Russia Party Conference re-elected Lenin as the Party representative to the Bureau.

Lenin's official report to the Bureau regarding the Conference that took place was distributed in Circular No. 4 of the I.S.B. to all the socialist parties on March 18, 1912 by its Secretary, C. Huysmans, with a request that it be published in their respective organs. It appeared in the central organ of the Belgian Labour Party *Le Peuple* of March 23, 1912, and in the central organ of the German Social-Democratic Party *Vorwärts*, No. 72 of March 26, 1912 (Supplement No. 1). *Vorwärts* accompanied this notification with a scurrilous commentary by Trotsky (see Lenin's article "The Anonymous Writer in *Vorwärts* and the State of Affairs in the R.S.D.L.P." in this volume, pp. 533-46). p. 503

[189] Lenin wrote *"The Election Platform of the R.S.D.L.P."* in Paris, early in March 1912, shortly after the Prague Conference. "The Election Platform" was published in Russia by the Central Committee of the Party as a separate leaflet and distributed in 18 localities including the main working-class centres. Reprinted from the leaflet, it appeared as a supplement to No. 26 of *Sotsial-Demokrat*. It was also reprinted by many local Bolshevik organisations and by the Russian Bureau of the C.C. of the R.S.D.L.P. in Tiflis. The significance of this document is dealt with by V. I. Lenin in his article "The Platform of the Reformists and the Platform of the Revolutionary Social-Democrats". p. 506

[190] *Khodynka Tsar*—at Khodynka Field on the outskirts of Moscow, a carnival was arranged on the occasion of the coronation of Tsar Nicholas II on May 18, 1896. Criminal negligence on the part of the authorities led to a tremendous crush in which about 2,000 people lost their lives and tens of thousands were injured. p. 506

[191] *The law of March 4, 1906*—temporary regulations providing for a certain freedom of associations, unions and meetings, but which at the same time laid down a number of obstacles, and in fact reduced the law to a scrap of paper. It gave the Minister of the Interior the right not only to suppress associations and unions, but also to refuse official recognition to new unions. p. 508

[192] This document is a postscript to the authorised copy of the leaflet "The Election Platform of the R.S.D.L.P." As the manuscript had no heading it has been provided by the Institute of Marxism-Leninism of the Central Committee of the C.P.S.U. p. 513

[193] *"Put Your Cards on the Table"* was written in Paris in March 1912 for publication in the Bolshevik newspaper *Zvezda*, but was not

printed at the time. It was sent to the Editorial Board with a
covering letter intended as a postscript.   p. 514

[194] *The language of the Duchy of Monaco*—the language of gambl-
ing.   p. 514

[195] This refers to the book *The State Duma, Third Convocation. Handbook*, 1910.   p. 520

[196] The pamphlet *Voter's Handbook (Our Election Law)* was published
in St. Petersburg in 1912.
    Lenin attached great importance to the publication of the *Vo-
ter's Handbook* and compiled and edited the material for this book.
In a letter to the Editorial Board of *Zvezda* dated April 9 (22),
1912, he recommended that the 2nd and 3rd chapters of his article "The Campaign for the Elections to the Fourth Duma" be
included (see pp. 372-84 of this volume). He urged that they issue a
"serious work" which "would be of value as an effective guide to
the elections". However, the *Zvezda* editors were able to issue only
the first part of the book which dealt with the electoral law and
the regulations concerning the elections to the Duma.   p. 520

[197] In February 1912, the Menshevik-liquidator T. O. Belousov,
deputy to the Third Duma from Irkutsk Gubernia, notified the
Social-Democratic group of his withdrawal from the group. The
group unanimously demanded that Belousov immediately resign
his seat, and published this demand in *Zvezda*, No. 12, February 23,
1912. Two days later, Belousov published a letter in *Rech*, which
also appeared in *Zhivoye Dyelo*, in which he criticised the statement of the group and tried to justify his withdrawal from it. The
Irkutsk Stock-Exchange Committee at its meeting of February 29
(March 13) discussed the question of Belousov's resignation from
the Duma, and these representatives of commerce and industry
asked him to continue as a member of the Duma. Belousov expressed his thanks to the Committee "for their support and faith in
him". When he wrote his article Lenin was unaware of Belousov's
correspondence with the Irkutsk Stock-Exchange Committee, but
on its publication *Zvezda* informed its readers of the contents of
this correspondence.
    Following the appearance of Lenin's article in *Zvezda* Belou-
sov sent a new statement to the group full of abuse of the revolutionary Social-Democrats.   p. 521

[198] The pamphlet is a reply to an anonymous, scurrilous article by
Trotsky in *Vorwärts* against the Prague Conference and its decisions.   p. 533

[199] This refers to the anti-Party, slanderous resolution adopted on
March 12 (N. S.), 1912 in Paris at the meeting of the representa-
tives of the Bund Committee Abroad, the *Vperyod* group, *Golos
Sotsial-Demokrata*, Trotsky's Vienna *Pravda*, and of the pro-

Party Mensheviks and conciliators. This resolution was adopted in opposition to the All-Russia (Prague) Party Conference and its decisions. It was published as a separate leaflet in the Vienna *Pravda*, and in *Informatsionny Listok* No. 4 of the Bund. Lenin, as the representative of the R.S.D.L.P. on the International Socialist Bureau wrote an official statement on this and then a letter to Huysmans, Secretary of the International Socialist Bureau (see pp. 547-50 of this volume).   p. 535

200 This refers to the resolution of the Fifth Conference of the R.S.D.L.P. (All-Russia Conference of 1908) "On the Amalgamation of Local National Organisations".   p. 539

201 *Prosveshcheniye* (*Enlightenment*)—a monthly theoretical, legal, Bolshevik magazine, published in St. Petersburg from December 1911 to June 1914. It was founded on Lenin's initiative to replace the Moscow Bolshevik magazine *Mysl*, suppressed by the tsarist government. The circulation of the new magazine reached 5,000 copies. V. V. Vorovsky, A. I. Ulyanova-Yelizarova, N. K. Krupskaya, M. S. Olminsky, M. A. Savelyev contributed to its columns. In response to Lenin's request, Maxim Gorky assumed the responsibility for the literary section of the magazine. While in Paris, and later in Cracow and Poronin, Lenin took an active part in the work of the magazine, edited articles published in it and regularly corresponded with the members of the Editorial Board. Among his articles published in the magazine, are the following: "Fundamental Problems of the Election Campaign", "The Three Sources and Three Component Parts of Marxism", "Critical Remarks on the National Question", "The Right of Nations to Self-Determination", "Disruption of Unity Concealed by Shouts for Unity", "The Methods of Struggle of the Bourgeois Intellectuals Against the Workers", and others.

The magazine exposed the opportunist-liquidators, otzovists, Trotskyites, and also bourgeois Nationalists, and threw light on the struggle of the working class in the conditions of a new revolutionary upsurge; popularised the Bolshevik slogans in the election campaign to the Fourth Duma; it attacked revisionism and centrism in the parties of the Second International and gave news of the international working-class movement. The magazine played an outstanding role in the international Marxist education of the advanced workers in Russia.

On the eve of the First World War the magazine was suppressed by the tsarist government. Its publication was renewed in the autumn of 1917, but only one double number appeared; it carried Lenin's articles "Can the Bolsheviks Retain State Power?" and "A Review of the Party Programme".   p. 544

202 Lenin's letter was sent to all socialist parties on April 12 (N. S.), 1912 by the International Socialist Bureau with a request that it be published in their press.   p. 547

[203] This refers to the expression "His Majesty's Opposition" used by P. Milyukov, the leader of the Cadet Party. In a speech delivered at a Lord Mayor's luncheon in London on June 19 (July 2), 1909, he stated: "As long as there is a legislative chamber that controls the budget in Russia, the Russian opposition will remain His Majesty's Opposition, and not an Opposition to His Majesty". (*Rech*, No. 167, June 21 [July 4], 1909.)   p. 551

[204] *F. L—ko, W. Frey*—Lenin's pseudonyms.   , p. 557

[205] The law of December 11 (24), 1905, convening the "legislative" State Duma was published by the tsarist government during the height of the Moscow armed uprising. The law ensured a tremendous majority of landlords and capitalists in the Duma. The First Duma, elected on the basis of the law of December 11, 1905, was a Cadet Duma.   p. 570

[206] *Zaprosy Zhizni (Demands of Life)*—a weekly magazine published in St. Petersburg from 1909 to 1912. Among its contributors were Cadets, Popular Socialists, and Menshevik-liquidators.   p. 574

THE LIFE AND WORK
OF
V. I. LENIN

Outstanding Dates
(December 1910-April 1912)

1910

Prior to December 15 (28)	While in Paris, Lenin writes a letter to the Russian Collegium of the C. C. of the R.S.D.L.P., on the state of affairs in the Party.
December 23 (January 5, 1911)	Lenin's article "Certain Features of the Historical Development of Marxism" is published in *Zvezda* No. 2.

1911

After January 2 (15)	Lenin writes the note "Judas Trotsky's Blush of Shame".
January 5 (18)	Lenin delivers a lecture on Lev Tolstoi in Paris.
January 13 (26)	Lenin's article "The Career of a Russian Terrorist" appears in *Sotsial-Demokrat*, No. 19-20.
January 22 (February 4)	Lenin's article "Lev Tolstoi and His Epoch" is published in *Zvezda*, No. 6.
After January 22 (February 4)	Lenin writes the article "Marxism and *Nasha Zarya*", which is published on April 22 (May 5) in No. 3 of *Sovremennaya Zhizn.* (Baku).
January	Lenin's article "Those Who Would Liquidate Us (Re: Mr. Potresov and V. Bazarov)" is published in *Mysl*, No. 2.
February 8 (21)	*Rabochaya Gazeta*, No. 3, publishes Lenin's articles "The Fiftieth Anniversary of the Fall of Serfdom" and "Paul Singer".
Between February 17 and 26 (March 2 and 11)	Lenin writes the article "Comments (Menshikov, Gromoboi, Izgoyev)". This article appears in *Zvezda*, No. 11, February 26 (March 11).
February 22 or 23 (March 7 or 8)	In his letter to N. G. Poletayev, Lenin exposes the blackmailing tactics of the liquidators and demands decisive and consistent struggle against them.

February   Lenin writes a letter "To the Russian Collegium
                      of the C. C. ", on the splitting activities of the *Golos*
                      and *Vperyod* groups and Trotsky.

                      Mysl, No. 3, publishes Lenin's article "Apropos
                      of an Anniversary" and the conclusion of the arti-
                      cle "Those Who Would Liquidate Us".

March 19 (Ap-   Lenin's article "Wreckers of the Party in the Role
ril 1)   of 'Wreckers of Legends'" is published in *Sotsial-
                      Demokrat*, No. 21-22.

Between March   Lenin writes the article "The Cadets and the Octo-
23 and April 2   brists", published in *Zvezda*, No. 16, on April 2
(April 5 and 15)   (15).

Between April   Lenin writes the article "Conference of the British
8   and 16 (21   Social-Democratic Party", published in *Zvezda*,
and 29)   No. 18, on April 16 (29), 1911.

April 15   (28)   Lenin's article "In Memory of the Commune"
                      is published in *Rabochaya Gazeta*, No. 4-5.

Between April   Lenin writes the article "'Regret' and 'Shame'",
28 and May 7   published in *Zvezda*, No. 21, on May 7 (20).
(May 11 and 20)

April 29 (May   Lenin delivers a speech at a May Day meeting
12)   in Paris.

                      Lenin's article "A Conversation Between a Legal-
                      ist and an Opponent of Liquidationism" is pub-
                      lished in No. 3 of *Diskussionny Listok*, supplement
                      to *Sotsial-Demokrat*, the Central Organ of the C. C.

May 14 (27)   In his letter to Maxim Gorky, Lenin explains
                      his negative attitude to the unification of the Bol-
                      sheviks, pro-Party Mensheviks, and Social-Demo-
                      cratic Duma group around some press organ in
                      view of the Mensheviks' predominance in the Duma
                      group; criticises the *Zvezda* editorial board for
                      lack of a firm political line; informs him of rumours
                      about Stolypin's circular letter on suppressing all
                      Social-Democratic press organs, and writes about
                      the necessity to intensify underground activities.

                      Lenin signs a letter to the members of C. C. of
                      the R.S.D.L.P. living abroad, with an invitation
                      to participate in a meeting of the C. C. members.

Between May 19   Lenin writes a letter to the Meeting of the members
and 23 (between   of the C. C. of the R.S.D.L.P. abroad in which he
June 1 and 5)   exposes the intrigues of the liquidators, who sabo-

taged the convening of a plenary meeting of the C. C. of the R.S.D.L.P.

Lenin writes a summary (plan) for the report of three Bolshevik members of the C. C. to a private meeting of nine members of the C. C.

May 28 (June 10)

Lenin's article "The Results of the Duma Session. 'We Did This Together'" is published in *Zvezda*, No. 24.

May 28-June 4 (June 10-17)

Lenin guides the work of the Meeting of members of the C. C. of the R.S.D.L.P., called on his initiative in Paris with the object of working out measures to accelerate the convening of a plenary meeting of the C. C. of the R.S.D.L.P., and an all-Party conference.

June 11 (24)

Lenin's article "Old Truths That Are Ever New" is published in *Zvezda*, No. 25.

June 18 (July 1)

Lenin takes part in a meeting of the Second Paris Group supporting the R.S.D.L.P., and introduces the draft resolution on the state of affairs in the Party. This resolution is adopted by the Group and in July 1911 is published as a separate leaflet.

July 20 (August 2)

Lenin writes the introduction to the pamphlet *Two Parties*.

July

Lenin has a talk with M. A. Savelyev on the publication of the legal Bolshevik magazine *Prosveshcheniye*, and arranges for his participation in editing the magazine.

Spring and summer prior to August 17 (30)

Lenin and N. K. Krupskaya live in Longjumeau (near Paris).

Lenin arranges the organisation of a Party school there.

He gives a course of lectures at this school on political economy (29 lectures), the agrarian question (12 lectures) and on the theory and practice of socialism in Russia (12 lectures).

At the request of the students of the school Lenin reads 3 lectures on the materialist conception of history and a paper on the current situation and the state of Party affairs.

September 1 (14)

Sotsial-Demokrat, No. 23, publishes Lenin's article "Comment by *Sotsial-Democrat* Editors on

Statement by Commission Convening Plenary Meeting of C. C.".

September 2 (15) In a letter to Maxim Gorky, Lenin invites him to continue contributing to *Zvezda*.

September 9 or 10 (22 or 23) Lenin goes to Switzerland to take part in a meeting of the International Socialist Bureau in Zurich.

September 10-11 (23-24) Lenin participates in a meeting of the International Socialist Bureau held in Zurich, and defends Rosa Luxemburg's opposition to the opportunism of the German Social-Democrats.

September 12 (25) Lenin delivers a report on the state of affairs in the Party to a meeting of the local group of the R.S.D.L.P. in Zurich.

September 13 (26) Lenin reads a paper on "Stolypin and the Revolution" in Zurich.

September 15 (28) Lenin reads a paper on "Stolypin and the Revolution" in Berne.

September 19 (October 2) Lenin reads a paper on "Stolypin and the Revolution" in Geneva.

October 18 (31) *Sotsial-Demokrat*, No. 24, publishes Lenin's articles "Stolypin and the Revolution", "The New Faction of Conciliators, or the Virtuous", "The Election Campaign and the Election Platform", and "From the Camp of the Stolypin 'Labour' Party". Lenin reads a paper on "Stolypin and the Revolution" in Paris.

October 19 (November 1) Lenin sends an enquiry to the representative of the Czech Social-Democratic Party on the International Socialist Bureau on the possibility of convening a conference of the R.S.D.L.P. in Prague, and asks for assistance in its organisation.

October 23 (November 5) Lenin's article "The Grand Total" is published in *Zvezda*, No. 26.

November 5 (18) Lenin's articles "Two Centres" and "Old and New (Notes of a Newspaper Reader)" are published in *Zvezda*, No. 28.

November 14 (27) Lenin reads a paper on "A Liberal Labour Party Manifesto" in Paris.

November 20 (December 3) Lenin delivers a speech in the name of the R.S.D.L.P. at the funeral of Paul and Laura Lafargue. It is published in *Sotsial-Demokrat*, No. 25, on December 8 (21).

November 26 *(December 9)*	Lenin's article "Hyndman on Marx" is published in *Zvezda*, No. 31.
End of November-beginning of December	Lenin writes the article (report) "The Social-Democratic Group in the Second Duma." The article is published in the periodical bulletin of the International Socialist Bureau, No. 8, in December 1911.
December 3 (16)	Lenin's article "A Liberal Labour Party Manifesto" is published in *Zvezda*, No. 32.
December 8 (21)	Lenin's articles "The Slogans and Organisation of Social-Democratic Work Inside and Outside the Duma", "Agency of the Liberal Bourgeoisie", "The Climax of the Party Crisis", "From the Camp of the Stolypin 'Labour' Party", "Trotsky's Diplomacy and a Certain Party Platform" and "The Results of the Arbitration of the 'Trustees'" are published in *Sotsial-Demokrat*, No. 25.
December 10(23)	Lenin's article "Old and New" is published in *Zvezda*, No. 33.
December 10 (23)-January 6 (19), 1912	Lenin's articles under the general title "The Campaign for the Elections to the Fourth Duma" are published in *Zvezda*, Nos. 33, 34, 36, for 1911 and No. 1, 1912.
Not later than December 14(27)	Lenin prepares for a meeting of the Bolshevik groups abroad; works on the theses for a report on the state of affairs in the Party, drafts the resolution "Organisation of the Social-Democratic Party Forces Abroad and the Tasks of the Bolsheviks".
December 14-17 (27-30)	Lenin leads the Meeting of the Bolshevik groups abroad, in Paris.
December 14 (27)	Lenin opens the Meeting with a speech of welcome, and delivers the report on the state of affairs in the Party.
December 15 (28)	Lenin guides the discussion at the Meeting and delivers the concluding speech on his report.
December 16-17 (29-30)	Lenin participates in the discussion on the final text of the resolution. At Lenin's suggestion the Meeting elects the Committee of the Organisation Abroad, and empowers the Committee to draw up the Rules.

Lenin speaks in the discussion on support for the Russian Organising Commission and the holding of a Party conference. The Meeting adopts the resolution submitted by Lenin.

Prior to Decem-   *Prosveshcheniye,* No. 1, appears with articles by
ber 17 (30)   Lenin "Fundamental Problems of the Election Campaign" (beginning of the article), "First Exposure of Cadet Negotiations with the Cabinet", and "Three Questions".

December   22   Lenin's article "The Famine and the Black-Hun-
(January   4,   dred Duma" is published in *Rabochaya Gazeta,*
1912)   No. 70.

End of the year   Lenin writes an outline for a report on the political situation.

1912

January 5-17   Lenin plays a leading role in the Prague Confer-
(18-30)   ence of the R.S.D.L.P.; speaks at the opening of the Conference and delivers the report on the tasks of the Party in the present situation; takes the chair at sessions; drafts resolutions on the constitution of the Conference, on the tasks of the Party in the present situation, on liquidationism and the group of liquidators, on the tasks of the Social-Democrats in the struggle against the famine, on the political campaign, and drafts changes in the organisational Rules of the Party

January 5 (18)   Lenin speaks on the constitution of the Conference.

January   6,   7   At five sessions of the Conference Lenin takes the
and 10 (19, 20   minutes of the reports of the local organisations.
and 23)

January 7 (20)   At the fifth session of the Conference Lenin delivers a speech on the work of the Central Organ and a report on the work of the International Socialist Bureau; replies to delegates' questions and speaks in the discussion on the resolution dealing with reports of the local organisations.

At the sixth session of the Conference Lenin speaks twice in the discussion on his report on the work of the International Socialist Bureau.

January 8 (21)   At the eighth session of the Conference Lenin speaks in the discussion on the tasks of Social-Democracy in the struggle against the famine.

The draft resolution drawn up by Lenin on this question is adopted by the Conference.

Between January 9 and 13 (22 and 26)   Instructed by the Conference, Lenin draws up a message of greeting to the German Social-Democrats in connection with their success at the elections to the German Reichstag. This message was published in *Vorwärts* on January 27, 1912.

January 10 (23)   At the eleventh session of the Conference, Lenin takes part in the discussion on the question of Party work abroad.

January 11 (24)   At the twelfth session of the Conference Lenin delivers a speech on organisational questions.

January 12 (25)   At the fifteenth session of the Conference Lenin's draft resolution on the tasks of the Party in the present situation is adopted.

Between January 12 and 17 (25 and 30)   The Prague Conference elects Lenin to the C.C., the Central Organ, and as representative to the International Socialist Bureau.

January 19 (February 1)   Lenin meets the Social-Democratic deputies to the State Duma in Leipzig and acquaints them with the decisions of the Prague Conference.

End of January   Lenin leaves Leipzig for Berlin to receive Party funds from the "trustees" in accordance with the decisions of the Prague Conference.

February   In a letter to Maxim Gorky, Lenin informs him of the All-Russia Party Conference of the R.S.D.L.P. which has taken place, and asks him to write a May Day leaflet for publication in Russia.

February 19 (March 3)   Lenin's article "An Organ of a Liberal Labour Policy" is published in *Zvezda*, No. 11.

February 28 (March 12)   Lenin writes a letter to G. L. Shklovsky in Berne on the necessity of reading a paper in all Swiss towns on the results of the Prague Conference, informs him of its composition and proceedings, the steps taken in Russia to bring its decisions to the knowledge of the local organitsations, the break with the liquidators, the intention of the Bund and the Lettish Social-Democrats to convene a conference with the participation of the liquidators and the stand of the Duma Social-Democratic group.

February

Lenin edits the pamphlet *The All-Russia Confer-ence of the Russian Social-Democratic Labour Party, 1912*. The pamphlet was issued in February 1912 in Paris, published by the C. C. of the R.S.D.L.P.

Not earlier than March 2 (15)

Lenin writes the article "Against Unity—With the Liquidators", published in *Prosveshcheniye*, No. 3-4, in February-March 1912.

March 4 (17)

Lenin's article "Political Parties in the Five Years of the Third Duma" is published in *Zvezda*, No. 14.

March 5 (18)

Lenin's Report to the International Socialist Bureau on the All-Russia Conference of the R.S.D.L.P. is distributed to the socialist parties by the Secretary of the I.S.B., in Circular No. 4 of March 18, for publication in their party press.

Beginning of March

Lenin writes "The Election Platform of the R.S.D.L.P." It is published as a separate leaflet in March 1912 in Russia and abroad in April as a supplement to No. 26 of *Sotsial-Demokrat*.

March 12-13 (25-26)

Lenin writes "Put Your Cards on the Table". Lenin in a letter to the Editorial Board of *Zvezda* asks them to send him books on the electoral law of June 3 (16), 1907 and other materials essential for compiling and editing the pamphlet *Voter's Handbook (Our Election Law)*, enquires about the publication of a daily workers' paper, its size, etc.

March 13 (26)

Lenin's article "Deputy T. O. Belousov's With-drawal from the Social-Democratic Group in the Duma" is published in *Zvezda*, No. 17.

Between March 13 and 19 (be-tween March 26 and April 1)

Lenin writes the pamphlet "The Anonymous Writer in *Vorwärts* and the State of Affairs in the R.S.D.L.P." It was published in 1912 in Paris by the Central Organ of the R.S.D.L P., *Sotsial-Demokrat*.

March 15 (28)

Lenin in a letter to G. K. Orjonikidze and other members of the C. C. R.S.D.L.P. Bureau in Russia in Tiflis points out the necessity for strengthening the ties of the local Party organisations with the centre abroad, and urges that organisations be visited and the news of the Prague Conference be brought to them as soon as possible.

March 17 (30)	*Rabochaya Gazeta*, No. 8, publishes Lenin's articles "Famine" and "The Peasantry and the Elections to the Fourth Duma".
Between March 23 and 26 (between April 5 and 8)	Lenin writes the article "The Bloc of the Cadets with the Progressists and Its Significance". It is published in *Zvezda*, No. 23, March 29 (April 11)
Prior to March 30 (April 12)	Lenin writes a report and a letter to the Secretary of the International Socialist Bureau, Huysmans, in connection with the statement of the liquidationist and otzovist groups abroad against the decisions of the Prague Conference.
	Lenin's report is sent by the International Socialist Bureau on March 30 (April 12) to all socialist parties in Circular No. 7, to be published in their party press.
April 1 (14)	Lenin's article "A Poor Defence of a Liberal Labour Policy" is published in *Zvezda*, No. 24.
April 3 (16)	Lenin's article "The Second Ballot in Russia and the Tasks of the Working Class" is published in *Zvezda*, No. 25.
April 8 and 19 (April 21 and May 2)	Lenin's article "Liberalism and Democracy" is published in *Zvezda*, Nos. 27 and 32.
Prior to April 9 (22)	Lenin edits the *Voter's Handbook (Our Election Law)*
April	Lenin guides the organisation of the publication of the legal Bolshevik paper *Pravda*.

В. И. ЛЕНИН
СОЧИНЕНИЯ
Том 17

На английском языке